W9-APX-017

The psychology of personal constructs

The psychology of personal constructs

Volume one
A theory of personality

George A. Kelly

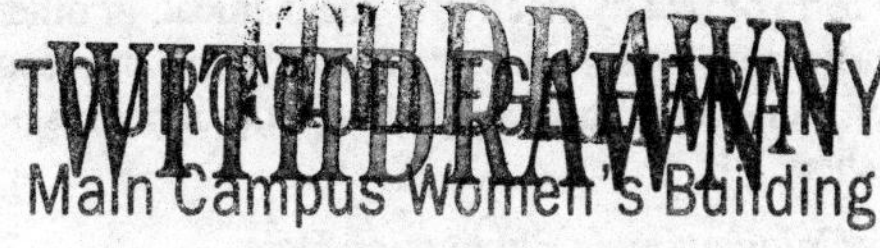

London and New York
In association with the Centre for Personal Construct Psychology, London

First published in 1991
by Routledge
11 New Fetter Lane, London EC4P 4EE

Simultaneously published in the USA and Canada
by Routledge
a division of Routledge, Chapman and Hall Inc.
29 West 35th Street, New York, NY 10001

Typeset by Michael Mepham, Frome
Printed and bound in Great Britain
by Mackays of Chatham PLC, Kent

British Library Cataloguing in Publication Data
Kelly, George, *1905–1967*
The psychology of personal constructs.
1. Man. Behaviour. Personal construct theory
I. Title
155.2

Library of Congress Cataloging in Publication Data
Kelly, George Alexander, 1905–1967.
The psychology of personal constructs/George A. Kelly.
p. cm.
Reprint. Originally published: New York: Norton, c1955.
Includes bibliographical references and index.
Contents: v. 1. Theory of personality — v. 2. Clinical diagnosis & psychotherapy.
1. Personal construct theory. 2. Personality. 3. Personal construct therapy. 4. Psychotherapy. I. Title.
BF698.9.P47K44 1990
155.2—dc20 90-39114
CIP

ISBN 0-415-03799-9
ISBN 0-415-03797-2 vol. 1
ISBN 0-415-03798-0 vol. 2

Contents

Figures and tables

Figures

Volume one

Tables

Volume one

Volume two

Preface to Volume One

This book started out twenty years ago as a handbook of clinical procedures. It was designed for the writer's students and used as a guide in the clinic of which he was the director. At first, the emphasis was upon specific ways of revealing and understanding the client's record of personal experience and of seeing clearly the milieu in which he was seeking to find his place. From this beginning the handbook was supposed to develop gradually into something which might have wider use. But, time after time, the writing bogged down in a morass of tedious little maxims. It was no good – this business of trying to tell the reader merely *how* to deal with clinical problems; the *why* kept insistently rearing its puzzling head.

So we started to write about the *whys*. It was encouraging to find words trickling out behind the typewriter keys again. Yet no sooner had we started than something strange began to happen; or rather, we discovered that something unsuspected had already happened. It turned out to be this: in the years of relatively isolated clinical practice we had wandered far off the beaten paths of psychology, much farther than we had ever suspected.

And now how far afield were we? Or, what was more important, could our readers ever find us? Obviously we had been making many basic assumptions implicitly – taking for granted our somewhat unusual convictions. Unless we now were able to become explicit about such matters could we ever hope to say sensible things to anybody about the *whys* of clinical practice? It seemed not.

We backed off and started again, this time at the level of system building. It was a half-and-half job; half invention of coherent assumptions which would sustain a broad field of inquiry, and half articulation of convictions we had already been taking for granted.

Now at last, the pages began to pile up. We had cut out for ourselves the job of first expounding a theoretical position – a new theory of personality – and then pursuing its practical implications right on out into the psychologists' workday world. This was no holiday task, as we were soon to discover. Even with the omission of originally projected chapters dealing with social organization, education, and the current status of relevant research, the bulk of manuscript assumed formidable proportions. At this moment the writer has, of course, not hefted either of the final printed volumes, but he can easily imagine that neither of them will be of a comfortable size to curl up in bed with.

A word about the writing job itself. When the chapters began to take shape the writer glibly offered to read first-draft manuscript on Thursday nights to any who would come, listen, and discuss. This weekly ordeal lasted for three long years. It was painfully stimulating. Attendance ran as high as thirty and pages covered in an evening ran as low as one. That either the writer or the manuscript survived at all is entirely due to the psychological perceptiveness of colleagues who, somehow, always found a way to strike a gentle balance between pity and realism.

To whom it may concern

It is only fair to warn the reader about what may be in store for him. In the first place, he is likely to find missing most of the familiar landmarks of psychology books. For example, the term *learning*, so honourably embedded in most psychological texts, scarcely appears at all. That is wholly intentional; we are for throwing it overboard altogether. There is no *ego*, no *emotion*, no *motivation*, no *reinforcement*, no *drive*, no *unconscious*, no *need*. There are some words with brand-new psychological definitions, words like *foci of convenience, preemption, propositionality, fixed-role therapy, creativity cycle, transitive diagnosis*, and *the credulous approach*. *Anxiety* is defined in a special systematic way. *Role, guilt*, and *hostility* carry definitions altogether unexpected by many; and, to make heresy complete, there is no extensive bibliography. Unfortunately, all this will make for periods of strange, and perhaps uncomfortable, reading. Yet, inevitably, a different approach calls for a different lexicon; and, under its influence, many old terms are unhitched from their familiar meanings.

To whom are we speaking? In general, we think the reader who takes us seriously will be an adventuresome soul who is not one bit afraid of thinking unorthodox thoughts about people, who dares peer out at the world through the eyes of strangers, who has not invested beyond his means in either ideas or vocabulary, and who is looking for an *ad interim*, rather than an ultimate, set of psychological insights. He may earn his living as a psychologist, an educator, a social worker, a psychiatrist, a clergyman, an administrator – that is not particularly relevant. He may never have had a course in psychology, although if he has not been puzzling rather seriously over psychological problems he will most certainly be unhappy with his choice of this book.

Readers and writers

Approximately a hundred copies of earlier drafts of the manuscript, not including the original handbook, have been duplicated and read. Readers of these copies, together with the Thursday-nighters, include nearly a hundred persons who have reacted to all or to a sizable portion of the book. It goes without saying that this pretesting of the reader audience has been of great help.

Following is a list of colleagues who were regular Thursday-night participants and who, perhaps better than the author, know what the psychology of personal constructs is about.

Dr. James Bieri	Dr. Robert E. Jones
Dr. Jean Burton	Dr. Alvin W. Landfield
Dr. Richard B. Cravens	Dr. Leon H. Levy
Dr. Robert E. Fager	Dr. Sue P. Lloyd
Dr. Alvin R. Howard	Dr. Richard M. Lundy
Dr. William H. Lyle, Jr.	Dr. Henry Samuels
Dr. Brendan Maher	Dr. Donald Shoemaker
Dr. Joseph M. Masling	Dr. E. Philip Trapp
Dr. James W. Rohrer	Dr. Jane H. Wooster

But this by no means completes the list of those whose ideas have been incorporated into the psychology of personal constructs. Dr. John Barry, through correspondence, kept up a running critical analysis of first-draft material. Dr. L. S. McGaughran's experimental study set the stage for the dimensional analysis of constructs. Dr. Harry Mason did some of the early work on experiential analysis, as did Dr. John Hemphill. Dr. John Hadley performed early experiments with some of the psychotherapeutic techniques discussed in the second volume. Mrs. Ethel H. Edwards and Mr. Alexandra J. Robinson conducted the first explorations with fixed-role therapy. And it was Dr. Harry J. Older who first suggested that the systematic position implied by fixed-role therapy should be expounded.

In addition, there are those colleagues whose writings have been quoted. These include:

Mr. Ibrahim Abou Ghorra	Dr. Joseph M. Masling
Dr. David E. Hunt	Miss Joyce Olhoeft
Dr. Sue P. Lloyd	Mr. Philip A. Preble

Dr. Jane H. Wooster

and, of course, that distinguished and insightful colleague of all personal-construct theorists, Mr. William Shakespeare.

In some cases their names are mentioned here, rather than in the context of the quotations, to protect the anonymity of the cases with which they were associated.

On a certain occasion nearly ten years ago there was a colleague who listened attentively to some of our impromptu mumblings about a theory of personality based on 'role constructs'. By happy coincidence that listener has turned out to be the psychology editor of this book, although he has probably long since forgotten the occasion on which he listened. Not only has he scrutinized the eighteen pounds of manuscript with an editor's eye, but he has reacted to it as if it were said for him to hear, sometimes responding with booming enthusiasm, sometimes with puzzled dismay. What more could an author ask for! The Sanfordized manuscript will make a far better book and the author is as grateful as he is awed.

There are those to whom the writer feels a special kind of debt. The purple-fingered brigade – Mrs. Virginia Brevoort, Mrs. Ruth Hedges, Mrs. Mabel Oakley, and Mrs. Mildred Waddell – typed, duplicated with a purple aniline dye process, and assembled two preliminary editions of the manuscript.

And, finally, there is the writer's wife, Mrs. Gladys T. Kelly, who spent long hours with the manuscript, many of them patiently reconciling the mysteries of English grammar with the vagaries of her husband's ideas. But where does one ever find words to express this kind of appreciation?

Road map for the itinerant reader

Now for the structure of the book. Unless the reader has a map in mind he is pretty sure to get lost, especially if he goes skipping around among the chapters. There is a customary pattern for writing books of this sort, but we have found it impractical to follow. Custom has it that the writer first expresses his misgiving about the way his colleagues are going about their business, then he expounds his theory, next he offers scriptural quotations from his profession's literature, and finally he illustrates how well he has solved the problems which have been bothering him.

The reader normally goes yessing through the complaining pages: he, too, is unhappy about the way things have been going. Then he jots down a mental note or two about the writer's theory, just so that he can keep it in mind. Finally, he thumbs through the last two sections to make sure the writing is legitimate and to see if the theory really makes any practical difference in the way the world is to be run.

But we have found, from experience, that this plan of writing and reading does not work for what we have to say. There are altogether too few familiar landmarks and altogether too many sweeping assumptions for the reader to keep oriented in the usual way. Besides, we have no serious quarrel to give vent to – either with psychoanalysis, Gestalt theory, neophenomenology, or with Hullian learning. Instead of starting with a complaint, we have simply offered an invitation to adventure. Instead of asking the reader to keep the whole theory in suspense until the second volume, the writing follows a spiralling approach. We have turned, time after time, to practical applications, only to return in later chapters to a further exposition of the more detailed aspects of the theory. Thus there is a kind of repetition from section to section, but each time at a more complex level. And, as for *post hoc* analysis of psychology's experimental scriptures, we believe that a theory is validated by the bets it lays before the races are run, rather than by its 'I-told-you-so'. We have therefore omitted all *post hoc* experimental evidence.

The writing starts with a philosophical position – to which we have given a special name – sketchily stated in Chapter 1. Next we get formal; we lay down a basic postulate, or underlying assumption, for everything that is to come. The postulate is immediately elaborated by a series of eleven statements, called corollaries. And that is Chapter 2.

Now we take up a job of elaboration so that the reader will have a better idea of what one of these personal constructs, about which this book is written, will look like when he meets it in our street. Here we deal with experience and with what, for so many psychologists, is man's fateful past. Following this we move to a descriptive level of exposition and say something about the field of service for which our theory is especially designed. And this, in turn, leads to the presentation of a clinical instrument, called the Rep Test, which illustrates the kind of practical gadget we ought to expect our theory to help us invent. Five chapters down!

In Chapter 6 we turn to the mathematical structure of psychological space. We discuss the interweave of concepts and figures giving substance to the fabric of society. Our mathematics is of the Bertrand Russell type, anchored firmly in psychology. This is primarily a researcher's chapter.

It is our conviction that theory ought to be kept busy at something. Hence, in Chapters 7 and 8, we try to show just what the psychology of personal constructs might lead one to observe in the spontaneous speech of a fellow human being and what it might lead the clinician to do about it. This is relatively down-to-earth material, but with systematic assumptions behind it. We think the reader may follow the later development of the theory better if he has seen it at work in a face-to-face situation.

The last two chapters of this volume, Chapters 9 and 10, were inserted here when it became apparent that the book would have to be published in two volumes, although, originally, they appeared later in the manuscript. This shift was made so that one volume would be mostly theoretical and the other mostly practical. The two chapters, offering a tentative repertory of diagnostic constructs for the practising clinician, are not absolutely essential to the development of the theory. But they are highly abstract and they are in the style of the first volume – the theoretical one.

The second volume is, as we have hinted, concerned with the implications of the psychology of personal constructs in the field of clinical practice. Here we have striven for extensive coverage of cook-book details rather than precise logical development and economical description. The volume discusses the role of the psychotherapist and some of his stand-by techniques, the cataloguing of experience and activity data, and a schedule of diagnostic procedures. Incidentally, its two chapters on experience and activity are the much shrivelled vestiges of our early manuscript efforts, years ago. After presenting two chapters describing how our novel system of diagnostic dimensions may be used to structure illustrative types of cases, we turn to a series of detailed discussions of psychotherapeutic techniques from the standpoint of personal-construct theory. Five chapters of this conclude the volume.

And now the reader is on his own. If Volume I, from this prefatory vantage point, appears to be too abstract, he can go on to Volume II, where he may expect to find somewhat more folksy reading.

G. A. K.

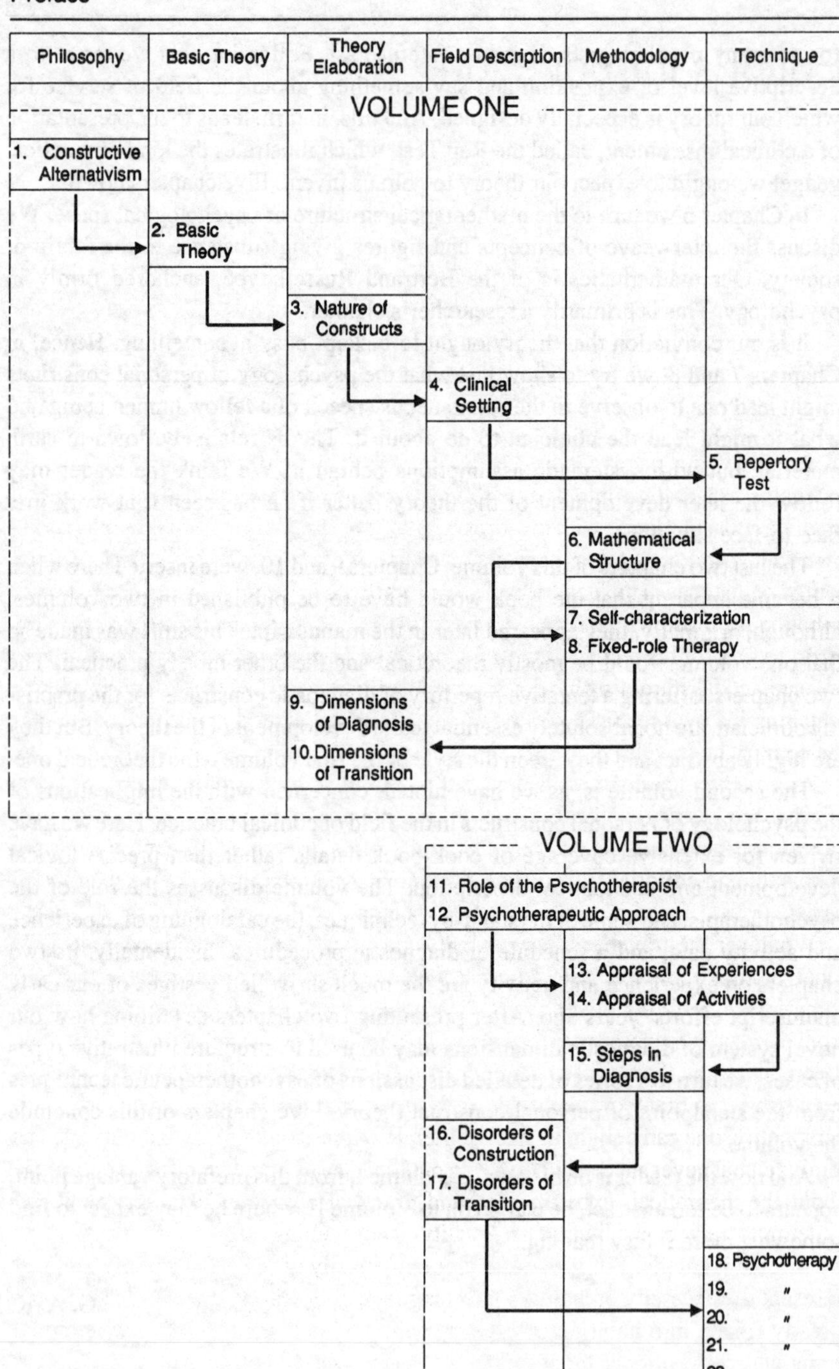
Philosophy
Basic Theory
Theory Elaboration
Field Description
Methodology
Technique
VOLUME ONE
1. Constructive Alternativism
2. Basic Theory
3. Nature of Constructs
4. Clinical Setting
5. Repertory Test
6. Mathematical Structure
7. Self-characterization
8. Fixed-role Therapy
9. Dimensions of Diagnosis
10. Dimensions of Transition
VOLUME TWO
11. Role of the Psychotherapist
12. Psychotherapeutic Approach
13. Appraisal of Experiences
14. Appraisal of Activities
15. Steps in Diagnosis
16. Disorders of Construction
17. Disorders of Transition
18. Psychotherapy
19. "
20. "
21. "
22. "

Figure 1 Diagram of chapter content

Editor's introduction

In the following pages George Kelly conducts, for all who care to follow, an extensive exploration into a strange new land of personality theory and clinical practice. In accordance with customary practice, Dr. Kelly, after mapping out his own routes and sequences, carried an editor with him on the trip he had planned for his colleagues. The idea behind such a test run seems to be that an editor, with empathy for those who will subsequently make the trip, can help the author in his effort to find for his reader-travellers the best of alternative pathways, to eliminate any syntactical stumbling blocks or lexical pebbles, to spare the reader the need for watching his own feet and hence free his attention for the significant contours of the country he travels.

An editor can perhaps further serve the reader by reporting his own impressions of what the journey is like. Such reporting, of course, must be accompanied by a caveat, for the editor has only one nervous system, subject to all the ills that such is heir to; and editorial travelling is done with eyes more to the paths than to the peaks.

Whatever the traveller's perspectives and filters, getting from one end to the other of this book can be a genuine adventure – a stimulating, absorbing and sometimes frustrating adventure. If one is in a mood to see familiar phenomena from a new viewpoint, old concepts in new dress, old relationships in new theoretical light, then he can take delight in following Dr. Kelly around. If one has been subject to many of the influences lying behind the author's new approach to personality, one can delight in finding literate expression of many insights one has dimly felt but never succeeded in saying out loud. If one is in a mood to be optimistic about the theoretical, experimental, and practical outcomes of a very new and systematic view of the human personality, the travelling will be very much worth the trouble it entails. But if one is either temporarily or temperamentally inclined to resent the necessity of learning new language or of learning new uses for words already frozen into habit, one will experience frustration; for both conventional terms and conventional modes of thought are politely but definitely shaken up. Sometimes one cannot even read along at one's wonted pace and stride, for the pathway takes unexpected turns – up, down, and sideways.

When one returns from this adventure and looks about the world to which one is accustomed, things are different. There is a difference in the day-to-day business of living with human personalities. One sees things one has not before noticed. One finds oneself making observations that are new to one, formulating new and unexpected sentences about human behaviour, including one's own. The adventure has resulted in changed perspectives. Such changes will probably happen to any reader, whether he is concerned with theory, with detailed testing of explicit research hypotheses, with clinical concentration on a single individual, or with everyday intricacies of relating with human beings.

It seems probable that many psychologists, of varied slants of interest, many psychiatrists, many social workers, and others who live in the world of human personality will find excitement, challenge, productive confusion, and some plain pleasure in exploring with Dr. Kelly this new land. Others, it seems safe to predict, will wish to pick up their intellectual household goods and establish residence here.

Fillmore Sanford

The psychology of personal constructs

Volume one
A theory of personality

Chapter one

Constructive alternativism

In this chapter, instead of starting immediately with a statement of our theoretical position, we reach back to uncover some of its philosophical roots. Constructive alternativism not only underlies our theory, but it is also an explicit and recurrent theme throughout our later discussion of psychotherapeutic techniques.

A. Points of departure

1. Perspectives on man

This theory of personality actually started with the combination of two simple notions: first, that man might be better understood if he were viewed in the perspective of the centuries rather than in the flicker of passing moments; and second, that each man contemplates in his own personal way the stream of events upon which he finds himself so swiftly borne. Perhaps within this interplay of the durable and the ephemeral we may discover ever more hopeful ways in which the individual man can restructure his life. The idea seems worth pursuing.

Neither the notion of man's march through the centuries nor that of his personally biased nature is especially new. The successive literature of the Old Testament portrays a well-known epic story of man's progress. Nor has the stream of the individual man's life escaped the attention of curious students. The highly articulate William James was fascinated by the currents and eddies in the stream of consciousness. The inarticulate Adolph Meyer urged his students to draw a time line through the facts in their patients' lives. The sensitive Sigmund Freud waded into the headwaters of the stream in a search for the underground springs which fed it. And the impulsive Henri Bergson jumped from the bank into the current and, as he was carried along, speculated that mind could be used as a yardstick for measuring time. As for personal ways of looking at things: Solomon, in writing about the worried man, said, 'As he thinketh in his heart, so is he.' And Shelley once wrote, 'The mind becomes that which it contemplates.' John Locke, struck by the unique imperceptiveness of each of his friends during an evening's discussion, sat down to write the *Essay Concerning Human Understanding* before retiring for the night – a task which, incidentally, he did not finish until twenty years later.

The long-range view of man leads us to turn our attention towards those factors appearing to account for his progress rather than those betraying his impulses. To a large degree – though not entirely – the blueprint of human progress has been given the label of 'science'. Let us then, instead of occupying ourselves with *man-the-biological-organism* or *man-the-lucky-guy*, have a look at *man-the-scientist*.

At this point we depart again from the usual manner of looking at things. When we speak of *man-the-scientist* we are speaking of all mankind and not merely a particular class of men who have publicly attained the stature of 'scientists'. We are speaking of all mankind in its scientist-like aspects, rather than all mankind in its biological aspects or all mankind in its appetitive aspects. Moreover, we are speaking of aspects of mankind rather than collections of men. Thus the notion of *man-the-scientist* is a particular abstraction of all mankind and not a concrete classification of particular men.

Such an abstraction of the nature of man is not altogether new. The Reformation called attention to the priesthood of all men in contrast to the concretistic classification of certain men only as priests. The democratic political inventions of the eighteenth and nineteenth centuries hinged on the notion of the inherent rulership of all men in contrast to the older notion of a concrete class of rulers. In a similar fashion we may replace the concretistic notion of scientists being set apart from nonscientists and, like the reformists who insisted that every man is his own priest, propose that every man is, in his own particular way, a scientist.

Let us see what it would mean to construe man in his scientist-like aspect. What is it that is supposed to characterize the motivation of the scientist? It is customary to say that *the scientist's ultimate aim is to predict and control*. This is a summary statement that psychologists frequently like to quote in characterizing their own aspirations. Yet, curiously enough, psychologists rarely credit the human subjects in their experiments with having similar aspirations. It is as though the psychologist were saying to himself:

> I, being a *psychologist*, and therefore a *scientist*, am performing this experiment in order to improve the prediction and control of certain human phenomena; but my subject, being merely a human organism, is obviously propelled by inexorable drives welling up within him, or else he is in gluttonous pursuit of sustenance and shelter.

Now what would happen if we were to reopen the question of human motivation and use our long-range view of man to infer just what it is that sets the course of his endeavour? Would we see his centuried progress in terms of appetites, tissue needs, or sex impulses? Or might he, in this perspective, show a massive drift of quite a different sort? Might not the individual man, each in his own personal way, assume more of the stature of a scientist, ever seeking to predict and control the course of events with which he is involved? Would he not have his theories, test his hypotheses, and weigh his experimental evidence? And, if so, might not the differences between the personal viewpoints of different men correspond to the differences between the theoretical points of view of different scientists?

Here is an intriguing idea. It stems from an attempt to consolidate the viewpoints of the clinician, the historian, the scientist, and the philosopher. But where does it lead? For considerable time now some of us have been attempting to discover the answer to this question. The present manuscript is a report of what has appeared on our horizons thus far.

2. *What kind of universe?*

All thinking is based, in part, on prior convictions. A complete philosophical or scientific system attempts to make all these prior convictions explicit. That is a large order, and there are few, if any, writers who can actually fill it. While we have no intention of trying to build a complete system at this point, it does seem to be incumbent upon us to attempt to be explicit about some of our more important prior convictions. The first of these convictions has to do with the kind of universe we envision.

We presume that the universe is really existing and that man is gradually coming to understand it. By taking this position we attempt to make clear from the outset that it is a real world we shall be talking about, not a world composed solely of the flitting shadows of people's thoughts. But we should like, furthermore, to make clear our conviction that people's thoughts also really exist, though the correspondence between what people really think exists and what really does exist is a continually changing one.

The universe that we presume exists has another important characteristic: it is integral. By that we mean it functions as a single unit with all its imaginable parts having an exact relationship to each other. This may, at first, seem a little implausible, since ordinarily it would appear that there is a closer relationship between the motion of my fingers and the action of the typewriter keys than there is, say, between either of them and the price of yak milk in Tibet. But we believe that, in the long run, all of these events – the motion of my fingers, the action of the keys, and the price of yak milk – are interlocked. It is only within a limited section of the universe, that part we call earth and that span of time we recognize as our present eon, that two of these necessarily seem more closely related to each other than either of them is to the third. A simple way of saying this is to state that *time provides the ultimate bond in all relationships*.

We can express the same idea through extrapolation from a well-known mathematical relationship. Consider the coefficient of correlation between two variables. If that coefficient is anything but zero and if it expresses a linear relationship, then an infinite increase in the variance of one of the variables will cause the coefficient to approach unity as a limit. The magnitude of the coefficient of correlation is therefore directly proportional to the breadth of perspective in which we envision the variables whose relationship it expresses. This is basically true of all relationships within our universe.

Another important prior conviction is that the universe can be measured along a dimension of time. This is a way of saying that the universe is continually changing with respect to itself. Since time is the one dimension which must always be considered if we are to contemplate change, we have chosen this particular way of saying that within our universe something is always going on. In fact, that is the way the universe exists; it exists by happening. Actually we tried to convey the same notion when we said in an earlier paragraph that the universe is really *existing*. Indeed, every day and all day it goes about its business of existing. It is hard to imagine what the world would be like if it just sat there and did nothing. Philosophers used to try to contemplate such a world, but, somehow, they never got very far with it.

The three prior convictions about the universe that we have emphasized in this section are that it is real and not a figment of our imaginations, that it all works together like clockwork, and that it is something that is going on all the time and not something that merely stays put.

3. What is life?

There are some parts of the universe which make a good deal of sense even when they are not viewed in the perspective of time. But there are other parts which make sense only when they are plotted along a time line. Life is one of the latter. This is a point about which we shall have a great deal to say later when we talk about ways to reconstruct personal lives. Whether it be the research-minded psychologist or the frantic client in the psychological clinic, life has to be seen in the perspective of time if it is to make any sense at all.

But life, to our way of thinking, is more than mere change. It involves an interesting relationship between parts of our universe wherein one part, the living creature, is able to bring himself around to represent another part, his environment. Sometimes it is said that the living thing is 'sensitive', in contrast to the nonliving thing, or that he is capable of 'reaction'. This is roughly the same distinctive characteristic of life that we envision. But we like our formulation better because *it emphasizes the creative capacity of the living thing to represent the environment, not merely to respond to it.* Because he can represent his environment, he can place alternative constructions upon it and, indeed, do something about it if it doesn't suit him. To the living creature, then, the universe is real, but it is not inexorable unless he chooses to construe it that way.

In emphasizing the prior conviction that life involves the representation or construction of reality, we should not imply that life is not itself real. Sometimes scientists, particularly those who are engrossed in the study of physical systems, take the stand that psychological events are not true phenomena but are rather epiphenomena, or merely the unreliable shadows of real events. This position is not ours. A person may misrepresent a real phenomenon, such as his income or his ills, and yet his misrepresentation will itself be entirely real. This applies even to the badly deluded patient: what he perceives may not exist, but his perception does. Moreover, his fictitious perception will often turn out to be a grossly distorted construction of something which actually does exist. Any living creature, together with his perceptions, is a part of the real world; he is not merely a near-sighted bystander to the goings-on of the real world.

Life, then, to our way of thinking, is characterized by its essential measurability in the dimension of time and its capacity to represent other forms of reality, while still retaining its own form of reality.

4. Construction systems

Man looks at his world through transparent patterns or templets which he creates and then attempts to fit over the realities of which the world is composed. The fit is not always very good. Yet without such patterns the world appears to be such an undifferentiated homogeneity that man is unable to make any sense out of it. Even a poor fit is more helpful to him than nothing at all.

Let us give the name *constructs* to these patterns that are tentatively tried on for size. They are ways of construing the world. They are what enables man, and lower animals too, to chart a course of behaviour, explicitly formulated or implicitly acted out, verbally expressed or utterly inarticulate, consistent with other courses of behaviour or inconsistent with them, intellectually reasoned or vegetatively sensed.

In general man seeks to improve his constructs by increasing his repertory, by altering them to provide better fits, and by subsuming them with superordinate constructs or systems. In seeking improvement he is repeatedly halted by the damage to the system that apparently will result from the alteration of a subordinate construct. Frequently his personal investment in the larger system, or his personal dependence upon it, is so great that he will forego the adoption of a more precise construct in the substructure. It may take a major act of psychotherapy or experience to get him to adjust his construction system to the point where the new and more precise construct can be incorporated.

Those construction systems which can be communicated can be widely shared. The last half century has shown much progress in the development of ways of making personal constructs and construction systems more communicable. We have developed a scientific psychological vocabulary. A better way of saying this is that our public construction systems for understanding other people's personal constructs are becoming more precise and more comprehensive.

Certain widely shared or public construction systems are designed primarily to fit special fields or realms of facts. When one limits the realm of facts, it is possible to develop a detailed system without worrying about the inconsistencies in the system which certain peripheral facts would reveal. We limit the *realm* and try to ignore, for the time being, the intransigent facts just outside the borders of that *realm*. For example, it has long been customary and convenient to distinguish between 'mental' and 'physical' facts. These are two artificially distinguished realms, to which two types of construction systems are respectively fitted: the psychological construction system and the natural-science group of construction systems. It is becoming increasingly clear, however, that we have on our hands two alternative construction systems, which can both be applied profitably to an ever increasing body of the same facts. The realms overlap.

Consider more specifically the realms of psychology and physiology. These realms have been given tentative boundaries based upon the presumed ranges of convenience of the psychological and the physiological construction systems, respectively. But many of the same facts can be construed within either system. Are those facts 'psychological facts' or are they 'physiological facts'? Where do they really belong? Who gets possession of them, the psychologist or the physiologist? While this may seem like a silly question, one has only to sit in certain interdisciplinary staff conferences to see it arise in the discussions between people of different professional guilds. Some individuals can get badly worked up over the protection of their exclusive rights to construe particular facts.

The answer is, of course, that the events upon which facts are based hold no institutional loyalties. They are in the public domain. The same event may be construed simultaneously and profitably within various disciplinary systems – physics, physiology, political science, or psychology.

No one has yet proved himself wise enough to propound a universal system of constructs. We can safely assume that it will be a long time before a satisfactorily unified system will be proposed. For the time being we shall have to content ourselves with a series of miniature systems, each with its own realm or limited range of convenience. As long as we continue to use such a disjointed combination of miniature systems we shall have to be careful to apply each system abstractly rather than concretively. For example, instead of saying that a certain event is a 'psychological event and therefore not a physiological event', we must be careful to recognize that any event may be viewed either in its psychological or in its physiological aspects. A further idea that we must keep straight is that the physiologically constructed facts about that event are the offspring of the physiological system within which they emerge and have meaning, and that a psychological system is not obliged to account for them.

It is also important that we continue to recognize the limited ranges of convenience of our miniature systems. It is always tempting, once a miniature system has proved itself useful within a limited range of convenience, to try to extend its range of convenience. For example, in the field of psychology we have seen Hull's mathematico-deductive theory of rote learning extended to the realm of problem solving or even to the realm of personality. Freud's psychoanalysis started out as a psychotherapeutic technique but was progressively enlarged into a personality system and, by some, into a religio-philosophical system. This kind of inflation of miniature systems is not necessarily a bad thing, but it does cause trouble when one fails to recognize that what is reasonably true within a limited range is not necessarily quite so true outside that range.

Any psychological system is likely to have a limited range of convenience. In fact, psychological systems may, for some time to come, have to get along with more limited ranges of convenience than psychologists would like. The system or theory which we are about to expound and explore has a limited range of convenience, its range being restricted, as far as we can see at this moment, to human personality and, more particularly, to problems of interpersonal relationships.

Not only do systems, psychological and otherwise, tend to have limited ranges of convenience, but they also have foci of convenience. There are points within its realm of events where a system or a theory tends to work best. Usually these are the points which the author had in mind when he devised the system. For example, our own theory, we believe, tends to have its focus of convenience in the area of human readjustment to stress. Thus it should prove most useful to the psychotherapist because we were thinking primarily of the problems of psychotherapy when we formulated it.

In this section we hoped to make clear our conviction that man creates his own ways of seeing the world in which he lives; the world does not create them for him. He builds constructs and tries them on for size. His constructs are sometimes organized into systems, groups of constructs which embody subordinate and superordinate relationships. The same events can often be viewed in the light of two or more systems. Yet the events do not belong to any system. Moreover, man's practical systems have particular foci and limited ranges of convenience.

5. Constructs as grounds for predictions

We started out with two notions: (1) that, viewed in the perspective of the centuries, man might be seen as an incipient scientist, and (2) that each individual man formulates in his own way constructs through which he views the world of events. As a scientist, man seeks to predict, and thus control, the course of events. It follows, then, that the constructs which he formulates are intended to aid him in his predictive efforts.

We have not yet tried to be very explicit about what a construct is. That undertaking is reserved for a later chapter. But we have already said enough to indicate that we consider a construct to be a representation of the universe, a representation erected by a living creature and then tested against the reality of that universe. Since the universe is essentially a course of events, the testing of a construct is a testing against subsequent events. In other words, a construct is tested in terms of its predictive efficiency.

Actually the testing of a construct in terms of its predictive efficiency may turn out to be a somewhat redundant affair. A man construes his neighbour's behaviour as hostile. By that he means that his neighbour, given the proper opportunity, will do him harm. He tries out his construction of his neighbour's attitude by throwing rocks at his neighbour's dog. His neighbour responds with an angry rebuke. The man may then believe that he has validated his construction of his neighbour as a hostile person.

The man's construction of his neighbour as a hostile person may appear to be 'validated' by another kind of fallacy. The man reasons, 'If my neighbour is hostile, he will be eager to know when I get into trouble, when I am ill, or when I am in any way vulnerable. I will watch to see if this isn't so.' The next morning the man meets his neighbour and is greeted with the conventional, 'How are you?' Sure enough, the neighbour is doing just what was predicted of a hostile person!

Just as constructs are used to forecast events, so they must also be used to assess the accuracy of the forecast, after the events have occurred. Man would be hopelessly bogged down in his biases if it were not for the fact that he can usually assess the outcomes of his predictions at a different level of construction from that at which he originally makes them. A man bets that a horse will win a certain race because it is black and he has recently won with a black hand at poker. When the race results are in, however, he is likely to construe the announced decision of the judges as being more palpable evidence of the horse's performance in the race than is the horse's colour.

When constructs are used to predict immediate happenings, they become more susceptible to change or revision. The validational evidence is quickly available. If they are used solely to predict an event in the remote future, such as life after death or the end of the world, they are not likely to be so open to revision. Besides, most people are in no hurry to collect validational evidence in such matters.

A good scientist tries to bring his constructs up for test as soon as possible. But he tries them out initially in test-tube proportions. If hazards appear to be great, he will first seek some indirect evidence on the probable outcome of his trials. This straightforward testing of constructs is one of the features of the experimental method in modern science. It also characterizes any alert person.

But there are times when a person hesitates to experiment because he dreads the outcome. He may fear that the conclusion of the experiment will place him in an ambiguous position where he will no longer be able to predict and control. He does not want to be caught with his constructs down. He may even keep his constructs strictly to himself lest he be trapped into testing them prematurely. This reluctance either to express or to test one's constructs is, of course, one of the practical problems which confront the psychotherapist in dealing with his client. We shall have more to say about these issues later.

Constructs are used for predictions of things to come, and the world keeps rolling along and revealing these predictions to be either correct or misleading. This fact provides the basis for revision of constructs and, eventually, of whole construction systems. If it were a static world that we lived in, our thinking about it might be static too. But new things keep happening and our predictions keep turning out in expected or unexpected ways. Each day's experience calls for the consolidation of some aspects of our outlook, revision of some, and outright abandonment of others.

What we have said about the experience of the individual man holds true also for the scientist. A scientist formulates a theory – a body of constructs with a focus and a range of convenience. If he is a good scientist, he immediately starts putting it to test. It is almost certain that, as soon as he starts testing, he will also have to start changing it in the light of the outcomes. Any theory, then, tends to be transient. And the more practical it is and the more useful it appears to be, the more vulnerable it is to new evidence. Our own theory, particularly if it proves to be practical, will also have to be considered expendable in the light of tomorrow's outlooks and discoveries. At best it is an *ad interim* theory.

B. The philosophical position

6. Statement of constructive alternativism

Enough has already been said to make clear our position that there are various ways in which the world is construed. Some of them are undoubtedly better than others. They are better from our human point of view because they support more precise and more accurate predictions about more events. No one has yet devised a set of constructs which will predict everything down to the last tiny flutter of a humming-bird's wing; we think it will be an infinitely long time before anyone does. Since an absolute construction of the universe is not feasible, we shall have to be content with a series of successive approximations to it. These successive approximations can, in turn, be tested piecemeal for their predictive efficiency. Essentially this means that all of our interpretations of the universe can gradually be scientifically evaluated if we are persistent and keep on learning from our mistakes.

We assume that all of our present interpretations of the universe are subject to revision or replacement. This is a basic statement which has a bearing upon almost everything that we shall have to say later. We take the stand that there are always some alternative constructions available to choose among in dealing with the world. No one needs to paint himself into a corner; no one needs to be completely hemmed in by circumstances; no one needs to be the victim of his biography. We call this philosophical position *constructive alternativism.*

We have now said enough about the testing of constructs to indicate that it is not a matter of indifference which of a set of alternative constructions one chooses to impose upon one's world. Constructs cannot be tossed about willy-nilly without a person's getting into difficulty. While there are always alternative constructions available, some of them are definitely poor implements. The yardstick to use is the specific predictive efficiency of the system of which it would, if adopted, become a part.

7. Philosophy or psychology?

Scholars customarily distinguish sharply between the forms of thought and the actual thinking behaviour of people. The study of the former is classified under *philosophy* – or more particularly, *logic* – while the latter is considered to be *psychology.* But we have taken the basic view that whatever is characteristic of thought is descriptive of the thinker; that the essentials of scientific curiosity must underlie human curiosity in general. If we examine a person's philosophy closely, we find ourselves staring at the person himself. If we reach an understanding of how a person behaves, we discover it in the manner in which he represents his circumstances to himself.

A person is not necessarily articulate about the constructions he places upon his world. Some of his constructions are not symbolized by words; he can express them only in pantomime. Even the elements which are construed may have no verbal handles by which they can be manipulated and the person finds himself responding to them with speechless impulse. Thus, in studying the psychology of man-the-philosopher, we must take into account his subverbal patterns of representation and construction.

What we are proposing is neither a conventional philosophy nor a conventional psychology. As a philosophy it is rooted in the psychological observation of man. As a psychology it is concerned with the philosophical outlooks of individual man. Upon this framework we propose to erect a limited psychological theory.

8. Relation to philosophical systems

Constructive alternativism represents a philosophical point of view, but we have no intention of trying to elaborate it into a complete philosophical system. It may, however, be useful to attempt to plot its position roughly with respect to some of the types of philosophical systems with which scholars are familiar.

Realm-wise, constructive alternativism falls within that area of epistemology which is sometimes called *gnosiology* – the 'systematic analysis of the conceptions employed by ordinary and scientific thought in interpreting the world, and including an investigation of the art of knowledge, or the nature of knowledge as such'. The emphasis upon the constructs through which the world is scanned suggests *positivism*, although most of the criticisms that are levelled at Comte are not applicable here. Comte's positivism is too often deprecated in terms of some of his concrete proposals rather than evaluated in terms of the abstract features of the system.

Our emphasis upon the testing of constructs implies our reliance upon the principles of *empiricism* and, more particularly, *pragmatic logic.* In this respect we are in the tradition of present-day American psychology. But, because we recognize that man approaches his world through construing it, we are, in a measure, *rationalistic.* Moreover, since we insist that man can erect his own alternative approaches to reality, we are out of line with traditional *realism*, which insists that he is always the victim of his circumstances.

Ontologically, our position is identifiable as a form of *monism*, although, in view of the many complex varieties of ontology, the differentiation of its monistic from its pluralistic aspects is hardly worth the effort. If it is a monism, it is a *substantival* monism that we are talking about; yet it is *neutral*, and, like Spinoza, we are prepared to apply *attributive pluralism* to the substance whenever our purposes might be served thereby.

Two classical issues remain to be discussed: *determinism vs. free will*, and *phenomenology*. Since both problems have to be with our design specifications for a theory of personality, we reserve the discussion of them for the next division of this chapter.

9. The realm of psychology

The realm of psychology is limited practically to that which can be spanned by whatever psychological theory we happen to be using at the moment. The theory's range of convenience is what determines the boundaries of the discipline. A range of convenience is that expanse of the real world over which a given system or theory provides useful coverage. Those features of the universe which do not fit neatly into the system are left out of the psychological realm for the time being. If we are reasonably good psychologists, there should still be enough of the universe remaining for us to make ourselves useful by structuring it. Later, if our theoretical reasoning is extended, further areas may fall within our ken.

There are, of course, various psychological construction systems. These systems differ primarily because the people who developed them were focusing their attention upon somewhat different events. Psychological systems have not only ranges of convenience but also characteristic foci of convenience: points at which they are particularly applicable. Thus stimulus–response theories are particularly convenient at the focal point of animal learning, field theories at the focal point of human perception, and psychoanalytic theories at the focal point of human neurosis.

There is no clear criterion by which a theory can be labelled 'psychological', and not 'physiological' or 'sociological'. There is much interrelationship. The stimulus–response theories in psychology bear a close family resemblance to the interaction theories of physiology. There are field theories in physiology which resemble the psychology of Gestalt. Whether a theory is called 'psychological', 'physiological', or 'sociological' probably depends upon its original focus of convenience.

10. The function of a theory

A theory may be considered as a way of binding together a multitude of facts so that one may comprehend them all at once. When the theory enables us to make reasonably precise predictions, one may call it scientific. If its predictions are so elastic that a wide variety of conceivable events can be construed as corroborative, the theory fails to meet the highest standards of science.

A theory need not be highly scientific in order to be useful. All of us order the daily events of our lives by constructions that are somewhat elastic. Under these constructions our anticipations of daily events, while not scientifically precise, nevertheless surround our lives with an aura of meaning. Because life does not seem wholly capricious we are prepared by our personal construction systems to take each day's new experience in our stride.

But this is not all. A theory provides a basis for an active approach to life, not merely a comfortable armchair from which to contemplate its vicissitudes with detached complaisance. Mankind need not be a throng of stony-faced spectators witnessing the pageant of creation. Men can play active roles in the shaping of events. How they can be free to do this and still themselves be construed as lawful beings is a basic issue in any psychological theory.

The answer lies, first of all, in our recognition of the essentially active nature of our universe. The world is not an abandoned monument. It is an event of tremendous proportions, the conclusion of which is not yet apparent. The theories that men employ to construe this event are themselves incidents in the mammoth procession. The truths the theories attempt to fix are successive approximations to the larger scheme of things which slowly they help to unfold. Thus a theory is a tentative expression of what man has seen as a regular pattern in the surging events of life. But the theory, being itself an event, can in turn be subsumed by another theory, or by a superordinate part of itself, and that in turn can be subsumed by another. A theory is thus bound only by the construction system of which it is understood to be a part – and, of course, the binding is only temporary, lasting only as long as that particular superordinate system is employed.

11. Determinism and man's free will

A theory binds or determines the events which are subordinated to it. It is not determined by the events themselves; it is determined by the superordinating point of view of the theorist. Yet it must conform to events in order to predict them. The number of alternative ways of conforming are, as far as we know, infinite, but discriminable from the infinite number of ways which do not conform.

A person is to cut a pie. There is an infinite number of ways of going about it, all of which may be relevant to the task. If the pie is frozen, some of the usual ways of cutting the pie may not work – but there is still an infinite number of ways of going about it. But suppose the pie is on the table and there is company present. Certain limiting expectations have been set up about how a meal is to be served. The pie is construed as part of the meal. There are also certain conventions about serving wedge-shaped slices with the point always turned toward the diner. If one accepts all the usual superordinating constructions of the situation, he may, indeed, find his course of behaviour determined and very little latitude left to him. He is not the victim of the pie, but of his notions of etiquette under which the pie cutting has been subsumed.

But suppose the pie makes him sick. Is he not then a victim of circumstances? We might then ask why he ate it in the first place. We could even suggest that his illness need not rob him of his freedom. The illness may even increase his scope of action, as many children and hypochondriacs have discovered.

The relation established by a construct or a construction system over its subordinate elements is deterministic. In this sense the tendency to subordinate constitutes determinism. The natural events themselves do not subordinate our constructions of them; we can look at them in any way we like. But, of course, if we wish to predict natural events accurately, we need to erect some kind of construction which will serve the purpose. But the events do not come around and tell us how to do the job – they just go about their business of being themselves. The structure we erect is what rules us.

Actually there are two forms of determinism which concern us. The one is the determinism which is the essential feature of any organized construction system – the control of superordinate constructs over subordinate elements. The second is implied in our notion of an integral universe. The universe as it flows along is not essentially divided into independent events like cars on a railroad train. It is an essential continuity. Because of this continuity we may consider that there is determinism operating between antecedent and subsequent events. This is the continuity which is assumed in the so-called First Postulate of Logic, the Postulate of Cosmic Connectedness.

But the second kind of determinism is, to our way of thinking, relatively unimportant. The universe flows on and on. While one may abstract certain repetitive features in its course, it never actually doubles back on itself. Matters would become enormously confused if it ever did. (The very idea of a universe that doubled back on itself is highly amusing and might even have some relativistic significance for a cosmic theorist.) Since we assume that the universe does not double back on itself, any sequence of events is the only sequence of its exact identical sort that ever occurred. It is inconceivable, then, that any sequence could have occurred in any way other than that in which it did without losing its identity. Since no event could possibly have happened otherwise and still have been itself, there is not much point in singling it out and saying that it was determined. It was a consequent – but only once!

We are left with one important kind of determinism, the control of a superordinate construct over its elements. It should now become clear what is not determined. For one thing, an element does not determine the constructs which are used to subsume it; for another, an element which falls outside the purview of a construct is independent of it. The latter type of independence or freedom is relatively unimportant to us; it is only the freedom of chaos. The former type of independence or freedom is highly significant, for it implies that man, to the extent that he is able to construe his circumstances, can find for himself freedom from their domination. It implies also that man can enslave himself with his own ideas and then win his freedom again by reconstruing his life. This is, in a measure, the theme upon which this book is based.

One thing more: since determinism characterizes the control that a construct exercises over its subordinate elements, freedom characterizes its independence of those elements. Determinism and freedom are then inseparable, for that which determines another is, by the same token, free of the other. Determinism and freedom are opposite sides of the same coin – two aspects of the same relationship. This is an important point for a man to grasp, whether he be a scholar or a neurotic – or both!

Ultimately a man sets the measure of his own freedom and his own bondage by the level at which he chooses to establish his convictions. The man who orders his life in terms of many special and inflexible convictions about temporary matters makes himself the victim of circumstances. Each little prior conviction that is not open to review is a hostage he gives to fortune; it determines whether the events of tomorrow will bring happiness or misery. The man whose prior convictions encompass a broad perspective, and are cast in terms of principles rather than rules, has a much better chance of discovering those alternatives which will lead eventually to his emancipation.

Theories are the thinking of men who seek freedom amid swirling events. The theories comprise prior assumptions about certain realms of these events. To the extent that the events may, from these prior assumptions, be construed, predicted, and their relative courses charted, men may exercise control, and gain freedom for themselves in the process.

C. Design specifications for a psychological theory of personality

12. Theoretical models and foci of convenience

American psychology has recently turned much of its attention to the problems of theory building. There has been a revival of interest in philosophy, particularly in the philosophy of science. Just as philosophers have begun to look around to see what various kinds of thinking men are actually doing, so psychologists have begun to look around to see what kinds of theories scientists in other realms have actually been producing. This is new. To be sure, psychologists used to look to the methodology and the content of physiology as grounds upon which to build their own new structure. Then physiology was accepted because its facts were presumed to be real and its methods appeared to be validated by the palpability of its facts. But now psychologists have begun to compare and contrast the theoretical structures which characterize a variety of other disciplines. From this examination of what is going on elsewhere some of them hope to discover a still better theoretical model for psychology.

But we are sceptical about the value of copying ready-made theories which were designed for other foci of convenience. Psychology has already achieved some success in developing its own theoretical and methodological approaches. It might now be a good plan to start abstracting the scientific principles which are beginning to emerge from our experiences as well as others', instead of poking about in the neighbours' back yards for methodological windfalls. If we learn something of the principles of theory construction, we can start building psychological theories which are adapted to psychological foci of convenience. Our position, then, would be that we should examine a variety of scientific theories, not to find one which can be copied concretely, but to discover common principles which can be applied to the building of brand-new theories especially designed to fit psychology's realm of events.

At this point there should be no doubt about our stand on two things that it takes to build a psychological theory. The perspective should be broad and should take cognizance of principles which emerge in the comparison of various theoretical structures. And the theorist should also have something to theorize about. Otherwise, he may spend his time building a fancy theory about nothing: his theory will have no focus of convenience. He should be intimately aware of a range of problems to be solved if he is not to waste his own time and that of his readers with the exposition of his theory.

The focus of convenience which we have chosen for our own theory-building efforts is the psychological reconstruction of life. We are concerned with finding better ways to help a person reconstrue his life so that he need not be the victim of his past. If the theory we construct works well within this limited range of convenience, we shall consider our efforts successful, and we shall not be too much disturbed if it proves to be less useful elsewhere.

13. Fertility in a psychological theory

We have already noted that a theory may be considered as a way of binding together a multitude of facts. But a good theory also performs more active functions. It provides an explicit framework within which certain deductions may be made and future events anticipated. It also provides a general framework within which certain facts may be held in place, pending one's induction of some specific principle among them. In both senses the theory acts as a tool for the man who actively seeks to anticipate the future and to explore its possibilities.

One of the criteria of a good scientific theory is its fertility in producing new ideas. It should lead to the formulation of hypotheses; it should provoke experiments; and it should inspire invention. In the field of psychology a good theory should suggest predictions concerning people's behaviour in a wide range of circumstances. It should lead to extensive psychological research to determine whether or not those predictions can be substantiated. It should also encourage the invention of new approaches to the solution of the problems of man and his society.

14. Testable hypotheses

Another criterion of a good psychological theory is its production of hypotheses which are testable. In contrast to other construction systems, any scientific theory should enable one to make predictions so precise that they are immediately subject to incontrovertible verification. This means that the hypotheses which are deducted from the theory should be brittle enough to be shattered whenever the facts they lead one to anticipate fail to materialize.

The theory itself need not be so fragile as its offspring hypotheses. If it is a comprehensive theory it is likely to possess some degree of elasticity even though the hypotheses deduced from it are brittle. Rarely does a scientific theory wholly stand or fall on the outcome of a single crucial experiment. Especially is this true in the field of psychology, where theories must necessarily be written at a high level of abstraction.

15. Validity

An acceptable scientific theory should also meet another requirement. While it need not itself have the palpable truthfulness of a cold fact, it should, in the hands of thoughtful people yield a succession of hypotheses which, in the light of experimentation, do turn out to be palpably true. When a theory produces a hypothesis which turns out to be verifiable, it is in a strict sense the hypothesis only which is substantiated and not the theory. As we have already indicated, it is difficult ever to say that one has validated a theory; the most that one can ordinarily say is that the hypotheses turned out by a certain theory usually prove to be valid. But who knows; the same hypotheses might have been produced by other theories. In that case the other theories are at least as valid as the first one.

Sometimes scientists design experiments so that hypotheses derived from different theories are tested in competition with each other. The hypothesis which received the more clear-cut support scores in favour of its sponsoring theory. Suppose, for example, a researcher is eager to determine whether the psychoanalytic theory of Freud, with its attendant therapeutic procedures, is better than the self-concept theory of Rogers, with its attendant client-centred procedures. Suppose he sets up an elaborate experiment, controlling such tricky variables as type of client, type of therapist, type of clinical setting, type of society, and so on. Suppose, also, he finds a suitable yardstick for measuring results – one which is not biased towards either theory and its implied standards of what constitutes mental health. Then suppose – what is, of course, highly unlikely – the experiment comes off without a hitch and the results indicate a greater therapeutic success with one of the procedures than with the other. While this provides some important evidence in favour of the favoured theory, it does not necessarily provide grounds for abandonment of the less favoured theory. There are always other issues which can be formulated and considered. The populations sampled in the study may not represent all the kinds of person to whom the theories relate. The relative economy of training a group of therapists under the aegis of one theory may give it certain practical advantages which outweigh its disadvantages in the controlled experiment. Indeed it is almost impossible to give any comprehensive theory the final *coup de grâce*.

Occasionally an experiment is designed in which the rival hypotheses are mutually incompatible. For example, one theory might lead us to hypothesize that a certain kind of client would commit suicide immediately and the other to predict that he would continue to live a long and productive life. Obviously he cannot do both. In this kind of experiment one of the two hypotheses is likely to collapse, although there is always some little ground left for equivocation. But what happens to the theory behind the discredited hypothesis? Not necessarily very much. As we have already indicated, a comprehensive theory is so formulated that the fragile hypotheses which are deduced from it are not inescapable. The deduction of a hypothesis is always a somewhat loose affair, and the next experimenter who comes along may not agree that the discredited hypothesis was a necessary derivative of the theory in the first place.

By and large, however, a theory continually yielding hypotheses that lead experimenters up blind alleys is not to be considered valid, even though one may argue that some of the blame rests with the experimenters. A theory is an implement in man's quest for a better understanding of the future. If it does not serve its purpose, it is meaningless to say that it is valid. The theory becomes valid only when someone is able to make use of it to produce verifiable hypotheses.

16. Generality

Sometimes people make the mistake of assuming that a theory is the same as the accumulation of a certain body of facts, rather than a set of principles which appertain to the facts. It is easy to make this mistake, since often the facts assume their particular shapes only in the light of a certain theory. But the essentially abstract nature of the theoretical structure is lost sight of when the facts which it yields are simply classified and concretistically designated.

For example, the Kraepelinian nosological system in psychiatry is generally used as a set of diagnostic pigeonholes into which to stuff troublesome clients. The principles which originally gave it its dimensional structure have long since been discarded or lost sight of altogether. Almost without exception the system is used concretistically. Now contrast with current usage of the Kraepelinian system the use of the psychoanalytic system. Here the diagnosis is in terms of features of the case rather than its categorical classification. The diagnostician can see the case from more than one angle at once. Hence he is not so likely to confuse the abstraction of dynamics, with which each case is shot through, with the concrete lumping of the case with others of its kind.

Yet even psychoanalytic psychodynamics are often handled concretistically by adherents to the system. A patient is seen as 'having Oedipal strivings', as if the strivings had taken possession of him. If the concept of Oedipal striving were used more abstractly, the patient would be evaluated with respect to the Oedipal striving dimension rather than described as 'having it'. The difference may seem obscure, but perhaps an analogy from physics will help make the point clearer. Suppose the physicist lifted an object and said, 'By golly, this has weight!' This would not be a very meaningful statement since, presumably, all bodies have weight. Actually, he is treating the abstract property of weight as if it were a commodity. A careful physicist is much more likely to say, 'The weight of this body is greater than the weight of that one.' The property of weight is abstracted and the other features of the two bodies are disregarded for the time being. It is a system composed of this kind of abstraction that modern psychological theory builders seek to devise.

A good psychological theory should be expressed in terms of abstractions which are of a sufficiently high order to be traced through nearly all of the phenomena with which psychology must deal. It should concern itself initially with properties rather than with categories, although the properties may subsequently be used as grounds for isolating categories. If the abstractions are well taken, they will possess a generality which will make them useful in dealing with a great variety of practical problems. For example, if there should be abstracted within the field of psychology a property which had the generality that *mass* has in the field of physics, it might prove immensely useful. Moreover, any psychological theory that possesses generality throughout its structure is likely to be more valuable than one which is essentially a grouping of specific categories of persons and behaviours.

17. Operationalism

The writing of the physicist Bridgeman has recently had considerable influence among psychological theorists. There has been a new emphasis upon the need for operational definition of the variables envisioned in one's experiments. Carried to the extreme that some psychologists would carry it, this would mean that no theoretical statement could be made unless each part referred to something palpable. It is this kind of extremism which has led to the quip that while psychiatrists would rather be abstruse than right, psychologists would rather be wrong than abstruse.

Operationalism also implies something else. It implies that scientific constructs are best defined in terms of operations or regular sequences of events. Thus, whatever it is that links an antecedent to its consequent may be called an intervening variable, and merely a statement of the antecedent–consequent linkage is all the definition the variable ever needs. MacCorquodale and Meehl suggest that it is better for psychologists to stick to this way of conceptualizing variables lest they forget themselves and think they have to start looking for some unknown objects which constitute the variables. For example, a not too bright physiologically minded psychologist might go looking for the IQ with a microscope. Not that he wouldn't be successful; he might even win the Nobel Prize by pointing to something like a kink in a chromosome.

Variables may be operationally conceptualized by psychologists in different ways. In a time-and-motion study a variable may be a therblig – a unit of motion of some part of the body. The antecedent and consequent conditions are relatively easy to identify. But in some experiments the operational definition of the principal variable is more complex. In personnel selection and training studies the identification of the criterion – the measure of what it is we want to improve through selection and training – is itself a difficult problem. Yet the criterion has to be settled upon before one can get down to brass tacks. Even after the experimenters have agreed on what they will use as a criterion, the value of the ensuing study is limited by the way in which the definition has to be written. For example, in studies dealing with the selection and training of aircraft pilots it has been customary to use the so-called *pass–fail criterion* – the consequent condition is whether or not the selectee or trainee eventually gets his wings. But it is quite appropriate for a critic to complain that getting one's wings does not necessarily mean being a good pilot.

Sometimes the antecedent and consequent conditions, which are agreed upon as giving a variable an operational definition, are themselves in need of operational definition. In the field of personality the term *anxiety* is used to explain all kinds of different behaviours. Indeed, asking a psychiatrist to explain neurotic behaviour without recourse to the concept of *anxiety* is like asking a jockey to win a race without riding a horse. Yet how can *anxiety* be given an operational definition? We may say that the antecedent and consequent conditions are stress and disorganization, respectively. But then we are faced with the need for defining *stress* and *disorganization*. If, eventually, we end up saying that stress is what causes anxiety, and disorganization is what is produced by anxiety, we are back at our starting point and slightly out of breath from having expended a few thousand well-chosen words. Since *stress* and *disorganization* are both rather high-level abstractions, it is necessary, in dealing with any client or in performing any experiment involving anxiety, to find, in turn, more concrete operational definitions for the antecedent and consequent conditions.

As we see it, operationalism interposes no ultimate objection to the use of such a term as anxiety; it means only that when one seeks ultimate proof of some anxiety function through experimentation one will have to define one's operations explicitly. Operationalism is of primary concern for the experimenter; it is of only secondary concern for the theorist. The terms in which a theory is stated do not need to carry their own operational definitions on their backs, though if the theory is to be productive it should, in the hands of experimentally minded psychologists, lead to research with operationally defined variables.

One of the hazards of operationalism is its tendency to make researchers think concretistically. It encourages experimenters to see things rather than principles. Yet, it is not things that a scientist accumulates and catalogues; it is the principles or the abstractions that strike through the things with which he is concerned. Thus a good scientist can penetrate a bewildering mass of concrete events and come to grips with an orderly principle. The principle is not the aggregate of all the events; it is rather a property, so abstracted that it can be seen as pertinent to all of them.

For example, in designing an experiment having to do with intelligence, a psychologist may have to give *intelligence* an operational definition in terms of specific scores obtained by his subjects on a certain test. This is a practical expedient. Yet, if he gets his nose too close to his data sheets, he may forget the abstractive nature of the concept and think that *intelligence* is just another name for the scores he has written down. Originally intelligence was abstracted as a property of many different behaviour situations and it owes no special allegiance to a test. It was the headlong urgency of writing an operational definition that distracted the psychologist into thinking so concretively about intelligence.

18. Modifiability

There is another feature of good scientific theorizing which is not so much a property of theories themselves as it is of those who use them. A theory should be considered as modifiable and, ultimately, expendable. Sometimes theorists get so pinned down to deductive reasoning that they think their whole structure will fall down if they turn around and start modifying their assumptions in the light of their subsequent observations. One of the characteristics of modern scientific theorizing is the opening it leaves for inductive reasoning following the outcome of experiments.

To be sure, experiments are designed around hypotheses which are temporarily assumed to be true. From these tentative hypotheses one hazards specific predictions. If the predictions do not materialize, and if the scientist sees no other angle, he is free to abandon his hypotheses, and he should lose no sleep when he does. How long one should hang on to his assumptions in the fact of mounting contrary evidence is pretty much a matter of taste. Certainly he should not abandon them the first time something turns out unexpectedly. To do that is to make himself the victim of circumstances. Generally one holds on longer to those assumptions which have more sweeping significance and readily abandons those which have only momentary relevance.

If we apply this principle to perseverance in a theoretical position, it would mean that we would consider any scientific theory as an eventual candidate for the trash can. Such an outlook may save the scientist a lot of anxiety, provided he has flexible overriding convictions that give him a feeling of personal independence of his theory. It may also prevent him from biasing his experimental results in favour of a theory which he dares not abandon.

19. What can be proved?

The function of a scientific theory is to provide a basis for making precise predictions. These predictions are formulated in terms of hypotheses and are then subjected to test. The outcome of the test may be essentially that which was predicted. If the test or experiment is properly designed, one may then conclude, with a limited amount of confidence, that the hypothesis is substantiated. The substantiation of hypotheses is really not quite as simple as this. The catch is in the design of the experiment. If the experiment is so designed that other obvious hypotheses would have expressed the same prediction, the question arises as to which hypothesis was verified. As a matter of fact, in scientific research, one never finds the ultimate proof of a given hypothesis. About the time he thinks he has such proof within his grasp, another scientist comes along with another hypothesis that provides just as plausible an explanation of the experimental results.

The usual practice is to design the experiment so that the results, whatever they may turn out to be, can best be expressed as the outcome of either of two hypotheses: the *experimental hypothesis* or the *null hypothesis*. The experimental hypothesis is the one derived from one's theoretical position or from some other systematic source. The null hypothesis represents one's prediction under random or chance conditions. If the data furnished by the experiment turn out to be rather unlikely outcomes of chance conditions, which is what one usually hopes for, one can turn to the experimental hypothesis as the most likely alternative explanation. For example, if the data are such as would be expected less than one time out of a hundred under the regime of chance, the experimenter reports that he has evidence at the coveted 1 per cent level of confidence. This is all very well until some imaginative experimenter cooks up a third hypothesis under which the same predictions would have been made.

The relevant point for the purposes of this discussion is that even the precise hypotheses which one derives from a good scientific theory are never substantiated with absolute finality, no matter how many experiments are performed. For one thing, we are always dependent upon the second-hand proof that the unlikelihood of the null hypothesis provides; for another, the null hypothesis never wholly relinquishes its claim on the data; and finally, some other plausible hypothesis may turn up unexpectedly at any time.

20. Where do hypotheses come from?

There are roughly three ways of coming up with a testable hypothesis: (1) one may deduce it from explicit theory; (2) one may induce it from observation – for example, from clinical experience; (3) one may eschew logical procedures and go after it with a statistical dragnet.

Each of these methods circumvents some of the disadvantages of the other two. The hypothetico-deductive method proceeds from a theory which, for the time being, must be considered inflexible. Sooner or later, however, the impact of unexpected experimental results must affect the logical structure, either at the hypothetical level or at the level of the theory itself. In scientific practice the question becomes one of deciding upon the stage in an experiment or in an experimental programme at which one must bow to facts. That stage, wherever it is, marks the point at which one ceases to be wholly deductive.

The hypothetico-inductive method yields to facts from the outset. Even hypotheses are formulated as minor generalizations of observed facts, and the explicit theoretical superstructure is allowed to take shape more or less as an afterthought. Again, in practice, it seems to be impossible to adhere faithfully to the hypothetico-inductive method. Facts can be seen only through the eyes of observers and are subject to whatever selections and distortions the observers' viewpoints impose upon them. Realistically, then, the hypotheses formulated are personally construed facts. They may be thought of as being deduced from the observer's implicit personal theory as much as from phenomenal events.

The statistical-dragnet method also appears to accept the priority of facts. It differs from the hypothetico–inductive or clinical method in two principal ways: the logical structure, both of hypotheses and theory, is minimized; and the facts that are brought into focus have been made available by a variety of prior observations with a variety of biases.

Dragnet hypotheses are usually stated in a much less general form and, even though supported by a cross-validation procedure, cannot be extended to other situations unless certain precarious assumptions regarding the representativeness of the known samples are made. The hypotheses are usually no more than single items on a test which are predicted to be discriminative between two subsamples separated solely on the basis of a 'criterion'.

A dragnet picks up whatever is lying around loose. The statistical method of formulating hypotheses does just that. Variables which do not account for a sizable proportion of the measured variance in the sample are not picked up by the method, even though they may be extremely significant in bringing about personal readjustments or social changes. The hypotheses which are dredged up reflect the massed bias in the status quo.

In psychology all three methods of formulating hypotheses are employed. The hypothetico-deductive method is represented in the work of the followers of Hull's learning theory. The clinico-inductive method is represented in the work of the more scientifically minded psychoanalysts. The statistical-dragnet method is represented in the bulk of current personnel-selection test research and in the work of the Minnesota group with such tests as the Strong Vocational Interest Blank and the Minnesota Multiphasic Inventory. As long as good scientific methodology is used in checking the hypotheses, all three methods are acceptable. In using them, however, one should be aware of the bias of literalism of the hypothetico-deductive method, the personal bias in the clinico-inductive method, and the popular bias in the statistical-dragnet method.

Progress under the hypothetico-deductive method is likely to be restricted to a narrow realm for some time because of the method's inherent rigidity. The clinico-inductive method, because it aligns itself with the personal-construct system of the investigator from the outset, is likely to give the impression of very rapid progress, to lead to sweeping conclusions and to cults of like-minded clinicians who establish apostolic successions for themselves through a 'laying on of hands'. The statistical-dragnet method provides a quick and sure exploitation of ideas that have already been expressed or applied. It tends to be sterile from the standpoint of developing new ideas, and it commonly falls into the error of assuming that the greatest volume defines the greatest truth.

21. Mental energy in theory design

Once the fundamental postulate of a theory is laid down, the variables, dimensions, and constructs with which one must be concerned start to become fixed. Also the knotty problems which sooner or later trick the scientist into intellectual contortions or into torturing his data with fancy statistical computations are likely to be traceable to the theory's fundamental postulate. It is therefore important that the fundamental postulate be chosen with the greatest of care.

In developing an alternative theoretical approach in the field of psychology it seems desirable to this writer to formulate a fundamental postulate which will obviate three of the particularly knotty problems which tend to entangle psychologists who use current theoretical approaches. The first and most important of these is the problem of explaining the impetus of psychological changes or the genesis of psychological processes. Here, most of us have unknowingly fallen heir to the physicists' ancient and implicit assumption of inert objects, objects which had to be conceived as being or as being ready to be pushed about by something. Not wishing to be animistic, the physicist called the something 'energy'. The scheme worked – for the physicist.

This construct of 'energy' has caused particular difficulty when imported from physics into the realm of psychology. Originally introduced to explain physical change, it has been a vital feature in a variety of other scientific theories. But in the realm of psychological phenomena it has caused confusion from the outset. It has never been possible to make a very literal translation of the concept of physical 'energy'. It is difficult to conceive of mental 'energy' as operating in anything like the closed system of economy which has been one of the useful features of its physical counterpart. In its practical application to the realm of psychology mental 'energy' bears an uncomfortable resemblance to animism or even demonology.

The construct of 'energy' is really an outgrowth of certain fundamental assumptions that physicists have found it convenient to make. By assuming that matter is composed basically of static units it became immediately necessary to account for the obvious fact that what was observed was not always static but often thoroughly active. What made the units active? Why 'energy' of course! Psychologists, therefore, by buying the notion of 'energy', had implicitly bought the same assumption of static units which had first made 'energy' a necessary construct for the physicists.

For a time psychologists had trouble deciding what it was that was propelled by 'energy'. Was it ideas or people? At last, most psychologists agreed that it was people. But what were the vehicles for the energy which prodded these obviously inert objects into action? On the verbal level it was a simple matter to ascribe energetic properties to the elements of one's personal environment by calling them 'stimuli'. Or, if one preferred, he could ascribe energetic properties to aspects of the person himself; these were called 'needs'. Thus psychology developed *push* theories based on 'stimuli' and *pull* theories based on 'needs'. But both approaches tended to be animistic, in that it was the 'stimuli' or the 'needs', rather than the person, which accounted for all the work that was done.

After berating themselves for their *naïveté* over a period of years, push psychologists now aver that the objects in one's environment do not really provide the energy for human acts: the notion is obviously preposterous. Instead, environmental goings-on have 'stimulus functions'. This means that 'stimuli' are not imbued with energy – not really – it just happens to work out that way! The pull psychologists, on the other hand, insist that the 'needs' and 'motives' which they talk about are really no more than abstractions of human behaviour. Yet these are treated as internal irritants in a creature who would otherwise continue in quiescent repose. Both theoretical groups, in their efforts to avoid an animistic interpretation of man, fall to using animistic conceptualizations of his 'stimuli' and of his 'needs'.

Lest this appear to be a captious criticism, let it be said that any theory, scientific or opportunistic, may be considered as built upon postulates and constructs which are treated as if they were true. The acceptance of the prior assumption permits tentative formulations of conclusions and opens the way for scientific experimentation. The notions of 'stimulus energy' and 'need energy' do not work out too badly in this setting: they have led to many verifiable hypotheses. In this light even outright animism, in spite of its bad repute, has at times shown its worth.

There have been attempts to give a more mechanistic slant to the notions of push and pull psychology. Yet the prior assumption of the inertness of psychological objects probably makes some form of animism almost inevitable. It seems time to reconsider this prior assumption and give life back to the person who lives it.

The purpose of this discussion is to lay the groundwork for the consideration of a fundamental postulate which would obviate the necessity for a construct of mental energy. Such a postulate may make it possible to circumvent many of the knotty problems that have entangled psychologists with the constructs of 'stimulus' and 'stimulus function', special 'needs' and 'motives'. One of the possibly distressing outcomes of this venture will be the discarding of much of what has been accumulated under the aegis of learning theory, perhaps even the abandonment of the concept of 'learning', at least in its present form.

Instead of buying the prior assumption of an inert object, either on an implicit or explicit basis, we propose to postulate a process as the point of departure for the formulation of a psychological theory. Thus the whole controversy as to what prods an inert organism into action becomes a dead issue. Instead, the organism is delivered fresh into the psychological world alive and struggling.

Such a notion of the object of psychologists' curiosity may eventually produce an analogue for physicists to conjure with in their own domain. Indeed, some already have. The construct of matter as motion–form has already been explored by some physicists, though the yield of new testable hypotheses has not yet made the venture clearly profitable.

22. Which way will a man turn?

Next to the problem of what accounts for the fact that a man moves at all is the problem of the direction his movement will take. This is the second of the knotty problems which tend to entangle psychologists who use current theoretical approaches. Generally psychologists have approached it with the same set of constructs which they have used to explain the fact that he moves at all. The push psychologists have assumed that each stimulus, or some resultant vector of all past stimuli put together, accounts for the direction the person takes when he is prodded into action. Similarly the pull psychologists have assumed that each need and motive carries its own special directional tendency. Thus each group derives its notions of directionality from its particular corollary to the inert-object postulate.

Field theory or Gestalt theory in psychology is an exception. Here there are certain principles which are used to account for the direction in which a man will turn, and these are more or less distinct from those which account for his merely being active. The directionality of a man's behaviour is described at a higher level of abstraction than in other current theories, and some provision is made for the way the man himself structures his field.

Psychoanalysis takes no consistent theoretical stand with respect to this issue. It is perhaps best described as a theory of compromises: the compromise between the reality principle and the pleasure principle, between Todestreib and the Eros instinct, between repression and anxiety, between filial and connubial love, between action and reaction formation. Perhaps we see a Hegelian influence towards building a theory out of thesis and antithesis; perhaps we see an attempt in psychoanalysis to build a clinical theory so elastic that no hypothesis could ever be invalidated and no therapist ever discomfited.

In developing a fundamental postulate for a psychological theory of personality it would seem desirable to state it in such a way that there would always be some basis for inferring which way a person will turn when confronted with a choice situation. In this connection the psychological theorist faces an interesting problem. He must write a theory about people and what they produce. His own theory is a human production, hence it too would need to be accounted for. Any psychological theory is therefore somewhat reflexive; it must also account for itself as a product of psychological processes. Thus, if the theory is to account for the way in which a man turns, it should also account for the way its author turned when he wrote it. This is what we were thinking of when, in an earlier section of this chapter, we proposed that we be consistent about what we conceived to be mankind's goals and what we conceived to be scientists' goals.

23. Individuality in theory design

The third perplexing problem which may be obviated by the careful choice of a suitable basic postulate is that of explaining individual differences in a lawful manner. Psychology made rapid strides after it turned its attention to plotting the group dimensions along which men could be distinguished from each other. Progress, however, was ultimately limited. The psychology of individual differences turned out to be a psychology of group differences. Its actuarial predictions, while useful in personnel management for telling us how many students would fail, how many pilots would wash out, or even which ones had a greater likelihood of failing, nevertheless left us with few cues as to what more constructive ways could be devised for reducing failure rates, for improving instruction, for maintaining morale, for making psychotherapy more effective, or for increasing men's output of worthwhile ideas.

The problem requires some constructive approach to the relationship between private and public domains. If a man's private domain, within which his behaviour aligns itself within its own lawful system, is ignored, it becomes necessary to explain him as an inert object wafted about in a public domain by external forces, or as a solitary datum sitting on its own continuum. If a man's existence in the public domain is ignored, our painstakingly acquired knowledge of one man will not help us understand his younger brother, and our daily psychological efforts will yield no increment to the cultural heritage. If both John Doe and Homo sapiens are to be construed within the same system of laws, we must lift the data from John Doe at a higher level of abstraction. It is presumptuous to construe John Doe's agitated behaviour patently as 'anxiety', just because it is agitated, and to bring it into the public domain as such. It may, in his particular case, be far more adequate to understand his personal construct of 'kick' or 'guts' or 'lift' and construe it within the public domain as a form of 'aggression' or 'reality testing'. Richard Roe's agitated behaviour may, on the other hand, when proper account of his personal-construct system is taken, be lifted into the public domain as a construct of 'anxiety'. By conceiving the individual person as himself operating under a construct system, the psychologist can lift his data from the individual case at higher levels of abstraction. It then becomes possible to build publicly a truly scientific theory around the psychology of personal constructs.

Recently there has been a resurgence of the *phenomenological* viewpoint in psychology. The original phenomenology of Husserl and Stumpf was largely swallowed by Gestalt psychology or, more generally, by field theory. The neo-phenomenological point of view is perhaps best expressed by Snygg and Combs, whose basic postulate is: 'All behaviour, without exception, is completely determined by and pertinent to the phenomenal field of the behaving organism.' The position emphasizes the fact, basic to the concept of psychology as an objective science, that the outlook of the individual person is itself a real phenomenon, no matter how badly he may misrepresent the rest of reality to himself. Since it is a real phenomenon, the psychologist is concerned with the formulation of laws and principles which explain it, and he should not assume that an erroneous view lacks any substance of its own. Moreover, the psychologist should not necessarily infer that what one person thinks has to be like what another would think in the same circumstances, nor can he accurately infer what one person thinks from what is publicly believed to be true.

Today's neophenomenology relates itself closely to what is called *self-concept theory* – the latter perhaps most clearly expressed by Raimy and Bugental. These writers are concerned with the self's position in the person's phenomenal field or, in other words, with the person's perspective of himself. Lecky's *self-consistency* position is closely allied. He emphasizes a person's urgent need for the maintenance of structure, particularly as regards himself. Thus he applies the Gestalt *law of pregnancy* to the self's seeking of integrity, and the *law of figure and ground* to the relatively greater emphasis upon self-consistency and the lesser emphasis upon consistency in external matters. On the practical side, it is Rogers who has demonstrated the fertility of these points of view in a psychotherapeutic situation. Yet here is a situation in which the inventions appeared before the theory became articulate. Rogers' *client-centred therapy* – or nondirective therapy, as it was originally called – was in full swing at Ohio State University when Raimy and Combs were students there, and Bugental was later a student of Raimy in the same department.

Rogers' systematic position, while mainly consistent with the group of positions which we have classified as neophenomenological, actually has not been stated in terms of a psychological theory. Perhaps he has been reluctant to attempt such an exposition. From his more recent writings his position appears to be more deeply rooted in certain philosophical convictions regarding the nature of man, and society's proper relationship to him, than in a set of psychological postulates.

Allport, aligning himself with Stern's later writings, has incorporated a neophenomenological type of viewpoint with the emphasis upon its methodological implications. Accepting Windelband's separation of the *nomothetic* and *idiographic* disciplines as a useful abstraction, but not as a concrete classification, he advocates a broadening of the approaches of psychology to include idiography. It is not altogether clear how logically Allport envisions the distinction between the nomothetic and the idiographic methodological approaches. Superficially the former appears to be the study of *mankind*, while the latter is the study of a *man*. Windelband considered any nomothetic discipline to be one which was concerned with general laws and which used the procedures of the exact sciences; an idiographic discipline was essentially descriptive – for example, history and biography. But the historian, in contrast to the chronicler, also derives general laws and principles which run through the mass of events that have happened. If he did not, he would be hopelessly bogged down in his newspaper files. The psychologist, too, when he describes a case, may be conducting an idiographic study; but if the description is to have any thread of meaning running through it, he must relate his selection of relevant facts to principles of human behaviour. The principles, of course, may be derived within a realm no larger than the individual case, but they are still principles – they are abstractions of events.

It would be interesting and profitable to pursue further the implications of these important contributions and to pay proper respect to those who have pioneered where we have followed. But we have set out to propound a particular psychological position which seems to be promising and we must get on with it. If we stopped to pay our respects to all the thinking which has preceded and influenced what we have to say, we would never get it said. While we do not wish to appear to be historically unoriented, our plan is mainly to delineate a theoretical position for what it is and not for what its ancestry may be.

What this adds up to is that we believe it is possible to combine certain features of the neophenomenological approaches with more conventional methodology. We cannot, of course, crawl into another person's skin and peer out at the world through his eyes. We can, however, start by making inferences based primarily upon what we see him doing, rather than upon what we have seen other people doing. We have already emphasized the need to abstract behaviour within the realm of the individual before making it a datum in any study of a group of individuals. Of course, when it comes to be viewed within the framework of many other individuals, it may have to be further abstracted before the useful properties begin to emerge. Thus we would be sceptical of the value of lifting a single muscle twitch as a datum from each of a thousand individuals in order to see what is happening psychologically. We would be more hopeful of abstracting the essential features in a sequence of muscle twitches in the same individual and then comparing the resultant construct with abstractions similarly anchored in other individuals' twitchings. This means, of course, that each study of an individual becomes a problem in concept formation for the psychologist. After he has conceptualized each of his cases, he next has the task of further abstracting the individual constructs in order to produce constructs which underlie people in general.

24. Summary of design specifications

We are ready to commit ourselves to a fundamental postulate but, before we do so, let us review the broader framework within which theory generated by the postulate must operate.

Mankind, whose progress in search of prediction and control of surrounding events stands out so clearly in the light of the centuries, comprises the men we see around us every day. The aspirations of the scientist are essentially the aspirations of all men.

The universe is real; it is happening all the time; it is integral; and it is open to piecemeal interpretation. Different men construe it in different ways. Since it owes no prior allegiance to any one man's construction system, it is always open to reconstruction. Some of the alternative ways of construing are better adapted to man's purposes than are others. Thus, man comes to understand his world through an infinite series of successive approximations. Since man is always faced with constructive alternatives, which he may explore if he wishes, he need not continue indefinitely to be the absolute victim either of his past history or of his present circumstances.

Life is characterized, not merely by its abstractability along a time line, but, more particularly, by the capacity of the living thing to represent its environment. Especially is this true of man, who builds construction systems through which to view the real world. The construction systems are also real, though they may be biased in their representation. Thus, both nature and human nature are phenomenologically existent.

The constructs which are hierarchically organized into systems are variously subject to test in terms of their usefulness in helping the person anticipate the course of events which make up the universe. The results of the testing of constructs determine the desirability of their temporary retention, their revision, or their immediate replacement. We assume that any system may, in proper time, have to be replaced. Within the structure of a system determinism and free will are directional aspects of the same system; that is, a construct is determined by that with which one judges it must always be consistent, and it is free of that which one judges must always be subordinated to it.

A good psychological theory has an appropriate focus and range of convenience. It suffers in usefulness when it has been transplanted from one realm to another – as, for example, from physiology to psychology. It should be fertile in producing new ideas, in generating hypotheses, in provoking experimentation, in encouraging inventions. The hypotheses which are deduced from it should be brittle enough to be testable, though the theory itself may be cast in more resilient terms. The more frequently its hypotheses turn out to be valid, the more valuable the theory.

A good psychological theory should be expressed in terms of abstractions which can be traced through most of the phenomena with which psychology must deal. In this connection, operationalism, when applied to theory construction, may interfere with the psychologist's recognition of the abstractive implications of his experimental results – he may become a laboratory technician rather than a scientist.

A psychological theory should be considered ultimately expendable. The psychologist should therefore maintain personal independence of his theory. Even experimental results never conclusively prove a theory to be ultimately true. Hypotheses are always related to some theoretical structures, but psychologists may produce them by induction or by dragnet procedures, as well as by deduction.

An attempt will be made to design a theory which will avoid the problems which are created by the implied assumptions of mental energy in push and pull theories of psychology. Such a theory would also provide a universal accounting for the alternative a man selects in a choice situation. It would recognize individuality by lifting each datum from the realm of the individual man at a relatively high level of abstraction.

Our next task is to formulate the assumptive structure which would undergird such a theory. The most basic assumption, upon which all subsequent statements must stand, is to be called a postulate. The elaboration of this statement into further related assumptions is pursued by means of corollaries.

Chapter two

Basic theory

In this chapter we lay down the Fundamental Postulate of our psychology of personal constructs. The theory is then elaborated by means of eleven corollaries.

A. Fundamental Postulate

1. Fundamental Postulate: a person's processes are psychologically channelized by the ways in which he anticipates events

Let us try to lay down a postulate which will meet the specifications we have outlined. In doing so we shall have to recognize certain limitations in our theory-building efforts. The postulate we formulate will not necessarily provide a statement from which everyone will make the same deductions. The system built upon the postulate will therefore not be completely logic-tight. Rather, we shall strive to make our theoretical position provocative, and hence fertile, rather than legalistic.

The initial statement, *a person's processes are psychologically channelized by the ways in which he anticipates events*, seems to meet our specifications. Before we go on to examine the explicit meanings and the ensuing implications of this rather simple declarative sentence, let us have a brief look at what we mean by a fundamental postulate in a scientific theory. A postulate is, of course, an assumption. But it is an assumption so basic in nature that it antecedes everything which is said in the logical system which it supports.

Now, a person may question the truth of a statement which is proposed as a fundamental postulate; indeed, we are always free, as scientists, to question the truth of anything. But we should bear in mind that the moment we do question the truth of a statement proposed as a postulate, that statement is no longer a postulate in our subsequent discourse. A statement, therefore, is a postulate only if we accord it that status. If we bring the statement into dispute, as well we may in some instances, we must recognize that we are then arguing from other postulates either explicitly stated or, more likely, implicitly believed. Thus, in scientific reasoning nothing antecedes the postulate, as long as it is a postulate, and the truth of a statement is never questioned as long as that statement is in use as a postulate.

What we have really said, then, is: let us suppose, for the sake of the discussion which is to follow, that a person's processes are psychologically channelized by the ways in which he anticipates events. Let it be clearly understood that we are not proposing this postulate as an ultimate statement of truth. In modern scientific thought it is always customary to accept even one's postulates as tentative or *ad interim* statements of truth and then to see what follows.

2. *Terms*

Let us look at the words we have carefully chosen for this Fundamental Postulate.

a. Person. This term is used to indicate the substance with which we are primarily concerned. Our first consideration is the individual person rather than any part of the person, any group of persons, or any particular process manifested in the person's behaviour.

b. Processes. Instead of postulating an inert substance, a step which would inevitably lead to the necessity for establishing, as a corollary, the existence of some sort of mental energy, the subject of psychology is assumed at the outset to be a process. This is akin to saying that the organism is basically a behaving organism, a statement which has been emphasized by certain psychologists for some time now. But our emphasis, if anything, is even more strongly upon the kinetic nature of the substance with which we are dealing. For our purposes, the person is not an object which is temporarily in a moving state but is himself a form of motion.

c. Psychologically. Here we indicate the type of realm with which we intend to deal. Our theory lies within a limited realm, which is not necessarily overlapped by physiology on the one hand or by sociology on the other. Some of the phenomena which physiological systems seek to explain or which sociological systems seek to explain are admittedly outside our present field of interest and we feel no obligation to account for them within this particular theoretical structure.

As we have indicated before, we do not conceive the substance of psychology to be itself psychological – or physiological, or sociological, or to be preempted by any system. A person's processes are what they are; and psychology, physiology, or what have you, are simply systems concocted for trying to anticipate them. Thus, when we use the term *psychologically,* we mean that we are conceptualizing processes in a psychological manner, not that the processes are psychological rather than something else.

Psychology refers to a group of systems for explaining behaviour, all of which seem to offer similar coverage. Thus, when we identify our system as psychological, we are loosely identifying it with certain other systems because it has a similar realm and range of convenience.

In theorizing, some people think that one ought to start out by defining the boundaries of the field of psychology. But we see no point in trying to stake out property claims for psychology's realm. The kinds of realms we are talking about are not preemptive at all – what belongs to one can still belong to another. The thing for one to do is simply erect his system and then set out to explore its range of convenience, whether that be large or small.

d. Channelized. We conceive a person's processes as operating through a network of pathways rather than as fluttering about in a vast emptiness. The network is flexible and is frequently modified, but it is structured and it both facilitates and restricts a person's range of action.

e. Ways. The channels are established as means to ends. They are laid down by the devices which a person invents in order to achieve a purpose. A person's processes, psychologically speaking, slip into the grooves which are cut out by the mechanisms he adopts for realizing his objectives.

f. He. Our emphasis is upon the way in which the individual man chooses to operate, rather than upon the way in which the operation might ideally be carried out. Each person may erect and utilize different ways, and it is the way he chooses which channelizes his processes.

g. Anticipates. Here is where we build into our theory its predictive and motivational features. Like the prototype of the scientist that he is, man seeks prediction. His structured network of pathways leads towards the future so that he may anticipate it. This is the function it serves. Anticipation is both the push and pull of the psychology of personal constructs.

h. Events. Man ultimately seeks to anticipate real events. This is where we see psychological processes as tied down to reality. Anticipation is not merely carried on for its own sake; it is carried on so that future reality may be better represented. It is the future which tantalizes man, not the past. Always he reaches out to the future through the window of the present.

We now have a statement of a fundamental postulate for which we have high hopes. Perhaps there can spring from it a theory of personality with movement as the phenomenon rather than the epiphenomenon, with the psychological processes of the layman making the same sense as those of the scientist, a dynamic psychology without the trappings of animism, a perceptual psychology without passivity, a behaviourism in which the behaving person is credited with having some sense, a learning theory in which learning is considered so universal that it appears in the postulate rather than as a special class of phenomena, a motivational theory in which man is neither pricked into action by the sharp points of stimuli nor dyed with the deep tones of hedonism, and a view of personality which permits psychotherapy to appear both lawful and plausible. Let us call this theory *the psychology of personal constructs.*

B. Construction Corollary

3. Construction Corollary: a person anticipates events by construing their replications

In building the system which we call *the psychology of personal constructs* we have chosen to rely upon one basic postulate and to amplify the system by stating certain propositions which, in part, follow from the postulate and, in part, elaborate it in greater detail. These propositions are termed *corollaries*, although, logically, they involve somewhat more than what is minimally implied by the exact wording of the postulate. Our corollary introduces the notions of construing and replication.

4. Terms

a. Construing. By construing we mean 'placing an interpretation': a person places an interpretation upon what is construed. He erects a structure, within the framework of which the substance takes shape or assumes meaning. The substance which he construes does not produce the structure; the person does.

The structure which is erected by construing is essentially abstractive, though the person may be so limited in the abstraction that his construing may, in effect, be relatively concretistic. In this connection we shall need to say much more later about the forms of construing. For the present, however, since we are sketching the psychology of personal constructs in preliminary outline only, we shall not go into great detail.

In construing, the person notes features in a series of elements which characterize some of the elements and are particularly uncharacteristic of others. Thus he erects constructs of similarity and contrast. Both the similarity and contrast are inherent in the same construct. A construct which implied similarity without contrast would represent just as much of a chaotic undifferentiated homogeneity as a construct which implied contrast without similarity would represent a chaotic particularized heterogeneity. The former would leave the person engulfed in a sea with no landmarks to relieve the monotony; the latter would confront him with an interminable series of kaleidoscopic changes in which nothing would ever appear familiar.

Construing is not to be confounded with verbal formulation. A person's behaviour may be based upon many interlocking equivalence–difference patterns which are never communicated in symbolic speech. Many of these preverbal or nonverbal governing constructs are embraced in the realm of physiology. That is to say, they deal with elements which fall within the ranges of convenience of physiological construction systems. Thus they may have to do with such matters as digestion, glandular secretion, and so on, which do not normally fall within the ranges of convenience of psychological systems.

If a person is asked how he proposes to digest his dinner, he will be hard put to answer the question. It is likely that he will say that such matters are beyond his control. They seem to him to be beyond his control because he cannot anticipate them within the same system which he must use for communication. Yet digestion is an individually structured process, and what one anticipates has a great deal to do with the course it takes.

What we are saying is that the notion of construing has a wide range of convenience, if we choose to use it that way. It may even be used within borderland areas of the realm of physiology. To be sure, it operates somewhat less conveniently there, but the overlapping functions of psychological and physiological systems in this regard help to make it clear that psychology and physiology ought not to try to draw preemptive boundaries between themselves. We recognize that the psychological notion of construing has a wide range of convenience, which is by no means limited to those experiences which people can talk about or those which they can think about privately.

Construing also transcends disciplinary boundaries in another manner. A person develops a physiological construct system. We say it is a physiological construct system because it is designed around the same foci of convenience as other 'physiological' systems. We are perfectly willing, therefore, to call it a 'physiological' system. But that does not prevent us from examining the person's private system from a psychological point of view. Why, psychologically, did he find it convenient to look at matters this way rather than that? When we examine the personal thinking which takes the form of a physiological construction system, we may find it useful to appraise it from a psychological point of view. Thus, we may subsume a person's physiological construction system within our own psychological system.

The physiologist may turn around and do the same thing to the psychologist. He may, if he wishes, try to subsume a person's psychological system within his own professional physiological system. He may interpret ideas of grandeur in terms of physiological constructs of circulation, cortical topography, and so on. One person may subsume the constructs of A and B under the construct of C. Another may subsume B and C under A. In fact, this kind of upsetting of the hierarchical apple cart characterizes much of our day-to-day thinking, as we shall see later.

b. Replications. The substance that a person construes is itself a process – just as the living person is a process. It presents itself from the beginning as an unending and undifferentiated process. Only when man attunes his ear to recurrent themes in the monotonous flow does his universe begin to make sense to him. Like a musician, he must phrase his experience in order to make sense out of it. The phrases are distinguished events. The separation of events is what man produces for himself when he decides to chop up time into manageable lengths. Within these limited segments, which are based on recurrent themes, man begins to discover the bases for likenesses and differences.

Consider a day. Concretely, today is not yesterday, nor is tomorrow today. Time does not double back on itself. But after a succession of time man is able to detect a recurrent theme in its ever flowing process. It is possible to abstract the recurrent theme in terms of the rising and the setting of the sun. Moreover, the same theme does not recur when time is segmented in other ways. Thus, the concept of a day is erected along the incessant stream of time – a day which is, in its own way, like other days and yet clearly distinguishable from the moments and the years.

Once events have been given their beginnings and endings, and their similarities and contrasts construed, it becomes feasible to try to predict them, just as one predicts that a tomorrow will follow today. What is predicted is not that tomorrow will be a duplicate of today but that there are replicative aspects of tomorrow's event which may be safely predicted. Thus man anticipates events by construing their replications.

5. Mathematical implications of the Construction Corollary

The statistics of probability are based upon the concept of replicated events. And, of course, they are also contrived to measure the predictability of further replications of the events. The two factors from which predictions are made are the number of replications already observed and the amount of similarity which can be abstracted among the replications. The latter factor involves some complicated logical problems – for example, representative sampling – and, in practice, it is the one which usually makes predictions go awry. Since the abstractive judgement of what it is that has been replicated is the basis for measuring the amount of similarity, we find that the concept-formation task which precedes the statistical manipulation of data is basic to any conclusions one reaches by mathematical logic.

The old arithmetic adage that 'you can't add cows and horses' holds here. An event is replicative of another only if one is willing to accept the abstracted similarity of the two. Thus a person who owns one *cow* and one *horse* may say that he owns two *animals* – if he is willing to accept the *animal-like* abstraction of the two of them.

At a more complicated level one may average the results of two test performances of the same person, provided, again, one is willing to accept the abstraction of the similarity in both of them. For example, one test may be a *performance* type of test and the other a *verbal* type of test. If one averages the results, what one gets is an expression of the underlying feature in both of them. If one uses a weighted average, what one gets is an expression which is a more concrete representation of the more heavily weighted test score.

We may think of it this way. All mathematical expressions, when applied to real events, are, at best, approximations. One can always question the appropriateness of the use of a statistical measure, such as chi-square, regardless of the context. The events to which this non-parametric statistic is applied must be assumed to be replications of each other. We can enter the cells of a chi-square table with cows and horses, but when we do so the cow-ness must be dropped from the cows, the horse-ness must be dropped from the horses, and only the animal-ness in both of them allowed to remain. Thus, whenever one uses the chi-square statistic, he must be aware of the abstractive implications in his data. What one could conclude from a chi-square computation from a table in which both cows and horses had been entered is that, *in the sense that cows and horses are replicated events, such and such is true of them.*

We have been talking about the mathematical expression of chi-square. What we have said might have been said about simple enumeration. We point to each of a series of things and count: *one, two, three....* The counting makes sense if the things are distinguishable from each other, and it makes sense only in the respect that they are alike. Before we can count them we must construe their concrete difference from each other, their abstract likeness to each other, and their abstract difference from other things which are not to be counted. We must be able to construe where one thing leaves off and another begins, which one is similar enough to the others to be counted, and what is extraneous. What we count depends on which we abstract to be counted; thus, any mathematical expression relies upon the concept-formation task which has preceded it. Mathematical manipulation does not reify data, though it often provides a handy way of testing the adequacy of our conceptualizations.

What we are saying is that when a person anticipates events by construing their replications, he lays the ground for mathematical reasoning. All mathematical reasoning is utterly dependent upon the premathematical construing process which gives it something to enumerate. We think this is important.

C. Individuality Corollary

6. Individuality Corollary: persons differ from each other in their construction of events

Since our Fundamental Postulate throws our emphasis upon the ways in which a person anticipates events, it provides grounds for a psychology of individual differences. People can be seen as differing from each other, not only because there may have been differences in the events which they have sought to anticipate, but also because there are different approaches to the anticipation of the same events.

Persons anticipate both public events and private events. Some writers have considered it advisable to try to distinguish between 'external' events and 'internal' events. In our system there is no particular need for making this kind of distinction. Nor do we have to distinguish so sharply between stimulus and response, between the organism and his environment, or between the self and the not-self.

No two people can play precisely the same role in the same event, no matter how closely they are associated. For one thing, in such an event, each experiences the other as an external figure. For another, each experiences a different person as the central figure (namely, himself). Finally, the chances are that, in the course of events, each will get caught up in a different stream and hence be confronted with different navigational problems.

But does this mean that there can be no sharing of experience? Not at all; for each may construe the likenesses and differences between the events in which he himself is involved, together with those in which he sees that the other person is involved. Thus, while there are individual differences in the construction of events, persons can find common ground through construing the experiences of their neighbours along with their own. It is not inevitable that they should come upon such common ground; indeed, where the cultural identifications are different or where one person has given up seeking common ground with his neighbours, individuals can be found living out their existence next door to each other but in altogether different subjective worlds.

D. Organization Corollary

7. Organization Corollary: each person characteristically evolves, for his convenience in anticipating events, a construction system embracing ordinal relationships between constructs

Different constructs sometimes lead to incompatible predictions, as everyone who has experienced personal conflict is painfully aware. Man, therefore, finds it necessary to develop ways of anticipating events which transcend contradictions. Not only do men differ in their constructions of events, but they also differ in the ways they organize their constructions of events. One man may resolve the conflicts between his anticipations by means of an ethical system. Another may resolve them in terms of self-preservation. The same man may resolve in one way at one time and in the other way at another. It all depends upon how he backs off to get perspective.

8. Terms

a. Characteristically. Again we emphasize the personalistic nature of the process: here in the case of the system. Not only are the constructs personal, but the hierarchical system into which they are arranged is personal too. It is this systematic arrangement which characterizes the personality, even more than do the differences between individual constructs.

b. Evolves. The construction system does not stand still, although it is relatively more stable than the individual constructs of which it is composed. It is continually taking new shape. This is a way of saying that the personality is continually taking new shape. Deep psychotherapy may help a person with this evolvement and thus possibly accomplish important readjustments in a person's style of life.

c. Construction system. A system implies a grouping of elements in which incompatibilities and inconsistencies have been minimized. They do not disappear altogether, of course. The systematization helps the person to avoid making contradictory predictions.

d. Ordinal relationships between constructs. One construct may subsume another as one of its elements. It may do this in either of two ways; it may extend the cleavage intended by the other or it may abstract across the other's cleavage line. For example, the construct *good vs. bad* may subsume, respectively, among other things, the two ends of the intelligent–stupid dimension. In this sense, 'good' would include all 'intelligent' things plus some things which fall outside the range of convenience of the *intelligent vs. stupid* construct. 'Bad' would include all the 'stupid' things plus some others which are neither 'intelligent' nor 'stupid'. This is what we mean by extending the cleavage intended by the construct *intelligent vs. stupid.*

An example of abstracting across the *intelligent vs. stupid* cleavage line would be the construct of *evaluative vs. descriptive.* In this case the *intelligent vs. stupid* construct would be subsumed as a dimension. The construct would itself be identified as an 'evaluative' type of construct and would be contrasted with other constructs such as *light vs. dark,* which might be considered 'descriptive' only. Both *good vs. bad* and *evaluative vs. descriptive* may thus be used as superordinating constructs, the former in what some writers would call an 'absolutistic' sense and the latter in what they would call a 'relativistic' sense.

Within a construction system there may be many levels of ordinal relationships, with some constructs subsuming others and those, in turn, subsuming still others. When one construct subsumes another its ordinal relationship may be termed *superordinal* and the ordinal relationship of the other becomes *subordinal.* Moreover, the ordinal relationship between the constructs may reverse itself from time to time. For example, 'intelligent' may embrace all things 'good' together with all things 'evaluative' and 'stupid' would be the term for 'bad' and 'descriptive' things; or, if the other kind of subsuming is involved, 'intelligent' might embrace the construct *evaluative vs. descriptive* while 'stupid' would be the term for the *good vs. bad* dichotomy. Thus man systematizes his constructs by concretely arranging them in hierarchies and by abstracting them further. But whether he pyramids his ideas or penetrates them with insights, he builds a system embracing ordinal relationships between constructs for his personal convenience in anticipating events.

9. Implications of the Organization Corollary

The pursuit of implications arising out of our assumptive structure is the major objective of the chapters which follow. However, it may be helpful to offer some passing hints as to the practical implications of our corollaries. The Organization Corollary is basic to our understanding of that most common of all clinic commodities, anxiety. It also sets the stage for the way we shall look upon the clinic client's mirrored image of himself.

Thus far we have said that the person is bent on anticipating events. His psychological processes are channelized with this in mind. Each person attunes his ear to the replicative themes he hears and each attunes his ear in a somewhat different way. But it is not mere certainty that man seeks; if that were so, he might take great delight in the repetitive ticking of the clock. More and more he seeks to anticipate all impending events of whatsoever nature. This means that he must develop a system in which the most unusual future can be anticipated in terms of a replicated aspect of the familiar past.

Now it so happens that a person must occasionally decide what to do about remodelling his system. He may find the job long overdue. How much can he tear down and still have a roof over his head? How disruptive will a new set of ideas be? Dare he jeopardize the system in order to replace some of its constituent parts? Here is the point at which he must choose between preserving the integrity of the system and replacing one of its obviously faulty parts. Sometimes his anticipation of events will be more effective if he chooses to conserve the system. It is precisely at this point that the psychotherapist may fail to understand why his client is so resistive. It is also at this point that he may do his client harm.

Lecky has emphasized a person's need for self-consistency. In doing so he has thrown particular emphasis upon the preservation of those aspects of one's system which have to do with the self. Certain essential features of what Lecky says are, in effect, reiterated here, and we are indebted to him. However, our view is that it is not consistency for consistency's sake nor even self-consistency that gives man his place in the world of events. Rather, it is his seeking to anticipate the whole world of events and thus relate himself to them that best explains his psychological processes. If he acts to preserve the system, it is because the system is an essential chart for his personal adventures, not because it is a self-contained island of meaning in an ocean of inconsequentialities.

E. Dichotomy Corollary

10. Dichotomy Corollary: a person's construction system is composed of a finite number of dichotomous constructs

We have already said that a person anticipates events by noting their replicative aspects. Having chosen an aspect with respect to which two events are replications of each other, we find that, by the same token, another event is definitely not a replication of the first two. The person's choice of an aspect determines both what shall be considered similar and what shall be considered contrasting. The same aspect, or the same abstraction, determines both. If we choose an aspect in which A and B are similar, but in contrast to C, it is important to note that it is the same aspect of all three, A, B *and* C, that forms the basis of the construct. It is not that there is one aspect of A and B that makes them similar to each other and another aspect that makes them contrasting to C. What we mean is that there is an aspect of A, B, and C which we may call *z*. With respect to this aspect, A and B are similar and C stands in contrast to them. This is an important notion, for on it is built much of the technical procedure that characterizes the psychology of personal constructs.

Let us pursue our model further. Let us suppose that there is an element O in which one is unable to construe the aspect of *z*. O then falls outside the range of convenience of the construct based on *z*. The aspect of *z* is irrelevant in that part of the realm occupied by O. Not so C, however. The aspect of *z* is quite relevant to C. It is *z* that enables us to differentiate between C and the two similar elements, A and B. The aspect of *z* performs no such service in helping us discriminate between O and the two similar elements, A and B.

Suppose, for example, A and B are men, C is a woman, and O is the time of day. We abstract an aspect of A, B and C which we may call *sex*. Sex, then, is our *z*. Sex is not applicable to O, the time of day; at least most of us would not so abstract it. The time of day, O, does not fall within the range of convenience of the construct of sex, *z*. Now, with respect to sex, *z*, the two men, A and B, are alike and in contrast to the woman, C. Moreover, the construct is no less applicable to the woman, C, than it is to the two men, A and B.

But suppose we say that the construct is not sex, *z*, but masculinity, *y*. Then is not the woman, C, just as unmasculine as the time of day, O? Our answer is no. She is much more relevantly unmasculine than is the time of day. The notion of masculinity is predicated upon a companion notion of femininity, and it is two of them together which constitute the basis of the construct. Masculinity would mean nothing if it were not for femininity. There would be no point in using the term *man* in the masculine sense if it were not for the notion of sex.

What we propose to do is to assume that all constructs follow this basic dichotomous form. Inside its particular range of convenience a construct denotes an aspect of all the elements lying therein. Outside this range of convenience the aspect is not recognizable. Moreover, the aspect, once noted, is meaningful only because it forms the basis of similarity and contrast between the elements in which it is noted. In laying down this assumption we are departing from the position of classical logic. But we suspect that this comes nearer representing the way people actually think. In any case, we propose to pursue the implications of this assumption and see where we are led.

11. Terms

a. Composed. By this we mean that the system is composed entirely of constructs. It consists of nothing but constructs. Its organizational structure is based upon constructs of constructs, concretistically pyramided or abstractly cross-referenced in a system of ordinal relationships.

b. Dichotomous constructs. The construct denotes an aspect of the elements lying within its range of convenience, on the basis of which some of the elements are similar to others and some are in contrast. In its minimum context a construct is a way in which at least two elements are similar and contrast with a third. There must therefore be at least three elements in the context. There may, of course, be many more.

c. Finite number. Man's thinking is not completely fluid; it is channelized. If he wants to think about something he must follow the network of channels he had laid down for himself, and only by recombining old channels can he create new ones. These channels structure his thinking and limit his access to the ideas of others. We see these channels existing in the form of constructs.

12. Implications of the Dichotomy Corollary

But do people really think in terms of dichotomies? Do they always abstract on the basis of both similarity and contrast? These are questions which are bound to be asked. Since they challenge a part of our assumptive structure, we would have to step outside our system in order to try to answer them. We can, however, clarify the assumption somewhat further and thus perhaps make it more acceptable for the time being.

Not long ago a client said, in effect, to her therapist, 'I believe that everything in the world is good. There is nothing bad. All people are good. All inanimate things are good. All thoughts are good.' These statements, faintly suggestive of Voltaire's *Candide*, alerted the clinician to a probable underlying hostility. Obviously the client's statement was intended to mean something; the therapist's task was to find the implied contrast which she was unable to put into words.

The client could have meant several things. She could have meant that everything is now good whereas formerly it was bad. She could have been denying the good–bad dimension as a meaningful dimension and have chosen to do so by asserting the universality of one end of the dimension. She could have meant that everything other than herself was good. Or she could have meant that she was one who saw good in everything whereas others were seers of the bad. As matters turned out, she was expressing her construct in the latter two senses. She meant, 'I suspect that I am bad and I suspect that you see me as bad, even though I have the compensating virtue of myself being willing to see everyone as good.' There is a suggestion of what the clinicians call 'an idea of reference' here, and the way the client expressed it suggests what some clinicians call 'acting out'.

Perhaps this illustration will suffice, for the time being, to indicate how the Dichotomy Corollary affects the clinician in dealing with his client. Instead of seeing his client as the victim of submerged conflict between opposing instinctual forces, he sees the dichotomy as an essential feature of thinking itself. As he seeks to understand what his client means, he looks for the elements in the construct context. As long as he approaches man's thinking from the standpoint of formal logic, it is impossible for him to comprehend any thinking which man is unable to verbalize. But as we approach man's thinking psychologically, using both the clinical and the more fragmentary methods of investigation, we can see the operational dichotomization of his constructs into similarities and contrasts.

Much of our language, as well as of our everyday thinking, implies contrast which it does not explicitly state. Our speech would be meaningless otherwise. If we proceed on this assumption, we may be able to gain insights into the psychological processes which have long been concealed by a formal logic which was altogether too much shackled by words.

How does our notion of dichotomous constructs apply to such 'class concepts' as *red*? Is *red* a statement of contrast as well as of similarity? We might point out that, according to one of the prevalent colour theories, red is the complement of green. Among the hues it stands in sharpest contrast to green. But *red* is used in other ways also. When we say that a person has red hair we are distinguishing it from the nonredness of white, yellow, brown, or black. Our language gives no special word for this nonredness, but we have little difficulty in knowing what the contrast to red hair actually is.

Similarly other constructs, such as *table*, express, within their ranges of convenience, both likenesses and differences. The differences are just as relevant as the likenesses; they are applicable within the constructs' ranges of convenience. Unlike classical logic, we do not lump together the contrasting and the irrelevant. We consider the contrasting end of a construct to be both relevant and necessary to the meaning of the construct. It falls within the range of convenience of the construct, not outside. Thus the construct of *table* has meaning, not merely because a series of objects, called *tables*, are similar to each other in this respect, but also because certain other objects of furniture stand in contrast in this same respect. For example, it makes sense to point to a chair and say, 'That is not a table.' It makes no sense to point to a sunset and say, 'That is not a table.'

The Dichotomy Corollary assumes a structure of psychological processes which lends itself to binary mathematical analysis. The concepts of modern physics, particularly electron theory, and the devices, such as the vacuum tube, which have been developed as the implements of those concepts, are having a far-reaching influence these days. The practical task of reducing information to a form which can be handled by electronic computing machines has forced scientists to reconsider the mathematical structure of knowledge itself. Psychology, for a half century an initiator of mathematical inventions relating to human behaviour, is now itself caught up in the new nonparametric mathematics. Personal-construct theory, with its emphasis upon the dichotomous nature of the personal constructs which channelize psychological processes, is in full accord with this modern trend in scientific thinking. But personal-construct theory would not lose sight of premathematical construct formation. A sorting machine, no matter how complex, is not a thinking machine as long as we have to select data to feed into it.

F. Choice Corollary

13. Choice Corollary: a person choose for himself that alternative in a dichotomized construct through which he anticipates the greater possibility for extension and definition of his system

If a person's processes are psychologically channelized by the ways in which he anticipates events, and those ways present themselves in dichotomous form, it follows that he must choose between the poles of his dichotomies in a manner which is predicted by his anticipations. We assume, therefore, that whenever a person is confronted with the opportunity for making a choice, he will tend to make that choice in favour of the alternative which seems to provide the best basis for anticipating the ensuing events.

Here is where inner turmoil so frequently manifests itself. Which shall a man choose, security or adventure? Shall he choose that which leads to immediate certainty or shall he choose that which may eventually give him a wider understanding? For the man of constricted outlook whose world begins to crumble, death may appear to provide the only immediate certainty which he can lay hands on. And yet, in the words of Shakespeare's *Hamlet*:

> But that the dread of something after death –
> The undiscover'd country, from whose bourn
> No traveller returns – puzzles the will;
> And makes us rather bear those ills we have
> Than fly to others that we know not of?

Whatever the breadth of his viewpoint, it is our assumption that man makes his choice in such a fashion as to enhance his anticipations. If he constricts his field of vision, he can turn his attention toward the clear definition of his system of constructs. If he is willing to tolerate some day-by-day uncertainties, he may broaden his field of vision and thus hope to extend the predictive range of the system. Whichever his choice may be – for constricted certainty or for broadened understanding – his decision is essentially elaborative. He makes what we shall call hereinafter *the elaborative choice.*

14. Terms

a. Chooses. Not only is a person's construction system composed of dichotomous constructs but, within the system of dichotomies, the person builds his life upon one or the other of the alternatives represented in each of the dichotomies. This is to say that he places relative values upon the ends of his dichotomies. Some of the values are quite transient and represent merely the convenience of the moment. Others are quite stable and represent guiding principles. Even the stable ones are not necessarily highly intellectualized – they may appear, rather, as appetitive preferences.

b. For oneself. When one makes a choice one involves oneself in the selection. Even if the choice is no more than a temporary hypothesis explored in the course of solving a mathematical problem or in looking for a lost screwdriver, one must perceive oneself as being modified through the chain of ensuing events. Some of one's choices will seem to be major turning points in one's life; others may appear to be no more than a passing impulse – a decision to glance to the left rather than to the right.

c. Alternative. If a person sets up the construct of *black vs. white*, an object cannot, for him, be both black and white. The construct tends to force upon him either one or the other of the two alternatives. If it were not so, the construct would have no meaning.

What about shades of grey? While the construct of *black vs. white* is composed of mutually exclusive alternatives, this does not preclude the use of the construct in a relativistic manner. Relativism is not the same as ambiguity, although some persons try to construe it that way. Of two objects, one may be blacker than the other; but it cannot be blacker than the other and at the same time the other be blacker than it is. As we shall see later, dichotomous constructs can be built into scales, the scales representing superordinate constructs which are further abstractions of the separate scalar values. Thus, *more greyness vs. less greyness* is a further abstraction of the construct *black vs. white.*

d. Through. We must keep in mind that constructs have to do with processes and not merely with the spatial arrangement of static objects. The use of the constructs is itself a process also. Thus the use of constructs is a matter of choosing vestibules *through* which one passes during the course of his day.

e. Anticipates. Since we have postulated that all human movement is based on anticipations, the choice of an alternative through which to move is itself a matter of what one anticipates.

f. Greater possibility. Not only is one's choice based upon the anticipation of some particular thing, but it may also be based upon one's anticipation of things in general. A person does not have to know specifically what it is that he expects in order to make his elaborative choice. He can go fishing, choosing only a well-stocked stream.

g. Extension. Instead of saying that one makes his choice in favour of the alternative that seems to offer the greater possibility for extension and definition, we might have said that he makes his choice in favour of the greater possibility for further elaboration of the system. But we wish to make it clear that elaboration of one's construct system can be in the direction either of extension or of definition, or of both. The extension of the system includes making it more comprehensive, increasing its range of convenience, making more and more of life's experiences meaningful.

h. Definition. The principle of the elaborative choice also includes a person's tendency to move towards that which appears to make his system more explicit and clear cut. As we have already indicated, this may, in some instances, appear to call for constriction of one's field – even to the point of ultimate constriction, suicide. Internal conflict, as in the case of Hamlet, is often a matter of trying to balance off the secure definiteness of a narrowly encompassed world against the uncertain possibilities of life's adventure. One may anticipate events by trying to become more and more certain about fewer and fewer things or by trying to become vaguely aware of more and more things on the misty horizon.

i. One's system. Here we emphasize the assumption that, while it is events that one seeks to anticipate, one makes one's elaborative choice in order to define or extend the system which one has found useful in anticipating those events. We might call this 'a seeking of self-protection', or 'acting in defence of the self', or 'the preservation of one's integrity'. But it seems more meaningful to keep clearly in mind what the self is, what it is designed to do, and what integral function is served. Thus we hope it is clear that what we assume is that the person makes his choice in favour of elaborating a system which is functionally integral with respect to the anticipation of events. To us it seems meaningless to mention a system *qua* system. It must be a system *for something*. From our point of view a person's construction system is for the anticipation of events. If it were for something else, it would probably shape up into something quite different.

15. Implications of the Choice Corollary

The Choice Corollary lays down the grounds upon which we can make some predictions regarding how people will act after they have construed the issues with which they are faced. Frequently the therapist finds it difficult to understand why his client, in spite of insights which would appear to make it clear how he should behave, continues to make the 'wrong' choices. The therapist, seeing only the single issue which he has helped the client to define, often fails to realize that, within the system of personal constructs which the client has erected, the decision for action is not necessarily based on that issue alone but on a complex of issues.

For example, no matter how obvious it may be that a person would be better off if he avoided a fight or spoke pleasantly to his boss, it may so happen that such a course of action would seem to him personally to limit the definition and extension of his system as a whole. He may, therefore, in spite of the neatest psychotherapeutic interpretations, continue to quarrel with his neighbours and to snub anyone who seems to be invested with authority. The Choice Corollary, therefore, suggests ways in which a therapeutic programme can go beyond mere intellectual insight and how it might enable the client to enter the experimental phases of the programme.

Under the Choice Corollary we are able to reconstrue some of the issues for which hedonism and motivational theory provide awkward answers. Stimulus–response theory requires some sorts of assumptions to explain why certain responses become linked to certain stimuli. In certain theoretical structures this is managed by some supplementary theorizing about the nature of motives or need satisfactions. But in our assumptive structure we do not specify, nor do we imply, that a person seeks 'pleasure', that he has special 'needs', that there are 'rewards', or even that there are 'satisfactions'. In this sense, ours is not a commercial theory. To our way of thinking, there is a continuing movement towards the anticipation of events, rather than a series of barters for temporal satisfactions, and this movement is the essence of human life itself.

G. Range Corollary

16. Range Corollary: a construct is convenient for the anticipation of a finite range of events only

Just as a system or a theory has its focus and range of convenience, so a personal construct has a focus and range of convenience. There are few if any personal constructs which one can say are relevant to everything. Even such a construct as *good vs. bad,* in its personalized form, is not likely to be considered by the user to be applicable throughout the range of his perceptual field. Of course, some persons use the construct more comprehensively than others; but, even so, they are inclined to erect boundaries of convenience beyond which elements are neither good nor bad. A construct of *tall vs. short* is much easier to see as having a limited range of convenience. One may construe tall houses versus short houses, tall people versus short people, tall trees versus short trees. But one does not find it convenient to construe tall weather versus short weather, tall light versus short light, or tall fear versus short fear. Weather, light, and fear are, for most of us at least, clearly outside the range of convenience of *tall vs. short.*

Sometimes one is surprised to learn how narrowly a certain person applies some of his constructs. For example, one person may use the construct of *respect vs.*

contempt to apply broadly to many different kinds of interpersonal relationships. Another person may use it to apply only to a very narrow range of events, perhaps only to the choice of words in a formally structured situation, such as a court proceeding.

As we have indicated before, in our discussion of the Dichotomy Corollary, our position here is somewhat different from that of classical logic. We see relevant similarity and contrast as essential and complementary features of the same construct and both of them as existing within the range of convenience of the construct. That which is outside the range of convenience of the construct is not considered part of the contrasting field but simply an area of irrelevancy.

While we have not said so before, it is probably apparent by now that we use the term *construct* in a manner which is somewhat parallel to the common usage of 'concept'. However, if one attempts to translate our *construct* into the more familiar term, 'concept', he may find some confusion. We have included, as indeed some recent users of the term 'concept' have done, the more concretistic concepts which nineteenth-century psychologists would have insisted upon calling 'percepts'. The notion of a 'percept' has always carried the idea of its being a personal act – in that sense, our *construct* is in the tradition of 'percepts'. But we also see our *construct* as involving abstraction – in that sense our *construct* bears a resemblance to the traditional usage of 'concept'. And finally, we prefer the use of the term *construct* because, as a term, it has emerged more within the context of experimental psychology than within the context of mentalistic psychology or of formal logic.

Now when we assume that the construct is basically dichotomous, that it includes percepts, and that it is a better term for our purposes than the term 'concept', we are not quarrelling with those who would use it otherwise. Within some systems of logic the notion of contrast as something distinct from irrelevancy is not part of the assumptive structure. We, on the other hand, are simply assuming that this is the way people do, in fact, think. We shall operate upon this assumption until it begins to appear that our theory is failing to measure up to the standards we outlined in the preceding chapter. We do not insist that people ought to think in this way, nor are we greatly concerned if others believe that people ought to think in the classical way. Ours is simply a psychological theory, and the nature of personal constructs is built into the assumptive structure.

17. Implications of the Range Corollary

The Range Corollary, together with the Dichotomy Corollary, provides a somewhat new approach to the analysis of human thought processes. Consider a given person's use of the construct of *respect vs. contempt*. Under conventional logic one would consider these as two separate concepts. If we wished to understand the person's use of the term 'respect', we might seek to find out how broadly he applied the term – how he 'generalized the concept'. We would want to know what acts he considered to be characterized by 'respect' and what acts he did not consider 'respectful'. Thus we might be able to discover by the method of varying concomitants just what abstraction among the acts he had been able to make.

But when we approach the thinking of a person, say a clinic client, in this way, we miss a great deal. We miss it because we are tacitly assuming that everything which he does not construe as 'respect' is irrelevant. Yet his use of the construct may be particularly meaningful because of what he excludes rather than because of what he includes. When we approach his thinking from the standpoint of the psychology of personal constructs, we do not lump together what he excludes as irrelevant with what he excludes as contrasting. We see the construct as composed essentially of a *similarity–contrast* dimension which he strikes through a part of his field of experience. We need to look at both ends of it if we want to know what it means to him. We cannot understand him well if we look only at the similarity – 'respect' – end of the dimension. We cannot understand what he means by 'respect' unless we know what he sees as relevantly opposed to 'respect'.

The psychologist who employs the approach of the psychology of personal constructs is led always to look for the contrasting elements of his client's constructs as well as the similar elements. Until he has some notion of the contrast, he does not presume to understand the similarity. He would therefore seek to understand what his client construed as the opposite of respect and what the range of convenience of the whole construct covered. As his client continues to talk about the construct of 'respect', the psychologist may discover just what it is that the client is condemning, by implication, as contemptuous or contemptible.

Freud found that he needed to understand what his client meant by what they *did not say.* He used the notions of 'repression' and 'reaction formation' to explain what he observed. These he saw as perverse tendencies, somewhat characteristic of all men but particularly of certain disturbed persons. Our position is that contrast is an essential feature of all personal constructs, a feature upon which their very meaning depends. We would agree with Freud that there are instances in which the person is so self-involved with a construct that he avoids expressing its contrasting aspect lest he misidentify himself.

In practice, then, one looks not only for the similarities but also for the contrasts in understanding a client's construct. Moreover, he looks to see how extensive is the range of convenience of the construct, both for the similar elements and for the contrast elements. Until he understands how extensively the contrast is construed, he cannot realize the full import of the client's thinking.

H. Experience Corollary

18. Experience Corollary: a person's construction system varies as he successively construes the replications of events

Since our Fundamental Postulate establishes the anticipation of events as the objective of psychological processes, it follows that the successive revelation of events invites the person to place new constructions upon them whenever something unexpected happens. Otherwise one's anticipations would become less and less realistic. The succession of events in the course of time continually subjects a person's construction system to a validation process. The constructions one places upon events are working hypotheses, which are about to be put to the test of experience. As one's anticipations or hypotheses are successively revised in the light of the unfolding sequence of events, the construction system undergoes a progressive evolution. The person reconstrues. This is experience. The reconstruction of one's life is based upon just this kind of experience. We have tried to express this implication of our Fundamental Postulate in the Experience Corollary.

19. Terms

a. System. We have already indicated that a system implies a grouping of elements in which incompatibilities and inconsistencies have been minimized. We have also indicated that a person's construction system involves ordinal relationships between constructs. Construction is systematic in that it falls into a pattern having features of regularity. Since construing is a kind of refinement process involving abstraction and generalization, it is a way of looking at events as having a kind of identity with each other and as not being wholly unique. These features of identity and regularity are given shape through construction, which itself has been shaped up as a system.

b. Varies. The changes in the construction system are not always 'for the good' nor do they necessarily always tend to stabilize. They do vary, however. The variation may disrupt the system and lead to further and more rapid variation. It may precipitate a major shake-up in the system. Contrariwise, the variation may stabilize the system and make its basic features resistant to further modification.

c. Successively. Construing, like all processes, may be chopped up into segments having beginnings and endings. Construing may itself be considered a sequence of events. Segmented in this manner it is proper to speak of construing as taking place successively. Like other features of life, its principal dimension is time, and it is itself a process, a phenomenon. The events of one's construing march single file along the path of time.

d. Replications of events. As new events are added to the record of those which have passed, the person has an opportunity to reconsider the replicative aspects which link the recent with the remote. What is it which has been repeated? What now constitutes the recurrent theme? Concretely, the new events are unique; it is only by abstracting them that the person finds that which is replicated.

20. Experience, orderliness and time

By calling this corollary the Experience Corollary we indicate what we assume to be the essential nature of experience. Experience is made up of the successive construing of events. It is not constituted merely by the succession of events themselves. A person can be a witness to a tremendous parade of episodes and yet, if he fails to keep making something out of them, or if he waits until they have all occurred before he attempts to reconstrue them, he gains little in the way of experience from having been around when they happened. It is not what happens around him that makes a man experienced; it is the successive construing and reconstruing of what happens, as it happens, that enriches the experience of his life.

Our corollary also throws emphasis upon construing the replicative features of experience. The person who merely stands agog at each emerging event may experience a series of interesting surprises, but if he makes no attempt to discover the recurrent themes, his experience does not amount to much. It is when man begins to see the orderliness in a sequence of events that he begins to experience them.

The notion of an organized and potentially lawful universe has not been easy for men to accept. How can one accept lawfulness unless one can state the law? Must not one resort to anthropomorphism whenever one's predictions go awry? Should we not attribute all such unexpected events to 'manlike' caprice? There are actually some scientists who see great orderliness within their physical frames of reference but who throw up their hands and say, 'There must be a psychological factor', whenever they fail to find orderliness. This might be all right if what they meant was that it was time to apply some psychological constructs. But what they usually mean is that the phenomena are disorderly.

Sometimes the notion of the world as an orderly development of events seems downright threatening to a person. Particularly is this likely to be true when he deals with psychological events. If he sees orderliness in the behaviour of a friend or in his own behaviour, it seems to preclude the possibility of seeing the actions of either as being free. This is a personal problem that the psychotherapist must frequently face in trying to help his client. If the client perceives himself as an orderly succession of events, he feels trapped by his own structure or by the events of his biography. Yet, if he sees himself as deciding each moment what he shall do next, it may seem as though one little false step will destroy his integrity.

In spite of the personal hazards and the difficulties of construing the succession of events which make up his universe, man has gradually extended his constructs of orderliness through the centuries. Perhaps he first perceived orderliness in the stately procession that marched across the night sky. Perhaps he first saw replication in the rolling of a stone along the ground and, from its rapid succession of events, was able to construct the notion of cycles and epicycles. Perhaps it came much earlier, as he detected the beating of his own pulse. But wherever it started, man's widening awareness of the universe as an orderly unfolding of events gave him increased capacity to predict and made his world more and more manageable.

Even rare cataclysms assumed the familiarity of *déjà vu*. Man gradually discovered that he could lay a sight on the future through the experience of the past.

The essential referent dimension along which all orderliness and organization must be construed is that of time. Except as there is a seasonable replication of events or aspects of events, no organization whatsoever can be ascribed to the universe and there is no such thing as experience. The discovery of replicative themes is not only the key to experience, it is the key to natural law.

21. Experience and learning

The Experience Corollary has profound implications for our thinking about the topic of learning. When we accept the assumption that a person's construction system varies as he successively construes the replications of events, together with the antecedent assumption that the course of all psychological processes is plotted by one's construction of events, we have pretty well bracketed the topic of learning. What has been commonly called 'learning' has been covered at the very outset. Learning is assumed to take place. It has been built into the assumptive structure of the system. The question of whether or not it takes place, or what is learned and what is not learned, is no longer a topic for debate within the system we have proposed. Of course, if we wish to step outside the system and argue within the framework of some other system, we can take sides on these topics.

The burden of our assumption is that learning is not a special class of psychological processes; it is synonymous with any and all psychological processes. It is not something that happens to a person on occasion; it is what makes him a person in the first place.

The net effect of incorporating learning into the assumptive structure of a psychological theory is to remove the whole topic from the realm of subsequent discourse. Some readers may be dismayed at this turn of events. Psychology now has a considerable investment of research effort in the topic. But psychology's investment is not altogether depreciated by the new set of assumptions, even though much of the research is ambiguous when viewed in the new light. If it is any comfort to do so, one may say that learning has been given a pre-eminent position in the psychology of personal constructs, even though it has been taken out of circulation as a special topic. In the language of administrators, it has been 'kicked upstairs'.

Now what happens to the venerable laws of learning and to the family of notions which have more recently grown up in the household of learning? Much! Let us take a look again at what we mean by 'construing' and 'system'. Construing is a way of seeing events that makes them look regular. By construing events it becomes possible to anticipate them. To be effective, the construction system itself must have some regularity. The palpable feature of regularity is repetition, not mere repetition of identical events, of course – in a strict sense that would deny the idea of time its rightful place in the scheme of things – but repetition of some characteristic which can be abstracted from each event and carried intact across the bridge of time and space. To construe is to hear the whisper of recurrent themes in the events that reverberate around us.

The subject in a learning experiment is no exception to our psychological rule. He too directs his psychological processes by seeking the recurrent theme in the experiment. If he segments the experience into separate 'trials' and then further separates the 'trials' into 'reinforced trials' and 'unreinforced trials', he may hear the same repetitive theme which the experimenter hears. On the other hand, he may not be so conventional. He may listen for other kinds of themes he has heard before. He may not even segment his experience into the kinds of trials or events the experimenter expects. In the language of music, he may employ another way of phrasing. Viewed in this manner, the problem of learning is not merely one of determining how *many* or what kind of reinforcements fix a response, or how *many* nonreinforcements extinguish it, but rather, how does the subject phrase the experience, what recurrent themes does he hear, what movements does he define, and what validations of his predictions does he reap? When a subject fails to meet the experimenter's expectations, it may be inappropriate to say that 'he has not learned'; rather, one might say that what the subject learned was not what the experimenter expected him to learn. If we are to have a productive science of psychology, let us put the burden of discovery on the experimenter rather than on the subject. Let the experimenter find out what the subject is thinking about, rather than asking the subject to find out what the experimenter is thinking about.

A more adequate discussion of the role of learning in personal-construct theory is reserved for another section on experience presented at a later point in our exposition of the psychology of personal constructs. The present remarks may suffice to suggest the possible extent of the implications of our basic assumptions.

I. Modulation Corollary

22. *Modulation Corollary: the variation in a person's construction system is limited by the permeability of the constructs within whose range of convenience the variants lie*

If we are to see a person's psychological processes operating lawfully within a system which he constructs, we need also to account for the evolution of the system itself in a similarly lawful manner. Our Experience Corollary states that a person's construction system varies as he successively construes the replications of events. Next, we must note that the progressive variation must, itself, take place within a system. If it were not so, we would be in the position of claiming that little everyday processes are systematically governed but that the system-forming processes are not subordinate to any larger, more comprehensive system. We cannot insist upon the personal lawfulness of the *elements* of human behaviour and at the same time concede that the *patterns* of human behaviour are unlawful. Nor can we insist that the elements follow a personal system but that the patterns can evolve only within a suprapersonal system.

The problem is a special case of the problem of determinism and free will, which we discussed in an earlier section. There we indicated that we assumed that determination and freedom are two complementary aspects of structure. They cannot exist without each other any more than *up* can exist without *down* or *right* without *left*. Neither freedom nor determination are absolutes. A thing is free *with respect to something*; it is determined *with respect to something else*.

The solution proposed for the problem of determinism and free will provides us with the pattern for understanding how persons can vary and still be considered as lawful phenomena of nature. A person's construction system is composed of complementary superordinate and subordinate relationships. The subordinate systems are determined by the superordinate systems into whose jurisdiction they are placed. The superordinate systems, in turn, are free to invoke new arrangements among the systems which are subordinate to them.

This is precisely what provides for freedom and determination in one's personal-construct system. The changes that take place, as one moves towards creating a more suitable system for anticipating events, can be seen as falling under the control of that person's superordinating system. In his role identifying him with his superordinating system, the person is free with respect to subordinate changes he attempts to make. In his role as the follower of his own fundamental principles, he finds his life determined by them. Just as in governmental circles instructions can be changed only within the framework of fixed directives, and directives can be changed only within the framework of fixed statutes, and statutes can be changed only within the framework of fixed constitutions, so can one's personal constructs be changed only within subsystems of constructs and subsystems changed only within more comprehensive systems.

Our position is that even the changes which a person attempts within himself must be construed by him. The new outlook which a person gains from experience is itself an event; and, being an event in his life, it needs to be construed by him if he is to make any sense out of it. Indeed, he cannot even attain the new outlook in the first place unless there is some comprehensive overview within which it can be construed. Another way of expressing the same thing is to say that one does not learn certain things merely from the nature of the stimuli which play upon one; one learns only what one's framework is designed to permit one to see in the stimuli.

23. Terms

a. Permeability. Here we introduce a special construct within the psychology of personal constructs which we shall have occasion to use quite frequently in later sections. Particularly in the sections dealing with psychotherapy and the ways of helping persons reconstrue their lives, we shall expect to invoke the notion of *permeability of superordinate constructs.*

A construct is permeable if it will admit to its range of convenience new elements which are not yet construed within its framework. An utterly concrete construct, if there were such a thing, would not be permeable at all, for it would be made up of certain specified elements – those and no others. Such a construct would have to be impermeable.

There are, of course, relative degrees of permeability and impermeability. One person's construct of *good vs. bad* might be sufficiently permeable to permit him to see many new ideas and new acquaintances as good or bad. Another person's construct of *good vs. bad* might include many things but not be open to the inclusion of many new things; most of the good things and most of the bad things have already been labelled – and he has almost run out of labels.

The notion of permeability as a feature of conceptualization stems from the painstaking research of L.S. McGaughran, who approached the problems of conceptualization empirically and inductively. As a result of his investigation he was able to show that certain highly abstracted characteristics of a person's verbal behaviour were predictive of his nonverbal behaviour when dealing with palpable objects. While he does not use the term in his writings, in a conversation he once did propose the word *permeability* as a symbol for one of the aspects of conceptualization which he had abstracted. For his purposes, he found *permeability* to be a more useful dimension on which to plot conceptualization than the classical *abstract–concrete* dimension.

In our own usage a permeable construct is not necessarily loose, inconsistent, comprehensive, or tenuous. It may be quite definite; it may have little tendency to vary; it may embrace elements which are similar in other ways; and it may be persistently held. When we say that a construct is permeable we refer only to the particular kind of plasticity we have described – the capacity to embrace new elements.

It must be admitted that when new elements are added to the context of a construct there is a tendency for the construct itself to change somewhat. The abstraction of A and B versus C is likely to change when D is taken into consideration. For this reason permeable constructs may show a tendency to shift slightly from time to time. But the shift may be minimal, and shifting is not what we have in mind when we speak of permeability.

In earlier formulations of the theory of personal constructs we used the term 'stable aspects' instead of 'permeability'. Permeable constructs, because they possess resiliency under the impact of new experience, do tend to be stable, but 'permeability' is a more precise and operationally useful mark of identification for the kinds of constructs we have in mind than is 'stability'.

We do not necessarily refer to stability in the sense of longevity or lasting qualities, although a certain permeability in one's constructs gives them durability. Nor do we refer necessarily to a construct's intransigent rigidity in the face of its repeated systematic failures to anticipate events adequately. We refer rather, to those aspects of the system which can span a greater variety of new subordinate variations, which are less shaken by the impact of unexpected minor daily events.

A construct, or an aspect of one's construction system, can be called permeable if it is so constituted that new experience and new events can be discriminatively added to those which it already embraces. A construct which 'takes life in its stride' is a permeable one. It is under the regnancy of such constructs that the more subordinate aspects of a person's construction system can be systematically varied without making his whole psychological house fall down on him. Sometimes, of course, the house does fall down. Frequently, on a clinical basis, we can see the so-called 'decompensation' taking place in a client in the space of a few days or weeks. We are able also to see how the brittleness and impermeability of his construction system failed to support the alterations which he was finding it necessary to make. But more about this later!

The kind of construct which is permeable has more of the qualities of a theoretical formulation, as contrasted with a hypothetical formulation, in science. A hypothesis is deliberately constructed so as to be relatively impermeable and brittle, so that there can be no question about what it embraces and no doubt about its being wholly shattered or left intact at the end of an experiment. A theory is not so inflexibly constructed. It is stated in relatively permeable terms so that it may, in the future embrace many things which we have not yet thought of. It is stated in an open-ended form. A theory, then, both provokes and accepts a wide variety of experimental ventures, some of which may even be antithetical to each other.

Just as a scientific experimenter's formulations of successive experiments may undergo progressive changes in a manner which is always subordinate to the more theoretical aspects of his system, so any person, scientist or not, may vary his construction system in a manner which is subordinate to certain more permeable aspects of his system. The way the scientist uses his theory to accomplish this is a special case. We have tried, in this corollary, to state the more general case.

b. Variants. The constructs which replace each other may be considered to be the variants. Suppose a person starts out with a construct of *fear vs. domination* and shifts it to a construct of *respect vs. contempt.* Whereas once he divided his acquaintances between those he was afraid of and those whom he could dominate, he may, as he grows more mature, divide his acquaintances between those whom he respects and those whom he holds in contempt. But, in order for him to make this shift, he needs another construct, within whose range of convenience the *fear vs. domination* construct lies and which is sufficiently permeable to admit the new idea of *respect vs. contempt*. The two constructs, the old and the new, are the variants.

The permeable construct within whose range of convenience the variants lie may be such a notion as that of *maturity vs. childishness.* The attitude of *fear vs. domination* may be construed as a 'childish' notion and the attitude of *respect vs. contempt* may be considered to be a relatively 'mature' idea. Or it may be that both old and new constructs are seen as similar with respect to *maturity vs. childishness.* In the former case the person will see his new attitude as contrasting with the old in this respect; in the latter case he will see the new attitude as essentially similar to the old in this respect.

The psychotherapist who is concerned with his clients' psychological reconstruction of their lives runs across both types of transition in the course of his practice. The essential feature, from the standpoint of the assumptive structure of this theory, is that any transition needs to be subsumed by some overriding construction which is permeable enough to admit the new construct to its context. It is extremely difficult in practice to accomplish extensive psychotherapeutic results in a client whose superordinate structures are impermeable and most of whose basic conceptualizations are rooted exclusively in the past.

The client whose overriding structures are all permeable also presents certain therapeutic problems. Some of the structures which might better have their contexts closed out so that they will not be used to deal with new ideas may cause difficulty for the client as he construes the changes which are taking place in himself. But we are getting ahead of ourselves in this exposition of the psychology of personal constructs! The technical problems in the psychological reconstruction of life are reserved for a later discussion.

J. Fragmentation Corollary

24. Fragmentation Corollary: a person may successively employ a variety of construction subsystems which are inferentially incompatible with each other

A person's construction system is continually in a state of flux. Yet, even though it is fluctuating within a superordinate system, his successive formulations may not be derivable from each other. It is possible that what Willie thinks today may not be inferred directly from what he was thinking yesterday. His shift, nevertheless, in the light of our Modulation Corollary, is consistent with the more stable aspects of his system. What we are being careful to say now is that new constructs are not necessarily direct derivatives of, or special cases within, one's old constructs. We can be sure only that the changes that take place from old to new constructs do so within a larger system.

Now those larger systems may have been altered (within a still greater system, of course) by the impact of the old construct. In that case and in that sense the old construct is a legitimate precursor of the new construct. The relationship is still a collateral one, however, rather than a lineal one. The old and the new constructs may, in themselves, be inferentially incompatible with each other.

This is an important corollary. It should make even clearer the assumed necessity for seeking out the regnant construct system in order to explain the behaviour of men, rather than seeking merely to explain each bit of behaviour as a derivative of its immediately antecedent behaviour. If one is to understand the course of the stream of consciousness, one must do more than chart its headwaters; one must know the terrain through which it runs and the volume of the flood which may cut out new channels or erode old ones.

This is the point where statistical sampling theory may lead us astray if we are not careful to use it discriminatingly. If we are making an idiographic study by analysing a sample of the population of previous behaviours, we may make the mistake of assuming that a sample of future behaviours would be drawn from a universe having exactly the same parameters. From this kind of inference we would be led to believe that a four-year-old child who sucks his thumb fifteen hours a day would grow up to be a man who most likely would suck his thumb about fifteen hours a day. If we turn to sampling theory in a nomothetic framework, we may make another kind of mistake. We may assume that since most men do not suck their thumbs at all, this child will also grow up to be a man who will have no unusual habit of this type.

We are less likely to make a mistake if we are careful to look at the problem in the manner which was suggested in the preceding chapter. If we study the sample of past behaviours and extract our abstraction generalization, not in terms of a quantitative prediction of behaviours of the same order, but rather in terms of an abstraction or regnant construct of those behaviours, we may be able to solve our problem. We may come up with some such answer as the following: a sample of this particular child's behaviour appears to be drawn from a population of behaviour whose average is fifteen hours of thumb sucking a day. Up to this point we shall have used sampling theory within the idiographic frame. Now let us form a concept. Sampling theory will not help us do that; indeed, there is no reason to expect it to. Let us look at the child's other behaviours in a manner which will enable us to construe them, to form a construct, or, better still, to discover the child's own construction, verbalized or unverbalized, under which these different behaviours emerge. We look at the other behaviours. We sample them also idiographically. Since a construct is a way of seeing some things as being alike and, by the same token, as being different from other things, we shall seek the way in which some of the child's behaviours are alike and at the same time different from other behaviours. To use the common notion of 'abstraction', we shall *abstract* his behaviour, and, possibly, come up with such a construct as 'oral behaviour', or 'ingestive behaviour', or 'comfort behaviour', or 'narcissistic behaviour'. At this second stage in our reasoning process we shall have used concept formation, not sampling theory.

As a third step, let us move over into the nomothetic frame and try out our newly formed construct. Let us see whether it fits other children, whether their behaviour can be similarly construed as having elements some of which consistently fall into the category of our construct of oral behaviour and others of which clearly do not. Again, this is concept-formation or sorting procedure, not statistical sampling in the ordinary sense.

The fourth step is to see whether the construct fits adult behaviours. Again the framework is nomothetic.

The fifth step is statistical sampling in the nomothetic frame. We see whether or not a sample of childhood behaviours, of the abstract type we have construed, is correlated with a sample of adult behaviours of the same construct type. Presumably we will want to study the same people – as children, then as adults – although, under certain assumptions, we may study the correlation by some indirect method, such as by matching children with adults on some relevant variables which are already known to remain fairly constant throughout life.

Let us note that sampling and concept formation are not wholly different processes, though, for the purposes of the preceding discussion, it was convenient to label them so. In sampling, one makes certain hypotheses (an experimental and a null) as to the way in which two samples are similar, and then tests them.

25. The problem of consistency

One of the difficulties which arise in propounding a system like the psychology of personal constructs is that the reader is likely to expect any true construct system to be logic-tight and wholly internally consistent. Yet a candid inspection of our own behaviour and our own thinking makes it difficult to see how such an ideal system could exist in reality. Consistency is not an easy concept to handle in a meaningful fashion. What is consistent with what? Is thumb sucking in childhood consistent with thumb sucking in adulthood? Is it consistent with pipe smoking in adulthood? Is it consistent with the accumulation of property? Is it consistent with financial success? Is there anything that it is not consistent with? Is anything inconsistent with anything else?

If everything can be reconciled and made to appear consistent with everything else, the notion of consistency fails to meet our standards for a construct – a way in which at least two things are alike and at the same time different from at least one other thing. If it is not a construct, it cannot help us anticipate events. If it cannot help us anticipate events, it is of no service to science whose goal is prediction. Unless we accord to the notion of consistency a special meaning that gives it the status of a construct, either in the eyes of the person who seeks to reconcile his own behaviours or in the eyes of the observer who seeks to understand those behaviours, the term might be better not relied upon.

Before discussing a particular way of understanding consistency, let us take time to mention the theme of self-consistency that underlies some of the neophenomenological systems of today: Raimy's self-concept theory, Lecky's self-consistency theory, Rogers' client-centred approach, and Snygg and Combs's phenomenal field approach. All of these contemporary theories have enough similarity to personal-construct theory to make it important, from time to time in this discussion, to distinguish their differences as well as their similarities.

Lecky's self-consistency theory treated consistency as if it were a property of the ideas one has. He said that one method of dealing with inconsistency is to try to injure or destroy the objects or persons in connection with which the alien idea arose. Another method is 'to reinterpret the disturbing incident in such a manner that it can be assimilated'. Another is 'to alter the opinion one holds of oneself'. This all seems reasonable enough, but one soon finds oneself wondering what constitutes consistency or inconsistency.

Part of the answer, probably anticipated by Lecky, although he did not express it in so many words, is that consistency and inconsistency are personal labels. What one person sees as inconsistent another may see as consistent. While Lecky was concerned primarily with the problem of consistency and inconsistency of new ideas with the underlying self-idea, his view of consistency *per se* was that it was a property attributed to experience by the person who has the experience. In our own terms, his 'consistency' is a construct, and it is a personal one.

But to say the *consistency–inconsistency* construct is a personal one is not enough to make it applicable. When we hold to two views which are consistent with each other we expect to choose similar, or at least compatible, courses of action under them. The two views are inconsistent if they require us to perform the impossible feat of riding off in opposite directions at the same time. They are inconsistent if they lead us to anticipate two incompatible events. The key to the proper labelling of consistency lies in our Fundamental Postulate: a person's processes are psychologically channelized by the way in which he anticipates events. The operational definition of consistency can be written in terms of the way events are anticipated. Do the wagers one lays on the outcome of life cancel each other out or do they add up?

Our Fragmentation Corollary avers that a person may *successively* employ a variety of construction subsystems which are inferentially incompatible with each other. This means that his subsequent bets on the turn of minor events may not always add up with his earlier bets. Does this mean that his personality is structured only with respect to his minor anticipations? No!

The Fragmentation Corollary is, in part, a derivative of the Modulation Corollary. We said in the latter corollary that the variation in a person's construction system is limited by the permeability of the constructs within whose ranges of convenience the variants lie. We did not assume that variation in a person's constructions is subordinate to all antecedent (in time) aspects of his system. Our assumption is simply that it is in the context of the more permeable aspects of one's system that consistency is the law.

Now that we have suggested a more operational definition of consistency, the intent of the Modulation Corollary should be more clearly communicated. The Fragmentation Corollary follows as an explicit statement of the kind of inconsistency which the Modulation Corollary implicitly tolerates. The Modulation Corollary tolerates inconsistency between subsystems. More specifically, it tolerates the successive use of subsystems which do not, in themselves, add up.

A few sentences back, when we stated that a person's bets on the turn of minor events may not add up with his earlier bets, we asked if this meant that his personality is structured only with respect to his minor anticipations. We gave an emphatic no. Looking at the Fragmentation Corollary in the context of the Modulation Corollary one can give a more comprehensive answer. Now we can say that while a person's bets on the turn of minor events may not appear to add up, his wagers on the outcome of life do tend to add up. He may not win each time, but his wagers, in the larger contexts, to not altogether cancel themselves out. The superordinate permeable features of his system may not be verbalized, they may be more 'vegetative' than 'spiritual', or they may be seen as what Adler would have called a 'style of life'; but they are part of a *system* and, therefore, may be considered from the viewpoint of their free aspects.

As in the case of the idiographic–nomothetic issue, and as in the case of the determinism–free will issue, it is by considering the relative levels of abstraction and generality involved, or the permeability–impermeability levels with which we are dealing, or, in brief, by considering our problem in terms of the individual's personal-construct system and the person's attempts to anticipate events, that we are able to come to a satisfactory answer to the important psychological question of how the human organism can be organized and still appear to behave in a disorganized fashion.

26. Further implications of the Fragmentation Corollary

Since the variation in a person's construction system is subordinate to certain more permeable aspects of his system, each time his behaviours or his ideas undergo a change he must invoke, in some way or other, the permeable construct which provides the thread of consistency in his behaviours. If that permeable construct is not too clearly patterned, or if it is not too permeable, he may have to abandon its use and seek frantically for new ways of making sense out of life. These frantic attempts at new large concept formation may yield some weirdly new constructs, as he attempts to find the respects in which the events of life have definite likenesses and differences.

There is no clearer example of the limitation of one's ability to adjust to the vicissitudes of life, due to the impermeability of one's superordinate constructs, than the case of a compulsion-neurosis client who is undergoing a marked decompensation process. The construct system of such a client is characteristically impermeable; he needs a separate pigeonhole for each new experience and he calculates his anticipations of events with minute pseudomathematical schemes. He has long been accustomed to subsume his principles. The variety of construction subsystems which are inferentially incompatible with each other may, in the train of rapidly moving events, become so vast that he is hard put to it to find ready-made superordinate constructs which are sufficiently permeable or open-ended to maintain over-all consistency. He starts making new ones. While he has very little successful experience with concept formation at the permeable level, these are the kinds of concepts he tries to develop. They may turn out to be generalized suspicions of the motives of other people. They may have to do with reevaluations of life and death. They may lead him to anticipate reality in very bizarre ways.

A person's tolerance of incompatibility in his daily construction of events is also limited by the definition of the regnant constructs upon whose permeability he depends to give life its over-all meaning. If those constructs are so loosely defined that he has trouble getting organized, as in an emotional state, we may see him shifting his behaviour pattern back and forth, or reducing it to a childlike pattern which, though not very applicable to the present situation, does appear to provide optimal anticipations at the moment. In this case, too, we see what happens when the permeability and definition of one's superordinate constructs ceases to provide consistency, and the person is thrown back upon a more primitive and less effectual system, albeit a more permeable one.

K. Commonality Corollary

27. Commonality Corollary: to the extent that one person employs a construction of experience which is similar to that employed by another, his psychological processes are similar to those of the other person

We come now to a discussion of the implications of our Fundamental Postulate in the field of interpersonal relations. As we have already indicated, it is possible for two people to be involved in the same real events but, because they construe them differently, to experience them differently. Since they construe them differently, they will anticipate them differently and will behave differently as a consequence of their anticipations. That there should be such differences seems to be a logical outcome of our Fundamental Postulate, and we have stated that fact in the Individuality Corollary. But if we have an Individuality Corollary, we must also have a Commonality Corollary.

As with the other corollaries the Commonality Corollary is little more than a clarification of what seems to be implicit in our Fundamental Postulate. If a person's processes are psychologically channelized by the ways in which he anticipates events, and if he anticipates events by construing their replications, it may seem obvious that we are assuming that, if two persons employed the same construction of experience, their psychological processes would have to duplicate each other. This seems like an innocent statement. But as we examine this corollary closely, we find it has some implications which are not generally accepted among psychologists.

It is important to make clear that we have not said that if one person has experienced the same events as another he will duplicate the other's psychological processes. This is the assumption of stimulus–response psychology and, in its way, a perfectly respectable assumption; but it is not our assumption, and because we have not chosen to make it, we are free to develop our theoretical position in ways in which the stimulus–response psychologist is not. We could say, with systematic consistency, that two persons with identical experience would have identical psychological processes. But such a statement might be misleading unless the reader kept clearly in mind just what we mean by *experience*. He might have to keep turning back to our discussion of the Experience Corollary to see wherein our position differs from that of stimulus–response theory. So we prefer to state it the way we have – that two persons' psychological processes will be as similar as their constructions of experience.

One of the advantages of this position is that it does not require us to assume that it would take identical events in the lives of two people to make them act alike. Two people can act alike even if they have each been exposed to quite different phenomenal stimuli. It is in the similarity in the construction of events that we find the basis for similar action, and not in the identity of the events themselves. Again, as in the matter of learning, we think the psychologist can better understand his subjects if he inquires into the way in which they construe their stimuli than if he always takes his own construction of the stimuli for granted. In the words of our Modulation Corollary, we think psychologists need to use more permeable constructs in their own systems so that they can better subsume the variant constructions of their subjects.

Phenomenologically speaking, no two persons can have either the same construction or the same psychological processes. In that sense our Commonality Corollary would be unrealistic. But what we mean is this: to the extent that we can construe the constructions of two other people as being similar, we may anticipate that their psychological processes may also be construed as similar.

28. Terms

a. To the extent. In our Individuality Corollary we committed ourselves to the view that persons differ from each other in their constructions of events. The Commonality Corollary may appear to imply a contradiction to this previous statement. But when we say that persons differ from each other we do not rule out the possibility that there may be certain respects in which persons can be construed as being like each other. To say that James differs from John is not to say that James and John have nothing in common. In fact, to say that two things differ from each other in every conceivable respect is to express the ultimate in particularism and to leave one's listener in a confused state of mind about the whole matter. It is also about as confusing to say that two things are like each other in every conceivable respect; one is left wondering how they can then be considered as two distinct things.

What we have said in our Commonality Corollary does not contradict what we have assumed in our Individuality Corollary. By using the term, *to the extent*, we indicate that we are designating a totality of aspects in which the two persons' constructions of experience may be construed as similar. That there will still be many respects in which the two persons will retain their individuality goes without saying – our Individuality Corollary took care of that.

b. Construction of experience. Experience, as we have defined it, is a matter of successively construing events. To construe experience, then, is to take stock of the outcome of this successive construing process. Thus, if two people take similar stock of their successive interpretations, their behaviour will exhibit similar characteristics. The historical development of their thinking need not be similar – only the stock-taking need be similar. Hence it is not the similarity of experience which provides the basis for similarity of action, but similarity of their present construction of that experience.

By construction of experience we do not necessarily refer to highly verbalized interpretations. We keep reiterating this point. A person may construe his experience with little recourse to words, as, for example, in certain conditioned reflexes. Even those constructions which are symbolized by words are not necessarily similar just because the words are similar. Conversely, two persons may be using essentially the same constructions of their experience, although they express themselves in quite different terms.

29. Implications of the Commonality Corollary

It is an observed fact that certain groups of people behave similarly in certain respects. Some of these similarities are associated with similarities in their ages, some with similarities in what is expected of them by their associates, some with similarities in experience, and some with other kinds of constructions of similarity. Indeed, if we wish, we can approach the matter of similarities between persons from any one of a number of angles.

One of the common and interesting approaches to similarities and differences between persons is that taken from the standpoint of culture. Usually, as the term 'culture' would imply, this means that we see persons grouped according to similarities in their upbringing and their environment. This, basically, means that cultural similarities and differences are understood in terms of stimulus–response theory.

Sometimes, however, culture is taken to mean similarity in what members of the group expect of each other. This is an interpretation of culture which is more commonly found among sociological than among psychological theories. Psychologists perhaps avoid this approach because it seems to require that one interprets the behaviour of more than one person at a time; they prefer an approach which permits them to derive their system from observations of the individual man.

When one does understand culture in terms of similarity of expectations, one can proceed from that point in one of two directions. One can consider the expectations of others as stimuli to which each person is subjected; or one can understand cultural similarity between persons as essentially a similarity in what they perceive is expected of them. The latter approach throws the emphasis back upon the outlook of the individual person. This is, of course, the kind of approach one would be expected to make if one employed the psychology of personal constructs.

The similarity-of-expectations view of culture is also consistent with personal-construct theory from another angle. Our Fundamental Postulate assumes that a person's psychological processes are channelized by the ways in which he anticipates events. That makes the psychology of personal constructs an anticipatory theory of behaviour. Some of the real events that one anticipates are the behaviours of other persons. Personal-construct theory would then understand cultural similarity, not only in terms of personal outlook rather than in terms of the impingement of social stimuli, but also in terms of what the individual anticipates others will do and, in turn, what he thinks they are expecting him to do.

In interpreting social behaviour we are confronted with a spiraliform model. James anticipates what John will do. James also anticipates what John thinks he, James, will do. James further anticipates what John thinks he expects John will do. In addition, James anticipates what John thinks James expects John to predict that James will do. And so on! We are reminded of the famous illustration of the cat looking in the mirror. In complicated social situations, as in psychotherapy, for example, one may find oneself looking at another person through such an infinite series of reflections.

Personal-construct theory approaches problems of the commonality of behaviour primarily from the point of view of the individual person. Furthermore, it sees his point of view as an anticipatory one. It follows, then, that our approach to culture and group behaviour is via the study of similarities and contrasts in a person's anticipations and the channels he constructs for making his predictions. We are interested, not only in the similarities in what people predict, but also in the similarities in their manner of arriving at their predictions. People belong to the same cultural group, not merely because they behave alike, nor because they expect the same things of others, but especially because they construe their experience in the same way. It is on this last similarity that the psychology of personal constructs throws its emphasis.

L. Sociality Corollary

30. Sociality Corollary: to the extent that one person construes the construction processes of another, he may play a role in a social process involving the other person

While a common or similar cultural background tends to make people see things alike and to behave alike, it does not guarantee cultural progress. It does not even guarantee social harmony. The warriors who sprang up from the dragon's teeth sown by Jason had much in common but, misconstruing each other's motives, they failed to share in a constructive enterprise and soon destroyed each other. In order to play a constructive role in relation to another person one must not only, in some measure, see eye to eye with him but must, in some measure, have an acceptance of him and of his way of seeing things. We say it in another way: the person who is to play a constructive role in a social process with another person need not so much construe things as the other person does as he must effectively construe the other person's outlook.

Here we have a take-off point for a social psychology. By attempting to place at the forefront of psychology the understanding of personal constructs, and by recognizing, as a corollary of our Fundamental Postulate, the subsuming of other people's construing efforts as the basis for social interaction, we have said that social psychology must be a psychology of interpersonal understandings, not merely a psychology of common understandings.

There are different levels at which we can construe what other people are thinking. In driving down the highway, for example, we stake our lives hundreds of times a day on our accuracy in predicting what the drivers of the oncoming cars will do. The orderly, extremely complex, and precise weaving of traffic is really an amazing example of people predicting each other's behaviour through subsuming each other's perception of a situation. Yet actually each of us knows very little about the higher motives and the complex aspirations of the oncoming drivers, upon whose behaviour our own lives depend. It is enough, for the purpose of avoiding collisions, that we understand or subsume only certain specific aspects of their construction systems. If we are to understand them at higher levels, we must stop traffic and get out to talk with them.

If we can predict accurately what others will do, we can adjust ourselves to their behaviour. If others know how to tell what we will do, they can adjust themselves to our behaviour and may give us the right of way. This mutual adjustment to each other's viewpoint takes place, in the terms of the theory of personal constructs, because, to some extent, our construction system subsumes the construction systems of others and theirs, in part, subsume ours. Understanding does not have to be a one-way proposition; it can be mutual.

For the touch and go of traffic it is not necessary for the motorists to have an extensive mutual understanding of each other's ways of seeing things but, within a restricted range and at the concrete level of specific acts represented by traffic, the mutual understandings must be precise. For the more complicated interplay of roles – for example, for the husband-and-wife interplay – the understanding must cover the range of domestic activities at least, and must reach at least a level of generality which will enable the participants to predict each other's behaviour in situations not covered by mere household traffic rules.

One person may understand another better than he is understood. He may understand more of the other's ways of looking at things. Moreover, he may understand the other at a higher level of generality. Presumably, if this is true of a certain person with respect to a group of people whose ways of seeing things have some commonality, he is in a strategic position to assume a leadership relation to the group. On the other hand, there may be still other factors which effectively deny him that opportunity.

A therapist–client relationship is one which exemplifies greater understanding on the part of one member than on the part of the other. As a therapist comes to subsume the client's construction system within his own, he becomes more and more facile in developing his own role in relation to the client. It then becomes possible for them to make progress jointly in a social enterprise.

Parenthetically it should be admitted that the therapist–client relationship can, in some instances, be effective with the client's understanding more about the therapist's construction system than the therapist understands about the client's. Some therapists conduct their interviews with so much elaboration of their own views that this kind of role relationship might easily be the outcome. Some clients try to manage the interplay of roles so that they can find out what the therapist thinks – as if that would help them get along in life – without letting the therapist in on what they think. If he accepts the flattery, the therapist may waste time confiding his views to the client.

Perhaps somewhat more legitimately, the therapist, in his relationship with the client, may carefully manage his own role and the constructions of experience which he permits the client to observe. In that way he may enable the client to develop a role under certain presumptions about the therapist. The therapist may tentatively present a carefully calculated point of view in such a way that the client, through coming to understand it, may develop a basis for understanding other figures in his environment with whom he needs to acquire skill in playing interacting roles. This is known as *role playing* in psychotherapy and there are many ways in which it may be effectively employed.

31. Definition of role

In terms of the theory of personal constructs, a *role* is a psychological process based upon the role player's construction of aspects of the construction systems of those with whom he attempts to join in a social enterprise. In less precise but more familiar language, a role is an ongoing pattern of behaviour that follows from the person's understanding of how the others who are associated with him in his task think. In idiomatic language, a role is a position that one can play on a certain team without even waiting for the signals.

This definition of *role* lays emphasis upon several important points. First, like other patterns of behaviour, it is assumed to be tied to one's personal-construct system. This implies that it is anchored in the outlook of the role player and does not necessarily follow from his congregate relationship to other members of a group. It is a pattern of behaviour emerging from the person's own construction system rather than primarily out of his social circumstances. He plays out his part in the light of his understanding of the attitudes of his associates, even though his understanding may be minimal, fragmentary, or misguided. This notion of role is, therefore, neither a typical stimulus–response notion nor a typical sociological notion. We believe it is essentially consistent with our Fundamental Postulate and with the various corollaries which have already been stated.

The second point to be emphasized is that this definition of role is not equivalent to the 'self-concept' as used in some psychological systems. Seeing oneself as playing a role is not equivalent to identifying oneself as a static entity; but rather, as throughout the theory of personal constructs, the role refers to a process – an ongoing activity. It is that activity carried out in relation to, and with a measure of understanding of, other people that constitutes the role one plays.

The third point to be emphasized is that this definition ties up the role with a social process. While the concept of role is appropriate to a psychological system which is concerned with individual persons, it is defined herein so that it is dependent upon cognate developments within a group of two or more people. It is not enough that the role player organize his behaviour with an eye on what other people are thinking; he must be a participant, either in concert or in opposition, within a group movement. This further restriction of the definition of a role places emphasis upon team membership on the part of the role player.

The fourth point to be emphasized is that, while one person may play a role in a social process involving the other person, through subsuming a version of that other person's way of seeing things, the understanding need not be reciprocated. Thus the one person is playing a role in a social process, but the other is not playing a role in that social process. This is the way we have chosen to define *role*. It does not mean that the other person is not a factor to be taken into account in explaining the social process.

The fifth and final point to be emphasized is that this definition of role does not insist upon commonality in the construct systems of the people involved in the social process or in the persons specifically involved in playing roles. Commonality between construction systems may make it more likely that one construction system can subsume a part of another, but that fact is incidental rather than essential in those cases where roles are played between people who think alike and understand each other. Moreover, commonality can exist between two people who are in contact with each other without either of them being able to understand the other well enough to engage in a social process with him. The commonality may exist without those perceptions of each other which enable the people to understand each other or to subsume each other's mental processes. As in the case in psychotherapy in which the clinician identifies himself so closely with his client's way of seeing things that he cannot subsume the client's mental processes, the role the clinician plays becomes impoverished and the social process or the productive outcome of the clinician–client relationship comes to a standstill. The management of both transference and countertransference in psychotherapy is an example of the development of roles for both client and therapist.

We have made the point that for people to be able to understand each other it takes more than a similarity or commonality in their thinking. In order for people to get along harmoniously with each other, each must have some understanding of the other. This is different from saying that each must understand things in the same way as the other, and this delicate point has profound implications in psychotherapy. To the extent that people understand each other or, stated in the language of our theory, to the extent that their construction systems subsume each other, their activities in relation to each other may be called *roles*, a role being a course of activity which is played out in the light of one's understanding of the behaviour of one or more other people.

Let us make sure, further, that we have not slighted the point that there is a difference between two people's holding the same construction system and two people's understanding each other so that they can play roles in relation to each other. Consider the differences in the characteristic approaches to life of men and women. None of us would claim, we believe, that men and women construe all aspects of life in the same way. And yet nature has provided us with no finer example of role relationships and constructive social interaction than in the sexes. If we look at the testimony of nature, we shall have to admit that it often takes a man to understand a woman and a woman to understand a man and there is no greater tragedy than the failure to arrive at those understandings which permit this kind of role interrelationship.

32. The leadership role

It is not intended to discuss all the implications of the Sociality Corollary at this point. However, it may be helpful to look at certain of its implications in order to suggest what impact this assumption might have in the field of psychology. For example, the Sociality Corollary has implications for the psychology of leadership which may prove useful. It will be necessary, however, first to clarify what is meant by 'leadership'. In studying groups sociometrically it appears that nominators may make their selections of 'leaders' quite differently, depending upon their understanding of what the situation demands. If ingenuity and originality appear to him to be required, a nominator may choose one person. If defence of the group against an outside threat or a superordinate authority is believed to be needed, quite another kind of person may be chosen. If devotion to duty and housekeeping activities are required, still another may be selected. If individual members of the group are afraid their own freedom of action may be constricted if the group becomes tightly organized along certain lines, they may choose as leaders those who promise optimal permissiveness in the group structure. If the nominators feel keenly their interdependence upon each other, and therefore wish to mobilize the group, they may choose still another type of leader.

While prestige or status may be common to nearly all leadership, the psychologist will be badly fooled if he overlooks the variety of leadership patterns because they hold this one feature in common. A leader is one who performs any one of the variety of jobs which are popularly recognized as leadership jobs. He may do the job because of the expectancies with which he is surrounded; in that case, he may 'perform better than he is able'. Again, he may do the job with such originality that his 'leadership' is recognized only in the pages of history.

Let us consider first what is involved in the leadership role of the mobilizing or rallying type of leader. The situation within which he operates tends to accelerate the social processes of the group as a whole, though it sometimes retards the social processes of subgroups or superordinate groups. The rallying leader's contribution to the acceleration of the group's social progress is dependent upon and proportional to his understanding of the relevant features in his colleagues' personal-construct systems. By 'understanding' we do not mean that he necessarily holds the common viewpoint, but rather that he has a way of looking at his colleagues' ideas that makes sense and enables him to predict their behaviour. Of course, a commonality of viewpoint may, to a certain extent, make it easier for him to subsume parts of the construction systems of his colleagues within his own, but commonality is not a necessary prerequisite to subsuming.

Simply stated, the point is that one does not have to be like certain people in order to understand them, but he does have to understand them in certain respects in order to rally them. While this sentence may require some additional modifiers, it does express the central theme of what the psychology of personal constructs has to say about the rallying type of leadership.

In a somewhat different sense the Sociality Corollary provides inferences regarding other types of leadership. The ingenuity leader may not be playing a role in a social process, as we have defined *role* here, but the people who select him may be playing roles in a social process which involves him. In choosing him they are anticipating his contribution to the group and subsuming it within their own constructions of the part he ought to play.

The defending leader may not be called upon to perform an intragroup role; his role in a social process is played out primarily in relation to persons outside the group. The housekeeping leader may or may not be playing a role in the sense we have defined it. On the one hand, he may, like the ingenuity leader, be the one in relation to whom others play out their own roles in a social process. On the other hand, he may, as in the case of an effective executive secretary of an organization, understand the explicit and implicit policies of the group so well that he is able, without specific mandate, to act in each newly arising situation just as the group would want him to act.

The compromise leader need not play a role as we have defined it, and the role value of the participation of the people who select him may be minimal. Since his selection implies a slowing down of social process in the particular group with which his leadership is identified, perhaps so that other social processes will not be stifled, it is expected that his role will be constricted. To be sure, as some vice-presidents have done, he may surprise his electors and play out a role which generates more social progress than they bargained for.

33. Testing the theory of personal constructs

Since a theory is an *ad interim* construction system which is designed to give an optimal anticipation of events, its life is limited by its period of usefulness. If this theory proves to be fertile in providing us with testable hypotheses and in suggesting new approaches to the problems psychologists face, it will have cleared its first hurdle. If, subsequently, it occurs that a considerable proportion of the hypotheses prove to be true, and many of the new approaches provide desired control over psychological events, the theory will have reached maturity. When its place is eventually taken by a more comprehensive, a more explicit, a more fertile and more useful theory, it will be time to relegate it to history.

It cannot be expected that we can accomplish any more than the partial clearing of the first hurdle in this presentation. An attempt will be made to show that the theory does provide us with some interesting new approaches to the problems psychologists face, particularly in the field of psychotherapy. Some hypotheses which are believed to be testable by more formal procedures will also be suggested. The establishment of real fertility in this respect, however, will depend upon what the readers of this manuscript come up with as a result of reading it.

M. Summary of Assumptive Structure

34. Fundamental Postulate and its corollaries

a. Fundamental Postulate: A person's processes are psychologically channelized by the ways in which he anticipates events.
b. Construction Corollary: A person anticipates events by construing their replications.
c. Individuality Corollary: Persons differ from each other in their constructions of events.
d. Organization Corollary: Each person characteristically evolves, for his convenience in anticipating events, a construction system embracing ordinal relationships between constructs.
e. Dichotomy Corollary: A person's construction system is composed of a finite number of dichotomous constructs.
f. Choice Corollary: A person chooses for himself that alternative in a dichotomized construct through which he anticipates the greater possibility for extension and definition of his system.
g. Range Corollary: A construct is convenient for the anticipation of a finite range of events only.
h. Experience Corollary: A person's construction system varies as he successively construes the replications of events.
i. Modulation Corollary: The variation in a person's construction system is limited by the permeability of the constructs within whose ranges of convenience the variants lie.
j. Fragmentation Corollary: A person may successively employ a variety of construction subsystems which are inferentially incompatible with each other.
k. Commonality Corollary: To the extent that one person employs a construction of experience which is similar to that employed by another, his psychological processes are similar to those of the other person.

l. Sociality Corollary: To the extent that one person construes the construction processes of another, he may play a role in a social process involving the other person.

Chapter three

The nature of personal constructs

We turn now to a descriptive elaboration of the psychology of personal constructs in an attempt to give greater palpability to what we have been saying earlier in abstract terms.

A. Personal usage of constructs

1. The basic nature of a construct

A construct is a way in which some things are construed as being alike and yet different from others. We have departed from conventional logic by assuming that the construct is just as pertinent to some of the things which are seen as different as it is to the things which are seen as alike. For example, suppose a person construes in terms of a *black vs. white* construct. His field comprises a number of things. Some of them, such as his shirt, his shoes, his house, the paper on which he writes, the skin of his neighbour, and so on, are amenable to the *black vs. white* construct. The construct may be misapplied; he may call his shirt white when his wife sees it as black. It may be inappropriate; merely to construe his neighbour's skin as black may not be a very enlightened way to look at his neighbour. But, all in all, the construct is applicable to those things which for him can be either black or white. Yet there are other things in the person's life. There is the time of day, his affection for his children, the distance to his office, and so on, for which the *black vs. white* is patently irrelevant.

a. Bipolar nature of constructs. Now conventional logic would say that *black* and *white* should be treated as separate concepts. Moreover, it would say that the opposite of *black* can only be stated as *not black*, and the opposite of *white* can only be stated as *not white*. Thus the person whose field we mentioned would have shoes which would be just as much *not white* as the time of day, and he would write on paper which would be just as *not black* as the distance to his office.

Some logicians take the further view that a concept is a way in which certain things are naturally alike and that all other things are really different. For them the concept is a feature of the nature of the things with which it is concerned and not an interpretative act of someone. We would agree that the concept is real, but its reality exists in its actual employment by its user, and not in the things which it is supposed to explain.

The conventional logic to which we have referred is perfectly respectable in its way. It is an approach to thinking which, for some centuries now, many careful thinkers have assumed to be a good one. Our view would admit it as one of the possible approaches to the problems of psychology. We would not admit that it is nature's ultimate revelation. In a manner which is compatible with the view of constructive alternativism, upon which the psychology of personal constructs is based, we have chosen, for the time being, to abandon the classical notion of concepts and to assume a somewhat different structure of thought.

While it is not absolutely necessary that one start out by defending the plausibility of his assumptions, our assumptions regarding the nature of constructs seem to correspond more closely to observation of how persons actually think than do the customary assumptions regarding conceptualization.

b. Lyle's study. While our view of constructs as dichotomous abstractions is in the nature of an assumption, and hence not something which needs to be tested within the framework of our theory, there is already some research evidence which supports the view. Lyle, in a study of selective perception, from the standpoint of the psychology of personal constructs, had occasion to factor analyse certain accuracy scores made by subjects who were asked to categorize groups of words. The categories were set up in terms of constructs commonly used by the population from which the sample of subjects was drawn. The list of words was carefully chosen and pretested in order to provide certain controls. These words were then presented to his subjects and they were asked to assign each word to one of the eight categories or to a ninth, or 'don't know', category. This was done under pressure of time, with a paced presentation.

Subjects were scored in terms of their accuracy in identifying words 'correctly' in each of the eight category groups. 'Correct' categorizations were based on agreement in a separately drawn sample of the same population of undergraduate college women. Since each subject produced eight accuracy scores, the data could be factor analysed.

Lyle's eight categories were chosen so as to represent four construct dimensions: *cheerful vs. sad, broad-minded vs. narrow-minded, refined vs. vulgar*, and *sincere vs. insincere*. However, as far as the selection of words to fit these categories and the experimental presentation were concerned, they were treated as entirely independent concepts.

The factor analysis produced five factors: a general factor which might be called verbal facility, intelligence, or something of the sort, and four factors each of which had a pair of heavy loadings on the contrasting ends of the original construct dimensions. While there was nothing in the selection of terms or in the mathematical procedure which would make the loadings pair off in this manner, it did happen that when persons made errors in assigning terms to Lyle's *cheerful* category they also tended to make errors in assigning terms to his *sad* category, but they did not necessarily make errors in connection with his *broad-minded*, *narrow-minded*, *refined*, *vulgar*, *sincere*, and *insincere* categories. In a similar manner the other pairs of terms showed up on the loadings of the other factors. This suggests that if *cheerful* corresponds to a construct in a person's personal-construct system, its antonym does also. Or, stated in other terms, if a person's personal construct of *cheerful* makes sense in a public system, his personal construct of *sad* will also make sense in the public system. This is what one would expect if one's personal constructs were essentially dichotomous. It is not what one would expect if the concepts of *cheerful* and *sad* were independently abstracted by the person.

(See Lyle's factor table, Table 3.1.)

Table 3.1 Lyle's factor table

	Factors				
Terms	*I*	*II*	*III*	*IV*	*V*
Cheerful	52	60*	01	02	−03
Sad	47	66*	−03	−04	22
Broad-minded	66	00	42*	05	12
Narrow-minded	72	−02	57*	03	04
Sincere	12	06	−10	75*	02
Insincere	27	−01	12	48*	−05
Refined	00	−04	−07	20	55*
Vulgar	43	03	23	−06	72*

Note: *Indicates highest pair of loadings on each of the specific factors

c. Personal range of convenience. From our point of view, each construct, as used by a person, has a limited range of convenience. Outside that range the person does not find it relevant, one way or the other, to the objects located there. For example, the time of day is an element most people would place outside the range of convenience of their personal construct of *black vs. white*. But within the range of convenience of the construct there is a relevant similarity and difference which together form the essence of the construct. The difference is not simply the outer boundary of relevance of the construct – that boundary is the limit of the range of convenience. Rather, the difference exists within the range of convenience, and it is just as important to the construct as is the similarity.

The elements lying within the range of convenience of the construct are said to constitute its context. For one person the construct of *black vs. white* may have a somewhat different context than for another. For example, one person may classify his moods as black or white, another may classify his fabrications as black or white, and another may use the construct to distinguish between cultures. Moreover, a person who frequently reads the dark-faced type and light-faced type in a railroad time schedule may come to deal even with the time of day within the range of convenience of his *black vs. white* construct. Finally, one person may classify as white what another, perhaps from a different cultural group, classifies as black. For example, in European cultural groups black is the colour of mourning, while in parts of the Orient white is the colour used to symbolize grief.

d. Usefulness of the dichotomous assumption. Have dichotomous construction systems proved useful in the field of science? This is an important question to ask, for we are ascribing a dichotomous quality to all human thinking. It is therefore quite relevant to ask whether or not previous attempts to ascribe dichotomy to phenomena have proved valuable.

Let us cite two cases in which dichotomous thinking has proved to be particularly useful. The first is in the field of electromagnetism, and later, electronics. Here the notion of positive and negative poles and charges has opened the door to many important discoveries and inventions. Yet the notion of *positive vs. negative* is only an assumption which was imposed upon the data; the atoms did not come around to the scientists and ask to be divided into positive and negative aspects. The second outstanding example of the successful use of dichotomy is Mendel's theory of genes. While no one has yet been able to point to a palpable gene of either the dominant or recessive type, the concept of *dominant vs. recessive* has proved to be remarkably fruitful.

It is important for us to keep in mind that it is not the accumulation of the elements in the context that constitutes the construct, nor is it the differential grouping of the elements. Rather, the construct is the *basis* upon which elements are understood. It is a matter of how the person construes the elements in order to deal with them, not where they happen to appear or where he decides to set them down. The construct is an interpretation of a situation and is not itself the situation which it interprets.

Our view of constructs makes it appear that all people's thinking must be abstract, and never absolutely concrete. We assume that is true. We do not envision the possibility of an entirely concrete psychological response. Even perception, long thought to be something quite different from conceptualization, is assumed to be an act of construing. But we do see some individuals who are much more concretistic in their outlooks than are others. They have difficulty making the bridge from element to element unless the elements are laid physically side by side. But even so, they must abstract the elements in some degree, else their lives would be hopelessly kaleidoscopic and there would be no possibility of internal organization.

2. *Do people mean what they say?*

It is not possible for one to express the whole of one's construction system. Many of one's constructs have no symbols to be used as convenient word handles. They are therefore difficult, not only for others to grasp and subsume within their own systems, but also difficult for the person himself to manipulate or to subsume within the verbally labelled parts of his system. The fact that they do not readily lend themselves to organization within the verbally labelled parts of the system makes it difficult for a person to be very articulate about how he feels, or for him to predict what he will do in a future situation which, as yet, exists only in terms of verbal descriptions.

A person may say that he will not take a drink if he is offered one tomorrow. But when he says so he is aware only of what he can verbally label; he is not fully aware of what it will be like tomorrow when tomorrow's situation actually confronts him. The situation which he envisions is, to be sure, one in which he would not take the drink. But the situation which actually rolls around may loom up quite differently and he may do what he has promised himself and others he would not do. There may be a failure of his structure, or, more particularly, that part of it which is verbally labelled, to subsume adequately certain aspects of the rest of the system.

There is another respect in which it may appear that one does not mean what one says. It may be impossible for one to express certain constructs in such a way that others can subsume them within their own systems without mispredicting one. They 'take him at his word', but he does not mean by his word what they think he means. It therefore appears that he does not mean what he says. Sometimes a person's verbal expression represents such a contamination of constructs that he himself, when he hears a transcription of his remarks against a different background of circumstances, may be amazed at what then seems to be the import of his verbal behaviour. This happens in psychotherapy when a client hears transcriptions of parts of earlier interviews.

a. Incomplete expression. Often people express their constructs incompletely. Let us keep in mind that a construct is a way in which some things are alike and yet different from others. In its minimum context a construct would be a way in which two things are alike and different from a third. It should be kept in mind that the *way* in which the two things are like each other should be the same as the *way* in which they are different from the third. We do not explicitly express a whole construct if we say, 'Mary and Alice have gentle dispositions but neither of them is as attractive as Jane.' We would have to say something like this, if we were to express a true construct: 'Mary and Alice are gentle; Jane is not.' Or we might say, 'Jane is more attractive than Mary or Alice.'

When we say 'Mary and Alice have gentle dispositions but neither of them is as attractive as Jane', we may be implying two different constructs: *gentleness* and *attractiveness*. The selection of an adjective to describe two persons, or even to describe one person, usually means that the speaker has formed a category which, for him, has the simultaneous inclusive and exclusive properties of a construct. To say that Mary is gentle is to imply that at least one other person is gentle also and that at least one other person is not gentle. Or it may imply that at least two other persons are not gentle.

The minimum context for a construct is *three* things. We cannot express a construct, either explicitly or implicitly, without involving at least two things which have a likeness and one which is, by the same token, different. To say that Mary and Alice are 'gentle' and not imply that somewhere in the world there is someone who is 'not gentle' is illogical. More than that, it is unpsychological.

Now a person may be heard to say, 'Mary and Alice are gentle and I cannot conceive of anyone's not being gentle.' Such a speaker may be attempting to avoid placing himself in the position of one who sees ungentleness. His statement may thus provide an important lead for the psychologist who is seeking to understand him. On the other hand, the speaker may be restricting the reference of the concept to the idiographic frame. He may, if we ask him, indicate that he means, 'Mary and Alice are gentle *now*, as contrasted with some other time' – in other words, that gentleness is not a construct which distinguishes people from each other, but rather one which distinguishes day-to-day variations in persons. This construction of gentleness may also throw considerable light upon the speaker's own pattern of day-to-day mood changes. It is certainly profitable to listen carefully to a speaker's use of constructs.

Sometimes a person will attempt to limit the context to two things which are unlike in some way. He may say, 'Mary is gentle; Jane is not. I know of no one else who is like either of them.' It may be a little more difficult to see, but this also represents a verbal distortion of conceptualization. Mary and Jane have already been distinguished when they entered the discussion identified by their names. To say that they are further distinguished by their gentleness or lack of it is to add nothing to the distinction, unless that further distinction, by indicating a kinship of at least one of them with a third person, classifies them. While this kind of conceptual distortion is not as common as that described in the previous paragraph, it does indicate that the speaker is having trouble communicating the kinship he covertly construes between Mary and Jane and the other people in his social world. The missing *like* element in the expression of his construct is quite possibly denied because he himself is it. To say that his conceptualization of Mary and Jane is concretistic is not enough; he is really in trouble about Mary and Jane.

One cannot help but be reminded, at this point, of those psychologists and others who insist that everyone is an 'individual' and that we cannot understand one individual through understanding other individuals. Here is a form of conceptual distortion which seems to betray the particular scientist's deeply rooted confusion about what to do about 'people'. The therapist who is really reduced to this sort of reasoning is likely to find that his therapeutic efforts extract a heavy toll from him, and the problem of transference and countertransference (because he himself covertly becomes one of the two missing figures in the constructural context) is one which he cannot face. The insistence upon the exclusive use of the idiographic frame is a further example of the attempt to reduce all social constructs to a context comprised solely of unlikenesses. That mistake, at least, is one which is avoided in the psychology of personal constructs by the recognition that the abstractions which are lifted from a sample of behaviours of a single person may, in turn, be used as data from which abstractions are lifted from a sample of people of a group.

We have spoken of the two types of instances in which a speaker may attempt to limit the context of his construct to two or more *like* things, and the second in which he attempts to limit the context to two or more *unlike* things. Next let us consider the case in which he attempts to limit the context to one thing only.

'Mary is gentle. I wouldn't say that anyone else was gentle and I wouldn't say that they weren't.' This is not even equivalent to the redundant statement that 'Mary is Mary'. By calling a person 'Mary', we are at least implying that all of her is 'Mary' and that other people are 'not Mary'. But the speaker who says that Mary is gentle but still insists that gentleness provides neither kinship nor distinction for Mary is failing to communicate a construct. It may be, of course, that he means that Mary is gentle now *like* she was at some other time and *unlike* she was at still a third time. More likely, he is unable to bring himself to the point of full expression of his construct. At the verbal level, at least, his construct has probably reached the point of complete impermeability. He is not in a position to use it for meeting new situations in life or for readjusting to old. He cannot organize other constructs under it. On the verbal level, the construct has become inoperative.

b. Names as personal construct symbols. Are proper names expressions of constructs? Yes. A name is a way of seeing a likeness in one group of events which distinguishes it from another group of events. Over here, we have a group of events which may be seen as being alike by way of being 'Mary events'. Over there are events, still within the range of convenience of the construct, which are 'un-Mary-like events'. 'Mary' is a construct of events. So, any name is a kind of construction of events. This is a partial answer to critics of Raimy's self-concept theory who, on logical grounds, claim that the term 'self-concept' is a misnomer; that it should be called 'self-percept' or 'self-identity'. In terms of classical logic, these critics are, of course, correct in their criticism. However, in terms of our functional definition of construct and our theoretical position in the psychology of personal constructs, it is quite appropriate to refer to a given person's self-construct, or to a class of constructs which can be called personal self-constructs.

c. Nondiscriminating universals. Finally, let us look at the instance in which an attempt is made to express a universal similarity. 'Mary, Alice, Jane, and everyone else are always gentle.' This reminds one of the common expression, 'Everything is good.' Taken literally, both statements deny their constructs. If everyone is gentle, the construct of gentleness has no meaning. But the speaker must mean something. The listener must look beyond the literal symbolism and construe the speaker's personal construction.

There are several possibilities. Suppose the contrast to 'gentleness' in the speaker's system is something we might call 'aggressiveness'. If the speaker says that 'everyone is gentle', he avoids pointing to anyone and labelling him 'aggressive'. He may do this because he does not want to be in the position of one who is known as a seer of aggressiveness. He may do it because he cannot deal satisfactorily with aggressive people and, for the moment at least, is trying to limit his population to people he can deal with. Then there may be an implied exception in the statement; he may mean, 'Everyone *except me* is gentle.' Another interpretation is that he may feel that if anyone in the world is aggressive it would have to be himself, his own latent aggression is so great. The only way, therefore, that he can escape being the prime example of aggressiveness is to insist that everyone is gentle.

A similar interpretation is that someone close to him, such as a parent, would have to be identified as aggressive if he admitted that anyone was aggressive. To construe the parent as aggressive may have such far-reaching consequences that the better elaborative choice would seem to be to include the parent with the gentle ones, even if it means universalizing 'gentleness'. Any other interpretation on his part might shake the whole construction system which gives shape to his life role.

Often a speaker, by his choice of constructs, indicates what he thinks of the listener. This happens continually in psychotherapy; the psychotherapist gets a pretty good notion of what the client thinks of him by what the client chooses to emphasize or even to talk about. For example, the client who says, 'Everyone is gentle', may be implying that the therapist is too prone to see aggressiveness. What he means is, 'You seem to keep looking for aggressiveness; please take the view, when dealing with me, that everyone is gentle.' Another similar interpretation is that he means, 'Look, I'm such a nice person that I am willing to call everybody gentle, whether they are or not. Now don't you think I'm saintly?' Or he may mean, 'So many people see aggressiveness around them and I am so upset by it that I try to exemplify the virtue of seeing gentleness'.

Another possible interpretation is that the client is trying to express movement. Whereas once he saw the world as aggressive, he now sees it as gentle. Or he may be warning the therapist of impending movement: 'So many people see the world as aggressive. I don't yet – but watch out!'

d. Special problems of interpretation. Since constructs are primarily personal, not all of them are easily shared. The peculiar nature of a person's construct or his unusual use of terminology may be misleading to his listener. For example, what one person means by 'gentle' may correspond more closely to what others would call 'dependent' or, perhaps, 'weak'. He may even have in mind some kind of refinement of manners, social status, or cultural grouping such as one might imply when he uses the term 'gentleman'.

Then one needs to be aware of the two-ended nature of the construct and the possibility that one person's 'gentle' may have quite a different continuum stretching away from it than does another person's 'gentle'. We have suggested that the speaker might be construing in terms of a *gentle vs. aggressive* continuum. But perhaps the contrast end of his construct is not 'aggressive' but something like 'tactless' or, perhaps, 'ingenuous'. In that case, his statement might mean something more like, 'Everyone is subtle', or, 'Everyone is sly.'

Sometimes a client is simply performing an experiment with his therapeutic role. He acts out a point of view in order to see how the therapist will respond or what the resulting situation will yield for him. He may mean, 'Let's see how you react to this statement: "Everyone is gentle".' The key to understanding this kind of statement is to note the implied quotation marks in what the client says. The client is experimenting. If the therapist appears either to accept or reject the statement, the client interprets it as throwing light upon the therapist. If, for example, the therapist appears to accept the statement, it may mean that he is ill-prepared to deal with the latent aggression which the client might be hoping to express. If the therapist appears to reject the statement, it will next be important to find out what he considers aggression to be and who the aggressive people are. Perhaps the therapist, in that case, is getting ready to be aggressive himself.

Sometimes the client makes his statements in reverse form. Like the experimental psychologist who, if he is precise, designs his experiments around the null hypothesis, which he really hopes will be rejected, the client may make tentative reverse bets. Instead of saying, 'Is *not* the whole world aggressive?' he says, 'The whole world is gentle.' He uses an affirmative antithetical statement instead of the *not*. Having laid down the hypothesis, he proceeds to see how many holes the data of his experience will shoot into it. Perhaps the client is experimenting with himself. He may mean, 'While I do not think so, I shall now pretend that the whole world is gentle; I wonder what preposterous things will happen *to me* in consequence of my taking this pose.' Persons frequently experiment in these ways, a fact which the therapist needs to keep in mind continually. It is also a fact for which conventional learning theory in psychology has no facile explanation.

It is not our intention to make an exhaustive analysis of what a person means when he makes a simple declarative statement. It is sufficient to make clear that the contrast aspects of an expressed personal construct must not be overlooked in interpretation, and to point out that there is a great variety of possible interpretations that a listener may place upon such a simple statement as we have used for our illustration.

3. Implied linkages in the interpretation of personal constructs

In the practical interpretation of personal constructs we need to be alerted to another feature of the way people express themselves. Let us take our original illustrative statement, 'Mary and Alice have gentle dispositions but neither of them is as attractive as Jane.' While it may appear that the speaker is invoking two different constructs in order to avoid mentioning the contrast end of one of them, he may have actually contraposed the ideas so that his construct functions as a *gentle vs. attractive* continuum. Gentleness and unattractiveness may be undifferentiated from each other in the speaker's construction system; also attractiveness and ungentleness. It may be that they have never been differentiated; or it may be that recent experience has, through construction, linked them, so that they now function as a single personal construct.

This kind of linkage is a common problem in psychotherapy. It is found in stereotypes and in the global *figure transferences* through which clients see their therapists and others during certain stages of treatment. This kind of linkage is sometimes interpreted by the therapist, in whose own system the terms seem clearly to refer to separate constructs, as 'conflict'. He does this because he has not yet entered into the client's thinking perceptively enough to see the singularity of the construct as it is used personally by the client. The 'conflict' may be more the experience of the therapist than of the client. What the client experiences, assuming that the construct fails to work for him, is *anxiety*. But more about anxiety later!

The statement about Mary, Alice, and Jane may imply another kind of linkage, which stems from the person's own identification of himself with the context of the construct he uses. 'Mary and Alice have gentle dispositions *but* neither of them is as attractive as Jane.' The speaker may be using the two different constructs of *gentleness* and *attractiveness*. If he says simply that Mary and Alice are not as attractive as Jane, he will have identified himself as a detractor of Mary and Alice; so he first identifies himself as maintaining a pleasant relationship with Mary and Alice. Our social discourse is full of the *yes, but...* types of construction. They represent our efforts to be objective, not by keeping ourselves detached from the context of our discussion but by allying ourselves with all parties in the context. 'John is a nice fellow', 'Jim is a swell guy', 'Some of my best friends are Jews', are common prefaces designed to give immunity to the speaker against the consequences of what he is about to say.

Finally, there is the possibility of a kind of linkage which stems from the speaker's attempt to set up a *system* of constructs. The construct of *gentleness* is seen as subsuming the construct of *attractiveness*. Mary and Alice, by virtue of being gentle, are attractive. Jane is also attractive, but not because she is gentle.

We have pointed out the minimum context of three things out of which a construct can be formed, and the minimum of two relationships, one of likeness and one of difference, which must be implied. We have offered some introductory interpretations of the conceptual breakdown which may be implied in a speaker's simple statement; and, finally, we have suggested the linkage of constructs. One should not infer from this discussion that it is possible for a clinician, even though highly skilled, to assure himself that his client's conceptual system is breaking down in some area, merely from listening to one simple sentence of the type used in the illustration. As we have tried to illustrate, there are several possible interpretations of the personal constructs implied by the illustrative sentence. The alternatives are not so vast as to be unmanageable, however, and the skilled clinician may be able to tease out the meanings and linkages of the client's personal constructs, as expressed in such a sentence, without too great difficulty.

When conceptual distortion is detected, through noting the client's inability to accept at least a threefold context or a twofold relationship in expressing his construct, we have seen that the clinician may want to pay particular attention to the missing *opposites* implied by the construct, the implied momentary *role* in which the construct would force the speaker to cast himself in relation to the listener, the kind of *world* or cast of characters in relation to which he must establish a life role, the kind of experimental *venture* he may be attempting, and the kinds of subsuming relationships, or *system*, in which the client's constructs are ordered. With these points in mind, we can now turn our attention to some further basic implications of the psychology of personal constructs.

4. Constructs and anticipations

From what we have said thus far about the nature of constructs one might easily conclude that they are designed to set in order a universe composed of inherently static objects. Yet our Fundamental Postulate envisions a universe of processes. Indeed, it may seem as though we have inadvertently exposed our *construct* to the same modern criticism that is levelled at the Aristotelian *concept* – that it fails to deal with antecedence and subsequence. It is time, therefore, for us to take up more explicitly the part that construing plays in an anticipatory system of psychology.

We have said that a person's processes are psychologically channelized by the ways in which he anticipates events, and that these ways exist in the form of constructs. A construct, in turn, is an abstraction. By that we mean it is a property attributed to several events, by means of which they can be differentiated into two homogeneous groups. The invention of such a property is the act of abstracting. To construe events is to use this convenient trick of abstracting them in order to make sense out of them. Each person goes at it in his own way, more or less, and that is where the title of this book, *The Psychology of Personal Constructs*, comes from.

Now what about prediction? We have said that events are set apart from each other by the construing of their replications. That is to say, we look at the undifferentiated stream of circumstance flowing past us, and we try to find something about it that repeats itself. Once we have abstracted that property, we have a basis for slicing off chunks of time and reality and holding them up for inspection one at a time. On the other hand, if we fail to find such a property, we are left swimming in a shoreless stream, where there are no beginnings and no endings to anything. Thus the first step in prediction is to get hold of a solid fistful of something to predict. And this is done by construing, as we have assumed in our Construction Corollary.

Setting off an event so that it can be predicted is one step; but the moment we take this step we commit ourselves even further. By the very process of identifying the event as something replicated, we imply that it may happen again. Or, rather, we imply that its replicated properties may all reappear in another event. Thus it is impossible not to imply prediction whenever one construes anything. Certainly there is nothing static about a world which is construed in this manner.

a. What is it that is predicted when one predicts? When one abstracts replicated properties in the events he has already experienced, it becomes possible for him to chart events to come in terms of these same properties. A navigator who has never been to the North Pole may yet know its coordinates so well that he can predict the event of his arrival there. In a sense he does not conjure up the event itself, but rather its properties. Sure enough, twenty-nine days after he makes his prediction he does experience an event having all the predicted properties – time, declination of the sun, and so on – all occurring in conjunction with each other. With this evidence of the converging properties of time and space, he shouts to his companions, 'Here we are; this is it!' His prediction is satisfactorily confirmed.

Let us make sure that we are explicit about this. What one predicts is not a fully fleshed-out event, but simply the common intersect of a certain set of properties. If an event comes along in which all the properties intersect in the prescribed way, one identifies it as the event he expected. For example, a girl in her teens anticipates eventual marriage. There are few men in her life and the system of constructs which she uses to keep them arranged is fairly simple. The predicted husband does not exist for her in the flesh, but simply as the intersect of a limited number of conceptual dimensions. One day a young man comes along and plumps himself down more or less on this waiting intersect. Her prediction, like the navigator's, is confirmed and, before anyone realizes what is happening, she marries him.

But take the old maid. She, too, has predicted a husband in terms of the intersect of a number of conceptual dimensions. But there are altogether too many dimensions involved and nobody ever lands on the precise point where all of them converge. Her long-standing anticipation is never fulfilled; she continues to be a spinster.

b. Concretizing constructs. We have taken some pains to point out that to understand whole events we have to abstract them. Now let us point out, in turn, that to understand constructs we have to concretize them. Thus to make sense out of concrete events we thread them through with constructs, and to make sense out of the constructs we must point them at events.

Here we have a full cycle of sense-making, the first phase of which is embedded in the traditions of rationalism, but the second phase of which conforms to the basic tenet of modern scientific experimentalism. Any theory, such as our theory of personality, must make good through both phases of the cycle. Not only must it give us a rationale of the events of human behaviour, but it must result in predictions having their counterparts in tomorrow's reality.

The prediction in terms of which constructs are concretized is itself entirely hypothetical. It is the imagined intersect of several construct dimensions. Once it is made, it can be validated only if an event comes along which can be construed like the intersect. This is the experimental evidence one usually looks for. Through the accumulation of such evidence a theory gradually gets its feet on the ground.

c. If-then relationships. Let us turn from the structure of a prediction and look next at the process of arriving at it. This, too, is a construing process which starts with an abstraction. But a special kind of abstraction is involved. The construct one forms is a construct of trend or movement perceived amid the context of elements. As in the case of all constructs, the possibilities are twofold; the tendency can be in one direction or the other. The two poles of the construct establish the line along which the movement may take place.

Consider again our illustration of the navigator. Ever since he left his point of departure he has been observing various events. He has made records of chronometer readings, of the declinations of astral bodies, of magnetic and gyroscopic compass readings, and of track. To these events he applies constructs from his professional repertory. For example, he may apply the constructs of longitude and latitude. Next, in relation to these navigator's coordinates, he creates a special construct of movement, tailor-made to the situation. The construct will be dichotomous, of course; one pole refers to the direction of which he is going and the other to the direction he is coming from. With this construct in hand, together with the coordinates of the hypothetical North Pole and certain other constructs, he arrives at a prediction that twenty-nine days hence he will reach the Pole.

To predict is to construe movement or trend among surrounding events. The particular movement construed is always a construct tailor-made for a particular situation; nevertheless, it is one based on a standing system of coordinate axes having more general applicability. The point of convergence of all relevant constructs – time, the movement construct, and the coordinate readings of the hypothetical event – constitute the prediction. The next step is to see whether any event falls smack on this imaginary point so as to fulfil all of its presupposed conditions. That is validation.

Consider another illustration. A child predicts that if he breaks his mother's necklace he will get a spanking. He seems to perceive an *if-then* relationship between the breakage and the spanking. But this is never a simple one-to-one relationship, even to a child. To predict the spanking it is necessary for him to construe a considerable variety of events: his mother's disposition and mood, the value she places on the necklace, his own part in the breakage, the discovery of his act, a previous spanking or two, and the circumstances which surrounded the previous spankings. From these he abstracts a trend. At one pole of his trend construct are those events which lead away from a spanking; at the other are those which lead towards it. The events now confronting him look like those which lead towards the spanking. The child's construction does not have the mathematical qualities of the navigator's, but the process is basically identical.

d. The contrasts implied in prediction. Since a prediction is based on bipolar constructs, it tends to have an *if-then-but-not* quality. To have solid meaning the prediction must make a clean distinction between what will occur and what will not occur. This is what we mean by *differential* prediction. The child in our illustration predicted that he would get a spanking. But, in doing so, he also ruled out the opposite trend as a likelihood in his case; he predicted that he would *not* get a nod of approval from his mother.

To say that one thing will happen is also always to say that certain other things will not happen. Otherwise, our predictions would not be discriminating. A prediction always involves a negative forecast as well as a positive expectation. The range of convenience of the particular predictive system the person employs determines how extensively he implies, by his prediction, that certain things will not occur. Often in clinical work the therapist overlooks the specific negative implications of his clients' forecasts. When he does he is likely to be unduly surprised and confused by the clients' reactions to what appear to be extraneous events.

e. Deductive use of constructs. There is an if-then relationship implied in deduction. Since a construct is a two-ended thing, one would, in using our illustration of Mary, Alice, and Jane, say, '*If* this person is gentle, *then* she could be Mary or Alice or – *but not* Jane or –.' Under our view of constructs the structure becomes an if-then-but-not form of reasoning. The elements which follow the *then* are the *like* elements in the context and the elements which follow the *not* are the *contrast* elements in the context. Elements outside the context are not touched by the construct, nor are they involved in the prediction. If Mary, Alice, and Jane constituted the entire context of the construct – that is, if the construct did not cover any other persons in its context – then our statement would become simply, 'If this person is gentle, she is Mary or Alice, and she is definitely not Jane.' She could even be both, if those were her two names. She may or may not be Elizabeth, Ann, or Joan – those might be her other names also. But of this much we are sure, if she is *gentle*, and the complete context of *gentle* is Mary-like-Alice-in-contrast-to-Jane, then she is Mary or Alice, but not Jane.

The construct may be employed inductively, although, as everyone who has tried to draw generalizations from research knows, this involves practical difficulties. In this case the form is slightly changed. We may say, '*If* this person is Mary or Alice *but not* Jane, *then* this person is gentle.' This is an if-but-not-then form of reasoning.

Suppose the context of *gentle* is limited to Mary, Alice, and Jane. Then we must come to the somewhat startling conclusion that any contextual arrangement of these three figures, and these three figures only, in which Mary and Alice are linked in contrast to Jane, is, in fact, the construct of *gentle*. There would be no basis for the existence of any other construct – that is, any other construct would thus be identical with *gentle*. If, however, on one occasion Mary and Alice were linked in contrast to Jane, and on another Mary, Alice, and Elizabeth were linked in contrast to Jane, then there would be operational grounds for distinguishing two different constructs.

Our if-then-but-not relationship takes on an interesting connotation when we see such a term as 'Mary' as itself the symbol of abstraction. This involves the notion of superordination. Suppose a series of events is construed in terms of its Mary-ness. Indeed, that is what a person really is – an abstraction of a series of events. Let us suppose that *Mary-ness* is further abstracted as *gentle*. Then we may, as we have in our illustration of the deductive use of a construct, use our if-then-but-not form. *If* this is Mary-ness, *then* gentle things *but not* aggressive things are to be expected.

Sometimes, as all of us know, even such a paragon of gentleness as Mary has turned out to be in our series of illustrations fails to act in a gentle manner. Actually Mary is abstracted at several levels. In her more material abstraction she is sometimes known to act in an ungentle manner. We say then that she is revealing the 'human side of her nature'. Or we may say, 'Mary is not herself today.' Or we may say, 'This is not the Mary I was referring to.' What we mean is that the Mary-ness that we construe as gentle is not a feature of today's events; what we have today is a lower order of Mary-ness, a person abstracted in a somewhat different manner.

5. Constructs as controls

Constructs are the channels in which one's mental processes run. They are two-way streets along which one may travel to reach conclusions. They make it possible to anticipate the changing tides of events. For the reader who is more comfortable with teleological terms it may be helpful to say that constructs are the controls that one places upon life – the life within him as well as the life which is external to him. Forming constructs may be considered as binding sets of events into convenient bundles which are handy for the person who has to lug them. Events, when so bound, tend to become predictable, manageable, and controlled.

Let us recall what we said about determinism and free will. We described them as essentially complementary aspects of the same hierarchical structure. That which is subsumed by a construct may be seen as determined by it; that which subsumes the construct is free with respect to it. Now we may approach *control* as a special case of the aspect of determinism. If we explain the goings on in nature in terms of theological constructs, it is God who determines everything that happens and it is He who controls our destiny. If, for the moment, we take a series of more constricted views, we may see the control vested in geophysical processes, or in social forces, or in the national economy, or in local business conditions, or in the administration of our university, or in the orneriness of a certain man. Control, like determinism, is not an absolutistic construct; it depends on which way one is looking. If he looks up the street, he sees control; if he looks down the same street, he sees spontaneity.

But does a man control his own destiny? Our answer to that is that he may control it to the extent that he can develop a construction system with which he identifies himself and which is sufficiently comprehensive to subsume the world around him. If he is unable to identify himself with the system, he may be able to predict events determinatively, but he can experience no personal control. If he is able to develop the system as a self-system as well as a not-self-system, and can make it work – in other words, predict – he may exercise control. According to this view, mankind is slowly learning to control his destiny, although it is a long and tedious process. Furthermore, this view, since it is framed within the position of constructive alternativism, does not necessarily negate the view of man as the result of social forces or of man as the servant of a supreme being.

It is no accident that the intellect has been classically described as the controlling feature of the human mind. The intellect has been associated with communicable constructs. When a person communicates the construct under which he is operating, we too can see what he is doing. His behaviour then makes sense to us; we understand him. When he fails to communicate his construct, his behaviour is likely not to make sense, and we say that he is stupid and his behaviour is uncontrolled. Usually we can see more clearly the patterns into which another person's behaviour falls in those instances in which he is able to convey to us a clear understanding of the personal constructions which are governing it. It is not surprising, therefore, that we are inclined to assume that it is the communicable or intellectualized constructs which provide the neatest controls upon people's behaviour.

The term 'control' is frequently used in describing patients. Sometimes psychologists speak of 'overcontrol'. But to our way of thinking, control, in general, is a point of view from which we seek to explain any behaviour. To say that something is out of control is merely to say that we have given up trying to explain it. To abandon the notion of control, with respect to any behaviour whatsoever, is to abandon the notion of lawfulness.

Now what about 'intellectual control' or 'overintellectualized control' in the patient? The person who continually expresses, in some communicable form, the constructs under which he sees himself operating is likely to be described in a clinic as 'overintellectualized'. If he were less articulate, the clinician would probably not give him that label. Also, he would probably avoid the label if he expressed his constructs less clearly. Furthermore, and this is probably important in psychotherapy, if he had not shared his constructs with so many other people or with people with whom he is presently so closely identified, he might be able to reshuffle them without altering his basic role relationships.

One way to think of the construct is as a pathway of movement. The two-ended construct provides a person with a dichotomous choice, whether it be a choice in how he will perceive something or a choice in how he will act. One may say, therefore, that the system of constructs which one establishes for oneself represents the network of pathways along which one is free to move. Each pathway is a two-way street; a person can move either up or down the street, but he cannot strike out across country without building new conceptual routes to follow. Whether he goes up or down a particular street is a matter of choice, and we have indicated that this choice is governed by what we call the principle of the elaborative choice.

The network of pathways which is formed by the construction system may be considered as a system of controls, but each one represents an opportunity for a dichotomous choice. The choice, in turn, is controlled by the principle of elaborative choice. Thus, as we have already indicated, the deterministic and the free features of one's psychological system exist together. Since the construct does not pretend to say which of its two ends shall be chosen, it leaves the person free to choose; since it does say what its two ends are, it controls the possibilities of choice.

The principle of the elaborative choice, on the other hand, does control the choice that is made within a construct dimension, but it leaves the person free to decide what it is that will give him the greater opportunity for further definition and elaboration of his system.

When a person must move he is confronted with a series of dichotomous choices. Each choice is channelized by a construct. As he reconstrues himself he may either rattle around in his old slots or he may construct new pathways across areas which were not previously accessible. When he is under pressure he is not likely to develop new channels; instead he will tend to reverse himself along the dimensional lines which have already been established. If he is a client, and his therapist merely exhorts him to change himself, this will be the type of movement open to him. If the emergency is great and the pressure is intense, the movement is likely to be abortive. In that case he will show marked contrast behaviour along the major axes of his personality. If the therapist is willing to approach the treatment more circumspectly, it is often possible to develop some new channels within which the client can work out his readjustment. In that case the movement is often less drastic but more appropriate. But whether a client develops new constructs to channelize his movement, or whether he rattles around in the old slots, the constructs of his system may be considered both as controls and as pathways along which he is free to move.

Dewey emphasized the anticipatory nature of behaviour and the person's use of hypotheses in thinking. The psychology of personal constructs follows Dewey in this respect. From our position each construct represents a pair of rival hypotheses, either of which may be applied to a new element which the person seeks to construe. This thing that I hold in my hand: is it black, or is it white? Black and white are the rival hypotheses which are set up by the *black vs. white* construct. Thus, just as the experimental scientist designs his experiments around rival hypotheses, so each person designs his daily explorations of life around the rival hypotheses which are suggested by the contrasts in his construction system. Moreover, just as the scientist cannot foresee possibilities that he has not somehow conceptualized in terms of hypotheses, so any individual can prove or disprove only that which his construction system tells him are the possible alternatives. Again the construction system sets the limits beyond which it is impossible for him to perceive. His constructs are controls on his outlook.

There are many ramifications to this issue of control and they are particularly interesting, it seems to us, in the area of psychotherapy. Our main point, at this juncture in our exposition of the psychology of personal constructs, is that constructs are pathways of freedom of movement. Because they are two-way channels they provide freedom for the person who possesses them; because he can move only along these pathways they represent restrictive controls upon everything that he does. Moreover, our view of constructs does not limit them to those which are symbolized by words, or even to those which can be communicated by means of pantomime. Perhaps the psychology of personal constructs is an intellectualized theory. But if, by intellectual controls, one means that the constructs are communicated, then there are some kinds of controls which are not intellectual, since they are not communicated. A large portion of human behaviour follows nameless channels which have no language symbols, nor any kinds of signposts whatsoever. Yet they are channels and they are included in the network of dichotomous dimensions with relation to which the person's world is structured.

The psychology of personal constructs is built upon an intellectual model, to be sure, but its application is not intended to be limited to that which is ordinarily called intellectual or cognitive. It is also taken to apply to that which is commonly called emotional or affective and to that which has to do with action or conation. The classical threefold division of psychology into cognition, affection, and conation has been completely abandoned in the psychology of personal constructs.

While the psychology of personal constructs is concerned with personal constructs all of which may not be communicable, and hence is not really what some would call intellectualized theory, it is important that it be itself communicated and that it be intellectually comprehensible. Here we distinguish between the personal constructs about which the theory is concerned and the constructs which constitute the approach of the theory itself. The former may or may not be communicated; the latter must be communicated to make public sense. If the psychology of personal constructs turns out to be no more than the fulminations of the writer rattling around in his own personal-construct slots, it will scarcely be worth committing to print. The understanding of this manuscript will be one of the practical tests of whether or not the psychology of personal constructs can be communicated.

6. The personal construction of one's role

Let us turn our attention, more particularly, to the controlling effect one's constructs have upon oneself. As we have pointed out before, the *self* is, when considered in the appropriate context, a proper concept or construct. It refers to a group of events which are alike in a certain way and, in that same way, necessarily different from other events. The way in which the events are alike is the self. That also makes the self an individual, differentiated from other individuals. The self, having been thus conceptualized, can now be used as a thing, a datum, or an item in the context of a superordinate construct. The self can become one of the three or more things – or persons – at least two of which are alike and are different from at least one of the others.

When the person begins to use himself as a datum in forming constructs, exciting things begin to happen. He finds that the constructs he forms operate as rigorous controls upon his behaviour. His behaviour in relation to other people is particularly affected. Perhaps it would be better to say that his behaviour *in comparison* with other people is particularly affected. It is, of course, the comparison *he* sees or construes which affects his behaviour. Thus, much of his social life is controlled by the comparisons he has come to see between himself and others.

We have already discussed the distortion of conceptualization that occurs when one is reluctant to express the full context or relationships of one's construct and how, in some instances, the full expression of the construct would commit the speaker to a role which he does not want to play. For example, the statement, 'Mary, Alice, Jane, and everyone else are always gentle', may indicate that the distortion is at the point at which the person is on the verge of casting himself in the role of one who must deal with ungentle people. If the only counterpoise against aggression is aggression, and if aggression, in turn, is linked tightly in a personal chain of constructs which would inferentially deny the person his identifying role, he is likely to avoid saying that anyone is 'not gentle'. In very simple and tentative language, one does not ask to be seen in a role he cannot handle and he does not elaborate the role he is not ready to play.

The personal construction of one's role may also be inferred, as we shall see later in connection with a discussion of the Role Construct Repertory Test, from the construction he places upon other people. One of the clinical uses of Murray's Thematic Apperception Test is to make an analysis of the human figures portrayed as well as an analysis of the themes or story plots. Indeed, most clinicians tend to emphasize the figure type of analysis to the exclusion of the thematic type of analysis. From the figure analysis one is able to get some idea of what kind of people populate the client's world. By understanding the cast of the play, and, from a thematic analysis, by understanding the plot of the play, the examiner may infer the kind of role the examinee must see cut out for himself. Sometimes that role is even described explicitly by the examinee as he attributes ideas and actions to the principal actor in the story he makes up.

But this is not the only way in which the examinee's response to the test reveals his casting of himself; it is revealed in the constructs in terms of which he describes the people he reads into the pictures or weaves into his plot. Each construct has its contrast features. The clinician who administers the test needs to take account of the contrasts which are implied by the examinee's descriptions of the persons in the pictures. These contrast features also play a part in the examinee's construction of his role. This is a point which can easily be overlooked in the interpretation of Thematic Apperception Test performance.

When, in an intake interview, a client describes the other people who populate his intimate world, he is essentially stating the coordinate axes with reference to which he must plot his own behaviour. He is stating his personal-construct system. Too often the clinician does not realize what a rich source of potentially useful information about the client is being revealed. He may garble the interpretation of the interview by trying to find out whether or not Aunt Olga was really as mean an old buzzard as the client is describing her. Or worse still, he may simply identify the client's statement about Aunt Olga as a cold fact which is not subject to later reinterpretation by the client. The really important thing about the client's statement of Aunt Olga's sins may be that he is describing a role to which he is, at times, partially committed himself, or a role to which, even now, he must play an opposite or complementary part.

As a person construes other people, he formulates the construction system which governs his own behaviour. The constructs which have other people as their contexts bind oneself too. One cannot call another person a bastard without making bastardy a dimension of one's own life also.

But, again, let us remind ourselves that a construct is a *single* formulation of a likeness *and* a difference. To call another person a bastard is not necessarily to conceptualize oneself as a bastard. One may conceptualize oneself as definitely *not* being a bastard. The important point for the clinician to understand is that the client has ordered his world with respect to the dimension of bastardy.

A construct is a two-ended thing, not merely a category of likeness with no inferred difference in the offing. One cannot refer to the likeness aspect of the construct without simultaneously invoking the difference aspect of the construct. Many years ago Freud pointed out that in dreams ideas were frequently represented by the opposites. Since dreams also deal in constructs, it is not so surprising that in them the constructs sometimes remain intact but are merely turned end for end. The clinician who regularly applies the psychology of personal constructs should not be misled by this simple upending of a construct.

Now something very interesting happens when a person first seeks to readjust to life with the framework of his personal system of constructs. The dimensions, of course, tend to remain the same. His freedom of movement, therefore, at first appears to him to be possible only along the axes which he has already established for himself. Let us suppose, for example, that he has oriented his role with respect to the personal construct of *gentleness vs. aggressiveness*. Let us suppose he has classified himself as like the gentle people in his construct context. He is one of the gentle ones. Next, suppose the act starts to misfire. He misses his cues, bobbles his lines. Something has gone wrong with his anticipation system. There are too many rude surprises. It becomes apparent that he must do something about his role. The most obvious thing to do is to start reclassifying his role within the contexts of some of his personal role constructs. Suppose he decides to move it along the *gentleness–aggressiveness* axis. He does so. A few weeks later his friends remark, 'What's happened to Casper? My, how he has changed!'

The chances are that Casper has not really changed his adjustment system but has tried to reassociate himself within whatever limited construction system he had to work with. A study of so-called marked personality changes, such as the manic-depressive cycle, confirms the fact that most of the radical movements that we see appearing in people's behaviour do not represent basic changes in their blueprints of life, but rather an attempt to shift within the rigid frameworks which provide their only cues to the understanding of human relationships. If a clinician is aware of a client's dimensional system, he can make some prediction of the *directions* in which the client would have to move if he were required to jump quickly.

A psychotherapist who seeks to force his client to move too rapidly runs into just this type of problem. He forces the client to move along the only axes the client has previously established for himself and the results may be catastrophic. Even if the psychotherapist proceeds slowly, yet is not aware of what the personal construct system is, he may find his client moving in totally unexpected directions.

While one's personal constructs represent the controlling system in which one's role is played out or readjusted, it is possible, under favourable conditions, for the person to readjust the constructs himself. To use the mathematical expression, he can rotate the axes on life. This will give him a new set of dimensions and new obvious directions of freedom of movement.

A person's reconstruction of life is a process which goes on all the time. Actually it is impossible for a person to reverse his stance with respect to one of his role-governing constructs without changing the construct in some measure. In psychotherapy a concerted effort is frequently made to help the person formulate new and rather basic constructs with respect to which his conception of role may be reoriented. It is almost essential that these new basic constructs first be formulated in contexts that do not involve the client too intimately before such a fundamental system as that which governs his own role is challenged. The client who is suddenly told that he must change himself is likely to be seriously threatened, and may either become inaccessible to treatment or be panicked into making violent evasive movements within his old framework.

If the new constructs are first developed in contexts which do not involve the client or members of his immediate and present family, the paralysing threat of premature movement may be avoided. Very soon, however, the person himself must be involved in the new construct formation. If it is avoidable, his whole self should not be committed to the construct's context all at once. One approach is to commit only the client's past self to the context; let him re-sort himself as he was when he was a child. Another way is to sort out certain behaviours only, say those which can be observed wholly within the confines of the treatment room. Another way is to construct artificial roles and play them out.

But more of this later. The principal points are that construct systems control the role one plays in life, that they are revealed by the client whenever he talks about other people, as well as when he talks about himself, that the constructs which control one's role are two-ended or dimensional in character, that the most obvious freedom of movement that one can see is from one end to the other along the axes one has already personally construed for oneself, and that the construct systems that control one's role can, under favourable circumstances, be changed.

7. The real nature of constructs

We have long since committed ourselves to a point of view from which we see the world as being real and man's psychological processes as being based upon personal versions of that reality. The personal versions are personal constructs. Now we may ask ourselves the question whether, from this point of view, constructs are real. The answer is a qualified yes. Constructs are not to be confounded with the factual material of which they are personalized versions; they are interpretations of those facts. But constructs may be used as viewpoints for seeing other constructs, as in the hierarchical relationships of constructs within a system. In that sense the superordinate constructs are versions of those constructs which are subordinate to them. This makes the subordinate constructs a form of reality which is construed through the use of the superordinate constructs. The summary answer to our question of whether or not constructs are real is that a construct is indeed real, but its reality is not identical with the factual elements in its context. With respect to the factual elements it is representative, not identical. Its reality is not their reality. The construct has its own reality. The problem should not cause us trouble if we keep in mind that a construct and its elements are both real, but distinguished from each other.

Can a construct be communicated from one person to another without losing its reality? In a sense the answer is yes. It is not, of course, transferred from one person to another like the one eye of the three Graeae in Greek mythology: when one got it the other two lost it. The notion of communication is itself a construct and, just as we let a construct represent that of which it is a construction, we let a communicated construct represent the personal construct of which it is a construction. The communicated construct is the construing of the person who 'receives' it; one of its elements is the construct of the person who had it beforehand. The construct of the person from whom the communication takes place is real; so is the communicated construct, but the communicated construct is a construction of the original construct and hence not identical with it. In this sense the answer to our question about whether or not a construct can be communicated from one person to another without losing its reality is definitely yes. A construct does not change its allegiance when someone else gets a version of it.

B. Formal aspects of constructs

8. Terminology

a. Range of convenience. We have already indicated that a theory or system has a range within which it serves the user conveniently for the job of predicting events. We have also indicated in our assumptive structure for the psychology of personal constructs that a construct has a range of convenience. The range of convenience of a construct would cover all those things to which the user found its application useful.

b. Focus of convenience. A construct may be maximally useful for handling certain matters. The range of these matters is called its focus of convenience.

c. Elements. The things or events which are abstracted by a construct are called elements.

d. Context. The context of a construct is composed of all those elements to which the construct is ordinarily applied. It is somewhat more constricted than the range of convenience, since it refers to the circumstances in which the construct emerges and not necessarily to all the circumstances in which a person might eventually use the construct. It is somewhat more extensive than the focus of convenience, since the construct may often emerge in circumstances in which its application is not altogether optimal.

e. Pole. Each construct involves two poles, one at each end of its dichotomy. The elements associated at each pole are like each other with respect to the construct and are unlike the elements at the other pole.

f. Contrast. The relationship between the two poles of a construct is one of contrast.

g. Likeness end. When referring specifically to elements at one pole of a construct we have used the term *likeness end*, meaning that we are referring to the pole at which these elements are grouped by the construction.

h. Contrast end. When referring specifically to elements at the opposite pole of a construct, we have used the term *contrast end*, meaning that we are referring to the other pole.

i. Emergence. Here we borrow Lyle's construct. The emergent pole of a construct is that which embraces most of the immediately perceived context. For example, in the statement, 'Mary and Alice are gentle but Jane is aggressive', gentleness is emergent because it refers to two-thirds of the context. Frequently only the emergent pole is explicitly mentioned, as when a person says, 'Mary and Alice are gentle but Jane is not.'

j. Implicitness. Again we borrow from Lyle's thinking. The implicit pole of a construct is the one which contrasts with the emergent pole. It is frequently not mentioned by name. Sometimes the person has no symbolization for it; it is symbolized only implicitly by the emergent term.

9. Symbolism

Any one of the like elements in the context of one's construct may give the construct its name. A construct, formed in the context of A, B, and C, with A and B being the *like* elements, may be represented simply by the mentioning of A. Now A may itself, in turn, be a true construct, originating in a context of A_a, A_b, and A_c; we are not referring to A's use in this sense but rather to its use as a representative for or as a symbol of the construct formed out of a context comprising A, B, and C. A may then be used to represent a construct which is not A at all but really one which subsumes A, a higher-order construct which really has A as a part of its context only. This is the basic nature of symbolism.

Symbolism is a handy tool. Understood in the light of the above paragraph, it is not the sole tool for shaping thought but is certainly a very useful and commonly used one.

Man has developed a neat trick in the use of symbolism. He makes up sounds and shapes and introduces them artificially into the context of his constructs as one of the elements. Then he lets this sound or shape become a symbol of the construct. For example, he adds the word 'gentleness' to Mary and Alice so that now the context reads, 'Mary, Alice, and gentleness versus Jane.' From now on *gentleness* is used to represent the kinship of Mary, Alice, and the word 'gentleness'.

There is a simpler type of symbolism which does not involve the invasion of words into the context of a construct. We can let Mary become the symbol for gentleness and Jane the symbol for attractiveness. Mother can become the symbol for social belongingness. Father can become the symbol for maturity. In most people Mother and Father do represent personal constructs of a much higher order than their own identities necessitate. This kind of figure symbolism is characteristic of the personal constructs one forms in childhood. Moreover, these constructs are likely to be retained in terms of figure symbolism, an important fact for the psychotherapist. For a psychotherapist to say that a person 'introjects' his father and mother is to miss the point; rather, his father and mother are likely to have been contextual elements in a great many of the personal constructs which the person has formed, particularly his role constructs. They may or may not be employed actually as symbols of these constructs.

We have said that figure symbolism is characteristic of the symbolism used to represent personal constructs formed in childhood. It is possible to state the case more generally. The use of one of the original contextual elements as the symbol of a construct is characteristic of the early stages in the formation and use of any construct. The construct of *Mary-like-Alice-unlike-Jane* is likely to be symbolized in the person's thinking simply as *Mary* or *Mary-ness*.

As new members are added to the context of the construct, assuming that it is a permeable construct, or as he seeks to invoke Mary-ness behaviour in his friends, the person may contrive a verbal symbol. If the construct happens to be relatively impermeable or not communicated, except in the most intimate ways, it may continue to be represented symbolically simply by one of its original contextual elements. For example, if *mother* is the contextual element used to represent a certain personal construct which is relatively impermeable – for example, 'Now there is no one like my mother' – or if no effort is made to communicate the personal construct – for example, 'No one could possibly understand what my mother was really like' – then 'my mother' is likely to be retained as the symbol as well as one of the contextual elements of the personal construct.

Through most of this discussion of personal constructs we have been using people or 'figures' to illustrate the contextual elements of personal constructs. It is believed that such constructs are of paramount importance to the psychologist. But what we have said is also true of personal constructs about other things. The construct of *speed* may be symbolized by an automobile as well as by a word. The construct of *comfort* may be symbolized by a curve like that of the mother's breast; the construct of *rectitude* may be symbolized by the sound of a firm, masculine voice; or the construct of *virility* may be symbolized by an erect penis. The 'blood and guts' type of response on the Rorschach Test may, in certain instances, be a symbol of a personal construct lifted directly from a construct's context. In evaluating such a response it is essential for the clinician to find out (a) what the construct is and (b) what is its level of generality – that is, what order of elements it subsumes.

10. Communication

Having portrayed symbolism in the above manner, we have also committed ourselves to a point of view regarding the nature of communication. If symbolism is a matter of letting one of the elements in the context of a construct appear as the representative of the construct itself, then communication is a matter of reproducing the symbolic element in hopes of eliciting a parallel construct in another person. The neatest way is to use a word as a symbol. Of course, it may not work, for our listener may not have incorporated the word into the same kind of context, or have used it as a symbol of the same construct. Then we may have to trot out other elements of our personal construct's context, some of them words, some of them nonverbal acts. With luck we may succeed in communicating, at least at an approximate level.

The client who attempts to communicate his personal constructs to a therapist can rarely depend upon simple verbal statements to communicate the precise personal nature of his constructs. He has to bring out for display a long list of other contextual elements before the therapist can understand. It is particularly difficult to communicate with a therapist if the personal construct is relatively impermeable and there are no contemporary elements which can readily be used to illustrate the context. It is difficult to communicate with the therapist if he does not appear to understand the subordinate constructs out of which the construct is formed. Finally, it is difficult to communicate with the therapist if the construct is a role-governing one which cannot be communicated without distorting the role relationship the client has established between himself and the therapist.

The therapist, on his side of the table, must not be too ready to impose his own preexisting personal constructs upon the symbolism and behaviour of the client. He will first have to compile a lexicon for dealing with the client. Moreover, he will have to accept the possibility that the client's relations with him will vacillate markedly as the client illustrates, with naked realism, the contextual elements of his role-governing constructs.

11. Scales of constructs

From time to time we have used the notion of a construct as if it were an axis or a dimension. Since we have assumed that constructs are essentially dichotomous, it may appear that we have ruled out the possibility of scales or continua involving more than two steps. For example, Landfield, who performed interesting studies of threat from the standpoint of earlier formulations of personal-construct theory, had originally developed tailor-made scales of personal constructs for each of his subjects to use. He observed, however, that '"Dimensional scale" may be a misnomer, since it soon becomes apparent that many subjects who perceived people in degrees construed them, for example, not as a series of varying greys, but rather in terms of black, white and combinations of black and white.' Even though we envision the basic constructs out of which our systems are built as dichotomous, it is still possible to conceive of gradations, as Landfield did, along a dimensional line.

There are several ways in which this kind of conception can be presented.

a. Hierarchical scales. Just as it is possible to express an infinite number of gradations of value in terms of binary number systems, so it is possible to express an infinite number of gradations of value in terms of a dichotomous construct system. One may construct such a scale by assuming a hierarchy of construct. Consider a hierarchy of four constructs in the order of A, B, C, and D, each of which has two possible values, 0 and 1. A *hierarchical scale* of values may be built up from these four constructs. It will have $\log_2^{-1} 4$ or sixteen steps. The values of the sixteen steps can be represented by the first sixteen numbers of the binary system as follows:

0000
0001
0010
0011
0100
0101
0110
0111
1000
1001
1010
1011
1100
1101
1110
1111

Suppose we build a hierarchical scale of *integrity vs. disintegrity* out of the four basic constructs of *honesty vs. dishonesty*, *candour vs. deviousness*, *courage vs.*

defeatism, and *objectivity vs. subjectivity.* Suppose, also, that these constructs are arranged in that hierarchical order. Let the binary digit 1 represent the first of each pair and the binary digit 0 represent the second of each pair. A dishonest, devious, defeatist, subjective person would be represented by the scale value of 0000 and would be at the *disintegral* end of the scale. An honest but devious, defeatist, subjective person would be represented by the number 1000. Because of the high relevance of honesty to integrity, he rates in the upper half of the scale. A person who was dishonest, devious, defeatist, and objective would be represented by the number 0001 and would still be near the bottom of the scale.

b. Additive scales. Constructs can also be formed into an additive type of scale. Suppose we drop the notion of a hierarchy of constructs and simply add the binary digits representing the poles of the constructs. Now an honest but devious, defeatist, subjective person would score 1 for honesty and 0 for each of his other characteristics. His scale value would therefore be 0001. If he were also courageous instead of defeatist his score would be boosted to 0010. It is clear that this kind of scale would have only five steps instead of sixteen. The values would run from 0000 to 0100.

c. Abstracted scales. We can build another kind of scale by stepping up to a higher level of abstraction. Let us call it an *abstracted scale.* Suppose we construe *integrity vs. disintegrity,* not in terms of any concrete accumulation of the other four constructs, as we have in the two types of scale previously described, but as an abstraction of them. *Integrity vs. disintegrity* is now seen as a property which runs through the other four constructs. More particularly, it is a property of the relationship between any pairing of the constructs. For example, *honesty* in comparison with *dishonesty* is *integral* while *dishonesty* is *disintegral,* but mere *honesty* in comparison with *courage* might be considered *disintegral.* The construct of *integrity vs. disintegrity* is still dichotomous. Its abstraction, however, is relative, and in order to symbolize its application to shifting context one has to set up a whole row of symbols or numbers. This, of course, is a temptation to the user to employ the construct concretistically, and often that is precisely what happens.

We could depart from the central course of our discussion at this point and mention the difficulty many of us have in using a number system abstractly rather than concretely. For a child, a series of numbers is a concrete arrangement of named things. As he grows older he finds that his number system can be used to arrange many different kinds of objects, but his numbers may still be concretistically perceived as mileage readings on a speedometer or weight readings on a scale. Still later, if he is lucky, he may be able to use his number system relativistically; when he abstracts the numerical value of *four* it is its *moreness* in relation to *three, two,* and *one,* and its *lessness* than *five, six,* and *seven,* that he perceives.

d. Approximation scales. There is a fourth type of scale which is an artifact of people's trying to understand each other. Let us call this an *approximation scale.*

Suppose an experimenter has a notion of *integrity vs. disintegrity* which is essentially dichotomous. He asks his subject to rate certain acquaintances on this scale. The subject, not being sure that what he would call 'integrity' is the same as what the experimenter would call 'integrity', tends to give compromise ratings. Only in those instances where the acquaintance appears to exhibit some combination of characteristics which seems clearly to be what the experimenter has in mind, will the subject venture to give an extreme rating. From this point of view, indeed from the point of view of the psychology of personal constructs, a leptokurtic distribution of scores on a scale is a clear indication of its approximate nature. The less the subject feels that he understands what the experimenter has in mind, the more he will hug some point on the scale, such as the middle, which seems to commit him the least. We can use this idea to infer how well a person understands the scale on which he is asked to make ratings. When the often mentioned J-curve or U-curve phenomena are observed, as in cases of cultural agreement, one may infer that the rater understands the prescribed construct well enough to make dichotomous ratings.

e. Accumulation scales. There is still another kind of scale which happens to be related to the additive scale. Let us call it an *accumulative scale.* Suppose two people have been observed on twenty different occasions. The first person has shown integral behaviour nineteen out of twenty times while the second person has shown disintegral behaviour nineteen out of twenty times. Each person is given a score which represents approximately the proportion of occasions on which he has shown integral behaviour. The construct of *integral vs. disintegral* remains essentially dichotomous; it is the accumulation of occasions which gives us an opportunity to assign more than two values to the degree of integrity.

f. Other scales. There are other ways in which scales built upon dichotomous constructs can be conceptualized. One could, for example, evaluate critical incidents and, disregarding the *number* of occasions in which he showed integrity, give a person a high score if he showed integrity in a *single* highly critical incident. Again a person could be rated on an integrity scale in terms of the proportion of his friends who classified him as integral. But it is not our intent to make an exhaustive analysis of the kinds of scales which people build; we wish only to make clear that the notion of dichotomous constructs does not preclude the use of scales. The notion does, however, lead one to look closely at all one's scales and try to determine exactly what discriminative bases they may have.

12. Scanning by means of constructs

While we have not committed ourselves to following a cybernetic model in constructing the theory of personal constructs, our assumptions permit us to visualize certain psychological processes in terms of electronic analogues. When a person scans the events with which he is surrounded he 'lights up' certain dichotomies in his construct system. Thus construct systems can be considered as a kind of scanning pattern which a person continually projects upon his world. As he sweeps back and forth across his perceptual field he picks up blips of meaning. The more adequate his scanning pattern, the more meaningful his world becomes. The more in tune it is with the scanning patterns used by others, the more blips of meaning he can pick up from their projections.

Viewed in this manner the psychology of personal constructs commits us to a projective view of all perception. All interpersonal relations are based essentially on transference relations, though they are subject to validation and revision. All test performances are best understood as projective test performances. In psychotherapy it becomes important to retune the client's scanning pattern. In learning and teaching it becomes important to know just what dichotomies in the pattern are being validated.

We may also think of constructs as providing ordinal axes in psychological space, the abscissas being provided by the temporal events themselves. With both constructs and events providing axes, the person builds a grid within whose quadrants his psychological space takes on multidimensional meaning. With respect to the ordinates there are many personal versions of what the axes are, but with respect to the abscissa of time we have a common experience. We may not agree with each other as to what the essential nature of an event is, but we can usually agree, subject to retrospective falsification, as to what the sequence is.

In a later chapter we shall indicate how the Repertory Grid can be used to lay out certain areas of a person's scanning pattern, how it can be factor analysed by nonparametric methods, how certain problems of generalization of learning can be studied, and how the personal construct system can be related to public construct systems. It is sufficient for our purposes at this juncture simply to invite attention to the fact that the personal construct system can be viewed cybernetically.

13. Personal security within the context of a construct

We have mentioned the fact that the self may be used as one of the elements in the context of a construct (though we can imagine some constructs in which the self does not fall within the range of convenience). We have called attention to the governing effect of such a construct in the person's playing out his life role. In another section we pointed out the frequent use of figure symbolism, as contrasted with word symbolism, in the representation of a construct. For example, one's own mother might become the symbol of a certain role-fixing construct. Now let us consider what may ensue when various shifts in the elements of such a construct are attempted.

Suppose the elements on the like-mother side of a person's *mother* construct include, as they frequently do, a considerable variety of comforts, protections, and securities. As long as a person construes himself on the like-mother side of the construct, or on the like-mother-wants-me side of the construct, he may perceive himself as heir to these comforts, protections, and securities. But suppose the person's therapist attempts to shift the self from the like-mother side of the personal construct to the unlike-mother side. The unlike-mother context includes all of the relevant contrast features of the personal construct of *mother* – discomforts, hazards, and insecurities. What happens to the client?

Having come to see himself in this new global fashion, he may be expected to demonstrate new behaviours. He may abandon many of the constricted and cautious ways of comporting himself and start behaving in many ways that seem to him to be in contrast to the like-mother pole of his *mother* construct. He may become markedly adventuresome. His behaviour may also become more diffuse as he plunges into new experiences and finds that he must face the unfamiliar events into which the new role precipitates him. This may prove to be an exhilarating experience, provided he has enough well-defined structure remaining to avoid the confusion of anxiety and if he has permeable constructs which adequately span both the old and the new behaviour patterns. On the other hand, he may, through lack of structure to handle the new role, become markedly anxious.

If the client identifies himself with the unlike-mother side of his one mother-symbolized construct, he may, through the use of figure symbolism, find himself construed on the unlike-mother side of all mother-symbolized constructs. He may then show contrast behaviour along all the dimensional lines represented by constructs which happen to have the mother as a symbol. This may be more than the therapist bargained for. The effect upon the client's construction of his life role may be disastrous. In this case we can hope that the client will have had enough independence of the therapist to reject the whole idea at the outset.

Consider the opposite kind of shift. Suppose we try to get the client to perceive and 'accept' his likeness to his mother. We may think this is a matter of giving him a good dose of 'insight'. In other words, what we are asking him to do is to see himself at the opposite end of *our* personal construct of *his mother* and we may be unaware of what such a shift implies in *his* personal construct of *his mother*. Our efforts may threaten to bring the client under the regnancy of all the construct poles for which *his mother* is his symbol.

Sometimes the therapist, in suggesting that a client is like his mother, has in mind only the idea that the client is like his mother *in some respect*. But the therapist may be overlooking the complex symbolic meaning of *mother* in the client's personal system. What the client then hears the therapist say is that he should identify himself with everything for which *mother* is the symbol. Yet the therapist may have meant only, 'You get angry quickly like your mother', and not, 'You are one of the mother-kind of people.' After the client's mother has been relegated to her proper place as merely one of the contextual elements in a construct of *quick to anger* instead of being the quintessence of it, the client may be able to accept himself as representing one of the like elements in a context which also involves her. The process of lifting the symbolism from mother may require a considerable period of therapy, and yet it may have to precede any proffered interpretations or any significant therapeutic movement.

Suppose we attempt to shift the mother *as an element* from the like-self side of the context to the unlike-self side. This is usually an easy way to get an immediate appearance of movement. The client usually shows a lift of spirits, brightens up, and becomes more responsive. A conference or two later he may begin to show anxiety or reticence. As he begins to work through the implications of the shift, he may have found that his role has lost so much of its definition that it has ceased to provide him with a minimum level of personal security. The shift may have confused him. He cannot anticipate a regular enough sequence of life's events under the residual construction system.

What has happened in this case is that the client had previously become dependent upon the mother, not merely as the symbol for the role-governing construct of himself, but as the definition of it. It was her example which illustrated the construct in action. The 'lift' the client experienced when the shift was first proposed was essentially a freeing effect which appears, in this case, soon to have left him in an insecure position. This is a freedom which he cannot use until he has a construction within which it can operate in a way which will give him some preview of life. One has only to have experience in therapy with a child in a home which is in the process of breaking up in order to see this phenomenon in action. During the breakup period one or both of the parents is likely to try to dissociate the other from the like-self side of some of the child's personal role-governing constructs. The child faces freedom and insecurity through this enforced loss of his kinship with a role-exemplifying parent. It is quite understandable that the successful therapist in such a case will frequently find himself, instead, cast as the primary role exemplifier in the eyes of the child.

Last, let us consider the fourth kind of shift, still assuming that the client uses his mother-figure as the symbol of one of his role-governing constructs. Mother is to go from the unlike-self to the like-self side. As in the immediately preceding case, this kind of shift also tends to destroy the construct's usefulness through the loss of its stabilizing symbol. In practice it appears to be impossible to retain the mother's symbolism when she is thus translated within the same construct. What usually happens is that the construct itself breaks up, or the client deals himself out as one of the like elements. In either case the role-governing features of the construct are likely to be lost. If the client reacts by dealing himself into the unlike pile, while retaining the construct itself, we have a situation on our hands similar to that discussed above in connection with a shift of the self to the unlike-mother side.

Now the symbol of a construct is usually one of the like elements, although that does not have to be the case. The mother figure can be one of the unlike elements and yet symbolize a construct maintained by the client. The client identifies himself with his mother's antitheses and these antitheses are the like elements. This is rare, but occasionally it actually happens in clinical work. It is, of course, not so rare that a person sees himself as unlike his mother; what is so rare is that the mother is at once the symbol of one of the client's role-governing constructs in which he is one of the like elements, yet she herself is one of the unlike elements. For example, his mother, by her bustling industry, may be the antithetical symbol of the very indolence with which the client identifies himself.

We have discussed in the preceding paragraphs of this section role-governing constructs which are maintained through figure-symbolism. We have used 'mother' as the example of the figure-symbol in each instance. We have pointed out the disruptive effects upon the client's role when an attempt is made either to shift the self or the symbolizing figure in the context of the construct. What we have said is applicable to any contextual shifts in relation to a construct involving the self and a symbolizing figure. The use of a symbolizing figure gives the construct a kind of stability or rigidity. This may represent personal security for the child, or even for the adult whose construct system involves relatively few levels of abstraction and whose constructs must therefore be related directly to concrete behaviours or persons. Figure-symbolized constructs are characteristic of children. They lend clarity, and hence a measure of stability, to children's roles.

What we have said has some implications for psychotherapy which is carried out under the theoretical system of the psychology of personal constructs. Where figure symbolism is involved, or any symbolism for that matter, the self and the symbol cannot be shuffled with respect to each other without affecting the security provided by the construct. It may be necessary, and frequently is, for the therapist to help the client attach a new symbolism to his construct so that the element which was formerly the symbol can be shifted, or the self can be shifted with respect to it. If the symbol is a figure symbol – *mother*, for example – it may require a great deal of time and patience on the part of the therapist to replace the *mother* symbol, preparatory to bringing about shifts in the client's construction of his role. It may be more economical to starting building a new set of constructs to replace the old altogether. In fixed-role therapy – to be discussed later – this is what is done.

Let us turn now to a more general case of personal security within the context of a construct. Let us disregard the symbolism of one of the elements. Let us disregard even the possibility that the self is the symbol of the construct. Consider only that the self is one of the elements. Now, since the construct is a way of holding its elements in place, the self is held in place by any construct by which the self is construed. The self-governing construct, or, more specifically where other people's presumed constructs are elements, the role-governing construct, provides a way of anticipating one's own responses. The result is social poise.

Consider an even more general case of personal security within the context of a construct. Let us disregard the possibility that the self is one of the elements. Consider only that the construct, perhaps having to do only with inanimate elements, provides a way of anticipating events. Armed with such a construct the person can face, not only his world of people, but his world of physical events with equanimity. This is an even broader kind of personal security. We might say that it represents personal poise.

14. Dimensions of constructs

The personal constructs of others may be construed by ourselves as observers. We can even set up comprehensive dimensions against which other persons' constructs can be evaluated. One of the common dimensions for evaluating constructs of others is the familiar *abstract vs. concrete* dimension. While there are some who believe that *abstract* is not the antithesis of *concrete*, most of us use these terms as if they represented the opposing poles of the same construct. We have, in our discussion thus far, had occasion to use these terms quite frequently, and we have been content to rely upon the usual meanings which readers might be expected to ascribe to them. But now it may be helpful to take a closer look at the nature of constructs and construe the various general ways in which constructs resemble and differ from each other.

Now constructs can be classified according to the elements which they subsume. For example, a certain construct may be called a *physical* construct, not so much because it is subsumed with a 'physical' system of constructs, but because it presumes to deal with elements which have already been construed as inherently 'physical'. Frequently the term *abstract* is used in this manner. For example, there are those who insist that any mathematical construct, regardless of who is using it, is bound to be 'abstract' because it deals with symbols which have been defined as 'abstract'. But anyone who has done intensive psychodiagnostic work with scholarly people, including mathematicians, must have discovered that a man may be an excellent mathematician and yet actually handle his mathematics in a highly concretistic manner. There are some mathematicians who seem to have only the barest amount of capacity for abstract thinking. Their mathematical thinking is shot through with literalisms which are concretistic, legalistic, and scarcely abstract at all.

McGaughran has made a study in which he attempted to determine the functional usefulness of certain construct dimensions. He had not gone far before he realized that the classical scheme of *abstract vs. concrete* was not describing the thinking of his subjects in a manner that would enable him to predict how they would operate from one situation to another. The person who dealt abstractly with one kind of problem was as likely as not to deal concretely with another kind of problem. Furthermore, those who were more prone than others to use abstract approaches in one area might be less prone than others to use abstract approaches in another area.

McGaughran set for himself an experimental design in which he painstakingly sought to predict what kind of conceptualization a person would use in his language behaviour from the kind he used in his nonverbal behaviour, and vice versa. This was an ambitious undertaking. Language behaviour was elicited by use of the Thematic Apperception Test cards. Nonverbal behaviour was studied in the way the subject sorted the Vigotsky blocks. The task was to discover dimensions of conceptualization which would be applicable to both types of protocol and which would enable him to predict how a subject would perform in one situation from knowledge of his conceptualization in the other situation. In accepting this as his task he was introducing a functional criterion for the classification of constructs, certainly a novel idea in an area which philosophers have been accustomed to use only formalistic criteria.

McGaughran found eventually that he could make reasonably valid predictions and these predictions fell essentially in two dimensions. These were *communicability* and something which is essentially what we have been calling *permeability*. In fact, the term *permeability* was one originally suggested by McGaughran, although he did not choose to use it in reporting his study. By *communicability* he did not refer, of course, merely to verbal communication, since one set of protocols was, by definition, nonverbal. In other words, he found that the dimensions of *permeability* and *communicability* were not only operationally definable but were efficacious for predicting individual behaviour. While we have not followed McGaughran's dimensional scheme precisely, we are indebted to him, not only for demonstrating that there are probably more meaningful ways to analyse conceptualization than by use of the *abstract–concrete* dimension, but also for suggesting certain definite features of constructs which may be far more characteristic of the users than is abstractness or concreteness.

In addition to the *permeability vs. impermeability* dimension, which has been discussed in an earlier section, we propose to use a triad of notions which basically represent two construct dimensions. These notions are not altogether unlike certain others which have been proposed by recent psychological writers. They have to do with the nature of the control which a construct implicitly exercises over its elements.

A construct which preempts its elements for membership in its own realm exclusively may be called a *preemptive construct*. The species type of construct belongs to this category. It can be exemplified by the statement, 'Anything which is a ball can be nothing but a ball.' In this case the construct is *ball*, and all the things which are balls are excluded from the realms of other constructs; they cannot be 'spheres', 'pellets', 'shots', or anything but balls. This is a pigeonhole type of construct; what has been put into this pigeonhole cannot simultaneously be put into any other. It represents, of course, the extreme of preemption and actually few personal constructs are totally preemptive in their use. Yet in therapy the tendency of the client to use preemptive construction in dealing with certain topical areas is often a major problem for the therapist. The problem of preemption is also a major factor in interpersonal relations and in certain thick-skulled approaches to social conflict. But more of this later.

Preemption tends to show up in those who have particular difficulty in seeing the universe as an ongoing affair and insist that dealing with it is simply a matter of arranging its inert elements. The pre-Aristotelian philosopher Heraclitus had actually made a pretty good start in construing an active universe, which he could see epitomized in fire. But the import of what he had to say was masked by the substantialism of philosophers like Empedocles, and it was lost altogether when

Aristotle put science into pigeonholes and refused to countenance anything so dynamic as the performance of an experiment, lest it be a distortion of nature.

During the past century there has been some recovery from the preemptiveness of Aristotelian thinking and greater emphasis upon the functional approaches to reality. Dewey, whose philosophy and psychology can be read between many of the lines of the psychology of personal constructs, envisioned the universe as an ongoing affair which had to be anticipated to be understood. Such thinking stands in sharp contrast to the kind of realism which insists that if a thing is a spade, it is nothing but a spade: if a person is a schizophrenic, he is nothing but a schizophrenic; if the heart is a physiological organ, it is nothing but a physiological organ, and it cannot be construed as a psychological organ; if an event is a catastrophe, it is nothing but a catastrophe; if a man is an enemy, he is nothing but an enemy.

Preemptive construction is often exemplified in the polemic disputes between scientists. It is sometimes called the *nothing-but* criticism: 'The psychology of personal constructs is *nothing but* mentalism'; 'Psychoanalysis is *nothing but* anthropomorphism'; 'Christianity is *nothing but* passivity'; 'Communism is *nothing but* dictatorship.' When we laid down our basic position in terms of constructive alternativism we eschewed the nothing-but type of reasoning from the outset, and we played the hunch that the abandonment of this kind of outlook might do a great deal to help psychologists along, just as it often helps their clients to reconstrue life and find renewed hope among stark realities.

A construct which permits its elements to belong to other realms concurrently, but fixes their realm memberships, may be called a *constellatory construct*. A stereotype belongs to this category. For example, a constellatory construct is expressed in the statement, 'Anything which is a ball must also be something which will bounce.' Some investigators call this a 'complex'. In this type of construct it is conceded that a ball may also be considered as something other than a ball, but there is no latitude permitted as to what else it may be considered to be. A ball, if a ball, has to be certain specified other things too.

A construct which leaves its elements open to construction in all other respects may be called a *propositional construct*. For example, throughout our discussion of the psychology of personal constructs we have attempted to rely heavily upon propositional constructs, as contrasted with the entity thinking implied by the use of preemptive constructs and the dogmatic thinking implied by the use of constellatory constructs. In the case of the ball example the following illustrates a propositional construct: 'Any roundish mass may be considered, among other things, as a ball.' Such a construct is relatively propositional since it does not hinge upon anything except the 'roundish mass' and it does not imply that a ball has to be any particular thing except a 'roundish mass'. In personal thinking such pure abstraction is about as rare as the utter concretism implied in preemptive construction. The propositional construct, therefore, represents one end of a continuum, the other end of which is represented by the preemptive and constellatory constructs.

While propositionality may seem to be a universally desirable characteristic in one's personal constructs, it would actually be quite difficult to get along in the world if a person attempted to use propositional constructs exclusively. A superordinate construct, which subsumes other constructs, treats its subordinates as if they were constellatory. For example, if *sphere* includes *ball* together with certain other objects, then to say that something is a ball is also to imply that it is a sphere. Thus *ball* has a constellatory implication when it is subsumed by *sphere.*

Moreover, if a person attempted to use propositional thinking exclusively, he might have considerable difficulty in coming to any decision as to what the relevant and crucial issues were in any situation. In a game of baseball he might be so busy considering, from all conceptual angles, the sphere which was being thrown in his direction that he might overlook the necessity for dealing with it momentarily as a ball and nothing else. Preemptive thinking, in a moment of decision, is essential if one is to take an active part in his universe. But preemptive thinking which never resolves itself into propositional thinking condemns the person to a state of intellectual rigor mortis. He may be called a 'man of action', but his actions will always follow well-worn ruts.

We can summarize as follows what we have to say at this point about the dimensions of constructs:

a. An impermeable construct is one which is based upon a specified context and which will admit no additional elements – for example, proper names: 'If *ball* comprises certain things, then no other things can be balls'; 'These and these only are balls.'

b. A permeable construct is one which implies additional elements – for example, class names: 'If *ball* comprises certain things, then there must be still other things which are balls'; 'Anything like these is a ball.'

c. A preemptive construct is one which preempts its elements for membership in its own realm exclusively – for example, species names: 'Anything which is a ball can be nothing but a ball'; 'This is nothing but a ball.'

d. A constellatory construct is one which fixes the realm membership of its elements – for example, stereotypes: 'Anything which is a ball has got to be...' 'Since this is a ball, it must be round, resilient, and small enough to hold in the hand.'

e. A propositional construct is one which does not disturb the other realm memberships of its elements – for example, 'philosophical attitudes': 'Any roundish mass can be considered, among other things, as a ball'; 'Although this is a ball, there is no reason therefore to believe that it could not be lopsided, valuable, or have a French accent.'

Later on we propose to list many more dimensional lines along which personal constructs may be plotted. *Anxiety, hostility, loosening, preverbalism, transference, dependence,* and a number of other dimensions will be described. But we are eager to finish our preliminary sketch of the psychology of personal constructs, so that, as soon as possible, we may demonstrate some of the theory's more interesting practical applications to the solution of human problems. Further dimensions will have to wait!

C. Changing construction

15. Validation

When we laid down our Fundamental Postulate we committed ourselves to a particular view of human motivation. *A person's processes are psychologically channelized by the ways in which he anticipates events.* The direction of his movement, hence his motivation, is towards better understanding of what will happen. Where Dewey would have said that we understand events through anticipating them, we would add that our lives are wholly oriented towards the anticipation of events. The person moves out towards making more and more of the world predictable and not ordinarily does he withdraw more and more into a predictable world. In the latter case he becomes neurotic or psychotic, lest he lose that capacity for prediction which he has already acquired. In either case, the principle of the elaborative choice describes his motivating decision. Moreover, as we have indicated before, he lays his wagers on predictability, not merely on the certainty of the immediate venture, but in terms of what he sees as the best parlay. Often, too, he finds it necessary to compromise between comprehensiveness and specific accuracy in his construction system. Thus he may tolerate an obviously misleading construct in his system if it seems to have the comprehensiveness that a more precise construct appears to lack.

If man is concerned primarily with the anticipation of events, we need no longer appeal to hedonism, or some disguised form of it, such as 'satisfaction' or 'reinforcement', to explain his behaviour. We can, of course, redefine some hedonistic terms in the language of prediction and validation, and thus continue to use them – but why bother!

What follows from our Fundamental Postulate is a particular notion of the kind of pay-off man expects from his wagers. Let us use the term *validation.* A person commits himself to anticipating a particular event. If it takes place, his anticipation is validated. If it fails to take place, his anticipation is invalidated. Validation represents the compatibility (subjectively construed) between one's prediction and the outcome he observes. Invalidation represents incompatibility (subjectively construed) between one's prediction and the outcome he observes.

Sometimes the client in therapy will construe as invalidation of a prediction what the therapist has expected him to construe as validation. Sometimes this happens because the therapist is not fully aware of the nature of the client's prediction. Sometimes it occurs because the therapist construes prediction and outcome at a sufficiently comprehensive level to see them as compatible with each other, but the client, not having such an overview, is disturbed because he won $998.14 on his wager instead of the $998.00 he expected to win.

The notion of *validation* is quite different from the notion of 'reinforcement' as the latter term is commonly used. Reinforcement carries the implication of meeting the person's needs, of satisfying him in some way, or of gratification. Validation refers solely to the verification of a prediction, even though what was predicted was something unpleasant. For example, a person may anticipate that he will fall down the stairs and break his leg. If his prediction turns out to be true, or at least if it seems to him that he has fallen down the stairs and broken his leg, he experiences validation, no matter how unhappy he may be about the turn of affairs. But breaking one's leg is ordinarily not what one would call 'reinforcement', except, possibly, in certain disturbed patients. Of course, we could redefine 'reinforcement' to bring it into line with the theory of personal constructs; but most of the current meaning that 'reinforcement' has among psychologists would then have to be abandoned.

When a prediction turns out to be accurate, what is it which is validated? If it turns out to be inaccurate, what is invalidated? These are questions which assume considerable importance in the psychology of personal constructs. While they are, in some measure, important also in most of the current learning theories which deal with generalization, the psychology of personal constructs casts them in a somewhat different light.

Poch's research deals with this problem. She structured the issues in this way: when a person discovers that his prediction has gone awry, just what does he do about it? Does he change his prediction only? Does he turn to another construct in his repertory and base his next prediction on that instead? Or does he revise the dimensional structure of his construct system?

Conventional learning theory, based on the notion of 'reinforcement', normally concerns itself only with the first of these questions. Available research evidence indicates clearly enough that persons ordinarily do change their predictions when they find that they have made mistakes. But Poch's questions penetrate much deeper than this. Her evidence indicated quite clearly that her subjects tended to turn to other construct dimensions in their repertories when their predictions were invalidated. There was also a tendency for them to shift their construct system with respect to the aspects employed in the invalidated predictions.

We may see, then, that validation can be viewed as affecting the construction system at various levels. These levels can be seen as falling into gradients, with those constructs which are functionally closest to the constructs upon which the original prediction was based being most affected by validational experiences. Bieri has shown how this relationship can be measured, both for constructs and for figures in the person's life. He has shown how validation affects not only the particular constructs and the particular figures which were involved in the original prediction, but also affects functionally related constructs and figures.

Our Experience Corollary infers from the Fundamental Postulate that a person's construction system varies as he successively construes the replication of events. Validation points off the successive cycles in his construing. If a person makes only vague commitments to the future he receives only vague validational experience. If his commitments are incidental and fragmentary, he experiences fragmentary validation only. If his commitments are based on far-reaching interpretations of the situation, he may construe the outcome as having sweeping significance.

This kind of reasoning gives us an approach to the results of the so-called 'partial conditioning' experiments. It has been demonstrated variously that a 'response' will resist 'extinction' under conditions of 'nonreinforcement' longer if, during the original 'conditioning' period, not all of the 'trials' were 'reinforced'. This is somewhat awkward for most of the conventional learning theories to explain. From our point of view, however, it suggests that the validational cycle – from prediction to outcome – is not necessarily the single 'trial' as envisioned by the experimenter. The 'trial', from the subject's point of view, may be a cycle of several 'trials', from the experimenter's point of view. Just because the experimenter phrases his experience in a certain way is no reason for the subject to phrase it in the same way. Thus the partially 'reinforced' series may, from the standpoint of the subject, consist of a number of different cycles, all of which were 'reinforced', but some of which were longer than others. Even the total experimental series itself may be a cycle, as far as the subject is concerned, and it may be that he will give up making his prediction only when the 'extinction' series approaches, subjectively, the length of the 'conditioning' series – that is, from where the subject considered that the cycle began to where the subject considered that he received his terminal validation. Again, as we have suggested before, it is often more helpful to discover what the subject has learned rather than whether or not he conforms to what the experimenter has learned.

16. Conditions favourable to the formation of new constructs

At the end of the section on the personal construction of one's role, we pointed out that new constructs can be formed with less danger of paralysing effects if they are first approached in contexts which do not involve the client's self or members of his immediate family. In the section on personal security within the context of a construct we pointed out the disruption of one's role that may result from attempts to change certain figure elements in a construct when the construct is a role-governing construct and one of the figures – the mother-figure, for example – is the symbol of the construct. We suggested that in some cases it may be more economical to start from scratch and help the client form a new set of role-governing constructs altogether. Thus a person might first develop a new hypothetical cast of characters and only later find that they were like the people with whom he is living every day.

a. Use of fresh elements. In the first place, it is helpful if a fresh set of elements is provided as the context in which a new construct is to emerge. The elements, being relatively unbound by old constructs which would be seen as being incompatible with the new construct, do not involve the person with the old constructs until he has brought the new into a state of usefulness. In the common language of psychotherapists, 'resistance is temporarily circumvented'. This procedure includes such safeguards as developing new constructs in contexts which do not involve the self or members of the immediate family. It includes setting up a therapy situation which, at first, is insular as far as the rest of the client's world is concerned. The sanitarium or the private therapy room may provide the 'protected environment' so frequently mentioned in connection with psychotherapy. A therapist who is previously unknown to the client and who does not let himself become too fixed a figure in the client's world is an important fresh element upon which the client can start to develop wholly new constructs. In setting up fresh elements the therapist must be careful, however, not to introduce the client to so complicated a new world that he cannot make his moment-to-moment anticipations work at all. Even though the situation is insular, it must not be implausible.

There are various ways of developing new constructs upon fresh verbal elements. The development of tailor-made and carefully designed stories is a powerful tool in child psychotherapy and which, incidentally, has amazingly escaped systematic treatment by psychologists. The reading of Hawthorne's *The Great Stone Face* should suggest psychotherapeutic procedures beyond those which are commonly employed. We are familiar with the social-controlling effect of folklore, so important in the understanding of cultural anthropology; it is only a short step from folklore to the use of similar stories for special therapeutic purposes. In the clinical experience of the writer it has been relatively easy to develop new constructs for children in connection with story elements and thus give them form, definition, and usefulness before they come into conflict with the constructs which they are eventually to replace. In the use of stories the self is only gradually involved and the new constructs which are developed are allowed to replace only gradually those undesirable role constructs which have continued to exercise control in the client's life after having outlived their validity.

The composition and playing out of artificial roles, as elements upon which to create new constructs which in turn are later to have more vital meanings, is another example of the use of fresh elements to develop new constructs. The patent artificiality of the role is the very feature which prevents the tender shoots of new ideas from being trampled in the frantic rush to maintain oneself in one's previous role.

b. Experimentation. The next condition which is hospitable to the formation of new constructs is an atmosphere of experimentation. In more precise language this means the shifting of construct grounds upon which predictions are based and the checking of validating experiences to see which anticipations have corresponded to actual outcomes. It means even more. It means that the constructs are tried out in relative isolation from each other; this corresponds to the scientist's use of experimental controls. Constellatory constructs, as we have described them in a previous section, are tentatively avoided. The atmosphere of experimentation is one in which the consequences of one's experimental acts are seen as limited. One does not 'play for keeps'. Constructs, in the true scientific tradition, are seen as 'being tried on for size'. They are seen propositionally. In fact, the seeing of constructs as proposed representations of reality rather than the reality itself is propaedeutic to experimentation.

The client who is to form new constructs is encouraged by 'try out' new behaviours or to explore within a controlled situation, perhaps verbally only, the outcomes of asymptotic behaviour. His tentative constructs of the roles of other people may be tried out on the therapist. In the language of psychoanalysis this is 'transference'. Later we shall attempt to give *transference* an operational definition. At the moment it is sufficient to consider transference as a special case of experimentation with role constructs.

c. Availability of validating data. The third condition which is hospitable to the formation of new constructs is the availability of validating data. A construct is a framework for making predictions. If it does not work, there is a tendency to alter it – within the more permeable aspects of the construction system, of course. If returns on the prediction are unavailable or unduly delayed, one is likely to postpone changing the construct under which the prediction was made.

In the field of applied learning it has long been pointed out that 'knowledge of results facilitates learning'. This has been substantiated on a research basis. It needs rather careful interpretation, however. What the experimenter sees as 'results' may not be what the subject in the learning experiment sees as 'results'. If the subject is checking the results of his thinking within the larger aspects of his system, he may not consider the experimenter's 'results' as relevant.

Suppose a subject is attempting to solve a puzzle. He puts certain blocks together, knowing full well that eventually they cannot go together in that particular sequence, in order to get an idea of what the eventual volume of the completed puzzle will be like. He is developing an intermediate construct. The experimenter, with his forefinger on the phrase, 'knowledge of results', keeps nagging the subject by telling him that his 'trials' are unsuccessful. This is an instance in which the phrasing of the process for the subject is different from what it is for the experimenter. For the subject, the 'trials', as he sees them, may be 'successful'. This point has been previously mentioned in connection with the phrasing of experience.

Rather than throwing the emphasis upon knowledge of pre-conceived results, we have chosen to throw the emphasis upon availability of results in general as a facilitating condition for the formation of new constructs. In this manner the subject is permitted to phrase his experience in different ways. If he wishes to make long-range predictions, he is not plagued with moment-by-moment 'outcomes'. If he wishes to make a long-term investment, he is not compelled to keep reading ticker tape. If he wishes to develop intermediate constructs or 'tools', the fact that he is not yet anticipating the eventual outcomes successfully will not need to be interpreted as invalidating his efforts.

In the psychotherapeutic situation the availability of validating data implies skill on the part of the therapist. For the most part, this is verbal skill in expressing clearly facts and reactions, against which the client can check the results of his explorations whenever he is ready to do so. The therapist has to guard himself against producing facts which serve no purpose except to provide further confirmation of those constructs which ought to be replaced. Sometimes the client will ask, 'Don't you agree that my wife is impossible?' This is one the clinician will probably duck! Even if the clinician agreed, his agreement might not properly be considered as validating data for the construct the client really had in mind, although it would probably be construed in that way.

The clinician needs to be continually alert as to what constructs are being 'tried on', and try to govern the availability of data in terms of what is relevant to the construct actually being used. The client's question in the above paragraph may be indicative of various constructs other than the one explicitly expressed. For example, it may be interpreted to mean, 'I'm not such a bad husband, am I?' It may mean, 'You will help protect me from my wife, won't you?' It may mean, 'You are a better friend than my wife, aren't you?' It may mean, 'Everything will be all right if I get rid of my wife, won't it?' If a clinician gives an answer, it is a good thing for him to know what question he is answering. That, of course, is not always possible.

Sometimes clinicians like to emphasize 'objectivity'. They keep confronting the client with 'facts', in the hope that a continual steeping in such 'truthful' material will give the poor fellow a proper flavour. They usually succeed only in keeping the client in a stew. Many a clinician, under the guise of objectivity, gives his clients the 'right' answers to the wrong questions. In other words, 'objectivity' is altogether too frequently a disguise for literalism, and hence is not objective at all, merely verbal.

The role-playing exchange is an excellent way of enabling the client to try out new constructs which have immediate access to validating material. If it is carried out as a rehearsal, he has a preliminary round of validating data. If it is tried out in an extramural situation, he may have even more impressive evidence regarding the efficacy of this new construct.

The offering of interpretations of the client's attitudes of transference is an example of the use of validating data in the verification or falsification of constructs. The client tries out both old and new role constructs upon the therapist; the therapist both clarifies them and, by implication, makes it clear that, as regards some of them, appropriate results are not to be anticipated from them in any situation other than a childlike or a clinical one.

By providing validating data in the form of responses to a wide variety of constructions on the part of the client, some of them quite loose, fanciful, or naughty, the clinician gives the client an opportunity to validate constructs, an opportunity which is not normally available to him. This, of course, involves a good deal more than 'setting the patient right about things' or 'preaching'. It involves a careful prior analysis of the client's personal constructs and an opportunity for him to work them out in explicit forms. Again, it must be a way of giving the right answers to the right questions rather than the literal answers to the wrong questions.

It will be in order to say much more about the optimal conditions for the formation of new and regnant constructs when we discuss the techniques of psychotherapy. The preceding discussion is intended merely to be illustrative of the basic requirements involved in the propagation of new constructs.

17. Conditions unfavourable to the formation of new constructs

In general a failure to maintain conditions favourable to the formation of new constructs will delay their formation. There are, however, certain conditions which are especially inimical to the formation of new constructs. The most important of these is that in which the elements out of which the new construct is to be formed involve *threat*.

a. Threat. First, let us state rather precisely what we mean by *threat*. Basically, *threat* is a characteristic of a construct's relation to the superordinate constructs in a system. A construct is threatening when it is itself an element in a next-higher-order construct which is, in turn, incompatible with other higher-order constructs upon which the person is dependent for his living. The construct of danger is a *threat* when it becomes an element in the context of death or injury. There are circumstances when it is not a threat, at least not a very significant one. A roller-coaster elicits a construct of danger, but that danger is rarely placed in the context of death.

To continue our illustration: death, of course, is incompatible with living, at least in the minds of most people. There are people, however, who do not see life and death as incompatible. One may see death as an entrance to a phase of life beyond the River Styx. One may see death merely as a vestibule through which transmigration of the soul takes place. If death is incompatible with the construction system through which one maintains a basic orientation towards events and their anticipation, then the like elements in the context of death are threats. We shall have much more to say about threat later, for it is an important construct in the clinician's repertory.

Now if the elements out of which it is proposed to form a new construct commonly involve threat, that is, if they tend to elicit a construct or an issue which is basically incompatible with the system upon which the person has come to rely for his living – he may not readily utilize the elements for forming any new construct. The interpretation which makes them threatening may not even be as serious a matter as death. Its mere incompatibility with the construction system upon which one leans heavily in any way may make its elements threatening.

One may ask why a particular client is so insistent in construing the elements in such a way as to make them threats. The answer to this lies in the inherent nature of constructs themselves. One maintains one's construct system by clarifying it. Even one's own system is stabilized or controlled in the manner in which outside events are controlled. This means, among other things, that one controls one's system by maintaining a clear identification of the elements which the system excludes as well as those which it includes. The moment one finds oneself becoming involved in any way with the excluded elements of one's system, one becomes aware of the outset of incompatibility and sees these new clutching associations as threats. Like a wounded animal, one keeps facing one's enemy.

Now what happens when the client is presented with new elements which seek to ally themselves with his self in the formation of an intolerable construct? He may seek to disperse them or, as a last resort, he may turn his whole attention to the extrication of himself from the unholy alliance and to the rejection of the new elements in one big lump. The clinician can see this happen before his eyes. It is the very plausibility of the unwanted elements which makes them a threat to the person. If they seemed utterly alien to him, he would not be threatened by them; he could assume the part of a bystander.

It is clear that this kind of reaction to elements which are proposed as a basis for formulating new constructs would make them useless to their purpose. The effect of threat is to compel the client to claw frantically for his basic construct. Threat arouses the necessity for mobilizing one's resources. It should be borne in mind that the resources which are mobilized may not always be mature and effective. Therefore a threatened person may often behave in childish ways.

Another effect of introducing threatening elements, and frequently an undesirable one, is the tendency for the traumatic experience to act as further subjective documentation or proof of the client's own maladaptive conceptual framework. Not only may the traumatized client be thrown back upon older and more infantile constructions of life, but he is likely, through this further experience, to find 'proof' of those primitive constructions. It is correct to say of traumatic experience that it usually 'freezes people in their tracks'. It is important for the clinician to assess the freezing effect that may result from the introduction of certain new material in a therapy session.

b. Preoccupation with old material. There is another condition which is inimical to the formation of new constructs. That is an exclusive preoccupation with old material – what happens when a client in a psychotherapeutic series becomes unduly repetitive. Then the therapist begins to complain to his colleagues that he can see no movement. Old or familiar material tends to be fixed in place by old and childlike constructs; it is only as we let the client interweave it with new and adult material that he starts bringing his constructs up to date. The interlarding of new material with the old calls for new sorting of old material into new categories that will fit both the old and the new material.

Sometimes old constructs are impermeable. The events they subsume are the last of their kind. Such constructs are practically of no use in dealing with future events, and it may be just as well for the client that they are that way. In certain types of psychotic patients it may be desirable to let an old delusion lapse into impermeability rather than trying to resolve it by reconstruing the events it subsumes. The same may be true with respect to the outmoded but inaccessible constructs that one finds occasionally in less disturbed clients.

Sometimes one makes a deliberate effort to reduce a client's construct to a state of inoperative impermeability. Basically this is what happens in the establishment of a habit. The habit becomes a way of dealing with old material, but it certainly is not an alert way of dealing directly with new elements. There is nothing open-ended about a habitualized construct. That is not to say that habits are useless in helping one deal with the onrush of events. They do serve the purpose of stabilizing certain constructions so that one may be left otherwise free to deal intelligently, by contrast, with selected aspects of the new material. A habit may be considered as a convenient kind of stupidity which leaves a person free to act intelligently elsewhere. Whether he takes advantage of the opportunity or not is another question. Some people fail to seize the advantages offered them by their stupidity.

c. No laboratory. New constructs are not formed when one lacks a laboratory in which to try them out. This is just as true of any person as it is true of the scientist. A laboratory is a situation in which there is present, for the person to re-sort, a sufficient amount of the stuff out of which new constructs can be formed. It is difficult to form new social concepts out of situations which are barren of social relationships. It is difficult to form new parental constructs out of a situation which involves no parents. It is impossible to teach a prisoner who has had no relations with women for years how to play his sex role properly. It is impossible for a hospitalized patient to learn social poise in a situation which denies him the opportunity to assume a dignified position. A soldier, denied the privileges of democracy, learns little of how it operates – this, even though he may yearn for its advantages.

A laboratory also provides a convenient insulation from other variables, the complexities of which might swamp the person who is trying to form new constructs in a necessarily limited sphere. If one considers at once all the ramifications and ultimate consequences of each exploratory act, one will be overwhelmed and unable to formulate any new construct. One who has directed graduate students in their research efforts will have frequently seen this kind of intellectual drowning take place. Frequently the student sees so many implications of his study and so many possible variables to be considered that he is unable to design his experiment. A laboratory, however, permits a person to explore in a limited sphere. The bang that results from some of his inadvertent mixtures need not blow up his world. This is a way of saying what we have already said before on the affirmative side: that a person who is completely and continually involved in the ultimate consequences of his acts is in no position to experiment with new ideas.

Like the scientist who must form testable hypotheses and then try them out, the person who is to form new hypotheses needs to have data available in a form which his new constructs will either predict or clearly fail to predict. The person who lives in a completely elastic world can soon become discouraged in his attempts to measure it. The child whose parents are predictable only within a framework which is too complex for him to understand lives in such a world. He may be as maladjusted with respect to his parents as is the child whose parents would make all of his social constructs impermeable ones, or, to use the psychoanalytic notion, who attempt to organize all of his relations with them under 'superego' control.

D. The meaning of experience

18. The construed nature of experience

By now the reader is fully aware that the psychology of personal constructs sets itself against strong currents in the mainstream of psychological thought. Ours is an *anticipatory* rather than a *reactive* system. To many it will seem that we have herein abandoned a basic tenet of all modern science.

At the heart of this heresy is the delicate question of how a system such as ours is to deal with *experience*. Indeed, how does the person himself deal with experience? Is not man a product of his experience? Can he do other than *react* to it? Are not one's personal constructs always prefabricated by the disembodied hands of one's culture? Let us see.

There is a world which is happening all the time. Our experience is that portion of it which is happening to us. These two thoughts may be combined into the simple philosophical statement, 'The universe is existing and man is coming to know it.' In the sections immediately preceding this one, we have concerned ourselves with the knowing process; now let us turn our attention to that which is known.

Things happen to us personally only when we behave in relation to them. But we have already committed ourselves to the position that psychological response is initially and basically the outcome of a construing act. Experience, therefore, in this system, must be defined as the compass of fact which has fallen within a man's purview. It is a set of personally construed events. To study a man's experience, then, is to have a look at that upon which, rightly or wrongly, he has placed some construction.

Experience is the extent of what we know – up to now. It is not necessarily valid. We may 'know' a lot of things which are untrue, like the naval officer who was once described by a distinguished psychologist as having been gifted with a vast and versatile ignorance. Knowing things is a way of letting them happen to us. The unfortunate naval officer simply had allowed a lot of things to happen to him in a peculiar way. He had *variety of experience*, but his constructions were invalid. If his personal constructs continued to mislead him, he could be expected to sink a lot of whales and shoot down a lot of more or less friendly Air Force planes. But he had experience!

Just as the compass of experience is no guarantee of the validity of our personal constructs, neither does the *duration of experience* give us any such warranty. There is the case of the veteran school administrator, described by Dean Arthur Klein of Ohio State University, who had 'had only one year of experience – repeated thirteen times'. In this statement there is the implication that it is only the sequence of the construing process which gives both added range to one's experience and more comprehensive validity to one's anticipations. Presumably, the administrator, during his successive years of service, had not enlarged the scope of his vision or diminished the reaches of his misinformation.

Our Experience Corollary claims that a person's construction system varies as he successively construes the replications of events. If he fails to reconstrue events, even though they keep repeating themselves, he minimizes his experience. The person who takes events for granted, and who does not seek new light to throw upon them, adds very little to his store of experience as the years go on. Sometimes it is said that a person learns from experience. From the standpoint of the psychology of personal constructs, however, it is the learning which constitutes experience.

It is interesting to note the effect that reconstruing has upon the range of one's experience. Our Modulation Corollary states that the variation in a person's construction system is limited by the permeability of the constructs within whose ranges of convenience the variants lie. This is a matter of taking events in one's stride. If one tries to deal with one's world by legalistic book-keeping, one is likely to find that there is little one can do to adapt oneself to varying events. A person who approaches his world with a repertory of impermeable constructs is likely to find his system unworkable through the wider expanses of events. He will, therefore, tend to constrict his experience to the narrower ranges which he is prepared to understand. On the other hand, if he is prepared to perceive events in new ways, he may accumulate experience rapidly. It is this adaptability which provides a more direct measure of the growing validity of a man's construct system than does the amount of time he consumes in swatting at the events which buzz around his ears.

To summarize, our experience is that portion of the universe which is happening to us – that is, which is successively construed by us – and the increase of experience is a function, not of the hodgepodge of events which we have construed, or of the time spent in being aware of them, but of the successive revision of our construct system in the general direction of increased validity. An analysis of experience, then, becomes a study of the field of fact which one has segmented into meaningful events; the way those events, in turn, are construed; the kinds of evidence against which one has checked the validity of one's predictions; the progressive changes which the constructs have undergone; and, most of all, the more permeable and durable constructs which have subsumed the whole evolvement.

19. The interpretation of experience

Up to this point we have not developed any public diagnostic constructs for the clinician's use. This comes in a later chapter. Before we propose such constructs we want to discuss further man's experience and the personal way he structures it. We also want to illustrate how man can recover from his experiences, as, for example, in psychotherapy. The diagnostic constructs we propose need to be designed in relation to such recovery.

So far our approach to personal constructs has been almost phenomenological or descriptive. Yet our theoretical position is not strictly phenomenological, for we recognize that personal constructs locked up in privacy cannot be made the subject of a book designed for public consumption. What we attempt to do is to lift our data from the individual at a relatively high level of abstraction. This is a little like saying that we deal concretely with a person's abstractions rather than abstractly with his concretisms. Behaviourism, for example, did it the other way; it created elaborate public abstractions out of minute personal concretisms.

In practice, what we do is observe the individual's behaviours, using the lowest possible common denominators of description. Then, continuing to deal descriptively with the individual, we observe his personal abstractions of those behaviours – his *constructs*. Now these abstractions are not necessarily verbalized by him, nor are they necessarily immediately translatable by him into verbalizations, either in the public language or in his own babble. His abstractions of his own behaviour may be structured or construed by him solely in terms of anticipated continuities and cycles. They are still abstractions. They are isolated. There is still a construct-like discrimination of simultaneous likeness and difference in the way he thinks about them.

Now the personal-construct psychologist observes a person's own abstractions of behaviour, both as they are verbalised and as they are otherwise regularised by the individual. But the personal-construct psychologist initially deals with them as concretely, from his own point of view, as possible. He starts by taking what he sees and hears at face value. He even takes at face value what he sees and hears about his subject's constructs. In psychotherapy this is commonly called 'acceptance' of the client. For Sullivan it would be 'learning the language of the patient'. Our term, which we shall elaborate later, is *the credulous attitude.*

But the psychologist is himself a person; hence, his psychological processes follow his own personal constructs. Other psychologists are persons too. If there is to be a common understanding of the client, there must be commonality in the way he is construed. If there is to be a constructive social process involving the client – for example, therapy – the person who is to play the role of therapist must subsume the constructs of the subject rather than merely interpret his overt behaviour. All of this means that we cannot consider the psychology of personal constructs a phenomenological theory, if that means ignoring the personal construction of the psychologist who does the observing.

What the personal-construct psychologist does is first attempt to describe accurately the highest levels of abstraction in his subject's system at the lowest possible levels of abstraction in his own. This is what we meant when we said that data should be lifted at a relatively high level of abstraction. We were referring to a high level of abstraction *in the subject's system.* This could not, of course, have been taken to mean that the data themselves were to be considered as abstractions in the system in which they were handled by the psychologist. Data, when considered as such by the psychologist, are relatively concrete elements awaiting some sort of construction.

20. The ahistorical approach

The perceptual theories in psychology are frequently said to espouse the ahistorical approach to the understanding of behaviour. This approach is from the viewpoint that one's activity at a given moment is determined primarily by one's outlook at that moment. What has actually happened in the past can influence behaviour only through the perceptions which are operating at the present instant. Personal-construct theory takes a somewhat similar stand. In personal-construct theory, however, the basis of perception has been broadened to include 'nonconscious' as well as 'conscious' processes, and the manner of perception has been cast in the form of *constructs.*

It should be emphasized, also, that personal-construct theory does not ignore history, just as some perceptual theories do not actually ignore history even though they may consider it a remote rather than an immediate determinant of behaviour. Now history, as contrasted with chronology, is a method of study, not a definitive set of causes. In personal-construct theory one may be interested in a historical type of study because it helps to reveal the successive patterning of the elements for whose interpretation his client's personal constructs are formed. Sometimes it is only through the analysis of these elements that we can infer what the client's presently operating constructs must be like. This is a legitimate psychological use of the *historical method.* It is granted that our use of the method is indirect, and thus is in contrast with the direct approaches illustrated in the last chapter, but there are occasions when one must utilize such indirect ways of gaining access to personal constructs.

21. Group expectancies as validators of personal constructs

Among the many kinds of events in the world which one seeks to anticipate optimally, people and their behaviours are particularly salient. People, too, are events. One can have a set of constructs whose contexts comprise other persons as elements. The elements can also be specific bits of behaviour of the other persons. When one tries such a construct on for size one subjects it to a process of validation. If one's friends behave the way one expects them to behave, one accumulates supportive evidence for one's construct; if they do not, one's construct has, in this one instance, failed to provide that person with a precise anticipation of events.

This failure, of course, does not necessarily mean that a person will immediately discard his construct. The construct may, considering all of its elements, and not merely the single unfortunate event which has just been concluded, still provide him with what he considers to be an optimal basis for predicting the behaviour of most persons. In the long run, however, he must come to accept the total accumulation of evidence – or what he construes as evidence – which attests to the validity or invalidity of the construct under which he has been operating. In the case of constructs involving people, this evidence is the subsequent behaviour of the people with whom he comes in contact.

But let us take into account the fact that the behaviour which is taken as validating evidence is also itself psychologically generated. 'Other people' are persons too. They, in turn, act according to their anticipations. When one lives in a community in which the commonality of personal constructs is extensive, one finds people behaving similarly because they tend to expect the same things. In this sense, the expectancies which are common to the group actually operate as the validators against which the individual tends to verify the predictive efficiency of his own constructs. Broadly, this is what we mean by saying that group expectancies are validators of personal constructs.

There are some special cases of the way in which group expectancies operate as validators of personal constructs. First, let us consider a type of construct which is not about people at all, but for which the validating evidence is *ordinarily* available only by way of other people's opinions. Take, for example, the construct of *sphericity*, as applied to the earth. While certain features of curvature can be observed directly at sea, we are, for the most part, dependent upon other people's descriptions of their own experience for evidence of the earth's complete sphericity. If the people with whom we come in contact all expect the earth to be as flat as a pancake, all the validating evidence to which we must subject our construct of earth sphericity is negative. We may have to decide that the earth is flat after all. This is a particular type of case in which the opinions of other people operate as validators of one's personal constructs about nonhuman events.

Next, let us consider the case of the person who is construed by his neighbours in such a way that he is always expected to do certain things. Whenever he fails to perform according to their expectations he finds them acting as if he had threatened them. He has. Now he may start to fancy himself as an unpredictable person – unpredictable, that is, for other people. In that case he may go right on shocking the neighbours. His conceptualization of himself, at the same time, is markedly affected. In order to maintain his pose he may have to construe himself as a 'shocking' person. Thus, even though he rejects the expectancies of his neighbours as being invalid, he has had to construe himself in relation to those expectancies and has had to bring his behaviour under the reign of constructs which are carefully validated in reverse of his neighbours' expectancies.

This kind of perverse conformity can frequently be observed in children. A child attempts to establish himself in relation to his parents. He may do this by being negativistic. Yet, in order to be consistently negativistic, he must see the world the way his parents see it. Only by doing so can he be sure to place himself at the contrast pole of each of their constructs. He winds up using the very same dimensional system his parents use.

A third special way in which group expectancies may be considered as validators of personal constructs involves one's construction of one's role. *Role*, as we have tried to define it in a strict sense, was not necessarily involved in the example of the person who tried so hard to behave in contrast to his neighbours' expectations that he adopted their construct dimensions. The person who maintained himself as a shocking person may not have entertained any particular subsuming construction of his neighbours' construction systems such as would be required if he were to meet our criterion of role. He need only have observed his neighbours' reactions without trying to construe them as functioning within any system but his own. We have insisted that the term *role* be reserved for a course of activity which is played out in the light of one's construction of one or more other persons' construct systems. When one plays a *role*, one behaves according to what one believes another person thinks, not merely according to what the other person appears to approve or disapprove. One plays a *role* when one views another person as a construer. This, of course, is a restricted definition of the term. It is the definition specifically used in the psychology of personal constructs. The term is used much more broadly elsewhere.

It should be apparent at once that one's construction of one's role must necessarily be validated in terms of the expectancies of the persons with respect to whom one construes one's role. In this case, the ultimate validating criteria are themselves the operations of the construct systems which appear to govern our neighbours' behaviours. Our very definition of *role* commits us to this position.

We have attempted to state the general way in which group expectancies operate as validators of personal constructs, and to mention three special types of cases. The general way is the same as the way all psychologists validate their theoretical approaches – by checking predictions of people's behaviour against their subsequently observed behaviour. People's behaviour is taken as validating evidence for a considerable variety of personal constructs. Since people's behaviour is believed to be statable in terms of their expectancies, this is tantamount to saying that group expectancies operate as validators of personal constructs. We are saying, simply, that everyone uses this approach. The special cases are (1) the necessary acceptance of group judgments as validators of any construct for which more direct evidence is not available, (2) the implicit and inescapable acceptance of group expectancies as validators whenever one tries to maintain a pose, and (3) the acceptance, by definition, of group expectancy-governing constructs as validators of one's own *role constructs*. It is this last special case which is illustrative of the characteristic approach of the personal-construct psychologist to other people, for he, by his Fundamental Postulate, must seek validation of his understanding of other people by checking it against their personal-construct systems. The personal-construct psychologist thus seeks to establish for himself a role in relation to other people. Personal-construct theory might have been called 'role theory'. In fact, this was the term by which it was known among the writer's students during the earlier stages of its development.

The psychology of personal constructs, rather than being a system in which the study of individual behaviour leaves no place for the study of group participation, is one which keeps open vast areas of social relationships to be explored by adventurous psychologists. The concept of individual suggestibility need not be considered, as it once was, the sole basis for a social psychology. Within the present psychological system the phenomenal areas of traditionalism, social controls, law, cultural identification, and ethnic unity can properly be brought into the realm of psychology.

In this particular book the discussion of group expectancies as validators of personal constructs is preliminary to a discussion of what is believed to be one of the major areas of investigation in psychological clinical work: the analysis of the client's experience. It is hoped that it will serve to indicate that, while the theoretical point of view of the psychology of personal constructs is largely consonant with the ahistorical stand of perceptual theories, it is, in practice, very much concerned with the historical study of chronological elements upon which presently operating personal constructs are formed. It is particularly concerned with those chronological elements with respect to which the presently operating constructs cannot be directly elicited, in symbolic form or otherwise. The clinician must infer them by trying to form parallel constructs out of the same stuff.

22. Gaining access to personal constructs through the study of the culture in which they have grown

In psychotherapeutic practice one never ceases to be impressed both by the differences in the problems of clients who come from different cultural backgrounds and by the similarities in the problems of clients who come from backgrounds which are similar. To be sure, these differences and similarities seem more crucial in diagnosis and the early stages of therapy. Yet one cannot ignore them in establishing and maintaining an effective relationship with this client throughout the entire therapeutic series. As the therapeutic programme moves along, the therapist more and more comes to see his client as an individual and thinks of him less and less as a member of a class. But the cultural identification is there to be seen whenever the therapist backs off and looks at it.

A failure to understand cultural controls may make the therapist insensitive to the disruptive nature of some of the client's anxieties. A few months ago the writer was supervising a therapy programme in which the client was a Negro and the therapist was white. It was apparent that the client was avoiding the discussion of an extremely threatening topic, the nature of which was well enough perceived to enable him to skirt it consistently. After employing various techniques and assuring ourselves that the problem could probably be faced in the kind of therapeutic relationship already established, we put the client under a regime of physical tension during the interviews, and subjected him to a type of stress questioning ordinarily used only with the greatest of caution. At the third interview in this part of the series he told the therapist about his fantasies of intercourse with white women. His physical tension immediately became automatic; that is to say, he did not have to remind himself to keep his muscles tense or be reminded to do so by the therapist.

The client had discussed masturbation and sex fantasies before. The therapist, who was inexperienced in therapy with clients from this type of cultural background, had only one cue regarding the deeply disturbing nature of the material elicited; that was the motor behaviour of the client. Fortunately, this was so marked that the therapist, who was fully alert to this kind of semiotics in therapy, could not overlook the significance of the material associated with the change in behaviour. (If the client had been under a physical-relaxation regime at the time the material was elicited, it would have been much easier to have overlooked its traumatic nature. The relationship between a tension set and the clear-cut and obvious revelation of the traumatic nature of the material elicited is appreciated by trial lawyers who 'break down' certain kinds of witnesses on the stand.) The problem for this therapist, after the traumatic nature of the material had been so clearly revealed, was to understand the nature of the threat to the client's basic construct system. With the help of another therapist, who was familiar with the client's type of cultural background, it was possible to come to appreciate the way in which cultural controls, especially those against interracial sex behaviour, operated in the client's group.

The client had been forced to construe the crosscurrents of two different cultures. In his high school there were few other coloured students, and he had seen himself as more or less accepted by his white peers. His home, however, came wholly under the control system of a Negro culture. His fantasies of intercourse with white women threatened him with the loss of his basic role and he experienced painful guilt feelings. It was not surprising that he was, before and during the early period of therapy, frantically engaging in group organizational activity directed towards the improvement of the social status of his race.

There are other illustrations which can be cited to indicate the access which can be obtained to personal constructs via a study of cultural controls. The therapist who comes in contact with a series of rural clients for the first time may be struck and possibly baffled by their similarity. If he attempts to relate the 'run' of clients to his own diagnostic construct system, he may come up with some such notion as 'farmers tend to be schizoid'. This is stereotype, not diagnosis!

The Gentile therapist who comes in contact with a series of Jewish clients for the first time may also be baffled by the similarities he sees by way of contrast with his other clients. If he is to understand them as persons, rather than to stereotype them as Jews, he must neither ignore the cultural expectations under which they have validated their constructs – expectation of both Jewish and Gentile groups –

nor make the mistake of focusing on the group constructs to the exclusion of the personal constructs of each client. If he stops with group constructs, he does an injustice to his clients; if he sees group constructs as the elements upon which his clients must have had to form personal constructs about themselves and their companions, he may come to understand the obstacles and aspirations which play such an important part in their personal readjustment.

Moreover, the Gentile therapist who seeks to understand a Jewish client must have some appreciation of the family ties which are characteristic of the culture, and which the client must do something about, one way or another, if he is to develop a personal-construct system enabling him to get along in the world. This is not to say that the Jewish client, who thinks he needs to do so, cannot ever hope to differentiate himself from his family or from his culture; indeed, he may, if he considers it necessary, do an unusually decisive job of it. It means, rather, that if he does the job, he will have to have a formula for it, a construct or system of constructs which will permit him to see the surrounding contrary expectations as not necessarily invalidating his construct of independence. It may take a while to work out his formula for release, and he may apply it in a number of inappropriate forms before he gets the 'bugs out of it', but eventually there is no reason why he cannot be just as free of cultural conventionality as his capacity for forming new ideas will permit him to be. Indeed, in a sense, he may become more free – for his new personal construct may give him a clearly constructed path leading elsewhere.

What we have said with respect to a client's adjustment to his Jewish cultural background is equally applicable to any client's adjustment to any cultural system similarly well integrated. One does not escape from his cultural controls (assuming that there is ever any reason to escape) simply by ignoring them – he must *construe* his way out. Some people try to *fight* their way out by being perverse; but they, as we have already suggested, often end up by being more than ever like the persons whom they have rejected. Others concern themselves less with the problem of extrication and approach the matter from the standpoint of overriding principles. They are likely to be happier with their results.

We shall have much more to say later about the appraisal of a particular client's experiences and activities within the framework of his culture. We have discussed the topic here as a way of illustrating the broader implications of personal construing. We wanted to show how personal constructs are the tools of experience rather than its products merely.

As a whole, this chapter on the nature of constructs has had as its purpose the clarification of what is meant by *personal constructs*, their variations, their everyday uses, their communication, their simple dimensions, their propagation, and their experiential and cultural roots. It is hoped that, as a result of this clarification, the reader will understand and make some practical use of the rationale which underlies the psychological undertakings and procedures proposed in later chapters.

Chapter four

The clinical setting

It is time to pause in the development of our theory in order to set the stage for the presentation of a personal-construct psychologist's device. The further development of theoretical constructs is left for later chapters, when, perhaps, the reader will feel more comfortable with the everyday working of the new system.

A. Characteristics of the clinical method in psychology

1. Clinical psychology as a disciplinary area

When different groups of men attempt to accomplish different objectives they tend to develop varying procedures and unique outlooks. It is not surprising, then, that if one group of men sets out to anticipate certain events, they may develop, for example, a *psychological discipline*; while others, having their attention focused upon other events, may develop a *physiological discipline*. This is no more than one would expect if one assumed our Fundamental Postulate: a person's processes are psychologically channelized by the ways in which he anticipates events. Moreover, having developed a characteristic disciplinary approach which receives rather extensive validation in one area, it is quite natural, through application of the principle of the elaborative choice, for a man to try to extend its range of convenience. This is what happens when a physician bursts into the field of psychiatry after several years of preoccupation with medicine, or when a physicist, suspecting that the social scientists are not keeping up with him, decides to take a year off and bring 'scientific enlightenment' into the collapsing world of interpersonal relations. Yet it may be some time after the man changes his letterhead before he begins to grasp constructs whose focus of convenience is in the area in which he has come to work. Some men, possibly because of personal identifications with their profession, continue throughout their lives to conduct psychotherapeutic interviews on the basis of physiological principles, or to manipulate groups of people in terms of Newtonian law.

The free movement of ideas from one area of application to another may, nonetheless, provide healthful mixtures. The notions of cybernetics and servomechanisms have represented useful exchanges between physics and psychology. It is only in certain cases, such as professional medicine's attempt to preempt the field of psychiatry, that the invasion has introduced misanthropic elements of intellectual dictatorship and the suppression of free research.

As we have indicated before, the psychology of personal constructs is a system designed to have a range of convenience covering those events commonly covered by psychological theories but with a particular focus of convenience in the clinical area. Its intended focus of convenience sets it apart, for example, from Hull's learning theory but brings it close to the intentions of Rogers' theoretical rationale for client-centred therapy. Since the area upon which we are focusing our attention has a good deal to do with the form our theory takes and its practical utility, it is appropriate for us to have something to say about what we think clinical psychology is.

As we see it, the ultimate objective of the clinical psychologist is neither diagnosis nor research. It is rather the anticipation of actual and possible courses of events in a person's life. Thus, as in our theory, the emphasis is upon the future and its possibilities. If diagnosis helps us to anticipate what would happen under various imposed conditions, then diagnosis is an intermediate step in reaching the ultimate objective of clinical psychology. If diagnosis is no more than a plot of the person's present position or a log of his past navigation, then it occupies a relatively minor place among the intermediate objectives of the clinical psychologist.

Research, except as it is directed towards the anticipation of the future, is also a minor objective. Research may be nothing more than static diagnosis carried on at a higher level of abstraction and with a range of generality extending to more persons. Its generalizations may not embrace individuals' futures. Thus research, while generally accepted as meritorious, appears to us to be important in clinical psychology primarily because of the light it may throw upon what will happen to the clinical psychologist's clients under the various possible conditions which may be imposed.

It might seem that the point we are leading up to is that therapy is the ultimate objective of clinical psychology and that it is the point towards which our theory-building efforts are primarily directed. In a sense, possibly, this is true. But the term 'therapy' and its companion term 'patient' carry many implications which we are reluctant to buy. Most of all, they carry the implication that the person served is reduced to an ultimate state of passivity and that his recovery depends upon his submitting *patiently* and unquestioningly to the manipulations of a clinician. We think this is a badly misleading view of how a psychologically disturbed person recovers.

But if one is to communicate, one must use familiar words or else spend a great deal of time coining new ones. And when a person uses familiar words he invokes traditional meanings. He usually ends up compromising between saying what he means and letting the listener hear what he is already prepared to hear. In our case we have largely abandoned the term 'patient' in favour of Rogers' more expressive 'client', but we have submitted to the term 'therapy', even though what we mean by *therapy* is quite different from what is commonly called 'therapy'.

Our view of the ultimate concern of clinical psychology as a discipline, and our notion of *therapy*, is that of a psychological process which changes a person's outlook on some aspect of life. It involves construing, or, more particularly, reconstruing. That which is reconstrued is usually a person's own life or the role he envisions for himself through his understanding of others' outlooks. Not only does he construct life in an ordinary biographical sense, but he also reconstructs his own life processes, even those which are commonly called vegetative. The reconstruing is what some psychologists would call 'learning'; but again we are inclined to avoid a term because of its customary implications – in this case, because of its stimulus–response implications.

Since we see processes psychologically channelized by one's construction system, we can view them as being changed, either by rerouting through the same system of dichotomous constructs, or by reconstruction of the system of channels. In the clinic one is more apt to be concerned with the latter kind of readjustment. The former type is sometimes referred to as the 'Dean's Office treatment'. It could also be called, quite appropriately, 'lawyer treatment'. But the latter kind of readjustment is a much more ambitious undertaking and involves many technical difficulties, both in communication and in timing. Yet we see it as the ultimate objective of the clinical-psychology enterprise, and have used it as the basis for the theme of this book – *the psychological reconstruction of life.* We even considered using the term *reconstruction* instead of *therapy.* If it had not been such a mouth-filling word we might have gone ahead with the idea. Perhaps later we may!

2. *The clinician and the null hypothesis*

In psychology, as well as in a number of other disciplines, it has become customary to design research projects around rival hypotheses. In that way, instead of letting the data point to the 'truth' or 'falsehood' of a hypothesis, the researcher recognizes that truth and falsehood are not absolutes which can be determined with finality during his lifetime. This is an important practical attribute for one to take towards his research. But sometimes its significance is misinterpreted. When one comes to realize that truth and falsehood are *relative*, one may then take the view that there must be shades of grey between truth and falsehood and that the terms cannot be used categorically. To take this stand is to miss the basically comprehensive nature of the construct of *truth vs. falsehood.* It is to construct a scale of *truth vs. falsehood* out of a series of preemptive numeral-like constructs.

But *truth* and *falsehood* can still be used quite dichotomously even though, in their application, they must be considered relativistically. Our discussion of abstracted scales, composed essentially of dichotomous constructs, is pertinent here. The relativity applies, not to gradations between truth and falsehood, but to the contexts of the things which are construed. For example, in the context of A, B, and C, A and B might be relatively true as compared with C. The truth that applies to A and B is categorical; it is A and B in comparison to C which is relative. Thus when one says that A is true one means, not that it is a little bit true or a whole lot true but that it is categorically true in a sense in which B is also true and in contrast with C, which is, by the same token, categorically false in comparison to A and B. For the person who is not accustomed to using scales abstractly, this notion may be a little hard to follow, but it should really not give him too much difficulty after he gets the hang of it.

Now the scientifically minded psychologist does not ordinarily try to say simply that A is true; nor does he expect his data to tell him that A is true. Moreover, he does not expect his data to tell him *how much truth* there is in A, as if there could be an absolute measure of the amount of truth inherent in A, independent of its context of B and C. In order to make sense the researcher has to ask *which of two things, in comparison with each other*, is true. Actually his context implies at least three, rather than two, things, but the rest of the like elements in the context can often remain unmentioned. Thus the researcher nowadays usually designs his research around two rival hypotheses and asks the data to tell him *which, in a given sense and in comparison with the other*, is true.

All of this is very much in line with the epistemological position we have called *constructive alternativism*. For we must keep trying our alternative interpretations on nature for size, since she never offers to give us her measurements in advance. Only by comparisons of what we contrive to try on do we successively approximate the one ultimate hypothesis that is truer than any other. It should be clear, then, that what any scientist can hope to discover is not an absolute categorical truth, nor even a relative fraction of truth, but a categorical truth applied in a context of relationships. The relativity refers not to the truth – that is categorical – but to the hypotheses in the context of which truth is the abstraction.

There is a principle that most scientists try to follow with great devotion: the *principle of parsimony*. It asserts that the simplest interpretation of any phenomenon is always to be preferred over any more complex interpretation. As far as the writer knows, no one has come out with a very objective definition of what constitutes simplicity. It is likely to resolve itself into whatever the person finds more convenient, or, in terms of our theoretical position, into whatever is more consistent with his personal-construct system. Actually, if this is what simplicity means, it is not too bad a notion – except that we ought to keep clearly in mind what we mean by it. This line of reasoning leads us into the interesting position of restating the principle of parsimony as a principle of convenient consistency.

In order to use the principle of parsimony in their experimental designs psychologists often set up a *null hypothesis* in competition with a *theoretical* or *expected hypothesis*. Sometimes the latter is called an 'experimental hypothesis' to distinguish it from the null hypothesis. Actually, however, both hypotheses are experimental. The null hypothesis is deduced from mathematically formulated laws of probability or 'chance'. The theoretical or expected hypothesis is deduced from a psychological theory, or induced from prior observations. In some cases it is picked up opportunistically because it happens to be lying around; in that case, as we have already suggested, we may say that it is obtained by the dragnet method.

Having set up the null hypothesis and the theoretical or expected hypothesis as rivals, the psychologist usually reasons that the null hypothesis, if at all plausible, is the more parsimonious of the two. He therefore usually places a 20 to 1 or 100 to 1 handicap against his theoretical or expected hypothesis and in favour of the null hypothesis. If the null hypothesis would account for such an outcome as he obtains at the rate of more than one or five times out of a hundred (the 1 per cent or 5 per cent levels of confidence), he feels that the principle of parsimony requires him to give the preferential nod to the null hypothesis.

Now is the null hypothesis always the more parsimonious explanation? Does it deserve the 100 to 1 advantage that it is customarily given? To answer this question we need only refer back to what functionally constitutes 'parsimony' or 'simplicity'. The answer we get is that if one's basic construction of the universe is one of randomness, then the null hypothesis would tend to be more meaningful. It would be more meaningful because it would be more consistent with one's basic interpretation of nature. But if one's basic approach to the universe is systematic, then the null hypothesis may not represent the more parsimonious explanation, and it may conceivably be that the theoretical or expected hypothesis should be the one to be given the 100 to 1 advantage. It is from a background of this type of analysis that we turn to the clinical situation, and the kinds of problems the clinician faces, to see what should be the role of the null hypothesis in clinical thinking.

The clinician is faced with a client who is very much alive. Each moment the clinician delays his professional decision, the client moves along the course of his life. No matter what the clinician does, something is going to happen in the client's life. It is impractical to assume that the clinician's choice is between having some particular thing happen and having nothing happen. In the clinical situation the choice is between two somethings – not between a something and a nothing. In other words, in the clinical situation, in contrast to the usual research situation, none of the choices open to the clinician actually corresponds to the null hypothesis.

If a client is disturbed, the clinician's decision may be between hospitalization and sending the client back into his household. Both alternatives have important implications. Yet it may be that the clinician can marshal no evidence at better than the 5 per cent level of confidence that hospitalization will help the client or that returning to the household will do damage. Does this mean that the clinician should 'let nature take its course'? No, his obligation is to make *the better* of the two practical choices with which he is faced. Neither of them corresponds to the null hypothesis.

Consider another illustration. Let us suppose that, from a careful psychological examination of a client, it appears that there is only one change out of five that his condition will improve with lobotomy. This represents only the 20 per cent level of confidence – not a scientist's betting odds. But let us suppose, also, that the psychological examination leads the clinician to believe that the chances are nine out of ten that the client's condition will become permanently worse if he is not lobotomized. Taking this as a hypothetical case, and disregarding the actual merits or disadvantages of lobotomy for the moment, what should the clinician's decision be? Neither level of probability reaches the sacred '1 per cent', or even the semisacred '5 per cent', level of confidence. Yet, on the basis of this information, the conservative decision in the hypothetical case would be in favour of lobotomy. In this clinical situation, as in nearly all clinical situations, the null hypothesis has no practical counterpart in the choices between which the clinician must make a decision.

In other words, one of the unique features of the clinical method, whether it be in psychology or elsewhere, is that it rarely presents any alternative corresponding to the null hypothesis. This makes some psychologists unhappy, particularly those who want to make noises like those they suppose scientists must make, regardless of what issues are at stake. The clinical setting invites one to engage in just as rigorous thinking as any scientific laboratory, but it presents its issues in different, and often more baffling, forms.

3. Successive approximation and the clinical method

A second characteristic of the clinical method is its emphasis upon successive approximation. It is not that science fails to employ successive approximation in connection with all its methods, but rather that the clinical setting invites the psychologist to include a greater number of successive steps in his approach to his client. In a typical research setting, for example, the psychologist may design an experiment to last months, or even years, dealing with a single variable. Usually a definitive or lasting answer is sought to the question which has been propounded.

In the clinical setting, however, the psychologist develops both his answers and his issues in a swiftly moving sequence of inquiries. This feature of the clinical method can be noted especially in psychotherapy. The client makes a statement; instead of spending the next few weeks trying to determine precisely the truth or falsehood of the statement, or its range of generality, the clinical psychologist usually accepts or rejects it tentatively, on the spot, and goes on to the issues which emerge as a result of his interpretation of the statement. His interpretation is necessarily an approximate one, often reached at a low level of confidence, but he keeps moving along to other issues, or to subordinate issues, and to a continuous series of successive approximations. Often he comes back to an old issue on which he has once accepted an approximate answer. When he does, the old issue has usually taken on new meaning and the response he receives is interpreted with an enlarged frame of reference. Within an hour's psychotherapeutic interview the clinical psychologist may have successively formulated and accepted approximate answers to dozens of issues.

This feature of clinical methodology is disturbing to literal-minded psychologists who mistake their literalism for objectivity. What they are likely to overlook is that the clinical psychologist is in the process of developing hypotheses as he goes along, and that the emphasis of the method is on formulating appropriate questions whose answers may have relevance to the client's difficulty, rather than on extracting definitive answers to irrelevant questions. When one ponders the fact that mankind has probably spent more time trying to answer poorly posed questions than figuring out sensible issues, one wonders if this feature of the clinical method should not be more widely advocated in all human enterprise.

4. The clinical method and multivariant structure

One of the commonly accepted features of the clinical method is its recognition of the multivariant structure of its problems. The clinician, especially the psychological clinician, can rarely reduce the problem of his client to a single issue. He must see his client, not merely by successive approximations, as we have suggested in the last section, but simultaneously in terms of a considerable number of dimensions. This is not easy to do. Some clinicians do not even try; they attempt, instead, to reduce the problem to one single 'diagnosis' or 'disease entity'. Having thus construed the problem preemptively, they start doing to the client all of the things their book says should be done in this particular kind of case. When a client meets this kind of clinician, he should be very careful what kind of 'diagnosis' he lays himself open to.

At a later point in this book we shall suggest the use of certain over-all dimensions which should prove helpful in understanding clients. These are in the nature of propositional constructs, not preemptive nosological categories. They are designed to subsume at a comparatively high level of abstraction, and with great permeability, the complex shadings of meaning that one encounters in his clients' personal construct systems.

5. Simultaneous application of low levels of probability

Suppose that observations A and B are believed to be indicative of problem X. Suppose, however, that A is observed among people who do not have problem X (that is, 'normal' people) 10 per cent of the time. Suppose the same is true of B, although A and B are not associated. If John is observed to have A, the null hypothesis could be rejected at the 10 per cent level of confidence only. In other words, the chances are one out of ten that if he had been randomly drawn from a 'normal' population he would have symptom A. Likewise, if he were observed to have B, the chances would be one out of ten that he would have shown the symptom if he had been randomly drawn from a 'normal' population. However, if he were observed to have both A and B, the chances are $1/10 \times 1/10$ or only $1/100$ that this would have happened if he had been randomly drawn from a 'normal' population. Thus two observations, either of which was alone highly indicative that there was anything wrong with John, might be combined to suggest rather strongly that John was not 'normal'. Incidentally, we should note the particular kind of reverse logic that the scientist must use in drawing inferences from his data. We have not been able to say that ninety-nine persons out of a hundred who have John's symptoms have problem X.

We have assumed in our illustration that observations A and B are distributed independently in the population. This made our illustration somewhat simpler; but actually such 'diagnostic signs' are likely to be somewhat correlated. Therefore, the likelihood of a person, who was randomly drawn from a 'normal' population, exhibiting both A and B would ordinarily be somewhat greater than one out of a hundred.

Of course, all that we have shown by our observations A and B is the likelihood that John was *not* like a person randomly drawn from a population of 'normal' people. We have not demonstrated what his difficulty is. It still may be more reasonable to call him 'normal' than to throw him into one of the diagnostic pigeonholes we have constructed. In deciding how we ought to think about John the null hypothesis is not of much use to us.

We can think of the combination of low-level predictors in another way. Suppose observations A and B are each correlated with disorder X to the extent represented by a Pearsonian correlation coefficient of .20. This is not a very high coefficient; it permits the reduction of the standard error of estimate by slightly less than 2 per cent. But now suppose that A and B are uncorrelated with each other – in other words, that they approach disorder X from entirely different angles. Taken as a team, they enable the statistician to make a prediction on the basis of a multiple correlation of .28. This would permit the reduction of the standard error of estimate by almost 4 per cent. If several other independent and relevant observations can be made, the diagnosis of X may eventually be predicted with a fairly respectable level of confidence.

Of course, the clinician is not likely to have his normative data in such a form that he can compute his probabilities in terms of proportionate chances or in the form of a multiple regression equation. What he does is organize his constructs in a hierarchy of apparent relevance to the situation at hand, and make a sequence of judgements of the type if – then – but not –. It is a matter of some controversy between statisticians and clinicians as to whether or not the clinician is simply operating loosely as a multiple-regression equation when he combines probabilities in this manner. The problem is somewhat baffling.

It does seem to the writer that the clinician must do more than compute an implicit multiple-regression equation. Before he can start to do that he must determine the relevance of the data to his 'equation'. In terms of personal-construct theory, he must determine whether or not his observations fall within the range of convenience of his constructs. In this respect each client he sees or each situation he evaluates has a somewhat different relevance to his preestablished set of formulas. He must judge this relevance and assign regression weights accordingly: a somewhat different set of weights for each case. But this is an issue which will have to await more mature consideration.

6. Concept formation within an idiographic realm

In contrast with statistical approaches to psychology – except, perhaps, factorial analysis – the clinical method involves the formation of new constructs as one goes along. Both the clinician and, in the case of psychotherapy, the client are normally involved in reconceptualization of the situation at hand; not merely in computing outcomes within a predetermined conceptual structure. When we say this we do not mean to imply that the statistician does not ever reconceptualize; obviously he does, as attested to by the many new statistical inventions which continually come to light. What we mean is that the statistician, *in his application of his method*, does not ordinarily change his conceptualization of his variables. In contrast, the clinician, *in his application of his method*, does change his conceptualization of his variables. Indeed, many of his variables emerge as new constructs as he goes along. A clinician who cannot approach his client creatively in this manner is likely to have difficulty in his work, particularly in attempting to help his clients reconstrue their lives. If he cannot erect new structures himself, he is not likely to be able to help his clients erect new structures for themselves.

The new constructions which a clinician erects for himself in dealing with his case are ordinarily designed around the observed facts relating to that single person. Each newly formed construct is designed with a focus of convenience, just as all constructs, as we have said before, are designed with foci of convenience. In the clinical setting the psychologist forms many new constructs whose foci of convenience are in the realm of his particular case. The constructs are designed to enable him to predict what this particular person will do, and not necessarily what other persons will do. This is what we mean when we say that one of the features of the clinical method is the formation of concepts within an idiographic realm.

Some writers have considered the idiographic approach in psychology to be descriptive only. If by 'descriptive' one means that no concept formation is involved, we would not say that the clinician is making much of a contribution when he approaches a case idiographically. But if by 'descriptive' we mean that one shapes up new constructs which are tailor-made to a specified sequence of events – for example, a person's life – then we would say that the clinical method is characterized by description, and we would insist, furthermore, that much of the clinician's operation is within the idiographic realm.

Does the clinician operate exclusively within the idiographic realm? Our answer is emphatically no. The clinician approaches his client with a prepared set of professional constructs which are sufficiently permeable to embrace a client whom he has not yet seen. It is within the framework of these open-ended constructs and primarily within the realm of the individual person that new constructs are created to meet the particular situation at hand. The clinician approaches his client with a rich background of experience and with broad conceptualizations and then, within the matrix of the individual client's life, he casts up new constructs which are especially designed to deal with his particular case.

The constructs which are fabricated by the clinician for dealing with one particular client are not necessarily inapplicable elsewhere. Yet the range of convenience of a given construct, even though its focus was within one client's life, may be extendable into many other clients' lives. The construct which a clinician erects in order to predict what Archie will do may also prove to be useful in dealing with Algy or Percy.

7. Communication as a feature of the clinical method

All scientific methods emphasize observation; and some forms of communication, at least, may be considered as forms of observation. The clinical method emphasizes in particular the communication between the client and the clinician. Inasmuch as the clinician's observation of the client involves making sure that he understands what the client is trying to convey, the clinician's task is one of communication.

Much of a clinician's effort is bent towards listening attentively to what the client says and in trying to interpret his sign language. It is inappropriate for a clinician to assume that the client is not expressing anything at all or that his behaviour is lawless. If we take the view that all nature, including human nature, can eventually be interpreted lawfully, we should not abdicate our position at the outset by deciding arbitrarily that some human behaviour is lawful and other human behaviour is not. Whether or not the clinician despairs of being able to construe a given client's behaviour meaningfully is another issue. But the inadequacy, in that case, is the clinician's and not nature's. The clinician's approach is still one which should be characterized by perceptiveness.

The clinician must be considerably concerned with trying to catch the client's outlook, with trying that outlook on himself experimentally, and with explorations into the use of that outlook for predictive purposes. The clinician should test the outlook to see what predictions he would make if he were the client, and what he would do if he were in the client's shoes. He tests his understandings of the client's meanings, not only by direct inquiry, but also by anticipating what the client will do between interviews or in response to situations created in the interview room. Thus the clinician tries to reproduce the client's outlook, not merely to classify it in a prefabricated pigeonhole, such as that of 'schizophrenic thinking'.

8. The clinician's concern with nonlanguage and nonsymbolized constructs

There are various levels at which a clinician may listen to what a client says. He may concern himself with the public meaning of the client's words and assume that the words refer to the constructs of which they are the common symbols. He may study the private meanings of which the words are symbols. Then he may consider the words as elements in the construct contexts and not as symbols at all. In that case the constructs may have no stable symbolization in the client's lexicon. Or it may so happen that the symbols which stand for the client's constructs are not verbal symbols at all; they may be postures, objects, people, or even situations.

Finally, it may be that the constructs which are most important in a client's life have no kind of symbolization at all, either verbal or nonverbal. In that case the clinician may have to help the client create some kind of effective symbolization, both to enable him to communicate more effectively and to stabilize the client's own thinking in a fundamental area.

The clinical method is often characterized by its concern with these nonlanguage types of personal constructs. It is not only the constructs which have nonlanguage symbols which the clinician looks out for; it is also those which have no symbolization at all. While the clinician is characteristically more concerned with such constructs than are other psychologists, it is possible to approach nonlanguage symbolization and nonsymbolized constructs psychometrically. This is a matter which is discussed in a later chapter.

9. Assisting the client in creating new constructs

The eighth and last distinguishing characteristic of the clinical type of scientific method is its emphasis upon formation of new constructs by the client. This is more than is usually implied by merely teaching or education. Whereas in teaching or in education the principal task is usually conceived as that of putting at the disposal of the student certain concepts which society has generally accepted or has found particularly useful in certain situations, in clinical psychology the ultimate task is to help the client to fabricate for himself constructs which will serve his personal purposes and enable him to meet the particular kinds of situations which confront him. These may or may not be conventionalized constructs. The primary requirement, from the clinical point of view, is that they shall prove useful to the client.

All of this assures that the primary function of the clinical method is not merely to enable the clinician to predict certain things accurately but also to enable him to enlarge his scope of operation and help the client to reconstruct his life psychologically. Only as the clinician conceives his task in this way will he be able to realize the full scope of the field in which events may be anticipated.

B. The psychological test in a clinical setting

10. The accessibility of personal constructs

There is a sense in which a personal experience can never be shared. What happens is that personal experiences sometimes parallel each other; they sometimes have features of commonality. When a person seeks to convey a personal construct to another he may reproduce certain elements of the context upon which he has formed his construct. Usually at least one of the elements reproduced, and sometimes the only one, is the symbolic element. The other person bases a construct upon the elements provided him. It may be a new construct as far as the second person is concerned. Alternatively, if one of the elements provided is a word or some other thing which the listener is prepared to use as a symbol, he may simply use it to invoke one of his own ready-made personal constructs. Thus, for any of us, the sharing of personal experience is a matter of *construing* the other person's experience and not merely a matter of having him hand it to us intact across the desk. The psychology of personal constructs therefore lends itself quite conveniently to the handling of the theoretical problem of gaining access to private worlds.

As we have pointed out before, it is common practice to name or identify constructs after one or more of their elements. The element a construct is named after is called a symbol. Thus an element is made a representative of the construct though it is really not the construct but only an element in the context upon which the construct was formed. Words, when used as symbols, and they often are so used, are not the constructs they represent; they are representative contextual elements of those constructs.

The whole arrangement does not work out too badly in practice, the general semanticists notwithstanding. We understand what another person means when he says 'dog', not by taking his construct away from him or by making him relinquish a share in its ownership, but by using what he has said as an element, perhaps as a symbolic element, upon which we also form a construct. If we utilize what our friend has *meant*, as well as what he has *said*, as an element – that is, if we make his presumed *personal construct*, as well as his *behaviour*, an element in our construing – then *our personal construct can be considered a version of his personal construct.* Thus communication, at some more or less effective level, has taken place.

Personal constructs are accessible through the use of the same basic devices which make any other part of the real world accessible to us. We construe personal constructs. We have psychological constructs about people's personal constructs. We entertain both scientific and unscientific constructs about people's personal constructs. To the extent that we subsume other people's personal constructs or form constructs of them, we are able to play a role in a relationship with them, whether they, in turn, play roles in relation to us or not.

11. Types of approaches to personal constructs

Anything that we can observe about another person may be used as an element in forming a construct about him. We can note what he does, put it together with his name, contrast it with another person or another act, and come up with a construct of our friend. We can note something that he does, associate it with a consideration of why he did it, then contrast both act and construct with something he does not do, and, therefrom, form our own construct of the personal construct under which his behaviour is organized.

The simplest, and probably the most clinically useful type of approach to a person's personal constructs, is to ask him to tell us what they are. It is hard to persuade some psychologists that such a guileless approach will work. Yet the most useful clinical tool of the physician is the four-word question uttered audibly in the presence of the patient: 'How do you feel?' There is a similar golden rule for clinical psychologists. *If you don't know what's wrong with a client, ask him; he may tell you*!

Now, of course, a clinician may not want to believe what he hears. He may not be willing to accept the problem in the client's terms. He may want the client to lie down on a Procrustean couch and be 'psychoanalysed'. But if the clinician simply listens to the client, he may come to understand the personal constructs which the client is able to express in words under the clinical circumstances which are provided. Even the couch may help; that is, it may help until the clinician starts to make the client conform to the clinician's doctrines. Physical relaxation, freeing of the associative processes from supposed reality, removal of threat, and elicitation of dream or fantasy material, are all properly considered as supportive accessories for making a direct, rather than an indirect, approach to the client's personal constructs.

Even projective testing may properly be considered a direct approach to personal constructs. As we have all come to realize in recent years, new projective tests are 'a dime a dozen'. Anything a person does can be interpreted as a projection of his personal constructs. Indeed, the whole system of the psychology of personal constructs might possibly have been called 'the psychology of projection'. In some projective tests, such as the Rorschach, we attempt to provide less conventional elements upon which the subject may expound his constructs without hazarding his self-concept. In others, such as Rosenzweig Picture Frustration Test, an attempt is made to have the subject deal with more representative lifelike situations. Here the threat to the self-concept is allowed to increase in an attempt to get at constructs which one can be more certain actually govern the subject's day-by-day role. The possibility of involving the self or involving threatening elements is, of course, not wholly absent in any form of testing.

The less direct types of approach to personal constructs include the study of spontaneous activity patterns, interests, play, some forms of language exchange which cannot be described as symbolic expressions of constructs, vocational pursuits, the cultural milieu, the family pattern, and the client's own biography.

For purposes of the discussions which are to follow, we have divided the approaches to personal constructs into three types which, if we consider them in a clinical setting, might well be called: (1) elicitation and analysis of the complaint; (2) elicitation and analysis of the client's construction of events other than those manifestly involved in the complaint – for example, most of the commonly used 'tests'; and (3) analysis of behaviour which has already been exhibited – for example, 'case history' materials. The first of these we consider to be the most direct, the last the least direct. Viewed in this perspective the so-called 'objective' tests, while falling into the second category, should be considered as certain *dimensional measures* of personal constructs, such as cultural commonality, rather than direct revelations of the *constructs themselves*.

This part of the chapter is concerned with tests which may be used in a clinical setting and which are designed primarily to elicit the constructs themselves rather than merely their dimensions. The term 'tests' is conceived to embrace those direct approaches to personal constructs which involve a formal assigned task for the subject. Tests are here contrasted with procedures which involve a study of documents and events relating to the subject's life, on the one hand, and psychotherapeutic interviewing, on the other. The term 'clinical setting' is used to limit our discussion to tests which are given as part of a programme for helping the subject make an optimal adjustment to life, not those tests which are given primarily for the convenience of a personnel administrator.

12. Functions of a test in a clinical setting

There are two ways in which one can look at psychological measurement and clinical diagnosis. On the one hand, one can seek to fix the position of the subject with respect to certain dimensions or coordinates – such as intelligence, extraversion, and so on – or to classify him as a clinical type – such as schizoid, neurotic, and the like. On the other hand, one can concern oneself with the subject's freedom of movement, his potentialities, the resources which can be mobilized, and what is to become of him. From the point of view of the psychology of personal constructs, in which the emphasis is upon process rather than upon fixed position, the latter represents the more enlightened approach. Let us say, then, that the primary purpose of psychological measurement in a clinical setting is to survey the pathways along which the subject is free to move, and the primary purpose of clinical diagnosis is the plotting of the most feasible course of movement. As a whole, diagnosis may be described as the planning stage of therapy.

Perhaps we should take pains at this point to tie this statement firmly to what we have said about free will and the controlling nature of constructs. Freedom, it will be remembered, was described as an aspect of organization, the complement of which was determinism. Freedom and determinism were not considered to be antithetical, but rather, as functions of descendance and ascendance in a construct system. Freedom is a matter of what controls what. Psychology, in seeking to emphasize the pathways along which the person is free to move, therefore turns its attention to the formation and development of new constructs whose reign over subordinate elements will be sufficiently benevolent to permit new forms of new identities to emerge without undue anxiety. Therapy is concerned with setting up regnant personal constructs to give new freedom and new control to the client who has been caught in the vicelike grip of obsolescent constructs. Again, it may be appropriate to recall our Organization Corollary: each person characteristically evolves, for his convenience in anticipating events, a construction system embracing ordinal relationships between constructs. At this point we are concerned with implementing the evolving process.

a. The first function of a test which is to be used in a clinical setting is to define the client's problem in usable terms. It is not enough for a test to be 'valid'; it must be 'valid for something'. A test which does not define a client's problem in a way which helps the clinician to deal effectively with him is not valid for clinical usage, no matter how highly it correlates with certain 'external criteria'. This principle is an application of the *construct approach* to psychodiagnosis, in contrast with the *entity approach.* Usability, rather than accuracy, *per se*, is the minimum standard of a good clinical test. One might even argue that usability is a good operational definition of accuracy. Such an argument would make sense in terms of our philosophical position.

b. The second function of a test which is to be used in a clinical setting is to reveal the pathways or channels along which the client is free to move. We see these channels as laid out in terms of the client's personal constructs. A client who structures his role with respect to a personalized dimension of *quietness–agitation* may today see himself as quiet; but, if he is forced to abandon his position, the most obvious escape route, from his point of view, is 'agitation'. Personal constructs can thus be seen as pointing out the pathways along which the client is able to conceptualize movement for himself. A test should, if possible, reveal those pathways.

c. The third function of a test which is to be used in a clinical setting is to furnish clinical hypotheses which may subsequently be checked and put to use. This is important! In the clinical setting it is not always necessary for the test to present the clinician with *conclusive* findings. Like any other psychological process, therapy proceeds by the successive application of hypotheses and the observation of their outcomes. A test may serve a therapist well if it provides him with a rich source of likely hypotheses regarding his particular client. The verification of the hypotheses can come about through subsequent therapeutic experience with the client. If the client gets well, the therapist has evidence which is at least consistent with the hypotheses. In some clinics it is customary to speak always of 'clinical hypotheses' rather than 'findings' in reporting psychological test results.

d. The fourth function of a test which is to be used in a clinical setting is to reveal those resources of the client which might otherwise be overlooked by the therapist. It is a common thing among clinicians to express surprise at how much can be wrong with a client without impairing his ability to get along in the world. Some clinicians express it by saying that you have to know all about a client before you can say whether or not a given defect is incapacitating. One of the functions of a good clinical test is its usefulness in revealing resources which are mobilized or can be mobilized in meeting the client's problem.

e. The fifth function of a psychological test which is to be used in a clinical setting is to reveal those problems of the client which might otherwise be overlooked by the therapist. Clients frequently try to encapsulate their therapy by concealing certain positions from which they do not wish to be dislodged. Why they do this is a topic for a later discussion, but it is relevant to our present discussion to point out that one of the important functions of a test used in a clinical setting is to survey the client's psychological deployment so as to reveal all of his vulnerable positions.

13. Appraisal of the clinical utility of a test

We have mentioned the five functions of a test in a clinical setting. In order to appraise the functional utility of a test we can examine certain assumptions which underlie it and certain manifest characteristics of its performance. Let us do this frankly from the standpoint of the psychology of personal constructs, since our theoretical position has an important practical influence on our appraisal.

a. Whose yardstick does the test represent? When a psychologist attempts to understand a client, he is limited, of course, to those yardsticks which he has accumulated in his own repertory. Perhaps it is more accurate to say that he measures the client within his own set of coordinate axes. The so-called 'objective' tests are designed exclusively along the lines of psychologists' axes. The client is plotted with respect to these given axes and his own set of axes is ignored entirely. The test treats him as a first-order element and not as a higher-order element which is itself, in turn, a construction or a construer of still lower-order elements. The client stands still and is measured; he is not understood as a measurer himself.

When a 'projective' test is used, the clinician is presumably alerted to the possibility that the client may have some personal version of the universe which constitutes the basis of his actions. He is measured, not merely as an inanimate object, but as a fellow psychologist who has his own notions about the world and expresses them in his actions. In using a projective test a clinician concerns himself with his client's yardsticks.

Yet it must be admitted that the clinician cannot use the client's yardsticks as if they were his own. The clinician is human too, and he must depend on what personal yardsticks his training and experience have provided for him. But it makes a world of difference whether the clinician uses his yardstick to measure the client as a simple object or whether he attempts to measure the client's yardsticks. In the latter case the clinician may be able to build conversion tables for translating the client's personal measurements into the clinician's mensuration system. This is essentially what the projective-test expert attempts to do. He attempts not so much to measure the client's performance, as to embrace his outlook.

A test which is to be used projectively is ordinarily designed so that the tasks can be construed in different ways by different clients. The clinician is more concerned with what kind of answer the client offers to each item than he is with whether the 'correct' answer is offered. The items may be as 'unstructured', as the ink blots of the Rorschach Test or the blank card 16 of the Thematic Apperception Test. In some cases they may be highly structured, so highly structured that the client cannot possibly produce a perfect answer. His response then necessarily represents a personal deviation from reality, as in the copying of geometric forms presented in the Bender-Gestalt Test.

It is not so much the tests which are 'objective' or 'projective' as it is the way in which clinicians use them. It is possible to examine a client's performance on an 'intelligence' test not so much from the standpoint of its accuracy as from the standpoint of the client's interpretation of the test. Yet intelligence tests are carefully designed as 'objective' tests and the construct of *intelligence* is definitely a clinician-imposed yardstick.

As we have said before, the psychology of personal constructs invites each psychologist to examine his client's performance as a projection of the client's outlook. This does not mean that the clinician cannot also be objective. Indeed, we see this approach to the client as being *more objective* than that of the old-fashioned psychometrician. It is more objective, not because it is more legalistic – a feature which is often confounded with objectivity – but because it is more object-oriented. It recognizes that it is the client who is the primary object of the psychologist's investigation and not the test. Thus we would argue that the psychology of personal constructs *is more objective because it is more projective.*

In appraising a test which is to be used in a clinical setting it is appropriate to investigate carefully what professional yardsticks it enables the clinician to apply and what personal yardsticks it permits him to examine. Is it a test of intelligence, of anxiety, of permeability – all of them important clinician yardsticks? Is it also a test of the client's personal constructs – does it make those personal constructs manifest? Whose yardstick does the test represent?

b. Does the test elicit permeable constructs? A permeable construct is one to whose context new elements can be added. It is therefore one which can be used to embrace the future as well as to pigeonhole the past. Consequently, it is not particularly important for a clinical test to reveal the fact that a client believes in 'miracles', if it turns out that as far as he is concerned the age of miracles has been closed out and that the *natural–miraculous* dimension will not be considered relevant to anything he will meet hereafter.

This is another way of saying that the constructs elicited by a test should have some continuing relevance to the client's life. For example, we may, as some therapists do, spend a good deal of time attempting to see how a client structures his past, particularly his remote past. But this may not be as important as one might suppose.

There are two levels from which one may appraise a client's past. One may look at a client's past as the determinant of his present and of his future. This is a view we often find to be misleading when dealing with clients in a clinical setting. From the standpoint of the psychology of personal constructs, the events of the past are not the primary basis for predicting the future; rather it is the structure that one places upon the past that determines how he will let it influence his future. We say it another way too; we say that a person is not the victim of his biography but that he may be enslaved by his interpretation of it.

But is one's interpretation of the past always important? Even granting that his interpretation of the past is more relevant to his situation than are the actual events of the past, it may still be that neither is particularly relevant to his future. The constructs with which he structures certain events of the past may be so impermeable that they cannot, in any case, be employed to structure the future. If so, there is not much use in testing for them. One's time is better spent in testing for the constructs which are sufficiently permeable to be of continuing usefulness. One should examine one's tests, then, to make sure that they are designed to get at constructs which are likely to be used again, and not constructs which are of historical interest only.

c. Are the test elements representative of life's events? A test used in a clinical setting, whether used 'objectively' or 'projectively', should reveal the client's approach to various elements of his world, not merely to the items in the particular test. This means that the items of the test should be representative of the items the client faces in structuring his life. The psychometric task of the clinician is to elicit constructs in a form which will throw light upon the way they govern the subject's approach to elements of his world other than ink blots or pictures. The context of most projective tests is so restricted that it is often precarious to infer what the subject would do with other elements, such as people. It might be easier to predict what a subject would do with the Rorschach Test, for example, from a knowledge of how he deals with the people in his world than it would be to predict what he would do with the people in his world from a knowledge of how he deals with ink blots.

d. Does the test elicit role constructs? We have said that a role is a course of activity which is played out in the light of one's understanding of the outlook of one or more other persons. Role constructs are therefore constructs which have other persons as elements in their contexts. More particularly, they are constructs which have the presumed constructs of other persons as elements in their contexts. While not all clinical services to a client are concerned with the reconstruction of role, a large portion of them are, and it is important for the battery of tests used in a clinical appraisal of a client to include some which are primarily directed at role constructs.

In this respect the Thematic Apperception Test provides the clinician with a clearer understanding of how the client will relate himself to others than will such a test as the Rorschach. This would be true of the Thematic Apperception Test whether it were subjected to 'figure interpretation' or to 'thematic interpretation'. In our opinion, it would be profitable to go even further and set up a test around the actual persons with whom the client lives. We have attempted to do this, and the description of such an approach constitutes the major portion of the next two chapters of this manuscript.

But we do not wish to imply that such a test as the Rorschach, in which ink blots are used as 'stimulus' material, or the Vigotsky, in which coloured blocks of different sizes and shapes are sorted, does not have its place in the clinician's armamentarium. Sometimes the client's problem is so centrally located in his construction system that the very way he perceives and manages simple objects is affected. In such a case the client's performance on the Rorschach Test may reveal basic features of his thinking which, though they are deviant, may or may not upset his role relationships. It is a well-known clinical fact that one may be deeply disturbed in such matters as are approached through the Rorschach Test and yet be able to work out a good practical adjustment to life. It is also well known that a person may be disturbed in his role relationships, as in certain cases of paranoid states, and yet show little sign of his disturbance in his Rorschach or concept-formation test performance.

Yet our principal point is that a clinician should always appraise his test and his test battery with respect to the assumption of role regnancy. He should be careful about assuming that a test which is concerned with the perception of ambiguous forms or the sorting of objects will reveal all that he needs to know about how the client manages his life in a social setting. Even a mind which seems to strike a healthy balance between imaginativeness and reality awareness can seriously misconstrue its relations with other persons whose outlooks are strange and culturally alien. This we can see in international relations, where it would be folly to assume that those with whom we disagree so violently would all show the error of their outlook on a Rorschach Test.

e. What is the balance between stability and sensitivity? Later in this book we shall emphasize the importance of utilizing professional constructs in dealing with clients, with respect to which the clients can be perceived as moving. If a clinician uses a set of coordinate axes – or professional constructs – with respect to which it is impossible for the client ever to change his position, he accomplishes little more than to paint himself and his client into a corner. Psychotherapy, for a clinician who thinks in such terms, can be little more than a matter of persuading the client to subside into the niche that fate has destined for him.

Yet if the clinician uses a set of coordinate axes with respect to which the client's behaviour is utterly capricious, he is not much better off. What the clinician needs is a set of axes within which the client will show some day-by-day consistency, but with respect to which the deeper flow of his life can be plotted. He is more concerned with the tides and currents than he is with oceanic boundaries, on the one hand, or the slapping of waves, on the other.

In view of the clinician's need for setting up dimensions which are appropriate for the phenomena in which he is interested, he should select his tests in terms of his dimensions. If he lays out a base line along which the client can be expected to move during the course of psychological treatment, he should also select a test which will enable him to plot the client's position from time to time with respect to this base line. Again we may emphasize the stand we took in laying down our philosophical position of constructive alternativism: the facts of life take shape only as we plot them within the framework of a construction system, and the dimensions of that construction system are always subject to revision. We can express the same idea mathematically by saying that facts are the intersects of constructs. Any fact is a fact in the sense that the North Pole is a fact. It is, among other things, the intersect of the meridians we have laid down in order to understand what is going on in the world. Thus a clinician should select his tests with his psychological dimensions – or meridians – in mind. The facts he learns about his client through testing assume their positions in terms of these dimensions.

Sometimes this compromise is stated in terms of properties of the tests clinicians use. We say that a clinical test needs to strike some reasonable balance between stability – as measured by test–retest reliability – and sensitivity to quotidian changes. But the problem is more basic than the mere characteristics of tests. It is a problem in psychological-conceptualization: what kind of dimensional structure shall the psychologist choose to employ in dealing with his client? Once that dimensional structure has been assumed, the psychologist next turns to his instruments to see if they are designed to measure along the selected dimensional lines.

We have been talking about the balance between stability and sensitivity in the professional-construct system of the clinician. By implication we also need to consider the balance between the stability and the fluctuation in the client's personal constructs which we choose to measure. The client's construct which is here today and gone tomorrow is not likely to be worth measuring with an elaborate test. The clinician, then, ordinarily wants a test to measure those constructs which tend to continue in operation for protracted periods of time, but which are not so 'reality-bound' and so conventional that there would be no point in trying to revise them.

f. Will the test reveal constructs which are communicable to other clinicians? Again we are concerned both with the clinician's dimensions and with the personal constructs of the client. Clinical psychologists working in a mental-hygiene team setting, in collaboration with representatives of other disciplines, frequently experience difficulty in presenting the results of psychological tests in a way that has any practical bearing on how clients will be handled. To some extent this is a problem of words and syntax. Somewhat more fundamentally it is a problem arising out of the differences in the construct systems employed by psychologists on the one hand and psychiatrists and social workers on the other. Most fundamentally of all it is a problem arising out of the inadequacy of current psychological and psychiatric theories which are either laid out with an eye to the client's immobility or which presume, as in the case of psychoanalytic theory, that there is only one acceptable kind of psychotherapeutic procedure for producing mobility.

The Rorschach Test, and later the Thematic Apperception Test, have done much to bring into the clinical setting a new and interdisciplinary appreciation of the measurability of personalized constructs. The notion of projective testing, which in a sense is not testing at all, is built basically upon the idea that the client's own constructs are to be *revealed* rather than his efficiency in using the examiner's constructs *tested.*

It is not enough, however, for constructs to be revealed or for *the dynamics* of the case to be determined. To apply again our basic conception of science as a set of tentative construct systems, we need to concern ourselves with the *system* of dynamics, in terms of which we attempt to describe a client, and the *framework* within which we plot his personal constructs. For example, the problem of the 'validation' of the Rorschach Test is, at this moment, one of the most exasperating that clinical psychologists face. They can neither justify its continued use on scientific grounds, nor can they bring themselves to abandon it.

Yet it is likely that this is a problem of *what system* of 'dynamics' or construction is useful, not one of what is 'valid' or 'true'. Can the systematic deployment of Rorschach variables be used effectively? Can they serve any predictive function other than that of increasing the comfort and self-esteem of the Rorschach examiner? Can other features in the case record be structured systematically with respect to them, and thus a system built up around the Rorschach axes within which scientific predictions can be made? How about 'validating' the Rorschach by predicting its scores from case material structured in compatible terms, rather than by validating its predictions against evidence incompatibly structured? Why not see whether the Rorschach *system* is one within which validity can be obtained rather than continuing the seemingly futile effort to validate the Rorschach simply as a test? Systems are matters of convenience, and it is not impossible to change them when they have outlived their usefulness. The client is not himself inexorably bound by a system of 'dynamics' existing in the mind of the clinician; only a clinician is. It is up to the clinician, therefore, to reconsider the usefulness of his *system* from time to time.

Collet has used this approach in studying the effectiveness of the Rorschach Test in predicting other kinds of client data. She structured the non-Rorschach data in terms of Rorschach dimensions and then developed formulas for predicting the Rorschach scores that each subject would make. These were cross-validated in a design that was carefully worked out to avoid contamination of either criterion or predictor. Her results were gratifying and provide considerable corroborative evidence for the view that tests need to be validated within compatible systems.

The ideas we are propounding here, together with Collet's research, are derivable from the philosophical view of constructive alternativism and from the psychological theory of personal constructs. Moreover, they have important bearing upon the problem of communicability of psychological test findings in an interdisciplinary clinical setting. If the psychologist attempts to communicate his hypotheses regarding the client, as he has inferred them from test data, he may find that the systematic frame in which he is making his presentation has no parallel axes among the frames used by his colleagues who represent other disciplines. It then becomes necessary for him to consider whether or not he can rotate the axes of his data in such a way as to bring them within the ken of his colleagues. If he cannot, he may decide that it is more practical to change his test and operate more nearly within their system from the outset.

The system implied by any test may be checked from time to time. We have proposed that one of the criteria for evaluation of various clinical tests is their capacity to define the client's problem in *usable* terms. By 'usable' we mean helpful in planning therapy, in determining client management, or perhaps even for statistical records. If a test does not meet this criterion, it can be abandoned, altered, or a new type of scoring system may be developed for it.

Finally, the functional communicability of the constructs elicited by a test should not be overlooked. Not only should the constructs elicited in the clinician who administers the test be communicable, in other words, not merely impressionistic – but there should be a reasonably good exposition of the client's personal constructs. In the case of the client's constructs, this does not mean that precise word symbols which can operate as complete vehicles for expressing the client's personal constructs should be produced; that is not always possible. Rather, it means that the client's constructs, either in words, gestures, or in other representative terms, are communicated to the examiner in relatively unequivocal forms.

g. Will the test serve its basic functions? We have said that a good clinical test should reveal the pathways along which the client is free to move. In a clinical setting this is also, in part, a matter of usability. More is implied, however. The clinician may be interested in what the client will do under stress. If he finds he must abandon some of his positions, what routes of retreat or redeployment are clear to him? We may refer to these as 'latent tendencies'; but, within the psychology of personal constructs, these 'latent tendencies' are functions of the very same constructs by means of which the client maintains his present position. The client who says he is feeling 'high' today has a 'latent tendency' to feel 'low'. This 'latent tendency' is revealed by the very dimensionality of his description of himself.

There are various levels at which a test can reveal the pathways along which the client is currently free to move. When confronted with a context which is not bound by interpersonal or social demands, the client may employ constructs which, if translated into interpersonal or role terms, would prove disastrous. Thus a person, in his responses to the Rorschach Test, for example, may employ constructions of experience which, if used analogously in the interpretation of people, would result in marked distortions of his perception of his own role. The crucial question in such a case is, of course: are the constructs revealed on the Rorschach available to him in construing people; and, if so, what are the implications for his own role?

A good clinical test should furnish clinical hypotheses which may subsequently be checked and put into use. In this respect the Thematic Apperception Test has generally proved to be more satisfactory than the Rorschach Test. Both thema and figure constructs can normally be checked in therapy with profit in terms of therapeutic goals. Morton has shown quite effectively how collaboration with the client in scoring his own TAT protocol may achieve therapeutic results. Therapists who believe in the efficacy of selecting topics for discussion in therapy sessions, rather than assuming an utterly passive role, find a well-analysed TAT protocol quite useful in providing initial clinical hypotheses and in delineating areas of interpersonal relations which need new constructions and interpretations if the client is to adjust to them. Even in vocational guidance the thema, or life plots, throw considerable light upon how the client may make use of the vocational information provided him by the counsellor.

A good clinical test should reveal those resources of the client which might otherwise be overlooked by the therapist. The Rorschach Test, for example, may reveal modes of control, a balance between permeable and impermeable constructs, and a use of time and continuity, as revealed by movement responses, which the clinician may take as encouraging signs against the turmoil revealed in the day-by-day therapeutic sessions. The TAT may reveal stable, well-defined figures and regnant plot constructs which may provide the client with a substantial role model to follow and a firm assuring of eventual outcome in spite of present difficulties.

Sometimes a client is willing to reveal problems in a test situation which he attempts to rule out of a therapy situation. The TAT is particularly useful for searching out such problems which might otherwise not be discovered. The Incomplete Sentences Test is also useful in this respect.

Unless the constructs which are elicited by a test are permeable, their meaning tends to be limited to the subject's handling of the specific elements which appear in the test. There would be little point in administering a Rorschach Test, for example, if the constructs elicited referred to the way in which the subject construed ink blots and nothing else. As suggested before, this is precisely the point at which extrapolation from the Rorschach Test situation to social situations may fail. It is possible for a person to express some quite vicious constructs in a Rorschach Test, and yet those constructs may be so impermeable as to leave his social relations unjeopardized. It is, furthermore, possible for a subject, even on the TAT, to reveal constructs which have serious social implications; and yet the therapist may find, on more careful study, that the constructs are limited to the particular figure elements on which they were first propounded.

Not only is it possible that the constructs elicited by a test are sufficiently impermeable as to be inapplicable to other contexts, it is possible also that they have a certain degree of impermeability which limits their application to figures known in childhood or to people in the home community. Similarly, the protocol may show, after therapy, the continuance of certain constructs in relation to events of the past, whereas the current evidence seems to indicate that the therapy has reduced the constructs to obsolescence so far as future events are concerned. In that case something of importance has happened to the client as the result of therapy which is not revealed by the comparison of before-and-after test protocols.

As in the case of any scientific instruments from which generalizations are to be drawn, the sampling should be adequate. It is on this score, perhaps more than any other, that current projective tests are open to criticism. The Rorschach is particularly vulnerable since it samples elements which may be entirely construed as not human, and since it is used as a basis for inferences regarding the client's role. Now the way the client sees the inanimate features of his world is not unimportant. Not all of the problems which drive men to distraction are social problems or problems involving human figures. It may be important to learn how a client deals with the inanimate features of his world as a means of gaining insight into the way he anticipates such events. Even so, however, the question remains as to the adequacy of ink blots as sample elements of whatever world they are supposed to represent.

14. Conclusion

The purpose of this chapter has been to define more clearly the focus of convenience of the psychology of personal constructs. We have discussed the clinical setting, the characteristics of the clinical method as one of the scientific methodologies employed by psychologists, and, particularly, the functions of a test in a clinical setting. Thus we have laid the ground for devising instruments from the standpoint of the psychology of personal constructs. The next step is to describe instruments and procedures which stem from this kind of thinking about this kind of problem.

Chapter five

The Repertory Test

In this chapter we present a new diagnostic instrument which illustrates how our theoretical thinking can be applied to the practical needs of the psychotherapist.

A. Structure of the Rep Test

1. An instrument for eliciting personal constructs

As an example of the type of testing which emerges as a result of the thinking generated by the psychology of personal constructs, the *Role Construct Repertory Test* (Rep Test) is here reported for the first time. It is designed as a test to be used in a clinical or preclinical setting. Five functions of a clinical test were described in the preceding chapter. This test is designed primarily for the function which has to do with a preliminary list of clinical hypotheses. These hypotheses are later to be used by the therapist who is to work with the examinee.

The test is aimed at role constructs. Since role constructs are of particular importance in psychological practice, it seems appropriate that we should make a direct approach to the elicitation of such constructs in the subjects whose personal–social behaviour we wish to understand.

Methodologically the Rep Test is an application of the familiar concept-formation test procedure. It uses as 'objects' those persons with whom the subject has had to deal in his daily living. Instead of sorting *Vigotsky blocks* or *BRL objects* the subject sorts people. The technique bears some resemblance to the sorting employed in the Horowitz Faces Test. It is also somewhat similar to Hartley's later procedure in which he used pictures in a sorting test. Rotter and Jessor have also experimented tentatively with the formation of 'social concepts' in the sorting of the paper dolls of the Make a Picture Study (M.A.P.S.) Test.

Unlike the traditional concept-formation test, the Rep Test is concerned with how the particular items are dealt with, not merely the level of abstraction involved. Unlike the picture-sorting tests, the Rep Test is concerned with the subject's relations to particular people.

2. Procedure for designating figures

The subject is given a Role Title List. This may be presented either orally or in written form. He is asked to respond to the list by designating, by name or otherwise, the personal identities of the people in his own realm of experience who fit the role titles. He may be asked to write his responses either upon cards or within rectangular spaces on a single blank form. In the Minimum Context Form the procedure is as follows:

> The examiner instructs the subject, 'Here are some titles which should suggest to you some people you know. You are asked to write the names of these people on these cards. On this first card it says, "A teacher you liked".' The examiner hands the subject a numbered 3" × 5" card bearing the role title. 'If the name of that teacher happens to be Smith, then write his or her name in the blank space on the card.'
>
> On presentation of the third card the examiner says, 'You find as you go through this list that you will think of someone whose name you have already listed. When this happens write down the name of another person who seems most like that person, so that, when you are through, you will have all *different* names.'
>
> If, for example, the subject has difficulty recalling a teacher he liked, the examiner may say, '... or the teacher of a subject you liked'. The alternative titles are indicated in parentheses below.
>
> The remainder of the role titles are presented in a similar way. Following are the role titles used in a current form of the test:

1. A teacher you liked. (Or the teacher of a subject you liked.)
2. A teacher you disliked. (Or the teacher of a subject you disliked.)
3. Your wife or present girl friend.

3a. (for women) Your husband or present boy friend.

4. An employer, supervisor, or officer under whom you worked or served and whom you found hard to get along with. (Or someone under whom you worked in a situation you did not like.)
5. An employer, supervisor, or officer under whom you worked or served and whom you liked. (Or someone under whom you worked in a situation you liked.)
6. Your mother. (Or the person who has played the part of a mother in your life.)
7. Your father. (Or the person who has played the part of a father in your life.)
8. Your brother nearest your age. (Or the person who has been most like a brother.)
9. Your sister nearest your age. (Or the person who has been most like a sister.)
10. A person with whom you have worked who was easy to get along with.
11. A person with whom you have worked who was hard to understand.
12. A neighbour with whom you get along well.
13. A neighbour whom you find hard to understand.

14. A boy you got along well with when you were in high school. (Or when you were 16.)
15. A girl you got along well with when you were in high school. (Or when you were 16.)
16. A boy you did not like when you were in high school. (Or when you were 16.)
17. A girl you did not like when you were in high school. (Or when you were 16.)
18. A person of your own sex whom you would enjoy having as a companion on a trip.
19. A person of your own sex whom you would dislike having as a companion on a trip.
20. A person with whom you have been closely associated recently who appears to dislike you.
21. The person whom you would most like to be of help to. (Or whom you feel most sorry for.)
22. The most intelligent person whom you know personally.
23. The most successful person whom you know personally.
24. The most interesting person whom you know personally.

3. Procedure for sorting

Following the completion of the responses to the Role Title List the procedure is this:

> The examiner says, 'Now I would like you to tell me something about these three people.' The examiner hands the subject cards 18, 20, and 21. 'In what *important way* are two of them alike but different from the third?'
>
> The examiner records the subject's response on a blank form opposite 'Sort Number One – Construct'. Usually the subject will indicate spontaneously which two cards are being judged as alike. If he does not, the examiner asks him.
>
> Then the examiner points to the odd card and says, 'How is this person different?'
>
> The examiner records the subject's response to the second question in the blank marked 'Contrast'.
>
> The remaining 'sorts' are elicited and recorded in the same fashion.

Occasionally a subject uses a role construct in such a way as to make it difficult to handle systematically. Hunt, who has made some of the necessary preliminary consistency studies of the Rep Test, has established standard procedures by which the examiner may deal with such responses. Following are the classes of constructs, slightly modified, which he believes require a follow-up procedure on the part of the examiner.

(1) *Situational constructs.* Sometimes a subject may say, 'These two are alike: they're both from the same town.' In instances of this kind the examiner records the response but follows up by saying, 'That is *one* way in which they are alike. Can you tell me how their being from the same town makes them alike, or can you tell me any *other* way in which they are alike?'

(2) *Excessively permeable constructs.* Sometimes a subject may say, 'These two are alike; they're both women.' The examiner follows a procedure similar to that above.

(3) *Excessively impermeable constructs.* A subject may say, 'These two are tool makers and the other one is a die maker.' The examiner uses the same procedure as above.

(4) *Superficial constructs.* A subject may say, 'They have the same colour eyes.'

(5) *Vague constructs.* 'They're both OK.' When this occurs, the examiner asks the subject to explain further and to cite possible examples of other people who are 'OK'.

(6) *Constructs which are a direct product of the role title.* For example, the subject may say, 'Both are hard to understand.' The examiner then may say, 'Is there something about their being hard to understand which seems to be alike?'

In each case of the use of a construct which is difficult to handle systematically, the examiner makes a full record of the constructs proposed by the subject.

Table 5.1 overleaf is a list of some sorts which may be useful in administering the Role Construct Repertory Test.

As the sorting progresses the examiner may substitute or add special combinations in order to test the subject's handling of certain figures or types of figures or to check the permeability of certain constructs.

4. Forms of the rep test for individual administration

The Rep Test may be administered in the Minimum Context Stencil Form. In this form the Role Title List is printed on a single sheet with each title in a separate rectangle. The subject writes the names in the blank portion of the rectangles. The examiner elicits the sorts by placing a window stencil or templet over the Role Title Sheet so that three names only are exposed at a time. It is considered important to expose only those names which are to be identified as elements in the sort. The procedure beyond this point is otherwise the same as in the Minimum Context Card Form of the test.

Much more information about the subject's personal role constructs can be learned by the skilled clinician if he administers the test in one of its more flexible forms. The Full Context Form of the test involves the use of the cards rather than the single sheet.

Table 5.1 Suggested sorts for the Role Construct Repertory Test

Number of sort	*Cards used*	*Number of sort*	*Cards used*
1	18, 20, 21	17	2, 6, 20
2	2, 22, 23	18	5, 13, 15
3	9, 10, 24	19	8, 10, 16
4	8, 12, 19	20	4, 11, 12
5	4, 11, 21	21	14, 17, 18
6	1, 3, 15	22	2, 19, 23
7	5, 14, 17	23	5, 13, 22
8	7, 13, 16	24	15, 16, 24
9	6, 9, 18	25	1, 12, 21
10	1, 8, 22	26	4, 5, 17
11	3, 21, 23	27	7, 20, 24
12	7, 14, 20	28	6, 8, 16
13	3, 6, 7	29	2, 9, 15
14	1, 9, 24	30	3, 10, 11
15	10, 12, 17	31	13, 14, 18
16	4, 11, 19	32	19, 22, 23

All of the cards are spread out before the subject and the examiner says, 'I want you to consider the important ways in which groups of these people are alike. Will you arrange these cards so that the people who are alike in some important way are together?'

As soon as the subject selects two cards to be put together, the examiner says, 'How are those two alike?'

When a third or any subsequent card is added the examiner says, 'Are these still the – ones?'

When a card is taken away from a group the examiner asks, 'Why did you take that one away? Are you still thinking of that pile as the – ones now?'

The examiner records the way in which the piles are built up in sequence, by using numbers to indicate the cards which are added or removed from groups. When the subject indicates that his sorting is complete, the examiner rechecks the constructs which identify the groups and checks the constructs which identify the cards left in isolation, if any. A record is kept of the final classification of all cards, whether grouped or not, as well as of the running record of intermediate constructs and their elements.

The Rep Test can be made a more exacting test of the functional adequacy of a person's constructs if it is administered in the Sequential Form. This form also requires the use of the cards rather than the single sheet. The procedure is as follows:

Cards 24, 23, and 22 are presented to the subject in the same manner as in the Minimum Context Card Form. In the second sort the examiner says, 'Now let me take this one away (removing card 24) and add this one (adding card 21).

Now what would you say is an important way in which two of these people are alike but different from the third?'

The sequence of sorts is as follows:

24, 23, 22
23, 22, 21
22, 21, 20
21, 20, 19
———
———
3, 2, 1
2, 1, 24
1, 24, 23

The test can be made a more direct indicator of the constructs which the subject verbalizes as identifying himself if it is given in the Self-identification Form. A card marked 'Myself' is introduced. The procedure is:

Cards 24, 23, and the Myself card are presented to the subject in the same manner as in the Minimum Context Card Form. The administration is like that of the Sequential Form except that the Myself card remains as one of the three cards presented in each sort.

The test becomes one under which role-governing constructs can be elicited by giving it in the Personal Role Form. The sequence of presentations is the same as in the Self-identification Form. The examiner says, however:

'Now suppose that the three of you were all together by yourselves for an evening. What kind of place might it be? What would happen? How would you yourself be likely to be acting? How would each of the others be likely to be acting?'

Other types of situations can be envisioned: an automobile trip, for example, if the examiner wishes to pin down the subject's construction of his own behaviour in relation to the two given figures and to no others. By using the 'evening' situation, however, the subject is given a chance to reject the necessity of functioning in certain threesomes by describing himself as withdrawing, or by interpreting the instructions in a way that permits him to add other figures to the group.

One other way in which the test can be administered is to superimpose the Personal Role Feature in the Full Context Form.

After the subject has completed his sorting in the Full Context Form the examiner lays the Myself card beside one of the groups and says, 'Suppose that you were to spend an evening with this group, what would be likely to happen? What kind of place might it be? How would you all get along together? What

would you talk about? How would you, yourself, be likely to be acting? How would each of the others be likely to be acting?'
The Myself card is laid beside each of the groups in succession, including the isolated cards, and the same questions asked.

5. Group form of the Rep Test

It is possible to utilize a Group Form of the Rep Test, although exploration along this line has not proceeded far enough to describe its usefulness with a high level of confidence. Following is one Group Form which is currently being used.

Role Construct Repertory Test – Group Form
Part A: Role Title List

Instructions:

Write the name of each of the persons indicated in the blanks provided below. If you cannot remember the name, but do remember the person, simply make a check mark or some other note of identification.
If you cannot remember the person, substitute the name of a person whom the role title suggests to you.
Do not repeat names. If a role title appears to call for a duplicate name, substitute the name of another person whom the second role title suggests to you.

1. Your mother or the person who has played the part of a mother in your life
2. Your father or the person who has played the part of a father in your life
3. Your brother nearest your age. If you have no brother, the person who is most like one
4. Your sister nearest your age. If you have no sister, the person who is most like one
5. A teacher you liked or the teacher of a subject you liked
6. A teacher you disliked or the teacher of a subject you disliked
7. Your closest girl (boy) friend immediately before you started going with your wife (husband) or present closest girl (boy) friend
8. Your wife (husband) or closest present girl (boy) friend
9. An employer, supervisor, or officer under whom you served during a period of great stress
10. A person with whom you have been closely associated, who for some unexplainable reason, appeared to dislike you
11. The person whom you have met within the past six months whom you would most like to know better
12. The person whom you would most like to be of help to, or whom you feel most sorry for
13. The most intelligent person whom you know personally

14. The most successful person whom you know personally
15. The most interesting person whom you know personally

Role Construct Repertory Test – Group Form
Part B: Construct Sorts

Instructions:

[Supply your name and the date]

The sets of three numbers in the following sorts refer to the numbers, 1 to 15 inclusive, in Part A.
In each of the following sorts three numbers are listed. Look at your Part A sheet and consider the three people whom you have listed opposite these numbers.
In what important way are two of these three people alike and, at the same time, essentially different from the third?
After you have decided what that *important* way is, write it in the blank opposite the sort marked Construct.
Next encircle the numbers corresponding to the two people who are alike.
Write down what you believe to be the opposite of the construct in the blank marked Contrast.

Sort	*Numbers, Part A*	*Construct*	*Contrast*
1.	10,11,12	________	________
2.	6,13,14	________	________
3.	6, 9,12	________	________
4.	3,14,15	________	________
5.	4,11,13	________	________
6.	2, 9,10	________	________
7.	5, 7, 8	________	________
8.	9,11,15	________	________
9.	1, 4, 7	________	________
10.	3, 5,13	________	________
11.	8,12,14	________	________
12.	4, 5,15	________	________
13.	1, 2, 8	________	________
14.	2, 3, 7	________	________
15.	1, 6,10	________	________

In summary, the forms in which the Role Construct Repertory Test has been used include the following:

1. Minimum Context Card Form
2. Minimum Context Stencil Form
3. Full Context Form

4. Sequential Form
5. Self-identification Form
6. Personal Role Form
7. Full Context Form with the Personal Role Feature
8. Group Form

These forms are only suggestive of Rep Test approaches. The procedure can be varied in a great many ways. In a later chapter we shall describe some of the more elaborate approaches, both to personal- and to public-construct systems.

6. Assumptions underlying the Rep Test

While it is never possible to be fully aware of all of the logical assumptions which are implicit in the use of a psychological instrument, it is profitable to do what one can in the way of stating underlying assumptions. There are at least six assumptions which should probably be taken into account in interpreting the results of the Role Construct Repertory Test.

a. The first assumption is that of the permeability of the constructs elicited. A construct is permeable if it is open to the addition of new elements, or elements beyond those upon which it has been explicitly formed. In the Rep Test the elements are persons who are believed to have been important figures in the subject's life and with respect to whom, principally, he would have carved out his own role. More precisely, it is believed that the role titles represent people of whom the subject has a measure of personal understanding, and that that understanding, right or wrong, provides a context of elements out of which the constructs governing his own role take shape. The constructs governing his own role would have to be sufficiently permeable to permit him to add new figures to their contexts, and thus to provide him with an outline for anticipating the part he is to play.

It may be well to recall our Fundamental Postulate at this point: a person's processes are psychologically channelized by the ways in which he anticipates events. We hope that the subject reveals, in taking the test, those channels through which new experiences, as well as old, may run. We assume that the constructs he verbalizes are ones which can be applied to people an interpersonal situations which he has not yet confronted. In other words we assume that the constructs elicited by the tests are permeable.

b. The second assumption is that pre-existing constructs are elicited by the test. While the method of sorting is frequently associated with concept *formation*, it does not seem likely that, where the elements are obviously familiar, the constructs used to sort them must all be concocted on the spot. The possibility of there being some new developments in the subject's constructs is not ruled out by the design of the test; but, if the test is to be useful, some lingering degree of permanence in the constructs elicited by it must be assumed.

c. The third assumption is that of the representativeness of the elements. If the test is to indicate how the subject develops his role in the light of his understanding of other people, it is necessary that the other people appearing as elements in the test be sufficiently representative of all the people with whom the subject must relate his self-construed role. The list of role titles is designed with this in mind. Representative figures, with respect to whom people seem normally to have formed the most crucial personal role constructs, are incorporated in the list.

d. The fourth assumption is that constructs will be elicited which subsume, in part, the construction systems of the element figures. We have limited our definition of *role* to a course of activity which is played out in the light of one's understanding of the personal constructs of one or more other people. The test assumes that a usable number of the constructs elicited by it do represent the subject's understanding, right or wrong, of the way other people look at things. If the subject gives only responses which describe his relationship to other people as if they were unthinking animals, the test has failed to elicit *role constructs.* The subject's measure of understanding of other people may actually be inadequate or preposterous; but, if it is the basis of a real social interaction with them, it is indeed related to his role construct system.

e. The fifth assumption is that of the role regnancy of the constructs elicited. If the subject entirely dissociates his own identity from the figures, or fails completely to organize his own behaviour under the constructs elicited with respect to the figures in the test, then the constructs cannot be considered to be *role constructs.* This seems unlikely, and therefore it should be safe to assume that the constructs elicited by the test are regnant over the subject's own role.

f. The sixth assumption is that of the functional communicability of the constructs elicited. This is the most precarious assumption. It involves believing that the words a subject uses in naming his constructs, and the explanations he gives, are adequate to give the examiner some practical understanding of how he is organizing the elements in the test. This is, in some measure, a function of the skill and perspective of the examiner.

There are certain uses to which the test can be put which do not involve this assumption. Landfield, for example, in his research on the threat hypothesis, has not had to make this assumption. His data have been lifted into the nomothetic frame at a different level of abstraction. He has had only to assume that the name of the personal construct remains constant over a short period of time and through certain variations in the elements. When we discuss the use of the Repertory Grid in a later chapter we shall have occasion to mention usages of a similar type of procedure which does not imply this assumption.

7. Consistency of the Rep Test

It seems more suitable to discuss the *consistency* of the Rep Test than to discuss its 'reliability'. The term 'reliability' has, for some readers, a very precise meaning. When one considers the many ways in which a test can be consistent it is difficult to subsume them all under the term 'reliability'.

Hunt has made some of the necessary preliminary studies of the consistencies of the Rep Test. He found tentative evidence for believing that by the time a subject has made forty sorts of twenty given figures he has expressed nearly all of the constructs which will have been expressed when he reaches his eightieth or one hundredth sort. He found, also, that when the number of sorts is held constant, twenty figures will produce as many constructs as thirty figures.

Hunt also studied a small sample of college students and a small sample of hospitalized patients to see what consistency could be expected when a new set of elements was used and a week's time was allowed to elapse. He used two different sets of twenty figures and administered the test in the Minimum Context Stencil Form, using an essentially different Role Title List in each administration. The two Role Title Lists were balanced as to sex, liking–disliking, relatives, authority figures, and persons known in adolescence. He developed a careful technique for determining the equivalence of constructs as used by the subject. He used forty sorts, except in cases where more than twenty constructs were elicited; in such cases he continued until the number of constructs fell below half the number of sorts.

Among hospital patients, Hunt found that the average per cent of agreement in *constructs used* on the two occasions and with the two different sets of elements was 69. The standard deviation was six. Among college students the average per cent of agreement was 70 and the standard deviation was a little less than eight. While Hunt was not particularly concerned with the problem, the per cent of agreement, in terms of the *number of sorts* involving the same constructs on the two different occasions, appears, from inspection of his data, to be considerably higher. The constructs which were used on both occasions tended to be used on more different sorts on those occasions than were the constructs which were used on one occasion only.

B. Methods of analysing Rep Test protocol

8. Clinical analysis of Rep Test results

Rep Test results can be subjected both to formal analysis and, in case the examiner is a skilled clinician, to a clinical analysis. The constructs themselves can be analysed as to content or tone and as to more abstract features, such as permeability and communicability. The figures also can be taken into account – that is, the kinds of people they are construed to be. From such an analysis one can get some insight into the facets of the subject's role – what he sees himself called upon to do in certain types of situations: at home, at work, and so on. Some judgment of the extent and flexibility of the subject's constructs can be made; also of the difficulties the subject has in construing some figures within his construct system.

a. Number of constructs elicited. This may give the examiner some idea of the range of the client's role construction system. It does not appear to be correlated with *intellectual ability*, but is probably correlated with the use of *intellectualization*. It may then, in some instances, be a preliminary indicator, either of compulsivity or of excessive striving for a definition of role.

b. Overlap. When the test is used by a skilled clinician some effort may be made to determine the equivalence of constructs, and thus to throw light upon the really effective range of the subject's constructs, as contrasted with his possible verbal expansiveness. The verbal expansiveness, in turn, may reflect a kind of privacy in the use of constructs which makes it difficult for the subject to use precise symbolism in communicating them. The following procedure for determining overlap is based upon Hunt's study of consistency.

> When the clinician suspects that two constructs are functionally equivalent in the mind of the subject he performs four tests for equivalence. For example, suppose that in one sort a subject gives 'honest' as the construct and 'dishonest' as the contrasting construct. In another sort he gives 'trustworthy' as the construct and 'not trustworthy' as the contrasting construct, perhaps involving the same person in the 'honest' and 'trustworthy' categories.
> The examiner then re-presents the figures which elicited the construct of 'honest' and asks, 'Which two of these are the more trustworthy?'
> Next the examiner re-presents the figures which originally elicited the construct of 'trustworthy' and asks, 'Which two of these are the more honest?'
> Next the examiner asks, 'Is a person who is honest almost always trustworthy?'
> Finally he asks, 'Is the person who is trustworthy almost always honest?'

If the subject gives positive evidence of functional equivalence on all four of these standards, the two constructs are classified by Hunt as being the same.

c. Permeable and impermeable constructs. Constructs which are repeated on different figures can be considered as showing evidence of permeability, at least within the limits of the test context. The number of figures to which the construct is applied suggests the range of permeability. Permeability is an indication of the availability of a construct for meeting varied situations in life. It is not a measure of a construct's effectiveness except in this one respect.

Impermeability is more difficult to establish positively than is permeability. A construct which is used once only in the test may still be a permeable one. The clinician may, if he considers it important in the case, check the possible impermeability of a construct by asking the subject if he knows 'anybody else that the category fits'.

d. Fields of permeability. If the Role Title List is divided into types of figures, the examiner may get some idea of special restrictions upon the range of the construct's permeability. The Role Title List can be divided according to sex, age at which the subject came to know the person, intimacy, and nature of contact situation. It can also be divided into acceptable and unacceptable figures, although permeability in one of these ranges does not have the same significance as in the other fields. A construct which is applied to women only cannot be considered to have the same kind of permeability as one which is applicable both to men and women. A construct which is applied only to people known in childhood may not be available for use in an adult situation. In general, those constructs can be interpreted as being more permeable which bridge the boundaries of these classifications.

During the course of psychotherapy the clinician is always interested in the development of impermeability in certain constructs which have caused difficulty for the client. It is as if the client were closing out his file. When he says 'I was' instead of 'I am' some clinicians consider the change a possible healthy development of impermeability, with respect to the construct involved. Impermeable constructs are partly unavailable to the client and, as far as adjusting his role to new people is concerned, inactive.

e. Contrasting constructs. Some constructs are used as descriptions of the contrasting figures only. When they are repeated upon different figures they may be considered permeable. The subject's use of a permeable construct in the contrast sense may indicate only a reluctance to employ it. Usually the clinician will find that the subject does not consider the figure so placed as wholly belonging to the category.

The permeable contrasting construct may be particularly important in predicting what the subject will do under stress. If such a construct as *aggressive* is used as the contrasting construct for several constructs or for several sorts, it may be considered as one which provides the client with a fairly clear alternative path to be taken, if the contrasting poles of the constructs with which it is linked cease to be useful. If the *aggressive* construct is not used as a basis for associating two figures in the sort, the subject may be considered as keeping his attention turned away from its use, but its use still tends to be implicit in his thinking. If the constructs of *nice, gentle, thoughtful*, and the others to which *aggressive* has been the contrasting pole, begin to break down, the subject may turn to *aggressive*, both as a way of seeing many other people, and as a way of behaving himself. This, incidentally, is an illustration of how the psychology of personal constructs handles the phenomena which, in other systems, are handled by the concepts of 'reaction formation' and, in a sense, the concepts of 'repression', 'inhibition', and 'unconscious impulses'.

Contrariwise, contrasting poles of constructs which are not repeated cannot be considered with certainty to be anything more than minor constructs.

f. Contrasting poles of constructs repeated on one figure only. When a contrasting pole is repeated, but on one figure only, the examiner may suspect impermeability. The pole may be one which is applicable to that person only, and hence be unavailable for dealing with other people. The clinician can check this by setting up special sorts to see whether the construct will be used as a basis of likeness between that person and some other person in the Role Title List who seems to be a likely candidate. He may also ask the subject to suggest the names of other people who are like the person in respect to the contrasting construct. When the Full Context Form is used, the impermeability of certain constructs becomes easier to determine.

g. Unique figures. These are figures which, in the limited context of the test, are associated with contrasting poles only. A unique or 'one and only' person, who is never seen as being like any other person, is hard to understand. The subject's adjustment to him is likely to be fixed and immobile, though not necessarily unpleasant. His role in relation to the person is likely to be highly stereotyped. In a sense, it is the figure, and not the construct, that is impervious in this instance.

One can check the uniqueness of any given figure by presenting it in context with two figures from another sort in which one of the same contrasting poles was used. One of these figures should have been associated with the contrasting pole and the other not. If the subject refuses to link the suspected figure with either of the two new candidates, the clinician has evidence of the figure's uniqueness.

When the examiner uses the Personal Role Form of the test he can check the difficulty the subject has in adapting his own role to the unique figure. It must be kept in mind, however, that the subject may have a clear pattern of adaptation to the unique figure – his wife, for example – but may not be flexible *in changing* his adaptation pattern with respect to her. She may appear to be such an utterly fixed figure that his own role is stagnant in relation to her. For example, he may refuse to see her as a maturing women and insist that she is still the charmingly irresponsible adolescent she was when he married her. If this is accompanied by marked changes or adaptations in other facets of his role, the examiner can suspect impending trouble, even though the subject currently expresses no difficulty in dealing with his wife. By construing his wife inflexibly the client puts himself in a rut in his interactions with her – a rut from which he may eventually wish to escape.

h. Linkages of constructs through contrasts. Two or more constructs may be reported by the subject as having the same contrasting pole, or two or more contrasting poles may be associated with the same likeness pole. This may indicate that the subject is having discrimination difficulties in utilizing his construction system. Linked constructs may be considered as partially equivalent. They are usually associated with 'ambivalence'.

Within the psychology of personal constructs, all ambivalence is seen basically as being a linkage problem. The construct of linkage is much more operationally definable than is the construct of ambivalence.

By noting the linkages the perceptive clinician can also get an inkling of the directions of future movement the client may take as a result of the breakdown in the use of any one of a number of his constructs. Where the linkages are complex the alternative movement, resulting from pressure, is likely to be more diffuse. As we have indicated before, one of the contributions of the psychology of personal constructs is the development of a way of predicting how a person will behave if he suddenly throws his present pattern of behaviour overboard. By seeing a client's constructs and their opposites as channels of potential movement for him, the clinician has some basis for forecasting what adjustments will appear to the client to be available when he finds himself up to his ears in people.

i. Linkages of constructs through figures. A less definite type of linkage of constructs is implied when several different constructs are identified with the same figure. Not much importance can be attached to this if the linkage is in terms of likeness. In that case more than one person is involved in the linkage. If the linkage is altogether in terms of contrast poles, however, one may suspect equivalence of constructs or possibly the same kind of discrimination problems which are indicated by the type of linkage described in the preceding paragraph.

j. Identification of figures. If the Role Title List is the case of characters, then the Role Construct Repertory Test reveals the subject's casting of parts in the play in which he has the lead. It is this casting which is of particular interest to the clinician who is to be of assistance to the subject. It gives structure to the part the subject must see himself as having to play, and to the eventual developments he must see in the plot. The examiner will want to see how figures with certain characteristics are identifiable as to their degree of intimacy with the subject, and what is the locus of their influence in the life cycle of the subject.

From noting the subject's identification of figures and his unique theory of interpersonal relationships the clinician may get some idea as to what constructs can be left operative, what constructs need to be closed out or made impermeable, and what constructs must be replaced if therapy is to be successful. The replacement of constructs, or development of 'insight', is a slow job and not always necessary. Sometimes it is simpler to close out a construct by helping the client make it impermeable. The client may then come to rely upon other, more useful constructs which are already in his repertory, or the clinician may help him add new constructs to his repertory. Such addition of constructs to take the place of ones relegated to impermeability is a supplementation job rather than a substitution job and does not correspond to what is sometimes called the attainment of 'insight'.

The identification of figures in the result of the test gives some idea of what new constructs may have to be introduced to explain these persons. Alternatively, if the old constructs revealed by the test are believed to be adequate, and if some of the figures seem to need to be reclassified with respect to these existing constructs, the clinician can make an initial decision regarding this issue also. Both of these decisions have to do with what is commonly called 'interpretive therapy'.

k. Situational constructs. These were defined in connection with the description of the examiner's procedure. In general, they indicate either that the subject is unable to deal meaningfully with the figures involved, or that he is unable to communicate his construction of them.

Inability to deal meaningfully with the figures may be the result either of the uniqueness of all three figures or the impermeability of the constructs which the subject actually uses to deal with the figures. If the inquiry proposed by Hunt is used to follow up the appearance of a situational construct, one may get clearer evidence of one or the other of these two interpretations.

If the subject is unable to communicate his construction of the figures, it does not necessarily mean that he has no useful construction of them. He may not be able to find the communicative words or he may be unable to cast himself in the role of one who sees the construct. In the former case he is likely, if he is not too much threatened in the test situation, to make some attempt to explain his construct in response to inquiry. If he does, the clinician may learn, for example, that 'being from the same town' is, for the subject, a permeable construct which has rich behaviour implications, perhaps of a subcultural nature. If the subject responds to the inquiry by suggesting a construct which appears to be unrelated to the situational construct, there is tentative evidence for believing that he did not, at first, wish to be caught saying such a thing.

l. Preemptive constructs. These may have the appearance of being excessively permeable. For example, the subject may say, 'They're both women.' Inquiry may reveal that the subject sees all women as being alike and no woman as being like any man in any way. This carries the further implication that when one has said that a person is a women he has said all that can be said about her. The alert clinician will hypothesize that the client is having difficulty dealing with women and that, as a consequence of this and regardless of his own sex, he may be having difficulty in establishing an adequate sex role for himself.

m. Superficial constructs. These are more likely to turn out to be preverbal or childlike in character. The meaning is likely to be highly personalized and difficult to communicate. The inquiry may throw some light upon the nature of the construct.

n. Vague constructs. These are more likely to indicate reluctance to cast oneself in the role of a user of the construct.

o. Dependency constructs. These are the constructs of the type 'These two are both nice to me.' They indicate the subject's dependency upon people and his probable use of persons as symbols of constructs. Some of the implications of this kind of symbolism were discussed in the preceding chapter.

p. Conventionalized constructs. Sometimes a subject will list a preponderance of constructs which are commonly considered as good or bad. The test can be scored in such a way as to indicate the proportion of obvious value constructs. Moreover, the number of figures associated with 'good' constructs can be compared with the number of figures associated with 'bad' constructs. This provides a measure of the subject's rejection of the figures in his Role Title List and the likelihood that he has sought or will seek a new social milieu.

q. Vocabulary level. The symbols the subject uses in conveying his constructs yield a by-product in the form of an indication of his vocabulary level. As we have pointed out before, however, the range of vocabulary with respect to role constructs is not necessarily a measure of the range of operating constructs.

r. Ambiguous figures. Some figures may appear on opposite sides of the same constructs when they are used in different contexts. While this may indicate that the subject is confused with respect to them, alternatively he may simply be using his construct system as a scale in the manner described in an earlier chapter. If he is using a construct as a scale, it is some indication of the position the construct holds in the hierarchy of constructs in his system, since a scale is a construct of constructs. An inquiry will help the examiner determine whether such a scale is in use whenever a figure is placed on opposite sides of the same or similar constructs.

s. Power constructs and figures. Since the notion of force, energy, or power is one commonly employed by subjects, it is useful to score the results of the Rep Test in terms of the proportion of constructs falling in this category and in terms of the number of figures seen as strong or weak. To recognize that 'force' is a feature of many personal-construct systems is, of course, not tantamount to embodying the notion of force in the psychology of personal constructs.

t. Other culture categories. Other categories, such as success, education, occupation, or strength types, may be used as grounds for grouping constructs.

u. Rejections. Some of the sorts may be rejected by the subject. As in the case of the situational constructs, this may mean that the subject is confused regarding the figures, that he has impermeable constructs regarding them, or that he does not wish to cast himself in the role of one who expresses aloud his view with regard to them.

v. Perseverations. When the Sequential Form is used the examiner may take account of perseverations: the tendency to use the same construct when one figure is taken away from the context and another put in its place. These may indicate the dominant figures in the contexts; but, even more, they suggest a kind of situational approach to the handling of figures which may express an inability to cope with them. The sequential mode of presentation provides a more rigorous test of the subject's use of role constructs. It is more likely to reveal their breaking points.

w. Self-identification. When the Self-identification Form is used, the examiner will want to tabulate, not only the full statement of position that the subject describes for himself, but also his position as to (a) the number of times he associated himself with the contrasting construct – in other words, his uniqueness; (b) his association with figures in the sex, recency, intimacy, and contact-situation brackets; (c) his identification with 'good' and 'bad' and 'strong' and 'weak' constructs, et cetera; and (d) his linkages and the constructs he falls heir to by virtue of them.

x. Inefficacies. If the Personal Role Form is administered, a tabulation should be kept as to the number of times the subject sees himself as the 'left out' person in the context and the number of times he sees one of the other persons as 'left out' of the activity. In either of these types of situations, the subject's inability to structure the role in such a manner as to provide interaction between all the parties is implied. The range of topics which he mentions as a possible basis for discussion, or the range of activities which he mentions as a basis for the group interaction with himself as a participant, gives some idea as to the breadth of the facet of his role which could be exposed in such a situation.

9. Tabular analysis of a sample protocol

The following protocol was obtained on an earlier revision of the Group Form of the Rep Test. (See Table 5.2.)

Table 5.2 Raw protocol of Mildred Beal

Sort no.	*Similar figures*	*Similarity construct*	*Dissimilar figure*	*Contrasting construct*
1	Boss Successful Person	Are related to me Not at all the same	Sought Person	Unrelated
2	Rejecting Person Pitied Person	Very unhappy persons	Intelligent Person	Contented
3	Father Liked Teacher	Are very quiet and easygoing persons	Pitied Person	Nervous Hypertensive

Table 5.2 cont. Raw protocol of Mildred Beal

Sort no.	*Similar figures*	*Similarity construct*	*Dissimilar figure*	*Contrasting construct*
4	Mother Sister	Look alike Are both hypercritical of people in general	Boy friend	Friendliness
5	Ex-flame Pitied Person	Feel inferior	Boy friend	Self-confident
6	Brother Intelligent person	Socially better than adequate	Disliked teacher	Unpleasant
7	Mother Boss	Hypertensive	Father	Easygoing
8	Sister Rejecting Person	Hypercritical	Brother	Understanding
9	Rejecting Person Ex-flame	Feelings of inferiority	Disliked teacher	Assured of innate worth
10	Liked Teacher Sought Person	Pleasing personalities	Successful Person	High-powered Nervous
11	Mother Ex-flame	Socially maladjusted	Boy friend	Easygoing Self-confident
12	Father Boy friend	Relaxing	Ex-flame	Uncomfortable to be with
13	Disliked Teacher Boss	Emotionally unpredictable	Brother	Even temperament
14	Sister Rejecting Person	Look somewhat alike	Liked Teacher	Look unlike
15	Intelligent Person Successful Person	Dynamic personalities	Sought Person	Weak personality

Following are tabulations (Tables 5.3–8) which are made preliminary to the interpretation of the protocol.

Table 5.3 Descriptions of figures

	Figure	*Constructs used to describe it*
1	Mother	*Looks like sister*
		Hypercritical of people in general
		Hypertensive
		Socially maladjusted
2	Father	*Quiet*
		Easygoing
		Relaxing
		Easygoing
3	Brother	*Socially better than adequate*
		Even temperamentl
		Understanding
4	Sister	*Looks like mother*
		Hypercritical of people in general
		Hypercritical
		Looks like rejecting person
5	Boy friend	*Relaxing*
		Easygoing
		Self-confident
		Self-confident
		Friendliness
6	Liked Teacher	*Quiet*
		Easygoing
		Pleasing personality
		Looks unlike sister and rejecting person
7	Disliked Teacher	*Emotionally unpredictable*
		Assured of innate worth
		Unpleasant
8	Boss	*Related to me*
		Hypertensive
		Emotionally unpredictable
9	Rejecting Person	*Very unhappy*
		Hypercritical
		Looks like sister
		Feelings of inferiority
10	Ex-flame	*Feels very inferior*
		Feelings of inferiority
		Socially maladjusted
		Uncomfortable to be with
11	Sought Person	*Pleasing personality*
		Weak personality
		Not related to me
12	Pitied Person	*Very unhappy*
		Feels very inferior
		Nervous
		Hypertensive
13	Intelligent Person	*Socially better than adequate*
		Dynamic personality
		Contented
14	Successful Person	*Related to me*
		Dynamic personality
		High-powered
		Nervous

Note: Constructs which were used as bases of similarity are italicized

Table 5.4 Construct constellations

Linking sort	*Sort no.*	*'Plus' construct*	*'Minus' construct*
Constellation A-1			
	3	*Easygoing*	Nervous
		Quiet	Hypertensive
3	7	Easygoing	*Hypertensive*
3	11	Easygoing	*Socially maladjusted*
		Self-confident	
3	10	*Pleasing*	Nervous
		personalities	High-powered
10–11	6	*Socially better*	Unpleasant
		than adequate	
11	5	Self-confident	*Feel very inferior*
5	9	Assured of innate worth	Feelings of inferiority
Constellation A-2*			
(11)	2	Contented	*Very unhappy*
(10)	15	Weak	*Dynamic*
(6)	12	*Relaxing*	Uncomfortable to be with
Constellation B			
	4	Friendly	*Look alike*
			Hypercritical
4	8	Understanding	*Hypercritical*
Separate construct C	13	Even temperament	*Emotionally unpredictable*
Separate construct D	14	Look unlike	*Look alike*
Separate construct E	1	Unrelated	*Are related to me*
			Not at all alike

Note: The terms 'plus' and 'minus' have no value connotation
*This constellation is ancillary to A–1 and is not internally consistent in a literal sense

Table 5.5 The nature of the basic constructs used

A+	People who are easygoing, pleasing, and socially better than adequate. Seven people were described in this way.
A–	People who feel inferior, are hypertensive, socially maladjusted, very unhappy, and dynamic. Eight people were described in this way.
B+	People who are friendly and understanding. Two people were described in this way.
B-	People who are hypocritical. Three people were described in this way.
C+	People with even temperament. One person was described in this way.
C–	People who are emotionally unpredictable. Two people were described in this way.
D+	People who look unlike. One person was described in this way.
D–	People who look alike. Three people were described in this way.
E+	People who are unrelated to me. One person was described in this way.
E–	People who are related to me. Two people were described in this way.

Note: Italicized terms from Table 5.4 are used

Table 5.6 Figures falling under the rubrics of the principal constellation

Figures classed as A+	*No. times classed A+*	*Figures classed as A–*	*No. times classed A–*
Ex-flame	4	Father	4
Pitied Person	4	Boy friend	4
Successful Person	3	Liked Teacher	3
Mother	2	Sought Person	2
Rejecting Person	2	Brother	1
Boss	1		
Disliked Teacher	1 or 1*	Intelligent Person	2 or 1*
Intelligent Person	1 or 2*	Disliked Teacher	1 or 1*
Totals:			
Persons classed	8		7
Characterizations	18		17

Note: *Mixed classification of figure: for example, the Intelligent person was characterized twice with a construct falling in the A– group and once with a construct falling in the A+ group

Table 5.7 Some figure constellations

Figures linked	*Constructs linked*
Constellation 'Mother'	
Mother was described in terms of	*Looks like sister*
	Hypercritical of people in general
	Hypertensive
	Socially maladjusted
She was described as similar to Sister, Boss, and Ex-flame, one or more of whom were additionally described in terms of	*Looking like rejecting person*
	Related to me
	Emotionally unpredictable
	Feels very inferior
	Feelings of inferiority
	Uncomfortable to be with
Constellation 'Father'	
Father was described in terms of	*Quiet*
	Easygoing
	Relaxing
	Easygoing
He was described as similar to Liked teacher and Boy friend, one or both of whom were additionally described in terms of	*Pleasing personality*
	Looks unlike sister and rejecting person
	Self-confident
	Friendliness
Constellation 'Boy friend'	
Boy friend was described as	*Relaxing*
	Easygoing
	Self-confident
	Friendliness
He was described as similar to the Father only who was additionally described in terms of	*Quiet*

Table 5.7 cont. Some figure constellations

Figures linked	*Constructs linked*
Constellation 'Sister'	
Sister was described in terms of	*Looks like mother*
	Hypercritical of people in general
	Hypercritical
	Looks like rejecting person
She was described as similar to Mother and Rejecting Person, one or both of whom were additionally described in terms of	*Socially maladjusted* *Very unhappy* *Feelings of inferiority*

Table 5.8 Tallies

Sorts	15
Construct symbols used	28
Sorts in major primary constellation (A–1)	7/15
Sorts in major secondary constellation (A)	10/15
constructs in major primary constellation	12/28
Constructs in major secondary constellation	18/28
Primary constellations	2
Secondary constellations	1
Figures involved in major primary constellation	13/14
Figures involved in major secondary constellation	13/14

The construct constellations in Table 5.4 were built up by starting with a construct dimension which, on the basis of inspection, appeared to be used more times than any other. In this protocol this was the dimension appearing in sort 3: *easygoing, quiet, vs. nervous, hypertensive.* Next, one looks for sorts in which one or more of the same terms were used. In this case sorts 7, 11, and 10 employed one or both of the construct poles mentioned in sort 3. Next, we look for terms in these sorts which may be repeated in additional sorts. This introduces the terms of sort 6, which is linked to the constellation through sorts 10 and 11 – already part of the constellation. Sort 5 next comes into the constellation by virtue of its linkage with sort 11; and sort 9 rides in on the coat-tails of sort 5.

If we drop our literalism slightly and infer similar meanings of slightly different terms, we may add sorts 2 (via sort 11), 15 (via 10), and 12 (via 6).

This ends our linkages for the A constellation, so we start over again with the remaining sorts. All we get is constellation B, in which sort 8 is linked with sort 4. The remaining sorts appear to represent separate constructs.

In setting down the terms, we are careful to keep the poles of the constructs aligned. Thus construct 7, which is linked to construct 3 through the term 'hypertensive', is reflected so that 'hypertensive' appears in the 'minus' column under the 'hypertensive' of construct 3.

In order to keep clear which terms referred to the two like figures in the construct context and which referred to the odd figure, the terms referring to the like poles are italicized.

C. Checking clinical hypotheses

10. Clinical hypotheses derived from an analysis of sample protocol

Mildred Beal took the Group Form of the Rep Test as a classroom exercise. She made the comment, after looking at her protocol, that she had probably revealed herself as a rather inadequate person. It turned out that she had recently requested psychological counselling. This provided an opportunity to check clinical hypotheses against therapeutic outcomes. The therapist was not given the protocol, however, nor was she provided with the clinical hypotheses derived from the protocol. The following clinical hypotheses were therefore not subjected to a running check during the course of treatment. At the conclusion of the series, however, the therapist did provide the writer with comments relating to certain specific questions he had formulated on the basis of the hypotheses. After the therapist replied to the questions, the more detailed hypotheses were made available to her. Following are the clinical hypotheses which were derived from the brief protocol produced by Mildred on the Group Form of the Rep Test.

In spite of the large number of symbols used (28) one is immediately impressed by the linkages which reduce Mildred Beal's repertory to four dimensions, two of which are constellations. One of the constellations seems to carry the burden of her dealings with people in her interpersonal world. Thirteen of the fourteen figures in her Role Title List were dealt with by means of this principal construct: the fourteenth figure, the sister, is so threatening that she can scarcely be handled at all. This suggests that the subject has little real versatility in handling the figures in her interpersonal world even though the number of construct symbols used is large. This would be the first hypothesis to be entertained by the therapist who would hope to be of assistance to this client.

The superficially large number of construct symbols suggests a kind of intellectual striving which, at this stage of Mildred's development, does not involve much more than a glib use of symbols. The nature of the striving can be further hypothesized from examining the italicized terms which go to make up the A– constellation: *hypertensive, socially maladjusted, feelings of inferiority, unhappy*, and *dynamic*. The representative italicized terms in the contrasting A+ constellation are *easygoing, quiet, pleasing personalities, socially better than adequate*, and *relaxing*. This should provide the therapist with an initial hypothesis that Mildred's personal world is dichotomized between unhappy striving on the one hand, and pleasant, comfortable quiescence on the other. If we consider this A+, A– constellation to mark the broadest highway, which is visible to her, we would expect that, under pressure, she would use it herself as a route of movement. If the movement attempted in one direction did not enable her to establish a suitable role, she could be expected to vacillate between unhappy agitation and easy self-indulgence. The therapist would therefore approach the case expecting the subject to attempt, initially, to establish a comfortable and superficial relationship with him. She might talk much of striving but actually do very little of it in an effective manner.

The third therapeutic hypothesis also stems from her glib use of symbols. Her repertory is so limited, yet so cluttered up with miscellaneous terms, that the therapist would expect to have considerable difficulty in getting points across in a way that would make them stick. Mildred might be expected to agree readily with suggestions and then foul them up completely in attempting to carry them into action. Insights might be glibly stated but not precisely retained. She might talk a great deal in the therapeutic sessions, but in an abstruse fashion; that is to say, she would use abstract words concretistically.

The subject's B constellation suggests that the therapist will initially be seen as either friendly and understanding or 'hypercritical'. The possibility of offering friendly and understanding criticism may seem plausible to the therapist; but, for the subject, friendliness and criticism appear to be antithetical. While the subject is engaging in the process of evolving something more useful out of this construct, she may be expected to cast the therapist in alternating 'friendly-uncritical' and 'hypercritical-unfriendly' roles. In this alternation the therapist may be able to see quite readily the transference of father and mother roles upon himself. These figures are currently seen by the subject as presenting such sharp contrasts that the therapist will have to exercise considerable care in the transference relationship not to become identified with one of them to the exclusion of the other.

The protocol suggests some important topics for discussion which the subject should be ready to handle fairly early in the therapeutic series. The most important of these, as far as the protocol is concerned, is the relationship with the sister, although it is not necessarily the topic to be discussed first. While the sister is likened to certain other figures, the construct of the sister as a person approaches preemption. The scoring of the protocol which yields constellation 'Sister' indicates, first of all, that the subject was twice hard pressed to find a construct which described the sister and had to fall back upon 'looking alike' to describe the similarity which she felt applied to these contexts. The unavailability of symbols for this figure, in a subject whose repertory is generally cluttered up with symbols, suggests that the subject's construction of the sister's role is difficult for her to verbalize and therefore quite difficult to manage. There is the possibility also that the construction of the sister's role is patterned after some childhood, possibly preverbal, construct system. The hypothesis for the therapist is that here is an area of discussion in which much loose thinking of the preverbal type will have to be elicited and verbalized before the subject can handle this figure in her personal-social world or orient herself to other figures whom she feels are similar to it. The task should not prove insurmountable, since there is a certain tone of sympathy associated with constellation 'Sister' by way of additional descriptions of the 'similar' figures.

Constellation 'Boy friend' can be hypothesized as a profitable topic of discussion, primarily because of the light it may shed for the subject upon her formation of her own role. The only additional similar figure in this constellation is the father and the only additional construct brought into the constellation by the father figure is 'quiet'. If the therapist is psychoanalytically oriented, it may be that he will see this as an indication that certain phases of the Oedipal problem are immediately available for discussion.

An additional therapeutic hypothesis stems from an analysis of constellation B. This, if supported by therapeutic experience, may prove to be quite important in helping this client to adjust her role. The two sorts in constellation B involve similarities seen between the mother, the sister, and the rejecting person and contrasts with the brother and the boy friend. The linking construct in this constellation is 'hypercritical'. If this means – and well it may – that this subject has guilt feelings which are easily triggered by the mother and the sister, it becomes relevant to study the constructs in the mother and sister constellations further, to get some clue as to what features in her own status generate a feeling of guilt. (The relationship between guilt and role threat are discussed in more detail in a later section.) The additional constructs associated with these two figures are *hypertensive* and *socially maladjusted*. 'Hypertensive' in this subject's lexicon obviously means 'nervous', 'dynamic', et cetera. This suggests that the guilt which is aggravated effectively by the mother and sister has to do with her failure to strive as her sister and mother are seen to strive. The subject keeps this guilt from consistently controlling her behaviour by pointing out to herself the nervousness and social maladjustment of the mother. Thus she protects herself, after a fashion, by punishing one of the guilt-revealing figures. The sister is not so easy to pass off, however, and the guilt in her case may be associated with the preverbal construction of the sister which was hypothesized in a preceding paragraph. (Since, at this point, we have not yet presented our system of diagnostic constructs, many of these hypotheses are couched in the more familiar psychoanalytic framework.)

The construction patterns of the father, brother, and boy friend suggest that the subject seeks a childlike dependency relationship to males in which she will be made comfortable and will not have to strive. She may feel guilty in such a relationship, however, for she sees her mother and sister as effectively critical of the quiet easygoing life. The record suggests that she was pampered as a child by the male members of the family and sees herself as reaping the resultant jealousy of the female members of the family.

The protocol suggests an initial formulation of the therapeutic goal of first establishing a somewhat more adult basic repertory of role constructs for Mildred. The clear-cut recognition of varying behaviour patterns in other people and the adjustment of her own role to such patterns would be a step in this direction. The clinician would expect to be particularly on guard against being misled into thinking that conceptual changes were occurring when actually nothing but verbal agitation might be taking place. The dependency relationship, while childlike and superficial at first, would probably have to be kept under constant scrutiny by client and therapist, and continually converted into forms of constructive action.

11. Description of Mildred Beal by her therapist

Since we have insisted that a test used in a clinical setting be considered, among other things, as a source of clinical hypotheses to be validated in therapy, it is of interest to see what Mildred Beal's therapist had to say. Mildred did seek therapy, although it was precipitated in connection with an entirely different situation. It was therefore not in connection with therapy that she took the Group Form of the Rep Test. In her case the therapist did not have access to the results of the test until after the therapeutic series reported below was terminated.

The therapist was asked to prepare a summary of the therapeutic series and to react specifically to the following eleven questions regarding Mildred. Her reaction does not, of course, constitute a validation of the hypotheses or of the test, qua test. It does, however, serve illustrative purposes.

1. How versatile is she in dealing with people?
2. How does she react to social pressure?
3. What kinds of alternations (not necessarily cyclical) can be observed in her behaviour?
4. How readily does she accept interpretations from the therapist and how effectively does she carry them out?
5. In what role or roles does she cast the therapist?
6. What persons does she find particularly hard to relate herself to?
7. What underlies her relationship to her present boy friend?
8. What is the nature of her guilt feelings?
9. What protections against guilt does she adopt?
10. What has been her relation to men in general?
11. Did she develop new basic concepts during therapy?

The writer is greatly indebted to Mildred's therapist and would like to acknowledge that person's substantial contribution at this point. However, it seems desirable, in order to provide complete protection of Mildred's anonymity, not to mention the name here. The therapist's name appears in connection with acknowledgements of unspecified contributions.

Following is the therapist's account. Certain editorial deletions have been made in order to protect the client's identity.

> Mildred Beal was referred to the Student Counselling Service by her former academic advisor, a professor in the psychology department, after she had requested counselling from him. She had had about four contacts with him over a period of a year and a half. Despite the fact that she had asked for counselling, she did not try to make an appointment at the Counselling Service until about two weeks after the referral. When she did appear for the first interview, she

was seen to be a dark, rather attractive girl of average height, dressed in the latest style. She brought with her a partially completed referral blank, on which she had written answers to questions describing her past history and present college situation, but she had not answered the questions asking for a statement of her problem. The first interview was on 1 May and the last on 29 May, there being a total of six interviews lasting about fifty minutes each.

From the referral blank and the conversation during the interviews, the following history was obtained. She was almost twenty-two years old at the time she sought counselling. She was born and reared on a farm near a small farming village in a nearby state. In that area about half the people belong to a closely knit socio-religious sect, but the counsellee's family is Lutheran. (Since coming to college she has attended Episcopalian services, although she stated no reason for the change.) She has three siblings: Charles, aged twenty-six, Geneva, aged twenty-five, and Sanford, aged nineteen. The family financial situation has always been good, the family obtaining a comfortable living from the farm. Initially she described the family relationship as 'close', but later her comments suggested that, although she felt close to her brothers, she does not feel close to her parents or sister. Education is stressed in the family; both parents are college-trained, and it was taken for granted that all the children would obtain college degrees. But despite the stress on education, intellectual interests apparently are not emphasized. Apparently education is stressed for vocational and social reasons.

Mildred reports that when she was a small child she was shown off by her mother frequently and given a great deal of attention by her. She did not play much with other children, she said, because of being nearsighted. At first, she said, she could not see well enough to play their games, and after she was given glasses at the age of six or seven she was cautioned not to run and break them. In talking about this she seemed to regard her poor eyesight as a severe handicap and to censure her mother for not realizing it sooner and obtaining glasses for her. Except for her eyesight, health does not seem to have been a problem during her childhood; she stated that she had the usual childhood diseases, but otherwise she did not talk about the subject.

She attended a consolidated school from Grade One through Grade Eight. In general her marks were high average. She disliked school intensely, chiefly because she found 'social contacts very frustrating'. She had only one or two friends in addition to her two brothers. Her mother continued to be the 'centre' of her life. At the time when Mildred was twelve and pubescent, her mother had the first of four 'nervous breakdowns'. Then the mother became very critical of Mildred, in contrast to her former attitude of praise and attempts to keep Mildred close to her. According to Mildred the mother has maintained this critical attitude constantly for the past ten years, and her sister has imitated her mother in this respect.

When Mildred entered high school in a nearby town, she found the first two years even more difficult socially than the elementary school years. She did not want to associate with the girls of the closely knit socio-religious sect; and, she said, the other girls were snobbish. She believed she looked different from these other girls, because her mother made her wear long stockings during the winter while the others wore anklets. She expected criticism from everyone, she said, because of her mother's criticism. She had no girl friends and only two boy friends, with whom she often spent lunch hours away from the other children.

At the beginning of her junior year she rebelled against her mother's restrictions and began to wear anklets, use lipstick, etc. During the last two years of high school she made a few more friends and entered into more activities (newspaper, music, dramatics). This period, she said, was 'relatively happy'. Following graduation from high school she attended X College for two years, intending to become a veterinarian. However, she found chemistry too difficult and decided to drop that ambition. For one semester she worked part time in the college library; this is the only work she has ever done except work on the family farm. She did not say much about social life at X College other than that all the girls were required to join a sorority, but that she did not do so because she intended to transfer to a state university.

Eighteen months prior to the first interview she transferred to this university and began to major in psychology. However, after talking with her original academic advisor – the psychology professor who later referred her for treatment – about vocational plans, and learning that she could not work as a psychologist without a graduate degree, she changed her major to speech and hearing therapy. Although she stated once that she likes this as a major, she said at another time that she is afraid of a professional career, and several times she mentioned that she has a chronic throat infection that makes her tire easily when talking. Although her college aptitude is good (she scored at the ninety-seventh percentile on the university's group test for scholastic aptitude), she has a low B average and worries about grades. Her studying is unplanned, being sandwiched between extracurricular activities.

At one time she pledged a sorority (the only one on campus to which she *did not* get a recommendation from X College sororities, she said). But before she went active she was blackballed following a 'stab in the back' by a sorority pledge sister whom she had tried to help. In view of her mother's emphasis on social life, this failure to be elected to a sorority was probably a great blow to her, although now she extols the values of being an independent. She has lived in off-campus rooming houses with a succession of room-mates, none of whom she has chosen herself. She merely rents half a double room and then takes as a room-mate whoever rents the other half.

She has entered into many campus club activities, but has concentrated most of her attention on a dramatic club, of which she was properties chairman for one year. She regards this as an important organization and has tried to convince her mother of its importance through telling her about activities of the club and the amount of money spent by the club on each production. She says she has about twelve girl friends, who are members of this club, and 'many boys who are just friends, not beaux'. She dates and goes to parties frequently, in contrast to her high-school period. Also, she regards herself as 'Dan Cupid' because of obtaining dates for other girls. She seems to try to keep busy all the time and to avoid free moments. Since coming to this university she has 'gone steady' with several boys, but has become dissatisfied with nearly all and has broken off the relationship. At the time this series of conferences ended she had been dating Gerald for six weeks; she said she liked him but had become critical of him and wondered whether that relationship would last, especially after she took him home to visit her family.

Mildred came to the Counselling Service only a month before the close of the spring term. During the first interview it was planned that she would come for interviews twice a week for the rest of the quarter, but after the first week she came in only once a week. She stated that she did not have any free time when the clinic had openings for appointments. She began the first interview by asking whether the counsellor (a woman) would 'use the directive or nondirective technique'. She stated that she had 'taken a couple of courses in counselling'; questioning indicated that she had taken an introductory course in counselling techniques and was currently auditing a survey course in clinical psychology for nonpsychology majors.

At first during the first interview she made broad and vague references to problems with her family and her boy friends, but then suddenly turned to giving a detailed, chronological account of her life history. When asked during this and subsequent interviews about the nature of her problem and her reason for coming to the Counselling Service, she had much difficulty in giving an explanation. During the first interview the counsellor extracted from her conversation complaints of lack of self-confidence, worry about grades, and a feeling that she needs to prove to her family that she is a 'success' socially, together with a fear that she will not be able to do this. In one later session she mentioned 'restlessness' as a problem. At the time of the fourth interview she brought in a completed copy of the Mooney Problem Check List (she had been given a copy as a sample in one of her speech therapy classes). On this she had checked 121 specific problems and had circled 32 as being of special importance. Her written summary of the problems was as follows:

> Insecurity, lack of self-confidence, and just plain anxiety about everything and everone pretty well summarize the problem. The main problem is learning to take a more objective, less emotional, and more sensible attitude toward my mother and sister. I resent them too much – although I do like them in many ways. And yet I am not even sure the above is the problem.

Neither before nor after this was she able to make any statement about her problems that was as definitive as this. Frequently she asked the counsellor, 'Do I have a problem?' She appeared to want to put her problem in the counsellor's lap without actually admitting that she had a problem. Towards the end of the series of conferences she was able to recognize her desire to have the counsellor take responsibility both for telling her whether she had a problem and for solving the problem. Her manner most of the time during the first four or five interviews suggested an attempt to entertain the counsellor, rather than an attempt to understand herself.

After her initial difficulty in getting started (she indicated that she expected the counsellor to ask questions for her to try to answer), she talked rapidly and almost constantly. Most of this talk was concerned with detailed accounts of recent or past events; about-one third of the time these events were ones in which people other than herself were the chief characters. Because of the short time available for interviews the counsellor repeatedly brought up reminders about what she was doing and questions about the reason for this manner.

The counsellor also offered tentative interpretations of a wish to avoid facing her problems and a wish to obtain attention and affection such as she has wanted from her mother during the past ten years. Apparently in response to this pressure, she cried a little in the fifth interview and part of the time she talked somewhat less rapidly and less about other people. During the sixth interview, also, she chattered somewhat less than in the first few sessions; perhaps this was a continuation of her reaction in the fifth interview or perhaps it was a response to an immediate problem with her boy friend. At any rate, by the last interview she appeared to be a little more willing to look at herself instead of merely going to other people for help and then avoiding discussing problems. During the last interview she stated that she might return for further counselling in the fall.

The writer [Mildred's counsellor] was asked to answer certain questions about Mildred and her reaction to therapy. Further information about the interviews will be given in response to these questions.

a. How versatile is she in dealing with people? Most of the time during the six sessions Mildred smiled in a rather fixed manner and talked rapidly about a wealth of details in a way suggesting that she was trying to entertain the counsellor. She admitted once that her 'yaketty-yak', as she called her talking, was the way she talked with her brothers and most people. Even her choice of words appears to be rather limited. During one session, when she was asked to review what she had said in a previous session, she gave an account that closely resembled the first account, often using exactly the same phrasings as she had originally used. She stated that she had given the same information to a campus physician and to the Dean of Women (the particular information was about trying to help a room-mate who was in some difficulty); it appears that not only the content but the manner of giving the information in different settings to different people was highly similar. On three occasions during these interviews her manner changed and she became more thoughtful or a little sad, but the changes were involuntary. All this suggests that she shows little flexibility in dealing with people and that if she does respond to people in a changed manner, that manner is not under her voluntary control and cannot be actively used by her.

b. How does she react to social pressure? Mildred sees pressure as coming first from her family and secondly from her circle of acquaintances. She appears to give little thought to a wider society. She seems to see almost all situations in which she is present as involving some type of social pressure on her: praise as a sign of approval of her or criticism as a sign of rejection. She seems to need to guard herself constantly against disapproval. In one of her classes she obtained and completed a copy of the Rotter Incomplete Sentences Test, and on this test she stated. 'What annoys me is *being destructively criticized*', and, 'My greatest worry is *not succeeding in the eyes of my family.*' She appears unable to accept, ignore, or reject the standards of her family. Her understanding of the reasons for the actions of others and their reactions to her is rather poor for a person of her intelligence and training. For instance, when she refused to accept a ring from a man whom she was dating, she was surprised that his manner toward her changed. Apparently as a result of some of her courses in college she sometimes makes an attempt to understand the motives of others, but these attempts resemble a rather mechanical application of formulae. For instance, she stated that she supposed her father whipped her severely once because he was worried about her sick mother and did not stop to think what he was doing. When family or social group pressures are applied, she tends to think that she has been treated unjustly. She described her mother and sister as criticizing her a great deal without ever making any constructive suggestions, and she describes a sorority as blackballing her and believing another girl's accusations after she had tried to help the other girl. When she sees some person as blaming her for something, she sometimes admits being at fault but is quick to look for extenuating circumstances.

c. What kinds of alternations in her behaviour can be observed? Mildred's manner most of the time might be described as a stereotyped cheerfulness. She uses this manner whether talking about pleasant or unpleasant topics. She talks rapidly, reporting many details of events. Much of the time she seems to be playing to an audience, both by her actions and her dramatic way of speaking. During interviews she frequently rearranged her skirts, and once when she wore an off-the-shoulder blouse she kept trying to push it farther off her shoulders. Her tendency to dramatize herself is seen in such remarks as, 'You have a sad little girl on your hands today', and her referring to herself as 'blind' after she broke her glasses.

As has been mentioned previously, on three occasions she became somewhat more thoughtful than usual or even a little sad. At these times she talked less rapidly, smiled less, and once even cried a few tears. Part of the dramatic manner, however, continued. Two of the three times this change occurred it appeared to be precipitated by an immediate problem situation, one involving pressure from the counsellor and the other involving possible loss of a boy friend. The third situation that precipitated a more thoughtful manner involved memory of loss of a boy friend. It is notable that although she regards her mother as the source of her problems, her manner did not change from the usual 'cheerfulness' when she spoke of her mother and her criticisms. The only time when she described herself as acting in a manner different from her interview manner was once when she said that during group discussions about a philosophy of life she feels ignorant about this topic and is afraid to let the others in the group know what she believes for fear of ridicule.

d. How readily does she accept suggestions from the therapist and how effectively does she carry them out? Three suggestions of things which might be done during or between interviews were made by the counsellor. When the counsellor suggested that she write a self-characterization, she immediately agreed to the proposal but then quickly expressed doubt about whether she could be 'objective' in writing it. Apparently this was an indirect expression of resistance to the task. She never did write the self-description, but after adequate time had passed for completing it, she gave two excuses: first that she could not do it because she had broken her glasses a few days before, and later that she had a term paper to write.

At another time the counsellor asked her to write a summary of what she said during an interview. Again she agreed readily and again she explained later that she had had no time to do it. It should be noted that although she claimed not to have time to do this writing, she spontaneously filled out both the Mooney Problem Check List and the Rotter Incomplete Sentences Test during this 'busy' period. During the fourth interview she asked, 'When are you going to give me the TAT?' When the counsellor explained that the test would take too long in view of the fact that only two more interviews remained, she seemed disappointed. At the same time the counsellor refused the TAT she suggested that Mildred's conversation could be used as a projective device if she wished. Mildred made no comment about this and showed little interest in examining the significance of any of her statements. All these episodes suggest a strong desire to resist suggestions, an inability to do it openly, and a resort to rationalization.

Few suggestions in the nature of interpretations were made. Mildred readily accepted the mild interpretation that she was trying to put her problem in the counsellor's lap for the counsellor to solve. She resisted the interpretation that she was looking for approval and affection from the counsellor just as she did from her mother. She also resisted the milder interpretation that her description of talking with her mother sounded much like her conversation with the counsellor during these interviews. (She said that she was trying to prove to her mother that she could be a success but was not trying to prove anything to the counsellor.)

e. In what role or roles does she cast the therapist? During the last ten minutes of the last interview Mildred volunteered that in the beginning she had been rather wary of the counsellor because of her sex but had decided to 'give it a try' because a male counsellor was not available. For the most part she seemed to place the counsellor in the role of mother-figure. This was shown in her wish to depend on the counsellor and have the counsellor not only solve her problems but even tell her whether she had any problems. She tried to get the counsellor to take responsibility for her coming to interviews (after most of the sessions she asked, 'When do you want to see me again?'), despite the fact that a regularly scheduled time had been agreed upon. The role of the mother also seemed to be indicated by her resistance to suggestions made by the counsellor – a resistance suggestive of the hostility that she quite obviously has for her own mother. Her attempts at justification of her behaviour, particularly when she failed to carry out suggestions, appear to indicate an expectation of criticism from the counsellor such as she says she received from her mother.

Despite her spontaneous denial, she did not seem to try to prove things to the counsellor as she admittedly did to her mother. For instance, during the fifth interview, when she appeared to be trying to avoid tears, the counsellor asked her whether she could let herself cry. Mildred immediately responded by citing two other situations in which she had cried. Her description indicated that she rarely has a spur-of-the-moment conversation with her mother but that she deliberately plans to talk to her mother about some activity or person. The same deliberate planning of a topic was shown in these interviews, or at least the first four of them; at the beginning of the third interview she said, 'I've been wondering what to tell you today, and I hit on a sad story.'

f. What persons does she find it particularly hard to relate herself to? Mildred seems to find it harder to relate to girls and women than to boys and men. Outstanding is her admitted difficulty in getting along with her mother and sister. Her difficulty in relating to women was demonstrated during these interviews. It is also indicated by the fact that she reports that in both high school and college she has had more boy friends than girl friends. Although she seems to relate to men better than to women, she does not appear to relate to men well despite the fact that she tried to convince herself that she does so. She admitted once, after describing a whipping given her by her father, that she had never felt close to him although she favoured him over her mother. And although she apparently has many dates and has 'gone steady' with at least four men in the past two years, something has always happened to break up the relationship.

g. What underlies her relationship to her present boy friend? Shortly before the beginning of the series of interviews, Mildred began to date Gerald. Six weeks later, during the last interview, she brought up the problem of her relationship to him. She likes him, she said, because of his kindness, his calmness, and his ambition. Perhaps his kindness partially satisfies her wish for sympathy as opposed to criticism and her wish for dependence. Resemblance to her father is also a possible factor, since she described her father as a 'considerate' man. His calmness may be postulated to be the manner she would like to have instead of her present feelings of restlessness and lack of self-confidence. His ambition she may relate to her own ambitions for social success and good grades. Perhaps she feels that if she dates and eventually marries a successful man she will achieve success through identifying with him and at the same time will be excused from making a personal effort after success. Gerald and she planned that he would drive her home from college at the end of the term, and she was worried about the reaction of her family to him and whether she would continue to like him after her family had seen him and possibly criticized him. Recently, she said, she has been 'looking at him through Mother's eyes' and has been silently critical of his slouch. These facts indicate that her ability to accept him is conditioned by her clinging to family values, particularly the values of her mother.

h. What is the nature of her guilt feelings? It is difficult to state the exact nature of Mildred's guilt feelings because the few interviews were devoted chiefly to preparation for therapy, rather than to therapy itself, and her defences were still high. She probably has considerable guilt over hostility to her mother and secondarily, perhaps, to her sister. She stated that last summer, in response to criticism by her sister, she 'blew up and told Sis what she and Mom had done to me', but at various times she assured the counsellor that she really loves and respects her mother. The latter statements appear to be a salve to her guilt feelings rather than a real expression of love, for she never made any other favourable comments about her mother. In view of her admitted favouritism for her father and her need to state that she loves her mother, perhaps she also has guilt feelings over this favouritism; this, however, can only be hypothesized, since there is no definite evidence of it. Although she usually maintained that she is very fond of her father, once she said spontaneously that she had never felt close to him, and once she related an incident involving punishment by him in which she was definitely afraid of him. In relating this incident she hastened too quickly to absolve him from blame. Perhaps at the back of the statements of fondness for him is some resentment, or even hostility about which she may feel guilty.

i. What protections against guilt does she adopt? One of Mildred's defences is keeping so busy with social and extracurricular activities that she does not have time to think. It is notable that she became uncomfortable enough to seek a series of counselling sessions only after her college work required that she drop some of these activities. Her habit of talking about a myriad of details without stopping to analyse the meanings of them or why she is saying them may well be another aspect of this escape into activities. During the interviews, when the counsellor asked about the significance of some of the trivia, she usually avoided answering. Another facet of this same situation is her practice, during counselling interviews, of repeatedly turning the conversation from herself onto other people. A second primary type of defence appears to be a form of rationalization in which she often tries to put the responsibility for her difficulties onto other people without actually seeming to blame them. And when she does accept blame herself, she nearly always brings up extenuating circumstances as if to remove the real responsibility from herself. For instance, she used her broken glasses as an excuse for not writing the self-characterization, even though she did not break them until several days after the counsellor had asked her to write it.

j. What has been her relation to men in general? Mildred's relationship to her parents appears to determine the nature of her present relationship to men more than is usual in a girl of her age. She seems to see every man as a potential husband for herself or one of her friends, but she seems to be looking for an ideal man for herself. The ideal man must have the kindness and considerateness that she wished (but possibly did not always get) from her father. The strong wish for considerateness may also be a function of the criticism received from her mother. Lawrence and Carney (former boy friends) both lack this quality, according to her, and it should be noted that she eventually broke the relationship with both of them. She stated that she liked both Gerald and Don (another former boy friend) for their kindness.

Physical appearance, also, seems to be an important element in determining whether she likes a man. This emphasis appears to be based on her mother's preferences. Her mother once told her, she said, that she (the mother) supposed that Mildred would 'bring home some little shrimp to marry', and Mildred has commented in all cases about the height of the men she has gone with recently. (Don is tall, but Lawrence is a 'little rooster'; although Gerald is tall, she is silently critical of his slouch.) Other physical characteristics also appear to be important, in that she wants men to be good-looking though not necessarily handsome. Although she denied that good looks are important to her, she listed it as one of the reasons for having liked Carney and has mentioned it also when talking about the other men.

Mildred's mother has also emphasized getting ahead and being a social and vocational success. Mildred has picked men who were 'ambitious', although she has disliked having them talk to other people about their ambition or success. Perhaps she is trying to feel that she has succeeded (she is afraid she will not succeed) through identifying with a man who succeeds. When she meets a man who appears to fit all these requirements, she is likely to be 'swept off her feet' immediately. Following this initial period, she stated, there is likely to be a 'cooling-off period' in which she 'gets used to him as a person'. She described this sequence in regard to her present boy friend (Gerald), but she did not mention it with regard to other men, and so the regularity of its occurrence is not known.

In the last interview she wondered whether she could allow herself to 'get close to any man' (a statement she attributed to the counsellor). In this connection it should be remembered that she once said she had never felt close to her father, and it may well be that she does keep a barrier between herself and men. A barrier to a close relationship with a man, such as is involved in marriage, is suggested in one answer on the Rotter Incomplete Sentences Test: 'Marriage is *a wonderful thing if approached with the right attitude.*' Here the reservation at the end of the sentence seems important.

k. Did she develop new basic concepts during therapy? Only a beginning at therapy was accomplished in these six interviews. The development of new concepts appears to be in an embryonic stage, and the new concepts as formed at this time can hardly be called basic. For over half the sessions she vacillated with regard to the question of whether she had any problem requiring counselling. By the last interview she seemed somewhat more sure that she does have a problem, though still unsure what it is, and her conviction is not deep enough to prevent doubt. Her spontaneous statement that she might return for further counselling in the fall appears to bear witness to some change in attitude. She has a partial realization of a desire for help from other people, but it is not known whether this is a new concept or an old one. However, she seems to have no concept that the degree of her dependence is inappropriate for someone of her age (cf. her statement to the counsellor during the last interview that 'You have a sad little girl on your hands today.').

In the last interview she did less talking about other people and more talking about herself than in previous interviews. But it is not known whether this change reflected development of a concept of this behaviour as evidence of her own difficulties or whether it was solely a function of an immediate situation in which she believed that the counsellor disapproved of this action. In the last interview Mildred stated that she had some question as to whether she could let herself get close to anyone. Apparently this was a new idea for her although not one that was very firmly established. Also in the last interview she stated for the first time that she was 'seeing Gerald through Mother's eyes'. This statement suggests the beginning of a realization of her dependence on her mother's values, but her alternate affirmation and denial of adoption of her mother's values indicates that this insight exists in only rudimentary form. On the whole it might more accurately be said that the groundwork was laid for new concepts rather than that new concepts were actually developed.

The foregoing account should serve to illustrate what is meant by checking clinical hypotheses based on tests against psychotherapeutic experience. This is an *illustration* of the possible usefulness of the test, not an *experimental proof* of its validity.

12. Conclusion

In the presentation of the Role Construct Repertory Test in its various forms and the citing of an example of protocol analysis, we have attempted to illustrate the application of the five functions of a psychological test as used in a clinical setting. We have also attempted, by this means, to clarify further the possible applications of the theoretical viewpoint of the psychology of personal constructs to practical problems.

Chapter six

The mathematical structure of psychological space

This is a researcher's chapter dealing with the way constructs and figures are interwoven to give substance to the fabric of society. Methods of factorial analysis are described and computations are illustrated. The chapter is concerned with basic methodology rather than theory or technique. It employs a generalization of the technique described in the preceding chapter.

A. Grid Form of the Role Construct Repertory Test

1. Looking beyond words

The methods of analysing Rep Test protocol which we have suggested in the preceding chapter rely heavily upon one's interpretation of the client's language. But we can look beyond words. We can study contexts. For example, does the client use the word 'affectionate' only when talking about persons of the opposite sex? Does he apply the term 'sympathetic' only to members of his own family or only to persons who have also been described as 'intimate'? The answers to questions such as these may give us an understanding of the interweaving of the client's terminology and provide us with an understanding of his outlook which no dictionary could offer.

In the preceding chapter we discussed the analysis of protocol in terms of constellatory constructs. One approach was to observe the way in which constructs were linked by virtue of their being applied to the same persons. With the form of the test which we described it was not possible to take full advantage of this kind of linkage. By redesigning the test, however, it becomes much more feasible to study the relationships between personal constructs by analysing the way in which they are applied to the same persons or objects. If the test can be arranged to produce a kind of protocol which can be subjected to a meaningful analysis, independent of words, we shall have made progress towards a better understanding of the client's personal constructs.

2. The grid

One may construct a Grid Form of the Rep Test by listing role titles along one axis and letting the client enter his personal constructs along the other. At the intersection of each row and column is a cell in which the client may place a check mark or not, depending upon which pole of his construct dimension applies to the figure. Thus all constructs in the repertory are presumed to apply, one way or the other, to all figures in the Role Title List.

The grid is comprised of f figures, c constructs, and $f \times c$ intersects. Each intersect, when the client has completed his task of filling out the grid, becomes either an *incident* or a *void.* It is an incident if one pole of the construct is checked as applying to the figure, a void if the figure is assigned to the opposite pole by the omission of a check mark.

In order to provide a context for the formulation of a succession of constructs the client is asked to consider successive groups of three persons. For example, each of the intersects of the first construct row with the columns representing the Self, the Father, and the Mother may be marked with a circle on the printed test form. The client would be asked first to consider these three figures only: in what way two of them are alike and yet different from the third. The two that he construes as alike may be so indicated by his placing check marks at their intersects. The intersect of the third figure and the construct row is represented by a void, indicating that the contrasting pole of the construct dimension is applicable to that figure.

Suppose the client checks the cells in the Father and Mother columns as incidents but leaves the cell in the Self column as a void. The next step is to have him label the construct which was used as the basis for the sort. Suppose he writes the word *mature* at the head of that row. He construes his parents as 'mature' – whatever that means to him. Next he is asked to label the contrasting pole of the construct, the one which is relatively applicable to the Self figure. Perhaps he writes the word *childish.* We infer then that he considers his parents as 'mature' and himself as relatively 'childish'; and that these terms personally represent for him the contrasting poles of a relevant construct dimension. Thus each construct in the grid is produced from the client's repertory primarily on the basis of its applicability to a prescribed trio of figures.

Lyle has proposed that the pole which represents the similarity of the two 'like' figures be called the *emergent* pole and the contrasting pole be called the *implicit* pole. He believes that emergence and implicitness have important implications for clinical diagnosis and for understanding the client's value system. We shall adopt Lyle's terminology and, when appropriate, refer to the poles of constructs produced on the Rep Test in these terms.

After the client has labelled the emergent pole of his construct and its contrast, the implicit pole, he is asked to consider each of the other figures and indicate, with an appropriate check mark, the individuals to whom the emergent pole is relatively applicable. Thus the construct, while selected for its applicability to a prescribed trio of figures, is subsequently considered in relationship to all the remaining figures listed along the margin of the grid. When all the sorts are completed the client has produced a protocol in which he has labelled both the emergent and the implicit poles of each construct and has indicated the incidents, by means of check marks, where the emergent poles apply to figures.

Some clients produce a protocol in which the grid is marked mostly with incidents. For them the emergent poles tend to be applicable to a majority of the figures in the sample. Other clients, perhaps more discriminating in their selection of emergent constructs, produce a protocol composed of very few incidents. While the clinical study of Repertory Grids has not yet progressed very far, our experience suggests that there are important differences between such clients.

An illustrative protocol is shown in Figure 6.1.

3. Assumptions

The Repertory Grid is an approach to relationships which has many possible applications. We have offered an illustration involving personal constructs along one margin and figures along another. But other kinds of data may be entered in the margins. For example, one may place behaviours along one margin and occasions along the other; one may place experiences along one margin and culturally prescribed constructs along another; or one may set up some other combination of axes. The possibilities of marginal entries are almost unlimited. Indeed, if one has a mind to do so, one may build a three-dimensional grid. The writer can say, however, on the basis of a moderate amount of experience that a three-dimensional grid is a formidable undertaking.

a. Representative figures. When the Repertory Grid is used as a framework for the Rep Test it is important for the psychologist to be aware of certain assumptions which he must make. First he must assume that the sample of figures is representative of those around whom the client must structure his life role. But it is not enough to say that the sample must be representative – it must be representative with respect to certain dimensions. It is only as a sample is representative along essential dimensional lines that it can be called representative of a population – but this is no place to launch a discussion of sampling theory from the standpoint of constructive alternativism! What we must assume here is simply that the figures elicited by the Role Title List are representative of those with whom the client must interact and that the dimensions of their representation are relevant to those lines along which he has chosen to structure his life role.

b. Representative sorts. Here again one must assume that the sorting problems proposed for the client are representative of those with which he must deal in structuring his life role. This does not necessarily mean that he must meet all three figures in the same social situation at the same time; it means, rather, that the trio calls for the kind of discrimination which invokes one of the personal dimensions in terms of which his psychological space is structured.

1 Self	2 Mother	3 Father	4 Brother	5 Sister	6 Spouse	7 Ex-flame	8 Pal	9 Ex-pal	10 Rejecting Person	11 Pitied Person	12 Threatening Person	13 Attractive Person	14 Accepted Teacher	15 Rejected Teacher	16 Boss	17 Successful Person	18 Happy Person	19 Ethical Person	SORT NO.	CONSTRUCTS: EMERGENT POLE	CONSTRUCTS: IMPLICIT POLE
						√			√		√					⊗	⊗	O	1	*Don't believe in God*	*Very religious*
			√	√			√						⊗	⊗	O	√			2	*Same sort of education*	*Complete different education*
√		√	√	√	√			√	⊗	O	√	⊗	√			√			3	*Not athletic*	*Athletic*
	√				⊗	⊗	O					√							4	*Both girls*	*A boy*
√	⊗	⊗	O	√	√		√						√	√	√	√	√	√	5	*Parents*	*Ideas different*
			√	O			√						⊗	√			⊗		6	*Understand me better*	*Don't understand at all*
	⊗	√	√					O					⊗	√	√			√	7	*Teach the right thing*	*Teach the wrong thing*
	√	O	√										√		⊗	⊗	√	√	8	*Achieved a lot*	*Hasn't achieved a lot*
			⊗	√			√		O				√	⊗	√	√			9	*Higher education*	*No education*
				⊗		√			⊗					O					10	*Don't like other people*	*Like other people*
√	√	√		⊗	√		√			O	√		√	√		√	√	⊗	11	*More religious*	*Not religious*
√	√	√	⊗			√	√	O	√	√	⊗	√	√	√	√	√	√	√	12	*Believe in higher education*	*Not believing in too much education*
	√		√		O				√	√	⊗		√		√		⊗		13	*More sociable*	*Not sociable*
	O				⊗	⊗						√							14	*Both girls*	*Not girls*
	√	O			⊗	⊗						√							15	*Both girls*	*Not girls*
√	√	√	√	√			⊗	O				⊗	√	√		√	√	√	16	*Both have high morals*	*Low morals*
⊗			⊗	O	√		√		√		√	√	√	√			√	√	17	*Think alike*	*Think differently*
			√	√										√	⊗	⊗	√	O	18	*Same age*	*Different ages*
	⊗	⊗		√						√	O		√	√	√	√	√	√	19	*Believe the same about me*	*Believe differently about me*
				√		√	⊗	⊗	√	√	√	O							20	*Both friends*	*Not friends*
						O	√						⊗	⊗	√	√	√	√	21	*More understanding*	*Less understanding*
⊗			√		O	√	⊗					√		√		√		√	22	*Both appreciate music*	*Don't understand music*

Figure 6.1 An illustrative protocol

	FAMILY					INTIMATES				VALENCES				AUTHOR-ITIES			VALUES		
	Self	Mother	Father	Brother	Sister	Spouse	Ex-flame	Pal	Ex-pal	Rejecting Person	Pitied Person	Threatening Person	Attractive Person	Accepted Teacher	Rejected Teacher	Boss	Successful Person	Happy Person	Ethical Person
1							√			√		√					⊗	⊗	O
2				√	√			√						⊗	⊗	O	√		
3	√		√	√	√	√			√	⊗	O	√	⊗	√			√		
4		√				⊗	⊗	O					√						
5	√	⊗	⊗	O	√	√		√						√	√	√	√	√	√
6				√	O			√						⊗	√			⊗	
7		⊗	√	√					O					⊗	√	√			√
8		√	O	√										√		⊗	⊗	√	√
9				⊗	√			√		O				√	⊗	√	√		
10					⊗		√			⊗					O				
11	√	√	√		⊗	√		√			O	√		√	√		√	√	⊗
12	√	√	√	⊗			√	√	O	√	√	⊗	√	√	√	√	√	√	√
13		√		√		O				√	√	⊗		√		√		⊗	
14		O				⊗	⊗						√						
15		√	O			⊗	⊗						√						
16	√	√	√	√	√			⊗	O				⊗	√	√		√	√	√
17	⊗			⊗	O	√		√		√		√	√	√	√			√	√
18				√	√										√	⊗	⊗	√	O
19		⊗	⊗		√						√	O		√	√	√	√	√	√
20					√		√	⊗	⊗	√	√	√	O						
21							O	√						⊗	⊗	√	√	√	√
22	⊗			√		O	√	⊗					√		√		√		√
$1t_0$	7	⑩	7	⑫	⑩	7	8	⑪	2	7	4	7	8	⑭	⑬	9	⑬	⑫	⑩
$1t_1$	12	⑬	12	⑰	11	6	3	⑯	5	6	9	8	7	⑲	⑳	⑯	⑯	⑰	⑰
1F	X	X	X	X	X			X						X	X	X	X	X	X
$2t_0$	4	2	2	⑧	4	2	4	⑤	1	⑥	2	⑤	4	⑥	⑥	3	⑥	⑥	3
2F				X				X						X	X			X	
$3t_0$	④	2	2	⑤	2	2	④	3	1	⑥	2	⑤	④	④	3	2	④	④	3
$3t_1$							X			X		X					X	X	
$3t_2$	1	③	1	2	③	1	⑤	2	2	③	③	2	1	1	2	③	③	③	2
3F							X												
$4t_0$	③	1	1	④	1	②	1	②	1	③	1	③	③	③	②	1	②	②	②
4F	X			X		X		X		X		X	X	X	X			X	X
$5t_0$	②	1	1	②	1	1	1	1	1	②	1	②	②	②	1	1	②	1	1
5F	X		X	X	X	X			X	X		X	X	X			X		
6F		X		X						X	X	X		X		X		X	

	Σ	$1t_0$	$1t_1$	1F	$2t_0$	2F	$3t_0$	$3t_1$	$3t_2$	3F	$4t_0$	4F	$5t_0$	5F	6F
1	5	-10	-10	-13	16	11	15	19	14	15//		-11		-10	12
2	6	16	14	13	12	16///				12		-10		10	-10
3	11	-12	-14	10	10	-12	13	-10	-13	-12	13	11	15	19//////	-11
4	4	-11	-11	-14/		10				16///		-11		-11	-10
5	12	14	14	17////		10				-13		10		-11	-12
6	5	15	15	12	14	19//////				13		13		-12	12
7	7	13	15	14/		13				11		-10		-12	12
8	7	15	17	14/		13				11		-10		-12	14/
9	7	15	15	14/		15//				11		-10		-11	10
10	3	-10	-12	-13	12	11	11	15	14	17////		-12		-10	10
11	12	14	12	15//		10				-13		12		10	-12
12	16	10	12	13	-10	-11	12	-11	-10	-15//		12		-11	11
13	8	10	12	-10	13	12	12	12	13	10	10	10	12	-11	19//////
14	3	-12	-12	-15//		11				17////		-10		-10	-11
15	4	-11	-11	-14/		10				16///		-11		-11	-10
16	12	16	14	17////		12				-13		12		10	-12
17	11	11	11	10	12	13	13	-10	-15	-12	17	19//////		11	10
18	6	14	14	13	13	14/				12		-11		-11	11
19	10	14	14	15//		10				-11		-13		-13	11
20	7	-12	-14	-15//		-10				13		-12		-10	-10
21	7	15	17	14/		15//				11		11		-14/	10
22	8	12	12	11	11	12	12	10	-12	12	12	12	12	-11	-14/
$1t_0$		282	292	296		270				288		253		251	254
$1t_1$				42%		29%				38%		21%		20%	21%
1F						(130)				(93)		(52)		(41)	(33)
$2t_0$						(54%)				(40%)		(9%)		(44%)	(74%)

Figure 6.2 Sorting grid

FIG. NO.

22	21	20	19	18	17	16	15	14	13	12	11	10	9	8	7	6	5	4	3	2	1	FIG. NO.		
O		O			O																	1		Se
			O					O							O		O					2		Mo
			O				O							O			O					3		Fa
					O					O			O				O					4		Br
					O						O	O				O						5		Si
O							O	O	O									O				6		Sp
	O						O	O										O				7		XF
O						O												O				8		Pa
						O				O					O							9		XP
																						10	MF	Mi
																						11	MF	MD
																						12	MF	Ne
	O											O	O						O			13	MF	RP
	O	O									O								O			14	MF	PP
			O						O	O												15	MF	UP
		O				O													O			16	MF	AP
															O	O				O		17	MF	AT
												O	O							O		18	MF	RT
				O										O						O		19	MF	Bo
				O										O							O	20	MF	SP
									O							O					O	21	MF	HP
				O							O										O	22	MF	EP
22	21	20	19	18	17	16	15	14	13	12	11	10	9	8	7	6	5	4	3	2	1	SORT NO.		

Name

Number

Date

Construct

Contrast

CONCEPTUAL GRID

CONCEPTUAL GRID OVERLAY SHEET – FIGURE LIST

1. Write your own name in the first blank here.
2. Write your mother's first name here. If you grew up with a stepmother, write her name instead.
3. Write your father's name here. If you grew up with a stepfather, write his name instead.
4. Write the name of your brother who is nearest your own age. If you had no brother, write the name of a boy near your own age who was most like a brother to you during your early teens.
5. Write the name of your sister who is nearest your own age. If you had no sister, write the name of a girl near your own age who was most like a sister to you during your early teens.

*FROM THIS POINT ON DO NOT REPEAT ANY NAMES. IF A PERSON HAS ALREADY BEEN LISTED, SIMPLY MAKE A SECOND CHOICE.

6. Your wife (or husband) or, if you are not married, your closest present girl (boy) friend.
7. Your closest girl (boy) friend immediately preceding the person mentioned above.
8. Your closest present friend of the same sex as yourself.
9. A person of the same sex as yourself whom you once thought was a close friend but in whom you were badly disappointed later.
10. The minister, priest, or rabbi with whom you would be most willing to talk over your personal feelings about religion.
11. Your physician.
12. The present neighbor whom you know best.
13. A person with whom you have been associated who, for some unexplained reason, appeared to dislike you.
14. A person whom you would most like to help or for whom you feel sorry.
15. A person with whom you usually feel most uncomfortable.
16. A person whom you have recently met whom you would like to know better.
17. The teacher who influenced you most when you were in your teens.
18. The teacher whose point of view you have found most objectionable.
19. An employer, supervisor, or officer under whom you served during a period of great stress.
20. The most successful person whom you know personally.
21. The happiest person whom you know personally.
22. The person known to you personally who appears to meet the highest ethical standards.

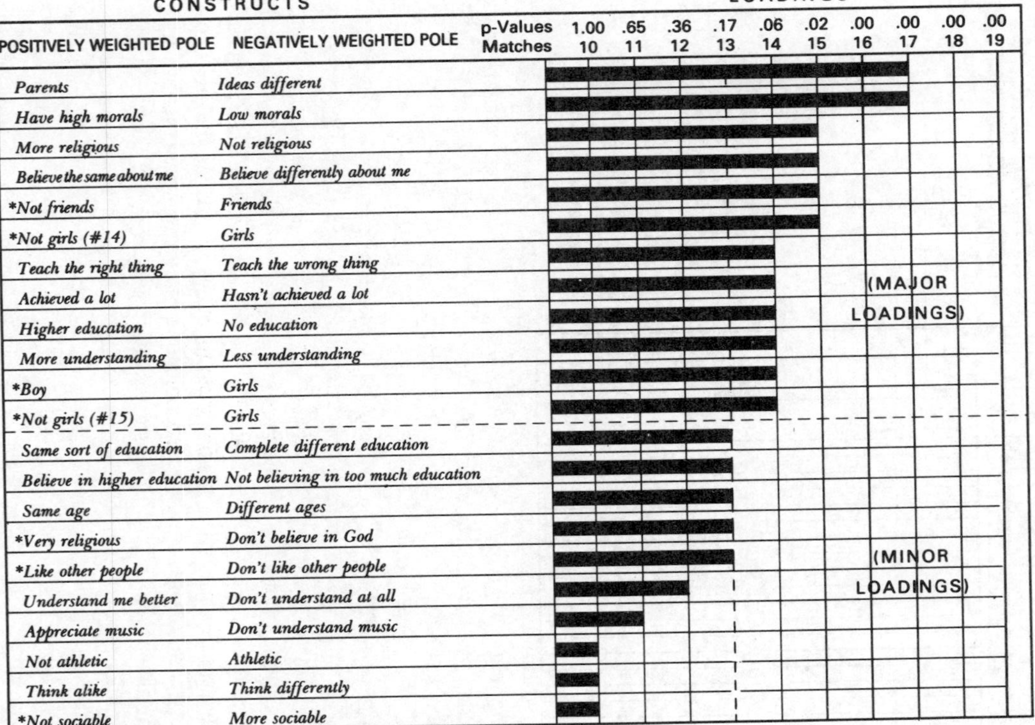

CONSTRUCTS
LOADINGS
POSITIVELY WEIGHTED POLE
NEGATIVELY WEIGHTED POLE
p-Values
Matches
1.00 .65 .36 .17 .06 .02 .00 .00 .00 .00
10 11 12 13 14 15 16 17 18 19
Parents
Ideas different
Have high morals
Low morals
More religious
Not religious
Believe the same about me
Believe differently about me
*Not friends
Friends
*Not girls (#14)
Girls
Teach the right thing
Teach the wrong thing
Achieved a lot
Hasn't achieved a lot
Higher education
No education
More understanding
Less understanding
*Boy
Girls
*Not girls (#15)
Girls
Same sort of education
Complete different education
Believe in higher education
Not believing in too much education
Same age
Different ages
*Very religious
Don't believe in God
*Like other people
Don't like other people
Understand me better
Don't understand at all
Appreciate music
Don't understand music
Not athletic
Athletic
Think alike
Think differently
*Not sociable
More sociable
(MAJOR LOADINGS)
(MINOR LOADINGS)
* Reflected constructs

Figure 6.3 Composition of the first construct factor, case A

POSITIVELY LOADED FIGURES	NUMBER OF INCIDENTS 12 11 10 9 8 7 6	NUMBER OF VOIDS 7 8 9 10 11 12	NEGATIVELY LOADED FIGURES
Accepted Teacher			*Ex-flame*
Rejected Teacher			*Attractive Person*
Ethical Person			*Spouse*
Boss			*Ex-pal*
Successful Person			*Rejecting Person*
Happy Person			*Pitied Person*
Father			*Threatening Person*
Brother			
Sister			
Pal			
Self			
Mother			

Figure 6.3a Composition of the first factor in terms of figures

c. Accessibility. One must assume – or hope – that one's client is sufficiently accessible to apply one's constructs to the paper and pencil task. Not all clients can do this. The names and words on the test form may fail to represent for him the figures and the sorts which they are supposed to represent. He may see the task, rather, as one of making marks or as one of pleasing the examiner.

d. Stability of conception. One must assume that the client does not shift ground between writing his emergent poles and listing his implicit poles. When a client does shift ground he gives the examiner what are essentially the emergent poles of two different construct dimensions. There are various clinical reasons for his doing this, which we shall not attempt to mention here.

e. Range of convenience. The assumption which is specific to the Grid Form of the test is that all the figures fall within the range of convenience of all the constructs. This assumption is implied when we insist on interpreting a void as specifying the implicit pole of the personal construct. This may not be a good assumption in all cases; it may be that the client has left a void at a certain intersect simply because the construct does not seem to apply, one way or the other, to this particular figure. Some of the writer's colleagues have proposed that the grid be marked in such a way as to avoid this assumption. For example, the client may be asked to mark a plus when the emergent pole of the construct applies, a minus when the implicit pole applies, and leave a void when the figure falls outside the construct's range of convenience. This would make the type of factorial analysis which is proposed later in this chapter considerably more difficult, though not

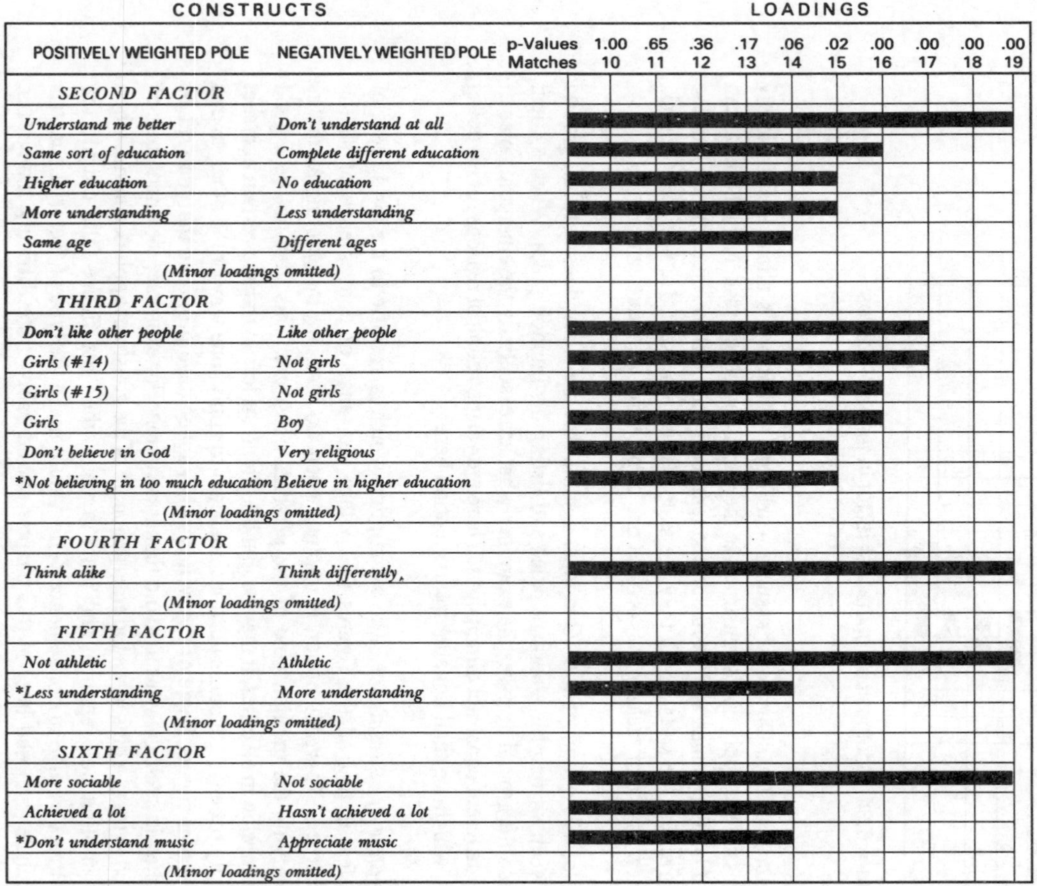

CONSTRUCTS		LOADINGS										
POSITIVELY WEIGHTED POLE	NEGATIVELY WEIGHTED POLE	p-Values Matches	1.00 10	.65 11	.36 12	.17 13	.06 14	.02 15	.00 16	.00 17	.00 18	.00 19
SECOND FACTOR												
Understand me better	*Don't understand at all*											
Same sort of education	*Complete different education*											
Higher education	*No education*											
More understanding	*Less understanding*											
Same age	*Different ages*											
(Minor loadings omitted)												
THIRD FACTOR												
Don't like other people	*Like other people*											
Girls (#14)	*Not girls*											
Girls (#15)	*Not girls*											
Girls	*Boy*											
Don't believe in God	*Very religious*											
**Not believing in too much education*	*Believe in higher education*											
(Minor loadings omitted)												
FOURTH FACTOR												
Think alike	*Think differently*											
(Minor loadings omitted)												
FIFTH FACTOR												
Not athletic	*Athletic*											
**Less understanding*	*More understanding*											
(Minor loadings omitted)												
SIXTH FACTOR												
More sociable	*Not sociable*											
Achieved a lot	*Hasn't achieved a lot*											
**Don't understand music*	*Appreciate music*											
(Minor loadings omitted)												

**Reflected constructs*

Figure 6.4 Major compositions of the second to sixth construct factors, case A

impossible. It would also suggest that the clinician should not interpret any of the constructs as having submerged ends – applications which the client does not admit to using.

f. Word labels. One assumption, which is quite important in the ordinary forms of the Rep Test, becomes less crucial in the Grid Form of the test. That is the assumption that the client's word labels for his constructs mean what the examiner thinks they mean. The use of the grid permits the psychologist to make a rather extensive analysis of the protocol without once looking at the terms which the client has employed. It is this advantage that argues strongly for the use of the grid, both in clinical settings and in research.

4. Illustrative Grid Form of the Rep Test

The current Grid Form of the Rep Test comprises three parts: (1) a sheet of instructions *(herewith)*, (2) a list of titles, and (3) a sorting grid.

Role Construct Repertory Rest (Rep Test)

Instructions

14–12–53

This test comprises three parts: (1) Conceptual Grid, (2) Conceptual Grid Overlay Sheet, and (3) this set of instructions. The test is designed to help the examiner to understand you and some of the people who have played a part in your life.

1. Start with the Overlay Sheet. Beginning with your own name, write the first names of the persons described. Write their names in the blanks provided. If you cannot remember a person's name, write his last name or something about him which will clearly bring to your mind the person's identity. You may keep this Overlay Sheet. The examiner will be interested only in what you write on the Grid.
2. Next, lay the Overlay Sheet sidewise across the top of the Grid so that the numbered blanks correspond to the numbered columns in the Grid. Note that the letters 'M' and 'F' appear at the heads of columns 10 to 22 inclusive. If the person whose name appears at the top of column 10 is a man, encircle the 'M'; if it is a woman, encircle the 'F'. Do the same in the remaining columns.
3. Now move the Overlay Sheet down on the Grid until it is just above the first row of squares. Note that the three squares at the extreme right have circles in them. This means that you are first to consider the three people whose names appear on your Overlay Sheet in the last three columns – columns 20, 21, and 22. Think about these three people. Are two of them *alike in some important way that distinguishes them from the third person?*

Keep thinking about them until you remember the important way in which two of them are alike and which sets them off from the third person.

When you have decided which two it is, and the important way in which they are alike, put an 'X' in the two circles corresponding to the two who are alike. Do not put any mark in the third circle.

Now write in the blank under 'Construct' the word or short phrase that tells how these two are alike.

Next write in the blank under 'Contrast' what you consider to be the opposite of this characteristic.

4. Now consider each of the other nineteen persons whose names appear at the heads of columns 1 to 19. In addition to the persons whom you have marked with a 'X', which ones also have this important characteristic? Put a check mark (✓) – not an 'X' – under the name of each other person who has this important characteristic.
5. Now slide the Overlay Sheet down to the second row. Think about persons number 17, 18, and 19 – the three who have circles under their names. In what important way are two of these distinguished from the third? Put 'Xs' in the circles to show which two are alike. Write the 'Construct' and the 'Contrast' in the blanks at the right just as you did before. Then consider the other sixteen persons. Check (✓) the ones who also have the characteristic you have noted.
6. Complete the test in the way you have done the first two rows. Write your name and the date on the Test Sheet and give it to the examiner. You may keep or destroy the other two sheets.

4. Rationale of titles and sorts

For the sake of brevity the titles are referred to, respectively, as follows:

Self
1. Self

Family
2. Mother
3. Father
4. Brother
5. Sister

Intimates
6. Spouse
7. Ex-flame
8. Pal
9. Ex-pal

Situationals
10. Minister
11. Physician
12. Neighbour

Valencies
13. Rejecting Person
14. Pitied Person
15. Threatening Person
16. Attractive Person

Authorities
17. Accepted Teacher
18. Rejected Teacher
19. Boss

Values
20. Successful Person
21. Happy Person
22. Ethical Person

Six of the seven groupings of the figures are taken into account in setting up the prescribed sorts.

The sorts are arranged into three brackets; sorts 1–5 being based on figures within a group. For example, sort 1 is based on the three figures in the Value Group; sort 2 is based on the three figures in the Authority Group; and so on. Sorts 6–13 involve three different figures from three different groups. Sorts 14–22 involve two figures from the same group and one from another group.

In the first bracket of sorts the client is somewhat more likely to produce constructs which follow along the lines of similarity and contrast suggested by the titles within a group – for example the Successful and Happy figures may both be construed 'happy'. However, the client is immediately confronted with the task of naming his contrast and applying it to the Ethical figure. It is at this point that the clinician becomes particularly interested in seeing how the client carries through his dimensional structure. Must he see the person whom he nominated as ethical as one who is relatively unhappy?

In the second bracket of sorts the client is more likely to draw his constructs along the lines of the manifest intergroup similarities and differences. In sort 8, for example, he may draw upon the idea that members of his family are more likely to understand him. In the third bracket of sorts the client is confronted with more searching problems, some of them involving the self, and some inviting comparisons between figures in manifestly contrasting roles.

We may take up the rationale of each sort as follows:

Sort 1: Value Sort. The client is asked to compare and contrast representatives of success, happiness, and ethics.

Sort 2: Authority Sort. The client is asked to compare and contrast a person whose ideas he accepted, a person whose ideas he rejected, even though he was expected to accept them, and a person whose support was badly needed at some period in his life.

Sort 3: Valency Sort. The client is asked to compare and contrast a person whose rejection of him he cannot quite understand, a person whom he thinks needs him, and a person whom he does not really know well but whom he thinks he would like to know better. All three of these are somewhat phantom figures and one may expect that in interpreting them the client relies heavily upon projected attitudes.

Sort 4: Intimacy Sort. This is a more difficult sort involving the Spouse, the Ex-flame, and the Pal. It tends to bring out features of personal conflict, both between the client's attitude towards two intimate figures of the opposite sex and an intimate figure of the same sex. (It is interesting to note how the client who produced our sample protocol had to break down into concretism in this sort.)

Sort 5: Family Sort. This sort involves the Father, Mother, and Brother figures. It is an invitation to form a construct which governs the client's relationship within his family.

Sort 6: Sister Sort. This is an invitation to construe a Sister figure. It provides an opportunity to see the Sister as like the Accepted Teacher and in contrast to the Happy Person, like the Happy Person and in contrast to the Accepted Teacher or in contrast to both of them.

Sort 7: Mother Sort. Here the comparison figures are the person in whom the client was once disillusioned and the person whose teaching was highly acceptable.

Sort 8: Father Sort. Here the comparison figures are the Boss and the Successful Person.

Sort 9: Brother Sort. The comparison figures are the person who appeared to reject the client and the teacher whom the client himself rejected.

Sort 10: Sister Sort. The comparison figures are the same as for the Brother sort.

Sort 11: Kindliness Sort. The Sister, Pitied Person, and Ethical Person are thrown into context.

Sort 12: Threat Sort. The client has an opportunity to construe threat in the context of the Brother, Ex-pal, and Threatening Person.

Sort 13: Spouse Sort. The Spouse figure is compared and contrasted with the Threatening Person and the Happy Person.

Sort 14: Mating Sort I. The Mother is placed in context with the Spouse and the Ex-flame.

Sort 15: Mating Sort II. The Father is placed in a similar context.

Sort 16: Companionship Sort. The Pal, Ex-pal, and Attractive Person are placed in context.

Sort 17: Sibling Sort. The Self, Brother, and Sister are compared and contrasted.

Sort 18: Achievement Sort. The Boss, Successful Person, and Ethical Person are placed in context.

Sort 19: Parental Preference Sort.

The Mother and Father are placed in context with the Threatening Person.

Sort 20: Need Sort. The Self is compared and contrasted with the Pitied Person and the Attractive Person. This gives the clinician an opportunity to study the relatively subjective and objective reference which the client gives to his personal needs.

Sort 21: Compensatory Sort. By placing the Ex-flame, the Rejecting Person, and the Pitied Person in the same context the clinician can sometimes get some understanding of how the client reacts to the loss of relationship.

Sort 22: Identification Sort. This is a crucial sort. It involves the Self, the Spouse, and the Pal. From it one sometimes gains an understanding of the client's domestic difficulties.

B. The factorial analysis of psychological space

6. Types of constructs

Let us examine the protocol shown in Figure 6.1 and see what we may learn from it regarding the subject's psychological space. What reference axes does he use? With what kinds of people is his world populated? These questions raise some important theoretical issues. Can we, as rank outsiders, crawl into this subject's skin and peep out at the world through his eyes? Perhaps not. But it should be possible to derive data from his protocol which can be meaningfully perceived within our own personal construct systems.

The kind of data we lift from the realm of the individual has a great deal to do with the kind of generalizations we are able to make regarding groups of individuals. What we lift can range all the way from muscle twitches to philosophical systems. If we lift muscle twitches we need only compare and contrast the muscle twitch of this person with the muscle twitch of that person and the muscle twitch of yonder person, and so on. But if we lift this person's whole philosophical system as a single datum, we are suddenly confronted with the breath-taking task of plotting it on continua with the philosophies of our other acquaintances. Does any of us have reference axes for such an undertaking?

a. The clinician's reference axes. Before we give a negative answer to such a question let us consider the relationship between a psychotherapist and his client. While successful psychotherapy apparently does not always require that the psychotherapist know what he is doing, it does seem that a better job might be accomplished in those instances when he does have an overview of his client's personal-construct system. Indeed some therapists do appear to have a pretty good set of reference axes against which to plot the complex outlooks of their clients. Let us therefore not give up too rapidly the hope that systematic methodologies can be developed for comparing and contrasting the psychological space structures of different persons.

Let us consider further the protocol shown in Figure 6.1 and see how we may analyse the particular set of reference axes our subject has used to plot his interpersonal relationships. Let us note, particularly, the constructs which he has invoked, and the ways in which he has drawn the contrasts between emergent and implicit poles. The term he has listed for the contrast side of his first construct is 'Very Religious'. This seems reasonable. Yet we must not jump to conclusions as to what he means before we have done what we can to make sure that we understand how it fits into the system as a whole.

b. Types of constructs used. As we go down his list of constructs it appears that some of them are situational rather than social or psychological in nature. This may be important. Rohrer's analysis of personal constructs showed that hospitalized patients who exhibit more 'psychological' constructs, as contrasted with 'physical-situational' constructs after they had been in the hospital for a time; this might not have been expected. Shoemaker has developed Rohrer's categories into five classes which yield a somewhat higher interjudge agreement. However, the purpose of this discussion is not to follow up Rohrer's and Shoemaker's interesting line of inquiry.

While some of our own subject's constructs appear to be situational in nature, it is possible that he actually applies them in a relatively abstract manner. We can also be alert to the possibility that constructs that appear to be duplicates of one another – for example, numbers 4, 14, and 15 – may be applied in different ways. Indeed numbers 14 and 15 apparently are applied differently. In the case of number 14 the mother is one of the 'Not girls', perhaps in the sense that she is not young, while in the case of number 15 the mother is one of the 'Both girls', perhaps in the sense that she is feminine. Another interesting feature of the protocol is the apparent fact that the person he named as the Sister was a male. We know that this subject does not have a sister and so it was necessary for him to select the name of someone 'who has played the part of such a sister'. There are other interesting features of the protocol which stand out when one inspects it from a clinical point of view but, again, let us pass up these lines of inquiry in order to follow one more interesting still.

c. Psychological space. If we look upon our subject's list of constructs as a set of reference axes with respect to which he plots the behaviour of those persons with whom he lives, we are immediately confronted with a notion of *psychological space.* Perhaps this is the sort of thing that Osgood calls 'semantic space', although it is more likely similar to Lewin's 'life space', since it is structured in terms of the subject's personal set of axes.

Now we can start asking ourselves certain types of questions about this subject's psychological space. What do we want to know? If he is one of many applicants for a position, we may want to compare him with the other applicants or with people who are already productively employed in such a position. We may want to predict how he will perform in a job situation. If he is a client undergoing psychotherapy, we will phrase our questions somewhat differently; for example, we will want to know what hypotheses the therapist should explore during his interviews. We will also want to know what alternatives this client is likely to see open to him if he should happen to be prodded into a premature decision, either by anxiety or by the exhortations of an overeager therapist. Certainly a test used in a clinical setting must meet certain practical issues which need not be met by a personnel test.

d. Emerging evidence. Some of the questions which arise when the Rep Test is used in a clinical setting have already been given tentative answers. Hunt found (1) that the number of constructs produced by a subject tends to be quite limited, (2) that a subject tends to give the same constructs on another occasion and with another set of role titles, and (3) that the test–retest reliability tends to be about the same for college students as for hospitalized patients. Shoemaker found that, under certain conditions of administration, the test protocol could be reliably matched with a subject's performance in five minutes of role playing. Landfield has shown that those personal axes with respect to which a subject perceives himself as moving and developing are those which reveal the lines along which he can feel personally threatened by other people. Poch has shown that certain types of experience produce a kind of rotation of personal axes, a conclusion which has important implications for therapy. Hamilton's study clearly indicated that Rep Test types of protocols could be reliably matched with Thematic Apperception Test types of protocols. Each of these studies involved rather extensive investigations; but, for our present purposes, these simple summary statements suffice to indicate the kind of evidence which is accumulating.

7. *Factor analysis of Rep Test protocol*

Is this subject's system of coordinate axes as complex as it would appear from an initial inspection of his test protocol? This question suggests factor analysis, and it is the type of question which led Levy and Dugan to undertake the laborious task of factorizing four different protocols by conventional procedures. Their exploratory study indicated that, regardless of the variety of words used by their subjects, the protocols tended to be factorially simple, in some cases reducible to two factors. The protocols analysed by Levy and Dugan involved fifteen sorts, hence required the computation of 105 correlation coefficients from each protocol before factor analysis could be begun. Even if tetrachoric *r*s were employed the amount of labour would prohibit the use of such a procedure in most clinical settings.

a. Simplified approach. Is there a simpler way to factorize a person's psychological space? After some exploration we have turned to what is essentially a nonparametric solution to the problem. It gives essentially the same answer that conventional factorial methods yield and in such a small fraction of the time that the method is quite feasible for clinical use. Essentially the method involves a form of scanning, analogous to that used in electronic computing machines. The procedure can be demonstrated on our sample protocol.

In Figure 6.1 the grid of nineteen figures and twenty-two constructs contains 418 cells, some of which contain check marks and some of which do not. In each row the incidents indicate those figures to which the construct applies and the voids indicate those figures to which the contrast to the construct is relatively applicable. Our data are therefore dichotomized with respect to each construct. If we wished, we could compute the 231 tetrachoric correlation coefficients between the twenty-two variables and proceed with a standard factor analysis. Or, if we preferred, we could do a transposed factor analysis and find loadings upon each of the nineteen figures. This would involve computing the 171 tetrachoric correlation coefficients between the nineteen figures. It would bear a relationship to the factorization of constructs analogous to that which the *Q-technique* bears to the *R-technique* in conventional factor analysis. At first glance the two methods may appear to be analogous to the *P*- and *O-techniques* described by R. Cattell, but that is not exactly correct. True, we have a problem of factorization of data taken from one individual but, unlike the *P*- or *O*-problem, we are not dealing precisely with trends or with a time sequence.

The method of factor analysis of Rep Test protocol which we have devised does not involve the computation of tetrachoric *r*s. Since the sum of the intersects in any two rows is always the same, we may simply count matchings of incidents and voids between any two rows. The number of matched pairs of intersects gives us a measure of the relationship (not a correlation coefficient) between the two variables represented by the rows. Moreover, the significance of the matching can be computed by a *p-value* (level of statistical significance) determined even more appropriately than in the case of a correlation coefficient.

b. First trial factor. The first step is to add the incidents in each column. In the sample protocol these totals are shown in the first row (1t) at the bottom of the grid in Figure 6.2. This gives us a trial basis for determining the nature of the most general factor or *row pattern* whose incidents and voids will match the greatest possible number of the 418 cells in the grid. This first trial factor (1t) is to be dichotomized. We therefore select the nine or ten (approximately half) largest of the column totals to represent the incident side of the trial factor, leaving the others to represent the void side of the trial factor. In our example these larger totals are encircled. It is as if we had set up a new hypothetical construct, a number 23, which appears as an incident in each of these columns and as a void in each of the others. We can treat this row as a scanning pattern and proceed, row by row, to see how well such a hypothetical construct would match each of the subject's constructs.

Before we do this, however, let us see how many of the 418 cells in the whole grid our trial construct will match. From the total of the individual construct incidents in the nine columns selected we can see that 1t will match incident with incident 105 times. By adding the incidents in all of the other ten columns and subtracting from the total number of intersects in all of those columns we can discover how many matchings of voids our 1t construct will provide. This gives a figure of 154 for void matchings or a total of 259 intersects matched out of the 418 in the grid. This is not a particularly impressive total, but reflection (interchanging *construct* and *contrast*) may increase this figure considerably. We shall see.

c. Scanning technique. A good technique at this point is to take a sheet of graph paper and lay the edge of it just under the row of incident totals. Mark an 'X' on the edge of the graph paper immediately under each of the encircled totals. Now slide the edge of the graph paper up to the top row of the grid. Starting with this top row (construct number 1), count the number of incidents appearing above the 'Xs' on the graph paper and add the number of voids appearing above blank spaces. In the first two this total is nine. Since chance matching would give us a figure of *nine and a half* (one half of nineteen), this first construct is obviously slightly negative correlated with our trial factor. We therefore subtract nine from nineteen and write *minus ten* in the first column marked $1t_0$ at the right of the grid.

d. Reflection. The next row gives us a total of sixteen matchings with our trial factor – well beyond what would be expected by chance. This personal construct is obviously highly matched with our trial factor. The procedure is continued through the twenty-two rows. Seven of the rows yield negative relationships. We shall therefore *reflect* these variables. After reflection we shall be able to match 282 of the 418 intersects with this pattern. (Note the arithmetic total of column $1t_0$.)

Since we are to reflect the constructs in the seven rows which yielded negative loadings, we should see what effect this has upon the incident totals at the bottom of the columns. The easiest way to make the correction is to use a piece of graph paper again. One may slide it across the grid from left to right after having marked *minuses* on the edge next to the rows to be reflected. Starting with the first column one finds that a void appears in the first column beside the minus. Since that row is being reflected, this means that the total of incidents in the first column should be increased by one. An incident appears opposite the next minus in row 3. This has the effect of decreasing by one the total of incidents in the first column. Continuing on down the column we find the total of seven incidents should be corrected to twelve when the reflections are taken into account. This number now appears in the second row of totals ($1t_1$). The other columns are corrected similarly.

e. Second trial scanning pattern. We may now re-consider our general factor. The Boss column now has one of the larger totals and the Sister column may be dropped from the incident list. Using a piece of graph paper as before, we may recompute the factor loadings on each of the twenty-two construct variables. These loadings appear in column $1t_1$ at the right of the grid. We need not concern ourselves with the reflections in counting the matches since we automatically convert any loading below *nine and a half* to a negative value by subtracting it from *nineteen*. It will be noted that the same constructs carry negative loadings as those we found on the trial run. Occasionally new negative loadings appear following reflection. When that occurs we must reflect additional rows.

f. Maximizing the algebraic loadings. Our second trial scanning pattern has boosted the total number of matches in the 418 cells of the grid to 290. We can do better than this. We have been using a nine incident scanning pattern for our two trial factors, since nine is approximately half of the nineteen cells in each row. This number of incidents in the trial scanning pattern tends to maximize the possibility of turning up negative totals at the ends of the rows. This we want in order to determine where our reflections should be.

Since we now appear to have our reflections taken care of, we next take a look at our scanning pattern to make sure that we have the optimal number of incidents in it. There are twenty-two cells in each column. We can see that the *algebraic* total of matches will be maximized if we use a scanning pattern with incidents in each column where the total is eleven or twelve or more. If no new negative signs turn up at the ends of our rows when we scan with such a pattern, we can be reasonably sure that we have developed a highly generalized scanning pattern.

The row marked 1F at the bottom of the grid contains the pattern which should maximize the algebraic total of the entries in column 1F at the right of the grid. The arithmetic sum of matches for the 418 cells of the grid has now climbed to 296. However, we face a new problem. The loading in Row 3 has switched back to a positive sign. Shall we rectify the reflection we have given it? In our original computation we did this and found that it made no difference, so the additional columns of computation are not shown in our illustration.

g. How general is our first factor? Our method of computation is one of successive approximations. It provides us with a scanning pattern that is optimal, or very nearly so. Occasionally a somewhat better scanning pattern can be developed. In the sample protocol we have discovered a scanning pattern that matches 298 cells – two more than the one shown in the illustration. However, the increased generality is scarcely worth bothering about and, besides, the method we have shown is comparatively simple.

h. Other generalized factors. As one works with conceptual grids one soon discovers there are numerous variations of the optimal scanning pattern that also have high generality. One should not look upon one's computations as revealing a hidden factor lurking in the protocol so much as simply the development of an economical and convenient way of representing the client's construct system.

i. Determining the level of significance. The level of significance of the loadings we have computed may be obtained by expanding the binomial $(p + q)^n$. These values are shown in Table 6.1. This gives us the probability that any number of matchings may be obtained by chance. We find our probability values (p-values) by reading down the left hand margin of the table until we come to '19', the number of cells in a row of this particular grid. At the right, on a line with '19', are the p-values for various possible numbers of matches.

Since we automatically consider any value of less than *ten* as being reflected, we may say that the chances of matching ten or more cells is perfect (p equals 1.00). The p-value for the fourteen matches found in the second row is 0.06, and so on. In order to show graphically where the loadings of this first factor are found, we have marked fourteen correct matchings with one vertical bar, fifteen with two bars, and so on. By referring to the list of this subject's personal constructs we see that the first factor now appears to be one which is most heavily loaded upon the subject's personal constructs of 'Parents' and 'Both have high morals'. This is also a loading on 'Understand me better', 'Teach the right thing', and so on. See Figure 6.3.

We may now set a fiducial limit upon what we shall consider an adequate loading of a factor upon a construct. For our purposes a 0.06 level seems appropriate. If we insisted on a more rigorous level we would probably come out with more factors than we care to deal with. Twelve of the constructs out of the twenty-two

Table 6.1 p-values for numbers of cell matches

No. of cells in row	Number of matches (arithmetic)																					
	1	2	3	4	5	6	7	8	9	10	11	12	13	14	15	16	17	18	19	20	21	22
1	1.00																					
2	1.00	.50																				
3		1.00	.25	*																		
4		1.00	.62	.12																		
5			1.00	.37	.06																	
6			1.00	.69	.22	.03																
7				1.00	.45	.12	.02															
8				1.00	.73	.29	.07	.01														
9					1.00	.51	.18	.04	.00													
10					1.00	.75	.34	.11	.02	.00												
11						1.00	.55	.23	.07	.01	.00											
12						1.00	.77	.39	.15	.04	.00	.00										
13							1.00	.58	.27	.09	.02	.00	.00									
14							1.00	.79	.42	.18	.06	.01	.00	.00								
15								1.00	.61	.30	.12	.04	.01	.00	.00							
16								1.00	.80	.45	.21	.08	.02	.00	.00	.00						
17									1.00	.63	.33	.14	.05	.01	.00	.00	.00					
18									1.00	.81	.48	.24	.10	.03	.01	.00	.00	.00				
19										1.00	.65	.36	.17	.06	.02	.00	.00	.00	.00			
20										1.00	.82	.50	.26	.12	.04	.01	.00	.00	.00	.00		
21											1.00	.66	.38	.19	.08	.03	.01	.00	.00	.00	.00	
22											1.00	.83	.52	.29	.13 *	.05	.02	.00	.00	.00	.00	.00

Note: *Boundary of fiducial limit, p = .10

carry this great a load. Our first factor, therefore, seems to be quite general. See Figures 6.3 and 6.3a.

j. Naming the factor. We may pause to see what two figures seem to be the best representatives of the poles of the factor. The Rejected Teacher scores incidents twenty out of twenty-two times on this construct. This suggests that the subject construed the Rejected Teacher as one which called for a person who may have been hard to accept at first but who may eventually have been admired and accepted. The contrast end of the construct seems best to be represented by the Ex-flame figure.

k. Extraction of a second factor. Our next task is to see whether we can extract a second general factor from the residuals. If we accept the loadings on the twelve rows as adequately explaining them, we may develop a new factor to fit the remaining rows. Using the edge of a sheet of graph paper again we can mark crosses next to the rows which are to be considered in forming the new factor. Incident totals for each of the columns – with these rows only taken into account – can be added up. These totals are shown at the bottom in the row marked '$2t_0$'. A $2t_0$ trial factor is set up and its matchings in the residual rows entered in the column at the right of the grid marked '$2t_0$'. No minus signs appear, so we could, if we wished, accept the trial scanning pattern.

l. Rotating the second factor to gain psychological meaning. Let us have a look at this second factor and see whether it is something we can consider to be psychologically meaningful. After all, it is one thing to express our subject's personal-construct system in a mathematical manner and quite another to subsume it within our own personal-construct system in a way which will enable us to deal with him psychotherapeutically. We note that $2t_0$ carries only two loadings (out of the ten) which meet our fiducial limits. The heaviest loading is on the construct 'Don't Believe in God'. The other loading is on 'Understand Me Better'. Before we conclude that the subject's own belief in God is something that must be understood as an essential part of himself, let us examine the factor in a more literal fashion. From a psychotherapeutic point of view we may wish specifically to know what the subject means by being understood. In order to rotate the axis all the way in this direction let us simply scan the whole grid with the pattern of 'Understand Me Better *versus* Don't Understand at All'. The loadings are shown in Column 2F. See, also, Figure 6.4.

m. Third factor. We may turn now to the extraction of a third factor. As before, only the residual rows are considered in determining whether reflection is necessary. A series of reflections brings us to the loadings shown in Column 3F. Figure 6.4 shows the composition of this factor graphically.

n. Remaining factors. We now repeat our procedure and seek to find a factor which will best match the patterns in the four rows which have as yet carried no significant loadings. The results shown in the column headed '$4t_0$' do not look very encouraging, so again we extract a unique factor from the residual pool. We could scan the grid with any one of the four patterns. Construct Number Seventeen looks like it was worth trying. The loadings are shown in the next column. A similar procedure is used in arriving at the Factors 5F and 6F.

o. Generality of the factors. It is interesting to note what proportion of the grid is matched by each of the factors we have induced. The number of intersects matched by each factor is shown at the bottom of the factor columns. Factor 1F, for example, matches 296 of the 418 intersects. While this represents seventy-one per cent of the intersects, we should probably make a correction for chance matchings. We may use the old familiar formula of 'rights minus wrongs'. This gives us a corrected figure of forty-two per cent 'nonchance' matchings.

p. Orthogonality of the factors. We may ask ourselves how much overlap there is between the six factors in terms of which we have chosen to interpret our subject's protocol. A check (computation not shown) shows that none of the matchings among the factorial scanning patterns reaches the fiducial limit we have set for statistical significance. The average number of matches is eleven and a half, exactly what one would expect from chance.

q. Special problems. There are alternative methods of inducing the factors. If the protocol contains relatively few incidents, it may be desirable to use scanning patterns containing proportionally fewer incidents. For example, if a protocol shows incidents in 150 or the 418 cells, we may use a scanning pattern containing only seven incidents – an equivalent proportion of the nineteen cells in a row. In cases where several rows are reflected, this proportion may change markedly.

Another problem arises in cases where the client has checked nearly all or almost none of the intersects in a row. Consider, for example, the twelfth row in the sample protocol. This row contains sixteen incidents. If one constructed a scanning pattern composed entirely of incidents or entirely of voids, he could secure sixteen – or minus sixteen – matchings of intersects. Does this mean that such a scanning pattern achieves spurious loadings on such rows?

r. The nonparametric nature of the analysis. Here we have to take account of the kind of factorial analysis which we are performing. Basically this is a nonparametric method; that is to say, it is based upon dichotomies rather than parameters or scales. The intersects in the scanning pattern either match or do not match the intersects in each of the respective rows. The factor which most economically represents a group of rows actually represents them in two ways, with respect to matchings of voids and incidents and with respect to the absolute proportion of voids and incidents. If it did only the former, it would be essentially a parametric factorial representation of the rows. But the factor is also balanced off proportionately in the same way the rows are. If a row contains seventeen incidents and two voids, the factor must not only tend to match incident with incident and void with void but it must also, in order to be significantly loaded on that row, carry a similar proportion of incidents and voids, say sixteen incidents and three voids or, perhaps, eighteen incidents and one void. The factor is not like a sliding scale which may be moved from side to side along the row; it is not equivalent to the factors one obtains by conventional factorial analysis. Indeed, for our purposes, it is even better suited to the kind of factorial representation we need to induce in order to understand the client's protocol.

We could digress at this moment and point out that the nonparametric method of factor analysis which we have proposed is quite in harmony with the conceptual system of the psychology of personal constructs. Our psychological system is itself a dichotomized system and it seems altogether appropriate that our mathematical methods should be based on a similar kind of reasoning.

If one discovers that the protocol which he is about to analyse contains several rows in which there are large numbers of incidents or large numbers of voids, he may decide that it is expedient to build his first factor in terms of an all-void scanning pattern. Such a pattern will show, for a grid having nineteen cells to the row, significant (fourteen or more) positive loadings on all rows in which there are fourteen or more voids and significant negative loadings on all rows having fourteen or more incidents. This amounts to pulling these lopsided constructs out of the grid before proceeding with the analysis.

As we shall indicate later, the grid procedure can be used in a great many different ways. This technique of lifting out the lopsided rows at the outset is more likely to be useful in connection with some of these other procedures than it is in the factorial analysis of Rep Test protocol.

s. Normality factors. When one uses this technique one needs to take some care in determining what the lopsided factor shall be considered to be. About the only conclusion one can safely reach is that one has extracted a *normality* factor. One's factor is loaded on all those rows in which the figures are quite unevenly divided. For example, if it is loaded on all those rows which have fourteen or more incidents out of a possible nineteen, it may be thought to represent rows in which a clear majority of the figures fall one way or the other. About all one can say of such a factor, then, is that it represents what is normal versus what is abnormal, or what is commonly found as against what is rarely found among the figures.

t. Sharpening factors. There is another interesting technical problem which should be mentioned – although we do not intend to take up space in this book to discuss all the issues which arise in connection with this factorial procedure. Sometimes one finds that the first factor one extracts is too 'flat' to carry psychological significance. For example, in the sample protocol the first factor has loadings on twelve different constructs. This makes it somewhat difficult to conceptualize, although the high loadings on numbers 5 and 16 suggest that it has to do with the morality of the subject's parents. We might be able to sharpen up the factor by building a scanning pattern to fit these twelve rows only, disregarding for the moment the other rows. We could set a higher fiducial limit on accepting the loadings of such a factor and thus, perhaps, we would come out with two factors instead of the single 1F shown in our computations.

8. Analysis of protocol in terms of generalized figures

There are other ways in which the grid can be scanned in order to superimpose our own structure on the subject's structure of his psychological space. Instead of scanning row by row, we may scan the protocol column by column, just as one does in inverted factor analysis. As before, this is done primarily on a basis of mathematical economy. But there is less occasion to rotate the axes to provide psychologically meaningful factors than there is in the case of the factorial analysis of the constructs. Each figure in the grid is a palpable person and it is entirely plausible that any two of them might be construed as similar. The work sheet is shown in Figure 6.5. The procedure is analogous to the one we used in dealing with Figure 6.2 except that what we did to columns we now do to rows, and what we did to rows we now do to columns. The first hypothetical generalized figure that emerges is shown in the row headed, '1P'. See also Figure 6.6. This figure has eight significant loadings.

The second generalized figure which emerges is a composite of the Self, the Pal, and, to some extent, the Father, the Rejected Teacher, and the Successful Person. See Figure 6.7. A check indicates some similarity to the pattern of loadings we obtained for the first generalized figure. The third figure gives us some trouble with reflections but, after two trials, the pattern of minus signs settles down and we get the figure 3P with significant loadings on six titles.

In 3P we have, for the first time, two significant negative loadings. This makes it somewhat more difficult to interpret. As we construe our subject's conceptualization of figures through mathematical analysis we see him inverting the Brother and the Boss. We may interpret this as an induced generalized figure which is largely the antithesis of these two figures.

Figure 4P completes the factorization of the grid.

If we wish to find some way of describing the generalized figures we have abstracted from the protocol, we may turn again to the scanning of rows. We may build a row pattern from the high *versus* low positive values of the loadings of 1P. For example, the incidents in this pattern are located by encircled numbers in Row 1P. Using this pattern to scan the grid, row by row, we get the construct loadings shown in the column headed 'F_{1P}' in Figure 6.5. This gives us some adjectives with which to describe 1P. Columns F_{2P} and F_{3P} give us similar information for the 2P and 3P hypothetical figures.

9. Self-identifications

Current personality theories place varying emphasis upon such factorial representations as 'the self', 'father figure', 'sex role', 'authority figure', and so on. Through the use of the Repertory Grid it is possible to discover, in the individual case, just how generalized such figure factors are. Let us examine our protocol and see what degree of generalization such figures have in this client's life.

a. The self as a factor. We may scan the protocol, column by column, in terms of the Self column as shown in Figure 6.8. When we do so we obtain the figure loadings as shown in row 1D, and in Figure 6.9. The statistically significant loadings are underscored. Of course, the Self receives the maximum loadings of twenty-two. Moreover, the Self pattern permits the explanation of 277 out of 418 cells of the grid (33 per cent 'true' matches). The next heaviest loading is on the Father figure and there are heavy loadings on the Attractive Person, Ethical Person, Spouse, Pal, and Threatening Person.

It is interesting to see how the Self compares with the factorial figures extracted by the procedure shown in Figures 6.5 and 6.9. The computations are not shown, but there are nineteen out of twenty-two possible matches with the first generalized figure – a proportion which more than reaches statistical significance (see Table 6.1). There are twenty out of twenty-two possible matches with the second generalized figure – a proportion which exceeds the 0.001 level of statistical significance (see Table 6.1). While our evidence is still fragmentary, this finding is somewhat consistent with the clinical observations of Mahrer, who reports that the second hypothetical role characterization produced by a hospitalized patient is much more likely to represent himself than is his first production. It also seems to tally with Bieri's finding that after a brief social interaction with a person one is likely to construe that person as more like himself than one did at the beginning of the interaction. It may well be that the Self is ordinarily a kind of latent figure pattern which is held in reserve.

b. Shadow figures. What does a negative loading mean? It will be noted that there are a few instances in the figure analysis of this protocol where significant negative loadings on figures are produced. When it occurred before, we reflected the column, although there are logical grounds for not reflecting columns as we reflect rows in the grid. Our experience indicates that this phenomenon does not occur frequently and that, when it does, it is likely to be in a protocol, such as this, which is produced by a person who seems to have very poor understandings of interpersonal relationships.

In scanning the protocol with the Self column we obtain a single negative loading on Boss. Again, does this mean that we must stand the Boss on his head in order to get at the relationship of the figure to the subject's Self? Or has the subject done this to his boss?

We must remember that, as far as our grid is concerned, the column headed Boss is simply a column of the subject's responses. It is not the boss in the flesh. What we have here is the fact that the subject identifies himself slightly with a percept of an 'anti-boss' or a shadow of the boss. We do not know whether the subject is actually acquainted with someone who corresponds to the 'shadow boss' or not. Indeed, it would be interesting to know whether one could ever identify with a shadow figure if it did not exist as a person in his perceptual field. But again we have no time just now to explore this by-path!

We have noted, in passing, that the Self figure matches 277 of the 418 cells, a proportion far beyond chance. Is this something generally to be expected? What is its significance for transference in therapy? Do men usually identify with father figures, and women with mother figures, as the analysts suggest? Do persons with 'sex-role misidentifications' tend to identify with parents of the opposite sex? It should not be hard to find out. But still again we must pass up some interesting issues and stay with our methodological topic.

c. Comparison of two women. It is interesting to contrast the identifications of different clients. Figure 6.10 shows a comparison of two college women, cases B and C. Case B is that of a young woman whose early life had prevented her from putting down roots. She had had relatively few peer relationships and her present boy friend represented to her the kind of life she had never had. It is not surprising, therefore, to find that she has few strong identifications and that the strongest one, that with her boy friend, is on the basis of a shadow. It is to be noted also that most of the figures she named were females and that she shows some interesting reflections.

Case C is that of another young woman, recently married, who complained that her parents had been overprotective. There was reason to believe that she was working out her problems in a healthy manner. There is a long list of strong identifications, not involving shadow figures.

10. Sex identification

We may examine the case A protocol to see to what extent the masculine–feminine dichotomy appears to match the patterns of response. Suppose we consider the four titles which we might reasonably expect would always elicit the names of female persons and the four titles which might always elicit the names of male persons. These titles are shown in columns 2, 3, 4, 5, 6, 7, 8, and 9. If we scan these eight columns only, row by row, with a pattern composed of incidents in columns 3, 4, 8, and 9 (since our subject is male) and voids in columns 2, 5, 6, and 7, we may get the loadings of each personal construct on this factor. This particular subject, as noted before, appears to have 'pulled a fast one' on us by naming a male in the Sister column in lieu of the sister he did not have. Inspection, however, indicates that the Attractive Person is a female, and so we have taken the liberty of substituting this as the fourth female title. With this revised scanning pattern we get the loadings shown in the first column on the right, MF in Figure 6.8.

We may now treat this first column of loadings as we treated the rows in Figure 6.2. The encircled numbers indicate constructs in which the males tend to be identified with the likeness side of the personal construct and the other numbers indicate the rows in which the males, as contrasted with females, tend to be identified with the contrast side of the construct. We therefore scan the grid, column by column with a hypothetical column which has incidents corresponding to the rows with encircled numbers. The matchings appear as loadings at the feet of the columns. If we set sixteen matchings as the minimum fiducial limit (see Table 6.1, page 208) we find that no figure, including the Self, stands out clearly in this subject's protocol as either masculine or feminine. Incidentally, this analysis of the protocol corresponds to the judgement of the subject's psychotherapist.

Figure 6.11 shows the comparison between sex-role perceptions of the two women whose self-identifications were shown in Figure 6.10. The form of Rep Test which they took provides a more complete definition of the masculine–feminine dimension, since every figure mentioned is identified by the examinee as either male or female.

The first woman sees ten of her figures as significantly loaded on the male–female dimension, though they are not all loaded in the direction one would expect from their sex. The father is seen as the most representatively masculine person. The sister, for example, is seen as having a significant loading on this dimension, but on the feminine side.

The other woman sees her most heavily loaded figures as feminine. Her spouse is not seen as markedly masculine (he is an artist) and neither her mother nor herself is significantly loaded on this dimension. Indeed, only five figures are significantly loaded on her masculine–feminine stereotype.

11. Authority figure

Therapists frequently concern themselves with their clients' 'authority relations' and 'authority figures'. Let us see what subject A's protocol might reveal if we project such a preconceived pattern upon it. The Rep Test is designed with an 'authority figure' grouping comprising the titles of Accepted Teacher, Rejected Teacher, and Boss. Presumably, in addition to the parents, these three persons have clearly stood in an authority relationship to the subject. If we add the incidents in these five columns row by row, we get the totals shown in the column headed 'Ay' in Figure 6.8. We now develop a column pattern from this column as we have done before, and scan the whole grid, column by column. This time, seven of the twenty-two figures stand out significantly. Furthermore, the hypothetical authority figure matches 279 of the 418 cells. It looks now as if we have something here which the therapist might well take into account. Incidentally, this stereotyping of authority patterns was also confirmed by the subject's therapist.

We can try something interesting at this point. Suppose we match the scanning pattern developed for the hypothetical authority figure with that developed for the first generalized figure. There are sixteen out of a possible twenty-two matches, a figure that reaches our fiducial limit.

When we try a similar procedure with the masculine–feminine scanning pattern we find it has a significant negative loading on the third generalized figure. This is not what one would expect in most adults who are undergoing therapy – the expectation would be for a matching on the first generalized figure. But our subject is said by his therapist to be only beginning to construe women with any kind of a coherent pattern, either healthy or otherwise, so our test analysis received some confirmation from clinical sources.

These approaches are only suggestive of the great variety of ways in which the Grid Form of the Rep Test can be subjected to analysis in the light of current personality theories. Yet we have not emphasized the clinical appraisal of verbal protocol in this chapter; nor have we emphasized the significance, personality-wise, of the factors yielded by the analysis. Much, indeed, remains to be learned about the test and its use in a clinical setting.

C. The Conceptual Grid as a generalized model in personality theory

12. What is a person?

We have seen how we may come to have an understanding of a client's outlook on his world of people by making an analysis of the way he builds up cross-references between constructs and figures. We have seen how the constructs may be used to explain figures and how the figures can be used to explain constructs. Each represents a different dimension of generalization: the one more palpable and externalized, the other more portable and subjective.

Presumably the child, as he initially structures his social world, depends more upon figures than upon constructs. But is not a figure itself a matter of construction? Does not the child's mother, for example, become a person in his world to the extent that she represents the intersect of certain personal construct dimensions which he sets up? Some of these dimensions are no more than minor discriminations of what has taken place versus what has not taken place. Yet their point of intersection becomes, in the child's eyes, the Mother figure. It is the permeability of this Mother figure that the child comes to rely upon as he seeks to incorporate new experience within his construct system. Whenever he meets a new individual, his first question may possibly be, 'Is she like my mother or is she in contrast to my mother?'

When the child uses a figure in this manner he actually develops two levels of meaning for *Mother*: the one referring to the actual behaviours of his mother, the other referring to *motherliness*. It is important, both in the study of conceptualization and in psychotherapy, to stand ready to discriminate between these two levels of figure conceptualization. It is especially important for the psychotherapist to be alert as to which he is dealing with, lest his relationship with his client bog down in his own concretism. This is a real problem among psychotherapists, especially among those who follow Freud concretistically with no real appreciation of the propositional use of many Freudian constructs.

Hall, in his excellent exposition, *The Meaning of Dreams*, presents a cognitive theory of dreams which takes account of the differences between figures used as entities and figures used as abstractions. He points out the importance of the therapist's understanding the client's dreams, not in terms of concrete symbols, but in terms of the properties which the dream elements represent. We have tried to say somewhat the same thing in our discussion of the understanding of constructs which have no literal symbols. We have said that the client must often communicate his constructs to us by lining up sample elements in the context instead of wrapping them up for us in terms of symbols. In order to understand him we must induce his constructs from the elements he provides.

In somewhat the same manner, the figures a person construes may become contextual elements in his constructs. They may come to stand for whole constructs in which they are also contextual elements. The Mother figure in the Rep Test protocol may stand for a construct and for an element in that same construct. The construct may be *motherliness*, while the person of Mother may be an element in the construct of *motherliness*.

a. The perceived person as a constructive intersect. From the standpoint of the psychology of personal constructs a person is perceived as the intersect of many personal-construct dimensions. In addition that person may come to represent, as in the case of certain familiar and important figures in the child's life, a dimension of construction in himself. It is in this sense that it is appropriate to factor analyse protocols, as we have done, in terms of factorial figures as well as in terms of factorial constructs. The identity of the factorial figure is expressed in terms of a derived set of incidents and voids, these constituting a mathematical statement of the hypothetical intersect of certain dimensions.

The notion of a person's being the intersect of a number of dimensions may be somewhat difficult to follow. Ordinarily a geometric group of lines is envisioned as having only one possible point of intersection. This is usually considered as the point of their origin. Does this mean that there can be only one real person in our client's world?

Let us keep in mind that we are talking about dimensions rather than lines in space. By a *dimension* we refer to an infinite grouping of lines all of which are parallel to each other. Lines which are not parallel to those in such a given group must necessarily belong to another dimension. Viewed in this manner, it is possible to conceive of an infinite number of dimensional intersects. Hence, our view does allow for many different persons in our client's psychological space.

Now in our psychology of personal constructs the dimensions are dichotomous. This notion is somewhat unconventional also, but altogether plausible. We could say that each line in the dimension has only two points on it. Considering all these two-point lines together, as they compose the dimension, we may say that the dimension has, not two points, but two poles. The pole is the locus of all the corresponding points in the grouping of lines which compose the dimension. We might say that the pole is a hemi-hypersphere, but perhaps such a word is more confusing than helpful.

b. Abstraction of dimensional poles. In order to accept the notion of dichotomous dimensions, rather than insisting on the view that any dimension must be composed of many gradations or scalar values, one must back off and take an abstract rather than a concrete attitude. Imagine that we have a foot ruler in our hand. As we look at its markings it seems obvious that it is a scale composed of many points, not just two. In a concrete sense that is possibly true – at least we shall concede that it is true for the sake of this discussion.

But how do we use the ruler? Suppose we decide to compare the length and width of the sheet of paper on which we are writing. Laying the ruler across the top of the sheet of paper, we find that the right-hand edge of the paper matches up with a point on the ruler which we call 'eight and one half inches'. Next, we lay the ruler along the left-hand side of the paper to check its length. Now the top edge of the paper extends beyond the 'eight and one half inches' point. We have thus applied a construct in the now familiar minimum context of three elements. The *width of the paper* and the *eight and one half inches* are alike in a way which distinguishes them from the *length of the paper*. The dichotomy or cleavage which we have made is one of the *same or more.* In this case the *length of the paper* is *more* and the *eight and one half inches* is the *same* as the *width of the paper*. The basic construction we have placed upon the situation is not that the width of the paper is concretely an 'eight and one half inches' fact – we could have used centimetres and obtained the same answer in different terms – nor is it concretely a certain point on our ruler – we could have used another rule or a plain stick – but that the length of the paper is *more* than the width. The dichotomy is the *same* or *more* pair of alternatives.

It is not our intention to launch into an extended mathematical discussion of the conceptualization of persons at this point. It is probably sufficient to offer this minimal defence of the notion of dichotomized dimensions, similar to the discussion we offered in our initial exposition of the Dichotomy Corollary, as a basis for understanding the construct of *person* within the psychology of personal constructs. When we say that a person is the intersect of many subjective dimensions, we mean, of course, that a person, *as construed by someone* such as ourselves, is a unique combination of dichotomous categorical interpretations.

Sometimes a somewhat similar notion is propounded by psychologists when they say that a person is a carrier of a unique combination of properties. Our only objection to this way of approaching the problem is that it does not take into account either the dimensional nature of the structure which is placed upon the person or the dichotomous nature of the constructs in terms of which the identification is made.

13. The Conceptual Grid

What we have been saying about the construing of persons can be generalized. Basically, construing is simply the erection and application of a system of grids, whereon the intersects between events may be plotted.

We have been talking about one type of grid, the Rep Test Grid. This particular grid is composed of the intersects between certain personal constructs of the person who takes the test and certain representative persons whom he knows. Both his constructs and the persons whom he construes are real events. But they are of somewhat different orders. The person-events are presumably reflections on real events, events which would take place even if the examinee were not alive; but, as far as the grid is concerned, they are themselves really the examinee's own acts of perception. On the other hand, the personal constructs which the examinee weaves through these person-events are also events; but, presumably, neither they nor their possible counterparts would exist if the examinee were not alive. Thus two different orders of events constitute the warp and weft out of which the pattern of the person's social life is woven.

We need only to extend this notion in order to arrive at a view of conceptualization in general. Our conceptualization of *poverty*, of *freedom*, or of *evil*, for example, may be viewed in the same manner. Certain events in our lives may be interwoven with the construct of *poverty*. This and this are *poverty*, while that and that are *not poverty*! These events are represented by *freedom*, while those events are represented by *enslavement*. Here and there we find the *good* which stands out in contrast to the intervening *evil*. It is by such interweaving that both the events of our lives and the constructs we use for dealing with them take on meaning. Each provides operational referrents for the other.

In this chapter we have suggested a type of analysis of Rep Test protocol which transcends both the subject's verbiage and the particular individuals who make up his personal–social milieu. The test protocol can be meaningfully analysed even if one clips off the names from the top of the test blank and the constructs from the side. What we have left is exclusively a geometric or a mathematical structure of the person's psychological space. The grid of intersects is speckled with incidents and voids. Some of the rows tend to match each other and some of the columns are almost alike. Moreover, certain rows are somewhat representative of all the rows, that is, all the constructs – and some of the columns are representative of all the columns – that is, all the figures.

Not only can the grid notion be generalized to all conceptualization, but this mathematical notion can also be generalized. The incidents and voids which populate a grid of intersects provide the binary numerical basis for a mathematics of psychological space. This cybernetic model permits us to scan any grid with a hypothetical scanning pattern and note the concurrences of incidents and voids, row by row or column by column. Thus we may have a mathematical basis for expressing and measuring the perceptual relationships between the events which are uniquely interwoven in any person's psychological space.

14. The mathematics of conceptualization

Scientists often refer to certain pairs or collections of events as 'alike' or 'identical', without bothering to specify just how they are alike. If we wish to be precise in our approach to conceptualization, we must recognize that no two events are ever so exactly alike that they are identical. To claim that they are is to fall into a logical fallacy: there has to be some distinguishing feature between them, else they would not be two separate events in the first place. One might say that if they were perfectly identical there would not be two of them; there would be only one! When we say that two things are 'alike' or 'identical', we obviously mean that they are alike *in some particular way or ways*, but, of course, never in every way.

Conceptualization has to be with the *way* in which certain things as alike. When a scientist, or anyone else for that matter, says that two things are 'alike', he implies that they are alike in some particular way, but that they are not wholly identical. Unless he is careful to specify just what that way is, we can only guess what his conceptualization is.

As we have pointed out in an earlier chapter, however, to say that two things are *alike* is also to imply that they are *different* from certain other things. Their *alikeness* makes no sense unless it also serves to *distinguish* them from certain other things. Thus likeness always implies a difference. The way in which two or more things are alike must necessarily be the way in which they are different from at least one other thing. Similarly, the way in which two things are different must, if it is to make any sense at all, be the way in which at least one of them is *like* a third thing.

Now let us see if we can make this simple! We started out this section by saying that if we claim that two things are 'alike', we obviously mean that they are alike only in a certain respect and that otherwise they are 'different'. For example, we can say that A and B are 'alike', in that they are letters of the alphabet, but that they are obviously 'different' letters. Or, if we want to sharpen our example, we might say that A and A are 'alike', in that they are the 'same' letter of the alphabet, but, of course, that they are obviously two 'different' As. If they were not two different As, about all we could do would be to mumble something about 'A being like itself'. Thus, to say that A and B are 'alike' is to imply that they are otherwise 'different'. This is one way in which likeness logically implies difference.

We have pointed out another way in which an expression of likeness implies a difference. Two paragraphs back we recapitulated some of what we had said in preceding sections about the nature of constructs. When we say that A and B are 'alike', we imply that they are different from another thing. For example, if we say that A and B are alike, in that they are *mathematical constants*, we may imply that they are different from X and Y, which are *mathematical variables*. This is the other way in which a construction of similarity implies difference.

Now we can go on from here. Just as construed similarity between A and B implies both a difference between them *in other respects* and a difference between them and X and Y *in the same respect*, so the construed difference between A and

X implies a similarity between them *in other respects* and a construed similarity between A and B (or X and Y) *in the same respect.*

What we are working up to is this: construing is never a single-dimensional proposition. There are always *the other respects* which are implied in the application of a construct. Therefore, no construct ever stands entirely alone; it makes sense only as it appears in a network. The conceptual grid is a way of representing that network and making it amenable to mathematical analysis.

It may not be immediately clear why this interweaving of construed likenesses and differences, or similarities and contrasts, is a precondition for mathematical analysis. Mathematics is, of course, a conceptual invention of man. It does not refer specifically to any particular class of events – as, for example, physics or sociology does. Rather, it is a rationale of man's thinking about events. Together with philosophy, logic, and so on, mathematics is an abstraction of man's psychological functioning. Its essential relation to psychology should never be overlooked.

As we have pointed out before, when the mathematician *enumerates* he applies a construction of the objects enumerated. Those objects must be conceptually differentiated in order to be enumerated. The objects must also be conceptually synthesized in order that their incorporation into the same numerical sequence can be justified. Moreover, as we have pointed out in the preceding paragraphs of this section, this premathematical conceptualization also calls for an interweaving of other construct dimensions. The conceptual grid, on which this interweaving is represented, is, therefore, a premathematical representation of an individual's psychological space, and it is designed to set the stage for a mathematical analysis of that space. As we see it, it is essentially multidimensional in character. We might even suggest, parenthetically, that the philosopher Herbart was probably struggling with some such problem as this when he arrived at the reluctant conclusion that psychology could never become a science because, among other things, it had only one dimension to work on. One might wonder whether he would have found it necessary to reach such a conclusion if he could have seen personal constructs as dimensions and had toyed with the notion of a conceptual grid.

15. What constitutes degree of similarity?

Scientists often refer to certain pairs of events as if they were naturally similar to each other. Aristotle attempted to use this patent similarity as a basis for classifying events. Classification schemes such as Aristotle's perform an important service for all man's thinking. But on what grounds do we judge the similarity which is the basis of any valid classification?

Our notion of a construct is that it is a *way* in which two or more elements are judged to be alike and, by the same token, different from one or more other elements. Until we discover, or think we have discovered, this way, we have no grounds for construing similarity. The discovery of the way in which two things are alike may turn out to be an undertaking of some considerable size. Sometimes about the best we can do is to say that A and B are alike because they appear at about the same time or in about the same place. This kind of construing by temporal or spatial association may not get us very far. Usually, if we want to do a really good job of predicting or anticipating, we have to abstract some other constructs with which to interlace the events.

But whether we can get no further than time-and-space classifications, or whether we interlace all life's events with a complicated weft of abstractions, the similarities which we are able to see are those which have some basis of pertinence. We do not see merely that some things are similar to each other: we see them only as similar with respect to something! Similarity does not exist, except as it has a reference axis. In this universe of ours it is the job of the perceiver to construct suitable reference axes with respect to which events may be neatly plotted and their outcomes reliably predicted.

a. Subsuming similarities. When we attempt to make a mathematical analysis of psychological space we measure similarity, from our particular point of view, with respect to the construct of *matching* – in other words, how many times incident matches with incident and void matches with void. Our subject, however, sees his similarities in terms of his particular personal constructs. He has his own personal axis system. We, in turn, attempt to subsume it mathematically with ours. If we do a good job, we shall be able to anticipate his behaviour and even establish a socially effective role relationship with him. Moreover, we may be able to make ourselves more predictable for him, and thus help him establish a more effective role relationship with us.

When we approach the problems of classification and association in this manner, our attention is attracted primarily to the constructs which underlie a client's groupings. A client associates two words as belonging together. What does he mean? Shall we say only that they are, for him, 'similar'? Or shall we look for the personal construction which provides the basis of the similarity? If we take this latter tack, we may find that the contrast the client construes between the words is quite as important as the similarity. It may be that the dimension of construction will be more important than the pole. As we shall point out repeatedly in later chapters, this emphasis upon dimensions of conceptualization as well as upon poles is in contrast to the current clinical emphasis upon concretistic groupings of ideas. Indeed, this particular emphasis is one of the principal features of the psychology of personal constructs, when it is applied to problems of psychotherapy and to a client's personal reconstruction of his own life.

b. Bases of similarity. We have been emphasizing the *basis* of similarity; now what about *degree* of similarity? With a conceptual grid it is a relatively simple matter to compute mathematically the degree of similarity between any two objects or between any two constructs. What we have to keep in mind is the point we have just elaborated – that similarity is not just 'similarity' but is similarity with respect to something!

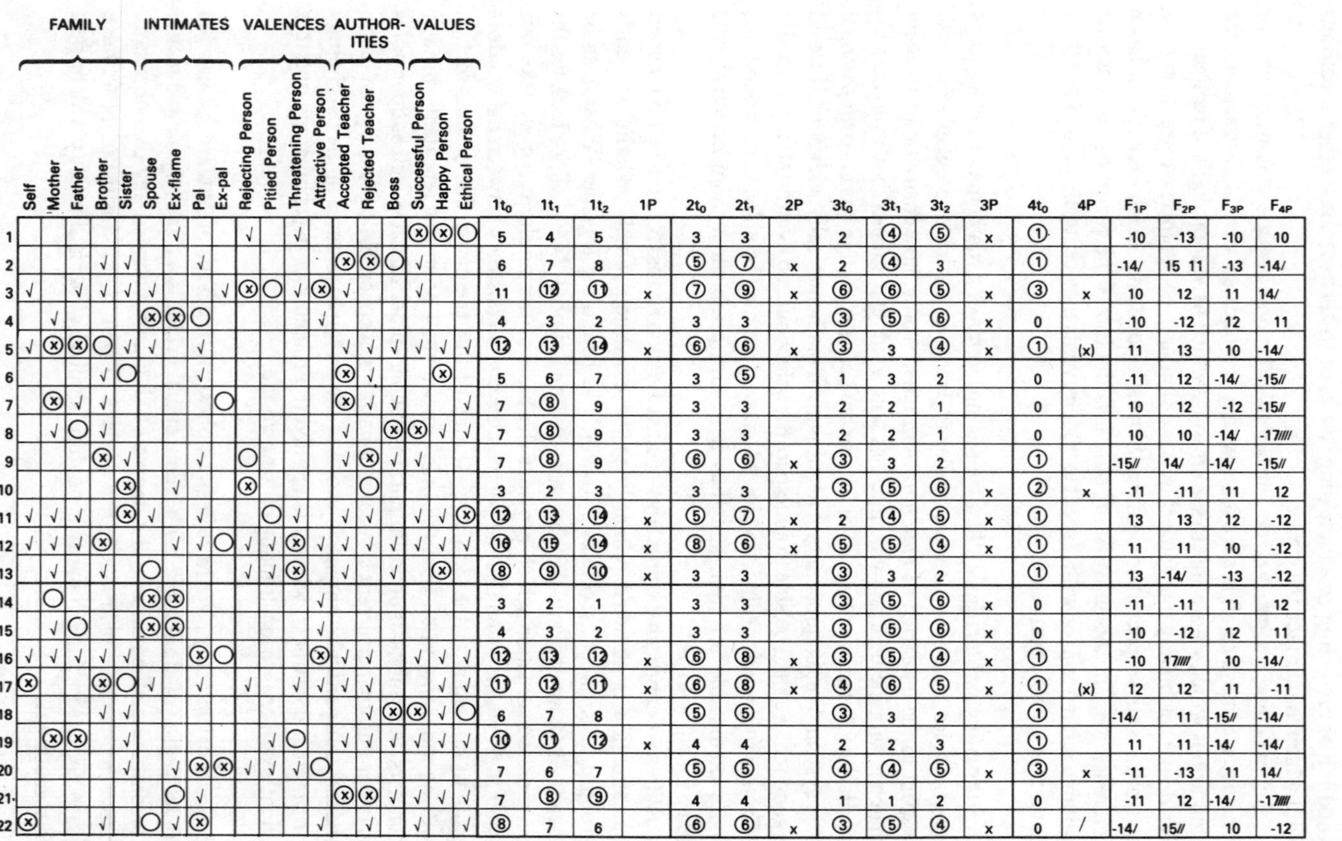

	FAMILY					INTIMATES				VALENCES				AUTHOR-ITIES			VALUES																			
	Self	Mother	Father	Brother	Sister	Spouse	Ex-flame	Pal	Ex-pal	Rejecting Person	Pitied Person	Threatening Person	Attractive Person	Accepted Teacher	Rejected Teacher	Boss	Successful Person	Happy Person	Ethical Person	$1t_0$	$1t_1$	$1t_2$	1P	$2t_0$	$2t_1$	2P	$3t_0$	$3t_1$	$3t_2$	3P	$4t_0$	4P	F_{1P}	F_{2P}	F_{3P}	F_{4P}
1							√			√		√					⊗	⊗	○	5	4	5		3	3		2	④	⑤	x	①		-10	-13	-10	10
2				√	√			√						⊗	⊗	○	√			6	7	8		⑤	⑦	x	2	④	3		①		-14/	15 11	-13	-14/
3	√		√	√	√	√			√	⊗	○	√	⊗	√			√			11	⑫	⑪	x	⑦	⑨	x	⑥	⑥	⑤	x	③	x	10	12	11	14/
4		√				⊗	⊗	○					√							4	3	2		3	3		③	⑤	⑥	x	0		-10	-12	12	11
5	√	⊗	⊗	○	√	√		√						√	√	√	√	√	√	⑫	⑬	⑭	x	⑥	⑥	x	③	3	④	x	①	(x)	11	13	10	-14/
6				√	○			√						⊗	√			⊗		5	6	7		3	⑤		1	3	2		0		-11	12	-14/	-15//
7		⊗	√	√					○					⊗	√	√			√	7	⑧	9		3	3		2	2	1		0		10	12	-12	-15//
8		√	○	√										√		⊗	⊗	√	√	7	⑧	9		3	3		2	2	1		0		10	10	-14/	-17////
9				⊗	√			√		○				√	⊗	√	√			7	⑧	9		⑥	⑥	x	③	3	2		①		-15//	14/	-14/	-15//
10					⊗		√			⊗					○					3	2	3		3	3		③	⑤	⑥	x	②	x	-11	-11	11	12
11	√	√	√		⊗	√		√			○	√		√	√		√	√	⊗	⑫	⑬	⑭	x	⑤	⑦	x	2	④	⑤	x	①		13	13	12	-12
12	√	√	√	⊗			√	√	○	√	√	⊗	√	√	√	√	√	√	√	⑯	⑮	⑭	x	⑧	⑥	x	⑤	⑤	④	x	①		11	11	10	-12
13		√		√		○				√	√	⊗		√		√		⊗		⑧	⑨	⑩	x	3	3		③	3	2		①		13	-14/	-13	-12
14		○				⊗	⊗						√							3	2	1		3	3		③	⑤	⑥	x	0		-11	-11	11	12
15		√	○			⊗	⊗						√							4	3	2		3	3		③	⑤	⑥	x	0		-10	-12	12	11
16	√	√	√	√	√			⊗	○				⊗	√	√		√	√	√	⑫	⑬	⑫	x	⑥	⑧	x	③	⑤	④	x	①		-10	17////	10	-14/
17	⊗			⊗	○	√		√		√		√	√	√	√			√	√	⑪	⑫	⑪	x	⑥	⑧	x	④	⑥	⑤	x	①	(x)	12	12	11	-11
18				√	√										√	⊗	⊗	√	○	6	7	8		⑤	⑤		③	3	2		①		-14/	11	-15//	-14/
19		⊗	⊗		√						√	○		√	√	√	√	√	√	⑩	⑪	⑫	x	4	4		2	2	3		①		11	11	-14/	-14/
20					√		√	⊗	⊗	√	√	√	○							7	6	7		⑤	⑤		④	④	⑤	x	③	x	-11	-13	11	14/
21							○	√						⊗	⊗	√	√	√	√	7	⑧	⑨		4	4		1	1	2		0		-11	12	-14/	-17////
22	⊗			√		○	√	⊗					√		√		√		√	⑧	7	6		⑥	⑥	x	③	⑤	④	x	0	/	-14/	15//	10	-12

Σ	7	10	7	12	10	7	8	11	2	7	4	7	8	14	13	9	13	12	10				
$1t_0$	20	15	18	13	13	14	-13	14	13	14	15	16	15	15	14	12	14	15	17	280			
$1t_1$	15	15	17	14	12	11	-18	13	-12	11	12	13	-12	20	15	17	15	16	18	276			
1P	19	16	19	12	14	15	-14	13	14	15	16	17	14	16	13	13	13	16	16	286	37%		
$2t_0$				15	17	12	-13	18	13	12			13		15	-12	16						
2P	20	11	16	15	15	14	-14	18	13	12	11	14	15	15	16	-12	16	11	15	273	31%	(160)	(32%)
$3t_0$				12	12	13	14		-12	13			16			-13							
$3t_1$				-13	11	14	17		-11	14			17			-20							
3P	16	11	12	-16	11	16	17	12	-11	14	-14	14	17	-15	-15	-18	-12	-13	11	265	27%	(120)	(36%)
$4t_0$						17			11	16													
4P	16	-13	14	-13	15	16	13	12	19	18	15	16	13	-13	-14	-13	-14	-13	11	271	30%	(53)	(61%)

Figure 6.5 Work sheet

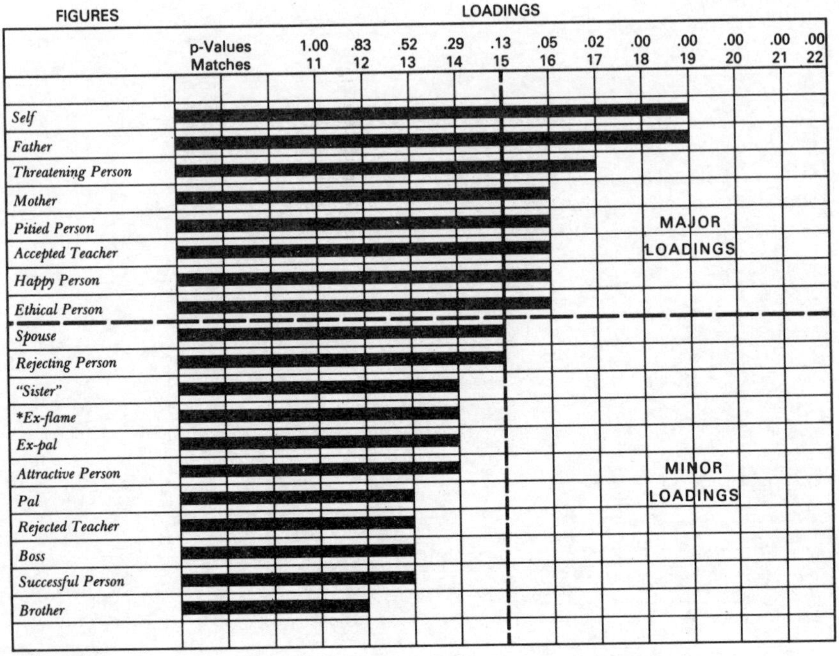

FIGURES

LOADINGS

p-Values	1.00	.83	.52	.29	.13	.05	.02	.00	.00	.00	.00	.00
Matches	11	12	13	14	15	16	17	18	19	20	21	22

Self
Father
Threatening Person
Mother
Pitied Person
Accepted Teacher
Happy Person
Ethical Person
Spouse
Rejecting Person
"Sister"
**Ex-flame*
Ex-pal
Attractive Person
Pal
Rejected Teacher
Boss
Successful Person
Brother

MAJOR LOADINGS

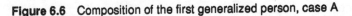

MINOR LOADINGS

* *Shadow figures*

Figure 6.6 Composition of the first generalized person, case A

We can compute the similarity between any two columns or rows on the conceptual grid simply by scanning one with the other in the manner described in connection with the factorial analysis of Rep Test protocol. Suppose, for example, we are dealing with a conceptual grid which shows the interlacing between certain culture-dictated constructs and certain current events reported in the newspapers. Along one margin of the grid we would have the culture-dictated constructs and along the other we would have a listing of the events. The examinee would be asked to fill in the incidents and voids in order to show how he weaves this particular warp with this particular weft.

Now we can compute the similarity between the current events, as he construes them, with the culture-dictated constructs – or his personal facsimiles of them. We may take the column representing event A and scan it with the pattern of incidents and voids representing event B. The number of matches gives us a numerical expression of the degree of subjective similarity between A and B. But we must not overlook one important consideration. This degree of similarity which we have

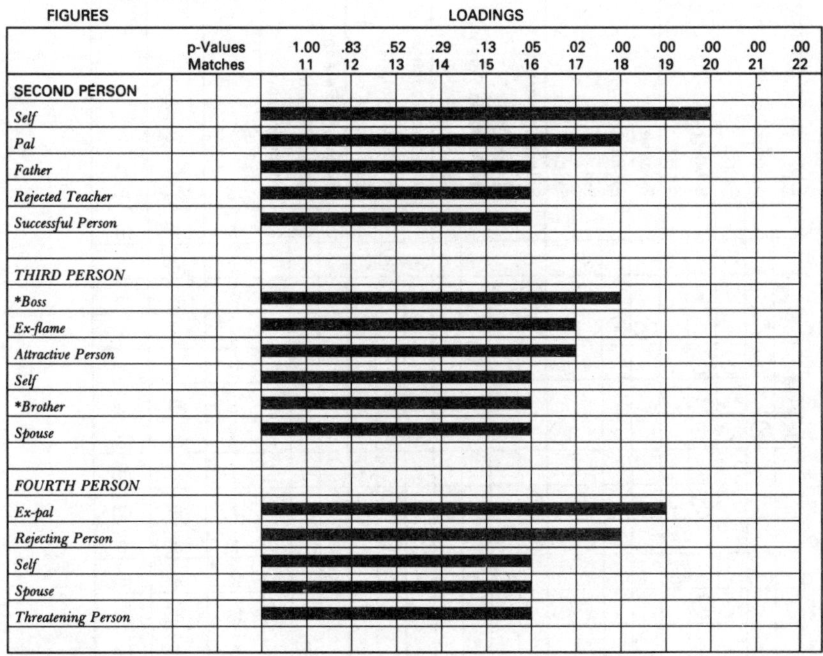

Figure 6.7 Composition of additional generalized figures, case A; significant loadings only

computed is solely *with respect to the specified constructs which are interwoven with events A and B.*

What we have done to columns we can also do to rows. But, again, we must be clear as to the basis of the similarity which we measure mathematically. The degree of matching that we compute between construct X and construct Y is solely *with respect to the specified events which are interwoven by our subject with these constructs.* Given another set of events of perhaps quite a different sort, the subject may weave a somewhat different design, and the pattern of similarities between constructs may turn out differently.

c. Similarity and gradient of generalization. What we have been saying has a bearing on the reasoning of scientists and goes considerably beyond the problem of making a mathematical analysis of a client's psychological space. For example, in setting up laws of generalization, psychologists have hypothesized that, under certain conditions, a subject's learning of certain responses will generalize to other possible responses in proportion to the similarity between the responses. Or, in the

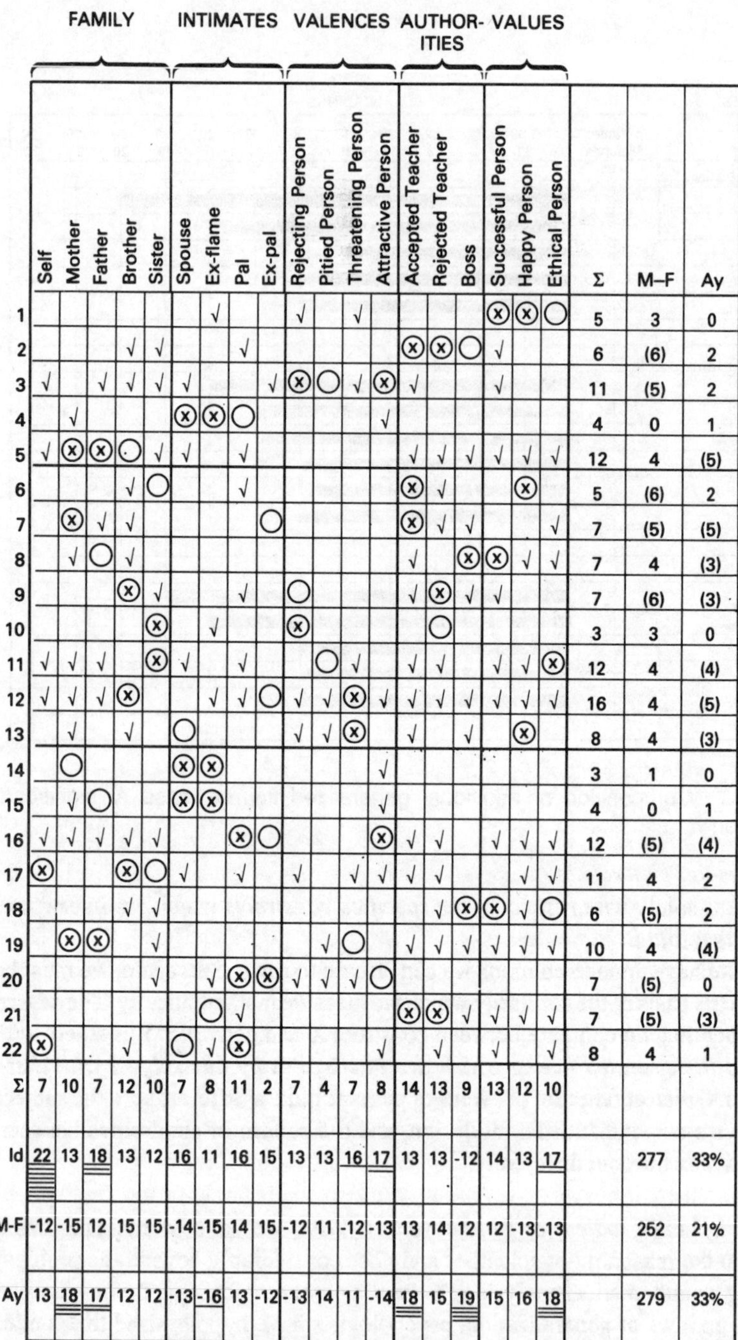

	FAMILY					INTIMATES				VALENCES				AUTHOR-ITIES			VALUES					
	Self	Mother	Father	Brother	Sister	Spouse	Ex-flame	Pal	Ex-pal	Rejecting Person	Pitied Person	Threatening Person	Attractive Person	Accepted Teacher	Rejected Teacher	Boss	Successful Person	Happy Person	Ethical Person	Σ	M–F	Ay
1							√			√		√					⊗	⊗	○	5	3	0
2				√	√			√						⊗	⊗	○	√			6	(6)	2
3	√		√	√	√	√			√	⊗	○	√	⊗	√			√			11	(5)	2
4		√				⊗	⊗	○					√							4	0	1
5	√	⊗	⊗	○	√	√		√						√	√	√	√	√	√	12	4	(5)
6				√	○			√						⊗	√			⊗		5	(6)	2
7		⊗	√	√					○					⊗	√	√			√	7	(5)	(5)
8		√	○	√										√		⊗	⊗	√	√	7	4	(3)
9				⊗	√			√		○				√	⊗	√	√			7	(6)	(3)
10					⊗		√			⊗					○					3	3	0
11	√	√	√		⊗	√		√			○	√		√	√		√	√	⊗	12	4	(4)
12	√	√	√	⊗			√	√	○	√	√	⊗	√	√	√	√	√	√	√	16	4	(5)
13		√		√		○				√	√	⊗		√		√		⊗		8	4	(3)
14		○				⊗	⊗						√							3	1	0
15		√	○			⊗	⊗						√							4	0	1
16	√	√	√	√	√			⊗	○				⊗	√	√		√	√	√	12	(5)	(4)
17	⊗			⊗	○	√		√		√		√	√	√	√			√	√	11	4	2
18				√	√										√	⊗	⊗	√	○	6	(5)	2
19		⊗	⊗		√						√	○		√	√	√	√	√	√	10	4	(4)
20					√		√	⊗	⊗	√	√	√	○							7	(5)	0
21							○	√						⊗	⊗	√	√	√	√	7	(5)	(3)
22	⊗			√		○	√	⊗					√		√		√		√	8	4	1
Σ	7	10	7	12	10	7	8	11	2	7	4	7	8	14	13	9	13	12	10			
Id	22	13	18	13	12	16	11	16	15	13	13	16	17	13	13	-12	14	13	17		277	33%
M-F	-12	-15	12	15	15	-14	-15	14	15	-12	11	-12	-13	13	14	12	12	-13	-13		252	21%
Ay	13	18	17	12	12	-13	-16	13	-12	-13	14	11	-14	18	15	19	15	16	18		279	33%

Figure 6.8 Special identifications, case A

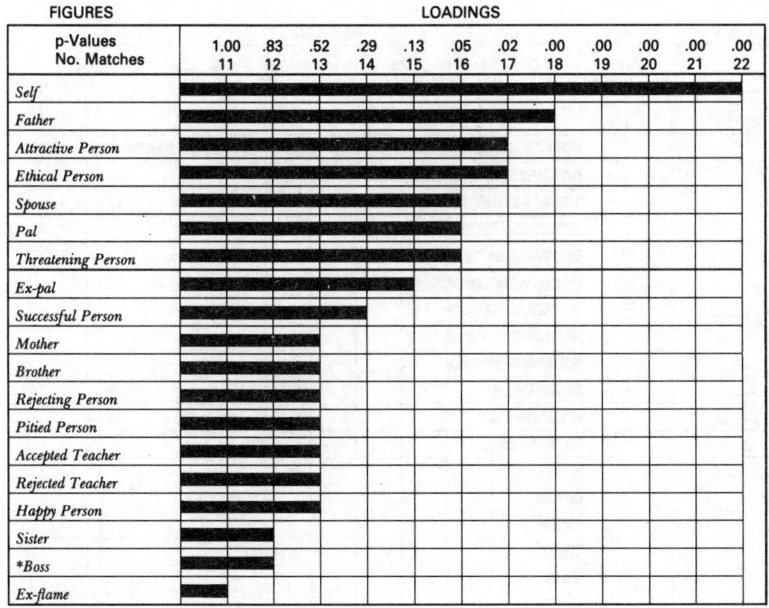

Figure 6.9 Identification loadings, case A

case of *stimulus generalization*, it is hypothesized that a subject will attach a newly learned response to other stimuli in proportion to the relative similarity of the other stimuli to the original stimulus.

But 'similarity' with respect to what? The psychology of personal constructs would lead us to look for the basis of similarity instead of taking it for granted or ignoring it altogether. Moreover, it would seek the basis of similarity in the psychological structure of the particular individual studied and not in an encyclopedia or in the latest book on physiology. Nor would the psychology of personal constructs throw up its hands if the subject of the experiment were unable to communicate his conceptual grid by means of conventionalized symbols. Indeed, theoretically, there is no reason why one could not establish a white rat's individual conceptual grid and from it determine what his generalization gradients might be expected to be.

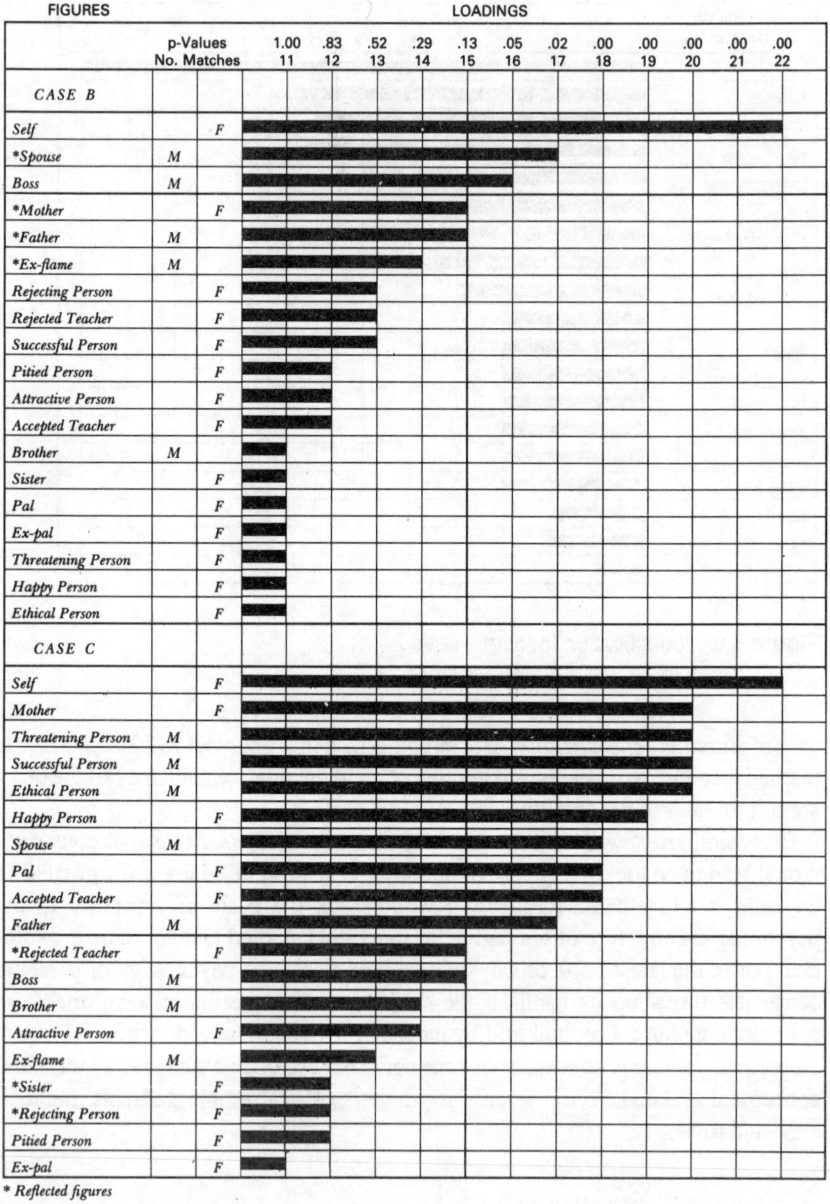

FIGURES			LOADINGS											
	p-Values		1.00	.83	.52	.29	.13	.05	.02	.00	.00	.00	.00	.00
	No. Matches		11	12	13	14	15	16	17	18	19	20	21	22
CASE B														
Self		*F*	■	■	■	■	■	■	■	■	■	■	■	■
**Spouse*	*M*		■	■	■	■	■	■	■					
Boss	*M*		■	■	■	■	■	■						
**Mother*		*F*	■	■	■	■	■							
**Father*	*M*		■	■	■	■	■							
**Ex-flame*	*M*		■	■	■	■								
Rejecting Person		*F*	■	■	■									
Rejected Teacher		*F*	■	■	■									
Successful Person		*F*	■	■	■									
Pitied Person		*F*	■	■										
Attractive Person		*F*	■	■										
Accepted Teacher		*F*	■	■										
Brother	*M*		■											
Sister		*F*	■											
Pal		*F*	■											
Ex-pal		*F*	■											
Threatening Person		*F*	■											
Happy Person		*F*	■											
Ethical Person		*F*	■											
CASE C														
Self		*F*	■	■	■	■	■	■	■	■	■	■	■	■
Mother		*F*	■	■	■	■	■	■	■	■	■	■		
Threatening Person	*M*		■	■	■	■	■	■	■	■	■	■		
Successful Person	*M*		■	■	■	■	■	■	■	■	■	■		
Ethical Person	*M*		■	■	■	■	■	■	■	■	■	■		
Happy Person		*F*	■	■	■	■	■	■	■	■	■			
Spouse	*M*		■	■	■	■	■	■	■	■				
Pal		*F*	■	■	■	■	■	■	■	■				
Accepted Teacher		*F*	■	■	■	■	■	■	■	■				
Father	*M*		■	■	■	■	■	■	■					
**Rejected Teacher*		*F*	■	■	■	■	■							
Boss	*M*		■	■	■	■	■							
Brother	*M*		■	■	■	■								
Attractive Person		*F*	■	■	■	■								
Ex-flame	*M*		■	■	■									
**Sister*		*F*	■	■										
**Rejecting Person*		*F*	■	■										
Pitied Person		*F*	■	■										
Ex-pal		*F*	■											

** Reflected figures*

Figure 6.10 Comparison of the self-identifications of two women

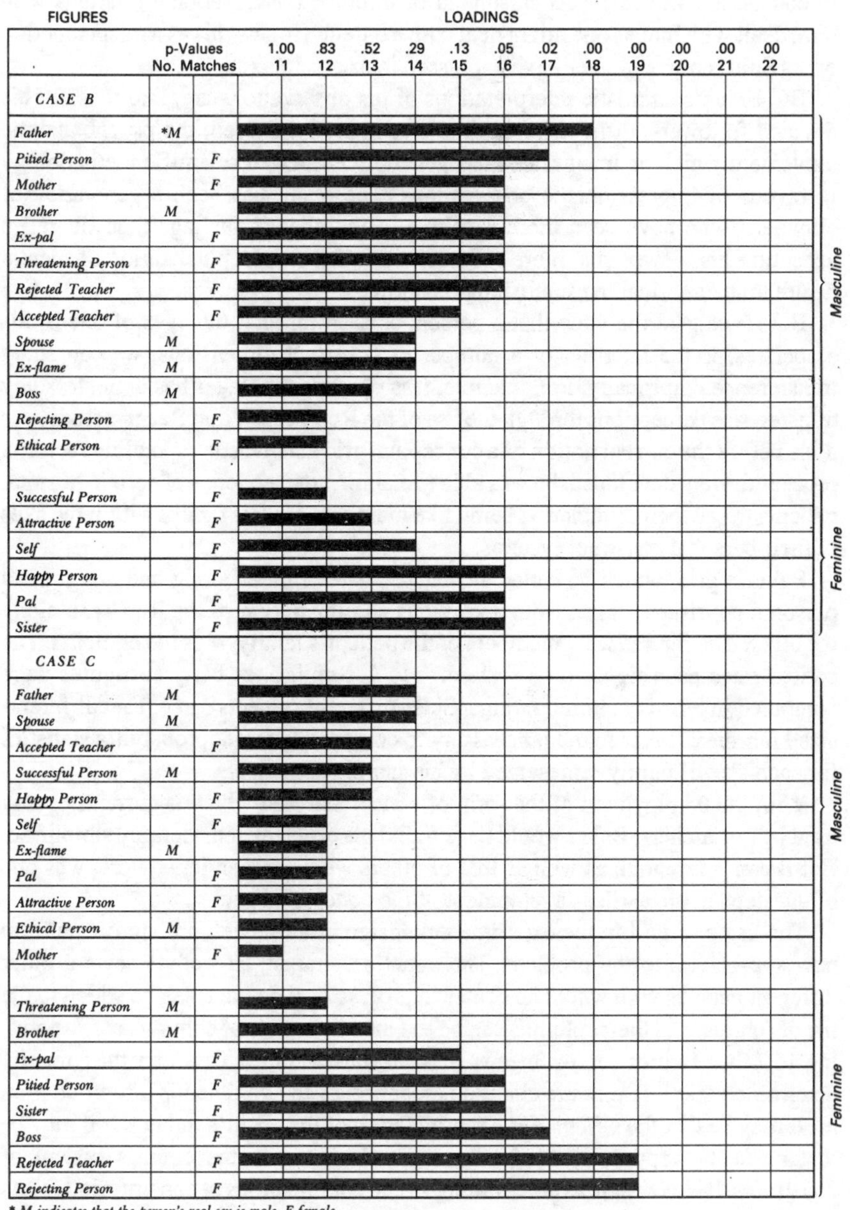

Figure 6.11 Comparison of sex-role perceptions of two women

16. Studies of transference relationships

Among the many astute observations which Freud has recorded are those which deal with what he called 'transference'. Freud clinically observed that his patients, in connection with their establishment of intimate conversational relations with him, dealt with him as one might deal with a parent. He saw this as a misperception or, as Sullivan would later have expressed it, as a parataxia.

But Freud's animistic interpretations of his observations are, like those of his devoted followers, difficult to explore scientifically. Indeed, the psychoanalytic movement which he inaugurated has generally eschewed scientific methodology in favour of impressionistic observations. The result has been a generation of clinicians who have been more sensitive to the client's feelings than liberal in accepting his viewpoints, more rationalistic in their conceptualization of mental health than empirical in establishing its norms.

But if we take the view that a person, as seen through the eyes of one of his associates, is the intersect of a number of construct dimensions, we can study transference empirically. For example, it is possible, as Baker has done, to study transference perceptions through the use of the Rep Test. While Baker's study was done before the current notion of a conceptual grid and the corresponding factorial procedure were developed, he was able to examine the tendency of certain hospital patients to see their clinician as being like members of their family within the axes of their personal construct systems.

Baker's grid, which he called a 'matrix', listed figures along one margin and personal constructs, taken from a previous administration of the Rep Test, along the other. The figures were members of the patient's family, plus the clinician. The patient rated each figure on a scale of 1 to 4. Similarities between figures were computed in terms of similar ratings. Since different subjects came from different-sized families, Baker found it necessary to compute different probability statistics for each size of family represented by his sample of subjects.

With the employment of the form of conceptual grid which is currently being used by researchers, Baker would have found his problem considerably simplified. But Baker's research, as well as that of others we have mentioned here, was one of the steps in the earlier development of the conceptual grid.

The use of a grid in the experimental design of a transference study opens up new approaches to the problem. The client's therapist, as well as several other different persons with whom he comes in professional contact, can be added to the list of figures, and their columns can be scanned by means of columns corresponding to other figures, or by means of factorial columns. One can thus readily determine what it is that the client's perception of the clinician is a reproduction of. It may be that the clinician is a reproduction of the client's father. Or it may be that he is the reproduction of a generalized person in the client's system of constructs. It is as simple as determining which combinations of construct intersects correspond to each other.

In his study Baker observed a tendency for some subjects to perceive the clinician as like some member of his family and for other subjects not to do so. This would not be surprising if it were not for the fact that the distribution was U-shaped rather than bell-shaped. Can it be that some persons tend to approach their clinicians and new acquaintances entirely in terms of generalized figures and others entirely in terms of generalized constructs? Perhaps it may not be too long before we know the answer to this question.

17. Studies of inverted figures

We have already mentioned the problem of interpreting the negative loadings which sometimes appear when one does a figure-factorial analysis of Rep Test protocol. Negative loadings cause us no trouble when we are dealing with the factorial structure of the constructs – but what is the antithesis of a known person in the client's life? Such evidence as we have leads us to suspect that negative loadings on figures indicate that the client does not have a very realistic idea of what his associates are like. Those clients who tend to set up negative loadings appear to be those who lack close relationships with others. The interpretation of these figures is another problem which can readily be brought to some kind of solution.

18. Studies of prescribed constructs

Joyce has used the constructs prescribed in the Minnesota Multiphasic Inventory as the marginal referents for a Repertory Grid. His subjects sorted selected cards from the inventory for themselves and as they thought each of several of their personal associates might sort them. After removing the lopsided rows Joyce was able to extract general and specific factors. The fact that many of the constructs specified in the inventory apparently do not fit the client's personal system makes the factorial analysis of the protocol particularly difficult to interpret.

Lyle selected constructs from a subcultural group and then asked his subjects, who were also members of that group, to use these constructs in classifying persons. This was an incidental methodological feature of his study of 'perceptual defence' from the standpoint of the psychology of personal constructs.

It is possible to use both prescribed constructs and personal constructs in the same grid. The person may take the Rep Test in the usual way and then go on to use certain prescribed construct dimensions in the last few rows of his grid. It then becomes a simple matter of scanning and factor analysis to see what his personal constructs mean, operationally, in terms of the prescribed constructs. Or, perhaps it would be better to say that this provides a way of understanding how he translates the prescribed constructs into the terms of his personal system.

Cravens and Fager have designed studies along these lines. Jones has used the approach to study the various identifications of his subjects. He has also studied the identifications of Japanese students in this manner. Goodrich has used a similar approach to the comparison of constructs.

Another approach is to place the prescribed constructs along one margin of the grid and the client's personal constructs (previously obtained) along the other margin. The client can then indicate the equivalences by checking in the cells. Factorial analysis, both obverse and inverse, may give the experimenter some idea of how the terms structure themselves.

19. Studies of generalization

Bieri, following up Poch's study of changes in constructs occurring after invalidating experience, has used the conceptual grid to study generalization of changes in figures and constructs. By scanning, he established the functional similarity of the subject's constructs and of the subject's figures within the dimensions of the matrix. He then introduced validating and invalidating experiences for the subject with respect to selected constructs and selected figures. Not only could he then study the changes in these constructs and figures, but he could also study the changes in functionally related constructs and figures. The grid gave him an opportunity, usually lacking in other studies of generalization, to measure the amount of similarity between constructs or between figures within the framework of the subject's own personal-construct system and in terms of their functional use.

Incidentally, Bieri's study showed that the gradient of generalization, as measured along the lines of similarity established on a conceptual grid, is by no means smooth. The gradients, both for construct change and for figure change, sloped sharply away from the critical construct or figure, then rose again before tapering away. This suggests a kind of 'framing effect' around constructs and figures which tends to make the generalization skip the adjacent construct or figure and affect, instead, constructs and figures which are somewhat more remote. But our purpose here is to expound a methodology rather than present the various kinds of evidence which the methodology is bringing to bear upon certain psychological issues.

Following Bieri's investigation and recent improvements in conceptual-grid methodology, Levy, who with Dugan was the first to factor analyse Rep Test protocol, has been able to design a series of studies dealing with the properties of personal constructs which make them amenable to modification or change. Such studies have an important bearing upon psychotherapy as it is conceived within the psychology of personal constructs.

20. Relations between situations and figures

Another use of the Repertory Grid has recently been under development by the writer in collaboration with Cromwell, Goodrich, Joyce, Lundy, Miller, Samuels, and Shoemaker. It has to do with an investigation of the client's dependencies: not whether he is strongly dependent or independent, but how he allocates his dependencies, and whom he depends upon for what. Incidentally, from the standpoint of the psychology of personal constructs, the former issue is meaningless, except as it is thrown into a context of situations and figures. Everyone is dependent; the problem is to make appropriate allocations of one's dependencies.

In this development there are two title lists. One refers to situations of different types which the client might be expected to have experienced as stressful. He designates where and when these situations were experienced. The other is a title list calling for figures of the types upon which one ordinarily leans at one time or another in his life. The intersects are checked according to whether or not the client feels that the persons nominated to represent the figures would be potentially helpful in the various specific stressful situations. In this manner one may use the grid to discover those areas of stress in which the client has few human resources and those figures upon whom he is inclined to depend for every conceivable kind of succour. Factorial analyses indicate the ways in which he groups his situations and the ways in which he groups his human resources.

The form of Rep Test grid shown earlier in this chapter can be used for this type of conceptual grid study. The same list of figures can be used and a revised list of instructions can be substituted for the Rep Test instructions. Here are the instructions for such a conceptual grid.

Situational Resources Repertory Test

Instructions

14-12-53

This test is composed of three parts: (1) Conceptual Grid, (2) Conceptual Grid Overlay Sheet, and (3) this set of instructions.

A. Start with the Overlay Sheet. Beginning with your own name write the first names of the persons described in the blanks provided. If you do not remember a person's name write something about him which will help you remember just whom you had in mind.

B. Lay the Overlay Sheet across the top of the grid so that the numbered blanks correspond to the numbered columns in the grid. Note that the letters 'M' and 'F' appear at the heads of Columns 10–22, inclusive. If the person whose name you have written at the top of Column 10 is a man, encircle the 'M', if a woman, encircle the 'F'. Do the same with the remaining columns.

C. The next step is to finish filling out the grid. Everyone faces some personal problems at one time or another in his life. Here are some very general types of problems that everyone comes up against in one way or another.

1. Think of the time in your life when you were most perplexed about what kind of job or vocation you ought to go into. Write the *year* when it happened in the first blank under 'Construct' on the Conceptual Grid. Now write the *place* where it happened, just to the right under 'Contrast'. This is to help you identify the incident later in the test.

Now suppose each of the twenty-two people whose names you have written at the tops of the columns of the grid had been around at that time. Which ones, if any, do you feel you could have turned to for help? Put an 'X' below each of their names in the first row of squares opposite the date and place.

2. Next, think of the time in your life when you had the greatest difficulty understanding how to get along with people of the opposite sex. Write the year and place in the second row. Then put an 'X' in the second row under each person you feel you might have turned to for help if he had been there.

NOW YOU CAN GO ON TO THE REST OF THE ITEMS. DO NOT REPEAT SITUATIONS. IF A SITUATION HAS ALREADY BEEN LISTED SIMPLY MAKE A SECOND CHOICE.

3. The time when things seemed to be going against you – when your luck was particularly bad.
4. The time when you were most hard up financially.
5. The time when you were in poorest health or had a long period of sickness.
6. The time when someone took advantage of you because you did not know what you were doing.
7. The time when you made one of the most serious mistakes in your life.
8. The time when you failed to accomplish something you tried very hard to do.
9. The time when you were most lonely.
10. The time when you felt most discouraged about the future.
11. The time when you wondered if you would not be better off dead or when you came nearest feeling that way.
12. The time when you felt most misunderstood by others or when it seemed as if people were ganging up on you.
13. The time when you lost your temper or got very angry.
14. The time when you hurt someone's feelings in a way he or she did not deserve.
15. The time when you felt most ashamed of yourself.
16. The time when you were most frightened or fearful about what might become of you.
17. The time in recent years when you acted childish or like a 'panty-waist'.
18. The time when you felt jealous of someone's affection.
19. The time in your life when you felt most mixed up or confused about things in general.
20. The time when you had serious trouble with your parents or came nearest having trouble with them.
21. The time when you had trouble with your brother, sister, or a close relative – or the time when you came nearest having trouble with one of them.
22. The time when you had trouble with your wife (husband) or girl (boy) friend – or the time when you came nearest having trouble with one of them.

NOW GO BACK OVER THE TWENTY-TWO SITUATIONS YOU HAVE LISTED AND PUT A CHECK MARK (✓) OPPOSITE THE *five* WHICH HAVE CAUSED YOU THE MOST WORRY DURING YOUR LIFE.

Trouble with	Date, Place	1. Mate	2. Father	3. Mother	4. Sister	5. Brother	6. Boss	7. Noncom. Officer	8. Com. Officer	9. Minister	10. Relative	11. Neighbor	12. Buddy	13. Confidant*	14. Physician	15. Advisor*	16. Self	Factor I Loadings Failure and Passivity	Factor II Loadings Shame	Factor III Loadings Discouragement	Factor IV Loadings Finances and Anger	Factor V Loadings Confusion
A. Finances	1947 Farm	.	x	x	.	.	.	.	.	.	x	.	.	x	.	x	.	10	12	12	14	10
B. Mate	1949	.	.	x	x	.	.	.	.	.	.	.	.	x	.	x	.	13	14	11	11	11
C. Police	(Omitted)																					
D. Neighbor	(Omitted)																					
E. Jealousy	(Omitted)																					
F. Parents	? ?	x	.	.	x	.	x	.	.	.	.	.	.	x	.	x	.	14	12	12	10	14
G. Sibling	(Omitted)																					
H. Loneliness	1952 Home	x	.	.	x	.	x	.	.	.	.	.	.	x	.	x	.	14	12	12	10	14
I. Anger	1953 N—	x	x	x	x	.	.	.	.	.	x	.	.	x	.	x	.	10	10	9	14	10
J. Fear of death	(Omitted)																					
K. Shame	1952 Home	.	.	x	.	.	x	.	.	.	.	.	.	x	.	x	.	13	15	13	11	13
L. Persecution	1953 N—	.	x	x	.	.	x	.	.	.	.	.	.	x	.	x	.	12	14	14	12	12
M. Discouragement	1953 N—	x	x	x	.	.	x	.	.	.	.	.	.	x	.	x	.	11	13	15	13	13
N. Sickness	(Omitted)																					
O. Suicidal thoughts	(Omitted)																					
P. Misunderstood	1952 N—	.	.	.	.	.	x	.	.	.	.	.	.	x	.	x	.	14	14	12	10	14
Q. Effeminacy	1953 N—	.	.	.	.	.	x	.	.	.	.	.	.	x	.	x	.	14	14	12	10	14
R. Cowardliness	(Omitted)																					
S. Stupidity	1952 N—	x	.	x	.	.	x	.	.	.	.	.	.	x	.	x	.	12	14	14	11	14
T. Hurting someone	1953 Home	.	x	.	x	.	x	.	.	.	.	.	.	x	.	x	.	14	12	11	10	12
U. Gullibility	1952 N—	.	x	.	x	.	x	.	.	.	.	.	.	x	.	x	.	14	12	11	10	12
V. Confusion	1953 N—	x	.	.	.	.	x	.	.	.	.	.	.	x	.	x	.	13	13	13	11	15
W. Failure	1952 N—	.	.	.	x	.	x	.	.	.	.	.	.	x	.	x	.	15	13	11	9	13
X. Women	(Omitted)																					
Y. Passivity	1953 Home	.	.	.	x	.	x	.	.	.	.	.	.	x	.	x	.	15	13	11	9	13
Z. Needed help	(Omitted)																					

*Same person named twice

Figure 6.12 Situational resources protocol, case X

Trouble with	Date, Place	1. Mate	2. Father	3. Mother	4. Sister	5. Brother	6. Boss	7. Noncom. Officer	8. Com. Officer	9. Minister	10. Relative	11. Neighbor	12. Buddy	13. Confidant	14. Physician	15. Advisor	16. Self	Factor I Loadings Misunderstood, Loneliness, Anger	Factor II Loadings Discouragement	Factor III Loadings Finances	Factor IV Loadings Sickness
A. Finances	1953 T—	.	.	.	.	.	.	x	.	.	.	.	x	x	.	.	.	−9	11	16	8
B. Mate	1953 Korea	.	.	x	.	.	x	.	x	.	.	.	.	.	.	.	.	11	13	10	10
C. Police	1952 Korea	.	.	x	.	.	.	.	x	x	.	.	.	.	.	.	.	11	13	10	10
D. Neighbor	(Omitted)																				
E. Jealousy	(Omitted)																				
F. Parents	(Omitted)																				
G. Sibling	(Omitted)																				
H. Loneliness	1953 Korea	x	.	x	.	x	x	.	.	x	.	.	.	.	.	.	.	15	11	8	12
I. Anger	1952 Korea	.	x	x	.	x	x	.	.	x	.	.	.	.	.	.	.	15	11	8	10
J. Fear of death	1952 Korea	x	x	x	x	x	.	.	.	x	.	.	.	.	.	.	.	14	9	−9	13
K. Shame	1951 M—	x	x	x	.	.	.	.	.	x	.	.	.	.	.	.	.	14	10	9	11
L. Persecution	1949 T—	x	x	x	x	x	.	.	.	.	.	.	x	.	.	.	.	12	10	8	13
M. Discouragement	1953 M—	.	.	x	.	.	.	x	x	.	.	.	.	.	.	.	.	9	15	12	10
N. Sickness	1953 T—	x	.	x	x	x	.	.	.	.	.	.	.	.	x	.	.	11	10	8	16
O. Suicidal thoughts	(Omitted)																				
P. Misunderstood	1953 M—	x	x	x	.	x	x	.	.	.	.	.	.	.	.	.	.	15	11	8	12
Q. Effeminacy	1951 R—	.	x	.	.	x	x	x	x	.	.	.	.	.	.	.	.	11	13	10	8
R. Cowardliness	1952 A—	.	.	.	.	.	x	.	.	x	.	.	.	.	.	.	.	12	10	11	9
S. Stupidity	1953 T—	.	x	x	x	x	.	x	.	.	.	.	x	.	.	.	.	10	12	11	11
T. Hurting someone	1951 T—	.	x	.	x	.	.	.	.	.	.	.	x	.	.	.	.	9	9	12	10
U. Gullibility	1953 Korea	.	.	.	.	x	.	x	x	x	.	.	.	.	.	.	.	10	14	11	9
V. Confusion	1953 T—	x	x	x	x	x	.	.	.	x	.	.	.	.	.	.	.	14	10	−9	11
W. Failure	1950 T—	.	x	.	.	x	.	.	.	x	.	.	x	.	.	.	.	12	9	11	9
X. Women	1953 T—	.	x	x	.	.	x	.	.	x	.	.	.	.	.	.	.	14	10	9	9
Y. Passivity	1950 T—	.	x	x	.	x	x	.	.	.	.	.	x	.	.	.	.	13	11	10	10
Z. Needed help	? ?	x	x	x	x	x	x	.	.	x	.	x	x	.	.	.	.	13	−9	−10	10

Figure 6.13 Situational resources protocol, case Y

Figures 6.12 and 6.13 reproduce protocols from two different subjects of similar age and background. One of them was undergoing extended psychotherapy. It is easy enough to infer, from his distribution of dependencies, which of the two he was.

21. Problems involving range of convenience

As we have indicated before, the use of the Grid Form of the Rep Test is based on the assumption that each figure falls within the range of convenience of each construct. Stated in a form which applies to the use of grids in general, the assumption is that each row has a psychologically true intersect with each column. If this assumption cannot be made, one may have to ask one's client to enter two kinds of incidents, a positive incident and a negative incident, on the grid. For example, if the emergent pole of the construct applies to the figure, he may mark the cell with a plus; and if the implicit pole applies, he may mark the cell with a minus. In this case the void is interpreted to mean that the figure falls outside the range of convenience of the construct. It is somewhat more difficult to compute a meaningful factorial analysis on such a grid, but the task is not wholly unfeasible.

22. Group factors

It is possible to use the Repertory Grid to derive factors common to individual members of a group, independently of the words they use to label their constructs. In such a case the figures must be assumed to be comparable from protocol to protocol. This may be assumed on the basis of similar relationships to the subjects' lives. Alternatively, one may set up the figures as persons known to all members of the group – for example, their fellow group members. The grids can be stacked one above the other and a common factor extracted, as if they all constituted one grid. If one wishes to extract a group stereotype figure, he may arrange the grids horizontally and extract a factorialized figure. It is possible to see to what extent each person's grid is matched by the group scanning pattern. This essentially provides a measure of the functional similarity between an individual's outlook and the common outlook of his group. Such an approach gives one access to a variety of issues relating to our Commonality Corollary.

The purpose of this presentation has been to sketch a methodological approach to the analysis of a person's psychological space. We have used the subject's own system of axes, yet we have abstracted them in ways which permit us to subsume them within our own system. Thus we have not bogged down in the particularistic approach, which has been the bane of the phenomenologists. The method we have employed involves various assumptions regarding the adequacy of this sampling of the subject's personal-construct system, its stability, the applicability of all of his constructs to all of the persons he names, the contrasting nature of the paired terms he has used, and so on. Yet, within such limits as the assumptions dictate, it is possible that the method provides a way of answering some of the questions that arise in dealing with a client psychotherapeutically, and a way of bringing evidence to bear upon some of the common but untested notions held by psychotherapists. In addition, the nonparametric approach to factorization may be a useful tool in other situations requiring the reduction of binary data to simple structure.

Chapter seven

The analysis of self-characterization

We are still trying to bring our theory down to earth before elaborating its abstractive aspects further. In this chapter, and in the one following, we show the working of the psychology of personal constructs in the realm of interpersonal relations.

A. Approaches

1. Pursuing the implications of the Basic Postulate

We have taken the position that a scientific theory should be not only precise and parsimonious but also fertile. In our discussions of the Role Construct Repertory Test and the Repertory Grid we presented some of the products of the psychology of personal constructs. Let us now continue with some of the practical outcomes of our theoretical position. Since our theory was designed primarily with the area of clinical psychology as its focus of convenience, let us turn to a point of application which is a particularly clinical one. How does one approach a clinical understanding of a client's self-characterization? Is it by the method of 'impression' only? Or are there formal procedures which, if carefully followed, will always yield a somewhat similar picture of the case, no matter who the clinician is?

a. The role relationship in the clinical setting. We have already discussed the clinical method as one of the various methods of science. We hope that our definition of the method has sufficed to indicate that it rests upon firm logical grounds. Our task in this chapter is to elaborate clinical methodology in greater detail, as it would be applied to raw verbal protocol, particularly the protocol produced by a client when he is asked to characterize himself. The outline of the procedure applied to this particular kind of data should help to clarify the distinction between a scientific application of the clinical method and its impressionistic misuse.

In our discussion of the functions of a psychological test used in a clinical setting we emphasized the fact that the test was useful primarily because it yielded likely hypotheses which, during the course of the client's treatment, could become the bases of inquiry and exploration. A test which yields cut-and-dried *findings*, in contrast to *clinical hypotheses*, is not as likely to be helpful; it usually fails to outline any way in which the client's situation can be improved. A good clinical test – and a good clinical analysis of any kind of protocol – should suggest many further approaches to the practical problems to the client. These approaches arise as hypotheses. The hypotheses are tested in the clinician's subsequent dealings with the client. If they are good hypotheses, they will lead the clinician to follow a line of experimentation which will eventually be helpful to the client. If they are irrelevant hypotheses, they may, even though 'true', lead the clinician into abandoning his client as an incorrigible neurotic.

Let us further consider the Fundamental Postulate: *a person's processes are psychologically channelized by the ways in which he anticipates events.* If we pursue the implications of this assumption we shall seek, not only to describe a client's acts, but to understand the anticipatory implications involved in the channels through which he initiates them. As we have indicated in our Construction Corollary, we envision these channels as existing in terms of constructs. Therefore, our clinical appraisal of a client's self-characterization protocol would be concerned, not only with the protocol as his concrete verbal act, but also with the anticipatory personal constructs which may be inferred from it. Because we would be concerned with his channelizing constructs, and not merely his terminal acts, we would, in accordance with our Sociality Corollary, be taking the first step towards establishing a role for ourselves in relation to him. This role relationship between psychologist and client is one of the features which distinguishes the clinical psychologist from others. Furthermore, we would like to think that the psychology of personal constructs is an approach which particularly lends itself to the establishment of just such a role relationship between psychologist and client.

Perhaps an analogy would be helpful. A teacher examines her pupils' arithmetic papers. She may approach the task in either of two ways: she can look at the answers only, and mark them right or wrong, or she can look at the methods by which the individual pupil obtained his answers. In the former case she operates as a test-scoring machine and reflects only validating evidence for the pupil to make use of. In the latter case she undertakes a role relationship with each pupil and joins with the pupil in establishing a miniature society with mutual efforts and objectives. A similar possibility is open to the psychologist in his relations with his client. He can exhibit himself to his client as a stalwart representative of 'Truth, Justice, and the American Way', or he can take a second look at his client's own personal outlook to see how the two of them might work together for a common purpose.

b. Anticipation. There is another important implication of our Fundamental Postulate. If we pursue it, we shall place an emphasis upon anticipating events rather than containing them. A meaningful construct is one which is designed to embrace the future rather than merely catalogue the past. The clinician, then, has not necessarily arrived at an adequate understanding of his client when he has precisely structured all of the events and behaviours which have already transpired. He should ask himself if his conceptualization of the client is permeable enough to account for what might happen in the future. Even the neatest diagnostic or nosological system may fail to meet this criterion.

c. The credulous approach. The third important implication of our Fundamental Postulate is that the clinician should maintain a kind of credulous attitude towards whatever the client says. He never discards information given by the client merely because it does not conform to what appear to be the facts! From a phenomenological point of view, the client – like the proverbial customer – is always right. This is to say that his words and his symbolic behaviour possess an intrinsic truth which the clinician should not ignore. But this is not to to say that the client always describes events in the way other people would describe them or in the way it is commonly agreed that they did happen. It is not to say that he always describes events in the presence of one person in the way he would describe them in the presence of another. He may use one level of description in talking to the clinician, yet use another level of description in construing events for his own purposes. He may even describe events in a way that is intended to lead the clinician to make false inferences.

But this does not mean that the phenomena of the client's speech, and what he says, are nonexistent, and therefore to be disregarded. The perceptive clinician always respects the content of his client's 'lies', although he is equally careful not to be misled by them. When he discovers that what a client has said does not agree with what has actually happened, he is careful to lay out both versions side by side and not erase the client's version in order to replace it with the 'true' version. He is even inclined to ponder over the client's version more than he is to derive conclusions from the 'true' version. Indeed, the perceptive clinician may be quite as much concerned with the client's version of an event which happens to be 'incorrect' as he is with the event itself or with the fact that the client has not told the 'truth'.

2. The self-characterization as an application of the credulous approach

As we suggested previously, there is a useful adage for clinical psychologists to follow on occasion: if you do not know what is wrong with a person, ask him; he may tell you. The clinician who asks such a question will have to be prepared to do some careful listening, for the answer will be couched in terms of the respondent's personal constructs, not only of himself but of the psychologist and of the situation. He may say in effect, 'I don't think you would understand if I told you.' Or he may say by means of polite conventions, 'Nothing is wrong with me that the elimination of people like you wouldn't remedy.' Or he may launch into an elaborate explanation whose very complexity suffices to make it clear how difficult and laboured must be every decision by which he maintains himself from day to day.

There is a simple approach which has proved useful in arriving at a clinical understanding of clients. It is the request that they write a character sketch of themselves. One may say:

> I want you to write a character sketch of Harry Brown, just as if he were the principal character in a play. Write it as it might be written by a friend who knew him very *intimately* and very *sympathetically*, perhaps better than anyone ever really could know him. Be sure to write it in the third person. For example, start out by saying, 'Harry Brown is...'

The phrasing of this request has gone through a great number of revisions. The term 'character sketch' seems to permit the client more latitude in using his own construction system for describing himself than do such phrases as 'self-description', 'self-analysis', and the like. The term 'sketch' suggests that the structure rather than the detailed elements are to be emphasized.

The emphasis upon the third person conveys the idea that the wholeness of the character sketch is important, rather than that the client should attempt to pick out certain things to confess or that he should attempt to catalogue his faults. He is to make himself seem plausible.

The same intent lies at the back of the phrasing of the second sentence. Since the client is writing as if in the role of a friend he is somewhat freer to conceptualize himself as if from an external point of view. The effort is to get him to see himself in some sort of perspective.

The terms 'intimately' and 'sympathetically' were chosen after a great deal of exploration. The first term indicates that something more than superficial appearances is to be covered. The second term indicates that the client is to consider himself acceptable and thus dwell upon what he is, rather than upon what he is not or what he ought to be. Some clients will feel, out of a respect for realism, that they are required to write a self-incriminating or threatening description of themselves. The term 'sympathetically' helps unfreeze such a client from the paralysis that sometimes accompanies the feeling of threat, and often lets him get on with the writing of the character sketch.

The phrase, 'perhaps better than anyone ever really could know him', while not particularly good syntax, tends to free certain literalistic clients from feeling that they must write the sketch as some actual, known person would write it. Without this phrase – sometimes even with it – some clients will choose a person known to them and write the sketch as they surmise that person would write it. Thus they hide from the task of expressing their own views behind the guise of literalism or behind some person version of 'objectivity'.

The omission of a suggested outline is intentional. Some explorations into the use of topical headings, such as 'family background', 'social characteristics', 'vocation', 'childhood history', and so on, have been attempted and abandoned. The result of imposing such an outline upon the client is a considerable loss of spontaneity and, more important, a failure to discover what his own outline of conceptualization about himself happens to be.

The object of this kind of inquiry is to see how the client structures a world in relation to which he must maintain himself in some kind of role. It is his personal construction system, then, in which we are primarily interested. We have, in addition, a secondary interest in where he places himself with respect to the personal categories and dimensions which structure his world. Least of all do we have an interest in where he would hit or miss in placing himself in a world we would structure for him. It is not merely his self-identification that we seek – certainly not his self-identification within a field we have first dimensioned for him with our own constructs. Rather we start with his own personal dimensional system, and after we understand that we concern ourselves with his self-percept in relation to that particular system.

This emphasis upon having the client use his own outline is the first of several ways in which personal-construct psychology differs from self-concept psychology. The relationship between the two systems is close, but the differences are important. Personal-construct psychology emphasizes the *constructs* and the *construct system* with respect to which the self is located. Self-concept psychology, if the writer understands it properly, emphasizes the location of the self within an externally imposed system of dimensions. Both approaches are to be distinguished from those requiring the psychologist to impose both the construct system and the placement of the client within the system.

It should now be clear that the instructions by means of which the self-characterization is elicited are intended to avoid prejudicing the over-all framework within which the client is to identify himself. They are instructions, however. They do, therefore, impose a measure of structure upon the situation. Their purpose is simply this: the client is invited to lay down only those constructs with respect to which he identifies himself; not those which are irrelevant to the characterization of himself. Constructs which have to do with the way he solves arithmetic problems or repairs his car are not sought, except as he may choose to report them as being in some fashion related to a proper characterization of himself.

There is a second purpose in structuring the situation in the way we have. It is to minimize threat. Here we are referring to the threat which the client's own sense of candour imposes on the situation, rather than the threat which he identifies with the clinician. The latter will have to be minimized by other means. The former is approached by the use of the term 'friend', by the combination of the terms 'intimately' and 'sympathetically', and by the suggestion that the sketch be written in the third person. To this extent, then, an effort is made to place the client initially in a protected spot within a loosely construed system which has the given dimensions of first, second, and third persons, friendship, intimacy, and sympathy.

Now there are occasional indications that even this attempt to allow the client to take off from a protected spot may threaten him. Some clients have a feeling of disorientation when it is even suggested that anyone could stand in a friendly or intimate relation to them. Some are threatened by the idea that they could be the object of sympathy – as they understand sympathy. The phrase, 'perhaps better than anyone ever really could know him', helps to provide an out for such people. Even so, they may still be threatened. We simply take this risk.

3. An illustrative self-characterization

The following self-characterization was written by a university student who had requested psychological services in connection with generalized complaints regarding academic, vocational, and social adjustments. At the time he wrote the self-characterization he had had about nine psychotherapeutic interviews, during which the clinician felt he had not shown a great deal of progress. The term was drawing to a close and the client was committed to a plan for going immediately to another university some thousand miles away. It was decided to employ *fixed-role therapy* for the remainder of the psychotherapeutic series. Since an analysis of the client's self-characterization is the first step in planning such a therapeutic programme, the following protocol was elicited.

a. Character sketch of Ronald Barrett. The following self-characterization is reproduced with its original misspellings and grammatical errors.

> An overall appearance of Ronald Barrett would give one the impression that he has a rather quite and calm personality. Furthermore, he dislikes doing or saying anything that will draw unfavorable attention in public. (Even if he isn't the 'disturbing' one in a group, he dislikes to be seen as one of the group.) However, he has been known to flare up (not in public, though) very easily and often gets quite worked up or frustrated over something done or spoken by (usually not his friends or anyone with him) someone that he feels should know better, or should have more sense than to do what he did. He very rarely shows signs of anger towards his friends. On the other hand, he is apt to be inconsistent in that it sometimes take a lot to get him worked up over some subject at hand, while other times he will very easily get very worked up over or bothered by something which is quite often of minor importance. One might say that his actions and attitudes depend on his mood, which shows great extremes. On the whole, he tries to impress people, especially his elders, with his knowledge, poise, and sincerity.
>
> One might be tempted to say that he litteraly hates inconsideration on the part of anyone and this fact is often the reason for him flaring up over the actions or words of other people. He is generally quite considerate of others and also shows great sincerity in what he does or says. Conscienciousness seems to be one of his main tributes where his morals and ethics seem to be his guide. A feeling of guilt often comes over him if he thinks he has not been kindhearted enough. He considers that he has very good common sense and good use of logic in analyzing or explaining many aspects of life and matereal things.
>
> His tendency to criticize and correct people, esp. in his family, on major as well as minor issues, shows some decrease outside his family, but not too much

within. Proving his point, or arguing his point, and arguing against other people's points, seems to be one of his major 'hobbies'. He is apt to be too gullable for what he reads/or has been told/as being factual or positive proof of something, and a result will sometimes argue himself 'blue in the face' over some issue that he thinks he has positive proof of. However, he has acquired the ability to stay away from this undesirable aspect to a great extent.

He puts much stress in technicalities and the importance of being accurate. On the average, he tries very hard to be errorless, /or/to do everything right and nothing wrone. When he does do something wrong, he may give excusses for his action, depending entirely on the situation, or he will get very mad at himself or very discouraged in himself. If he does make an error that he feels he knew better than to do, he will, in some way or another, let everyone around know that he knew better through his exclamations of disgust and anger that he has for himself. Inotherwords, when he does something wrong that he feels he knew better than to do, he gets very angry with himself and is generally bothered by such an error, if it be of major importance, for some time after.

It may be said that he is a materialist and a realist. He is quite apt to criticize or 'run down' things that appears too artificial or unpractical, or improbable, by saying that they are not realistic enough (especially in movies). He also possesses a feeling that there is a reason for the existence of most everything and often tries to find this reason and tell his conclusions to whomever he is with. As a result, (if proper to call this a result) he believes only what he wants to believe, even in religion, and it is usually difficult to change his beliefs or opinions unless the person attempting such shows equal or greater authority on the subject in question, or uses similar reasoning in arriving at conclusions. Another point that should be brought out, that he does not coincide with that of other people, especially his friends. However, he does waste time, even in his own mind, in deciding or thinking about what he will wear.

He has some ideas concerning girls that seem odd or just plain crazy to most people. He completely refrains from calling a girl 'beautiful'. She may be cute, pretty, attractive, or some other such adjective in his mind, but he uses the word 'beautiful' only describe material things that have no 'feeling' as humans have. Although he listens attentively to stories or general discussion about sex, he rarely enters into the conversation. One may say that he puts too much meaning and thought into kissing a girl. If he has gone out with a girl a couple of times, or even once, and doesn't continue to go out with her or to call her, he is very hesitant about asking her for a date again, say two or three months later. He is usually lost for conversation when meeting someone new, or seeing a girl he knows, but if he once 'breaks the ice', he can usually talk freely. However, when he calls a girl on the telephone, no matter how well he knows her, he hates to have anyone around him or even within hearing distance. Furthermore, he doesn't like to practice anything, such as a musical instrument, anyplace when he can be seen or heard.

b. First reactions to the protocol. It will be difficult for the clinician who is used to more conventional methods of approach to defer his categorization of this case. The protocol reeks of 'compulsivity'. The 'aggressive and sexual impulses' are close enough to 'the surface' to cause the clinician some concern. The following phrases, among others, stand out with painful clarity.

... impression that he has a rather quite [*sic*] and calm personality.

... inconsistent...

... his mood, which shows great extremes.

Consciencioussness [*sic*] seems to be one of his main tributes [*sic*]...

... logic in analyzing...

... angry with himself...

... realistic...

... he does waste time, even in his own mind, in deciding or thinking about what he will wear.

... beautiful only [to] describe material things that have no 'feeling'.

But let us attempt to see the world through Ronald's eyes. We shall use the *credulous approach.* Quite obviously we shall not depend primarily upon a verbal or syntactical analysis, as in the methods employed by Dollard and Mowrer in computing the Discomfort–Relief Quotient, or by Raimy and Bugental in categorizing Positive, Negative, Neutral, and Ambivalent Feelings in relation to the Self and Nonself, or by Barry in computing the Strength–Threat Ratio in relation to Topical Areas, or the method employed by Stern and Busemann in computing the Verb–Adjective Ratio. We shall listen to 'Nature babbling to herself', and see what Ronald offers as his own dimensions along which the protocol can be scored. We shall successively underscore his phrases and sentences and juxtapose with them similar themes from other parts of the protocol. Furthermore, we shall presume that his use of words is somewhat personalized, and that we can better understand what they mean in his lexicon by studying the contexts and sequences in which they appear.

But before proceeding to draw conclusions from the Ronald Barrett protocol, let us outline the techniques and objectives which govern the clinical appraisal of a self-characterization from the standpoint of the psychology of personal constructs. After these have been sketched in outline form we shall return to Ronald Barrett and seek to understand what he has told us about himself.

4. Techniques in the analysis of self-characterizations

A verbatim protocol, such as we have presented, is, to many psychologists, a baffling accumulation of raw data. One cannot 'score' the protocol as one might wish. When a 'scoring' is attempted it is likely to take the form of a vocabulary or syntactical analysis. If one attempts to score content, as in the use of the aforementioned strength–threat ratio, the scoring may have the disadvantage of representing itself along one dimensional line only. It is even more difficult to bring the client's own personal dimensional system into play in one's evaluation of the protocol.

Basically we start with the credulous approach, which has already been described. We then use various techniques, not to 'score' the protocol in a conventional sense, but to bring it into focus.

a. Observation of sequence and transition. The clinician starts by reading the protocol through to establish the context within which his more detailed examination of parts of the protocol will be conducted. Next, he reads the protocol from the standpoint of the sequences of content and the transitions from topic to topic. He assumes, for the moment, that the protocol represents a true continuity, as far as the client is concerned, and that the apparent 'breaks' in the continuity are not really discontinuities, but are either unexpected elaborations of subjectively similar content or are contrast elaborations. He assumes, for the moment, that the same construct dimension carries through each 'break'. He may revise this hypothesis later. For example, in the Barrett protocol, the apparent 'break' between the last two sentences is seen as a true continuity, as far as Ronald is concerned, and, as such, is interpreted as throwing light upon a construct dimension about which Ronald is relatively inarticulate.

The sequence of paragraphs and of generalizations and specifications is also noted. For example, it is noted that Ronald chooses to talk about sex in the last paragraph, rather than in the first, and that he chooses to point out the social mask which he is wearing at the very outset of his self-characterization. Moreover, the Barrett protocol is full of contrasts and particularizations. When his sequences and transitions are noted it becomes apparent that he tries to balance himself on a continual seesaw. This is pointed up by his use of parenthetical phrases.

b. Observation of organization. After examining the sequence and transition the clinician turns attention to the organization of the protocol. He seeks the topic sentences, both in terms of first sentences of paragraphs and in terms of sentences which seem to carry the greatest generality. He always pays particular attention to the opening sentence of the protocol and assumes, for the moment, that it is intended as a statement having either the greatest level of generality for the client, or that it represents the safest ground to use as a point of departure. For example, in the Barrett protocol, if the opening sentence is tentatively assumed to the one having the greatest range of generality, the clinician is immediately alerted to the possibility that the calmness in Ronald's personality is a superficial covering. If the rest of the paragraph and the rest of the protocol is read as if this were the topic sentence, it becomes clear that Ronald is indeed describing a situation of inner turmoil behind a very thin mask of calmness.

c. Reflection against context. Next, the clinician can take each statement and consider, not only what it means merely as an independent declaration, but what it might mean in the context of the protocol as a whole. This is something like saying to oneself, 'If all the rest of the protocol might be considered an explanation or an elaboration of this one statement, what would the statement mean?' This approach may also enable the clinician to circumscribe each statement by means of context. Thus, instead of extending the range of generalization of each statement, the clinician may consider what it might mean particularly within a circumscribed area as defined by the context. One may take each sentence in turn and mentally lay it beside each other sentence, then ask himself, 'What does each of these sentences mean in the context of the other?'

Take, for example, Ronald's statement in the third paragraph about his tendency to argue himself 'blue in the face'. Consider first what the statement might mean if all the rest of the protocol were momentarily taken as an elaboration of it. Is not the whole story one of how he argues himself 'blue in the face?' Is it not also a story of how his own arguments operate to make him look ridiculous or bring him to the point of apoplexy? Next, consider what the statement might mean within the more limited context of the paragraph. The paragraph has to do with his relations to his parents. The 'blue in the face' phrase in this context suggests a child having a temper tantrum. It also suggests that his disputatiousness arises primarily as a defence within the area of the family.

d. Collation of terms. The clinician should be alert to terms which are repeated and to linkages between terms. Consider the sequence of terms in the second paragraph: 'inconsideration', 'considerate', 'sincerity', 'conscientiousness', 'morals', 'ethics', 'guilt', 'kindhearted'. Here he is using a variety of terms in an attempt to communicate some construct which has no clear-cut symbolism. One can trace these linkages throughout the protocol, both by noting where certain terms are repeated and where their personal equivalents are repeated.

e. Shifting emphasis. When a clinician reads a protocol he tends to throw emphasis upon his own choice of sentences and words. In order to correct for his bias he needs to experiment with alternative emphases and inflections in reading each sentence and paragraph. For example, in evaluating the last sentence of the first paragraph, the clinician may come to understand what the client meant by reading it seven times, each time emphasizing a different one of the units we have noted below.

On the whole,
he tries
to impress people,
especially his elders,
with his knowledge,

poise,
and sincerity.

It may be noted that it was the term 'sincerity' which was picked up out of his sentence for elaboration in the next paragraph. Perhaps that is the term Ronald intended to underscore.

In judging where the inflection should be placed, the clinician may take particular cognizance of those terms which are repeated in the protocol. These are likely to refer to constructs which not only have a wide range of convenience for the client but also which he cannot be sure he is able to communicate by mere words. The same applies to repeated themes and sentence structure. The repetition is a clue to personal emphasis.

f. Restatement of the argument. The clinician can come to a better understanding of the protocol if he tries, from time to time, to express the same theme in his own words. This is much as if the clinician were to play the role of client. In using this technique the clinician attempts to subsume the client's point of view, not merely memorize or categorize it. To the extent that he attempts to understand the client by putting himself in the client's shoes and by attempting to stand and walk like the client, he is taking the first step towards playing a role in relation to the client. In the analysis of the Barrett protocol, which appears in the latter part of this chapter, we have used this technique freely, partly because it helps us understand what Ronald is trying to say, and partly because it helps us communicate to the reader what we infer that Ronald is trying to say.

5. Analysis of contextual areas invoked by the protocol

The clinician will want to pay attention to the topical areas which the client mentions during the course of his self-characterization. Some clients dwell upon their personal appearance, others upon their ancestry, and still others upon their vocation. The Barrett protocol deals largely with Ronald's communication and behaviour in face-to-face situations with people. One of the reasons for not specifying for the client the topical areas which he should cover in his self-characterization is that the clinician is interested in discovering the client's own selection of context within which he characteristically identifies himself. The self-characterization is read with this point in mind.

The contextual areas chosen by the client indicate where he sees himself as being distinguishable from other people. If, for example, he sees himself as being pretty much the run-of-the-mill type of person, as far as physical appearance is concerned, he is not so likely to mention physical appearance, unless, of course, he is disturbed by the fact that he does not stand out from the crowd in this respect, or unless he believes that the clinician expects him to cover this topic. On the other hand, if he sees himself as being unusual because of his red hair, he is likely to mention this feature of his appearance.

The areas indicate also those grounds upon which he feels secure enough to be able to elaborate his personal-construct system. If Ronald had felt completely at a loss to understand what was going on between him and his conversational companions, he would probably have been unable to put sentences together in this topical area. Even as it was, he had a pretty hard time with his syntax, as the reader will have noticed. Most clients do. It is not easy to find words and sentences to express the deeply rooted constructs by which the self is fixed into place. In the more crucial moments of a psychotherapeutic series, for example, syntax, grammar, and orthology all take a bad beating.

Some clients write their entire self-characterizations on comparatively safe ground. Others, more venturesome, take their chances in areas in which they are not so certain about where they stand. But we always know this much: the areas chosen are those in which the client sees enough uncertainty to make exploration interesting and enough structure to make it meaningful. Like the client who is permitted to choose his own topic in a psychotherapeutic session, the self-characterizing client may be assumed to have selected an area in which he has enough structure to sustain him while he inches forward into uncertainty. To ask him to plunge far beyond such solid ground is to precipitate him into confusion; to demand that he be more explicit is to force him to be trite.

As in the case of vocational choice, the choice of topical areas within which to plot the self is an indication of where the client has permeable constructs upon which to rely. And permeable constructs bespeak the capacity for change! The area analysis of the protocol gives the clinician one of his best cues as to the kinds of places and occasions where the client is probably ready to experiment with new outlooks and new approaches to his problems. The topical analysis also suggests the nature of the elements for whose ordering the client's constructs must be designed. It also provides some preliminary indication of the ranges of convenience of the constructs which are mentioned.

The clinician takes note of the sequence of areas discussed. Usually these represent a progression either from the well-structured to the more problematical, or from the general to the specific. The areas of relative security and those of relative striving are noted. The shifting of areas is noted – and where the shifts take place. Circular approaches to areas are noted; either the return to an area which was abandoned in an earlier part of the self-characterization, or the skirting of an area with which the writer never quite comes to grips.

Places, occasions, incidents in the personal history, undertakings, objects, property, group memberships, intimacies, and so on, are noted. Particular attention is paid to the persons who are mentioned. They are a sample of the figures which populate his world. The range of interests can be noted. Awareness of the reader, and the situation in which the self-characterization was requested, suggest the extent to which the client is bound to local circumstances in writing his sketch.

6. Thematic analysis

The clinician may turn his attention from topics to themes, or to cause-and-effect relationships. The client's reasons and explanations can be noted. Does he rely upon historical explanations, upon personal influence, upon chance, or upon his own actions in attempting to understand what has happened? What, implicitly, does he see as an efficacious cause? For example, in the Barrett protocol, 'results', 'reasons', 'conclusions', and 'ifs' loom conspicuously. Take the interesting sequence in the fifth paragraph:

> ... He also possesses a feeling that there is a reason for the existence of most everything and often tries to find this reason and tell his conclusions to whomever he is with. As a result, (if proper to call this a result) he believes only what he wants to believe, even in religion, and it is usually difficult to change his beliefs or opinions unless the person attempting such shows equal or greater authority on the subject in question, or uses similar reasoning in arriving at conclusions....

Here the client expresses the interesting notion that what leads him to become dogmatic is his firm belief that there must be a reason behind all existence. This may not seem to many of us to be a very logical explanation, but for the client the 'cause' and 'effect' are psychologically connected with each other. Our client, of course, is not the first person in the world to take the view that, if everything has its cause, the only approach to understanding that cause is through dogmatism via rationalism. Many philosophers have used this kind of reasoning to support a particular religious outlook.

If the therapist understands something of the cause-and-effect constructs of the client, as revealed by a thematic analysis of the protocol, he will have a better understanding of how the client will insist upon approaching therapeutic change. For example, if the client is firmly convinced that only physical treatment will eliminate the pain in his back, psychotherapeutic efforts to relieve that symptom will be handicapped. If he believes that his hatred for certain members of his family is caused by certain harsh treatment he received from them years ago, it may be hard to convince him that his attitudes are subject to modification on his own.

The client's objectives, purposes, and feeling of progress may be explored in the protocol. So may his obstacles, handicaps, and difficulties, as well as solutions to past problems and already accomplished readjustments. Persons who are described as difficult and persons who are described as helpful may be mentioned in the protocol. Powerful figures may be noted; idealized figures may also appear.

The client's values and his tendency to moralize also suggest his view of cause-and-effect relationships. One may look, also, for the devices he uses to maintain self-control. Sometimes the client reveals his themes, or cause-and-effect ideas, by means of deprecations of persons, values, and objects. The client's tendency to apologize for himself or his circumstances is also a clue to understanding what he thinks leads to what.

The client's expression of attitudes of strength and threat in the selection of words may also throw light upon how he views cause-and-effect relationships. One may use the approach of Barry in tabulating these items. The client's approach-withdrawal patterns can be observed similarly, by examining the protocol bit by bit.

Finally, one may note the way the themes are distributed through the protocol. What is the opening theme? What is the closing theme? What theme is repeated or returned to, time after time? What theme is perseveratively expressed with long explanations and elaborate detail? What themes appear to run counter to each other? Which ones are ambivalently expressed? For example, the ambivalence of theme is particularly outstanding in the Barrett protocol. As the clinician adapts himself to this kind of analysis, he can become quite adept at teasing out the themes and viewing them as the cause-and-effect relationships perceived by the client.

7. *Dimensional analysis*

Valuable as *area analysis* and *thematic analysis* are to the clinical understanding of self-characterization protocol, the dimensional analysis is, from the standpoint of the psychology of personal constructs, even more meaningful. It is here that the clinician begins to understand the lay of those channels through which the client's psychological processes flow in search of the future. Emphasis is placed upon similarities and contrasts so that the clinician may understand the dichotomized alternatives between which the client must continually and consecutively choose.

The clinician looks for the principal dimensions and the constellations of dimensions. He looks for dimensions which are commonly found among other clients. For example, the dimension of *sincerity vs. artificiality* is very commonly expressed in the Rep Test protocols of young people in later adolescence, and the dimension of *people-who-like-me vs. people-who-dislike-me* is commonly expressed in early adolescence or in adults who are considered to be immature in their social outlooks. It is to be noted that Ronald dwells at considerable length on the *sincerity vs. inconsideration* construct dimension.

The clinician looks, not only for the manifestly contrasting poles and the use of subjective equivalents, but also for the poles which are implicit but not stated. For example, if a person keeps emphasizing 'logic', as Ronald has done, one is immediately alerted to the issue of what is personally viewed as the contrast to 'logic'. Ronald never comes right out and says that he finds himself vacillating between 'logic' and impulsivity, but that seems to be a very likely hypothesis checked by the therapist. Moreover, the protocol suggests that the therapist, if he were to attempt 'insight therapy', might have to deal with this topic extensively.

Not only does the clinician look for the contraposed poles of the client's constructs, but he looks also for how the client characterizes himself with respect to these poles. For example, Ronald describes himself as 'logical', but he makes it clear that his behaviour is impulsive. He is logical by conviction, he thinks, but much of what he does is in contrast to his conviction. Certainly, in his case, we see his dimension as a kind of construct slot in which he rattles back and forth, as he tries to work out a moment-by-moment adjustment to his problems.

The clinician notes movements and changes the client describes in himself. These changes imply the existence of available construct channels. Their directional lay within the system may be important to know when the time comes to prod the client into making some important decision. Contrasts of past, present, and future may be noted. In the Barrett protocol, for example, there is only one such contrast mentioned: the one at the beginning of the third paragraph. This, however, is an important contrast and it is to be observed that the movement he notes with respect to it is mainly outside his family.

The clinician can note the sequence and repetition of the use of construct dimensions. What dimension is laid out first? For example, in the Barrett protocol, the first dimension laid out is the contrast between the 'appearance' of Ronald and the actual Ronald. The shifting dimensions, or choices of additional axes, can be noted as one reads through the protocol.

There is not likely to be as much shifting in most protocols as one might logically expect. Ronald certainly does very little shifting; mainly he elaborates his principal construct into a comprehensive constellation. The terminal construct, since it usually deals with a more intimate, and sometimes less articulate theme, often provides the clinician with an idea of the dimension with which some of the more advanced psychotherapeutic sessions will deal. If Ronald were to go through a continued psychotherapeutic series, for example, his attitudes along the 'beautiful' construct line would probably have to be explored. Moreover, we would be inclined to believe that, in Ronald's case, this construct of 'beautiful' would be explored with considerable caution. The term may not imply anything very intimate or volatile for most of us, but we would be inclined to suspect that it does for Ronald.

Next, the clinician should look carefully at the language structure – where it remains intact and where it breaks down, how words are redefined in the client's personal lexicon, how he compartmentalizes his thinking by means of punctuation, and so on. Ronald's use of punctuation, for example, is genuinely exciting. His attempt at compartmentalization of ideas is as clear from his punctuation as it is from his text. One may also take note of the client's choice of terms, his meticulous qualification of terms, his use of sweeping terms, of colourful terms, and the like. One needs to be especially alert to the implied equivalences and contrasts between his terms. A literalistically minded clinician, who does not realize that he is setting out to learn a new language, may seriously misinterpret what his client means, simply because he presumes that the client agrees with the dictionary.

Finally, one may note the client's vocabulary level and cultural identification from his choice of words. Disregarding Ronald's spelling, we may note that he has used a fairly complex vocabulary, although, with the exception of such terms as 'realist' and 'materialist', the words are rather trite. The choice of words does not indicate a very high level of discrimination and sensitivity, especially in the area of feeling and human attitudes. One would suspect that, on a moonlight night,

Ronald might be much more perceptive of the problems arising under the hood of an automobile than of those arising in its back seat.

8. Professional subsuming of personal constructs

After the clinician has identified the constructs the client appears to be using in his self-characterization, he turns his attention to his own professional system of constructs and makes a definite attempt to subsume the client's personal constructs under that system. At this point in the development of the psychology of personal constructs we have not expounded the system of professional constructs which we propose to use in clinical work. That discussion comes later – out of order, perhaps; but, since it is more interesting for the reader to see a few practical applications in the early stage of an exposition, we have chosen to delay presenting these more elaborate ramifications of the system.

We have already mentioned such professional constructs as *permeability, constellation, range of convenience*, and so on. It is obvious, then, that the clinician, upon reviewing the client's self-characterization, will need to appraise the personal constructs from the standpoint of those basic constructs which make up the clinician's psychological system. The professional constructs of *loosening, dilation, aggression, hostility, anxiety, guilt, the C–P–C Cycle, the Creativity Cycle*, and several others are described in a later chapter. These are important in the armamentarium of the clinician who uses the approach of the psychological system we are developing. We shall do no more than mention them now, however, and suggest that when the clinician has gone over them, he may wish to come back to the Barrett protocol and make a more sophisticated analysis than we are able to offer in this chapter.

B. Illustrative first-order analysis of a self-characterization

9. What is Ronald Barrett trying to say?

a. First paragraph. There are several different common approaches to writing a self-characterization. There is the 'personal-record approach': name, age, sex, marital status, residence, and so on. There is the 'outside-to-inside approach', which goes from superficial appearance to inner reality. There is also the 'problem approach', which starts with a statement of the principal problem which the client sees himself as facing. Ronald uses a combination of the latter two. He starts by saying:

> An overall appearance of Ronald Barrett would give one the impression that he has a rather quite [sic] and calm personality.

The principal initial self-construct used here is expressed in the word 'quite [quiet] and calm'. Let us see if he elaborates this construct immediately, draws contrasts, or abandons it to return later or to give a setting in which it may make more sense. The next phrase suggests that he has chosen a combination of all three approaches.

> Furthermore, he dislikes doing or saying anything that will draw unfavourable attention in public. (Even if he isn't the 'disturbing' one in a group, he dislikes to [be] seen as one of the group.)

He has linked 'drawing unfavourable attention' to his construct by making it a disliked act. The unfavourability of the attention drawn to him in 'public' is important enough to be mentioned in the second sentence of the sketch. This is apparently also an elaboration of the appearance idea. He is genuinely concerned both with 'appearance' and 'public'. The term 'public' tentatively suggests that other people are seen collectively as peering spectators rather than as approachable persons who are understanding and who may be understood.

Note that he has not said that he *does not* do anything that will draw unfavourable attention in public. He has said that he *dislikes* doing or saying anything that will draw unfavourable attention in public. This gives us a hint that he sees himself, at least on occasion, as drawing unfavourable attention.

The appearance and conspicuousness theme requires a parenthetical elaboration. He cannot let the statement in the preceding sentence stand by itself. Yet the sentence which he is about to add is not central enough to be made a part of the body of the description. Perhaps this is a way of emphasizing his disidentification of himself from 'disturbing' behaviour and from the 'group' – using parentheses around the sentence and quotation marks around 'disturbing'.

Taken together, the first three sentences indicate Ronald's vehement asseveration that he ought to have the appearance of a quiet and calm personality, suggest his sensitivity to the public, and reveal his willingness immediately to disidentify himself with any group that makes him appear disturbing.

Now we come to the contrast elements of his initial construct as applied to himself. This is what makes the issue poignant.

> However, he has been known to flare up (not in public, though) very easily and often gets quite worked up or frustrated...

Here he clearly expresses the feeling of sitting on the lid of explosive behaviour, which would be conspicuous and distasteful for him. He does 'flare up' but, so far, he has been able to avoid doing so in public.

It is important to note what he 'flares up' about.

> ... over something done or spoken by... someone that he feels should know better, or should have more sense than to do what he did.

This is the very kind of behaviour he sees in himself and rejects (cf. below). He loses his own intellectual control over people who lose their intellectual controls. Even his choice of verbs is appropriate to the meaning he seems to be trying to convey: 'Someone that he *feels* should *know* better'. He feels – but they should *know*. When we come to deal later with Landfield's *threat hypotheses* we shall see that people are seen as threatening when they exemplify behaviour which is an all too plausible alternative to that means by which the client is currently maintaining his identity. Ronald's control of his spontaneous behaviour is so precarious that he can be disturbed even by the exemplification of spontaneous behaviour in other people. This is not an uncommon problem, but rarely does one see it so clearly expressed in the first paragraph of a self-characterization protocol.

Let us have a look at the parenthetical phrase which is inserted into the sentence which deals with the contrasting elements in his principal construct.

> ... (usually not his friends or anyone with him). ... He very rarely shows signs of anger towards his friends.

He does not flare up against those present. He rarely shows *signs* of anger. Again *appearance*! It is the immediate situation which enables him to keep his behaviour under control. Even though we are beginning to suspect that he has no rich, warm role relationships with other people, apparently his conspicuous position in a world of people with eyes which keep him under observation has a restraining effect upon his behaviour. We should, of course, be careful not to leap to the conclusion that there is a paranoid strain in this protocol. *He has not told us that*. And we using the *credulous approach* in the analysis of this protocol.

Now he goes on to express a point which is particularly revealing for the clinical psychologist who is a student of explosive behaviour.

> On the other hand, he is apt to be inconsistent in that it sometimes takes a lot to get him worked up over some subject at hand, while other times he will very easily get very worked up over or bothered by something which is quite often of minor importance.

It is as if he were expressing the nature of his psychological confusion in the language of the psychology of personal constructs. He is saying that he cannot adequately anticipate the events of his own behaviour. He is saying that the superordinate construct system upon which he has sought to make sense out of his world seems to be breaking down. This is not to say that behaviour, not adequately expected under this system, is not expected at all. It is rather to say that the relatively less verbal and less explicit system of anticipations which governs this impulsive behaviour is inferentially incompatible with the system which he customarily verbalizes. It would be a serious mistake to infer that there was no systematic lawfulness to the behaviour which appears to be incongruous to him. Some day the whole pattern of currently unverbalized behaviour may snap into place with surprising suddenness – and bring with it a set of verbalizations to match. But we are allowing our attention to wander away from what Ronald is now saying!

Next he tells us that his inconsistent behaviour does have a frame of reference.

> One might say that his actions and attitudes depend on his mood, which shows great extremes.

He has only one word to describe it – 'mood'.

Now, he says:

> On the whole, he tries to impress people, especially his elders, with his knowledge, poise, and sincerity.

The phrase, 'on the whole', suggests that this is another attempt at writing the topic sentence of the paragraph. 'He tries to impress people' – he has already made that point clear; 'especially his elders' – this is new! The audience to which he is playing is made up mainly of 'elders'. We shall listen for more about this. 'With his knowledge, poise, and sincerity' – we are ready for his association of knowledge and poise, but is the term 'sincerity' a part of this precariously operating control system? Will he tell us what his personal construct of sincerity is? He does!

b. Second paragraph. The second paragraph helps explain what he means by sincerity.

> ... he ... hates inconsideration on the part of anyone...
>
> He is generally quite considerate of others and also shows great sincerity in what he does or says.
>
> ... if he thinks he has not been kindhearted enough

Sincerity is linked with consideration and kindheartedness into a constellatory construct.

Now when we deal with a construct we must keep in mind that its use invokes both its *similar* and its *dissimilar* aspects. Ronald is not only talking about sincerity, consideration, and kindheartedness but, by implication, about insincerity, inconsideration, and unkindheartedness.

He does a good job of attempting to explain the setting under which his turbulent behaviour makes some sense, though he appears to be unable to elaborate extensively upon its implications.

> ... he litteraly [*sic*] hates inconsideration on the part of anyone and this fact is often the reason for him flaring up over the actions or words of other people.

For one who has already indicated that he attempts to order his life on a literalistic basis and who tries to impress people, especially his elders, with his sincerity (implying considerateness and kindheartedness), both the terms 'literally' and 'hates' are strong expressions.

Now let us take a look at an interesting and important choice of words in this paragraph. It is as though he is telling us why he cannot express the frame of reference under which his explosive behaviour makes sense. We have italicized the key words.

> One might be *tempted* to say that he litteraly [*sic*] hates...
>
> *Conscienciousness* seems to be one of his main tributes [*sic*] where his *morals* and *ethics* seem to be his guide.

> A feeling of *guilt* often comes over him if he thinks he has not been kindhearted enough.

He appears to be saying that he cannot give full vent to his feelings without being guilty of the same kind of behaviour which he finds so distressing in others. If he were a child and more concretistic in his conceptualization, he might be able to see flare-ups, hate, and inconsiderateness in *himself* as the opposite of inconsiderateness in *others*. But he is an adult and inconsiderateness is inconsiderateness, whether it appears in himself or in others. Its opposite is quietness, calmness, and poise. But wait! Let us check this. Yes, but not altogether! The next sentence is:

> He considers that he has very good common sense and good use of logic in analysing or explaining many aspects of life and matereal [*sic*] things.

This is more than the mere passivity that one might infer from the terms 'quietness', 'calmness', and 'poise'. This is a highly structured self-control. 'Considerateness' is not quite what we would normally have expected. He has not said that it is the opposite of aggression. While he speaks of feeling guilty when he has not been kindhearted enough, the sentence elaborates the personal construct. It is a constellatory construct, of which *consideration* is one of the symbols, and it links together quietness, calmness, favourable attention of elders, knowledge, poise, sincerity, considerateness, kindheartedness, common sense, and good use of logic. His idea of consideration and kindheartedness is bound up with a highly intellectual process. Over and over, he tells us about this intellectualization. For him 'to consider' is 'to think logically'; 'to be considerate' of a person is 'to think logically' about him.

Now the basic oscillation which his construction system sets up in his behaviour becomes clearer. He can meet inconsiderateness in others with inconsiderateness in himself; in which case, instead of banishing inconsiderateness, he only lays it on his own doorstep. Or he can establish an intellectual control, a measure which, unfortunately, applies only to himself, and which other people will not abide by. He is caught in his own construct. If he becomes inconsiderate himself, he falls heir to all of the hate which he has heaped upon others for being inconsiderate. In his attempt to find a way out he does what any person tends to do: he vacillates from one side to the other. First he attempts to construe himself as one of the *similar* elements and then as one of the *opposite* elements. Neither construction establishes an adequate role of himself. We have already pointed out that a construct delineates a path of action which is obviously open, and along which a person is therefore free to move. Here indeed is a path which Ronald has worn smooth!

Now Ronald might be freed from this pacing back and forth in his own intellectual cage if he could reformulate his construct. There are several ways in which this might be done. One might follow the line suggested by the general semanticists and make the construct more specific. This would mean that Ronald would be helped to see that *only certain* people are specifically inconsiderate, and that they are that way *only on certain specific occasions*. This would tend to reduce the construct to relative impotence by making it relatively impermeable to events in the train of the future. Alternatively, one might seek to resolve the constellatory construct of *inconsideration, insincerity, and unkindheartedness vs. knowledge, poise, and calm appearance in the presence of elders* into, say, two propositional constructs which could operate independently of each other. One of these might be *inconsideration vs. personal understanding*. The other might be *feelings, enthusiasms, and intellectual curiosity vs. restraint and superficial appearances.* There are, of course, other approaches, but these two suggest what might be the eventual outcome of our credulous approach to Ronald's self-characterization.

We might have gone further in elaborating the terms which were italicized in the quotation about Ronald's feeling of guilt, but our theoretical position on the nature of guilt has to await elaboration in a later chapter. There is, nevertheless, a relevant minor point which might be made. While the credulous approach does not permit us to take many liberties in altering a person's statements regarding himself, it does seem as though the context and the general theme of Ronald's second paragraph might permit us to change the phrase, 'One might be *tempted* to say that he litteraly [*sic*] hates...' to 'One might say that he is literally *tempted* to hate....' A more adventurous hypothetical reconstruction would be, 'I am tempted to say (and for my kind of person to *say* is to *be*) that I literally (actually) hate.' Shortened this reads, 'My temptation is to hate.'

Ronald has used a term in his second paragraph which may be seen as a slip in spelling but which is so freighted with plausible meanings that one cannot ignore it.

> Conscienciousness seems to be one of his main *tributes* where his morals and ethics *seem* to be his guide.

One wonders whether this is a confounding of 'tribute' with 'attribute' and, even if so, whether it is tangential to our analysis. Does Ronald feel that his conscientiousness is a form of servile peace offering which is superficially ('seem') guided by a ritual of morals and ethics? The phrase comes in the context of a discussion of sincerity – ordinarily considered to be the opposite of mere making of an appearance. Is Ronald telling us that hating inconsideration on the part of others and flaring up over the actions or words of others is the nearest that he can come to actual sincerity, that such behaviour is the only propitiating tribute that he can make for his excessive superficiality? There is a further possibility of interpreting the meaning of Ronald's 'tribute', which will be discussed in connection with the sixth paragraph of the protocol.

c. Third paragraph. In the third paragraph Ronald begins to tell us of the movement which he perceived in himself. The presence of *a construct of movement* is, for the personal-construct psychologist, one of the indications that a person may be amenable to psychotherapy. At the time Ronald wrote this sketch he had had either nine or ten (our records do not clearly show which) psychotherapeutic sessions. While the therapist did not feel particularly sanguine about the progress which had been made, Ronald does express a construct of movement which is probably associated with his perception of the therapeutic series up to this point.

> His tendency to criticize and correct people, esp. in his family, on major as well as minor issues, shows some decrease outside his family, but not too much within.

One should be careful not to read sentences like this as self-contradictory. Our basic approach requires us to look for the consistent meaning in what the person says rather than to label certain statements as conflicting and to try to decide which ones should therefore be dismissed as false.

Ronald seems to be saying that his tendency to criticize and correct people has been particularly apparent in his family but that it is showing some decrease outside the family. His phrasing, 'major as well as minor issues', is noteworthy. We might have expected him to say, 'minor as well as major issues'. What he may be saying is that criticizing on major issues is the more extreme behaviour. Ronald's general approach to his problems may be hypothesized to be a critical circling of minor issues before coming to grips with a major issue. He appears not to be the kind of person who would feel free to criticize straightforwardly on major issues. Yet he is one who would consider criticism of minor issues as unworthy of him.

Ronald is having more difficulty achieving movement in relation to his family than in relation to the outside. That is usually the case in psychotherapy. One's family sees him in a long-term perspective and their expectations – and hence the validators upon which he must check the appropriateness of any new constructs he tries – are based upon relatively immutable perceptions of him.

The psychotherapy sessions up to this point had not wholly employed techniques derived from the psychology of personal constructs. They had been conducted along the general lines of Rogers' client-centred approach, except that the reflections had, at times, been recast into the therapist's terminology and therefore had had a strong interpretative flavour. The conferences were not electronically recorded, hence it is a little difficult to know precisely how the client's personal constructs were handled. The therapist was experienced, however, and a keen observer of the effects of his interaction with the client. It appears that the therapeutic goal, as seen by Ronald at this stage of therapy, was to 'decrease' 'his tendency to criticize and correct people'.

We can now see why, within Ronald's particular construction system, this kind of movement was difficult to accomplish. Criticism and correction is the very intellectual process by which he maintains 'poise', 'considerateness', 'sincerity', 'logic', 'common sense', 'appearance', and 'knowledge'. If he shifts himself as an element from the *like* side of the construct to the *unlike* side, he will get 'worked up', will 'flare up', will be 'frustrated', will be seen as 'disturbing', will draw 'unfavourable attention', and so on. Now this is not to say that when he engages in 'criticism' he successfully achieves calmness or that when he 'flares up' he leaves off criticism. It is rather to say that 'criticism' is the method by which he seeks stability and 'flaring up' is what inevitably happens when criticism ceases to operate successfully. To abandon logical criticism, therefore, appears to leave him at the mercy of its alternative – 'flaring up'. In the home, where 'major' as well as 'minor' issues are at stake, the potential 'flare-up' is too big a threat for him to handle at this stage in therapy. At this point, Ronald faces the problem which every client faces when his therapist nudges him into making some kind of movement within his currently operating construct system.

Ronald is, however, showing some signs of 'insight' – that is, using the therapist's construct system.

> Proving his point, or arguing his point, and arguing against other people's points, seems to be one of his major 'hobbies'.

The transition from *proving* his point to *arguing* his point suggests that he is becoming aware of the ineffectuality of his intellectualizing approach. He develops the idea in the next sentence by tying it up with a form of concretistic literalism (presumably the use of preemptive constructs) and the misuse of symbolism (substitution of the word for the truth – or, more accurately, the substitution of the word for the construct).

> He is apt to be too gullable [*sic*] for what he reads/or has been told/as being factual or positive proof of something, and [as] a result will sometimes argue himself 'blue in the face' over some issue that he thinks he has positive proof of.

It may be a surprise to hear him describe himself as gullible. Yet he is saying what he means to say. He is indeed the victim of his own literalism. He is misled into thinking the written word is the proof, and then he argues. At least now he is coming to distinguish between having the proof (which he is beginning to doubt) and presenting the argument (which he nevertheless persists in doing).

> However, he has acquired the ability to stay away from this undesirable aspect to a great extent.

The therapist scores!

d. Fourth paragraph. Now Ronald tries to make it clear that his use of literalism and intellectualism is a way of justifying himself. It has to do with the fundamental issues of right and wrong.

> He puts much stress in technicalities and the importance of being accurate. On the average he tries very hard to be errorless, /or/to do everything right and nothing wrone [*sic*].

We may say that Ronald's stress upon technicalities is much more than a perseverative habit – it is a way of leading a righteous life. Moreover, it is not a wholly negative thing. Note what follows the '/or/'.

This is a good point at which to call attention to Ronald's orthography and syntax. His misspelling, and his awkward syntax in the very protocol which indicates such a complete reliance upon intellectual controls should serve to make clear the fact that intellectualism is not necessarily the equivalent of academic proficiency. It is not even the equivalent of intelligence, and when it is found in the intellectually unproficient person it poses especially baffling problems in therapy. Intellectualism in the intellectually proficient person, on the other hand, provides an exhilarating test of the clinician's verbal skill.

The student who is interested in a more detailed analysis of the protocol than that which we have undertaken here will want to examine Ronald's misspellings to locate the precise points at which anxiety is beginning to have erosion effects upon his intellectual structure. His misspelling of the word 'wrong' will be noted in this connection.

Ronald's misspelling and awkward syntax in the same context with the assertion of his firm belief that technical accuracy is equivalent to the righteous way of life is a contradiction which cannot fail to arrest our attention. Perhaps it typifies the anachronistic confusion that he faces on many sides. It certainly suggests that his reliance upon technical accuracy has an untrustworthy support. And is this not what he is telling us throughout the protocol?

Perhaps, also, this is as good a place as any to call attention to Ronald's use of parentheses, slants, quotation marks, and qualifying clauses. Here is a kind of meticulousness which, considering the context, seems to indicate a need to justify himself in the presence of other people more than it does a spontaneous preoccupation with detail. This hypothesis would fit in with what we have just said about the technical accuracy with which Ronald has expressed his dependence upon technical accuracy.

One should not be too critical of the awkward syntax. Personal constructs tend to be idiosyncratic and when one tries to express them one creates strange and unfamiliar combinations for the reader to ponder over. Ronald has taken us at our word and is trying to say how *he* sees himself, not how we expect him to express himself.

Again Ronald tells us what the alternative to intellectualization is.

> When he does something wrong, he may give excusses [*sic*] for his action, depending entirely on the situation, or he will get very mad at himself or very discouraged in himself.

Note the spelling of 'excusses'. Well, he probably does 'cuss'! On the surface, however, for a person of Ronald's temperament, wrongness is something which must be immediately rationalized. The excuses, he says, depend entirely on the situation. They are an attempt to relate himself to the facts rather than frankly to placate those who may have been injured by his mistakes. If he fails to tie his behaviour rationally to the situation, he says he will either 'get very mad at himself or very discouraged in himself'. The aggression is turned inward. His expression, 'discouraged *in* himself' (italics ours), which he uses instead of the more common expression, 'discouraged *with*', minimally suggests a pervasive discouragement rather than a localized disappointment.

> If he does make an error that he feels he knew better than to do, he will, in some way or another, let everyone around know that he knew better through his exclamations of disgust and anger that he has for himself.

Here is *appearance* again. In berating himself is he beating other people to the punch? Is he not afraid that other people will be as circumstantial in their judgements of him as he is in ordering his own world? Not only must he be a rational being, but he must be on guard to make sure that no one else will see him as irrational. Even the phrase, '*knew* better than to do' (italics ours), suggests that all his errors must be construed as failures of the mind rather than failures of the heart.

> Inotherwords [*sic*], when he does something wrong that he feels he knew better than to do, he gets very angry with himself and is generally bothered by such an error, if it be of major importance, for some time after.

Perhaps the phrase, 'in other words', has been so much a part of his thinking and his attempts to structure his life by words that it has become a single word for his oft repeated personal experience of compulsive equivocation.

e. Fifth paragraph. Ronald further expresses his attempt to find a solid and rationalizable foundation for his construct system.

> It may be said that he is a materialist and a realist.

Let us see whether he will tell us what he is able to avoid by being a 'materialist and a realist'.

> He is quite apt to criticize or 'run down' things that appear too artificial or unpractical, or improbable, by saying that they are not realistic enough (especially in movies).

For one who depends so helplessly upon the intellectual process, he shows a remarkable unwillingness to live in a world of imaginative ideas. But this is not an uncommon case. Ronald is seeking firm ground upon which to base a set of *preemptive* constructs. He is not a *propositional* thinker in the main, nor even a very successful *constellatory* thinker. What propositional constructs he has leave him with no feeling of stability, and he cannot even formulate stereotypes with which to freeze his relations with other people into a rigid structure. He is dissatisfied with anything other than a concretistic formulation of his beliefs. Note his spelling of 'matereal' in the second paragraph. The constellation of material and real is carried out even in this spelling.

But we were asking ourselves what he was able to avoid by being a 'materialist and a realist'. The parenthetical phrase, '(especially in the movies)', offers us a hint. Is it romantic love? Is it sex?

> He also possesses a feeling that there is a reason for the existence of most everything and often tries to find this reason and tell his conclusions to whomever he is with.

The 'reason for existence' seems to be what he is seeking in realism and materialism. It may be, then, that it is not so much a matter of what he is avoiding as it is a matter of seeking a palpable answer to his question about existence. We should have realized that he is not an 'avoider' from what he has said before. He is critical of the movies because they do not answer his question. Since he wants the reason for existence explained so realistically and materialistically, we suspect that the question is a very old one, dating from childhood days when answers were things or observable acts, rather than words and ideas. Perhaps, as he grew into the language-using stage of childhood, words became a kind of unsatisfying substitute for the facts he vainly sought, rather than tools for exploring his environment.

Although his quest may have grown so old that he has almost forgotten what it was that he was seeking. Ronald is still asking questions by making assertions. He is checking his constructs against the reality of other persons' opinions, even though, once those opinions are obtained, he rejects the evidence as inconclusive. He reminds us of the mythological Greek hero, Cadmus, who spent much of his life seeking the lost little Europa. Perhaps someone in the weary world will tell Ronald where little Europa has gone.

> As a result, (if proper to call this a result) he believes only what he wants to believe, even in religion...

This is an *outcome* of his quest, but not the *result* he is seeking. Like Cadmus, he has asked the question so often that he cannot hear the answer.

> ... and it is usually difficult to change his beliefs or opinions unless the person attempting such shows equal or greater authority on the subject in question, or uses similar reasoning in arriving at conclusions.

Cadmus again! He appears to be saying to the clinician, 'Either show me that you have more facts behind your answer, or work out the answer within my personal-construct system.'

> Another point that should be brought out, is that he does not coincide with that of other people, especially his friends.

Here we are at a loss to pick up the thread of his discourse. To what does the third 'that' refer? If we look to the preceding sentence, we might infer that he is referring either to 'reasoning' or to 'conclusions'. In any case, there is a way in which he is unlike other people, especially his friends. Something in his personal-construct system is relatively private. But why 'especially his friends'?

Let us take a second look at the term 'coincide'. Does he equate the expressions 'to coincide' and 'to side with'? Is he saying that he finds it especially difficult to agree with anyone with whom he is closely associated? Is this a resistance which the therapist must expect to deal with?

The next statement has a clear implication for the clinician who deals in psychodiagnostic terms directly, rather than via personal constructs.

> However, he does waste time, even in his own mind, in deciding or thinking about what he will wear.

What is this sentence doing in a paragraph dealing with such lofty matters as reasons for existence? The word 'however' suggests that it is a contrasting construct to something which preceded. Perhaps it is in contrast to the firm opinions about which he argues with his friends. Perhaps the cultural conformities involved in dress bother him. In any case here is *appearance* again!

His use of the expression, 'he does waste time', suggests that there is an urgency about his intellectual quest. The expression, 'even in his own mind', suggests that the delay is a delay in thinking, rather than a delay caused by exploratory action, such as trying on clothes. His immobility in the face of an urgent task is not merely a preoccupation with the manipulation of details, but an ataxic sort of immobilization which blocks his action even before it reaches the exploratory stage.

f. Sixth paragraph. Quite appropriately in his last paragraph Ronald gets around to the topic of 'girls'. He has talked about 'movies' not being realistic enough. He has spoken of his 'feeling' that there is a 'reason for existence', a question whose original form probably was, 'Where do babies come from?' Can he link such a term as 'feeling' with the opposite sex?

> He has some ideas concerning girls that seem odd or just plain crazy to most people.

Here is a specific area of disagreement. Is it not, therefore, the focal area about which all of his arguments with his friends revolve? Here again he does not 'coincide'. The expression, 'just plain crazy', suggests the deeply disturbing nature of his ideas.

> He completely refrains from calling a girl 'beautiful'. She may be cute, pretty, attractive, or some other such adjective in his mind, but he uses the word 'beautiful' only [to] describe material things that have no 'feeling' as humans have.

Note the sharply delimited range of convenience of the construct of 'beautiful'. He does link 'feeling' with girls, but in doing so he makes them ineligible to be called 'beautiful'. Here is a 'tribute' which he refuses to pay. His use of terms suggests that he sees girls, and all feeling things, as inherently imperfect. Is this why he could never see the female sex as having anything to do with 'the *reason* for existence' (italics ours)? What happens to his argumentative intellectualism when he deals with such feeling creatures?

> Although he listens attentively to stories or general discussion about sex, he rarely enters into the conversation.

What! No disputation here? When sex is involved can he not 'tell his conclusions to whomever he is with'? The answer is no. Here is a topical area in which his thinking gives little guidance to his actions. It even interferes.

> One may say that he puts too much meaning and thought into kissing a girl.

Such an occasion is not one for meaning and thought – at least not one for as much meaning and thought as he tends to give it. Furthermore:

> If he has gone out with a girl a couple to times, or even once, and doesn't continue to go out with her or to call her, he is very hesitant about asking for a date again, say two or three months later.

Not only does he have trouble rationalizing his attention to a girl, but he has trouble rationalizing his inattention.

> Frequently he is even at a loss for words in talking to a girl he knows.
>
> He is usually lost for conversation when meeting someone new, or seeing a girl he knows, but if he once 'breaks the ice', he can usually talk freely.

With some encouragement he can respond to an intersexual situation.

In the last two sentences of the sketch he is presumably still talking about his trouble in dealing with free-flowing feeling.

> However, when he calls a girl on the telephone, no matter how well he knows her, he hates to have anyone around him or even within hearing distance.

One is reminded of the reaction of members of an earlier generation (notably Queen Victoria) to the introduction of the telephone. They were embarrassed at being overheard carrying on one side of the conversation only. Is the breaking up of the wholeness of a discussion so destructive of Ronald's verbal system that he cannot bear to have people overhear his side of a telephone conversation? Is it particularly disruptive when he is trying to keep his thinking lined up while in conversation with a girl? Does this apply to other phases of effective living?

> Furthermore, he doesn't like to practice anything, such as a musical instrument, anyplace when he can be seen or heard.

If music is an expression of affective living, it does appear that any behaviour which is structured at less than the verbal or literal level is threatening to Ronald. To be seen or heard practising is to be observed as imperfect and poorly structured.

We have come a full cycle from Ronald's initial statements about himself. The appearance he tries to maintain is one of calmness. He is concerned with appearances. He must maintain structure in the presence of other people. Feeling, whether it be in the form of a 'flare-up' or in the form of a telephone conversation with a girl, gives him an unsteady sensation. It is like making discordant and ridiculous sounds on a musical instrument.

g. Recapitulation. As a whole, Ronald's self-characterization holds together remarkably well. In the first paragraph he says that his intellectually structured pose in the presence of his elders is interrupted by outbursts whenever other people exemplify nonintellectually structured behaviour. In his second paragraph he indicates that intellectually structured behaviour is his closest approximation of morality, sincerity, and kindheartedness. In other words, if he were to abandon it, he would become immoral, insincere, and cruel. In his third paragraph he reports limited progress within the framework of this construction system. In his fourth paragraph he tells how disturbed he gets when he finds his constructs are inadequate. In the fifth paragraph he describes his urgent and disputatious search for substance which even tricks him into arguments with himself over such minor matters as to what to wear. In his sixth paragraph he tells of his inability to encompass the world of feeling within his verbally structured system.

Now there are alternative ways in which the above protocol could have been interpreted. Indeed, it will be surprising if the skilled clinicians who read this analysis do not come up with more perspicacious alternatives. If their analyses are different, but not contradictory, we shall not be greatly disturbed; if they are in conflict – that is, lead to incompatible predictions of events – we shall be forced to maintain that there are important issues yet to be resolved. In other words, our construction of this case is principally in terms of *propositional* constructs rather than in terms of *constellatory* and *preemptive* constructs, and therefore admits the possibility of other clinical constructions being just as 'true'.

We have tried to see matters through Ronald's eyes by underscoring and elaborating what he has told us about his construct system. We have not dismissed what he has said on the grounds that he does not possess 'insight'. *Insight*, as we see it, is too often applied by clinicians only to those clients who adopt the clinician's pet constructs. It is granted that Ronald may see things much differently after he has successfully completed a course of psychotherapy, but that is not to claim that the way *he will see* matters later is the way matters *are* now. Strictly within his personal world, matters *are* as they *are now seen.* Since, first of all, it is Ronald whom we wish to understand, rather than the world which is external to Ronald, we study *the way Ronald sees that world.* After we have understood the phenomenon of Ronald's viewpoint we can, if we wish, turn to an analysis of the validators against which his new constructs would have to be checked (the analysis of experience), then to the hypothetical constructs which might be proposed as alternatives to the ones he is now dependent upon, and, finally, to the means by which a therapist might seek to make the new constructs available to him. Particularly in these two last steps, we should be supervening in the case with an approach which goes beyond that of classical phenomenology. In the next chapter let us see if we can go directly to the third step without any further analysis of Ronald's personal construct system or of his experience.

Chapter eight

Fixed-role therapy

Now we follow our last chapter immediately with a description of one type of psychotherapy derived from our theoretical position and emerging from the type of analysis we have just described. Our primary purpose is to illustrate the working of the theory rather than to advertise a particular technique.

A. Reconstruction of the self

1. Development of a therapeutic approach based upon the self-characterization

In 1939 the writer began to piece together his interpretation of Korzybski and Moreno with certain observations arising out of his own clinical experience. Shortly before, he had begun to question the economy of certain psychoanalytic types of insights upon which he had been relying largely in his psychotherapeutic work. It was not that psychoanalytic theory appeared to lack practical utility. It had been far more useful in helping to predict developments during a course of psychotherapeutic conferences than had his previous systematic psychological thinking. That thinking had been influenced by Scottish analytic psychology, as represented by such writers as Stout, and in part by his teachers, such as James Drever, Sr. Their thinking, by the way, had seemed more Darwinian than associationistic. Moreover, psychoanalytic theorizing had seemed to fit clinical observation in a far more useful manner than had the mathematic-associationistic thinking of Godfrey Thomson, another teacher with whom the writer was fortunate enough to come in contact. Thomson's thinking, in turn, had struck a familiar note among recollections of an earlier interest and brief experience in aeronautical engineering where vector analysis of stresses was a useful conceptual tool.

Yet, in spite of its obvious utilitarian value within the four walls of the psychotherapeutic conference room, psychoanalysis had never quite seemed to be the answer to psychological problems obviously arising in a social, economic, or educational setting. Perhaps it was impossible to forget the technological approaches of Carl Seashore and L.E. Travis, or the social philosophies of the educational sociologist W. R. Smith, the labour economist Gagliardo, the sociologist W. S. Ogburn, the naturalist Edwin Teale, and the Quaker religious educator J. B. Mills, all teachers who had demonstrated that it was possible to strike quite new dimensions of thought through the world of ordinary facts. Perhaps it was the recollection of experiences in teaching speech making to students in a labour college, or perhaps it was teaching Americanization in a class for recent immigrants; whatever it was, something made psychoanalysis seem faintly out of tune with the circumstances. Perhaps it was the type of adjustment problems coming to the writer's attention during the decade prior to 1939. There had been school and preschool children. There had been adjustment difficulties among rural adolescents who, though they were only one generation removed from pioneer stock, were psychologically paralysed in the face of prolonged drought, dust storms, and economic depression. The writer recalls, for example, that at one time more than 60 per cent of the population of a neighbouring county had to have some type of direct public assistance.

Now, while it was possible to see these individuals as the victims of overflowing libido, and sometimes very helpful to do so, it often seemed incongruous to attempt to encompass their problems in such terms. They were not Park Avenue neurotics trying to maintain that particular social pace, nor were they in the midst of a waning Viennese authoritarian culture. It was not enough, of course, to describe them solely in terms of provincial clinical concepts. An adequate theory of personality, while taking account of individual and subcultural experience, should transcend such variations and be applicable to persons wherever they are found and whatsoever they may have become.

a. Observations of the lasting effects of dramatics experience. Four types of personal clinical observations set the stage for reading Moreno's writings. It had been observed that the experience of taking a particular part in a dramatic production had frequently had a lasting effect upon the behaviour and manner of adjustment of a particular student. For example, there was the high-school friend in a midwestern community who, when he went to college, was given the opportunity of playing a part of the English Lord in the play *Dulcy*. While the part might have been seen to call for burlesque, this friend apparently construed it as having broad implications. He 'lived the part', perhaps at the behest of the dramatics coach, for the two or three weeks the play was in rehearsal. He wore spats to school, carried a cane, and affected a British accent. Twenty years later he still had the incongruous accent and, as it seemed to the writer, many mannerisms dating precisely from the play.

While it is customary to ridicule such behaviour on the grounds that it is 'sheer affectation', a sober appraisal suggests that it was actually a faithful expression of his general outlook. The fact that he learned the manner of speech relatively late in life does not make him any more of an artificiality than those of us who learned our mannerisms relatively early. The fact that he chose to misidentify himself with the manner of speech of his friends need not make him less commendable than those of us who establish our individualities in other ways. Granted that many of us do become disturbed when one of our number abandons a cultural norm, it may be that we could profitably see the disturbance as residing in ourselves rather than in the person who has chosen to make himself somewhat unpredictable by the old patterns of perception.

What would happen if we simply said of this man: he is psychologically what he represents himself to be? He may have been reared in Kansas rather than in London, but that is incidental. The point is that his image of the character he portrays is his image of himself, or at least an image by means of which he maintains a measure of identity. His behaviour is not without substance. It is not false; it is only ahistorical. It is not to be ignored. It must be accepted as expressive of his real outlook if we are to understand him. What would happen if we took the general view that what people *do* is a feature of what they *are*; that the extent to which a person *behaves* in a certain way is a measure of the extent to which he *is* that kind of person?

b. Self-expression in dramatics. There was a second observation made in connection with plays. It appeared that certain persons were able to express themselves in certain parts with a spontaneity and vehemence which could not wholly be explained on the basis of their understanding of the playwright's intent. It was as if they had just found a verbal vehicle not ordinarily available to them for expressing ideas and elaborating upon the derivatives. In most instances this new behaviour, carried out within the containment of the rehearsal situation, seemed to be followed by a general influence in fluency, both verbal and behavioural.

The writer recalls an early experience in coaching a cast of students for the play *The Enemy*. There was a brief part to be played of a shell-shocked Austrian soldier. The writer's choice for the part was a young man who was considered to be unusually shy, socially rigid, and inarticulate. Other members of the cast were sceptical of the choice. Yet in the very first rehearsal the young man played the part so convincingly and so spontaneously that his friends could hardly believe their eyes and ears. He seemed to have become another person. The trauma of shell-shock was something he was already prepared to elaborate upon. Did this mean that there were traumata in his own life which needed to be elaborated within the protective limits of a rehearsal situation? We never knew.

c. Clinical exploration of enactment techniques. The third type of observation which paved the way for reading Moreno was made in connection with certain variations in psychotherapeutic technique which had been tried out from time to time, more or less on the spur of the moment. For example, there was the client who had repeatedly complained that she was 'afraid' that she did 'not love her husband'. She seemed to be unable to elaborate upon the idea or free-associate with it in a manner which appeared to be helpful. Thinking in psychoanalytic terms, we might say that, while obviously she could face the simple idea that she might not love her husband, her ego could not deal adequately with the flood of libido which would be released if she unwrapped the whole package. Was there not some protective screen behind which the package could be partly unwrapped and dealt with by the ego in the white light of reality?

We decided to employ the oldest dodge for releasing reality-bound thoughts known to man – make-believe.

> All right! Let us suppose for the next few minutes that you do not love your husband; that there is no longer any doubt about it. What do you think of next?... What would you be doing today?... Then what might happen?... And after all that, what?... What would be your thoughts?...

And so on. While the technique is not quite as simple as this account might imply, it is one which, in this case as well as in others, opened the door to further exploration of ideas by the client, and which eventually enabled her to 'bind' her libido in ways acceptable to her ego. Incidentally, her relations with her husband were markedly improved, both from her point of view and from his, although he was never aware, as far as the writer knows, that she once doubted her affection for him.

d. Establishment of a social function. The fourth type of observation relevant to thinking about roles occurred quite by accident in connection with the writer's college teaching experience, though he might have made the same observation initially by looking about himself in almost any direction. It was particularly impressive because of the context in which it came. As the local psychological clinic became known as a place where students could get 'straightened out about things', the requests for consultation services rapidly grew out of proportion to the writer's time for this type of extracurricular activity. However, instead of routinely saying to each applicant, 'Come back next semester and I'll see if I can work you in', the writer attempted in some cases to outline a course of activity and interests for the applicant to follow while he awaited his turn at therapy.

In several instances when the writer followed up the student at a later date he was met with some such reply as the following: 'I did need help when I first came to you and I suppose I still do but it does not seem quite so important now. I don't know why, but the things you told me to do have made me see things in a different light'; or, 'I don't need help as badly as some of the other people I know who are waiting. It's all right with me if you see them first.' Results such as this have led to the following types of comments in the writer's clinical group: 'If you just stand people on their heads, something will happen to them psychologically.' 'Anything may be a cure if the client is disposed to think of it that way.' Years later Morton, in connection with a doctoral dissertation written under the direction of Rotter, was able to show more precisely that significant changes took place in clients who were 'awaiting treatment'.

Whether we call it *active therapy, occupational therapy, vocational adjustment*, or just *guidance*, there does appear to be a stabilizing effect that accrues from seeing oneself in a functional relationship to one's surroundings, whether those surroundings be things or people. Moreover the effect seems to be much more marked than one would expect on the basis of statistical regression, although this is a matter which could be checked, and indeed ought to be.

e. Naming one's characteristics. In 1938 Guthrie published his *Psychology of Human Conflict.* He pointed out how it was possible for a person's role to be changed accidentally and that poor training in childhood can be an important factor in poor role formation. He described instances in which individuals had changed their conceptualization of themselves and thus their behaviour also changed. He suggested that it is unwise for parents, in correcting their children, to say they have been 'lying', 'cheating', and the like, since such terms may have a serious effect on the role the child builds for himself. His ideas were not wholly novel, but he was able to express in systematic form what many less scientific writers were also beginning to sense.

Also there were some simple observations which seemed to lend plausibility to what Korzybski was saying in 1939. It seemed that people tended to have the symptoms they had read about or had seen in other people. Was not the 'inferiority complex', so popular during the twenties and thirties, a socially contagious disease which had reached epidemic proportions? Many of the older persons with whom the writer worked had been insulated from this kind of cultural importation. They were people whose culture was familiar and, in certain nonverbal ways, they were quite progressive; yet their ideas about psychology were exceedingly hazy. It was a long time before they were able to figure out what kind of problem should be referred to a psychological clinic. Their complaints were couched in strangely unsophisticated terms. 'He acts like a horse who has got worms.' 'I feel skittish and jumpy.' 'He ain't crazy, is he?' 'I never was much of a talker.'

Yet, when the children of these people came in contact with psychological terminology through their high-school and college classes, they began to 'have inferiority feelings' with all the trimmings. They began to 'have anxieties' rather than to 'be worked up over something'. To what extent was this the learning of new terms for old complaints which came neatly wrapped in symptom bundles?

It seemed to the writer, in comparing the complaints of psychologically sophisticated people with those of the psychologically naïve, that there was a definite tendency, once a person had chosen a psychological name for his discomfort, to display all of the symptoms in whatever book he read, even if he had to practise them diligently. It suggested that psychological symptoms may frequently be interpreted as the rationale by which one's chaotic experiences are given a measure of structure and meaning. While it is not our intent to pursue this thought to great lengths, it is perhaps apparent to all of us that here is a line of reasoning along which one might go far. As a result of such investigation, our notions of suggestibility and culture conflicts, for example, might be profoundly altered.

f. Naming oneself. We have been talking about the effect of naming and defining symptoms. There is also the effect of naming and defining oneself. What happens, for example, when one changes one's name? There are some answers at hand in the history of our culture. Does not the fact that a woman changes her name when she becomes a wife make it easier for her to adopt new adjustment patterns and new ways of seeing herself? Does not the bride normally accomplish a more profound readjustment than does the groom? We recall that in various cultures the establishment of new adjustment patterns has customarily been accomplished simultaneously with the assumption of a new name. Religious orders employ the device freely. Saul became Paul in one of the most spectacular about-faces in history, though there was much in his earlier training under the liberal teacher Gamaliel that presaged his Pauline career. Changing one's name appears to be not only a way of escaping the social expectancies in which one has become enmeshed, but even a way of stabilizing the changes one assays to make in himself.

The making of a military officer is an amazing example of the adaptive effect of new symbolism when applied to the self. The rank, command title, and insignia all combine to create for the young man, who may otherwise have never been able to establish any claim to leadership and 'officer-like' qualities, a pattern of adjustment and behaviour far more effective than his biography would lead one to expect. The undiscriminating navy practice of creating officers for more responsible duties en bloc by a form of mass promotion known as an *AlNav* is the result of many decades of sheltered precedent. Yet shocking as it is to find such an obsolescent personnel policy applied at a point where national safety is at stake, it is just as amazing to discover that it works no worse than it does. Even men who are literally on the borderline of feeble-mindedness make fairly convincing officers. Perhaps it is because they *construe* themselves as officers. If they realized how stupid they really were, they might become less 'officer-like'.

g. New roles for the self. Without pursuing this topic further let it be said, in summary, that the tendency of people, in seeking a readjustment, both to seize upon an 'artificial' role and to seize upon a new label for themselves had been observed. Thus we were prepared to read both Moreno and Korzybski with a mind which had been somewhat opened by personal experience. The next question was what some of the practical outcomes of adding this kind of thinking to a background already badly cluttered with miscellany might be. (The task of arranging it into some sort of cognate whole was to come later.) What would happen, for example, if a client who came to the clinic for assistance on certain verbalized 'problems' were offered, instead, a new self, a new role, and a new name? What hazards were involved? Was what was commonly called 'insight' a prerequisite to basic psychotherapeutic change? How much therapeutic change was it possible for a client immediately to embrace semantically? What protective screening could be offered during the interim between one's losing of one's old identity and one's assuming of another? Certainly these are questions which suggest a whole host of research problems. We decided to explore.

2. *Writing the fixed-role sketch*

The original explorations in fixed-role therapy (originally called, simply, 'role therapy') were carried out in 1939 by a group comprising Edwards, McKenna, Older, and the writer. Edwards undertook the responsibility for carrying out the psychotherapy sessions and wrote the first thesis. A second study was undertaken by Robinson a year later.

The original procedure involved Edwards' taking the referral so that the identity of the client would not be known to the other three members of the group. She then had the client prepare a self-characterization and sort the cards of the Maller Personality Sketches (an early card-sorting type of personality inventory). In addition to the usual trichotomous sort, she used what would now be called 'Q-sort' procedure. It involved having the client select five cards which seemed to him to be most applicable to himself and five which seemed to him to be least applicable. The cards were laid out on a desk before the three other members of the group. They were arranged so as to indicate how the client had sorted them. The personality sketch was read and reread several times until the panel felt that it was able to establish some structure for the client's case, more or less in the client's own terms. Some years later we used the Rotter Incomplete Sentences Blank as an adjunct to the self-characterization, since it permits the client to verbalize his own constructs, rather than merely manipulate the normative phrases prescribed in a personality inventory.

The panel then attempted to write a new personality sketch suitable for enactment by the client. This was then called a *role sketch*, although at that time it did not always meet the definition of *role* we have chosen to employ in the present writing. One written nowadays would be called a *fixed-role sketch* and it would come nearer meeting our criterion of role. Edwards then presented the fixed-role sketch to the client and asked him to act it out continuously over a period of several weeks. In later practice this period of enactment was reduced. But more about that later!

a. Development of a major theme other than correction of minor faults. The method of writing the fixed-role sketch has undergone some changes. In the beginning we took the view that, as much as possible, the person should be accepted in the way in which he already saw himself and that he should be asked to make minor readjustments only. Our thinking was that we would not devise the fixed-role sketch to correct all the client's faults; rather, we would attempt to mobilize his resources. We looked for features in his self-characterization sketch which might be generalized and put to good use. We then attempted to put them into the fixed-role sketch in their more permeable and useful form. Thus, even in our earlier efforts in connection with fixed-role therapy, we made an effort to recognize the uniqueness of the client, even if that meant an implicit approval of his imperfections. The object was not to make a model human being out of him or even to make him into an approximation of a model human being, but to accomplish realistic therapeutic ends with as little disturbance to the client's personality as possible.

b. The use of sharp contrast. In the second place, it was not long before we began to realize that there is a kind of all-or-none characteristic in individuals' readjustments. It may be easier for a person to play up to what he believes to be the opposite of the way he perceives himself than it is to play *just a little less* in the way he perceives himself. We have attempted to embody this clinical observation into the psychology of personal constructs by using the notion of constructs as the basic units of adjustment rather than scales, dimensions, or axes. We recognize that this may at first seem archaic and not in line with modern quantitative thinking, and we have dealt with this issue elsewhere. Be that as it may, it is a common experience in therapy, when the client begins to report his first exploratory excursions into areas of behaviour where he has not previously been free to adjust, to observe that his efforts are essentially jerky and crudely contrasting rather than modulated and consistent. Even his thinking tends to have an all-or-none 'So it's black – no, it's white!' characteristic to it. Members of the client's family are likely to have an uncomfortable time of it during this 'jerky' stage of psychotherapeutic readjustment. If what we have said about a scale's being a built-up hierarchy of dichotomous constructs is a meaningful notion in general, it makes sense that the client would tend first to move in an 'either or' manner among his constructs rather than in an 'only so much' manner along a finely graduated scale.

Our experience indicated that clients tended to 'forget' about minor differences between their own conception of themselves and the conceptualization proposed in the fixed-role sketch. To be sure, they protested less in the initial stage about the 'a little less this way and a little more that way' readjustments which were proposed for enactment, but in the end *they did more* about the more shocking and sharply contrasting readjustments. There are limits, of course, to the contrasts which can be enacted by the client. These limits are not determined by the sharpness of the contrasts but by the constellatory nature of the constructs upon which the proposed movements are based. When a clinician proposes new behaviour to a client and structures it along certain lines, he may not be aware of how much other behaviour would, to the client's way of thinking, have to be swept along in its wake. Fortunately for the clinician, and for the client too, the client is likely to balk until he can differentiate the constructs in his constellation sufficiently clearly to be able to move in one respect without dislodging himself in all respects.

Soon we began to write fixed-role sketches which deliberately invited the client to explore certain sharply contrasting behaviour. An effort was made to define this behaviour so that its limits would be sharply perceived and the client would not shake down upon his head a whole closetful of carelessly stored ideas. The fact that the new sketch was to be played out behind the protective screen of make-believe tended to limit the constellatory implications of the constructs involved.

c. Setting ongoing processes in motion rather than creating a new state. The third consideration in writing the fixed-role sketch was to set the stage for a resumption of growth rather than to accomplish a major psychotherapeutic relocation during the interview series. Just as the psychoanalytically oriented therapist has to spend considerable time setting the stage for psychotherapeutic activity by developing a particular kind of relationship between his client and himself, and by training the client in free association and in a self-controlled tightening and loosening of conceptualization, so any therapist needs to give careful consideration to the way in which he prepares his client for readjustment. The psychoanalyst may have to spend months in what should be called pretherapeutic training. In fixed-role therapy the clinician conceives his job as one of preparing the client to resume the natural developmental processes of which he is capable.

In writing a fixed-role sketch the clinician is particularly sensitive to the constructs in the self-characterization sketch which imply immobility – that is, the impermeable constructs in which the self is one of the elements. The new sketch is written and the interview series undertaken in order to shake the client loose from these constructs – in order to jounce him out of his rut. In terms of another figure an attempt is made to loose him from the semantic chains with which he has bound himself. This is done primarily not by the methods of particularization, as usually proposed by the general semanticists, but by the instigation of movement within constructural frames already erected and by the introduction of new and more permeable forms of conceptualization. Movement in oneself is subject to construction, and once a person can say, 'Look, I have changed, haven't I?' he is more likely to be able to say, 'I can change.'

d. Testable hypotheses for the client. The fourth consideration in writing the fixed-role sketch has been to introduce conceptualization which can be immediately and widely checked against reality. This is akin to saying that a new scientific theory should provide testable hypotheses. The new role should not be merely an 'academic' one but should be freighted with implications for action and response. In other words, it should be a partial construction system by which a wide variety of the events of everyday life can be anticipated. Thus it becomes amenable to validation within a short span of time during which it is proposed that the client utilize it. Another way of saying the same thing is to describe the new role as being in fact exploratory and experimental.

e. Emphasis upon role perceptions. The fifth consideration, and one which has developed more recently in our thinking about the writing of fixed-role sketches, is that it should provide a conceptual basis for a new role relationship with other people. This means that the new constructs proposed as a basis for enactment should be the kinds of constructs which enable one to subsume the construction systems of other people. There is now, therefore, much more emphasis upon the way in which other people are to be construed during the enactment period. It was, in fact, because of our clinical observations that this feature lent life to a new role that we came to adopt the particular definition of *role* which we have chosen to use consistently in this book. Fixed-role therapy is, therefore, more than the introduction of new patterns of behaviour; it is a rationale for new patterns of behaviour and, more particularly still, it is a way of introducing concepts enabling a person to subsume the rationales under which other people operate.

f. The protective mask. The final consideration which is important to fixed-role therapy, though it bears only indirectly upon the actual writing of the fixed-role sketch, is that the client is to be given the full protection of 'make-believe'. As we have said before, this is probably man's oldest protective screen for reaching out into the unknown. The test tube and the scientific laboratory are outgrowths of this cautious approach to life. They enable man to explore his world without wholly and irrevocably committing himself. Fixed-role therapy is aligned with this ancient and respectable tradition. We shall have much more to say about the use of this protective screening, not only in connection with the fixed-role interview sequence, but also in our discussions of other psychotherapeutic techniques in later chapters.

In summary, it should be said that the writing of the fixed-role sketch taxes the ingenuity and perceptive capacity of the therapist far more than does the conduct of the interviews. While there may be concretistic formulas for writing the fixed-role sketch, it has been impossible, so far, for the writer and his associates to discover them. Certainly it appears that there should be a kind of *acceptance* of the client running through the theme of the fixed-role sketch. 'Acceptance' as it appears in most current psychological and psychiatric writings seems to be a pretty vague term. We have attempted to make it communicable by defining it as a willingness to see the world through the other person's eyes. It thus becomes a precondition to the intentional adoption of role relationships. Since the psychology of personal constructs lays great stress upon the interpretation of the regnancy of the constructs under which acts may be performed, rather than upon the mere acts themselves, and since it lays great stress upon *personal* constructs rather than *formalistic* constructs, it does demand of the psychologist that he have an acceptance of other persons. One might even say that the psychology of personal constructs is, among other things, a psychology of acceptance.

Now it takes skill and ingenuity to put acceptance into practice. It also takes courage. Some clinicians are so afraid of 'being taken in' by their clients that they are afraid to accept them. Such clinicians may even be shocked by the notion of the credulous clinical approach we have proposed. If a clinician finds it difficult to maintain his own integrity without rejecting the client's ideas, he will have difficulty writing a fixed-role sketch that the client can enact with any degree of spontaneity. Acceptance does not mean seeking mere commonality of ideas between clinician and client, it means seeking a way of *subsuming* the construct system of the client. One must retain his integrity in order to be of help to the client. But he must first be a client's clinician, not a clinician's clinician, a psychiatrist's psychiatrist, a doctor's doctor, or a psychologist's psychologist.

With these considerations for writing the fixed-role sketch in mind, let us turn to an illustrative example.

3. An illustrative fixed-role sketch

The following sketch was written by a panel of clinicians for Ronald Barrett, the writer of the self-characterization discussed in the preceding chapter. As an aid to the 'make-believe' context in which the role was to be enacted, the sketch was given another name, 'Kenneth Norton'.

Kenneth Norton

Kenneth Norton is the kind of man who, after a few minutes of conversation, somehow makes you feel that he must have known you intimately for a long time. This comes about, not by any particular questions that he asks, but by the understanding way in which he listens. It is as if he had a knack of seeing the world through your eyes. The things which you have come to see as being important he, too, soon seems to sense as similarly important. Thus he catches not only your words but the punctuations of feeling with which they are formed and the little accents of meaning with which they are chosen.

Kenneth Norton's complete absorption in the thoughts of the people with whom he holds conversations appears to leave no place for any feelings of self-consciousness regarding himself. If indeed he has such feelings at all, they obviously run a poor second to his eagerness to see the world through other people's eyes. Nor does this mean that he is ashamed of himself; rather it means that he is too much involved with the fascinating worlds of other people with whom he is surrounded to give more than a passing thought to soul-searching criticisms of himself. Some people might, of course, consider this itself to be a kind of fault. Be that as it may, this is the kind of fellow Kenneth Norton is, and this behaviour represents the Norton brand of sincerity.

Girls he finds attractive for many reasons, not the least of which is the exciting opportunity they provide for his understanding the feminine point of view. Unlike some men, he does not 'throw the ladies a line' but, so skilful a listener is he, soon he has them throwing him one – and he is thoroughly enjoying it.

With his own parents and in his own home he is somewhat more expressive of his own ideas and feelings. Thus his parents are given an opportunity to share and supplement his new enthusiasms and accomplishments.

A word might be said about the choice of name for the character to be portrayed during the enactment period. Generally we have chosen a name which will permit a person to continue to identify himself with his racial or national group. It is conceivable that there would be instances in which the role might well extricate the person from this type of identification. However, since we hope that the client can find abundant day-by-day validations for his trial role, we are inclined to accept these long-standing identifications. This seems to us to involve a much higher level of acceptance of the client than to commiserate with him regarding an 'unfortunate' patrimony or to attempt to 'redeem him from an ugly past'.

The fixed-role sketch of Kenneth Norton is written around a relatively simple theme: *the seeking of answers in the subtle feelings of other people rather than in literalistic dispute with them.* It might also have been written for a person who was to try out being a clinician.

The choice of language is calculated to enhance this emphasis upon feelings: for example, in the first paragraph, 'somehow', 'feel', 'know you', 'intimately', 'understanding way', 'knack', 'sense', 'catches', 'punctuations of feeling', 'little accents of meaning'. One might say that these are *textured* words rather than precise *form* words.

This construct of Kenneth as the sensitive listener is a relatively permeable one; it will permit him to embrace the future, not merely to pigeonhole the past. As a matter of fact, it is probably not a very good construct for structuring the past. We are assuming that in Ronald's case it is not particularly necessary for him to restructure his past in a fundamental way. We hope that if his adjustment processes can be freed, they will eventually take care of the past. If he were sixty-five years of age, instead of twenty or thereabouts, it might not be so easy for him to utilize this kind of concept unless it could, in some way, be tied up with, say, a sense of judiciousness born of rich experience.

Ronald's day-by-day circumstances provide a rich background against which to try out this kind of construction of himself. Being a university student, he has many opportunities for conversation with new people. Since most of them are away from home and in their late adolescence, they tend to be willing to confide their feelings to anyone who will listen. Moreover, the eagerness to talk about one's feelings is universal enough to make it feasible for Ronald to do some frequent listening in the role of Kenneth.

It is therefore to be noted how we have attempted to apply the six specific considerations which were discussed in the preceding section: (1) ignoring minor difficulties, (2) proposal of a 'radical' change, (3) release from impermeable constructs, (4) availability of validational experience, (5) a new framework for construing other people – that is, a basis for a true role, and (6) protection of make-believe as well as the general consideration of acceptance. For example, we have not countermanded Ronald's 'flaring up' by mentioning it or its opposite in the case of Kenneth; the 'flaring up' seemed to be a minor and incidental issue. We have proposed, instead, a different, a radical change; Kenneth attends to that which is warm and animate whereas Ronald could find beauty only in the inanimate. We have suggested permeable constructions. We have taken into account the availability of day-by-day validations of the Kenneth role. We have suggested ways in which he can come to understand other people. And, of course, we have preserved the protection of his make-believe by assigning a new name to the role and avoiding any literal comparisons or contrasts with Ronald. In general, we hope we have been *accepting* – but that is for the reader to judge.

Certain implications of the principal construct in the role have been spelled out. It has been given a preemptive touch in the first sentence of the second paragraph.

> Kenneth Norton's complete absorption in the thoughts of the people with whom he holds conversations appears to leave no place for any feelings of self-consciousness regarding himself.

This was our attempt to deal with the 'appearance' theme which ran through much of the Ronald Barrett protocol.

One of the dangers of setting up a preemptive construct in a fixed-role sketch is that the client is likely to abandon the whole effort when he finds that one of the elements has slipped out of place. What would happen to Kenneth if his absorption in the thoughts of other people were initially accompanied by sharp pangs of self-consciousness? We decided to set a safety valve.

> If indeed he has such feelings at all, they obviously run a poor second to his eagerness to see the world through other people's eyes.

Now there is the possibility that Ronald, considering the way he flagellates himself verbally in the presence of other people in order to keep himself from appearing shamefully stupid, may take this as meaning that he must swallow his shame rather than regurgitate it in words. Hence the next sentence.

> Nor does this mean that he is ashamed of himself; rather it means that he is too much involved with the fascinating worlds of other people with whom he is surrounded to give more than a passing thought to soul-searching criticisms of himself.

In other words, both the feelings of self-consciousness, and the shame for which we suspect that the feelings were a kind of propitiation, are to take a second place. But again we set a safety valve.

> Some people might, of course, consider this itself a kind of fault. Be that as it may, this is the kind of fellow Kenneth Norton is, and this behaviour represents the Norton brand of sincerity.

Here we have invoked a construct name from the Ronald Barrett protocol and have applied it to the construct which we have chosen to elaborate in the Kenneth Norton sketch. We suspect that the symbol 'sincerity' is one which has lost a great deal of its original meaning for Ronald Barrett under the continuous strain of keeping up appearances. It might therefore be revitalized and put to good use in the Kenneth Norton role.

The principal construct in the Kenneth Norton role is also spelled out in relation to his perception of girls. In the fourth paragraph we decided not to attempt a complete reconstruction of his approach to interpersonal relations. It appeared that he would spend the next few years of life at considerable distance from home. His relations with his family would therefore be carried on principally by correspondence. Why not let him continue to try to express his strivings by means of written words? The flare-ups might not be so likely to interfere in such a long-range dispassionate exchange.

As a parting shot we attempted to set the stage for his seeing the parents who read his letters as Kenneth Norton would see them rather than as Ronald Barrett perceives them.

> Thus his parents are given an opportunity to share and supplement his new enthusiasms and accomplishments.

Thus by construing his self-expression as a bid for the parents' sharing and supplementing, rather than as an attempt to correct their thinking (the Barrett brand of 'consideration'), Kenneth is offered the opportunity of finding some validation of his construction of his role even in an area where interpersonal relations appears to have been badly damaged.

4. The clinician's view of the fixed role

We learned early in our experience with fixed-role therapy that a few slips on the part of the therapist who conducted the interview sequence could completely destroy the effectiveness of the approach. The easiest way to destroy it, and a typical mistake of clinicians who try it for the first time, is to remove the protective screen of make-believe. Psychologists are frequently so bent upon being 'realistic' that they overlook the phenomenological realism with which it is possible for a person to exercise his imagination. Before he knows it the therapist is likely to find himself saying, in effect, to a Ronald Barrett, 'Here, this is the way Ronald Barrett *ought* to be', instead of saying, 'Let's just *pretend* for two weeks that you are a fellow by the name of Kenneth Norton.' Even among her original ten cases Edwards found that whenever the role smacked of being an admonition the client's response was reluctant and the procedure tended to be ineffective. In her studies, as well as in later experience, the most effective results seemed to be obtained when the client considered himself merely to be 'acting' in the earlier part of the therapeutic sequence. As soon as a client begins to take the fixed roles 'seriously' he is likely to begin to have difficulties and his progress is likely to slow down. In the successful case it is when the client begins to say in some way, 'I feel this is the way I really *am*', rather than, 'I feel this is the way I *ought* to become', that the clinician notes other evidences of real progress. Sometimes this kind of 'emotional insight' is voiced as, 'I feel as if this had been the *real me* all the time but that I had never let myself realize it before.'

Nor is it advisable for the therapist to try to hasten this kind of insight by direct suggestion. He must himself be so responsive and accepting of the new character that the client becomes aware of a wholeness to his new personality while he acts out his role, a wholeness which he had not experienced before in his old role. One might say that it is Kenneth Norton, *the client*, who establishes a warm relationship with the clinician, and not so much the *Ronald-Barrett-who-ought-to-become-a-Kenneth-Norton* who relates himself to the clinician. Kenneth Norton becomes the temporary reality, not merely the ideal. Kenneth Norton emerges in the present; his past slips into place as an afterthought.

If the therapist is precipitate in urging the client 'to see that Kenneth Norton is the real you', he may only succeed in convincing the client that Kenneth is merely another name for a part which is construed in the old Ronald Barrett way, and the fresh personality of Kenneth will never be born. It is important that the personality of Kenneth emerge free and unblemished by vestiges of Ronald. He must be an integral character in his own right, not merely a made-over Ronald. He must be made to live and breathe in the present and not be a facsimile of someone else.

Kenneth must be 'acted'. He must enter the world as a pure artifact. He is, in a sense, a comprehensive hypothesis which is not accepted until it meets the test of experience. The therapist, being a true scientist at heart, does not argue for this hypothesis; rather, he helps the client formulate it, conduct the experiment, and find every available bit of validating evidence which bears upon it. *Fixed-role therapy is a sheer creative process in which therapist and client conjoin their talents.* Any attempt to make it a *repair* process rather than a *creative* process seems to result in some measure of failure.

What we have been saying about the application of fixed-role therapy may, with some real significance, be extended to all types of psychotherapy, and thence to all types of scientific reasoning. As long as any client is inclined towards undoing the mistakes of his past rather than creating a constructive system which does not call for the repetition of those mistakes in the future, very little psychotherapeutic movement is likely to take place. The psychotherapist who allows his client to become wholly embroiled in his past on the theory that catharsis, abreaction, purging, punishment, expiation, or any of the exorcistic devices is, by itself, an efficacious act, is indulging in primitive thinking.

There are only three ways in which dealing with the past can be considered therapeutically defensible: (1) it may clarify the constructs under which the client has been operating and thus enable the client and the therapist to judge what the implications for the future are, (2) it may enable the client to reduce certain constructs to a state of inoperativeness by making them concrete – that is, impermeable to the embracing of additional elements – or (3) it may provide an array of elements out of which new constructs may be *created*. In this section we are emphasizing creativity. The acts of magic by which the primitive thinker tries to expiate his past sins are not creative. Rather, it is the future which counts. The teachings of Jesus, which so forcefully emphasized 'repentance' as a rethinking process rather than as an expiation process, and which urged men to embrace the future through a 'rebirth' or creative process, rather than by means of a retaliatory expedition, represent a long-standing formulation of this same point of view.

What we have said about the creative process applies to the way hypotheses are formed in any kind of scientific reasoning. They are formed as *predictions*. That is to say, they are designed to embrace the future rather than to embalm the past. The formulation of useful hypotheses requires the use of creative talent. They are designed to predict what will happen in the future. Even the archaeologist formulates his hypotheses to see whether he can predict what he will dig up next. The scientifically minded historian, as contrasted with the chronicler, formulates permeable constructs by means of which one may accomplish an optimal anticipation of events. And now again we drive our point all the way back to our Fundamental Postulate: *a person's processes are psychologically channelized by the ways in which he anticipates events*!

5. Introducing the fixed role

Fixed-role therapy may be used either in conjunction with other therapeutic procedures or by itself. We have had somewhat more experience with its use as the sole therapeutic effort. The cases have been, for the most part, college students with some variety of adjustment problems, usually involving anxiety regarding interpersonal relationships. It has been applied, with various modifications, by Blume to institutionalized children. As indicated in a later section of this chapter we have attempted some exploratory work in group fixed-role therapy, with tentatively encouraging results.

a. Presentation. When the fixed-role sketch is presented to the client who has just completed the diagnostic phase of therapy, it is usually presented in some such manner as the following:

> Before we go into the problems which brought you here to the clinic I would like you to spend at least two weeks doing some preparatory work. This will be something unusual. If it seems strange, so much the better.
>
> Here is a character sketch of a person by the name of 'Kenneth Norton'. In some ways he is, of course, quite a different kind of person from you. In other ways, I suppose, he may be a little like you. But whether he is or isn't is not important. Let's go over this together. It says...

b. Acceptance check. During the reading and at the end the therapist answers briefly any spontaneous questions raised by the client. If the client has not already expressed himself, he asks:

> What's your impression of this fellow Kenneth Norton? ... Does he sound like the kind of person you would like to know? ... Does he sound like a real person?

This is the *acceptance check stage* of fixed-role therapy. The purpose of the questions is to determine whether or not the client feels threatened by the kind of person portrayed in the new sketch, and to discover if there are any passages which are unclear or which seem implausible. The client is not asked if he would want *to be* like the person portrayed in the sketch. The answer to that question is likely to be negative. He is not asked if he would like to try *to act* like that person. His answer is likely to be a protest of his inability. The question, 'Is he the kind of person you would like to *know*?' seems to be the one which elicits the kind of response we need at this stage of the procedure.

c. Threat. In order to explain the reasoning behind this choice of language we need to refer to our conceptualization of *threat*. When a perceptual pattern is somewhat cohesive within itself, and at the same time tends to fall into a subordinate place under a type of construction system which has generally proved itself to be invalid, the person identifies the subordinate pattern as a threat. If it made no sense at all, it would not be a threat. But because of its limited plausibility, and because of the invalidity of the larger pattern by which it must be construed, it becomes a thing to be avoided. If a man meets a seductive blonde whose behaviour as well as form 'stacks up', but who, if she is to be construed within the larger framework of his family, his neighbours, and his community, would require an arrangement which has already proved itself to be invalid and one which casts him in the role of an unperceptive fool, he is likely to perceive her as a threat. Now this is not to say that a threat is something which is always avoided. Men who find seductive blondes threatening are likely to alternate between seeking them out and running away from them. They may spend a great deal of time trying to fit these luscious creatures into their pattern of life. If they are successful, they may marry one or may reconstrue them within a generally valid construction system. If they are unsuccessful, they may continue their ambivalent exploration or try to encapsulate them in some sort of impermeable construct, and try to avoid adding any more elements of experience to its context. In short, they wrap up Daphne, Hildegard, Katrinka, and Hedda, label the package 'sucker bait', and stop trying to 'understand' them.

Now, in presenting the fixed-role sketch the therapist needs to discover whether or not the very presence of a character such as Kenneth Norton is so threatening that the client has suspended his explorations in that direction and has started to avoid such people. If the new sketch is carefully written by an accepting therapist, the likelihood of its being a threat is minimal. If it is written by a therapist who is punitive and unaccepting, the client is likely to sense threat in the way the new character is portrayed. Indeed, one test of the acceptance which a therapist is able to show for his clients is the way in which they respond to the fixed-role sketches he writes.

Asking the client whether or not he would like to try to be like the character portrayed in the fixed-role sketch is another matter, however. Many clients have become so threatened on every hand that they have ceased to explore themselves. Their construction of themselves has become relatively impermeable. They devote their efforts so exclusively to *being themselves* that they have no time left for *discovering themselves*. To present these individuals with the responsibility of actually *being* anything additional to what they have already encapsulated in their self-concept is to confront them with a threat. In the language of our theory the typical client has such an impermeable construct of himself that the prospect of identifying himself with new ways of behaviour is threatening. When a client says, 'I feel as if I were insincere', or, 'I feel like a hypocrite', he is saying that his basic identity is being tampered with. It is the same kind of threat that would be experienced by a nun who was asked to portray the part of a prostitute, or a criminal who was asked to live like a conforming citizen.

d. Plausibility. The second part of the acceptance check stage is the clinician's effort to determine how plausible the new role seems to the client. Does it make sense or does the character seem unreal? Are there incongruities within the sketch? Frequently there are and the therapist has to decide, on the spot, whether to rephrase the sketch in certain places or come back the next time with a new sketch, written, of course, with a new name label.

Sometimes the client says in effect, 'I can imagine someone's being like that all right but I just don't see *how* they do it.' This does not necessarily mean that the client is threatened by the new role, except as he envisages himself trying to enact it. It is a matter of clinical judgement based on experience whether or not this type of response calls for modification of the sketch. If the clinician is skilful and has a clear idea of how the part can be played day by day among the people with whom the client lives, he may decide to go ahead. If not, he may have to make some changes.

6. The rehearsal sequence

a. The initiation stage. Following the acceptance check the therapist presents the therapy procedure. This is the *initiation stage.*

> For the next two weeks I want you to do something unusual. I want you to *act* as if you were (Kenneth Norton). We will work it out together. For two weeks try to forget that you are (Ronald Barrett) or that you ever were. You *are* (Kenneth Norton)! You *act* like him! You *think* like him. You *talk* to your friends the way you think he would talk! You *do* the things you think he would do! You even *have his interests* and you *enjoy* the things he would enjoy!
>
> Now I know this is going to seem very artificial. We expect that. You will have to keep thinking about the way (Kenneth) would do things rather than the way (Ronald) might want to do them.
>
> You might say that we are going to send (Ronald) on a two weeks' vacation and let him rest up. In the meantime (Kenneth) will take over. Other people may not know it but (Ronald) will not even be around. Of course you will have to let people keep on calling you (Ronald), but you will think of yourself as (Kenneth). After two weeks we will let (Ronald) come back and then see what we can do to help him.
>
> Let us arrange to talk this over every other day. (The clinician sets up the schedule of appointments.)
>
> Now that copy of Kenneth's character sketch is for you to keep. Keep it with you all the time and read it over at least three different times a day, say, when

you get up, some time during the day – perhaps when you eat lunch – and when you go to bed.

Now let us do some rehearsing.

The method of initiating the enactment of the fixed role can vary from situation to situation, but the preceding account illustrates the important features of the procedure. Almost without exception, clients are initially sceptical of their ability to enact the role. This feeling of scepticism and the accompanying reports of failure to enact the role are likely to continue through the greater part of the interview sequence. The therapist who is inclined to judge the effectiveness of fixed-role therapy in terms of the ease with which the client grasps it, and the faithfulness with which he enacts the part, will miss the point of the procedure and become discouraged himself. The role which is picked up too easily by the client may be ineffective, simply because it was written in a manner which did not require any fundamental readjustment of the client's outlook. If the role is picked up easily in the first week of the sequence, the therapist should recheck all phases of his work carefully. He may even have to ask for another self-characterization sketch.

If the therapist finds that the client is beginning to approach his problems in unexpected ways during the course of the interview sequence, he should not become unduly alarmed. He may keep on interpreting the new role in the manner he originally intended or he may introduce very slight modifications consistent with the interpretation the client is inclined to place upon the role. It should be emphasized that it is not essential for the client to do exactly what the clinician tells him to do. The main thing is for the client to abandon in large measure his old conceptualization of himself, and to launch out with new conceptualizations which have some possibility of proving themselves valid. The therapist's job is to make sure that new behaviour is kept bound by some kind of rationale, whether it be the kind he originally envisioned, or one the client is seeking to formulate. If the client starts behaving in a way which is like neither the self-characterization nor the fixed role, the therapist may assume that some possibly useful movement is taking place, even though he may continue to try to bind the new behaviour with the constructs set up in the fixed-role sketch. At all times, however, the clinician tries to keep the new behaviour, whatever it may be, bound with communicable constructs.

One way for the therapist to judge the effectiveness of the client's response to the interview sequence is by the degree to which the new role promises to open up new avenues for exploration to the client. Does the role show possibilities for enabling the client's personality to resume a natural process of growth and development? Does the role require the client to anticipate events and people in new ways which can be subjected to the validation that everyday experience can provide? It is this release of the client into a real and palpable world that the therapist seeks.

Sometimes a client will ask at the initiation stage, 'Do you mean you think I ought to *be* like (Kenneth Norton)?' Here is a real test of the philosophy of therapy. If the therapist really does think that the client *ought* to become the kind of person he has prescribed, he will have to make an insincere reply. A good therapist, however, does not think of himself as the dictator of what people should be like. His job is to help people to create new hypotheses and to experiment with them as a means of growing. He does not tell people what they should eventually *be*, he only suggests what they may now *try out*. What they shall eventually *be* is a matter that lies far beyond his ken.

The therapist who assumes this philosophical position regarding his work will candidly respond to the client's question in some such manner as the following:

> No; it is not for me to judge what you should be like. Right now I am not even going to try. We can talk about the question later, but I can tell you now that, when the time comes, *you* will have to help answer it. I am only suggesting that *for the present* – for two weeks – you *act out* the part of (Kenneth Norton).

b. Rehearsals. The next stage in fixed-role therapy is a series of rehearsals. While the client is asked to enact the role at all times and in every kind of situation in which he finds himself during the period, he is given special help in meeting situations which fall into the following five categories: (1) work situations, (2) situations involving casual social relationships with companions of his own sex, (3) situations involving the spouse or a person of the opposite sex, (4) situations involving parents, and (5) situations involving life orientation and plan. The usual procedure is to devote the first interview session to rehearsing the fixed role as it might apply to various types of specific work situations, the second interview to the next category, and so on, reserving the last interview of the series for a more general discussion.

c. Work situation. In the case of a student client the first type of situation may be considered to include relations with teachers. The client may be asked to describe a course he is taking, the kinds of discussions which take place in his classroom, and the kind of person his teacher appears to be. The therapist can then propose that he and the client consider how Kenneth Norton, or whatever the name of the fixed-role character is, would approach the next session of class. An interchange of discussion during or after class can be role played with the therapist and the client alternating between the parts of Kenneth Norton and the teacher. During the discussion the sketch of Kenneth Norton is reread and the client is encouraged to infer from it how Kenneth would react in the situation.

Other situations relating to work may be similarly rehearsed with a considerable amount of free comment on both sides as to how faithfully the part of Kenneth Norton is being portrayed. The client is encouraged to criticize the therapist's playing of the part. The therapist suggests and illustrates revisions in the client's playing of the part. Sections of the exchange are repeated in order to achieve greater verisimilitude.

If the client shows too much tendency to lapse back into his Ronald Barrett role, the therapist may insist on addressing him as Kenneth Norton and responding to him as if he were Kenneth Norton. This is a way of pushing Ronald Barrett out of the picture in order to make room for Kenneth Norton. The therapist can adopt various other measures to make sure that the new role is enacted throughout the greater portion of the interview. Of course, it is customary for the therapist always to address the client by his fixed-role name during the period of the interview sequence.

At the end of the first interview the therapist reminds the client that he is to play the role continuously – 'eat it, sleep it, feel it' – that he is to reread the sketch at least three times a day, that he is not to concern himself about what he ought to do in each situation he meets but rather ask himself how the new character would meet it, and that he is to try actually to create the kind of scene with his teacher or work supervisor which has been rehearsed.

The second interview in the therapeutic sequence can be opened with a discussion of the client's actual experience in creating the scene which was anticipated in the last interview. The difficulties encountered can be discussed and the scene, or some similar one, actually played out again. The therapist then turns to a rehearsal of the companionship type of setting. The typical kinds of conversational discussions with which the client is familiar can be worked through. The character of Kenneth Norton can be introduced into a typical scene. The fixed-role sketch can be reread. Parts can be interchanged as before, and the client can be urged again to inject the Kenneth Norton personality into an analogous scene during the ensuing twenty-four hours.

d. The client's initial reactions. During this period the client is likely to give the therapist very little encouragement. Usually the first clue the therapist has that the role is being undertaken seriously is when the client begins to make independent inferences as to how Kenneth would have played his part at a certain point. The therapist may seize upon such spontaneous efforts to elaborate the fixed role and offer to let the client role play them out with him immediately. During this period the therapist must move back and forth between generalized verbalisms about the role of Kenneth and the portrayal of Kenneth in action. During this period the therapist should not expect too much in the way of verbal fluency on the part of the client. While the enactment may be attempted in terms of words, the role playing is a much more comprehensive experience. The client who, for a few moments, says nothing, but who, for those moments, feels like a new person and sees things as if he were a new person, is engaging in exploratory behaviour just as truly as if he were reciting lines. It is important for the therapist to keep the interview pitched to a point which maximizes the possibility that some time, during the course of the hour, the client will *feel* like Kenneth Norton, if only for a few fleeting moments.

It is also important during this period for the therapist to indicate from time to time his approval and understanding of Kenneth Norton. The therapist who shows that he understands how Kenneth Norton feels is showing an acceptance of Kenneth Norton, and the client cannot help but feel that acceptance whenever he sees the therapist responding to him as if he were Kenneth Norton. As most therapists discover sooner or later, there are some clients who are deeply threatened by the therapist's apparent acceptance of them as they are. The psychologist who claims that acceptance by the therapist is always reassuring to a client simply has not been as sensitive as he might be. The threat of being accepted stems from the threat one sees within himself. If he sees a therapist accepting that portion of himself which he finds so threatening, he may become anxious lest the therapist join forces with the other validators in his life experience and convince him that 'what is must be'. Yet everyone ultimately seems to want acceptance from others, provided it can be an acceptance of the kind of self which is acceptable to oneself. Now, in accepting the client in the role of Kenneth Norton, the therapist is able to avoid some of the *threat of acceptance* of an unacceptable self. At the same time he is offering the client the kind of acceptance that makes it possible for him to feel that he can interact with the therapist. He shows his willingness to play a role.

e. Remaining situations. The other types of situations are rehearsed in succeeding interviews. In the second enactment interview, after the client's experience with the role in the work situation is reviewed, the therapist rehearses a companionship situation. The third situation, involving a friend of the opposite sex, is frequently the one which is succeeded by some slight encouraging sign that the client has taken hold of his part. The situation involving the parents frequently has to take the form of a letter to them, written in the vein of Kenneth Norton. The rehearsal having to do with life orientation and plan can usually be played out as a discussion of philosophical or religious matters in a group. It may involve participation in a religious group, if that is consistent with the character of Kenneth. The effort here is to see what anchorage in more regnant and permeable constructs can be found for the new role.

The final interview can be a frank withdrawal of the Kenneth Norton role, with the client being offered the opportunity to discuss any topic he wishes. Usually there is a great deal of spontaneous speech in this interview, and it is not normally necessary for the therapist to play an active part in the interview. Certainly he should not resort to moralizing or to urging the client to adopt the new role. The therapist has had his innings. If the client has found the new role effective, he will buy it, regardless of the name that is attached to it or of the therapist's sales talk on its behalf. This is the interview in which the therapist should listen, limiting his remarks to safe restatements of what the client has told him, and making only rather general remarks of encouragement. He will have to judge at this point whether he should continue therapy by some other method or trust the momentum of the processes which have already been unleashed to carry the client through a period of reorientation followed by continuing personality development. If the client proposes it, the therapist may agree to continuing the rehearsals for some extended period of predetermined length. In some cases we have continued fixed-role therapy for periods as long as three months. However, since one of the purposes in developing the method was to find an economical way of rendering psychological assistance, we have tried to reduce the interview sequence to an absolute minimum.

Six sessions in a two-week period, including the presentation session seems to be the least amount of time in which therapeutic results of any value can be achieved.

B. The use of fixed-role therapy

7. Excerpts from a therapist's account of fixed-role therapy

Almost any type of therapy appears to work in some cases. Not only that, but almost any type of therapy will work in some degree in a majority of cases. This is an interesting fact not always recognized by clinicians. It will be discussed in detail in a later section. Now it might be appropriate to cite some particularly encouraging examples of apparent success resulting from the use of fixed-role therapy: say, the girl in teachers' training who was initially judged by her supervisor to be too stupid to be encouraged to prepare herself for anything but a one-room country school job, but who, within a year, was urged by others to continue towards a Ph.D. degree, and who subsequently did build an exceptionally successful career for herself in teaching. Or the young man who was considered a bad risk by the college, both because of his low grades and because he rated at the eighth centile on the college intelligence test; at the end of an eight-week course of fixed-role therapy he stood at the twentieth centile on an alternate form of the test and fifteen weeks after the conclusion of therapy stood at the fortieth. Regression effect, possibly! Yet his grades and his social adjustment showed even more marked improvement.

These, of course, are selected instances. Since the purpose of this whole book is primarily to expound rather than to defend – let subsequent experimentation determine validity – we have selected an account which seems to illustrate some of the problems which arise in the application of fixed-role therapy in a case. The 'treatment' cannot be judged, on the basis of this account, to have been particularly successful.

The Ronald Barrett case was chosen partly because the self-characterization sketch clearly revealed a type of thinking which is more or less familiar to experienced clinicians, regardless of whether or not they are accustomed to the analysis of this type of protocol. Moreover, it was planned to select a case which would serve to illustrate both the analysis of self-characterization protocol and the application of fixed-role therapy.

In a sense, Ronald's case is not typical. He had already had some therapeutic help, as we have mentioned before. The interview series was cut short. He was the type of person who does not make sweeping and dramatic changes in his manner of generalizing. He would need considerable experience in any new role before he could feel comfortable in it. He had many unverbalized questions to ask. Furthermore, the therapist had never attempted this type of therapy before and was somewhat sceptical of its appropriateness to the case and its professional respectability in general.

On the positive side this was a case in which the therapist obviously had to terminate the treatment in a given length of time. The client was going into a new situation in which exploratory behaviour of the type sought in fixed-role therapy would be more feasible than it would be if he were to stay on the beaten paths around his home. Because there had been a number of other clinical contacts, enough was known about the case to make it reasonably sure that it was not significantly different from the way we construed it to be on the basis of the self-characterization protocol.

The therapist was a keen and sensitive observer who could be expected to make relatively impartial comments on the procedure. It was also a case in which the therapist appeared to make some typical mistakes, some of which he recognized immediately, and others of which possibly escaped him because of his lack of grasp of the full theoretical position from which the methodology stems. His training had led him to be deeply appreciative of client-centred therapy. For that reason he was perhaps more sensitive than many therapists in picking up the overtones of feeling in the verbalizations of the client. But, like most nondirectivists, he saw different therapeutic methodologies as lying along a continuum between 'nondirectivism' and 'directivism'. Because he construed therapy to some extent in this manner, his attempts to alter his procedure tended to move along this avenue only. His attempts to change himself within his current construct system were analogous to those we have already discussed in connection with psychological readjustment in general. He was willy-nilly forced into seeing fixed-role therapy as a kind of directive therapy or as a kind of compromise between directive and nondirective therapy. It therefore seemed to him to be primarily a method which involved some degree of admonishment and assertion rather than pure organized exploratory behaviour.

It is not always easy to approach therapy from a scientist's point of view and see it as a means of helping the client formulate and test out hypotheses without being overly ego-involved in them. It is easier to take the position that either the client or the therapist must decide what is the 'right' thing to do. If it is the therapist, then the method is 'directive'. If it is the client, then the method is 'nondirective' or 'client-centred'. But is not the scientist's point of view something quite different from either of these? Is not his point of view that the facts must be manipulated into making the ultimate decision rather than assigning the responsibility to either person? Does he not formulate his hypotheses in terms of make-believe and then see what happens to them in the white light of experience? Does he not formulate his hypotheses systematically and then follow through with an enactment of a fixed role – commonly called an *experimental design*? Does he not merely treat his hypotheses *as if* they were true during the course of the experiment? Even for one who has a degree of scientific sophistication, as indeed Ronald's therapist had, this perspective of therapy comes into focus only slowly.

Ronald Barrett

a. Eleventh interview. The first part of the interview was not devoted to fixed role. Rather it was a free interview situation in which I tried to determine his attitudes towards the effects of his role playing the previous week. He stated that he had had some trouble in understanding exactly what the role had meant. Specifically, he had trouble with the phrase, 'a passing thought to soul-searching criticisms of himself', and with the phrase, 'somewhat more expressive of his own ideas and feelings in his own home'. These he did not understand, but seemed to grasp the idea when I explained them to him.

The role did not go too well. He did try Kenneth Norton out with his foreman, Carl, and with a girl he knew, a former high-school classmate. All in all, though, it was not too successful. He kept repeating that he did not understand what he was supposed to do. I asked if he had read the role three times a day as I had asked the previous time and he said that he had tried, but generally it was twice a day, once in the morning and once at night. It seemed pretty clear that the resistance extended all the way up and down to the notion of this role. In the midst of all this discouragement of the failure of the role to work there was one bright note. He did meet this former classmate after a movie. The girl works in the candy counter in the lobby and he and she had a twenty-five- to thirty-five-minute talk. She seemed quite interested in him and the role worked better with her than with anyone else. In fact, by the time the conversation was finished she was paying him several compliments, saying that he had changed since he had gone away to college, obviously implying a change for the better. The conversation was so rewarding to the client that he did not leave until the manager of the movie came along and implied that he was taking too much of her time.

The remainder of the session was devoted to role-playing situations with his peers. Since the client knows a great deal about automobiles and cares about them, we role played a situation in which he and his friend were discussing cars. It was in this situation that he did the best work. In other situations where he was less competent and less comfortable, he would quite often lapse back into dominating the conversation by long soliloquies, by interruptions, by constant personal references. I was quite active all during this part, interrupting when I thought he did particularly well, complimenting and rewarding him when I thought he was getting into the knack of Kenneth Norton. We spent a great deal of time on techniques, on how to get the other person to talk. He remembered much of what had been done in this vein during the previous week, but we worked again on the incomplete sentence and on the ability to throw the conversation back into the lap of the other person. He seemed to be catching on to the technique, but it was still without spontaneity and without warmth. It almost seemed as though it were a lesson in speech.

Since the client was due to carry a passenger with him back to his home town, we worked considerably on the things that they could talk about, he and his passenger. The passenger, unfortunately, is pretty much of a Silent Joe and the client kept interrupting me as I would try to portray what his friend would be like. Whenever the client is resistant it takes the form of petty corrections or infinite explanations of his own feelings over a small point. I was probably somewhat nonpermissive at this point, stating that I did not want to get drawn into a discussion of whatever point it might be, but that we were mainly interested in getting into the swing of Kenneth Norton.

The whole interview lasted about one hour and twenty minutes. Towards the end of it he seemed to be going fairly well and fairly automatically, but he still did not have too much confidence in the role. He stated very clearly and unequivocally that he did understand what was expected of him. He stated that Kenneth Norton did make sense to him. Though he may have had difficulties during the past week he did seem as though he would give it all he had and for all the world appeared to have sold himself on the idea of giving Kenneth Norton a fair trial.

b. Twelfth interview. We devoted some time to a summing up of the things we had done during the course of the interviews. The client stated that he was much less insecure in social situations and that there was some diminution of day-dreaming. Especially evident, he said, was the fewer number of quarrels that he had at home, though he still engages in this behaviour. For example, a few days ago he and his mother had a quarrel about why he no longer quarrelled so much. He seemed to think this was quite funny.

In response to my question of what would he consider to be his problem if he had to come today for the very first interview, he responded that he might not ever come. The first time he came it was due to the fact that he was extremely uncomfortable and inadequate in presenting speeches to a group of people. Since this is no longer true, he felt that he might not have felt the need to arrange interviews. This in itself, though it was stated negatively, is one indication of diminished anxiety and increased security in the client. The first time he came in he was terribly anxious, the whole world looked gloomy to him, and he insisted on starting the therapeutic process. When I asked for specific situations where he felt more secure he cited the party he went to Christmas night. In the first place, he was able to call a girl on the telephone and when she asked him over to her house to meet some friends of hers, he was able to go and enter this situation which formerly would have frightened him off. During the party they played a game in which people took turns at being 'it'. When he was 'it', involving having to stand in front of the group and guess who had something hidden in their hands, he at first felt very uncomfortable but later started to feel more at ease. I asked how he got along with the other members of the party. He said, 'Well, not too well. It was kind of awkward.' At this point, I asked, 'How do you think Kenneth Norton might have handled this situation?' He perked up immediately and evinced great interest. 'Yes', he said, 'how would he have handled *that situation*?'

With this as a clue we started back into the fixed-role situation playing Kenneth Norton at this particular Christmas party. For the first time the client expressed an interest and need to see how Kenneth Norton would react. I acted out various strangers there in the group and he would be Kenneth Norton. For the first time since I had first seen the client he was relaxed, warm, and to some degree achieved spontaneity. This was more true with the male roles with whom he was interacting than with the females. He even cracked one joke, which is the first time I had heard him do such a thing.

We concentrated on how Kenneth Norton would behave with these strangers. When he behaved particularly appropriately, I stepped out of role, congratulated him, and tried to reinforce this new behaviour. He was altogether quite satisfactory in his new relationships with a strange male. However, with a girl that I structured for him he was somewhat more tense and much less comfortable. Again, his old habits of interrupting, of stammering, of going into long monologues reappeared. However, even here there was some improvement over his previous role playings. He did so well that I thought there was time to go on and play some of the family situations. The first situation I picked was when Kenneth Norton would return home. I tried to portray the mother as I understood her from his descriptions, but Kenneth Norton became immediately antagonistic towards her. When I, as the mother, said something about the fact that the father and I never really understood him, he became very upset, shook his finger at me, and said, 'Yes, that's what I want to know. Why didn't you ever understand me?' His whole behaviour was in that same vein. He seemed argumentative, hostile, and belligerent. I expressed the thought that Kenneth Norton would not behave like this and I tried to take over the situation, but he kept trying to point out how he was right.

On later contemplation it would appear that the client was being somewhat more expressive at home as the role had indicated. However, all I could see was the extreme aggressiveness towards the mother and, unfortunately, I tried to sit on him. I did coach him and encourage him in some of the techniques which he used in talking with his mother and I tried to reinforce whatever new behaviour I saw in him.

Towards the end of the interview we broke roles and I tried to undo some of the damage I had previously done when I had emphasized the change which would have to take place in him. I said that we did not want to throw Ronald Barrett in the ash can. Rather, Kenneth Norton was in a sense supposed to be another Ronald Barrett, a different version of him. I used the analogy of the onion skin where one layer comes off revealing another layer. I said that was the relationship between Barrett and Norton. Or, I said, that at least was the intention when we wrote the role. He seemed to understand this quite well and reacted with some feeling. He said, 'Oh, it's just like a diamond ring. It's just another facet of the same personality.' I nodded yes and expressed complete agreement with his analogy. The interview had lasted about one hour and a half. As we stood to leave, he shook my hand, called me 'Jack' for the first time, and thanked me for my efforts. I told him that I had enjoyed talking with him and that I appreciated how hard he had worked at this thing. I said it seemed that he had made great progress and that I hoped he would keep it up. He left feeling quite happy about the whole thing.

8. Clinical skills required in fixed-role therapy

Although the writer has had experience with fixed-role therapy during a sixteen- or seventeen-year period, he has never been comfortable in trying to write a fixed-role sketch without the aid of a panel of clinicians who are present during the actual drafting. Perhaps this is because the task involves so much more than assigning the case to a diagnostic category. More likely, it is because the fixed-role sketch requires more ingenuity than one man can easily muster at a sitting. The clinicians who write the sketch together must be able to envision a wide range of situations in which the client will have to enact the role, and to understand the kinds of verbal generalizations which are likely to have a wide range of applicability. A panel of clinicians is much more likely to give the sketch the necessary scope than is one clinician drafting the sketch by himself.

Another function of the panel is to provide a test of the communicative effectiveness of the composition. Since the sketch is to provide a basis for communication between the therapist and the client over a period involving several hours of intensive interviewing, and since it is to be read and reread dozens of times by the client, it is important that each word and phrase carry its full quota of perceptual freight. The panel can therefore provide a test group by means of which the communication potential of the sketch can be gauged.

We have already mentioned the need for the person who writes the fixed-role sketch to be accepting of the client and of the hypothetical person whom he is to portray. The therapist who conducts the interview sequence must be no less accepting. During the interviews he has to enact various parts ad lib. Most of these will be scenes in which the new role is portrayed by the therapist. Some will be scenes in which members of the client's family are portrayed by the therapist. The therapist must be accepting of all, for if he is not, he will, just as sure as the world, exhibit a burlesque rather than a role. And in exhibiting a burlesque he will fail miserably to provide the client with the kind of construct-subsuming interpretation which will enable him to play an effective role in relation to those persons in real life. If the therapist makes the mistake of portraying the client's mother as the shrew the client has described her to be, rather than, say, as a guilt-laden solicitous parent, his portrayal will have an untrue ring to it. Even though the portrayal conforms literally to what the client has said about his mother and the client is vastly amused by the therapist's joining him in a deprecation of his mother, he will be quick to sense the implausibility of the act and its basically threatening nature. The therapist must be able to play any of the roles he is called upon to portray with depth and sympathy even though he cannot always be expected to play them with accuracy.

In other words, the enactment must be the portrayal of a role relationship, and not an exhibition of burlesque or a 'release of hostility'.

It seems important that the therapist who conducts the interview sequence has some measure of verbal fluency and acting skill. This is, in the writer's opinion, somewhat desirable in all therapists who deal in concept-formation therapy. But here all the words must be particularly available. The therapist talks much more than in conventional procedures. He must talk as if he were various persons. He must be quick to take a sketch, whether the fixed-role sketch or a thumbnail sketch of some other person described by the client, and flesh it out with lines in a dialogue. He must be quick to sense when his lines ring an untrue note in the ears of the client. He must be able to utilize the client's terminology of the particular way in which the client uses it. He must set scenes quickly, bring in supportive content, follow the movement of each scene to see where it is leading and what issues it skirts, readjust his lines in the light of the criticism of the client, and every moment play in strong support of an actor – the client – who is continually fumbling his lines and contaminating his role.

The therapist must have skill in converting generalized statements into concrete illustrations. Repeatedly, as the client describes feelings and events in vague terms, the therapist seeks to reduce the communication to a palpable illustrative form. Furthermore, the therapist must be alert to situations described by the client from which generalizations might be drawn by him if he were to act them out in the interview room. This is not to say that the therapist tries to sermonize from the role-playing sessions. That should be consistently avoided. It means that the therapist must always be immediately aware of the illustrative potential of material appearing unexpectedly in the interview and be prepared to weave it into the rehearsal.

The clinician must have a great deal of enthusiastic momentum. He cannot hope that his pessimism will be perceived by the client as 'permissiveness'. Any discouragement he feels is likely to be communicated to the client immediately. As in other forms of therapy, the therapist frequently becomes aware of a perverse and persistent 'need' on the part of some clients to drag him down to their own level of despair. With the touch and go of this type of therapy the response of the therapist to the drowning man's frantic clutching is immediate and sometimes disastrous.

Finally, as we have mentioned before in connection with the Ronald Barrett protocol, the therapist must be thoroughly cognizant of the essentially experimental nature of fixed-role therapy. Unless he is able to see therapy from this point of view and see his role integrally as scientist and clinician, he will be caught with inadequate constructs. What happens next is clearly illustrated in the clinician's account of the twelfth Ronald Barrett interview, when he found himself resorting to an older conceptualization of therapy – in this case, in terms of nondirectivism versus directivism. The clinician who sees the role of the scientist as being antithetical to or even independent of one's role as a clinician will not be able to operate comfortably as a fixed-role therapist. The basic position of the psychology of personal constructs calls for seeing psychotherapy as an application of basic scientific methodology, not merely as an exploitation of 'scientific findings'. Clinical psychology is no more *applied* than experimental psychology should be, for the essence of experimentalism is that one's reasoning should be applied experimentally to live situations to see what the outcome will be. Moreover, clinical psychology should be no less *scientific* than experimental psychology claims to be, for the purpose of therapy is to open to the client doors of exploration. The scientist lays wagers on an imminent future; the clinician asks his client to do the same.

9. Evaluations of progress in fixed-role therapy

In evaluating progress the therapist should keep in mind that his purpose is to help the client set in motion a healthful psychological process rather than to create a fixed state of well-being at the termination of therapy. In saying this we are reiterating still again the Fundamental Postulate of the psychology of personal constructs. The Rogerian school of client-centred therapists, commonly called the 'nondirectivists', postulates a 'growth principle' which also emphasizes the on-going nature of the changes set in motion during therapy. It seems to the writer, however, that there are important differences in the two theoretical approaches. In the psychology of personal constructs we have attempted to emphasize the form in which construing takes place, the directionality of the evolving process or growth, and the validation of the construction system in terms of predicted events which either occur or fail to occur. Thus the individual does not merely reach a terminal state of adjustment through the unfolding of an inner potentiality, but he is continuously adjusting to a changing scene by means of *an organized succession of formulated plans.*

This difference in point of view, while not necessarily representing a sharp semantic contrast, does result in some contrasting approaches to psychotherapy and, of course, in some different ways of evaluating progress in psychotherapy. The nondirectivist, because of his faith in the emerging being, asks the client to pay attention to himself as he reacts with his everyday world. Somewhere the mature *self* is waiting to be realized. The nondirective therapist is hesitant to say what that self is, so he prefers to hold a mirror before the client in which can be seen the reflections of those vague stirrings of life which are called *his feelings.* The personal-construct psychologist, because he sees life proceeding by means of a series of hypotheses and validating experiences, may hold the same mirror, but he sees that mirror, and the image of validating experience which it reflects, as setting up the succession of targets towards which the growth is directed. The personal-construct psychologist is probably more inclined to urge the client to experiment with life and to seek his answers in the succession of events which life unveils than to see them within himself. The personal-construct psychologist does not hesitate to assume a role relationship with his client and to ask the client, in turn, to experiment with varying role relationships with the therapist. He urges the client to articulate his efforts with the enthusiasms of other people so that they may undertake joint inquiries into the nature of life. He urges the client to see himself in terms of an ever emerging life role rather than in terms of a self which approaches a state of maturity.

The emphasis which the personal-construct psychologist places upon the never terminating nature of life, rather than upon the self's state of being, can be illustrated from Dickens' *A Tale of Two Cities*. In that classic, Dickens, who had an unusual gift for seeing people as ever emerging beings, creates the character of Sidney Carton. It is not until the end of the book, when it is climaxed by the famous line, 'It is a far, far better thing', and so on, that the reader becomes fully aware of the intrinsic wholeness of the character's life role. Yet at that moment everything that Carton has represented begins to fall into place. It becomes clear that his sense of values, previously appearing to be so inadequate and profligate, was the very ethical basis for his sacrificing his life as he had his substance. The difference was the worthwhileness of the cause at stake.

10. Evaluation in terms of new behaviours

The personal-construct psychologist tends to evaluate the progress of therapy in terms of new behaviours which, in turn, he takes as evidence of movement within the client's construction system. One is reminded of writings of James (2: 14–26) in the New Testament, which might be paraphrased to read: 'Your fundamental anticipations are revealed in what you do' and 'Can't you get it through your stupid head that there isn't any such thing as an expectation which is not expressed in terms of one's acts?' The personal-construct psychologist is also willing to take the position that a person is what he does; and, by fixed-role therapy, as well as by other procedures, he encourages the client to see himself in the light of this viewpoint.

Now this is not to say that one's inner construction system does not matter, or that indulgence in a set of compensatory acts will lend meaning to a life which is structurally shaky. It is, rather, another way of saying that a person is what he is now and is not necessarily precisely what he was yesterday. If one makes a good adjustment today, we assume that it occurs under the aegis of a good construct which is now operating. If he makes a bad adjustment tomorrow, we assume that a bad construct is operating at that time. If he makes a series of good adjustments, we assume that he is operating under a relatively permeable construct embracing a variety of situations.

Usually the first sign of improvement noted by the therapist in fixed-role therapy is a report by the client of some behaviour which is not consistent with his self-characterization. He is not likely to say outright that he has done something new, he just reports it as something sufficiently interesting to be mentioned in the interview. The fact that he reports it at all is a clue to the possibility that he found his behaviour to be somewhat novel.

As soon as new behaviour is noted, the therapist must take stock of it. How does the client construe the new behaviour? In the early stages he is not likely to construe it as wholly 'new'. If the client appears to consider the behaviour to be something which was specifically prescribed by the therapist or by the fixed-role sketch, he is still in the verbally planned enactment stage of therapy rather than in the spontaneous stage. If he reports the behaviour in a matter-of-fact manner as if it were the obvious thing to do, the therapist has evidence that the role is becoming spontaneous.

The therapist should not expect the client to keep bringing him little gifts in the form of anecdotes clearly labelled by him as 'new reactions'. Real movement is more likely to be reported first in terms of matter-of-fact experiences which the therapist detects as actually new, and later in terms of experiences which the client finds somewhat surprising and is not sure he fully understands. The earlier signs of movement are likely to be explained by the client in terms of unusual circumstances, or perhaps he does not feel that they need any explanation at all.

As the therapeutic movement begins to gather momentum, the client has to decide whether he will report behaviour which he cannot explain and which does not appear to make sense, or simply ignore what has happened on the grounds that because it did not make sense it must be irrelevant. Some clients 'hold out on the therapist' in reporting movement for quite a long time. This sort of thing is a more common occurrence in connection with a conventional type of therapy; but it does occur even in fixed-role therapy, in which one might expect that the client would be so prepared for new behaviour by the structuration of the fixed role that he could not possibly be perplexed by its occurrence.

11. Hazards

No therapeutic programme is without its hazards. At first we were quite sceptical of fixed-role therapy and concerned that it might unhinge the client by creating an aura of unreality about his life. Experience shows us that quite the opposite is the case, if the procedure is properly conducted. The therapist is careful to create, in the first place, a role which has many day-to-day implications. He sets up a situation wherein the client actually tests his role against the validators which are immediately available to him. The interview sessions are 'right down on the ground' instead of 'up in the clouds of abstruse thinking'. Rather than creating an aura of unreality, the role, if properly written and rehearsed, is likely to be much more practical and close to daily reality than the role the client originally construed for himself. The fixed role can be looked upon as a way of getting the client's feet on the ground so that he can make something out of his daily experience.

Now the hazard involved is that the therapist may let the client jump into his role and take off into the wild blue yonder. This is not likely to happen unless the therapist is himself unable to visualize the practical applications of the fixed role and is reluctant or incompetent in utilizing commonplace events in rehearsing the client for its enactment. If the therapist conducts all of the interviews in the same generalized vein in which the fixed-role sketch is written, rather than using the sketch as a generalized approach to little incidents and everyday events, he is likely to accomplish very little of benefit to the client and, conceivably, could abet the client's maladaptive construction system. The role must be enacted. It must be rehearsed incident by incident, line by line, cross by cross.

We have had a little experience applying fixed-role therapy to clients with schizoid tendencies. Our initial approach was one of extreme caution, for we feared that the make-believe might augment the schizoid condition. The results have so far been quite reassuring on this point, although we would by no means claim that fixed-role therapy is the treatment of choice for schizophrenia. What happens is that the schizoid client simply has difficulty applying the role consistently to everyday events. There is little indication that he makes any kind of sense out of the fixed-role sketch, other than the private kind of sense he makes out of anything else a person might say to him. One can agitate him by means of fixed-role therapy, but apparently one cannot alter his approach. The schizoid client appears to have developed his own immunity against any harmful effects that fixed-role therapy might incur.

We have, however, had clients with tendencies which might be judged to be schizoid who reacted favourably to fixed-role therapy. Apparently the favourable reaction came about because the fixed role actually helped put them in contact with reality. The responses of other people came to be predicted and the predictions validated so many times a day that the clients found themselves in possession of a construction system that obviously worked. They found themselves actually playing a role in relation to real people. Their lives were caught up into a social pattern in which they knew what to expect of other people and other people appeared to have clear notions of what they expected of them.

There is another kind of hazard which is much more to be guarded against than the hazard of unreality. That is the possibility that the therapist, in his eagerness to produce therapeutic movement, will prod the client into moving wholly within his old construct system. While this type of hazard is no greater, if as great, with fixed-role therapy than it is with other types of therapy, it is one which some clinicians do not seem to know how to avoid. For example, if a client characterizes himself as 'kindhearted' and appears to use that construct as a mainstay in his construction system, the therapist should be immediately alerted to the serious implications of the construct as a whole. What are the behaviours which the client has so carefully excluded in his choice of the construct of 'kindheartedness'? Are they in turn collected by the client under such terms as 'retaliation' or 'rebellion'? The therapist should keep in mind that a construct upon which a client leans heavily in characterizing himself is a broad avenue which has an opposite end. Furthermore, it is one on which there are likely to be few intermediate stopping points. The most fundamental constructs by which we maintain ourselves tend to be dichotomous rather than scalar. The constructs of femininity and masculinity, so important to most of us, are good examples.

Now if the therapist prods the client too eagerly or allows him to come under too great a stress, the resultant movement may occur along an avenue of retreat which the client's own construct system sets for him and on which there are so few intermediate stopping points. This is not to say that the first signs of movement will occur along the client's principal dimension. Fortunately clients tend to resist overeager therapists. But the therapist's vigorous efforts may force movement and there is always the danger that that movement may be catastrophic, because it has to take place within the construct system which the client had to begin with.

When the therapist first notices movement in the client he should immediately ask himself which one of the client's constructs appears to be involved. If the movement appears to be taking place along a dimension whose opposite end spells trouble, the therapist should take steps to slow it down and make some attempt to clarify the constructs in the fixed role which are judged to be safer channels for the movement the therapist hopes will eventually take place.

These are the general hazards which are the outcome of the therapist's reluctance or inability to hold up his side of the enactment. They may be a result of the therapist's scepticism, although there is no essential reason why scepticism should prevent one's giving the technique a fair trial. Mostly what happens when a nonscientifically minded therapist's scepticism gets in his way is that the conferences bog down, the client keeps reiterating his complaints, and the therapist resorts to an intermittent series of nagging exhortations.

There is another way in which the therapist may detect his inadequacy during the course of therapy. It is, of course, customary in many types of therapy to keep pointing out to the client that he is the one who must actively bring about the readjustment. Some therapists take this principle so seriously that they use it as a way of disengaging themselves from the problems the case presents. Sometimes it operates as a defence behind which a therapist will hide whenever the going gets rough. If the therapist has come to use this principle as a defence for himself, rather than as a means of rationing self-responsibility to the client, his weakness will show up the moment he tries to conduct fixed-role therapy. If the therapist frequently finds himself reverting to his role as a therapist, nagging the client to 'imagine how this scene will go' or saying, 'Come now, what would you say to that?' rather than continuing in the complementary role as much as possible and eliciting response by means of it, he might well start to examine his own defence system.

12. Just acting

A client may complain in the early stages of fixed-role therapy, 'Sure, it worked out all right, but I was just acting.' To begin with, this kind of reaction is altogether desirable. It means that the role is being enacted without serious threat to the self. The therapist should encourage it. If it persists to the end of the predetermined series, the therapist may well question whether or not the fixed-role sketch was written in a sufficiently comprehensive fashion and whether the constructs it employs are sufficiently permeable to take care of the events with which the client has trouble. It may also mean that the rehearsals have not dealt with crucial situations for which the client really needs a new answer.

If a client appears to pick up a new role quite deftly, the therapist may question whether or not he has written the role in a manner which enables the client to deal with crucial issues. The reaction the therapist first hopes for runs something like this: 'This fellow, Kenneth, is quite a guy. He is certainly interesting. I think I could see how other people could be like that, but I just can't see myself being that way.' Remarks of this type are likely to be accompanied by a spontaneous further study of the personality of Kenneth, simply because Kenneth is attractive. Sometimes the client may say, 'I feel silly trying to act like that.' The therapist can ask, 'Do you suppose other people think Kenneth is silly? Do you suppose Kenneth, being the kind of person he is, feels silly about himself?' If the answer to both of these questions is affirmative, the therapist may question the integrity of the character he has created in Kenneth.

Sometimes the client appears to challenge the therapist to play the part in a way which will work in practical solutions. This provides an excellent opportunity for the therapist to cast the client in the complementary role, say, of a threatening parent, and for the therapist to exemplify the part of Kenneth. Whenever the therapist is so challenged he should turn immediately to rehearsal. Even if the client appears to create a complementary character which is implausible, the therapist should not feel defensive, for he is being given a chance to show the adequacy of the new role, the permeability of its constructs, and the protection it offers against the most extreme threats. Furthermore, the client will himself be aware of the implausibility of the lines he is reciting, even though he does not admit it to the therapist. Sooner or later, because his need is great, he will seek to make the complementary role as plausible as he knows how in order to find out whether or not the fixed role really offers him a practical solution. He starts out, of course, by trying to prove that it will not be effective for meeting the unique situation which he faces. But in his efforts to prove that it will not, provided the therapist is quick to reduce the situations to role-playing scenes, he not only requires himself to subsume the construction systems of the complementary characters he portrays in order to keep them from appearing ridiculous or incoherent, but he sees the fixed role, played by the therapist, as coherent, poised, and effective. The client who challenges the therapist to make the role work is leading right into his partner's hands.

Since fixed-role therapy, as we see it nowadays, involves true role constructs, the therapist should judge progress, in part, by the interpretations of other people which emerge during the course of the interview sequence. There may be no way of knowing whether or not these interpretations are markedly different from those the client might have offered if he had been asked to portray them before therapy was started. The mere fact that he is beginning to exhibit a coherent version of them is in itself evidence that he is getting into position for establishing a true role relationship with them and with others whom he perceives to be like them. The therapist should feel encouraged by this kind of development.

In the early stages of therapy the client may not play his new role consistently. Of course, he lapses into his old role the greater part of the time. But even when he plays his new role he may play it quite differently on different occasions. We have not considered this a matter to be alarmed about; but the clinician, being interested in organized behaviour, does keep seeking a comprehensive constructive base upon which all behaviours can be developed, and not merely collective evidence of a set of isolated, though successful behaviours. The therapist is looking for much more than an item-by-item reinforcement of behaviour trials; he is seeking to establish a generalization. In fixed-role therapy he seeks to do this by a combination of induction and deduction, not by induction alone. He seeks to establish a breath-takingly comprehensive generalization in the form of a fixed role and, from it, help the client deduce hypotheses for every time and occasion. The client, in turn, may, in the earlier stages of therapy, fail to use the system comprehensively and his explorations may at times appear to be based more upon induction than deduction. This the therapist accepts, for no one can depend wholly upon pure deduction, nor can one depend wholly upon pure induction. Yet the clinician should be continually ready to help the client organize his behaviour comprehensively under the constructs expressed in the fixed-role sketch.

13. Spontaneous portrayal

In all types of role playing, therapists are accustomed to look out for signs that the client has forgotten that he is merely acting and has started to put his heart into it. In a previous chapter we dealt with the elaborative nature of spontaneous behaviour. When the client shows signs, either in rehearsal or outside, that he has momentarily forgotten that he was just acting, the therapist may assume that true elaborative behaviour is taking place. This means that a process is in motion which tends to interweave the client's new role constructs with the fabric of his main construction system. This is a good sign. The only thing the clinician needs to guard against is the possibility that the client, in looking back on the incident, feels that he reacted in an incoherent manner and resolves never to let the bars down again. The therapist has to judge what kind of material he will let the client deal with so spontaneously and how long during the interview session it is wise for the client to work on his spontaneous elaboration. The usual way to protect the client from the unfavourable consequences of too much spontaneity in the early stages of therapy is to break role and simply say, 'You acted out that part well. You made Kenneth seem like a real person.' By this means the therapist offers the client the screen of 'make-believe' so that he need not feel embarrassed when he looks back on the scene. This kind of protection can be offered both for spontaneous expressions occurring in the interview and for those reported as occurring on the outside.

Sometimes there are indications that the client is more spontaneous outside of rehearsal than in. In such cases it is hard to judge what protections he needs or what particular personal twists the new role is being given. As much as possible the therapist should attempt to have the client bring his version of the new role into the interview, although we have had some experience with persons who got along quite well by playing the role spontaneously on the outside and quite self-consciously and hesitantly in the interview room. Perhaps it was because they used the interview only to test out the role in the more difficult situations in which they had not as yet achieved spontaneity.

One of the landmarks of progress is the client's first report that someone has told him that he seems different. One can be reasonably sure that when the incident occurred the client did not rest until he found out just how he was being perceived as different. The awareness of movement and the acceptance of that movement by others seem to set up a construct of a moving, developing, and emerging self, which is so important in all forms of therapy. Fixed-role therapy makes maximum capital of the principle of the perception of movement in therapy. The client perceives movement almost before he is aware that he has done anything to accomplish movement. Once he has established a construct of change within himself, much of the threat that ordinarily accompanies the thought of ever being different is resolved and other signs of therapeutic change are likely to ensue.

One of the most interesting outcomes of fixed-role therapy is the adoption by some clients of a new role which is neither the fixed role nor like the one they described in their original self-characterization. Sometimes this begins to emerge perceptibly during the course of the interview sequence. The therapist may choose to adapt himself to the new development or he may choose to play out the two-week sequence as faithfully to the fixed role as possible. If the fixed-role sequence is to run through a period of two or three months, there is good reason not to thwart the client's exploratory efforts towards setting up a third role. In the short sequence, however, where it is understood at the outset that the fixed role is to be tried out for a two-week period only, it seems much more desirable to continue the experiment according to a fixed design. This need not militate against the client's ultimately adopting a third role. Indeed, it may be of assistance, for it may enable him to see what far-reaching possibilities any new construction of his world might have. We must always remember that we are not trying to set up a fixed state of adjustment which is never thereafter to be tampered with. We are, instead, interested in helping the client to realize the possibilities for changed modes of adjustment within himself and in giving him one good, rousing, construct-shaking experience along that line.

14. Perception of change in the situation rather than in the self

Sometimes the therapist has to settle for a therapeutic change which does not involve as much conceptualization of movement as he would like. The client may say something like this: 'Oh yes, I played out the role. I don't think it changed my outlook much. I really think the situation is somewhat different now and I believe I can handle it.' This poses a perplexing problem for the clinician. Is he dealing with a cyclic change, or a set of episodic moods, or has something happened which constructively changes the client's perceptual pattern? There is no sure way of finding out, but the usual approach is to ask the client to compare and contrast the way the situation looks to him now with the way it looked to him earlier. The permeability of the constructs used to describe the situational 'change' provides some clue as to the reliability of the new outlook. If the constructs are so impermeable that he will not be prepared for new events of a similar type, or if they are so preemptive that he will not be able to throw new light upon the situations which he already faces, the prognosis of permanent improvement is bad.

Sometimes the client will add to the above remarks a comment such as, 'Of course it may be that I am just seeing it differently.' Now here we have a tentative expression of a propositional construct. He is not calling a spade a spade as if he were applying a preemptive construct to the situation. If there are other indications that he is ready to meet situations with new and propositional constructs, the clinician may be somewhat reassured.

Sometime the client will go further and say something like this: 'I am beginning to see how things all along have been somewhat different from the way I described them when we started this series of conferences.' As the client documents this new construction of his situation with material from remote happenings and spontaneously offers new material with which to document his position, the therapist may assume that he has some evidence of the permeability of the construction under which the client is now operating. It embraces a variety of new things, some of which were not embraced in the original complaint. Now will it embrace the kinds of events which are likely to occur in the client's near and distant future? Some role playing of simulated future events may provide the answer to the question of whether or not the new construction will prove permeable.

We have already pointed out that in the earlier stages of fixed-role therapy it is not uncommon for the client to assign his successes to 'changed situations'. As a first approximation to therapeutic movement this development is altogether acceptable. It may be interpreted tentatively as meaning that the client does not yet trust the role enough to lean heavily upon it and prefers to say merely that the success he has had should more properly be attributed to diminished difficulties in the situations he faces.

One of the subtle signs of therapeutic change in fixed-role therapy, and one which is more or less specific to this type of therapy, is the tendency of the client to forget what he originally came for. If the therapy were based on the assumption that therapeutic progress depends upon the client's rational 'insight' into his complaints, this might not be considered a healthy sign. That is not the assumption upon which fixed-role therapy depends, however. Such 'insight' is not necessarily ruled out, but neither is it considered essential to therapeutic change. The wager that the clinician makes when he undertakes fixed-role therapy is that the client can eventually deal with his complaint as a closed incident with no permeable meaning for the future. The clinician places a bet that the client can be given a new way of dealing with future events, a way which will not require him to invoke the constructs underlying the complaint, or even to construe the complaint itself as an item which must replicate itself.

15. Additional negative signs

There are some additional negative signs which should be mentioned. If a client keeps reiterating his complaint in spite of everything the therapist is able to do to get him to reduce it to role-playing elements, and in turn, to embrace those elements by means of the new role, the therapist will have to recognize that the method is proving ineffectual in the case. If the client continues to divert the conference from the role in ways other than merely complaining that he does not understand the part, that he cannot play it, that it will not work in the kinds of situations *he* faces, the therapist may have to abandon the hope that fixed-role therapy will accomplish any worthwhile results. Before the therapist gives up, he should, of course, make sure that he has portrayed the role in as vivid and lifelike a manner as possible and that he has been ready to adapt the sketch in the light of the client's response. Sometimes the client will keep reiterating, 'I don't see what good all this is going to do me.' As a last resort the therapist can say, 'Perhaps not, but this is one way of finding out whether or not I can help you at all', or, 'If you can do this, I shall have a much better idea of how I can help you.' If the client then is still unable to construe the procedure in a manner which will enable him to act, the therapist may well consider the possibility that the client is not, at the moment, ready to respond to any form of therapeutic effort.

Continued vacillation in the role and the use of gross mixtures of old constructs and new is also an inauspicious sign for fixed-role therapy. If the person continues to be unable to see what the implications of the fixed-role sketch are, even when they are illustrated by the therapist, the whole job is likely to turn out badly. He must be aware of the *contrast* when he sees the role portrayed and must be able to express his awareness of that contrast if he is to construe the new role. In fact, what we have said about the fundamental nature of constructs in general must be taken into account. There must be a contrasting element in the context of a construct in order for the construct to take form. The new role must contrast with the old if it is to be perceived with any degree of clarity. Failure to see the contrast either in terms of words or in terms of acts simply means that the new role has not been construed at all and hence cannot be the vehicle for readjustment.

The therapist should not mistake the client's criticism of the role for a failure in communication. While the latter is definitely a discouraging sign, the former is not necessarily so. Criticism requires that the critic conjure up some version of the role he is criticizing. In the course of doing so, he is put in the position of having to construe the new role in some systematic fashion. The therapist can have him illustrate his criticisms of the new role in terms of an enactment. By the time the client has made his criticisms clear he has performed an experiment with the new role. While the procedure is not ordinarily followed, the same scenes can be played out at the end of therapy both in the new role and in the old role. The client is then put in the interesting position of having to 'act' like himself as he was only a brief time before. We shall have more to say about this later, but it is a potent device in various types of therapeutic undertakings. The overcritical client can, in some instances, be placed in the position of having to perform some crucial experiments with the role he criticizes and even to conduct his experimentation with control situations, analogously to the method employed in scientific research.

There is the possibility that the overcritical client has assumed that the new role has been presented to him as a 'right' role and that he is therefore considerably threatened by it. Again, the therapist must assure him that he is not being asked to play the role permanently and can even hint that other therapeutic exercises may be undertaken as soon as the fixed-role series is completed, as indeed they may have to be in such a case. Always the emphasis in fixed-role therapy is upon experimentation – upon trying out.

There is another construction which can be placed upon the behaviour of the overcritical client. He may be testing out the defences which the role offers. Since he is to defend himself by means of it he may wish to make sure that it is not vulnerable. He tries to do this by means of logical manipulation. The therapist's response to his criticism is to try out the role in the interview situation with both therapist and client exchanging parts.

Overcriticism may be a real negative sign. If the client insists on *talking about* the role but will never *experiment with* it, either as a participant in a dialogue in which the therapist enacts the role or in one in which he attempts to enact it himself, the whole therapeutic attempt may be doomed to failure. The judgement as to success or failure, however, should not be made until the two-week sequence has been played out. The therapist should keep in mind that the first three or four sessions are almost always accompanied by reports of failure and half-hearted attempts, and that this is even preferable to easy success in the early stages. The therapist's own discouragement and his own tendency to talk about the role instead of enacting it are the usual obstacles to be overcome.

16. Evidence of progress

The most exciting evidence of progress in fixed-role therapy comes when the client says, after some fumbling around with the role, 'I feel as if this were the *real* me.' While this does not always happen, it frequently does, and when it does it is almost always accompanied by other positive evidences or readiness in the client to make progress on his own initiative. This indicates not only that the client has a feeling of spontaneity in his enactment of the role but that the old role now seems cramped and unnatural. It means that he has accepted the point of view expressed in the fixed-role sketch or in his version of it. It means also that his perception of validating evidence may be somewhat altered and he is able to see validations for his anticipatory behaviour which he might previously have overlooked.

With this change in perspective there has never yet failed to occur a marked shift in the client's formulation of his problems. The old complaints, if mentioned at all, tend to be referred to in such terms as: 'When I came in here I *thought*....' The past tense will be used predominantly in describing an attitude: for example, 'I used to feel....' The client may even describe the old complaints with mild amusement, though if he does it repeatedly with explosive laughter the therapeutic value of the change is suspect.

Sometimes the client says, 'I feel now that this must have been the real me all the time and that I somehow thought I was expected to be something else.' Such a statement provides an interesting lead for the intellectually curious therapist, but it does not necessarily have to be followed up from the standpoint of the client. This is the kind of evidence therapists sometimes call 'emotional insight' or 'gut learning'. We would call it simply 'organized construction'. It can be contrasted with the verbal fastidiousness used by some disturbed people to keep their shaky construction systems from falling apart.

Perhaps the successful climax one hopes to reach by means of fixed-role therapy can be illustrated by the following account. In this case the self-characterization is represented by its analysis only, while the protocol from the Rotter Incomplete Sentences Blank and the fixed-role sketch are reproduced verbatim.

A. Ray Gibson: Analysis of self-characterization

Technical analysis

(1) Sequence and transition.

A protocol comprising seven short paragraphs of one to four sentences each, moving in the following sequence:

Par. I: Mild criticism of appearance due to overweight (5'–11' and 190 lbs.).

Par. II: Tendency to talk about himself in order to cover up 'self conscioness'.

Par. III: Lack of aggressiveness.

Par. IV: Preference for reading, music, dancing, and photography rather than sports.

Par. V: Not as active as most males. Used to drink too much but, after discontinuing altogether for a year, resumed moderate drinking.

Par. VI: Poor study habits are better since marriage. Needs work on 3 R's and spelling.

Par. VII: Well liked by most people; has few enemies, although 'some what of a boar at times'.

(2) Observation of organization.

Little range in level of generality from sentence to sentence. Sentences weak. Paragraphs not organized around topic sentences. Mostly a bill of particulars. There is no illustrative material.

(3) Reflection against context.

I: Overweight mentioned in context of personal appearance and of conversational settings.

II: Sports, dating, drinking, and shyness mentioned in same context.

III: Poor study habits mentioned in context of marriage.

(4) Collation of terms.

I: Equivalence between being 'well-versed', 'conversing easily', and using the word 'I' too much.

II: Equivalence between 'aggressive', 'Sports', dating 'other women', 'active as most other males', and 'for socile reasons he drank rather heavy'.

III: Equivalence between 'sloppy', 'careless', 'never studied hard', and 'hard for him to develope the Correct habits'.

(5) Shifting emphasis.

Illustrative cases in which the shifting emphasis throws light on the construction system are as follows:

I: 'Be fore he was married he liked a variety in women...'

II: 'At one time for socile reasons he drank rather heavy but it strated to get a hold of him...'

III: '... never studied hard untill he was married and now its hard for him to develope the Correct habits...'

(6) Restatement of the argument.

I am a little sloppy, but not too bad. In spite of shyness, I talk rather freely and I am a little egocentric, but not too bad. I am a little passive and fail to play a masculine role, but not too bad. I used to drink to overcome my passivity but I had to give it up. Before my marriage I was indolent so long that it is now too late to do much about my study habits. I avoid making enemies and I am a kind of bore, but not so bad that people dislike me.

Analysis of contextual areas invoked

The primary contextual area is that of the face-to-face conversational situation. This seems to be the arena in which he sees himself as a person.

He also mentions recreational activities, relations with the opposite sex, and studies.

Thematic analysis

(1) There are no strong themes involving cause-and-effect relationships. The only changes he mentions are his abandonment of his liking for a variety in women and his moderation in drinking.

(2) Apparently he tries to avoid being offensive to anyone but recognizes that he has surrendered most of his initiative.

(3) His marriage has tended to correct his indolence, but it is too late to do much about it.

(4) He attributes his egocentrism to his shyness.

(5) There is a mild self-criticism running throughout the protocol, generally ending with the mitigating fact that he is well enough liked by others.

Dimensional analysis

(1) Talking too much, boorishness, egocentrism vs. self-consciousness, shyness, introversion
(2) Passive, shy, interested in sedative recreation, letting things pass by without doing anything about them vs. aggressive, active, masculine
(3) Sloppy, careless, indolent vs. sharp-looking, self-controlled, studious
(4) Well-liked vs. (submerged pole)

This brief analysis of the self-characterization protocol may be checked against the following protocol.

B. Ray Gibson: Rotter Incomplete Sentences Protocol

COMPLETE THESE SENTENCES TO EXPRESS YOUR REAL FEELING. TRY TO DO EVERY ONE. BE SURE TO MAKE A COMPLETE SENTENCE.

1. *I like* good food.
2. *The happiest time* has been since my marriage.
3. *I want to know* more about everything.
4. *Back home* I worked in a Dairy.
5. *I regret* I had to waste time in the army.
6. *At bedtime* I sleep.
7. *Boys* are more masculine than ladies.
8. *The best* way to success is education.
9. *What annoy me* most are uniforms.
10. *People* are in most cases good.
11. *A mother* is kind to her children.
12. *I feel* that school is important.
13. *My greatest fear* failure.
14. *In High School* I filt I was a big wheel.
15. *I can't* read spell or write well.
16. *Sports* are body building.
17. *When I was a child* I was good.
18. *My nerves* fair.
19. *Other people* are generly good.
20. *I failed* Chem. and Math at State.
21. *I suffer* from bad eyes.
22. *Reading* is good for you.
23. *My mind* about average.
24. *The future* is up to me.
25. *I need* speed in getting started.
26. *Marriage* is good for a person.
27. *I am best when* talking.
28. *Sometimes* I'm to slow.

29. *What pains me* most is Socliate trend of U.S.
30. *I hate* Army and Soclism.
31. *This school* is the best I have seen.
32. *I am very* poor in reading writing and spelling.
33. *The only trouble* with school is it takes to long.
34. *I wish* I had more time to spend in school before work.
35. *My father* is Pres. of the Cheese Factory.
36. *I secretly* hoping to become a Zeta active.
37. *I* think Soclism is the Downfall of U.S.
38. *Dancing* is a very injoyable past time.
39. *My greatest worry* is finances.
40. *Most girls* are injobl to see and are injoyable company.

C. Dick Benton: fixed role sketch

Dick Benton is probably the only one of his kind in the world. People are always just a little puzzled as to how to take him. About the time they decide that he is a conventional person with the usual lines of thinking in religion, politics, school, etc., they discover that there is a new side to his personality that they have overlooked. At times, they think that he has a brand-new way of looking at life, a really *fresh* point of view. Some people go through an hour of conversation with him without being particularly impressed; while others find that afterwards they cannot get some of his unusual ideas out of their minds. Every once in a while he throws an idea into a discussion like a bomb with a very slow fuse attached. People don't get it until later.

At times he deliberately makes himself socially inconspicuous. Those are the times when he wishes to listen and learn, rather than to stimulate other people's thinking. He is kindly and gentle with people, even on those occasions when he is challenging their thoughts with utterly new ideas. Because of this, people do not feel hurt by his ideas, even when they seem outrageous.

He is devoted to his wife and she is the only person who always seems to understand what is going on in his mind.

His work in college is somewhat spotted and the courses are interesting to him only to the extent that they give him a new outlook.

All in all, Dick Benton is a combination of gentleness and intellectual unpredictability. He likes to take people as they are but he likes to surprise them with new ideas.

D. Ray Gibson: excerpts from therapist's report and verbatim transcriptions

S [= Subject] was rather tired when he came to the Clinic. There was sweat on his brow, his smile was faint and looked unhappy.

When C [= Clinician] greeted him and asked him in a friendly manner to go to the private room, commenting about the weather, S began to loosen and acted much happier. (The room was taken.)
C: At last we found a room. It's rather warm in here – do you like to have the window opened?
S: It might help. (S takes the responsibility to adjust the window to his desire.)
C: Well – how do you feel today?
S: (approximate words) Tired. I had much work to do.
C: Did you –?
S: You mean write notes on my role –? No, I did not. I did not have time to. I thought I could but I could not. But I can remember most of it – well let us see – I was here Thursday afternoon. In the evening – where did I go? I don't seem to remember – exactly. (Long pause.)
C: Well – how about telling me your general reaction and feelings about it? Then we go into details.
S: Frankly – I tell you – I have not been very successful but I tried – and am going to try – would you like to give me three weeks instead of two weeks?
C: Oh – yes – we might, but remember we are just interested in the trial and see how it works. If it does not work, why –?
S: I am trying. But sometimes, it seems that I forget that I am Dick Benton. Sometimes I think of him. My trouble seems that I am not able to dig out new ideas that would surprise the people. It might need special talent. (S puts his hands on his head and presses it.) I never made a statement that would make other people think of it later. I can't see how can anybody do it – and people don't get it until later, unless he is very exceptional. I tried. In couple instances – I thought I am successful but there was no extraordinary reaction from the other people.
C: You understand that extraordinary ideas are not the main thing. It is the intellectual unpredictability that matters. Dick Benton would offer more than possibility and suggestion for any problem. He does not hold himself from a single idea because he expressed it one time. If he sees in his further thinking that there might be another possibility, he would not hesitate to express his thoughts. This means that he is putting his thoughts and ideas in new light. This would be true when dealing with other people's ideas.
S: I understand – I understand – I think this is possible somehow. I had a chance to talk to the assistant in the lab yesterday – and I think that I offered him a surprising idea....

A few days later Ray reported experiences covering four types of situations. He had tried out the role with an instructor, with friends, with his wife, and with his brother-in-law. He had surprised his brother-in-law, whom he dislikes, as well as his wife and himself, by not meeting the brother-in-law at the station when he came to visit. The brother-in-law had to take a taxi. Ray felt that since he had done it in the role of Dick there was no need to feel guilty. He seemed quite amused and pleased with himself. Furthermore, he was able to talk the brother-in-law into joining the Book-of-the-Month Club, somewhat to his own surprise.

Ray complained, however, that while he thought he had noticed a little change in himself, he did not see himself becoming much more aggressive. Following is an excerpt.

> Silence.
>
> S: If a therapist could help you to feel ... that I am better, then I really think ... can you tell one if you noticed any change in me? Is it you who tells me...? I came to realize that Dick Benton is me. This is what I expected you to say.
>
> There followed a discussion in which Ray said he felt like he was getting out of a shell. At one point he said, 'I am getting better in carrying on the role. But I did notice a change in *me* although I *do* different things now.'

This perhaps illustrates how Ray was still distinguishing between what he enacted and what he did and what he was. His state of *being* was starting to follow after his *acts*. It is to be noted that he uses the term 'although' in the last sentence. It is as if the fact that he *does* different things may make it merely appear that he is different. This is a common early reaction to the perception of movement in oneself.

This client had shown his wife the self-characterization sketch he had written at the beginning of the interview series. When he was given the fixed-role sketch he suggested that he would prefer not to show it to her immediately. Towards the end of the series he asked his wife if she had noticed any difference in him recently. This, as well as the passage described above, indicates that he was quite dependent upon the responses he was able to elicit from other people. We had predicted as much from his self-characterization sketch and we had written the fixed-role sketch in a manner which we hoped would bring out frequent and clear interpersonal validations of his simulated outlook. His wife replied that she had noticed changes in him and that she thought he seemed quite a bit more 'aggressive'. He said he then showed her the Dick Benton sketch without comment. According to him her response was: 'This is a very good sketch of *you*.' When he said that he had been acting out the part she replied that the sketch described him as the kind of person she had always thought he really was. He reported the incident with great delight.

17. Indications for fixed-role therapy

Considerable further exploration is in order before one can state with confidence what surface appearances should be taken as indicating that fixed-role therapy may be effective. At least we have some clinical evidence that the technique is relatively safe, even when it is ineffective. The client's defences in the form of his symptoms are not destroyed before he has an alternative construction system with which to face life. His present integrity is wholly respected, since he is not even asked to change *himself* in any way. While the method enables the experienced and skilful clinician to make full use of his talents, it is one which a relative inexperienced clinician can undertake under supervision with relatively little danger of damaging the client. It is important, in using the technique, that the clinician maintain a scientific attitude. His failure to do so will offset even the greatest of clinical skill and experience acquired with other techniques.

Tentatively we may say that there are nine considerations which may lead one to employ fixed-role therapy in a case.

a. Limited time. The interview sequence can be accomplished in as little as two weeks' time. Much longer sequences are, of course, feasible.

b. Where strongly dependent transference relationships are to be avoided. While it is not claimed that the client–clinician relationship can ever avoid transference of some type and in some degree, transference is something which, if properly understood, can be controlled. Whenever the therapist plays a complementary role with the client he is, according to our understanding of the meaning of transference, accepting a transference relationship. But it is a specified transference which the therapist sets up. The perceptions which are transferred from other objects and applied to the therapist are contained as much as possible within the construction of the fixed role.

c. Unavoidable client–therapist relationships of a nonclinical nature. The client is not asked to show himself to the therapist in any unsympathetic light nor is he asked to confide in the therapist after the self-characterization is written. Hence it is possible for him to maintain outside the interview room a kind of interpersonal relationship with the therapist which is organized and valid. Throughout the interview series the client is never urged or even permitted to place himself in a highly vulnerable position with respect to the therapist.

d. Inexperienced clinicians. We have already mentioned the fact that the danger of an inexperienced clinician's harming the client is relatively less in this type of therapy than it is in more conventional types of therapy. The therapist does not try to place himself in an authority relationship with the client. He helps the client conduct verbal experiments. He can withdraw from any statement or position he has assumed by reminding the client that he was only role playing. Let us emphasize, of course, that this safety is only relative to other types of therapy. There are, as we have carefully tried to point out, hazards in all types of relationships with clients and there are characteristic hazards in fixed-role therapy.

Where inexperienced clinicians are under day-by-day supervision, the procedure enables them to serve along with the supervisor as members of the panel which drafts the fixed-role sketch. It is also easy for them to engage in role playing during staff conferences and thus clarify their own interpretation of the client's reactions.

While the fixed-role type of approach may be undertaken primarily because only inexperienced clinicians are available, this should not be taken to mean that experienced clinicians should not resort to fixed-role therapy. In many ways fixed-role therapy allows the creative imagination and clinical skill of the experienced clinician to make their weight felt in a manner which is impossible in the more passive procedures. It also permits the scientifically minded clinician to capitalize upon his enlightened point of view.

e. Obvious social and situational components in the case. The ultimate outcomes of fixed-role therapy are not limited to superficialities, since the processes unleashed may eventually penetrate as deeply into the client's personality as maturity itself. The clinician who decides to employ fixed-role therapy may assess the social and situational components and decide that they furnish a rich reservoir of validational material which he can help the client put to good use. He offers the client a new approach to the people and events with which he is closely surrounded and he makes a bet with himself that there will be a new outcome.

f. Need for termination of another type of therapy sequence. There is considerable clinical evidence that fixed-role therapy may be used as a termination procedure following any one of a wide variety of other types of therapy. It tends to close out complaints, as we have already seen. It throws the emphasis upon the present and the future and thus helps the client to recover from his preoccupation with the past during the seeking of 'insights'. It enables the client to implement his new construction system and judge for himself how it works out in practice. It permits him to perceive the therapist as relatively independent of the adjustment process and thus enables him to break any lingering dependency transference ties with the therapist. In a sense it opens the door of the therapy room and turns the readjustment process loose in the world of everyday life.

g. Need for establishment of contact with everyday reality. Clients who live in a highly symbolic world and whose therapy is otherwise likely to be too much cluttered up with words and verbal gymnastics may be put through a course of fixed-role therapy in order to help them establish a more practical relationship with the people and the events which surround them. These are the so-called 'intellectualizers' who have difficulty taking their problems out of a realm of words and setting them down in a world of actualities. Through fixed-role therapy, having established a more effective relationship with reality by means of which they may maintain themselves for a time, they can later return to a more introspective type of therapy, without continually dragging their therapist through a clutter of verbalizations.

h. Uncertainty of the client's readiness for change. Fixed-role therapy can be considered as a kind of test tube in which the client's readiness for any form of 'insight' therapy can be tried out. The investment of the therapist's time is relatively small. Without giving too many hostages to the future the therapist can get some notion of what the client's 'ego strength' is, his willingness to foresee change in himself, the ways in which he casts the therapist into roles – hence the potential transferences which might be expected to develop in a longer course of therapy –

and the way in which the client is able to utilize the material of his everyday life in any readjustment he might undertake.

i. Where the client seems to be defensive with respect to therapy. Role playing, in general, provides some protection to the sensitive client. Fixed-role therapy, by offering him a mask behind which to experiment, provides him with an opportunity to accomplish something therapeutically, without unduly exposing his vulnerable points.

C. Group fixed-role therapy

18. Preliminary explorations with group fixed-role therapy

It would seem that fixed-role therapy would provide an interesting and useful way of approaching group psychotherapy. In our explorations we have elicited the self-characterization sketches individually and then have presented the fixed-role sketches in the first group meeting. Thus, each participant hears the fixed-role sketches offered the others as well as the one designed for himself. We have used clients who volunteered from a mental-hygiene class and who presumably had some feeling of need for readjustment, although not necessarily an urgent one. Throughout the interview sequence clients have been urged to maintain their new roles, address each other by their 'new names', and generally rehearse with reference to their old roles. A systematic attempt is made to keep them from revealing themselves to each other in their old roles. The therapist responds to them throughout in terms of their new roles.

As the group, so far limited to three clients and a therapist, rehearses, each client is helped by other members of the group to construe his role in a meaningful way. Different members of the group play complementary roles, and even take over a demonstration of another member's new role. As with individual fixed-role therapy the therapist is quite active during the first interview, but he gradually allows his place to be taken by the client members of the group as they help each other develop their new roles. Following are the self-characterization sketches which a group of recent participants in group fixed-role therapy prepared.

A. Miriam Kolften

Miriam Kolften is, by standards of our culture, a comparatively honest person. She does not steal, seldom lies or cheats, and often frightens and disturbs people in her efforts to be sincere. She often 'soft pedles' this sincerity in a way so as to prevent hurting others. The concern for their feelings and reactions is perhaps merely a guard against retaliation rather than the concern displayed by a 'good person'. Miriam has been and is keenly, almost painfully, sensative to others' moods and has occassionally become enmeshed in situations where she could not efficently function in the face of other's suffering. Within the past two years she has become aware of this shortcoming and has tried to objectivy her thinking, which, she hopes, will enable her to cope more effectively with herself and others.

To know Miriam intimately you must acquaint yourself with her past experiences and associations – an biography is not however, the purpose of this paper. Let me state briefly that her life and goals have been dominated to a great extent by the strong personalities of her parents. It would not I believe, be too far wrong to state that Miriam's home was the first place she learned the meaning of fear. (Pardon, Dr. Freud, I did not know M. during her pre-natal era.) In M's home, as in many homes, children were taught that 'good girls' were loved and could stay and 'bad girls' might as well hit the road. Over a period of years the idea changed labels and connotations but the theme remained the same; only Miriam forgot what the point was and became pretty dam confused. Now fears are something like rabbits. Once you have two they begin to breed and multiply and you had better have a big supply of carrots to feed the ego or there going to start on any available material. Nerves are a tasty tidbit. Well one night while the rabbits were chomping on Miriam's spinothalamic nerve tract she realized she was afraid of being afraid. With some help she reset the table and has been enjoying rabbit for dinner ever since. Indigestion often results but a good dose of humor and objectivity usually alieviates the pain.

Miriam is by temperament addicted to the arts. She paints mediocre watercolours, enjoys books and music and writes a few bad poems completely lacking in any semblance of meter. She also has carried on a love affair with the theatre for the past six years. It has returned her affection occassionaly but of late has retired sulkily in the face of forced neglect.

M. is a combination of the tersely practical and giddy impractical. If money is in her pocket, it is spent on the most extravagant, useless, gifts for friends. (Her motives are quite selfish in that she delights in watching others open gifts which are carefully contrived to make them feel, for example, that they have not properly appreciated their 'femme fatele' qualities.) The last gift she gave me was a pair of black lace garters which I will never wear but often try on when no ones around.

On the other hand if she succeeds in making it to the bank with the loot, only an impending economic crash can make her withdraw it.

She is quite a good cook although her attempts at experimentation are frowned upon by her family. A previous escapade with a live lobster ended in mahem. The monster escaped and had to be beaten unconscious with a flyswatter. Her mother found the sittuation completely unhumorus.

Miriam is moody at times but not to the extent she used to be. She is loyal and will work hard for those who command her respect and trust. She is very fond of her work at school but would rather discuss other things in her leisure time. Miriam is ambitious but, often unrealistic; desires much affection but is wary of those who offer it, likes children, dogs, horses and people older than herself but has few friends her own age; loves the outdoors but dislikes sports.

The picture of Miriam is not complete but I am taking you at your work – 'sketch'.

> The bald little prompter shuts his book, as the light fades gently. The end, the end. They all go back to their everyday life – but the hero remains, for, try as I may, I cannot get out of my part: Sebastian's mask clings to my face, the likeness will not be washed off. I am Sebastian, or Sebastian is I, or perhaps we are both someone whom neither of us knows.
>
> *V. Nabokov**

B. Chester Ulrath

Chester is a very intelligent person and would possible be capable of considerable and noteworthy achievement if it were not for his undisciplined personality and personality problems. His emotional life is rather retarded due to his unfortunate experiences in youth, and he tends to be somewhat childish emotionally. He is sometimes disturbed by little distractions, such as irritating noises, people talking loud in the library, etc. His main emotional difficulty seems to manifest itself as a paranoic outlook towards life. Nothing infuriates him more than being treated as if he wasn't worth much or doesn't count. When he is disturbed, his paranoic tendency can be quite pronounced, and, for example, he may interpret the negligence or inadequacy of another person, in a situation, as a personal 'slap' at him, – although the offender may really not intend this at all. In justice to him, however, it must be said that hes paranoic tendencies do not appear too strongly unless he is provoked by a real incident or is in a disturbed or a depressed state. His other big emotional weakness is his tendency to become depressed for intervals of time. Something can depress him and he will remain depressed for a week or so. This interferes with his ability to concentrate and work well. Since marriage, however, this tendency to become depressed has not been as strong as it used to be. The depressive periods are not dangerous or especially involved, but they do interfere with his outlook and efficiency.

On the positive side of the picture, he has an excellent sense of humor much of the time; he has a sympathetic outlook towards other's problems, and he has very good insight into himself, which mitigates, somewhat, his emotional problems and undesirable tendencies.

*Miriam's quotation is from the concluding paragraph of Vladimir Nabokov's story, *The Real Life of Sebastian Knight*, published and copyright by New Directions, Norfolk, Conn., 1941. Used with the permission of the copyright owner. The passage reads,

> And then the masquerade draws to a close. The bald little prompter shuts his book, as the light fades gently. The end, the end. They all go back to their everyday life (and Clare goes back to her grave) – but the hero remains, for, try as I may, I cannot get out of my part: Sebastian's mask clings to my face, the likeness will not be washed off. I am Sebastian, or Sebastian is I, or perhaps we both are someone whom neither of us knows.

He is shy in his social behavior, especially towards some types of girls. He therefore does not associate socially as much as he should, and so he has few personal friends. He mistrusts many people he does not know well, and has inhibited relations with them. However, in recent years, he has deliberately tried to improve his social participation and has had some success. His understanding and attitude toward people has improved and is improving.

His early life was somewhat unfortunate. His mother – was a very neurotic but loving person who was extremely overprotective, and who interfered with his social development in play groups. His father was a very kind man who showered him with everything within his means, but who did not understand him very well. He got along quite well with his parents, but due to his mother's shielding, he rebelled from her supervision during his last years of grade school.

His school and college records were better than average, but did not reflect his real intelligence, due to his emotional disturbances and the resulting inability to concentrate or work consistently. However, since his marriage, his ability has manifested itself in a high level of college work. He excels the majority of students in his classes when he works well. He is confused about his future career, and is a little scared to go out and compete for success as the supporter of a family. He has the capacity and background for an academic career, but does not like the seclusion, withdrawal, and lack of human interest that is involved in many academic fields. This vocation also might interfere with his attempt to achieve a more effective adjustment to society, and for these reasons he may reject this career. On the other hand, he feels that his social inhibitions would interfere with his effort to reach the top in a more applied field such as the ministry. In any case, he will need independence in his work; he detests hierarchical systems with their petty rivalries and their petty tyrants.

His marriage is successful, and, for the most part, has been a source of increased security and happiness to him. There were many marriage problems at first, but the majority of them have been handled quite well. Although both he and his wife are somewhat neurotic, they are quite well matched in that they meet the vital personality needs of each other, and understand each other rather well. He is far from the ideal marriage partner, however, because he tends to be domineering, possessive, sometimes jealous, and overly sensitive. His possessiveness and jealousy, although he masters them fairly well now, may inhibit his capacity to be a good father. If he continues to become more secure, as he has been doing, he may be able to control these selfish tendencies more in the future.

C. Pauline Fields

Pauline Fields is a person one might feel it was difficult to get to know. In a new group or in a crowd, she is apt to be quiet and retiring. With friends she knows well, or in a group in which she is sure of her status, she is more outgoing, talkative and expressive.

Since she is the youngest child and the only girl in her family, she has received some pampering. Her two older brothers often made decisions for her and took responsibilities she might otherwise have assumed. Her father and mother are intelligent and have tried to build her independence, but until her initial break from home upon entering college and for some time thereafter, there was a great deal of dependence upon them. In the years since that time she has learned to depend on her on resources and is fairly independent of home ties. However, she is still occasionally bothered by indecision and wants to fall back into the rut of having someone else make decisions for her.

Her peers generally like her and think of her as an easy-going, genuine, understanding person. People she knows well regard her as a 'good listener' and often bring problems of an intimate and personal nature to her. She enjoys this contact with people and wants to be able to help them.

She chose teaching as a profession largely because of this desire to work with people, but also because of the strong influence of a father who teaches and whom she admires and respects very highly. In many phases of her personality and in the manner in which she taught in the two years she was engaged in this field, she copies her father. She entered Graduate School because she felt it would help her to get ahead in her profession, rather than standing still. She chose Speech and Hearing because helping defective children seemed to offer an even greater challenge than working with normal children and also because she had an interest in this type of work.

She is convinced that work with people will give her the greatest satisfaction and happiness. Her main goal in life is not a career, but the role of a wife and mother. She believes in marriage as the ultimate in human relationships.

Intellectually, she is slightly above average. She has always made good grades easily. She is not outstandingly attractive or vivacious in social situations, so has probably tried to compensate for this and gain recognition through academic work. Because she likes people more than books, she has also striven for and gained recognition in clubs and various activities – often being chosen the leader or president.

She has set her standards fairly high and when she does not live up to them, she suffers feelings of guilt. She is conscientious about tasks given to her and though they are usually carried out well, she worries about them. She is often delegated by teachers or friends to take over responsible jobs.

In her associations with others, she is sensitive (perhaps overly so) to the needs and desires of the other person. She hates to hurt another's feelings and often puts her own feelings and views secondary to the other person's in an effort to avoid this. She listens to and often accepts suggestions of other people, provided they do not violate a deep seated belief or code of ethics of her own. She prefers to agree with others rather than to have an open conflict. She tends to be hypocritical in this respect. She has an extremely even temper – sometimes to the point of letting others walk over her when she probably would have a right to be more forceful or lose her temper. She worries a great deal about what others may think of her.

She is methodical and likes routine. She likes to have a time for work and a time for play. She does not like unorganized activities or people.

She is conservative in her thinking, often taking the middle road on issues. She is embarrassed and uneasy in the presence of radical and narrow minded people. She picks out good points in nearly every one she meets, seldom violently disliking a person. She is slow in making close friends – but once established the relationship is usually lasting. She has a wide range of casual friends.

She is probably not too scientific in her manner of solving problems, but depends more on common sense. She is not a particularly abstract or deep thinker, but deals more in concrete and practical terms.

She enjoys beautiful sights in nature, good literature and music. She likes to have some time to herself. She enjoys simple good times with a few friends, rather than artificial or noisy social good times with a large group.

She is not highly emotional or excitable. She refrains from showing her real emotions or inner feelings to others. She takes set backs calmly and objectively – at least to all outward appearances. She sometimes is guilty of feeling sorry for herself – but this is usually done in solitude.

Her religious background has been fairly strict. She does not believe any one religious denomination is better than any other, but she believes a person should live by Christian principles. She believes the person who leads a 'good' life will always win out, even though at times the influences for 'bad' may seem to be achieving success. She has no strict set of ideas on what is good or bad – but judges her actions in terms of the possible harm they might bring to others and in terms of the thing that will be best in her achievement of a happy and beneficial life. She believes in the Church as a sacred institution to which she owes certain responsibilities and which affords her an opportunity for group worship – but she believes very much in the power of personal communion with God.

19. Fixed-role sketches

Following is the introduction which was attached to each fixed-role sketch when it was presented in the first group session.

> This role has been prepared as a kind of venture for the person who is to play it. It is by no means to be construed as psychologically 'correct' or ideally suited for the role player. Solely as a two weeks' adventure it may provide a vehicle for the role player to transport himself to new and interesting experience.
>
> It is suggested that the role be played out as completely as circumstances will permit during a two-week period. The role player should read it three times a day, eat it, sleep it, think of himself by the new name, feel as the new character

would feel, and generally commit himself wholly to the role. It is hoped that the role player will keep daily notes on his experiences.

It is suggested that group rehearsal periods of approximately one hour each, three times a week, be scheduled by the three people who are experimenting with new roles. The role players should represent themselves in their new roles in this situation as well as in others. Particular care should be taken not to discuss the original characterizations of themselves which were prepared by the role players. The role players should accept each other wholly in terms of the new roles and never let expectations based upon revelations of the old roles creep into the picture.

In the rehearsals each person should review his experience with his role during the preceding days, ask for suggestions and interpretations from the others, and rehearse situations likely to occur in the coming days.

Neither the analyses of the self-characterization sketches nor the rationale underlying the drafting of the fixed-role sketches is discussed here. The Judy Pearson sketch was written for Miriam, the Timothy Ellman sketch for Chester, and the Patricia Deems sketch for Pauline. The Judy Pearson sketch represented somewhat of a departure from the usual approach to fixed-role writing, but the reasons for which it was decided to experiment with this type of approach in this case are somewhat too involved to discuss here.

A. Judy Pearson

Judy Pearson is a twenty-eight-year-old mother who has won the complete confidence and spontaneous admiration of all those who know her. She is successfully building a new life out of fragments of the past. During the last twelve years there have been more changing scenes and more transition in her ways of looking at the world than most people experience in a lifetime.

As a high-school senior at the age of sixteen Judy was a straight 'A' student – sensitive, impressionable, lonely, and very much disillusioned with her militantly moralistic parents. She was also secretly very much in love with a man she saw as being no less lonely and no less misunderstood than herself. She resented the petty artificial social customs which prevented their expressing their love for each other openly.

As she looks back now upon that day in May, it seems as if it must have been a century ago, not just twelve years. There was the beefy-looking woman from the Juvenile Bureau coming to call; the painful scene at the Judge's office where, as it seemed to her then, her parents sat in speechless and impotent fury; the two strange girls who were said to have made 'charges'; poor Ralph sitting at the other end of the long table, frightened and helpless; his pale wife and the two babies whining in the corridor. She dimly remembers the awkward efforts at kindness; the unexpected release from the detention centre so that she could graduate with her class.

There were bitter moments as well as frightening ones – like finding her luggage at home already packed and waiting after the commencement exercises; the lonely days at the Florence Crittenden Home; the first time she had looked upon death, so tiny, so still, so much her own, with no ears to hear her cry. There was her first job at a defence plant and the all too infrequent letters from home, which each time she resolved not to read but always did, once, twice, or even three times.

Two years later Judy married Carl. There wasn't much time for wedding frills. Plans centred about a forty-eight-hour pass and a Justice of the Peace. There were the precious letters that came from overseas in threes and fours. There were pictures of little Jeanne to be sent each week to the father who would never see her. Then the letters from overseas suddenly changed their tone and became infrequent. Carl wanted a divorce. She could only agree to this.

Now Judy is completing her training for a professional career as a speech teacher. The four years of college have been spread out over six. By intermittent employment she has managed to support herself and nine-year-old Jeanne, as well as contributing to her parents' support after her father's stroke two years ago.

The most remarkable part of Judy's story is the way in which she has found a rich store of meaning behind each unfortunate experience in her life – meaning which has enabled her to build a formidable store of inner resources. These have enabled her to meet with poise and assurance those obstacles which would defeat less experienced women. All the fear, bitterness, and loneliness which nagged at the adolescent Judy have been replaced by gentleness and tolerance of the frightened people she has found on every hand who do not have her inner resources. She has made the important discovery that it is a clutching fear that makes many people threatening and insensitive to the feelings of others. Ralph was afraid he could not bear the responsibilities of parenthood. Carl could not face the sneers of people who knew of his wife's past. It was not until she saw her father helpless and defeated following his stroke and the stark terror in her mother's eyes that she realized that even her parents had been afraid. The stern discipline which they had imposed upon her during her childhood was merely a 'strength of character' born of fear, fear of confusion, fear of the unknown, and most of all, fear of guilt. As she faces the rearing of Jeanne she feels the clutching fear of guilt herself – the fear that she will be unable to impress upon Jeanne the lessons that will enable her to avoid her mother's mistakes.

Judy finds that others sense her store of resources and seem to expect of her that she will furnish them with stability to replace their uncertainties, with meanings to replace their feelings of emptiness, and with calmness to replace their turmoil. For Judy the past has become a precious key to the future.

B. Timothy Ellman

At least once a day Timothy Ellman has to pinch himself to make sure that what has happened to him is real. So much of what has happened to him he had never believed could really come true. Many a time as a child he used to daydream about going to a great university and sharing the exciting company of scholars but in his heart he never really believed it could come true. But for Timothy reality has outrun imagination!

One of the most surprising events in Tim's adventure has been the discovery of the fascinating person who consented to become his wife. Their marriage has provided a never ending source of new interests and new experience for both of them. He has come to see his wife as more fascinating than he had ever believed any woman could be, but even more surprising to him is his discovery that she appears to find him fascinating also.

Time faces the future with wide-eyed and simple trust. It would never occur to him to deface it by trying to carve his own initials conspicuously upon it. If the future from this point on is only half as generous as she has been in the past, he will continue to count himself as the most fortunate of men. He finds himself impatient for the future to reveal what she has in store for him next, career, responsibilities, family, children, new friends he awaits with breathless anticipation.

In this setting Tim's response to friends and social situations is one of rapt and spontaneous interest. Each new revelation of a colleague's ideas causes him to pause and think. Thus his conversation has a deep undertone of unhurried thoughtfulness and empathy with the other person.

His inner life is not wholly without turmoil. One of the things, for example, which causes him concern is the possibility that people will be misled into thinking of him as being a more technically competent and sophisticated person than he really is. He is constitutionally opposed to taking on any 'intellectual' front. For him 'intellectualism' comes perilously close to destroying the rich vitality of life.

C. Patricia Deems

Patricia Deems is a versatile specialist in expressing unexpected 'points of view'. She satisfies a deep-seated and scholarly curiosity by seeking out for herself new ways of looking at familiar 'facts', 'beliefs', and social 'values'. She has an ability and intellectual flexibility which permit her to see and put into words any issue from at least two different points of view. This versatility in seeing things from novel points of view enables her to contribute new meanings to any discussion, and to sense the basic and justifiable differences in thinking which lead people to disagree with each other on everyday issues. She thus becomes a valuable member of any discussion group because of her ability to loosen people from their set positions and to take into account new ways of looking at what they are talking about.

It is not surprising that Patricia Deems has chosen teaching as her major professional interest. She is a teacher in the best sense of the term; she is an initiator of new ideas, not merely a purveyor of facts. Her contributions to a discussion, whether it be a class discussion or something more informal, are always unexpected and usually challenging. She never says quite what you would expect her to say, and she effectively prevents all her friends from identifying her consistently with any easily identified stereotyped attitudes. In fact, her nimble approaches to life sometimes leave her colleagues with an exhilarating feeling that they are not so sure they know where they stand as they originally thought they were.

Patricia Deems' ability to see alternative viewpoints is not merely part of her social interaction pattern; it stems from a deep-seated conviction that most of the troubles that people get themselves into are like ruts in an otherwise broad highway of life. If people could get themselves out of the ruts, they would be freer to understand the world around them and freer to appreciate each other. Her fresh approach to life and its day-by-day social situations leads her to be both freely expressive in a never ending variety of ways, and generously accepting of her friends' opinions, no matter how deviant they may appear to be.

20. Reactions of the participants

There were five sessions in the sequence, each of which was electronically recorded. At the beginning of the series each participant was asked to prepare during the following ten days a report of his reactions to the series. Following are their accounts.

A. Judy

When I first received my role I was tense, wary, and a little frightened. A hundred questions seemed to buzz around my head. Why was the role constructed so deliberately to arouse emotional reactions? Why the pathetic background? Why the victorious banner at the end? What did all this mean in relation to what I had previously written? I liked Judy. It would not be a hard role to assume – sympathetic, kind, admired – understanding, strong, intelligent, mature – Who was I trying to kid? evidently myself. It was going to be a hard two weeks and I knew it from the minute I had finished reading the role. (Its very hard to write this Dr. Kelly, I can't forget that words are only what you say about experiences and feelings. Yet if I don't or can't make it clear you will only be able to write words about words and that is a waste of time and quite a useless product in the final analysis. I forgot my place, yours is the task of discernment.)

I have just left our second meeting and I feel wonderful. Merry Christmas everyone! I'm so happy and you must be too. Its a lovely day and I feel warm and loving. Today I met two interesting and charming people. We are going to be friends and I like them very much but best of all they like me and I can help them. It was a great deal of fun working out our roles since everyone turned out to be such nice, believable people. Everyone that is except me. How can I possibly be so dam well adjusted? I feel so competent. Bring on the lions! Am I or am I not in my role – I am.

Tried out my role this evening on my parents and it went over very well. I don't think they noticed too much of a difference in me but I did. They had both had a bad day at the store and we prepared to sink into an evening of depression. When they talk about business at the dinner table I usually listen but offer few comments or questions. It takes a lot of effort to prepare a meal, even though I like to cook, and I usually would rather they slow down, forget the store, and grasp some inkling of what they were stuffing down the oral passage. Tonight however, I asked questions and sympathized. They got up from the table feeling noticeably better. I felt like hell. Here they had all these problems and I couldn't do a thing to help them solve them. They still didn't know whether they had pork chops or egg foo yong for dinner. (It was shrimp creole.)

Another meeting today. Tim is having a tough time with his part, poor guy. I think he's having a tougher time than most of us think if he is really working on it outside of the meetings. Patricia is too, to some extent. I talked to her yesterday and I'm afraid she thinks of her role as an unreliable person. Today in the group she did much better.

I tried my role out today on the mother of one of my delayed speech cases. Until recently she has been unconcerned about the lack of speech in her son (age 5½) and would not cooperate with therapy at home. Last week a little shock therapy was administered by letting her view her son among the group of other delayed cases. His lack of contact with them finally opened her eyes. Today she was bursting with explanations and questions and Judy was just the person to take over. Among the mass of words which tumbled out I saw the woman was afraid – afraid because she was an orphan and she felt, although she did not come right out and say so, her son might be feebleminded. She knew Judy knew and would try to help. For tangible evidence at the success of the role in this case I will add that she asked the head of the Clinic to under no circumstances to change the clinician working with her son. Somehow I feel awfully humble about this not proud at all. She was taking her beating and I had only pretended mine. Hadn't I? What am I going to tell her the next time or the time after that? Sometime soon they're going to tell her that the son is feebleminded and she's going to have to take it and I'm going to have to watch it. Thanks for the classroom techniques Dr. All of a sudden I'm so tired.

Tried the role out at a party last night and it didn't work out too well. I am unsure as to how Judy reacts among groups, consequently I was more quiet than usual. My friends tease me a good deal and they expected me to respond in my usual manner. Last night however, I did not return their parries but only accepted them in a good natured way. The general impression they seemed to have of me was that I was 'off my feed'.

I am rather discouraged with my handling of the role at the present. I can't seem to gain the objectivity which Judy characterizes. It is not hard to listen and see the hurts and worries which almost everyone has – but when I see and hear my friends and family going through it everyday it becomes difficult to keep in mind that they are human beings who must settle their own problems in their own way. I worry about them and inwardly flinch.

I felt terribly cornered in our last meeting today. It was more personalized than it had ever been and it seemed to me that much of the conversation was directed towards me and how I felt. How could I honestly express what I felt about the role in front of Tim and Pat without making it so obvious that my true role, roles, were at odds with Judy on several sensative points? To begin with Judy's and Miriam's pasts are not so very different but that's where the similarity ends. Judy over a period of time sees herself and is to all intents and purposes the one who has triumphed. She is mature and capable and knows it. Miriam on the other hand has not been as successful. Her experiences have not made her more competent only more cautious and less confident in her decisions. There are many more such differences but the role was not assigned for the purpose of self medication. The role was hard for me to play at times and it has been even more difficult keeping notes of how I felt. I am rather sorry to stop playing Judy. I liked her better than I liked Miriam. Perhaps with some more practice and a few years I can adopt some of the qualities which I liked best.

B. Timothy

May 23 Wed. *First conference.* My first look at Timothy. I felt like I was trying on a new suit that was the wrong colour and size. I did not yet understand what kind of a person Timothy really is, and had some hostility to the role. The role seemed very incomplete. How does Timothy act in situations not covered by the role? Is Timothy a spineless, weak individual (has he character) or not? Is his wife really a 'fascinating' type of person? I felt difficulty in playing the role? How can I be concerned about being thought more competent than I really am?

May 24 Thurs. So far I have been unable to really 'be' Timothy or feel like I was Timothy – rather discouraged at lack of progress. I read role over very carefully and tried to see how Timothy was constructed and why he was created in that way. The result was that I began to actually appreciate the kind of person Timothy is. Chester would be a much happier person if he were more like

Timothy in many ways. Examples: Timothy is not over concerned with the future – he lives in the reality of the present and has little anxiety. Timothy does not feel that he has to 'make' himself socially accepted; he feels automatically accepted and projects his interests outward to others in social situations instead of being tied up with inner anxieties about his acceptance by others.

Second conference. I was rather nervous about the whole thing and thus was very much inhibited in participation. Dr. Kelly's portrayal of Timothy was of great help in understanding him. I left feeling that Timothy was not spineless, but really very mature, and thus liking him much more.

I now feel that I would like very much to be more like Timothy, but I seem to have difficulty in projecting myself in to Timothy's role – still discouraged.

May 25 Fri. Made these notes (above material). Is Timothy's wife really the fascinating type? How does he deal with her in every day life? Tried Timothy role with wife. It is almost natural in some situations, in others it was difficult. It is difficult to break some habit patterns that may interfere in the role.

May 26 Sat. While the aspects of Timothy personality can be applied, it is difficult to think of myself as Timothy because of the interference of old habit patterns. I played the role rather well with some of my wife's friends who visited us for the weekend. I felt rather at ease doing this. The social situation was good in this case and I felt relatively successful in acting as Timothy.

May 27 Sun. Same situation as yesterday. After the guests left, my wife complimented me on getting along with the guests so well. I felt that I was accepted by these people.

May 28 Mon. *Third conference.* I felt less inhibited this time. Role playing helped me greatly to understand and appreciate Timothy's relationship with his wife. This may enable me to play this aspect of Timothy role more adequately. I have actually been playing this aspect of the role to some extent since marriage, but perhaps I ought to emphasize this more (understanding, interest, and admiration of wife). The conference group is becoming more effective as the members overcome inhibition, become more accustomed to roles and support each other more. The role playing of specific situations is especially helpful in perceiving the spirit of the roles.

Last conference. In that this being written some time after the last conference, my feelings and memories of this meeting are somewhat vague and difficult to clearly recall. One feeling that I had was that I had been less able to take on my role effectively than the others in the group. Perhaps this was due to different problems that I faced in adapting the role, perhaps it was due to tensions that arose during the playing of the role. The important things that I got out of this experience are: one, that a person can improve his adjustment to life by emotionally redefining his world and his role in it, and, two, several specific ways in which I can redefine my world and my role in it, and, three, the actual experiencing of the results of such a redefinition, demonstrating to me, to some extent, that continued effort in emotionally redefining my world would bring increased happiness and emotional maturity. I could write a very considerable amount of material on my reactions to this experience that might be of value, but I shall have to conclude here. I should be glad to furnish any information omitted here if, for any reason that is desired.

C. Pat

May 23 – (Dr. Kelly's office) Today I received the written characterization of Patricia Deems. I was quite surprised at the role I had been asked to assume. In some ways, I felt I already had some of Pat's qualities. For example, I felt that I liked to see alternative viewpoints and was acceptant of my friend's ideas. However, unlike Pat I could see it might be difficult for me to try to 'loosen people from their set positions' and to 'effectively prevent my friends from identifying me consistently with any stereotyped attitudes'.

I had the feeling on first reading that I would not like the role. I felt I could see in Pat people I had known and dislike who had either talked too much or who had always wanted to argue or take the opposite viewpoint from that conventionally accepted. I felt Pat might be superficial and insincere and that she could surely not have many friends who felt really close to her. I perceived her friends as being hesitant to come to her with problems, because they might not find their ideas accepted. Rather Pat would be apt to throw a bombshell into their thoughts and upset their present way of thinking. I don't think people want that – they need someone to see *their* point of view, understand and seemingly agree.

May 24 Tried the Pat role in a class. The professor made the statement – 'People cannot think without having words for symbols.' I think he merely threw this out to get some reactions from class members. All the students who recited supported his statement and agreed. I stated that I felt a 'delayed speech youngster with no words certainly shows evidence of thinking'. I think this was a rather feeble attempt at Pat's role, and in a class situation as it was – was accepted as a good viewpoint and given further clarification by the professor. But it did give me a start at the idea of looking for a new slant – rather than only seeing the point of view of the majority.

May 24 – (Dr. Kelly's office) Today I learned to like Pat much better. I decided that though she might lack a few very close friends who thought of her as always dependable and understanding, she might gain a wider range of interests and friends and gain a great deal of confidence in herself knowing she could be interesting even to those who did not know her well. Even her close friends would still want to talk things over with her knowing they might get less sympathy – but perhaps might gain a great deal in insight and in being jolted into a new line of thought.

I find I still fear Pat's role. I believe in trying to use it, I may hurt my friends or may experience a feeling that people dislike me for my novelness. As explained in the session, I can perhaps avoid this by (1) the manner in which my remarks are made, i.e. avoiding personal interjection such as '*I* disagree', but rather saying, 'Have you ever thought', etc. (2) by keeping a 'twinkle in my eye' when trying a new twist, (3) by following up a seemingly preposterous statement with worthwhile suggestions that show some thought.

I discovered Pat's role can probably be fun, but it will take a lot of conscious prodding of myself to put me into the active vivacious role instead of the easier, more passive, good listener role. I suppose I fear it because I wonder – what will people think of me?

Already, I can see the fallacy in my statement of yesterday that people do not want someone to disagree. This is certainly true when a person is under a great deal of stress, but in ordinary situations, they admire a good conversationalist and a person with new ideas. Then, too, I realize now that Pat can be understanding, she can agree, but people will also like her because they can go to her for the new slant – the new approach to a problem they can see only one answer to.

In today's session, I learned a great deal more about Tim and Judy. In Tim, the objective listener, wide eyed and interested in Judy with her maturity, deep sympathy and understanding – I see much more of what I feel are real and good personal values, than I do in Pat. Pat still appears slightly superficial to me. On the other hand, I see something pretty gay and intriguing about Pat. I look at it as though, 'It certainly would be fun to be vivacious, sparkling and interesting instead of more stereotyped and conservative.' But I guess at this point, there seems to be something almost selfish or self centred about being Pat. Seems I would feel almost guilty in the role.

May 24 – Conversation between Pat and friend.
Friend: (after reading article in paper on student riot) (very sarcastically): I certainly am proud to be a student at Ohio State.
Pat: Well, why not – I think we should be.
Friend: very startled – Why?
Pat: Well – look at all the publicity we got. (laughing by both)

May 25 and 26 – I tried the role in various situations this week-end and usually got the reaction from others that I was trying to be funny. They would look startled for a minute, then (knowing I *must* be kidding) would laugh. (And I would, too) Perhaps I could have avoided this by not laughing myself or by coming out with some really concrete suggestion to follow up my initial remark. For example, in the conversation reported May 24 – I might have said 'Sure, we can be proud. Remember the majority of the students didn't even participate and possibly feel as we do.'

This week-end's attempts at playing Pat was rather fruitless. I only got the feeling that I was trying to 'be funny'.

May 28 In discussing my reaction of last week-end, it was decided to tone down my role a bit and make my suggestions less preposterous and always followed by something that makes them worthwhile and make the other think, 'Now maybe she has something there!' I think this change will help me in playing the role.

In today's session I learned more about Tim's role and how he would interact with his wife. I also got more insight into Judy's role. It was decided she should add more of a sense of humor and a more vivacious, active participation than had formerly been included.

May 29 In today's session, we had an opportunity to see Judy and Timothy interact. I had been interested in how this would work because it seemed to me they were both basically 'listeners'. (Judy more on the plane of sympathetic, understanding listening to personal troubles – Tim more objective, searching for new ideas, but still interested in 'what makes the other tick'.) In watching the two interact, I felt Judy did a superb job of combining her listening, sympathetic qualities with that of a mature, confident woman voicing her ideas. Tim, I felt, was a little too unemotional and stern when he could've accepted overtures of friendship with feeling. At points he tried to exert his ideas – or to restate Judy's when actually an understanding 'Yes' or 'I see' would've been more in character. Pitch level of the voice went up in these situation but went down to a more pleasant, well-modulated one when he was a fascinated listener and observer of this 'new person'.

Pat did not do much interacting today. She did make the suggestion that she would like to see Tim and Judy interact and this was in character to suggest the 'new slant' whether this was Pat or Pauline is hard to say – I have a feeling it was 'the old self' because I was not consciously thinking – 'what would Pat do?'

I have had the feeling that in some ways the Pat role hits fairly close to the old self. The 'Pauline' is interested in new ideas, and has a dread of ruts and stereotyped ideas. Pauline, however, seldom leaves her friends wondering what she will say or how they stand. I believe her friends can expect the versatility on an intellectual plane or in a conversation involving ideas or course work – but they receive a more passive, stereotyped reaction to personal problems. Perhaps, it is because Pauline feels it is safe to diverge from the middle role on an ideational plane – but in real life contracts she fears loss of friends or prestige might result.(?)

I perceive Pat as more daring and more willing to take this chance of appearing somewhat inconsistent or revolutionary to her friends. In a teaching situation –

Pauline has had novel ideas – but has not dared to experiment for fear of being labelled 'different' or 'progressive' by the parents or administration. I believe Pat would try the new ideas (being tactful about the way in which they were introduced) – and further – I believe Pat would be respected and admired for having been more versatile and different. I think this is a new slant I have gotten (or at least an old slant which has been greatly reinforced by playing this role. I think I often *thought* the novel idea – but was fearful of verbally expressing it or trying it.

The role playing gives me a good, light feeling of not having to be the old, serious, 'bring me your troubles Pauline' – but rather a chance to laugh lots, be interesting, vivacious, prevent things from becoming bogged down in dreariness and oversentimentality and at the same time an interesting new slant on helping others – 'give them a new idea' – 'don't just reinforce their old one' (the old idea may be right or wrong, of course). But give them some *new* way of looking at the problem.

This part of the role is very challenging and interesting to me.

May 30 Tried the role with friends. Tried to make my comments not quite so preposterous and with evidence of more thought behind them. Seemed to work much better. My comments accepted as interesting additions to conversation.

May 31 The role playing seems easier and more a part of me. I find myself contributing more to conversations – rather than passively listening. It's fun. Keeps me on my toes, though.

June 1 I really am getting much more enjoyment out of the role. It is almost like a game to me to see if I cannot keep my remarks interesting and challenging. With a group of friends this morning, I tried to see if I could not act in a more versatile manner, giving some retorts and suggestions that would not have been a part of the old role. The friends seems to enjoy it.

I really feel the role playing experience has been a fascinating and beneficial one. At first, I think I tried to 'over play' and thereby I felt and acted ridiculous. Then I found I could utilize parts of Pat in combination with lots of the old self without having to fear the part or worry about the reaction of others. I found to my surprise that other's reactions were usually good. In fact, I think they were pleasantly surprised. This, of course, gave me more confidence to continue.

It has been interesting to me to see how role playing can be used in therapy. But the main interest, I suppose, has been a personal one – in realizing how some changes in the 'old role' might be achieved and profitably carried out. It has been a new and fascinating experience for me. And although I know I have fallen short of really acting my role 24 hours a day – I have grown more and more to feel I am (or could be) Pat and thereby have felt more natural in acting in the manner she would.

Thank you for the interesting experience, Dr. Kelly!

June 1 (After our 2 o'clock meeting) The meeting today was interesting because it gave us an idea of some of the reasons behind making the new roles as you did. I had noticed, for example, the more or less depressing mood into which it had thrown Judy and had wondered at the time if this had been expected or desired – and why. I saw a few days ago in a session with you that one of the purposes of Tim's new role was release of tension and indirectly through this, a lowering of the voice pitch.

In thinking over the reasons you made my role as you did, I guessed that you felt the old self was perhaps too conservative, too fearful of really expressing herself and in danger of getting into a rut. You further explained this idea (and reinforced it) by explaining today that the role had been designed with the idea of getting me to use available intelligence, especially to use it verbally, and to avoid a stereotyped personality or avoid getting in a rut.

I think the role has been especially beneficial to me in this way: I think a few years ago I was taking a very active interest in trying to help myself to become an interesting person and was very open to new suggestions and new ideas of achieving the kind of adult personality I wanted. I did have a fairly happy and successful college life, followed by two years of teaching (which, according to some, was successful also). This has gone quite far in giving me confidence in myself which I previously lacked. However, it has perhaps been detrimental in making me figure that at age 24 I am probably the type of person I am going to be and therefore, since I've gotten along well that way, why try to change? I think this experience was the necessary jolt I needed to make me realize that even though perhaps there is no need or occasion for any *complete change* of character – by taking such an attitude I am in danger of being immobile or in a rut. Why not, then, try to *add* to (not necessarily change old self completely) my present self – some other attributed such as Pat's – so that I will not fall into the stereotyped schoolmarm role? I know that no one is so perfect or inflexible that he cannot change – I knew that before – but frankly, I hadn't applied it to myself – so I am glad I had this chance to be jolted into realizing it.

I have been very much aware of 'ruts' and frankly, that is the biggest single reason I am in graduate school at the present time – to get out of the rut of the high school English teacher while I was still aware of the fact I was falling into it. My way of getting out of the rut was to get back in contact with younger people and to get into a field with more future and inspiration – such as I think Speech and Hearing is. I guess you call that 'environmental manipulation' – but frankly, it never even occurred to me to manipulate the person till to-day! (Frankly, in the above situation I think the environmental change was also needed – but – it is very clear to me that I may get back in the situation of being in a rut someday again, and a person can't go on moving every 2 years, so the one thing that can 'save me' is to make myself so interesting and fascinating to others (and myself) that I am never stereotyped. (At least it certainly looks as though that would help!)

I do not think I will discard the Pat role yet – I may not be so actively thinking about it – but I do want to keep reading it and consciously trying it out. As a matter of fact, I would like to do it long enough that Pat becomes so much a part of me – I don't have to consciously use the role. I am glad to realize that I can retain most of the old role because I suppose I feel certain security in it – but it is necessary to discard to some extent the old ideas of passivity always listening and 'no need to bother thinking as long as this other person enjoys talking so much'. I certainly hope to retain the good qualities of listening and understanding – but would like to add to that a little more verbal demonstration of ideas, particularly a new or different slant on an old idea. I think this will help me by presenting a challenge which requires a little action and change on my part. In order to be a 'Pat' one has to be pretty well informed on many things, and one has to be pretty quick in picking up cues and in responding. If I played the role well, other people would probably not be bored with me or feel they always knew how I'd respond – and in turn it would be hard to get in a stereotyped way of thinking or be boring to myself. It seems I would be too busy thinking of 'new slants' to let myself be immobile or in a rut.

I might add that my closest friend knew I was playing some sort of role, but did not know what it consisted of until to-day. Before I gave her the role to read, I asked for her comments on what she thought it had been. She did not hit it directly, but she did relate several instances where she had noticed I was 'different' and had somewhat startled her. (But had not offended her.) After reading the role, she agreed that she thought it was a good one for me and felt that acceptance of some of Pat would be a valuable asset to me.

As stated before, I have enjoyed the opportunity to work with you on role playing, and I have gained a great deal of insight from you and from attempting to play the 'new role'.

21. Conclusion

It is hoped that this report of sample experiences with the analysis of self-characterization sketches and fixed-role therapy will suffice to indicate that these approaches to personal-construct psychology may open up many new understandings of personality and the ways in which readjustment processes can be set in motion. The techniques described are still in an exploratory stage. Precise validational evidence growing out of fixed experimental designs is still to be obtained. This chapter, like the book as a whole, is designed to be provocative rather than conclusive.

Chapter nine

Dimensions of diagnosis

We hope that the reader is now aware that the psychology of personal constructs does have some practical applications. If he has followed us this far he should be ready for some more elaboration of the theory's system. So we spiral back to more abstract writing again. In the following two chapters we propose a new repertory of diagnostic constructs for the clinician. How he puts the repertory to daily use is a matter to be covered in the next volume.

A. Design specifications

1. Introduction

The purpose of this chapter is to give the clinician a set of professional constructs within which he can subsume the personal constructs of his clients. Since we have emphasized the subsuming of personal constructs as the primary basis for role relationships, it can be seen that these diagnostic constructs are designed to help the clinician assume professionally useful role relations with his clients.

These professional constructs do not refer to disease entities, or to types of people, or to traits. They are proposed as universal axes with respect to which it is possible to plot any person's behaviour, at any time or at any place. They are also axes with respect to which it is possible to plot the changes that occur in a person's psychological processes. In themselves, they are neither good nor bad, healthy nor unhealthy, adaptive nor maladaptive. They are like the points of the compass; they are simply assumed in order to enable one to plot relative positions and chart courses of movement.

2. Problems in the design of psychological constructs

A diagnostic system, like a scientific theory, should be fertile as well as neat. It is not enough that we pigeonhole our observations of the human personality. The human personality, being a course of events that keeps flowing along, is not well adapted to receptacles. Only after one is dead is it possible to make a relatively static classification of one's personality. Even then the unfolding of subsequent events may throw one's life role into a new historical perspective and change many of the meanings previously assigned to it.

A good diagnostic system is a set of coordinate axes with respect to which it is possible to plot behaviour. It makes a great deal of difference, however, whether the axes are designed to catch our fellow men like a fly in a spider's web or are conceived as a system of streets and highways along which he can be encouraged to move in an orderly fashion. We have already discussed the plight of a disturbed person who is enmeshed in his own construct system and how the psychotherapist may help him to find new avenues of orderly movement by helping him redesign his network of pathways. Now we must make sure that we do not make the same kind of mistake in our thinking about the disturbed person that he has made in his thinking about himself. The coordinate axes we set up should represent many different lines of movement which are open to him and not a labyrinth of one-way passages from which he can never escape.

Consider the diagnostic construct of the Intelligence Quotient or I.Q. Through the first three decades of this century it proved to be a relatively useful construct. It was pitched at rather useful levels of permeability and propositionality. It had some implications for what might be done in teaching the child and what his rate of development might be. Gradually, however, it was realized that the construct has little utility in dealing with adults, not because the I.Q. of adults could not be 'measured', nor wholly because adult I.Q. failed to correlate with the range of adult performance. Rather, it was because adult I.Q. as a construct carried fewer implications for what adults could do about themselves and about each other. Then, as we began to reevaluate the notion of I.Q. as applied to the child, we began to see that even there it tended to put the teacher or the psychologist in the position of pigeonholing the child, rather than opening up a fertile source of plans, opportunities, and methods of teaching him.

Does the I.Q. of the individual remain constant? We psychologists have tried to make it a construct which would be so. That has been its principal design specification. We may have been successful. If so, our success may have been a misfortune. The child who is nailed down to the I.Q. continuum has just that much less chance of changing his teacher's opinion about him. If he is 'low', his unorthodox constructive ventures will never be given a thoughtful hearing; if he is 'high' his stupidities will be indulged as the eccentricities of genius. In formulating the construct of the I.Q. we may have become enmeshed in the same net that immobilizes many a patient; we may have been caught in the web of our own construct system. Having been so careful to pin all persons down to a continuum with respect to which they can never change, we may now be confronted with the product of our own handiwork – a world full of people whom we cannot conceive of as changing, whom we can do nothing about! Is not I.Q. a distressingly unfertile construct after all? Should we not, therefore, take better care when we create the design specifications for future diagnostic constructs?

In a later chapter on the analysis of experience we conclude by proposing some collective terms under which the client's experience record can be tentatively structured by the clinician. We call this kind of formulation a *structuralization* and we ask the reader to reserve the term, *construction*, for the better-organized formulation which would arrange the client's personal constructs. In structuralization we arrange the client's separate behaviours directly under our own system. In construction we first arrange his behaviours under the constructs which we infer are his personalized ones, and then, in turn, we arrange his constructs under our own clinical system – that is, we attempt to subsume them.

As we have attempted to point out before, if we construe only bits of behaviour we tend to limit ourselves to normative thinking. If we concern ourselves solely with the client's personal constructs we limit ourselves to phenomenological thinking. Instead, the psychology of personal constructs is a system in which the normative is superimposed upon the phenomenological. We attempt to use the phenomenologist's approach to arrive at personalized constructs which have a wide range of meaning for the given individual; then we attempt to piece together this high-level type of data with what we know about other persons.

Our task in this chapter is to make a beginning – and only a beginning is possible for us – of the system of constructs which can be used for the *subsuming construction system* by which each client's case can be brought into the public domain. We started by saying that our system must be fertile. We gave the I.Q. as an example of a psychological construct which seems to be not quite fertile enough. There are other constructs in current psychological use which are more satisfactory from the standpoint of fertility, but which are so loosely defined that they are difficult to use systematically. *Anxiety* is a common example. Perhaps we can redefine it, together with some of the other commonly used diagnostic terms, so that we may use it systematically within the psychology of personal constructs. Perhaps, also, we can add some new terms which may prove useful; although, for the most part, we should like to be parsimonious in coining new words.

Before we proceed let us state our point of view by making a definite list of ten specifications for a useful diagnostic construct. These are much like our specifications for a psychological theory as discussed in our first chapter.

3. Ten design specifications for a psychological construct

a. Fertility. A good diagnostic construct should suggest some variety of hypotheses regarding the arrangement of its elements. It should not be so preemptive that one is left free to say only one thing about each of the phenomena which it subsumes. It should open up various new approaches to the problems which are construed by means of it.

b. Propositionality. A good diagnostic construct should be propositional in nature. By that we mean that it should be one which can be applied to a case relatively independently of other diagnostic constructs. This means that each diagnostic axis needs to be drawn somewhat orthogonally to all others. The fact that it can be handled independently of other constructs, rather than having to be always part of a tightly knit constellation, makes it adaptable to experimentation.

Now this is always a relative matter. It may be impossible ever to construe anything as completely independent of everything else. Yet science does not progress by designing its experiments to rattle the whole universe in its sockets every time a simple test is performed. The wholeness of the universe need not interfere with the independent investigation of its parts. In order to carry on profitably this investigation of the separable parts of a whole universe we need to have constructs which lend themselves to propositional treatment.

Preemptive or partly preemptive constructs have a stultifying effect upon diagnosis. Take, for example, the notion, growing partly out of Kraepelinian thinking, that a person who is a psychotic cannot also be neurotic. This is a somewhat preemptive construction. It is the same kind of reasoning which leads some people to say that what is 'physiological' cannot be 'psychological', or that a given case 'belongs to' the physician rather than to the psychologist or to the teacher. This kind of pigeonhole reasoning prevents the formulation of new classes of hypotheses and the scientific testing of those hypotheses. It precludes propositional treatment of phenomena.

c. Dichotomy. The construct should distinguish solely between the *like* elements and the *unlike* elements. A trichotomous grouping tends to be preemptive – as, for example, the trichotomous grouping of *normal–neurotic–psychotic.* A dichotomous construct permits the setting up of experiments, while a trichotomous construct has first be broken down into dichotomous constructs which must then be treated propositionally before they can be subjected to experimental test.

The dichotomy must be clear cut. If it is not, the door is left open for its misuse. For example, if there is no clear-cut distinction between what constitutes *anxiety* and what does *not*, the diagnostician is likely to construe anything which fits his whims as *anxiety.* Now this is not the same as saying that the construct must always be easy to apply. There may be instances in which it is difficult to determine whether the phenomena best fit the category of *anxiety* or the category of *not-anxiety.* Ambiguous as the phenomena may be, however, the construct itself must not be ambiguous. It must relate to some clear-cut dichotomy.

d. Permeability. This specification could be inferred by the reader from what has already been said. If a diagnostic construct fits only certain specific phenomena which have already occurred in the lives of certain clients, or which are known to have occurred in the life of any client, it has little bearing upon further discoveries, either about the client's past or about his future. The diagnostic construct must be one which will embrace additional elements – elements which are yet to arrive on the scene. Our discussion of permeability in an earlier chapter is basic to this point.

e. Definability. Not only must the construct be dichotomous but it must be practically useful by being definable in terms of what people can observe and agree upon. Sometimes this is called 'operational definition'. Sometimes it is called 'observer agreement'. Now this means more than specifically cataloguing all the phenomena embraced by the construct and then asking whose who use the construct to memorize the catalogue. The latter approach, though commonly used, tends to produce definition at the cost of permeability. It tends also to produce a kind of professional sophistry among those who have memorized the lists of elements – a sophistry which closes the door to experimental research.

f. Temporality. A good diagnostic construct should place its elements on a time line. In mathematical language we might say that its axis should never be orthogonal to the time line. It should relate to a course of events. Thus it becomes a basis for construing processes rather than states.

g. Futurity. Furthermore, a good diagnostic construct should not be concerned exclusively with etiology but should have prognostic value. It should have implications as to what to expect in the future.

h. Ability to generate testable hypotheses. It is not enough for a diagnostic construct to be fertile; it should generate the kinds of hypotheses which can be tested. We might have subsumed this specification under one of those listed above, but it seems advisable to emphasize it by listing it separately. A hypothesis which is to be tested must be dichotomous, or reducible to dichotomies. It must be permeable to the as yet unwitnessed outcomes of the experiment. It must be practically definable. Ordinarily in psychology it should involve a time line that stretches into the future. But more than this it should be one which it is feasible to test. If it relates only to matters of such vastness that one can never encompass them in an experiment, it is not practically testable.

i. Ability to generate treatment hypotheses. Not only should hypotheses generated by a diagnostic construct be testable but they should reflect a degree of optimism regarding outcomes for the client. They should imply that something can be done to change matters for the better. This is altogether a practical requirement. The way we conceptualize our world does affect our ability to deal with it. Over and over the psychotherapist sees that lesson driven home. He sees clients coming to him with their problems formulated in a way that leads only to 'realistic' despair and leaving with both issues and 'realities' reconstrued in ways that lead to new hopes and adjustments. Moreover, this is a lesson which the scientist can learn as well as the client. He too can see what was 'impossible' under one system of construction become 'possible' under a revised system of construction. Is it not time to begin to question the dogma that it is nature which has forever imposed upon man a set of immutable impossibilities?

j. Sociality. A diagnostic construct should be one which permits the psychologist to subsume a part of the construction system of his client, not merely to construe his separate acts. It should be a construction of construction systems. Thus it deals with data which are originally abstracted within the idiographic frame and in terms of the inferred personal constructs of the individual.

By specifying that a diagnostic construct should provide for sociality we are setting the stage for the therapist to cast himself in a role relationship to his client and play it out in a constructive social enterprise. We might say that a diagnostic construct should have a social value. To say as much and leave it at that would be to depend too much upon the meretriciousness of the term, 'social value'. We have tried to be more explicit as to what we have meant by playing a role in a social process. Our earlier discussion of the Sociality Corollary is relevant here.

B. Covert construction

4. Preverbal constructs

Here is the first of our proposed set of diagnostic constructs. These are clinicians' constructs about clients' constructs. The reader will find an assembled list of definitions in the glossary at the end of the next chapter.

A preverbal construct is one which continues to be used even though it has no consistent word symbol.

a. Symbolism. The means by which constructs are symbolized has a great deal to do with the manner in which they are used and maintained. In our earlier discussion of symbolization we pointed out that constructs are usually symbolized by invoking one of their elements. The element stands not only for itself but also for the whole construct with which it is customarily construed. Thus one's mother may become a symbol for the services upon which one sees himself as being dependent for life and sustenance. It may even be that the immediate awareness of the physical presence of one's mother may become the only means by which one can invoke the conceptualization of sustenance. This imposes obvious limitations upon the ways one can come to see oneself as sustained and secure.

The use of words of other mobile vehicles as symbols of constructs opens vast new areas for the utilization, continuation, and modification of constructs. The trick of using words as symbols is neat and efficacious. The word is simply introduced as one of the 'like' (or 'unlike', in some cases) elements in the construct context. Then it is used as a symbol. It stands not only for itself – a word – but also for the construct of which it is one of the elements.

Words are easily invoked. One does not ordinarily have to go to a particular place or wait for a particular occasion in order to produce them. There are exceptions to this, of course – exceptions which have their inhibiting effect upon the modification of constructs having to do with sex and excreta, for example –

but, in the main, words, being ubiquitous, serve to make constructs readily available for use, test, and revision.

Now words used as symbols of constructs may have other words used as symbols of the elements. The elements, in this case, are themselves constructs which are symbolized by words and which are subsumed or supraconstrued by the first construct. As long as we are using constructs that have elements which are themselves readily conveyed by words or other readily available symbols, the revision of constructs is relatively feasible. We can sit in our rocking chair and twiddle our constructs to our endless amusement. We may even test out some of our convictions without rising from our comfortable position. With the elements all arrayed before us by means of words, we can reformulate our superordinate constructs on the basis of the outcomes of our anticipations.

But what happens when the elements cannot be invoked by means of such mobile vehicles as words? In that case other symbols may be used. But they are likely to be less definite. They are likely to be more cumbersome. The client has difficulty communicating either the elements or the constructs. He may be able to do no more than act out his representations of the elements. His actions may not convey much to the therapist. The client may just sit and have feelings which he cannot describe.

The therapist will have to infer, from the occasions on which the client claims he has the indescribable feelings and from such fragments of description as he is able to offer, what the elements are and how they are construed.

b. The origin of a preverbal construct. In dealing with a preverbal construct it is important to realize that, ordinarily, it is one which was originally designed to construe those elements of which an infant could be aware. One should therefore not expect his adult client to describe or portray a preverbal construct in a manner which is becoming to a mature person. The therapist has before him an infant who is speaking with the voice of an adult. The infant's thinking may be overlaid with the sophistication of adulthood; but as the overlay is thrown back, the wide-eyed, vaguely comprehending, dereistic child is revealed.

The child depends for sustenance upon certain people. It may not be particularly meaningful to say that he is *more* dependent than is an adult. An adult is dependent too, but he extends his dependency discriminatingly to more people, to more things, and to institutions. The child, whose dependency is closely tied up with certain people, is likely to have more constructs which deal with his dependency relations to those particular people. Thus it is that preverbal constructs, when revealed in an adult client, are often found to relate to the client's dependency, though that need not always be so. Generally, if the client construes the therapist, through transference, by means of an essentially preverbal construct, the therapist should be alert to the possibility that the client is envisioning some kind of childlike dependency relationship to the therapist.

Preverbal constructs may, in some instances, represent a kind of core of the client's construction system. They are likely to deal with the self as well as with other people and inanimate things. The therapist should therefore not be surprised to find a client using a preverbal type of construction to maintain his integrity and unique identity in the face of difficulties. Preverbal constructs are often found in the client's reserve lines of self-defence.

c. Misleading features. The preverbal construct may have an overlay of verbalized constructs which may mislead the clinician. The client may appear to be highly articulate. There may be a torrent of words. The vocabulary may be versatile, picturesque, and, in many respects, unusually apt. The clinician may initially believe that he is dealing with a person of such verbal fluency and intellectual acumen that the reformulation of his constructs should be fairly easy. He may be misled, also, by the client's initial appearance of pliability. Yet, after he has waded through a wallow of words, he may come to have doubts about his initial assessment of the case. The words are only elements which have lately been embraced by the permeable preverbal constructions. He has not yet actually come to grips with the basic constructs of his highly verbal client. This is likely to be a case in which certain important preverbal constructions are operating in a permeable fashion. The client's verbal quicksand is no ground upon which experiments can be erected to test the preverbal construction or to expose it to validating evidence. Yet the illusive preverbal constructions continue to govern the over-all aspects of the client's behaviour. The client gets into messy deals. His wordy rationalizations may appear to be logically defensible. He may even be able to show the therapist just how he was applying a construct which the therapist apparently found acceptable in the last interview. Again he may have a sudden burst of 'insight' and be able to verbalize, even better than the therapist can, why he now sees that he made a mistake. Throughout all this the alert therapist may have a growing awareness that he is dealing with a seething overlay of construing but that the basic structures are still unexpressed and untested.

Usually the preverbalized constructions which are covered with the overlay of verbalized constructs relate to the client's dependencies. The transference situation, in some respects quite useful, may make it particularly difficult for the therapist to detect the preverbal dependencies. He may gradually become aware that the client's 'own needs are interfering with his relationships'. Another clinician may say of the client's behaviour, 'His dependencies are interfering with his adjustment'. Still another may say, 'He is showing *oral dependency*'. Within their respective theoretical frames, each of these may be a meaningful descriptive statement. Within the theoretical frame of the psychology of personal constructs it is systematically meaningful to say that a preverbal construction governing dependency relations is operative.

d. Special problems. We have said that the preverbal construct tends to be one which was originally formulated to deal with the elements of which a preverbal infant could be aware. Fortunately, therefore, the elements subsumed are fairly easily inferred and limited in intellectual range. But some persons utilize their preverbal constructs in such a permeable way that many of the elements of adult life are added to the contexts of these infantile constructs. Indeed, a person who places great store upon spontaneity may elaborate his preverbal constructs to the point where he has a complicated unverbalized system which is particularly difficult for even the most experienced clinician to unravel. In a strict sense some of these constructs may not be preverbal. They may have been formulated after the client had the use of words; yet, because they are essentially like the preverbal constructs which all of us have, it is appropriate to lump them with the preverbal constructs.

The preverbal construct in the precocious child whose speech has been delayed or ignored may pose special problems for the therapist. The nonverbal symbolization may be mobile enough for testing in the interview situation, but the therapist may not be able to recognize it. Even if the client comes to the therapist after he has grown up, he may have no ready way of communicating his constructions to the therapist except by means of a series of behaviours which the therapist is not prepared to interpret. Such a client may say, 'It's no use. You couldn't understand. Nobody can understand. Nobody can ever understand. It doesn't make sense to other people.' Yet the constructs in this kind of client may involve much more complex and advanced matters than the simple dependency relations which preverbal constructs represent in most clients. As a child the client privately understood too many things before he had public words to contain them.

A similar problem arises in the client whose early training compelled him to construe certain complicated matters before he had a public language. He need not have been a precocious child, in the sense of having an unusual ability to make meaningful constructions; he may simply have been prematurely confronted with certain issues. For example, he may have been required to construe the behaviour of his anal sphincter muscle before he was able to relate it to other means of maintaining comfort and before he was able to label it with any useful verbal symbol. In the therapy room the clinician may note that the client is dealing with many matters in a manner similar to that with which one deals with bowel control; yet there is remarkably little in the client's verbalization that specifies an anal type of construction. Similarly, the client may have had to develop constructions of other complex issues before he had words with which to bind them appropriately or a sufficient array of elements with which to fill out the contexts. Any construction, even though permeable, which was sharply formed before the client had adequate contextual elements available to which he could relate it, and an adequate public vocabulary with which he could manage it, is likely to be puzzling to the therapist.

e. Acting out preverbal constructs. Some therapists decry 'acting out' on the part of the client. They want the client to verbalize all of his constructs. It would be nice if the client could. But he cannot. If the constructs are to be dealt with, the therapist must learn to utilize the client's own nonverbal semiotic system. This is where role playing and other 'non-intellectual' approaches must be utilized in dealing with preverbal constructs.

Sometimes it is possible for the therapist to help the client to establish a verbal symbolic system to replace a part of his preverbal system. This is not an easy task. If it is undertaken, the therapist must be prepared to deal with a great deal of difficult material. Sometimes the therapist seeks only to help the client find a few words for his preverbal constructs. Such labelling may be propaedeutic to later therapeutic reconstruction and experimentation.

Preverbal constructs can often be tested by the client in their unverbalized form. It is easier, of course, if the constructs are first identified in terms of verbal labels. Since that is frequently not practical, the therapist must be prepared to help the client identify his constructs by means of other symbols and then subject them to validating test.

f. Clinical signs. There are four kinds of clinical evidence which one may use in determining whether or not one is dealing with essentially preverbal constructions: (1) the client's efforts at verbalization repeatedly end up in an expression of confusion; (2) inability to verbalize the construct consistently but relatively better ability to illustrate the construct by producing the elements which make up its context; (3) appearance in dreams, the content of which the client claims he cannot remember but which, on questioning, appear to have some structure in terms of mood, number of people, movement, and so on; (4) 'recollections' of events which the client is not sure really happened. In the last case the therapist may consider that the 'recollection' is not the original 'memory' but a cue which stands for the original memory or a symbol of the context upon which the preverbal construct was originally formed. The therapist, of course, should not be so reality-bound that he discredits all 'recollections' of things which did not really occur. Whether or not the client remembers something which really happened, or 'remembers' something which actually did not happen, is less important than the question of what the 'remembered' event constructively stands for.

5. The unconscious

The notion of the 'unconscious' has been utilized in various psychological systems. In psychoanalysis it has occupied an important and useful position, albeit a too ready cover for ambiguity. In the psychology of personal constructs we have chosen to utilize several other explanatory constructs and to use the term 'unconscious', as we must use many imprecise unscientific words in public discourse, in an illustrative rather than in a definitive sense. In part, the notion of preverbal constructs is a substitute construct for dealing with some of the elements which are otherwise structured by means of the construct of the 'unconscious'. The construct of preverbal constructs has a better range of inconvenience, including, as it does, personal constructs which are communicable by means other than words, and including personal constructs which are only partly immobilized because of their poor symbolization.

But preverbalism is not a full translation of 'unconscious'. We are about to present some other terms which also cover some of the same ground. One of them is *submergence.* Another is *suspension.* In addition, we may consider the fact that some elements are outside a given personal construct's range of convenience. This also makes them unavailable to the client, at least unavailable in terms which the therapist construes them. Moreover, in some measure, the 'unconscious' is replaced by the constructs of *subordination, impermeability,* and *loosening,* terms which have particular meanings in our system. A client may fail to construe his behaviour in the meaningful way the therapist construes it because he is organizing it under minor, subordinate, and nonregnant constructs. His elements are personally arrayed in little collections only, whereas the therapist may be seeing them arrayed in larger collections to which the little collections are subordinate. Again, a client may have 'closed out' a construct – that is, made it impermeable – whereas the therapist may see it as capable of embracing many new elements. It is easy for the therapist to accuse the client of 'unconscious resistance' in such a case. Finally, the therapist may observe the apparent shifting that goes on under loose conceptualization, and, because he cannot follow it, hypothesize that some stable unconscious conceptualization is taking place.

The decision not to use the notion of an 'unconscious' follows from our systematic position. This is a psychology of *personal* constructs. We assume that personal constructs exist. If a client does not construe things in the way we do, we assume that he construes them in some other way, not that he really must construe them the way we do but is unaware of it. If later he comes to construe them the way we do, that is a new construction for him, not a revelation of a subconscious construction which we have helped him bring to the fore. Our constructs are our own. There is no need to reify them in the client's 'unconscious'.

If a client is today able to see hostility in his behaviour whereas yesterday he could not see hostility, that does not necessarily mean that he 'had' the idea of hostility all the time but has only now become aware of it. He had behaviour. The therapist saw it as hostile. Then the client came to construe it as hostile. The behaviour was there all the time. Was the hostility? From the therapist's point of view the behaviour could, at the outset, be construed as hostile. From the client's point of view the behaviour might not have been originally organized under a hostility pattern at all. Is it therefore fair to say that the client was unconsciously hostile all the time? In such a case we would say no.

But let us make no mistake about this: after the therapist is done with him the client with his new 'insight' cannot engage in many of the old behaviours without invoking the brand-new personal construct of 'hostility' which he bought from his therapist. Any therapist may provide 'hostility' as a personal construct for a client who was previously operating under such personal constructs as 'independence' or 'ambition'. The change may be for the good. But let us not be too sure that the personal hostility existed 'subconsciously' in the client before the therapist got hold of him.

6. Submergence

A construct is a two-ended thing. There is the *likeness* and there is the *contrast* end. Sometimes one of these two ends is less available than the other. When this is markedly true we may refer to the less available end as the *submerged* end.

In an earlier chapter we gave some illustration of the shenanigans that people play in order to avoid a complete expression of some of their constructs. We have emphasized the idea that a construct involves both a likeness and a difference, that it is a way in which at least two things are alike and, by the same token, different from at least one other thing. To say anything about anything is to imply that it could also be said about another thing and that it definitely could not be said of something else. Alternatively, it may be a statement that is the converse of one which particularly applies to two or more other things.

A client says, 'Everyone has always been good to me.' He denies that anyone has ever mistreated him and yet he continues to dwell on the point that everyone has always treated him well. This is a point at which the therapist may start a search for the submerged end of the construct. It may lie in any one of several directions. The contrast may lie in his belief that certain *other* people have been conspicuously mistreated. Perhaps his father mistreated his brother and the client feels guilty because of it. Perhaps his father mistreated his brother and the client keeps thinking it will soon be his turn to be mistreated.

The contrast may lie in the client's own behaviour. He may mean, 'Everyone has always been good to me but I have not been good' or 'I don't want to be good to certain other people.' Here one looks for the client himself as one of the elements in the construct's context and attempts to discover whether he fits in the likeness grouping or in the contrast grouping.

The contrast may involve the client in a somewhat different way. He may mean, 'Look at me. I am the kind of person who says that people have been good to him. There are some people whom I could name who go around saying that people are mean to them. I am not the kind of person who says such things.' Here one may understand that the client, in saying merely, 'Everyone has always been good to me', is 'acting out' his construction of himself as an uncomplaining person rather than verbalizing such a self-description. This is an illustration of how verbal symbols can be used for one construct but used demonstratively rather than symbolically for the more important construct. As far as this section in our discussion is concerned, however, we are not so much concerned with the 'acting out' as we are with the submergence involved. Suppose the submerged end of the construct is, 'There are some other folks who go around saying that people are not good to them.' As the psychologist explores the submergence further he may find implied the idea that the client sees himself as the victim of such complaining people. He may mean, 'I say people have been good to me but some people say I have been bad to them. This is not fair!'

The client in our illustration may be expressing a construct which is being maintained at considerable cost. He may mean, 'I keep *telling* myself that everyone has always been good to me.' Here he is resorting to 'word binding' or 'liberalism' in order to keep from construing himself as a person who has been mistreated. If this client yielded to his paranoia, his whole system might be disrupted and he might become anxious or guilty.

The client may be expressing uncertainty about the future. In this case the emphasis is upon the 'has' in the statement, 'Everyone *has* always been good to me.' He may mean, 'Up to now, everyone has been good to me, but I anticipate that from now on I shall be treated badly. Perhaps you are going to treat me badly.' The client may imply further that the therapist is hereby warned not to treat him badly. At this point we are going somewhat beyond the construct of submergence and are dealing with the action, or if-then, implications of constructs – another topic.

a. Which end is submerged? Ordinarily it is the contrast end of the construct which is submerged. In some cases it is the likeness end. Since constructs are usually symbolized by some element which is associated with the likeness end, it becomes somewhat more difficult to uncover the submerged likeness end of a construct. The client invokes the construct by citing in context the contrast elements. He may indicate that they are associated, but does not say how, for that would mean saying words about the forbidden end of the construct, and those words are necessarily unsayable. For example, the client offers a series of descriptions of incidents and people which, judging from the contextual grouping, are conspicuously nonsexual in content. Elements which could be subjected to sexual construction are consistently omitted. There are no slips of the tongue, nothing that could possibly be given a sexual interpretation; the client's language is always 'scrubbed up'. The client apparently allows himself to say nothing which might be given a sexual interpretation. Yet he does not protest openly that he ignores sex. One has to infer the submerged end of his sexual construct from the scrupulous contextual grouping of the contrast elements.

b. Submergence in dreams. In dealing with a client's dreams it is usually not difficult to recognize submergence features. A client whose therapist is short and fat dreams of a tall thin man who goads him into doing things that are wicked. The therapist whose thinking tends to be bound to the elements rather than to the constructs – in other words, is concretistic – confines himself to thinking about what is tall, what is thin, and what is wicked. The therapist who thinks in terms of constructs realizes that to say that one is thin is to imply that another is fat, that to see wickedness is to be aware of goodness. He therefore first considers what constructs the dream has invoked: the *tall–short* construct, the *thin–fat* construct, and *wickedness–goodness* construct. If he is looking for elements, he then looks for elements which are clearly within the range of convenience of these constructs. It should not take him too long to come up with the hypothesis that the client, in elaborating the transference relationship, is being loosened from some of his old moorings.

c. Submergence and the self. Usually when submergence is detected the therapist can expect to find that the client construes himself as a potential element for inclusion in the context of the construct at the submerged end. Submergence may be a handy way of keeping a construct from being tested. Just as the scientist cannot do good work unless he considers the alternative to his hypothesis (among psychologists the alternative is usually the null hypothesis), so the client cannot adequately test a construct, one end of which is submerged. Perhaps the client fears that, if the submerged end of a construct is uncovered, he will have to reconstrue himself, with far-reaching and devastating results. Perhaps he will have to test his construct. It may be invalidated. How much more of his little world would have to be reconstructed as a consequence? In what kind of disordered world would he have to live in the meantime? The therapist, in seeking to help a client uncover the submerged ends of his constructs, should make sure also that the client is helped to deal with them propositionally. Propositional constructs are those which can be dealt with and validated or invalidated, one at a time, without a person's whole construction system crashing down on him every time he shifts a pivotal beam.

7. Suspension

The phenomena which are popularly identified as 'forgetting', 'dissociation', and 'repression' can all be handled within the theoretical framework of the psychology of personal constructs in much the same way. In order for an experience to be remembered or perceived clearly it must be supported within a system of constructs. When one construct is resolved in favour of another one, some of the elements tend to drop out, especially those which do not fit so well into the new construct. Simultaneously, other elements which were once less available to the person are now more prominently displayed because the new structure provides a convenient peg to hang them on. When one structure is substituted for another, the range of convenience of the new one is not likely to coincide precisely with that of the other. The new range of convenience can almost always be expected to allow some elements to drop out and others to reappear.

When a client begins to make marked movement, involving the substitution of new constructs for old, the therapist can usually detect that now things are remembered which formerly appeared to have been forgotten. The therapist may conclude that the movement taking place is the direct result of the client's having 'remembered' certain things. In a sense this is true. However, it is also true that the elements newly recalled are made available through the instrumentation of the new structure. For example, it has been this writer's observation that changes in dream content in a client undergoing comprehensive therapy tend to follow the incipient signs of new constructs in the therapy sessions rather than the converse. Moreover, during the intermediate stages of comprehensive therapy, certain elements tend to drop out of the picture and the client has difficulty recalling what he was once able to discuss quite glibly. As he reaches the later stages of a comprehensive therapy programme, and develops an over-all structure which makes a kind of sense out of his old thinking as well as his new, some of these temporarily forgotten elements may become available again. Sometimes we can see this happen during a course of electroshock therapy, although the psychotherapeutic aspects of electroshock therapy are usually so badly handled that there is more destruction of recent structure than emergence of new ideas.

Now this is not to imply, as some therapists do, that dreams are useful in psychotherapy only to the extent that they furnish evidence that changes are taking place. The elaboration of dream material is useful as a psychotherapeutic technique for helping the client initiate new structure. We are simply documenting the point that the content of dreams is a function of the client's current construction system.

When an idea is mislaid because the person has no place to file it, it need not be forever lost. Usually there is enough systematic structure surrounding it to keep it from escaping altogether. It may turn up again by itself, or when the minor structure which gives it minimal meaning turns up. In either case the recollection will be a function of its incorporation within a more comprehensive current system.

Some constructs can be considered as elements within the context of more comprehensive constructs. During the constant revision process which characterizes healthy living, major constructs as well as little memory bits get temporarily mislaid. Of course, the little memory bits may be considered to be constructs, too, but they are so local and so impermeable that they constitute a relatively low order of structure. When a structure is rejected, because at the moment it is incompatible with the over-all system which the person is using, we may say that it has undergone *suspension*.

a. Incompatibility. Sometimes a minor structure is incompatible with a major portion of a person's over-all construction system. Yet the minor structure may itself be one which the person once used extensively and which he has sought to outgrow. A kind of forgetting takes place when such a structure is rejected as incompatible. An experience may be clearly contained, but the structure itself may constitute such a threat that it, together with the experiences it contains, may be held in abeyance (cf. the Landfield threat hypotheses). This kind of forgetting is called 'repression' in some theories. Here let us call it *suspension*.

Our theory does not place the emphasis upon remembering what is pleasant or forgetting what is unpleasant; rather, it emphasizes that one remembers what is structured and forgets what is unstructured. In contrast with some notions of repression, suspension implies that the idea or element of experience is forgotten simply because the person can, at the moment, tolerate no structure within which the idea would have meaning. Once he can entertain such a structure the idea may become available within it.

What we have been saying ties back to our Modulation Corollary: the variation in a person's construction system is limited by the permeability of the constructs within whose ranges of convenience the variants lie. Moreover, as the Fragmentation Corollary states, a person may successively employ a variety of construction subsystems which are inferentially incompatible with each other. Psychotherapy may help a client develop greater permeability in the superordinate aspects of his system, and thus enable him to recapture certain suspended constructs that belong to subsystems which, in turn, are inferentially incompatible with each other. The therapy removes the threat. The subsystem can now be articulated with the whole, even though it is inferentially incompatible with it. As likely as not, the once threatening subsystem is now viewed in a historical perspective whence it may be seen as sequentially though not inferentially compatible with the major operating system. The client may thus say of the subsystem, 'That was a stage I went through.'

b. Suspension because of implications. It is important to bear in mind that ideas are not suspended because of their intrinsic nature but rather because their implications are intolerable. For example, a client complains that he has an intense fear of water. He says that he knows exactly how it came about, but that knowledge does not help him control the fear. He recalls having fallen into the rain barrel at the age of three and having nearly drowned. He claims he can even remember the incident in detail: where the rain barrel was, what it looked like, the choking sensations, the recovery of consciousness.

The therapist, realizing that the incident alone, while fearful enough, cannot account for a lingering phobia, seeks to have the client elaborate the circumstances surrounding the incident. The client then recalls that a day or two before the incident his mother had severely reprimanded him for dropping his baby brother on the floor, and had told him that God would take his own life from him if he did such things. Later, when his mother was in another room, the client struck his brother. Sure enough, God did make a threatening gesture in his direction. That was what the rain barrel's implication originally was. But this is not all. Recently, the client has been having competition problems in his own home. His present resentment is not unlike that which he experienced at the age of three. And so on and on, as the therapist helps the client to work through an important area of suspended structure.

The rain-barrel experience was not suspended. It had enough structure around it which was compatible with the client's major structure to enable him to remember it. What he had forgotten were the feelings of sibling rivalry. Those were so wholly embedded in the threatening structure of hostility that they were temporarily suspended. The therapist, by setting up a therapeutic situation which encouraged greater permeability in certain aspects of the client's superordinate system, helped the client bring the suspended structure within the purview of his system as a whole.

c. Permeability of suspended structures. Suspended structures are not necessarily impermeable during the period of their suspension. New experiences may be incorporated within the suspended structure even though the structure may still remain largely unavailable to elaboration and modification. A suspended structure is not easily tested and hence not easily invalidated or reconstrued within a larger structure. It is therefore likely that a person will organize his behaviour uncritically when he sets it up in terms of a suspended structure. What is lost is the capacity to modify the structure in the light of the person's major outlook, to profit from the outcomes of wagers laid within the suspended structure, to communicate the structure to others, to elaborate the structure through successive definitions and modifications, and to maintain a stable course of action along any line which is partially governed by the suspended structure.

d. Range of convenience. We should distinguish between suspended constructs or structures and those which are not used in a given situation because their range of convenience does not cover the elements at hand. The range of convenience figures in some kinds of suspension, as we have already indicated, but in a different way. Constructs are suspended, not because of the limitations of their own range of convenience, but rather because of the limitations of the ranges of convenience of those constructs which might ordinarily be expected to subsume them. Constructs which are not used in a given situation simply because their own ranges of convenience make them inapplicable are not systematically construed as suspended structures within the psychology of personal constructs.

8. Level of cognitive awareness

In an earlier chapter we pointed out that a person's construction of events, by which those events become incorporated into experience, is not necessarily a highly verbalizable or conscious process. Thus far in this chapter we have discussed certain interpretive constructs which fall in the areas popularly known as the unconscious, preconscious, or foreconscious – preverbal constructs, submergence, and suspension. Let us introduce a scalar type of interpretive or diagnostic construct at this point. It should serve the purpose of identifying the direction of certain movements observed during the course of a psychotherapeutic interview or series of interviews. Let us call it the construct of *level of cognitive awareness.* The diagnostic constructs of *preverbal constructs, submergence,* and *suspension* all represent relatively low levels of cognitive awareness. The constructs which are readily verbalized, which do not have to be acted out in order to be communicated, whose alternatives are equally accessible, and which fall within the range of convenience of one's major construction system or belong wholly to substructures whose inferential incompatibility with the major system is not so great as to put them into suspense, represent a higher level of cognitive awareness.

But the level of cognitive awareness includes more. A person's construing is also at a low level of cognitive awareness when he deals with elements which lie at the outer extremities of the ranges of convenience of his available constructs. For example, a scientist construes at a low level of cognitive awareness when he attempts to apply certain scientific constructs to data which do not conveniently lend themselves to such constructions. A person using the construct of *homeostasis* to explain a client's vocational choice, a person using the construct of *suggestibility* to explain dental caries, and a person using the principle of *infinite progression* to explain heaven would all be construing at a low level of cognitive awareness. In each instance the marginal constructs invoked do not provide grounds for making precise discriminations. The wagers one might lay on the basis of construing these particular elements by means of these particular constructs would not pay off. The opportunity for achieving validation or invalidation of the constructs is minimized. The person cannot be very keenly aware of what he is up to.

C. Content of construction

9. Dilation and constriction

When, following a series of alternating uses of incompatible systems, a person broadens his perceptual field in order to reorganize it on a more comprehensive level, the adjustment may be called 'dilation'. The dilation may successfully eliminate the original incompatibility, as it was experienced, but it may or may not set the stage for new incompatibilities as the person attempts to rearrange an increased clutter of events. *When one minimizes the apparent incompatibility of one's construction systems by drawing in the outer boundaries of one's perceptual field, the relatively repetitive mental process that ensues is designated as 'constriction'.*

When a person moves in the direction of dilation he jumps around more from topic to topic, he lumps his childhood with his future, he sees vast ranges of events as possibly related, he participates in a wider variety of activities, and, if he is a client undergoing psychotherapy, he tends to see everything that happens to him as potentially related to his problem.

When a person moves in the direction of constriction he tends to limit his interests, he deals with one issue at a time, he does not accept potential relationships between widely varying events, he beats out the path of his daily routine in smaller and smaller circles, and he insists that his therapist stick to a sharply delimited version of his problem.

10. Comprehensive constructs and incidental constructs

While dilation may not actually involve the construing of many elements or a wide variety of elements within the same construct contexts, it is, as we have pointed out, a way to set one's stage for more comprehensive conceptualization. *Comprehensive constructs are those which subsume a relatively wide variety of events.* They are not necessarily highly regnant or superordinate constructs, for the events which they subsume may all be relatively low on the superordinate–subordinate scale. A permeable construct tends to move in the direction of comprehensiveness because its open-endedness enables it to embrace more and more elements in its context as time goes on. A comprehensive construct is likely to be one which has been in use a long time, although, in certain cases – some manics, for example – there is a dilation which sometimes appears to bring forth a matrix of comprehensive constructs in a relatively short time.

When we say that a comprehensive construct is one which subsumes a wide *variety* of events, we introduce an interesting problem for the personal-construct psychologist. What do we mean by 'variety'? If the events are construed as similar at the likeness end of the construct, are they not, from the standpoint of the client's own personal system, psychologically similar? How then can we define them as various?

We could invoke a normative definition of 'variety' and say that one has a comprehensive construct if it embraces as similar a great many events which other people consider to be different. This might mean, however, that a person in moving from one culture to another, where people see the same similarities he does, would suffer, by definition, a loss of the comprehensiveness of his system.

Alternatively, we could say simply that the gross count of elements subsumed by a construct would determine its relative level of comprehensiveness. But this, unfortunately, would mean that the construct of *hair*, for example, would always have to be interpreted as a comprehensive construct; there are a lot of individual hairs in the world and the person could be more or less aware of all of them at one time.

Actually, as we see it, a comprehensive construct is one which cuts across many other construct lines. The 'variety' in the elements is established by the person's having otherwise distinguished them as being different from each other by means of other constructs. Thus, when we use the term 'variety', we are referring to a 'variety' within the person's own construct system. Thus a constellatory construct would tend to be less comprehensive than a propositional construct which embraced precisely the same elements. The constellatory construct tends to fix its elements with respect to other realm memberships and hence they cannot be construed in the same variety as they would otherwise. A wholly preemptive construct could, of course, not be comprehensive at all.

In contrast to *comprehensive* constructs, we have *incidental* constructs. Together they constitute a diagnostic dichotomy – *Incidental constructs subsume a small variety of events.* This may come about because of the preemptiveness of the given construct or of another construct within which these events are construed. It may occur because there are so few of the events numerically. It may occur because of the impermeability of the construct. It may be simply that the incidental construct is a subordinate part of a hierarchical system, and is designed to deal only with a few 'special' instances. A mathematical construct might commonly be expected to be incidental. It is limited to the mathematical constellation. It is not likely to be used to order one's interpersonal relations (though perhaps there are instances in which it could be so used).

11. Superordinate constructs and subordinate constructs

In an earlier chapter we discussed the idea that some constructs are superordinate to others. We have said, for example, that the variation in a person's construction system is limited by the permeability of the constructs within whose ranges of convenience the variants lie (Modulation Corollary). By that we mean that for a new construct to be formed it must itself be acceptable within the context of some construction which is permeable to its inclusion. There must be a potentially superordinate construct which is hospitable to the new construct. Constructs are construed by means of other constructs, and those, in turn, by still other constructs. It is thus that a system is formed (Organization Corollary). Constructs can be compared by their relative positions on the superordinate–subordinate axis of a person's system.

A construct is construed as superordinate to another if the other is utilized as one of its contextual elements. A construct is construed as subordinate to another if it appears as one of the elements in the other's context. For example, in many persons' systems the construct of *good vs. bad* occupies a superordinate position with respect to a large proportion of their other constructs.

Does a subordinate construct, by virtue of its subordination, fix the realm membership of its elements within the constructs which are superordinate to it? In other words, is a subordinate construct a constellatory construct? Not necessarily. Take the proposition, 'This is a spade.' If all spades are implements, then to say that this is a spade is to say that it is an implement also. That makes *spade* constellatory with respect to *implement*. In this case the object's realm membership under *implement* has indeed been fixed. However, if some spades are implements and others are not implements, then only the object's susceptibility to the *implement–nonimplement* range of convenience has been established by calling it a spade. We know only that *spade* is subject to the *implement* range of convenience, but we do not know whether it is one of the like or one of the unlike elements. The realm membership is not fixed. *Spade*, while a subordinate construct to *implement*, is not necessarily constellatory with respect to it.

Subordination does not rule out propositionality. To be sure, if *spade* is treated propositionally it is not thereby committed to being anything else in particular. Its realm membership is not fixed; that is, it is not necessarily an implement. It may, however, be committed thereby to the range of convenience of some superordinate construct; that is, it may be one of the things which it is appropriate to classify either as implements or as not implements.

It adds up to this. A subordinate construct is an element in the context of a superordinate construct. It is one of the things with which the superordinate construct is concerned. The fact that it is subordinate tells us this and this only. We do not know, until we take a look at the superordinate construct itself, how the subordinate construct will be grouped, whether all on the 'like' side, all on the 'unlike' side, or divided. A construct's subordination carries no constellatory of nonpropositionality implications. It is committed only to the range of convenience of the superordinate construct.

12. Regnancy

Regnancy is something else. *A regnant construct is a kind of superordinate construct which assigns each of its elements to a category on an all-or-none basis.* That is to say, it deals with its elements nonabstractively. This is the kind of grouping one finds in classical logic. For example, the construct of *implement* would be regnant over the construct of *spade* if one were to say that spades were implements. The construction of *spade* is so regulated by the construction of *implement* that if one says, 'This is a spade', he has also implied that this is an implement. Calling something a 'spade' commits it to another classification too.

The regnancy may operate in a contrast fashion. If no spade may be considered an implement, then one rules out the possibility that something is an implement the moment he construes it as a spade. This is still regnancy.

A regnant construct has the effect of making its subordinate constructs constellatory. If all spades are implements, then the realm membership with respect to *implement* is fixed. The moment one applies the construct of *spade* to an object, he has implied that it is an implement.

We should keep in mind that constructs are individual ways of behaving. The construct of *implement* may be regnant over *spade* in one person's construct system but not in another's. The question is not: *is 'implement' of itself a construct which is regnant over 'spade'*? Rather, it is: *does this particular person use 'implement' as a regnant construct over 'spade'*?

A superordinate construct is not a regnant construct if it commits a subordinate element construct only to its range of convenience and does not invariably class the subordinate construct as one of the like elements or as one of the unlike elements. If spades are the sorts of things that the *implement–nonimplement* construct deals with, then the *implement–nonimplement* construct is superordinate to *spade* but is not necessarily regnant over it. If some spades are implements and some are not, then the construct of *implement* is superordinate to but definitely not regnant over the construct of *spade*. If spades are the sorts of elements that the *implement–nonimplement* construct places in its range of convenience, and, furthermore, if all spades are implements, then the construct of *implement* is not only superordinate, it is also regnant.

We have not attempted to give the term 'concretism' a precise definition within the psychology of personal constructs. To be sure, we have used the term, as we have had to use many others, in order to communicate within the presumed personal-construct system of the reader. As in any writing of this sort, we have had to rely, in part, upon definition by extension. In casting about to pick up the things to which our new concepts apply, we necessarily mention many things which are not used superordinately within the more precise outlines of our system. We trust that the reader will understand that, when we say that a regnant construct deals with its element constructs 'concretistically', we are using the term 'concretistically' in this extensive rather than in a systematically precise manner.

Regnancy accounts for the simplification of one's personal-construct system. If one construes all spades as implements, one does not have to waste time wondering whether the thing one holds in one's hand is an implement or not, as long as one 'knows' it is a spade. A child for whom the concept of *goodness* is regnant over *mother* never stops to question whether or not his mother is good. A man who believes that an *authority* is a person who is always *right* does not have to decide for himself what is right; he finds it is sufficient merely to identify the authority. This kind of simplified thinking, stemming as it does from ancient logical forms, accounts for a lot of wooden-headed conflict in the world, both between persons and within persons.

13. Core constructs and peripheral constructs

Core constructs are those which govern a person's maintenance processes – that is, *those by which he maintains his identity and existence.* In general, a healthy person's mental processes follow core structures which are comprehensive but not too permeable. Since they are comprehensive, a person can use them to see a wide variety of known events as consistent with his own personality. He can see himself as a complex but organized person. If his core constructs are too permeable, however, he is likely to see too many new events as having a deeply personal significance. He tends to be less detached and objective. He may become paranoid, as he interprets each new event as intimately relating to himself. Or he may merely become hypochondriacal, as he sees each new event as relating to his health.

Peripheral constructs are those which can be altered without serious modification of core structure. Some are comprehensive and some are incidental, some are permeable and some are impermeable. The reformulation of a peripheral construct is a much less complicated affair than the reformulation of a core construct. Peripheral constructs can be broken up in therapy without precipitating serious anxiety. It is not necessary first to provide a substitute structure when seeking to revise peripheral constructs. Peripheral constructs may be relatively objectively applied, since they permit the person to make judgements without involving himself deeply. For the most part, formal education deals with what presumably are peripheral constructs, while therapy deals with core constructs, or at least with constructs which start out by being core constructs.

Sometimes it is assumed that a given structure in a person is peripheral. Later it is discovered that the person uses it as a core construct. One's personal notion of how long it took the earth to be created might be an example. It might seem that this could be expected to be a strictly peripheral matter in which the identity of the thinker would be in no way involved. But there are instances in which this is not true. For some, the concession that the earth must have been created in an evolutionary manner is also a concession to immorality and is accompanied by marked behavioural changes and a reidentification of the self. The clinician needs to be alert to the possibility that any construction utilized by his client may turn out to be a core structure.

Core constructs do not necessarily represent dependency, as we have defined dependency in a previous chapter. Moreover, role constructs, those which involve one's own behaviour in the light of the understanding of other persons' outlooks, do not necessarily represent either core constructs or dependency constructs. They are somewhat more likely to represent the latter, but it is possible to play a role without being appreciably dependent.

14. Tight constructs and loose constructs

Tight constructs are those which lead to unvarying predictions. Even the elements which lie at the outer edges of the construct's range of convenience are consistently construed as belonging either to the like or the unlike grouping. There is more of a tendency to give precise structure to the unlike grouping than may be true in other types of construction. Moreover, the unlike grouping is more likely to have its own symbol or name.

In a healthy person the core structures tend to be tight. He has regular habits with respect to such matters as eating, sleeping, and so on. On the other hand, these processes are subordinated to other patterns in such a way that his integrity is not threatened when he finds that he must make exceptions to customary ways of doing things.

Loose constructs are those which lead to varying predictions but which, for practical purposes, may be said to retain their identity. Among other things, loose construction is exemplified by dreams. The loose construction is like a rough sketch which may be preliminary to a carefully drafted design. The sketch permits flexible interpretation. This or that feature is not precisely placed. The design is somewhat ambiguous.

The alternation between tightening and loosening of construction is an important feature of deep therapy. New constructs are formed by loosening up old ones and tightening up the tentative formulations which begin to take shape in the resulting disarray. One may handle dream material in this manner during therapy – but that is a matter for a later chapter. The loosening may be accompanied by anxiety, as we shall see later when anxiety is expounded from the standpoint of the psychology of personal constructs. The loosening, of course, is likely to be accompanied by erratic and sometimes bizarre behaviour. For that reason the therapist usually tries to confine loose construction to the therapy room and tends to tighten up construction before the client leaves for the day. Especially the therapist tightens up construction before a break in the therapeutic sequence.

Time binding and word binding, which are described elsewhere, are examples of tightening techniques which are useful for certain purposes in therapy. They also, as we have already pointed out, help reduce a construct to a state of impermeability. Particularly is this true of time binding.

Free association, induced fantasy, dream reporting, and intermittently broken silences are all techniques for construct loosening. Physical relaxation, perhaps developed progressively, helps the client loosen his constructions. The furnishings of the therapy room may also have a bearing on the client's ability to loosen his constructions temporarily.

Tightening can be facilitated by raising the voice slightly, by the use of grammatically correct sentences, or by reflecting 'feeling', as the client-centred therapists do, so that the client will have to express himself more precisely – a procedure which possibly accounts for the more coherent typescripts of verbatim protocol that one seems to get from the Rogerian type of client-centred interview. The continual tightening of the client's own personal constructs may also account for the fact that client-centred therapists seem to be able to cancel appointments or break off therapeutic series with relatively little damage to their clients. Tightening also occurs when the therapist takes notes, or apparently works from a prepared outline. But we are getting ahead of ourselves! This section is merely to develop the diagnostic construct of tightening and loosening, not to illustrate all its uses in therapy.

Note: *A glossary of diagnostic constructs appears at the end of the following chapter.*

Chapter ten

Dimensions of transition

This chapter concludes the presentation of the repertory of diagnostic constructs which have been systematically designed for the clinician's use. It also concludes our basic theoretical exposition. The chapters which follow in the next volume are all at the descriptive, methodological, or technical levels.

A. Constructs having to do with dislodgment

1. Personal constructs and life's vicissitudes

Constructs enable a person to hear recurrent themes in the onrushing sound and fury of life. They remain relatively serene and secure while the events above which they rise rumble and churn in continuous turmoil. Yet constructs themselves undergo change. And it is in the transitions from theme to theme that most of life's puzzling problems arise.

In the words of the Organization Corollary, each person characteristically evolves, for his convenience in anticipating events, a construction system embracing ordinal relationships between constructs. The Modulation Corollary takes off from this point by stating that the variation in a person's construction system is limited by the permeability of the constructs within whose ranges of convenience the variants lie. If a person is to embrace new ideas in his organized system, he needs to have superordinate constructs which are permeable – that is, which admit new elements. Without such permeable superordinate constructs he is limited to a more or less footless shuffling of his old ideas.

These are notions which have already been discussed in Chapter 2, where we stated the assumptive structure of the psychology of personal constructs. Now that we have introduced some of the diagnostic constructs of our theoretical system, we may turn to other characteristics of personal superordinate construction which have a bearing upon the way people adjust themselves to changing scenes.

Some people seem to have much more difficulty than others in setting up adaptive solutions to their problems. Any person is likely to be able to make his transitions more easily in some areas and at some times than at others. Whether we are comparing persons or comparing the various adjustment efforts of a single person, we see this problem, basically, as that of making a suitable transition in one's personal construction system.

Let us suppose a certain person's behaviour is organized largely in terms of *tight incidental* structures. Let us suppose also that the constructs which are *superordinate* to these tight incidental structures are *comprehensive* but *loose*. We can now see the *control* in his living as being worked out in two ways. Under the aegis of the tight incidental structures, he consistently chooses to wear a red tie, never allow himself to be late for an appointment, never drops ashes on the floor, always says 'sir' when talking to a man older than himself, and generally lives by little inflexible rules. He calls these 'high ethical standards'. But when he is faced with a situation which is not indexed in his rule book, his behaviour has to be guided by constructs which are superordinate and more comprehensive. But such constructs are, for him, more loose. Now his behaviour varies. His 'high ethical standards' are revealed as nothing more than a system of little incidental routines. His morality is manneristic and lacks the sweep of greatness.

Such a person may also find that his well-worn rule book gets out of date. Yesterday's 'right' answers to little problems no longer look so right today. Perhaps he should 'shoot the works' and wear a blue tie, or a yellow tie, or no tie. But which is right? Why should a blue tie be better than a red tie? It would be easier to wear a red tie. What would it mean to wear a blue tie? Has it been wrong all these years to wear a red tie? The red tie feels so right. But why should he be enslaved to a red tie? Yet one might as well be enslaved to a red tie as to a blue tie. One does have to wear a tie of some sort. Suppose he wears a blue tie and then, in the middle of the day, begins to feel uncomfortable without his red tie. He will be caught. He will not be able to get his red tie. But he seems to be caught anyway. Tedious? Of course! But how can he make important decisions when he cannot even decide which tie to wear? He is not free to decide anything, is he? He is in a cage. He cannot live outside his cage. Indeed, how can he go on living at all? And if he kills himself and the undertaker lays him out for the funeral – would it be better to be wearing a red tie or a blue tie? That is a question which ought to be decided before he takes the fatal step.

This illustration of rumination may seem overdrawn and ridiculous. Yet not long ago the writer's attention was called to the case of a client whose plans for suicide had bogged down in the problem of who should inherit his prized collection of guns.

There are other ways in which transition, or the prospect of a transition, in one's manner of construing the world may involve difficulty. One's construction system is never completely at rest. Even the changes which take place in it must themselves be construed. The successive stages of one's construction system need to be treated as elements, and this calls for superordinate construction. But will new constructions be acceptable as elements in one's superordinate construction? That is where the permeability of one's superordinate constructs comes in. One's variation is subordinate to certain more permeable constructions. One's variation, to the extent that it involves successive use of subordinate constructs which are inferentially incompatible *with each other*, is not tolerated unless one's superordinate constructions are permeable to the new outlooks, are tight enough to make them practically meaningful, and yet are loose enough to permit some reshuffling of elements.

There are four terms which have particular relevance to transition: *threat*, *guilt*, *fear*, and *anxiety*. As might be expected, all four of these terms are defined within the psychology of personal constructs as experiential or psychological phenomena. Thus, as we have already suggested, *threat* in our system refers to an interpretation which a person places upon some of the events of which he is aware, not necessarily to what someone else would construe as dangerous to the person. *Guilt* refers to a condition of the person's construction system and not to society's judgement of one's moral culpability.

The commoner definitions of these terms are not abrogated by their being given limited meanings within our system. It is not our intent to preempt the words, and it is important for the reader not to assume that we have. We have not said that threat is *nothing but* a person's interpretation of events. Nor have we said that guilt is all in a person's mind. What we have said is that, within our psychological system – which is only a part of our total personal construction system – these terms are assigned restricted meanings. We have particular systematic definitions to offer also for *fear* and *anxiety*.

In setting up these diagnostic constructs we have often been careful to label both poles of the dichotomy. Thus, for example, we described *comprehensive* constructs and *incidental* constructs, although these are terms for the same construct and refer, respectively, to its contrasting poles. The comprehensive construct pole makes sense only because it discriminates between itself and the incidental construct pole.

But we have not always given symbol labels to both poles of the construct. For example the *regnant* constructs described in the last chapter were not accompanied by a term such as *abstract* constructs used to designate the contrast pole. In the present chapter there will be more cases of this sort. Yet we are firmly convinced that a construct is always best interpreted as a discriminating dichotomy.

2. *Threat*

Threat is the awareness of imminent comprehensive change in one's core structures. In order for the threat to be significant, the prospective change must be substantial. Death is an example. Death is threatening to most people. We describe it as threatening to them because they perceive it both as likely to happen to them and as likely to bring about drastic changes in their core constructs. Death is not so threatening when it does not seem to imminent. It is not so threatening to those who see either their souls or the fundamental meaning of their lives as being unaffected by it. In such persons the core structures are not so likely to be affected by the prospect of death.

The prospective change must appear to be comprehensive. This means that the threat represents a multifaceted alternative core structure. One is threatened when that which he thought all along might happen to his core structure at last looks as if it was about to arrive. A prisoner of twenty years, while eager, is nevertheless threatened on the last day by the imminence of his release. Most persons are threatened by the likelihood of their showing infantile behaviour in certain situations. A new client about to undergo therapy is threatened by the prospect that he may *really* change his outlook. A client's community can be threatened by a too sudden readjustment in a client, if it seems to affect the essential features of their lives. Even a client who has made great strides in readjustment under a therapeutic regime is deeply threatened by the prospect of relapse under certain precipitating conditions. The old ways of looking at things are still so clear, so easily structured, so palpably available. A bit of confusion, a haunting situation not easily pictured in the new light, and *click*, everything might slip back into place in the old pattern! That, too, is threat.

a. Landfield's hypotheses. Landfield proposed and produced experimental evidence in support of two threat hypotheses. Both had to do with the perception of other persons as threatening. His *exemplification hypothesis* was that a person would be perceived as threatening if he appeared to exemplify what the perceiver himself once was but no longer is. The very plausibility of what the threatening person represents helps to make him a threat to the perceiver. The threatening person makes a nostalgic sense. It would be so easy for everything to fall back into the old patterns. For example, the perceiver would find it so easy to become a bawling brat again, for here is the familiar model materialized before his eyes.

The threat of the exemplified regression would be lessened if the perceiver still perceived himself as being like the example. In that case there would be no great change in core structure staring him in the face. But if he sees himself as changed, though not yet too secure in his new status, the example of the person who behaves in the old familiar ways, from which he himself has only precariously escaped, presents a threat. He is on the verge of moving backwards himself.

Landfield's second threat hypothesis was the *expectancy hypothesis.* A person is seen as threatening if he appears to expect the perceiver to behave in the old ways. The nature of the danger is much the same. Again it would be too easy to regress. Interaction with the threatening person would be easy, though not necessarily pleasant. 'This person thinks of me as being the kind of person I used to be. I am no longer that way, I trust – or am I? Yet it all comes back to me so vividly that I can feel myself slipping backward along the years.'

It is small wonder that some people find it difficult to revisit their old communities or that a young person who has made some readjustment in his personality while away from home finds it difficult even to revisit his parents. He has not yet consolidated his gains. The expectancies he sees in the old familiar faces threaten to make him forget that he is now grown, mature, and basically a different person. Since one tends to construe events in the manner which makes them optimally anticipatable, he is likely to regress when his perceptual field is flooded with material which is familiar to childhood's eyes. The over-all advantages of his adult outlook are momentarily lost from sight. He is expected to be a child; it almost makes sense to be a child. That, too, is threat.

b. Threat in therapy. Landfield's threat hypotheses have to do with seeing other people as threats in terms of reverse biographical movement. But there are other ways in which people can be seen as threatening. A therapist can be seen as threatening, not only if he appears to expect one to behave in a way in which one no longer wishes to behave – for example, in expressing doubts, in weeping, in loose conceptualization – but also if he appears to expect one to behave in other ways which are substantially different, even though they are not reminiscent of the past. The more the therapist's expectancies appear to involve sweeping changes in one's core structures, and the more plausible the new outlooks become, the more threatening the therapist appears to be.

Clients are frequently most threatened by their therapists just before making major shifts in their outlooks. They may appear to fight defensively against the therapist's efforts. They may complain that they are worse off. They may show hostility towards the therapist. They may appear to be unusually obtuse to obvious interpretations. They may generally thrash about in a disturbing manner on the eve of accepting a newly structured version of themselves.

Nowhere is this better illustrated than in fixed-role therapy. The fixed-role sequence is likely to be a battle, almost to the very end. The therapist gets no bouquets. He is rarely rewarded by the client's eager compliance with suggestions or his bringing gift offerings of 'clinical material'. The client is not likely to say, 'I was thinking about what you said yesterday, Doctor, and it certainly applies to me', or, 'Now here is something you will be interested in, although it makes me awfully ashamed to tell you.' Instead, the client in fixed-role therapy protests vehemently that he cannot enact the fixed role, that he just isn't that kind of person, that it seems insincere, that he doesn't know what to do, that people will think he is silly, that he couldn't get started in the external enactment, that he forgot how you told him to do it, that the prerehearsed situation did not turn out the way it was anticipated, and so on. In short, he is threatened because a change in his core structure is imminent. The new structure has already taken definite shape and it looms large in his perceptual field.

Indeed, in fixed-role therapy the threat would be so great that the client might never perform the experiment if it were not for one simple fact. That fact is the key to the technique of fixed-role therapy: the therapist has proposed the new role as make-believe only, and hence not a new core structure. The game lasts for two weeks (or some other prestated period of time) only. The client is never told that he should *be* like the new character, only that he is to *act* like the new character, on an experimental basis. He is not told that this will solve his problems, only that this is preparation for approaching his problems. The new character is not given his own name, it is given a fictitious name. The new structure is introduced as *peripheral* rather than *core*. Everything is done to control the threat by postponing, as long as possible, the interpretation of the new role as a new core structure for the client.

Threat involves the awareness of an imminent and comprehensive change in one's core structures. One cannot conduct fixed-role therapy successfully unless one appreciates this fact. Indeed, it is an important consideration in the conduct of any type of therapeutic sequence.

c. Other kinds of threat. Not all threats loom up in the shape of human beings. One can be threatened by the prospect of changing one's core structure comprehensively even though that change is neither exemplified nor expected by any other particular person. He can be threatened by a new 'realization' of what he has been doing. He can be threatened by the mounting proportions of an alternative interpretation of himself. A childless husband can be increasingly threatened as each year adds new weight to the evidence that he does not have what it takes to be a father. An unmarried woman in her late twenties can be threatened by her thirtieth birthday. A child is threatened by punishment, not so much because it is painful, but because of the alien interpretation it imposes upon his basic identity. Yet when he has been punished so often and his intrinsic wickedness described so convincingly that he has accepted the new core construction of himself, it is not the old familiar punishment that threatens him; it is any strange new praise and the complex internal reorganization it implies.

3. Fear

Fear is like threat, except that, in this case, it is a new incidental construct, rather than a comprehensive construct, that seems about to take over. The incidental construct is still a core construct, and hence the person's maintenance processes are at stake, just as they are in the case of threat. If, in driving a car, a person has been developing the tendency to give vent to all kinds of aggression, exuberance, and creative imagination, he may find himself *threatened* by these impulses as he suddenly realizes that soon he is likely to run over some child and the whole matter will add up to his being a criminal and having to live out the life of a criminal. We call it *fear*, on the other hand, if one day he is confronted with a specific situation that promises to put him and his car in the ditch. In both cases it is a core structure which is in danger of being altered. In the case of threat, however, it is a comprehensive restructuration which is imminent. In the case of fear it is an incidental restructuration – the car, the ditch, the crash, the driver's body, these and these only – whose impact on the core structure is perceived. A more involved or comprehensive anticipation of the imminent accident might give it the proportions of threat. At the moment, however, the narrow variety of events subsumed by the imminent structure defines it as a situation of fear only.

One tends to be threatened by that which he construes comprehensively and is only made fearful by that which he construes simply. What threatens us is that which we are likely to know a good deal about. What makes us fearful is that which we know less about. We are threatened by hauntingly familiar things and frightened by unexpectedly strange things. But whether the disturbance is seen as comprehensive or incidental, it is the imminent likelihood of a sudden reconstruction of the *core* of our personalities that makes it a disturbance.

A secure child may toy with that which seems to be fearful to him. This may puzzle his parents. But they might be reassured if they realized that this meant that his core structures are not so deeply involved as to endanger his system as a whole. He still feels that his basic identity is secure. He is seeking, as all healthily curious individuals do, to elaborate that which is partly strange. He is doing it within the over-all control of certain superordinate aspects of his system.

But is the child who continually toys with fears really secure? Perhaps not wholly. He has a problem about fears and he is working on it. He is weaving a rationale about those things which have been fearful. Perhaps he will gradually reorganize his core structure to bring it into line with the reality of dangerous things. Sometimes he can use some wise help at this juncture. The help may come from his parents, his teacher, or his therapist.

When a child is observed to be continually toying with fears, the psychologist infers that he has such a problem and the amount of his preoccupation with it is a measure of how large it looms up in his system. But let us suppose that the child's core structure is pervasively involved. Will he still dare to experiment? Probably not. He now must skirt the problem or run from it altogether. He does not have the solid superordinate structure with which to maintain over-all control. The variations and transitions which might come about as a result of his experimentation would have no pivots to swing from. In the language of the Modulation Corollary there are no suitable permeable constructs in his system to which his variations can be subordinated.

4. Anxiety

Anxiety is the recognition that the events with which one is confronted lie outside the range of convenience of one's construct system. Of course, if events lay entirely outside the range of convenience of one's construct system one could not even perceive them, nor could one be specifically anxious about them. What happens is that the anxious person has found that he has partially lost his structural grip on events. He is caught in the confusion of anxiety.

Our definition of anxiety is somewhat unusual. Most of the clinicians who use the term do not concern themselves with a precise definition. They tend to treat it as an obvious phenomenon which requires no particular definition within a theoretical framework. Some personality theorists prefer not to use the term at all, either because of the difficulty of describing it systematically, or because, during the years of its popular and clinical use, it has become so reified and anthropomorphized that it is hopelessly cluttered up with incompatible implications. Those who see anxiety as an overgeneralized response derivative of fear may find our definition somewhat puzzling.

Some clinicians use the term, 'free-floating anxiety'. Approximately what they mean is a fear which has lost its object referents. They visualize it this way because they have difficulty finding its precipitating stimuli. The anxious person appears to be upset, but he is unusually unable to say or to indicate just what it is that he is upset about. Our point of view is that anxiety is not necessarily so much the result of 'fear' as it is the recognition that one is inescapably confronted with events to which one's constructs do not adequately apply. It is this inability to construe certain impending events meaningfully which gives anxiety its characteristically ambiguous quality.

This failure of the construct system to embrace urgent events may accompany one's use of incompatible subsystems of construction. Most of us can tolerate some amount of incompatibility. Our Fragmentation Corollary assumes that one may successively employ a variety of construction subsystems which are inferentially incompatible with each other. The Modulation Corollary, as we keep reminding the reader, assumes that the variation in a person's construction system *is limited* by the permeability of the constructs within whose ranges of convenience the variants lie. Taken together, these two corollaries assume that one can tolerate some incompatibility, but not too much. The amount that can be tolerated depends upon the permeability of the superordinating constructs. If those constructs which would normally superordinate the variants are insufficiently permeable to admit the impending variants into their ranges of convenience, the person finds himself in an anxiety situation. His construction system fails him. The deeply anxious person has lost the serenity that comes from having a philosophical position that readily translates itself into everyday living. He is confronted with a changing scene, but he has no guide to carry him through the transition.

a. Loosening a defence against anxiety. People protect themselves against anxiety in various ways. One way is in a loosening of one's constructs. To some extent this can be tested by means of a conventional concept-formation test. The Repertory Test can be administered in such a way as to test the integrity of the role constructs as well as their substance. The loosening permits greater variety in the application of a construct while still retaining its essential identity. This loosening of conceptualization as a precursor or correlate of anxiety symptoms is a matter of common clinical observation. If it works, it prevents the invasion of anxiety from overrunning the whole system. Its protective effect can be seen in the thinking of certain schizophrenic clients. The conceptualization is so loosened that they seem to have a system that still covers everything. They are not caught short of constructs. But what constructs!

Yet, even in the conceptually loosened schizophrenic, the loosening does not always work. Constructs now and then may be tested against reality. They turn out not to be loose enough. The system breaks down. Anxiety appears. This is not altogether bad. It may be a sign that the client retains a modicum of 'contact'. Conventional psychotherapy may still be feasible in the genuinely anxious schizophrenic.

The loosening of constructs in order to ward off the chaos of anxiety usually manifests itself first with respect to one's superordinate structures. The superordinate structures are those which increase one's measure of tolerance for ambiguity. If they are loosened, it sometimes appears that the tolerance can be increased, at least temporarily. The effective way, of course, to increase one's tolerance for ambiguity is to redefine and increase the permeability of one's superordinate system (the Organization and Modulation Corollaries). But mere loosening may save the day.

Such loosening of the superordinate structures is frequently observed in 'the personality changes' which are said to be the early clinical signs of the onset of acute schizophrenia. One's thinking about religious matters becomes loosened. It varies more from day to day. Over-all principles of conduct, or marital fidelity, of social values, are subjected to a working over which appears to produce an unwonted variation. The client's wife is surprised, not so much by the client's acts, but by what he now appears to think is right and wrong. He feels some things are wrong which once he considered right and some things are right which once he thought wrong, yet there is a strange mixture of thinking about both which makes it hard for the wife to follow the newly loosened point of view.

b. Tightening as a defence against anxiety. Sometimes one reveals the imminence of anxiety by exhibiting another kind of protective behaviour. One may tighten his subordinate constructs and thus maintain a greater measure of organization at the lower levels of his system. He may become more meticulous about the little routines of living. A man whose home life is losing structure may spend more time at the office. He may work out his office routine in a highly structured manner. The effect of this type of protective step is usually to block the readjustive changes which might follow from being anxious for a while. He does not 'face his problems'; hence he does not find new solutions for them.

c. Extent of anxiety. From the standpoint of psychology of personal constructs, anxiety, *per se*, is not to be classified as either good or bad. It represents the awareness that one's construction system does not apply to the events at hand. It is, therefore, a precondition for making revisions. Now it does not follow that the more anxious one is, the more likely he is to make an effective revision. Sometimes a person is so generally anxious that he spends all his time running around putting out small fires and has no time to design any fireproof structures. A therapist usually has to spend considerable time repairing minor anxieties so that the client can do something about the chaos represented by a major area of anxiety. Sometimes a therapist has to create anxiety in a certain area by bringing invalidating evidence to bear upon the defences used there. Sometimes a therapist wastes time trying to bring all the anxieties under control in order to make his client comfortable.

Our definition of anxiety also covers the little confusions and puzzles of everyday living. The sum of a column of numbers does not check. Anxiety! We add it up again, it still does not check. More anxiety! We add it up another way.

Good adjustment. Ah, there was our error! If the column of figures has to do with a precarious bank balance, the anxiety may have been greater. If, in addition, one's domestic status is at stake, the anxiety might have been greater still. More of one's construction system would have been revealed to be faulty.

d. Invalidation and anxiety. There is a further point about anxiety which is a little more difficult to explain, although one's experience with psychotherapy makes it palpable. It is not merely the invalidation of a construct that produces anxiety. Anxiety appears only if the construct is abandoned – appears no longer relevant – and there is nothing to take its place. A person may be fairly secure, even though he knows that his system is not working effectively. At least it is working. It appears to be relevant. He will keep on testing it. Perhaps it needs only minor revision. Perhaps he has only made a mistake in reading the decimal point. If the mistake that one makes in totting up a column of figures is construed in this manner, the anxiety may not be appreciable. It is the person – perhaps in this case a child – who sees this as evidence that he does not know how to add, who becomes genuinely anxious. A person may not be very anxious if he fails to solve a word-analogies problem. But if that problem is an item on an intelligence test which he thinks determines his capacity to pursue a professional career, he may be anxious. The anxiety in that case will not stem so much from the fact that he will be administratively eliminated from the group of candidates – that is fear or threat – but from the fact that he is confused in general, that he doesn't 'know the score'.

We have said that anxiety is not the result of the retention of invalidated constructs but rather the result of not having sufficient structure with which to deal with a situation. One may have abandoned his constructs and thus be caught short. Or he may have some low-order constructs – enough to enable him to perceive elements of the situation multidimensionally – but not have the overriding constructs with which to deal with it as a whole.

While the invalidation of a construct does not necessarily produce an appreciable anxiety, it is the normal basis for abandoning the construct. Invalidation is used in therapy to help the client find just where his system breaks down. The psychologist who utilizes the psychology of personal constructs intentionally designs his therapeutic programme around a series of practical experiments which will yield validating and invalidating evidence. The invalidating evidence will normally lead to the abandonment of constructs, to anxiety, and thence to revision, with help in reformulation coming either from the therapist or from another source.

Sometimes experiments are designed with too much at stake. The person who takes invalidating evidence seriously may find the outcome devastating. The therapist needs to know pretty much just what of personal wager he is asking his client to make before he precipitates him into an experiment. The client may be staking his whole system of values on what might appear to the therapist to be a very simple and limited venture.

One who has directed graduate-student research extensively may have noted this fact. The graduate students who are anxious over research are often those who take their hypotheses too seriously. They are likely to be trying to 'prove' something which involves far more in their lives than what they have verbalized in their experimental hypotheses. A good director of graduate study will make some effort to discover what his students are covertly staking on the outcome of their experiments. Just as we have used the model of the modern philosophy of science in setting up a psychology of how all people individually make progress in life, so we may use the model of effective direction of graduate students' research as one which the therapist may follow in helping his client to discover new meanings. The discriminative evaluation and control of anxiety is an important feature both in the direction of research and in the conduct of psychotherapy.

e. Failure of construction. Anxiety is something less than the failure to anticipate events optimally. It refers to a particular kind of failure: the failure to produce a construction that appears wholly applicable to the events of which one is aware. Anxiety is one way in which the psychological processes mentioned in our Fundamental Postulate are impoverished. It comes when the facts at hand do not fit into one's construct system; at least do not fit into it in an organized way.

But let us suppose that the facts do appear to be relevant, that the construct system does lead to precise predictions, but that the outcomes invalidate the predictions. The person applies his system but loses his bets. Before we say that this will lead to an evolvement in his construction system, we must know how he construes the outcomes. He may not think that his bet has been lost. We should, therefore, not necessarily expect him to exhibit anxiety nor should we necessarily expect him to attempt any major revisions in his construction system.

If the person, however, does construe the outcome of his prediction as something which was not expected, it does not necessarily lead to an anxiety that is proportional to the construction which was used in making the prediction. The person may say, in effect, 'Oh! I missed! But of course my *system* still applies. The only trouble was I was unable to take into account one small factor. It probably won't happen again.' In such a case the anxiety is proportional only to the small factor for which the person had no adequate system, not proportional to the construct upon which the bet as a whole was laid.

In interpreting anxiety one needs to note what it is that the person feels he has no adequate construction for. If we know what the general locus of the anxiety is, we can better determine the extent of the psychological movement which might ensue, as the person attempts to apply structure to the chaotic area. For example, a client makes a mess out of his interpersonal relations. He admits that things are turning out badly. What is the nature of his anxiety? The therapist may suppose that his anxiety represents chaos in the whole area of his anticipations of other people. Not necessarily so. The client may insist merely that he has overlooked minor cues. The anxiety may be localized there only. The basic construction which actually led to his trouble still seems to him to be wholly applicable. That is not what has dissolved into anxiety. All of his trembling and tears have to do with the 'cues' which he thinks he cannot understand.

The situation with the client has its parallel with the graduate student whose research is being directed by an adviser. The student gets negative results. He insists that it was not his hypotheses which were wrong but that something went awry with his criterion data. Perhaps they are not representative. Perhaps they were unreliably observed. Perhaps the *n* should be increased. The student may be right. So may the client! But whether the student (or client) is right or wrong, the adviser (or therapist) should be cognizant of the locus of the anxiety.

5. Guilt

Within one's core structure there are those frames which enable one to predict and control the essential interactions of himself with other persons and with societal groups of persons. Altogether these constitute his conceptualization of *core role.* Taken separately they delimit the facets of his core role and explain a person's varicoloured reflections under changing social illumination. One's deepest understanding of being maintained as a social being is one's concept of one's core role. *Perception of one's apparent dislodgment from one's core role structure constitutes the experience of guilt.*

The conventional notion of guilt as man's awareness of the evil within him is not antithetical to this formulation; nor is the psychoanalytic notion of guilt as a kind of spanking administered by the superego. Our proposed formulation is designed to free the research-minded psychologist from the absolutism of 'evil' on the one hand, and from the anthropomorphism of the Freudian superego on the other. An absolute term cannot be employed in a scientific system unless it is embodied in the assumptive structure of the system. In science the task is to keep one's overriding assumptions at a minimum and work primarily with tentative inferences.

Guilt is an inference within the assumptive structure of the psychology of personal constructs. Alternatively, it can be inferred either deductively from our Fundamental Postulate or inductively from clinical experience. These are not wholly independent methods of inferring guilt, for the Fundamental Postulate was chosen for its apparent applicability to the writer's experience and, conversely, his experience was highlighted throughout by what he was basically assuming to be true.

a. Guilt and role. In an earlier chapter we pointed out that a role is a course of activity which is based upon one's interpretation of the thinking of the other people in relation to whom the role is enacted. It is thus based upon a construction whose elements are the presumed constructs of certain other persons. A core role involves that part of a person's role structure by which he maintains himself as an integral being. The more peripheral role structures are not included.

Basic maintenance is not altogether a self-centred matter. We are dependent for life itself upon an understanding of the thoughts of certain other people. The psychology of personal constructs emphasizes the essential importance of social constructions. It emphasizes the fact that a role is not always a superficial thing, a simple mask to be put on or taken off; rather, that there is a core role, a part one plays as if one's life depended upon it. Indeed, one's life actually does depend upon it. Finally, it is the loss of status within the core role constructions which is experienced as guilt.

A child construes himself as belonging to his family. He interprets his mother's behaviour. He interprets his father's behaviour. He enacts his presumed part in relation to this interpretation. Who is he? Who is he *really*? He is a child belonging to Mother and Father and he therefore does this and this and this. Some of the things he does are merely incidental or peripheral. He may mention them because they are easier to put into words. The more basic features of his role may exist for him in terms of preverbal constructs. When asked who he is he may be unable to put them into words.

Now let us suppose that the child discovers that he has not been acting as his parent's child. Let us suppose that the discovery goes deep. His identity is affected. He *really* is not cast in the core role. The maintenance of his identity rests, he finds, not upon the filial part he thought he was playing, but upon some other, possibly more obscure, ground. It is at this point that he feels guilt!

Another child depends upon a relationship with his parents which is based upon a construction of them as bovine creatures. He sees them as animals which are concerned primarily with giving milk and making money. He writes his role accordingly. He validates. He grows up with his core role structured in relationship to such presumed people. When people try to make him feel guilty by pointing out that he is selfish, cruel, or immoral, he may readily agree that he is and concede that it would be nice if he were different. However, he does not experience guilt, for these interpretations are not incompatible with his core role structure. His friends may call him a 'ne'er-do-well'. His psychiatrist may call him a 'psychopathic personality'.

Another child construes her identity in terms of becoming a nourishing mother. When she grows up she is a fertile being and lives primarily 'for her children'. Her household is her queenly realm. Then the children get married and leave home. She becomes infertile. She cannot even nourish her husband's sexual appetites. They move to a smaller apartment. Her realm has shrunk. Her core role construction of herself seems no longer applicable. She starts talking about her sins. She feels guilty about the most trivial things. Her doctor calls it 'involutional melancholia'.

Still another child sees himself as maintained by his enactment of a role based upon an interpretation of the thinking of a celestial being. He identifies himself as one of that being's children. Then he is told that he has been excommunicated. His core role status is lost. He feels guilty.

A man belonging to a preliterate culture establishes for himself a core role structure based upon his membership in a tribe. Then he breaks taboo. He no longer belongs. He may not even be able to sustain life in the face of this guilty loss.

b. Early core role structure. There are many ways in which guilt can enter the picture of a person's life. From the standpoint of the psychology of personal constructs the point which all of them have in common is this loss of core role structure. We have not found it necessary to invoke the notions of pleasure and pain nor their derivatives, reward and punishment, in defining guilt. We do not see such terms as representing satisfactory explanatory principles. It seems much easier to conceive the variety of ways in which guilt is manifested as all representing loss of core role structure than to try to explain them as reenactments of the punishment scene of a mother teaching her baby bowel control.

It may be, of course, that a mother teaching her baby bowel control contrives to give him his first lesson in enacting a role in connection with basic maintenance processes, and with due respect for her own fixed opinions in such matters. To accede comprehensively to her demands, not merely as they are voiced at the moment, but as they must be construed throughout the hours of the day, is to play a role. The fact that one must dramatize the part with his bowels implies that it is a core role.

The point is that the bowel-control situation is only one of many in which the stage is set for playing the core role. The feeling of guilt, when it comes, may be reminiscent of any or all of these primordial situations. Guilt is psychological exile from one's core role, regardless of where, when, with who, or in what scenes the part has been played.

c. Punishment and guilt. There is a relationship between punishment and guilt. But it tends to be an institutionalized one. By that we mean that punishment is not a necessary or fundamental motivating factor in human life. We see a relationship between punishment and guilt simply because certain groups of people have construed such a relationship. Yet it need not be.

What happens is this. People are threatened by 'evildoers'. We have described threat; in this case it is the exemplification of a way of life from which we have only precariously escaped. The 'evildoer' exemplifies what we might do if we dared, or what we might be if we behaved childishly, or what we would have been if we had not tried so hard to do better. We dare not interact with him on common ground lest we slip back into the unwanted ways. In order to take protective steps against the threat that his presence arouses within us we take symbolic measures called 'punishment' against him. By such measures we either destroy or symbolize the destruction of the core role relationship of the 'evildoer' with ourselves. That may make us feel a little safer from the looming shadow of ourselves as 'evildoers'. We treat the 'evildoer' as if *he* were experiencing guilt. That helps us convince ourselves that our own newly won position is secure. He really is not one of us. Even he now knows that he is not one of us. We are therefore not like him – we hope! We picture him as feeling guilty as a result of his being punished by us. From this point of view it is not the guilt which leads inexorably to the punishment, but rather the punishment which symbolically establishes the guilt. Punishment brands the threatening person. It banishes him into psychological exile. It thus protects a feeble society which is only half convinced of its system of morality.

We have described punishment as a measure taken primarily to protect the punisher from the threat of being like the punished person. It does have a deterrent effect against evildoing – our own evildoing! It helps to clarify our stand as a nonevildoer by making it clear that the evildoer is not one of us.

Punishment sometimes also affects the person who is punished. He may feel that he has lost his core role structure. He is guilty! In the anxiety of the resulting confusion he may seek to reestablish himself. He may do so along the old lines or he may attempt a new structure. If he attempts a new structure, it may still be no less threatening to other people.

Sometimes the punished person turns the tables on the punishing people. He construes his own society. He moves towards establishing a core role for himself which includes the very behaviour which others have found threatening. Now he can be threatened, not by his evil ways, not by his recently confirmed perversity, but by the prospect of losing his status as an 'evildoer'. In a very real sense that is the loss which would make him feel guilty. He may be threatened by the presence of a person who is virtuous in the way he used to be virtuous. He may seek to punish such a person in order to make it clear to himself that the virtuous person is truly different from himself and that he is in no danger of slipping back into the half-familiar ways of virtue. We can see this mechanism at work both in the ways a delinquent directs his aggressions against certain persons and in the hostile compulsive acts of certain psychasthenic patients. From the standpoint of the psychology of personal constructs this is more than a simple exchange of retaliatory acts; it is each person's attempt to accent the difference between himself and the other person who represents the ever impending and ever threatening shadow of his earlier self.

Administration of punishment is not so likely to be an attempt to make another person behave in an acceptable manner as it is an attempt to prove to oneself that the other person has behaved in an unacceptable manner. There are exceptions. Punishment may occasionally be used to make a person feel guilty and anxious in the honest hope that he will mend his ways. Sometimes we say that we 'punish the crime and not the criminal'. This is silly; the 'criminal' gets punished nonetheless. We hope, however, that he will see that it is only a part of him that is condemned. The epigrammatic slogan may be a semantic device for leaving the door open for him to reestablish his role in our society rather than going out and establishing a core role which is outside our society.

Sometimes punishment is rationalized as a way of making the punished person 'pay a debt to society'. The analogy is somewhat unrealistic in its assumption that society somehow recovers from its injury through the expiative discomfort of the punished person. From the standpoint of the punished person, however, the figure of speech may have the effect of putting a time limit on his loss of role. When 'his debt is paid', he returns from exile automatically. Yet the basic psychological fact is that his behaviour has been threatening to those whose own morality is insecure;

and as long as he is seen as having exemplified the tempting way of life, there are those who will need to punish him as a prophylaxis for their own temptations. He comes out of prison feeling that he is to be reinstated, having 'paid his debt'; but, realistically, he meets a society which remembers his behaviour and is still threatened by the idea of accepting him as one of them.

The diagnostic constructs of *threat, fear, anxiety*, and *guilt* are all essentially constructs having to do with the transitions in one's construction system. Threat is the awareness of an imminent comprehensive change in one's core structures. The Landfield threat hypotheses deal with an imminent regressive change which is exemplified or socially expected. Fear is like threat except that the change is construed incidentally rather than comprehensively. Anxiety is confusion in one's construction system. It ranges from the little momentary bafflements of everyday living to the 'free-floating anxiety' which betrays a breakdown in superordinate structures. Guilt is the loss of one's core role structure. We have talked about punishment too, but have not proposed it as a diagnostic construct nor as one which is necessarily relevant to transition. While we propose these diagnostic constructs as being particularly relevant to transition, there is a sense in which all proper diagnostic constructs have to do with transition, since they denote properties with respect to which persons can change within themselves as well as vary among themselves. No diagnostic construct is quite satisfactory if it serves only to stuff whole live people into an Aristotelian pigeonhole.

6. Aggressiveness

Aggressiveness is the active elaboration of one's perceptual field. We have discussed the principle of the elaborative choice, that tendency of all of us to choose that one of a pair of alternatives which promises the greater possibility of extending our predictive system without endangering it. There are some persons who are distinguished by their greater tendency to set up choice points in their lives and then to make their elaborative choices. They are always precipitating themselves and others into situations which require decision and action. We call them aggressive.

Within the realm of the individual there are those areas in which he is likely to be more aggressive than in others. These are the areas in which the person 'does things'. Some psychologists might describe these areas as 'interest areas'. Within such areas the person appears to be neither shy nor lazy. He moves through them with initiative and relative freedom.

In the business world aggressiveness is often labelled 'a good thing'. It is the mark of the 'coming' or the 'successful' man. Sometimes account is taken of the area of one's aggression. If it occurs in the area of interpersonal relations, the man is fitted out with a white collar and put to work in 'sales' or in 'personnel'. If it occurs in the area of inanimate things, he is put to work in 'the plant', perhaps in 'engineering' or 'production', and he is asked to use a different washroom. If neither of these ways of adjusting his work milieu to the kind of thing he would do anyway seems feasible, he is simply put to work for pay. Of course, in the end, that costs more because there is no spontaneous elaboration, no useful mobilization of the man's aggressions.

a. Aggression and anxiety. Within limits, a person may be particularly aggressive in the area of his anxiety. This is the area in which his constructs seem partially to fail to embrace the events at hand within their proper ranges of convenience. In his effort to explore the uncharted area, the person may set up a rapid succession of choices and select alternatives among them.

When a person is aggressive, he seeks out bits of confusion. He fusses over them, he tests out constructs which might possibly fit, and he rapidly abandons those which appear to be irrelevant. Indeed, one might say that the areas of one's aggression are those in which there are anxieties he can face.

A well-placed worker is not one who has no anxieties about his job; rather, he is one who has many moderate anxieties in connection with his job, all of which he is willing to explore aggressively. The man who had no anxieties about his job would passively let it go to pot. On the other hand, the man who had anxieties, but who was unwilling to attempt to replace confusion with untried structures, would soon find himself an unwitting 'victim of circumstances'.

b. Aggression and threat. Aggression in one person may be threatening to another. The aggressive person – for example the 'social pusher' – keeps plunging himself and his associates into ventures which unduly complicate their well-ordered lives. The very fact that he insists on construing himself as belonging to the social group is threatening to those who are already identified with the group. They see, in their impending reciprocal identification with him, a major shift coming up in their own core structures. That is threat. One might say that the aggressive person in this kind of setting is perceived as threatening, not because of what he does or because of any desire to be harmful, but because of what his behaviour signifies in the lives of his associates.

Some clinical psychologists apply the concept of aggression as if it were essentially an antisocial impulse. They see aggression as always being essentially destructive. The only way they see to manage it is to divert it into artificially 'constructive' channels. They may even equate aggression with 'overt hostility'. This, of course, is not the view of the psychology of personal constructs.

7. Hostility

Hostility is the continued effort to extort validational evidence in favour of a type of social prediction which has already proved itself a failure.

It is interesting to note how the psychology of personal constructs leads one into a series of definitions of common terms which appear, at first, to be markedly different from familiar concepts. This is particularly true in the case of terms such as 'hostility', which are ordinarily conceptualized hedonistically.

It is customary to think of hostility as the disposition to do someone harm – to hurt them. But in the psychology of personal constructs we seek a way of understanding hostility from the point of view of the person who feels it and what it is that he is actually seeking to accomplish. We see the injury he may imagine that he would like to inflict upon another person, not as a primary goal in itself, but as an incidental outcome of something more vital that he is trying to accomplish.

Let us review the way a person lays his wagers upon the events of life. When he puts his constructs to test by basing predictions on them, he invites validating evidence. If the evidence turns out to be something quite different from what he expected, he has essentially three courses open to him: (1) he can concede that he has lost this particular bet and that his construct needs to be replaced, (2) he can guess that perhaps he did not read his evidence properly and replicate the experiment, or (3) he can try to alter the events in an effort to make them conform to his original expectations. The third method is the method of Procrustes, who was always stretching his guests or cutting them down to a size to fit his bed.

Let us see what this third reaction to invalidating evidence means when the wager has been laid with respect to other persons. The individual construes another person; he makes a prediction about him when he turns up contrary evidence, he senses a twinge of anxiety as it appears that the other person may not fall within the range of convenience of his role constructs (or, perhaps, he is threatened by the major revision of his system which the experience indicates may be necessary); then, in order to protect himself either from the anxiety or the threat, he sets out to make the other person into the kind of creature he predicted he was in the first place. This is hostility. The other person is the victim, not so much of the hostile person's fiendishly destructive impulses, as to his frantic and unrealistic efforts to collect on a wager he has already lost.

a. 'Loving' hostility. This conception of hostility, which seems to us to be far more revealing and far more useful in therapy, permits us to understand certain hostile behaviour which is more 'protective' than 'destructive'. For example, a parent treats a child as if he were her doll. Yet he obviously behaves in undoll-like ways. Instead of revising her construction of him she takes steps to make him into a doll. If she succeeds – which, of course, she can't – she can make good on her original prediction; he will be the doll that she always said he was. This we would call hostility, no matter how much attention she may give him, how many playthings she may lavish upon him, how often she fondles him, or how much she is dependent upon him. From her point of view, it may be her only protection against the spreading confusion of anxiety that arises in the wake of her misperception of him, or it may be a frantic protective step to ward off the threat of a lurid, and all too plausible, reconstruction of herself. It may also be, for her, a protection against guilt, the loss of her own core role status, as she has construed her status.

b. Hostility and guilt. Hostility arises when one cannot live with the results of one's social experimentation. Hostility involves experiments undertaken with respect to people. Frequently role constructs are put to test, although that is not an essential feature. Moreover, in hostility, the person, instead of revising or anxiously abandoning the construction which has proved to be misleading, takes further active steps to alter the data to fit his hypotheses. If people do not behave the way he predicts, he will make them! That will validate his construction of them! He may protect himself from threat by means of his hostility, although his protection may often be leaky. He may keep his face turned away from the dark empty void of guilt by taking a hostile attitude towards people. Yet, as much as he insists that people must be made into what he has already construed them to be, he continually keeps stumbling over bits of evidence that he is wrong, that his core role is on shaky ground – in short, that perhaps he is guilty after all.

The person who has been hostile over a period of time and with respect to many people faces great guilt. The potential guilt is proportional to the enormity of his unrealistic hostility. The therapist who deals with a hostile person must not overlook this fact. It is a serious mistake on the part of a therapist to assume that all he needs to do with a hostile person is convince him that people are really friendly and that he is in no danger. A client who is viewed in this manner may give the therapist a rude shock by committing suicide. He has tampered with his evidence so much and so long that his core role structure falls apart when the therapist convinces him that people are not as he has been construing them. The client is overwhelmed by guilt. Now it is himself who must be altered. He takes action. He makes himself into the kind of thing guilt implies – a dead thing! Again he has manipulated his datum to fit his construct. But this time the datum was himself.

The principle for the therapist to bear in mind is that the interpretation of people as benign may threaten his hostile client with the loss of core role structure. A role is a structure based upon an interpretation of other person's constructs. A core role involves one's basic maintenance processes. If one suddenly finds that his interpretation of many other persons' construing has been totally wrong, one's own life falls apart. The therapist must make sure that the hostile person has at least the rudiments of a new core role with respect to some people, perhaps with respect to himself – the therapist – before he starts a wholesale interpretation of the world as a benign place.

One should bear in mind that the guilt one suffers when one's core role falls apart does not necessarily depend upon the realization of actual damage done to one's fellow man. The person who has long been misconstrued may be untouched by the client's hostility. Even the client may concede that he has not hurt the person whom he has misconstrued. Yet it is enough to give the client that 'feeling of emptiness' in terms of which he describes his guilt to realize that he has founded his core role upon a wholly misguided interpretation of that person.

Hostility is not the only ingredient in guilt. A child can be overwhelmed by guilt on the discovery that his parent was either a better person than he had always construed him to be or a worse person than he had always construed him to be. The guilt comes because the child finds that the ground upon which he built his core role was misperceived and his important relationship to his parent has suddenly become amorphous.

c. *Psychoanalysis and hostility.* Psychoanalysis handles the delicate therapeutic issue of hostility by treating hostility as an entity. The construct, like many others in psychoanalysis, is entitized if not actually vitalized or anthropomorphized. Yet, as a whole, psychoanalysis has held for a more functional system of constructs in psychotherapy than has traditional personality theory. The psychoanalyst sees hostility as based upon a type of energy which, in the economy of things, does not simply vanish as a result of an explanation. He would expect a client's hostility, which had long been turned against other people, to be turned against the client himself in the form of suicide if the therapist did anything abruptly to turn this hostility away from others.

But psychoanalysis must invent the concept of 'latent hostility' to account for the guilt felt by people who have always carefully avoided injuring others. Within the psychology of personal constructs the 'latency' is handled by pointing up the dichotomous nature of construction in general. Guilt, on the other hand, is not based solely upon the awareness of having injured someone but rather upon a state of affairs within the person's own psychological system – that is, the loss of core role. Psychoanalysis defines guilt in terms of the moral turpitude of accomplishing or seeking to accomplish injury to someone. Personal-construct psychology leaves the matter of moral turpitude *per se* to systems other than psychological. Psychoanalysis perceives hostility as a potentially destructive attitude. Personal-construct theory recognizes hostility as a persistent irrealism.

B. Cycles of construction

8. *Typical shifts in construction*

It should be kept in mind that the psychodiagnostic constructs which we have proposed are not traits which apply invariably to a given person, but are axes or dimensions with respect to which his construction processes can be plotted from time to time. They are dimensions of intraindividual differences as well as dimensions of interindividual differences. For example, not only may one individual tend to use tight constructions and another loose constructions, but each of them may use tight constructions on some occasions and loose constructions on others. Thus the *tightness–looseness* dimension is useful for plotting the shifts in the construction processes of a single person.

There are typical shifts in the sequence of construction which people employ in order to meet everyday situations. Two of these sequences invite particular attention: one has to do with action decisions and the other with a person's originality. The first we call the *C–P–C Cycle* and the second the *Creativity Cycle*. The C–P–C Cycle (Circumspection–Preemption–Control Cycle) has to do with decision making in which the self is involved. The Creativity Cycle has to do with the way in which a person develops new ideas. In some respects both cycles are related, since a new act often involves a new construct and one finds himself on the verge of new constructs as a result of his venturesome acts.

9. The C–P–C Cycle

The C–P–C Cycle is a sequence of construction involving, in succession, circumspection, preemption, and control, and leading to a choice which precipitates the person into a particular situation.

In order to understand the C–P–C Cycle let us review briefly some of our descriptions of types of personal constructs. We have said that a propositional construct is one which makes no commitments of its elements to other realm memberships. For example, having said that this 'is a spade' we have not committed it to being anything else – a tool, a palpable object, of a particular shape, or anything. We have said only that it 'is a spade'. Now when one construes *circumspectively* one employs a series of propositional constructs in dealing with the elements at hand. One may employ these constructs successively or more or less simultaneously. Yet, even if one employs them simultaneously, this does not mean that one sees them as linked into a constellation. In other words, the simultaneity is incidental.

A preemptive construct is one which preempts its elements for membership in its own realm exclusively. For example, having said that this 'is a spade', one implies that it is nothing but a spade, that no other construct may embrace it. These are extreme types – actually, it is rare to find a person consistently applying a construct either wholly propositionally or wholly preemptively.

Now we have described control too. It was described as a function of *superordination.* One may seek to establish a more precise control – that is, *superordination* – by construing something preemptively. This has the effect of ruling out the additional alternatives that one must consider if one construes in several different dimensions at the same time. Preemption also helps one to achieve control by making it easier to *submerge* one end of the preemptive construct. Moreover, the preemptive use of a construct may be temporary – only long enough to permit making a decision or embarking upon a course of action. The preemption may be preceded by *circumspection,* a process of looking at a situation in a multidimensional manner. This may be followed by the establishment of the *regnancy* of a certain superordinate construct. The person may then say that here is the crux of the various issues he has been considering, and that, for the time being, he will deal with his problem as if it were *this and this only* – that is, *preemptively.*

The C–P–C Cycle, then, starts with circumspection, which enables the person to look at his elements propositionally, or in a multidimensional manner. But because he cannot, to quote a classic phrase, 'mount his horse and ride off in all directions', he must choose the most relevant axis along which to construe his situation. He therefore selects what he believes to be the crucial issue and temporarily – or permanently – disregards the relevancy of all the other issues that may be involved. Thus, by preemption, he sets up a choice point, a crossroads of decision. He may say, like Hamlet, 'To be, or not to be: that is the question...' Or he may say, as one must often say when one finds one's nation committed to a war, 'Whatever other issues there may be in this conflict, economic, social, political, there is only one issue which is relevant here for me – am I on this side or that?'

The preemption of issues characterizes 'the man of action'. He is likely to see things in what may appear to his associates to be an oversimplified manner. He consolidates all the possible perspectives in terms of one dichotomous issue and then makes his choice between the only two alternatives he allows himself to perceive. Yet, because he tends to do this in times of emergency, he may, on such occasions, be accepted by his associates as a leader.

But the C–P–C Cycle does not end with preemption. There is still the choice to be made. Indeed, the final 'C' in our term might stand for *choice* as well as for *control.* As we have indicated before in our Choice Corollary, a person chooses for himself that alternative in a dichotomized construct through which he anticipates the greater possibility for extension and definition of his system. This is, of course, the point at which Hamlet stuck:

> For in that sleep of death what dreams may come ... there's the respect that ... puzzles the will and makes us rather bear those ills we have than fly to others that we know not of? Thus conscience does make cowards of us all; and thus the native hue of resolution is sicklied o'er with the pale cast of thought, and enterprises of great pith and moment with this regard their currents turn awry, and lose the name of action.

This, of course, is the point at which anyone may 'lose the name of action', for, even though he may succeed in preemptively construing his situation, he may find that his effort to make the final elaborative choice throws him back upon circumspection before the cycle has run its normal course.

10. A further discussion of control

Let us consider again an illustration of a preemptive construct. 'This is a spade. It is nothing but a spade.' We may describe preemption, whether used temporarily by a person for the sake of control, or as always characteristic of his use of a given construct, as the *this-and-this-only* point of view. It crops up in many a debate between scientists when one of them says of the other's formulation, 'This is *nothing but.*'... It is sometimes called 'the nothing-but retort'. For example, one might attempt to refute the Fundamental Postulate of personal-construct psychology by saying, 'This is *nothing but* a form of neo-phenomenology', or by saying, 'This is *nothing but* a return to mentalism.' On the other hand, one could say, 'Personal-construct psychology can be construed as neophenomenological in nature', or one could say, 'This is a return to mentalism.' The omission of the *nothing but* keeps the criticism from being necessarily in the nature of a preemptive construct. Of course, the writer would not agree with either of the constructions, even though they were not made preemptively, but that disagreement is another matter.

Preemption permits one to take a ready-made stand without having to consider other aspects of a situation or to exercise judgement. Thus it makes for control. The frightened person may concentrate on a single aspect of a situation in order to keep from vacillating and getting himself into trouble. He may seek control through temporary preemption. He may go rigid. He may see a problem in one way only. A person who is unsure of his own position in a controversial matter may also show control through preemption. On a Rorschach card he may see each figure 'realistically' (F+) and ignore less realistic interpretations of the same cards or the same portions of the cards. A client may also show *constriction* as a way of achieving control. On the Rorschach Test he may ignore certain cards or certain portions of cards altogether. This, however, is not precisely what is commonly called 'constriction' on the Rorschach Test.

A client may maintain his own precarious position by describing events preemptively – that is, with the this-and-this-only attitude or the nothing-but attitude. He may say, 'I broke up with my girl friend last night. That's all. I just broke up. This is the only thing that I can think of. It was nothing but a breakup.' The experienced therapist will recognize this verbalization as possible evidence of 'overcontrol' and will be alert to the submerged and contrasting end of the client's personal construct of having a girl friend. Ordinarily he will, if he feels that the extreme form of control exhibited is not absolutely necessary, take immediate steps to get the client to construe the event less preemptively.

a. Constriction and control. Clinicians commonly recognize another type of control. A client may describe a situation, such as that of breaking up with a girl friend, with considerable 'intellectual' spontaneity. In other words, he appears to deal with the situation propositionally. Yet he does not appear to be 'ego-involved' or to express 'feeling'. The clinician may also want to call this 'overcontrol'. While the terms 'intellectual' (in contrast to 'emotional' and the like), 'ego-involved', and 'feeling' are not assigned systematic meanings within the psychology of personal constructs, this kind of behaviour would, nonetheless, be considered suspect by the personal-construct psychologist. Rather than using the term 'control', however, he would suspect it of revealing 'constriction'.

In testing for constriction the personal-construct psychologist would note whether or not the client related himself, or any aspects of himself, to the situation. If he consistently refrained from construing himself as relevant to the situation, the clinician would suspect that part of his perceptual field was being ruled out, that the client was constricting. To be sure, the therapist would closely observe the client's gestural, as well as his verbal, behaviour. If the client wept, if his voice broke, if he expressed dependency, or otherwise presented personal elements to be construed along with the breakup situation, the therapist could be somewhat reassured that the client was not constricting his field in an unhealthy fashion.

There may, of course, be other areas of constriction which are more subtle. The client may, for example, be ruling out of the girl-friend breakup situation all the circumstances which once surrounded a rejection by his mother when he was aged five. But at least the client who shows the self-identifying behaviour mentioned above is not ruling *himself* out of the range of convenience of the constructs he uses to deal with the breakup situation.

We have digressed to this discussion of constriction because it applies to what some clinicians would call 'control'. Perhaps what is meant by control within the psychology of personal constructs can now be made clearer. Constriction and control can be handled propositionally with respect to each other. That is, what is constriction may or may not involve control and what is control may or may not involve constriction. Constriction may make control more feasible for a person. To return to our example, if the client refuses to consider any elements in the situation other than the bare events of the preceding evening – '*only these things* happened' (constriction) – he may stand a better chance of construing them all as one thing and one thing only – namely, '*nothing but* a breakup' (preemption), about which he '*can do one thing only*' (control).

The relationship between *constriction–dilation* and *preemption–circumspection* can, perhaps, be made even clearer. Preemption is a way of ruling out *other constructs*. 'All these are spades and nothing but spades.' Constriction is a way of ruling out *other elements*. 'Just these, and these only, are to be construed.' And if the person construes impermeably he implies, 'Just these, and these only are spades.' Circumspection is a way of considering additional constructions. 'These are spades. Now what else may we say about them?' Dilation is a way of considering additional elements. 'These spades, those weeds, this blister, that sun.' Permeability implies that there are more and more spades.

b. Uses of control. Therapy is not always directed against preemption. Therapy often seeks control. But it seeks to enable the client to achieve controls through preemption or constriction where and when controls are necessary, and to exercise circumspection at other times. The appropriate articulation of control and circumspection provides the maximum opportunity for a person to test his construction system experimentally and to work out its continued revision in the light of outcomes. Just as the scientist needs to be widely circumspective in formulating his hypotheses and tightly controlled in performing his experiments, so any person needs to articulate these two phases in the evolution of his mental processes.

Preemption commits one to handling a given situation at a given time in one way and in one way only. This is in contrast to circumspection, which allows one to see any situation in various ways. Circumspection is maximized when one deals with a situation propositionally. Control is maximized when one deals with a situation preemptively.

Control, or the choice of an alternative, is a function of the side of the construct which better permits elaboration – that is, permits the permeable addition of elements and sets the stage for a programme of testing and validation without undue loss of structure. This is true of one's control of external objects as well as of self-control. Object control is a matter of behaving so as to achieve greater freedom of movement for oneself, freedom of elaboration, freedom of testing, freedom to seek validating experience for tentatively held constructions.

Control is made feasible by treating one's regnant constructs preemptively. If a regnant construct is preemptive, it tends to limit the realm membership of its elements. Thus the person acquires *self-control* if he tends to construe himself in one way only. For example, in combat, the soldier usually performs most effectively if he construes himself as a soldier and as nothing else. To a large extent, military training is primitively designed to make the construction of oneself as a soldier so preemptive that there will be no doubt in time of emergency as to how the man will behave.

The control of external objects is similarly useful.

> This object is a weapon. It is nothing but a weapon. Therefore, treat it as nothing but a weapon – not as a walking stick, not as an ornament, not as a tent pole, but as a soldier's weapon. In an emergency a soldier is expected to use it as a weapon.

Control is therefore facilitated by a kind of simplification of one's construct system. It requires, at least, a temporary preemption in one's regnant constructs. Propositionality in one's regnant constructs, on the other hand, does not facilitate the making of quick decisions. The propositional construction of oneself opens up the possibility of one's acting in a great variety of ways, depending on how he looks at himself. The soldier in combat who remembers that he is also a father, a member of a club, a great guy with the ladies, and sundry other things, may find the decision to climb out of his foxhole at zero hour quite difficult to make. If he chooses to act in some manner other than as a soldier, he may find, as a result of his action, that he must construe himself in certain additional ways that he had not anticipated. He may be a 'coward'. He may be a 'disgrace to his children'. The ladies may make fun of him. The backwash of circumstances may even force upon him, eventually, the preemptive construct of being a coward, to the exclusion of the other constructs which he had originally used in construing himself propositionally.

c. What are the alternatives? Up to this point in the exposition of the psychology of personal constructs we have described primarily the ways in which a person could approach his world circumspectively. We have described construing as a process of setting up a system of paired alternatives. We have described one's construction system as a matrix of streets and avenues along which movement is possible, but we have not stressed the matter of which way the traffic is running. The question of a person's *choice* of alternatives has been approached from time to time, for example, in our discussions of controlled elaboration and spontaneity, but we have chosen to emphasize the fact that one's choice of a form of behaviour ought to be understood, first, in terms of what alternatives one has to choose from.

If a man commits suicide, one can best understand that act only by knowing what he conceived to be the practical alternative to suicide.

In science one does not verify hypotheses by using such terms as 'motives', 'demoniacal possession', or 'fate'. Rather, one sets up alternatives – usually an experimental hypothesis and a null hypothesis – and, having given the null hypothesis a certain handicap – called the *fiducial limit* – lets the data choose between them. One does not always need to use the null hypothesis as the alternative to one's experimental hypothesis; one can use another experimental hypothesis, or a traditional hypothesis if one prefers.

The man who ended up in suicide must have found data which discredited his particular alternative hypothesis. *What was the alternative hypothesis, from his point of view*? The psychology of personal constructs lays great stress upon knowing the answer to this kind of question. It lays stress upon the clinician's perceiving the client's system of alternatives. In so doing it follows closely the model of scientific methodology.

Control requires decision. One alternative is chosen over another. Other aspects of the situation or other pairs of alternatives have to be ruled out for some finite period of time. A man considers whether to get married or to stay single. He cannot do both at the same time. Moreover, the act of engaging himself to be married cannot be made on the basis of other dimensions of life which are independent of marriage. When the girl friend, after a tedious courtship, says, 'Well, how about it, Buster?' it is scarcely an act of control for the man to say, 'I am a Republican.' Such a response may be a sign of a monolithic intellect, but it is not likely to bring about a happy solution to the issue of marriage. Control requires either that the man stay single or that he jump in with both feet and get married all over! Being a Republican may have been one of the circumspective issues, but the girl friend is not likely, at this crucial moment, to consider it an answer to her exasperated question.

d. The choice. But when the alternatives are set, how does the man decide whether or not to jump? For the answer to this question let us return to our Choice Corollary: a person chooses for himself that alternative in a dichotomized construct through which he anticipates the greater possibility for extension and definition of his system. Our postulate and its corollaries do not say that a person always behaves in the manner in which outcomes are most predictable; rather, they say that a person extends and defines a system of processes in such a manner as to provide an ultimate way in which more events may be better predicted. He normally does not beat out a little circular path; he explores. He seeks the optimal anticipation of events. He works towards evolving a system. He does not necessarily seek merely those events which are already optimally anticipated.

In an earlier chapter we explained spontaneous activity as the elaboration of one's experiential field under the aegis of permeable constructs. We said that one may therefore select a part of the world about him and deal with it, rather than some other part, simply because he can deal with it. We said that one does control one's field of perception in order to keep it within limits which are both predictable and fertile. Man explores in order to evolve and sustain an optimal scheme for anticipating events. Other things being equal, the man confronted with the alternative of marriage will choose marriage if that appears to provide him with an opportunity to enlarge or secure his anticipatory system. While it carries some uncertain implications, eventually he hopes that through marriage his world will become more predictable.

But there are other considerations. The idea of marriage must itself be construed in some way. There must be room in his construct system for marriage. His constructs must be permeable to it. Our Modulation Corollary states that such a variation in the man's behaviour must be subordinate to such permeable constructions. If marriage is wholly outside his ken, he is likely to miss altogether the point of his girl friend's petulant question. In that case, he ignores the question or says something which seems to the girl to be utterly irrelevant.

Again, if the idea of marriage is construable by the man, but marriage itself is to him an impermeable construct, he is more likely to avoid the act. For him the events embraced by marriage are already limited and highly predictable. There would be no *evolving* in the direction of an optimal anticipation of events if he got married. Marriage would introduce him to no fascinating future. He already knows the woman. For her to be his wife would add nothing to his experience. He already knows all there is to be known about marriage. Married life is cut and dried. Why marry?

But there are limitations in the other direction too. Marriage might place the man in a world where everything would be unpredictable and where his carefully wrought prediction system would, as a system, be wholly obsolescent. If he thinks he can come to understand his girl friend better and better, he is challenged by the prospect of marriage. If he is persuaded that she would never make any kind of sense and that, if married to her, he himself would not either, his answer is likely to be, 'No! No! No!' A mysterious or unpredictable girl may evoke a passing interest; but if she shows no promise of ever making any more sense than she does at the moment, the man will not wish to bind himself to her. Furthermore, if he finds that he himself makes less and less sense while in her company, he is likely to seek to extricate himself from the relationship. A person's tolerance of incompatibility is limited by the permeability and definition of certain superordinate aspects of his system. The uncertainties and vicissitudes of married life require a breadth of viewpoint and an open-mindedness towards certain kinds of things. Without this kind of permeability in one's construction system, one's tolerance of incompatibility will be so limited that one will not attempt marriage, or, if one does acquiesce, may soon seek to dissolve it in divorce.

Control, as it relates to action, normally involves a chain of psychological processes – circumspection, temporary preemption (sometimes constriction), decision. The evolution of a fertile prediction system is the goal. Elaboration of the system is possible only if the superordinate constructs are permeable enough to tolerate the incompatibilities which will crop up as the aftermath of one's making one's choice. Control permits one to elaborate one's prediction system while maintaining its essential features.

e. Clinical interpretation of control. When a clinician finds that his client is doing unexpected things, he knows, of course, that he has misunderstood his client. The error is likely to lie at either of two points. The clinician may not have understood the client's personal construction system and thus may not have realized what alternatives the client was having to choose between. On the other hand, the clinician may have predicted what the alternatives would be but have incorrectly predicted which one of the alternatives the client would choose as a basis of action. The latter kind of prediction is, of course, inherently more difficult. To make it one must understand the permeability of the client's superordinate constructs. Is the kind of action which the client is about to undertake one which opens up to him a field of new experience which he thinks he can construe in some manner without destroying his basic prediction system? It must be. Otherwise he would not choose this course of action.

Some clients get themselves into a series of troubles. The therapist cannot understand why they keep inviting 'disaster'. The therapist becomes confused and unhappy. He is not amused by the client's whimsical adventures! From a hedonistic point of view, the client's behaviour does not make sense. The therapist, if he is a thorough convert of hedonism, decides that the simplest explanation is that the client is trying to 'destroy' himself. Perhaps the client is so hostile to himself, his associates, and the therapist that he takes a fierce joy in setting them at naught.

In a case of this sort, however, the therapist should first take a look at the permeability of the constructs under which the actions have been taken. Perhaps the client is not risking so much after all. He may see himself as an exotic person. Perhaps the 'painful' consequences of his acts are ones which he finds interesting, tantalizing, and well worth elaborating. Perhaps he is experiencing nothing that he cannot take in his stride. To be sure, he suffers 'pain' and 'inconvenience'. But that, too, he can partially understand, he can explore systematically, he can experiment with. He may run to the therapist sobbing or crying for help. That, also, is an adventure. One discovers more interesting therapist responses that way! In such a case the therapist should question whether or not the client is as confused as he looks – or as confused as the therapist is – or whether he is not elaborating a field of activity under the aegis of a highly permeable set of constructs. Certainly one can observe this type of behaviour more frequently among clients who tend to have all-inclusive or comprehensive constructs – that is, constructs under which almost anything seems to fit. Their constructs seem to come with a set of dishes, a Crackerjack prize, a horoscope, a false moustache, and a full year's subscription to *True Romance.*

11. Impusivity

Impulsivity is a form of control, not the absence of control. The field is preempted. A choice point is established. A decision is made. Action ensues. *The characteristic feature of impulsivity is that the period of circumspection which normally precedes decision is unduly shortened.* The preemption, upon the basis of which the decision is reached, is also likely to be of short duration. It is often followed by another period of circumspection. Thus, when a person behaves impulsively, he looks at the situation in a multidimensional manner for a short period of time only. He quickly narrows down the issues and makes a choice which commits him to a course of events. He may then follow this decision by an attempt to retreat to a point where he can look at the decision multidimensionally again and perhaps retract his decision.

Impulsivity is not a trait reserved for certain people only. It is a dimension of behaviour. All people behave with a measure of impulsivity. A person is more impulsive over one span of time than over another. A person is likely to be more impulsive about some matters than about others. Some people are impulsive about spending money. Some people like to gamble at the horse races. Some people find that when they are intoxicated they are able to simplify the issues which appear to confront them and act decisively. They may like that. Many people are impulsive in their sex behaviour. When confronted with the possibility of having sexual intercourse they find it difficult to examine the situation multidimensionally over a protracted period of time. They are likely either to press for action immediately or flee from the situation in panic.

A person caught in an anxiety situation may construe impulsively in order to bring some semblance of structure to bear upon his problems. The impulsivity is a quick attempt at solution. A person caught in a guilt situation may act impulsively to restore his role. He may return unexpectedly to his old group identifications. The social-drinking alcoholic is likely to exhibit this impulsive restoration of his group identifications. The organization called Alcoholics Anonymous may help prevent this by giving him a role in a new group. The role is not easy to establish at a sufficiently maudlin level to replace his old role relationships. The old role relationships are based upon childhood constructions and involve both core and dependency structures. The abandonment of the old alcoholic role actually involves guilt, a point which personal-construct theory contributes to the psychological understanding of certain forms of alcoholism.

A person whose sex role causes him some anxious confusion may tend to act impulsively in sexual matters. Even though he may have considerable and varied experience in sexual relations, his sexual identification of himself may be shaky. Sometimes such a person attempts to dissipate his anxiety by acting impulsively. Under some psychological systems this is seen as a counterattack against homosexuality. From the standpoint of the psychology of personal constructs it is more often seen as impulsive behaviour undertaken to resolve the confusion which has overrun an area of his life. Homosexuality may indeed be a threat, and the impulsive sexual activity may appear to commit the person to a course of action which rules it out. Yet homosexuality may not always be a part of the Don Juan picture, unless one insists on construing any confusion with respect to one's sex role as homosexuality.

Impulsivity may characterize many behaviours and stages of behaviour in the client who is undergoing psychotherapy. As we have reiterated so many times, psychotherapeutic readjustment requires that the client lay new bets on life. He must experiment if he is to find new truths and verify them. It is not surprising, therefore, to find him experimenting now and then outside the interviewing room in ways which seem unduly impulsive. Certainly he tends to be impulsive inside the interviewing room – at least, most clients do under most types of treatment sequences. The therapist ordinarily need not be disturbed by the impulsivity he sees inside the interviewing room. He can usually keep that under control. The impulsivity outside the interview room is a more precarious matter; yet it must be risked, in some measure, if the client is to make an eventual adjustment. The task for the therapist is to see his client often enough and open up his areas of experimentation cautiously enough so that the outside ventures do not have the ultimate effect of restricting his freedom of action. In other words, the therapist must himself exercise control without due impulsivity.

12. The Creativity Cycle

The Creativity Cycle is one which starts with loosened construction and terminates with tightened and validated construction. This is the second of the two important cycles which need to be understood by the psychologist who is concerned with helping clients reconstrue their lives.

Loosened construction is that which is characterized by varying alignment of elements, while tightened construction involves rigid assignment of elements within the construct's context. In the loosened construction with which the Creativity Cycle starts, the person shows a shifting approach to his problems which is often exasperating to his associates or to anyone who is trying to follow what he is doing. What makes this ambiguity meaningful in the Creativity Cycle is the person's ability to experiment minimally with each transient variation, then to seize upon one of the more likely ones, tighten it up, and subject it to a major test.

A person who always uses tight constructions may be productive – that is, he may turn out a lot of things – but he cannot be creative; he cannot produce anything which has not already been blueprinted. Creativity always arises out of preposterous thinking. If the creative person mumbles the first part of his Creativity Cycle out loud, he is likely to get sharp criticism from everyone who is within earshot. For this reason most creative persons keep their loose constructions in the earlier part of their Creative Cycles to themselves. This is not hard to do, since these loose constructions are often preverbal in nature anyway.

But, just as a person who uses tight constructions exclusively cannot be creative, so a person who uses loose constructions exclusively cannot be creative either. He would never get out of the stage of mumbling to himself. He would never get around to setting up a hypothesis for crucial testing. The creative person must have that important capacity to move from loosening to tightening.

Therapy is, for the client as well as for the therapist, a creative process. It involves a series of Creativity Cycles, each of which terminates in some well-planned, but novel, experiment. The therapist tries to help the client release his imagination and then harness it. If the therapist succeeds only in producing the loosening phase of the cycle, he may, as many therapists do, succeed only in precipitating a schizoid reaction. The loosening gets out of hand, either because the therapist has misjudged the amount of loosening which might result from some of his interview-room measures, or because he has misjudged the client's capacity to recover from loosened structure. If the therapist succeeds only in developing tightened construction, he may discover, to his distress, that the interviews produce an endless repetition of old complaints and conventionalized 'insights'.

One of the features of fixed-role therapy, as well as of other forms of reconstruction by enactment, is its utilization of the Creativity Cycle. Granted, of course, that fixed-role therapy does not involve a long period of teaching the client how to 'free-associate' loosely or 'produce dreams', it does, nonetheless start with the creative effort of the therapist who drafts the fixed-role sketch and carries the client through a Creativity Cycle. At first the client can only construe the fixed role loosely. Yet he must translate this loosely construed sketch into daily behaviour; this is the tightening phase of the cycle for him. We might add, also, that he must execute various successive C–P–C Cycles in the daily enactment of his part.

The psychoanalytic therapeutic procedure lays great stress on loosening. In emphasizing loosening the analysts believe that they are plumbing the depths of the client's personality. We see this, not so much in terms of a vertical dimension of *consciousness–unconsciousness*, but as a matter of invoking loosened construction to see what additional elements it may pick up and what new constructs may begin to take shape within the vague mass. The psychology of personal constructs sees the new constructs which arise out of loosened construction, not as the 'true thoughts' or 'insights' of the person, but as new hypotheses which must still be tightened up and tested before they are to be accepted as useful. Thus our approach, following as it does the paradigm of experimental science, emphasizes the hypothetical nature of the constructs which emerge from loosened thinking and insists that they be tested experimentally. In this respect the psychology of personal constructs stands in the same relation to psychoanalysis as modern science stands in relation to classical rationalism.

13. Conclusions

There are, of course, many different ways in which personal constructs may be dimensioned by the psychologist. For our part, we have chosen a set of dimensions which are systematically consistent with our theory and which seem to fit particularly the problems confronted by the clinical psychologist. Thus they represent lines along which a person may shift his outlook in an effort to reconstrue his life. They relate, in some measure also, to the ways in which individuals differ from each other, but that is altogether a secondary consideration.

It is important that the diagnostic constructs we have proposed should not be considered as traits. Anxiety, for example, is not primarily a characteristic which sets some people apart from others, even though some people are more often anxious than others. Nor is anxiety a scale to various points on which whole live people can be permanently affixed. It is rather one of the coordinate axes with respect to which a given bit of psychological process, in a given person, at a given time, can be plotted. So are the other diagnostic constructs we have proposed. None of them provide the psychologist with a ready-made category for classifying people.

It is intended that our diagnostic constructs be used by the clinician *propositionally* rather than *preemptively.* If a person is anxious, he may also be construing loosely or tightly, or comprehensively, or he may be guilty, or he may be hostile. We have proposed coordinate axes, and it is hoped that the clinician will find it feasible to use them that way.

The fact that these constructs are clinicians' constructs of clients' constructs may have caused the reader some difficulty. Thus, when we speak of *anxiety*, for example, we are describing a state of the client's construction system; but anxiety is our term for it, and not necessarily his. This is the sort of thing the therapist must do. He must play a role in relation to his client. In order to do that he must not construe his client as an unthinking object; he must construe his client's construings. This is the central theme of the psychology of personal constructs.

Given these axes, how does the clinician deal meaningfully with a given case? How does he decide what to do in order to be of service? These are questions which we shall attempt to answer in *The Psychology of Personal Constructs: Volume II, Clinical Diagnosis and Therapy.*

C. Glossary of diagnostic constructs

14. General diagnostic constructs

Preverbal Constructs. A preverbal construct is one which continues to be used, even though it has no consistent word symbols. It may or may not have been devised before the person had command of speech.
Submergence. The submerged pole of a construct is the one which is less available for application to events.
Suspension. A suspended element is one which is omitted from the context of a construct as the result of revision of the person's construct system.
Level of cognitive awareness. The level of cognitive awareness ranges from high to low. A high-level construct is one which is readily expressed in socially effective symbols; whose alternatives are both readily accessible; which falls

well within the range of convenience of the client's major constructions; and which is not suspended by its superordinating constructs.

Dilation. Dilation occurs when a person broadens his perceptual field in order to reorganize it on a more comprehensive level. It does not, in itself, include the comprehensive reconstruction of those elements.

Constriction. Constriction occurs when a person narrows his perceptual field in order to minimize apparent incompatibilities.

Comprehensive Constructs. A comprehensive construct is one which subsumes a wide variety of events.

Incidental Constructs. An incidental construct is one which subsumes a narrow variety of events.

Superordinate Constructs. A superordinate construct is one which includes another as one of the elements in its context.

Subordinate Constructs. A subordinate construct is one which is included as an element in the context of another.

Regnant Constructs. A regnant construct is a kind of superordinate construct which assigns each of its elements to a category on an all-or-none basis, as in classical logic. It tends to be nonabstractive.

Core Constructs. A core construct is one which governs the person's maintenance processes.

Peripheral Constructs. A peripheral construct is one which can be altered without serious modification of the core structure.

Tight Constructs. A tight construct is one which leads to unvarying predictions.

Loose Constructs. A loose construct is one which leads to varying predictions but retains its identity.

15. Constructs relating to transition

Threat. Threat is the awareness of an imminent comprehensive change in one's core structures.

Fear. Fear is the awareness of an imminent incidental change in one's core structures.

Anxiety. Anxiety is the awareness that the events with which one is confronted lie outside the range of convenience of one's construct system.

Guilt. Guilt is the awareness of dislodgment of the self from one's core role structure.

Aggressiveness. Aggressiveness is the active elaboration of one's perceptual field.

Hostility. Hostility is the continued effort to extort validational evidence in favour of a type of social prediction which has already been recognized as a failure.

C–P–C Cycle. The C–P–C Cycle is a sequence of construction which involves in succession, circumspection, preemption, and control, and leads to a choice precipitating the person into a particular situation.

Impulsivity. Impulsivity is a characteristic foreshortening of the C–P–C Cycle.

Creativity Cycle. The Creativity Cycle is one which starts with loosened construction and terminates with tightened and validated construction.

Bibliography

1 Baker, Charles T. *Patients' perceptions of psychologists*. Unpublished master's thesis. Ohio State University, 1953.

2 Benjamins, James. 'Changes in performance in relation to influences upon self-conceptualization'. *J. Abnorm. Soc. Psychol.*, 1950, 45, 473–480.

3 Bieri, James. *A study of generalization of changes within the personal construct system*. Unpublished doctoral dissertation. Ohio State University, 1953.

4 ___ 'Changes in interpersonal perceptions following social interaction'. *J. Abnorm. Soc. Psychol.*, 1953, 48, 61–66.

5 Bugental, J. F. T. 'A method for assessing self and not-self attitudes during the therapeutic series'. *J. Consult. Psychol.*, 1952, 16, 435–439.

6 Burton, Jean L. *A qualitative analysis of the Stanford-Binet Intelligence Scale*. Unpublished master's thesis. Ohio State University, 1951.

7 ___ *The effect and interaction of manifest anxiety and failure in concept formation*. Unpublished doctoral dissertation. Ohio State University, 1955.

8 Collet, Grace M. *Prediction and communication problems illustrated with the Rorschach Test*. Unpublished doctoral dissertation. Ohio State University, 1953.

9 Cravens, Richard B. *The psychology of personal constructs as related to group membership and leadership*. Unpublished doctoral dissertation. Ohio State University, 1954.

10 Cromwell, Rue L. *Constructive factors in serial recall*. Unpublished master's thesis. Ohio State University, 1952.

11 Edwards, Ethel H. *Observations of the use and efficacy of changing a patient's concept of his role – a psychotherapeutic device*. Unpublished master's thesis. Fort Hays Kansas State College, 1940.

12 Fager, Robert E. *Communication in personal construct theory*. Unpublished doctoral dissertation. Ohio State University, 1954.

13 Fenichel, Otto. *The psychoanalytic theory of neurosis*. New York: Norton, 1945.

14 Goodrich, Edward G. *The generality of self constructs*. Unpublished doctoral dissertation. Ohio State University, 1954.

15 Hadley, John M. 'Various role of realization in psychotherapeutics'. *J. Gen. Psychol.*, 1938, 19, 191–203.

16 Hamilton, R. Jane. *Generality of personal constructs*. Unpublished doctoral dissertation. Ohio State University, 1952.

17 Howard, Alvin R. *Psychological changes as revealed by self- descriptions*. Unpublished doctoral dissertation. Ohio State University, 1951.

18 Howard, Alvin R. and Kelly, George A. 'A theoretical approach to psychological movement'. *J. Abnorm. Soc. Psychol.*, 1954, 49, 399–404.

19 Hunt, David E. *Studies in role concept repertory: Conceptual consistency*. Unpublished master's thesis. Ohio State University, 1951.
20 Jones, Robert E. *Identification in terms of personal constructs*. Unpublished doctoral dissertation. Ohio State University, 1954.
21 Landfield, Alvin W. *A study of the relationship between overstatement and personal need*. Unpublished master's thesis. Ohio State University, 1948.
22 ___ *A study of threat within the psychology of personal constructs*. Unpublished doctoral dissertation. Ohio State University, 1951.
23 Lecky, Prescott. *Self-consistency: A theory of personality*. New York: Island Press, 1945.
24 Levy, Leon H. *A study of relative information value of constructs in personal construct theory*. Unpublished doctoral dissertation. Ohio State University, 1954.
25 Lundy, Richard M. *Assimilative projection in interpersonal perceptions*. Unpublished doctoral dissertation. Ohio State University, 1954.
26 ___ *Changes in interpersonal perceptions associated with group psychotherapy*. Unpublished master's thesis. Ohio State University, 1952.
27 Lyle, William H. *A comparison of emergence and value as determinants of selective perception*. Unpublished doctoral dissertation. Ohio State University, 1953.
28 Maher, Brendan A. *An investigation into the relationship between level of awareness and perception of error*. Unpublished master's thesis. Ohio State University, 1951.
29 ___ *Personality factors and experimental conditions as a determinant of rigidity in problem solving*. Unpublished doctoral dissertation. Ohio State University, 1954.
30 Masling, Joseph M. *The efficiently of three rigidity tests in predicting group behavior*. Unpublished doctoral dissertation. Ohio State University, 1952.
31 McGaughran, Laurence S. *Dimensions of conceptualization: A preliminary experimental analysis of relationship between 'conceptual areas' and language behavior*. Unpublished doctoral dissertation. Ohio State University, 1950.
32 Morton, Robert D. *A controlled experiment in psychotherapy based on Rotter's social learning theory of personality*. Unpublished doctoral dissertation. Ohio State University, 1950.
33 Poch, Susanne M. *A study of changes in personal constructs as related to interpersonal prediction and its outcomes*. Unpublished doctoral dissertation. Ohio State University, 1952.
34 Robinson, Alexander J. *A further validation of role therapy*. Unpublished master's thesis. Fort Hays Kansas State College, 1940.
35 Rogers, Carl R. *Client-centered therapy*. Boston: Houghton-Mifflin, 1951.
36 Rohrer, James W. *An investigation of changes in response to a personality questionnaire from one administration to another*. Unpublished master's thesis. Ohio State University, 1949.
37 ___ *A study of predictive utility of the role construct repertory test*. Unpublished doctoral dissertation. Ohio State University, 1952.
38 Rotter, Julian B. *Social learning and clinical psychology*. New York: Prentice-Hall, 1954.
39 Shoemaker, Donald J. *The relation between personal constructs and interpersonal predictions*. Unpublished doctoral dissertation. Ohio State University, 1955.
40 ___ *The relation between personal constructs and observed behavior*. Unpublished master's thesis. Ohio State University, 1952.
41 Trapp, E. Philip. *Role constructs applied to group analysis*. Unpublished doctoral dissertation. Ohio State University, 1951.

Index